Lecture Notes in Computer Science

Lecture Notes in Artificial Intelligence 14173

Founding Editor

Jörg Siekmann

Series Editors

The series Lecture Notes in Artificial Intelligence (LNAI) was established in 1988 as a topical subseries of LNCS devoted to artificial intelligence.

The series publishes state-of-the-art research results at a high level. As with the LNCS mother series, the mission of the series is to serve the international R & D community by providing an invaluable service, mainly focused on the publication of conference and workshop proceedings and postproceedings.

Danai Koutra · Claudia Plant ·
Manuel Gomez Rodriguez · Elena Baralis ·
Francesco Bonchi
Editors

Machine Learning and Knowledge Discovery in Databases

Research Track

European Conference, ECML PKDD 2023
Turin, Italy, September 18–22, 2023
Proceedings, Part V

Editors
Danai Koutra
University of Michigan
Ann Arbor, MI, USA

Claudia Plant
University of Vienna
Vienna, Austria

Manuel Gomez Rodriguez
Max Planck Institute for Software Systems
Kaiserslautern, Germany

Elena Baralis
Politecnico di Torino
Turin, Italy

Francesco Bonchi
CENTAI
Turin, Italy

ISSN 0302-9743 ISSN 1611-3349 (electronic)
Lecture Notes in Artificial Intelligence
ISBN 978-3-031-43423-5 ISBN 978-3-031-43424-2 (eBook)
https://doi.org/10.1007/978-3-031-43424-2

LNCS Sublibrary: SL7 – Artificial Intelligence

This Springer imprint is published by the registered company Springer Nature Switzerland AG
The registered company address is: Gewerbestrasse 11, 6330 Cham, Switzerland

Paper in this product is recyclable.

Preface

The 2023 edition of the European Conference on Machine Learning and Principles and Practice of Knowledge Discovery in Databases (ECML PKDD 2023) was held in Turin, Italy, from September 18 to 22, 2023.

The ECML PKDD conference, held annually, acts as a worldwide platform showcasing the latest advancements in machine learning and knowledge discovery in databases, encompassing groundbreaking applications. With a history of successful editions, ECML PKDD has established itself as the leading European machine learning and data mining conference, offering researchers and practitioners an unparalleled opportunity to exchange knowledge and ideas.

The main conference program consisted of presentations of 255 accepted papers and three keynote talks (in order of appearance):

- Max Welling (University of Amsterdam): Neural Wave Representations
- Michael Bronstein (University of Oxford): Physics-Inspired Graph Neural Networks
- Kate Crawford (USC Annenberg): Mapping Generative AI

In addition, there were 30 workshops, 9 combined workshop-tutorials, 5 tutorials, 3 discovery challenges, and 16 demonstrations. Moreover, the PhD Forum provided a friendly environment for junior PhD students to exchange ideas and experiences with peers in an interactive atmosphere and to get constructive feedback from senior researchers. The conference included a Special Day on Artificial Intelligence for Financial Crime Fight to discuss, share, and present recent developments in AI-based financial crime detection.

In recognition of the paramount significance of ethics in machine learning and data mining, we invited the authors to include an ethical statement in their submissions. We encouraged the authors to discuss the ethical implications of their submission, such as those related to the collection and processing of personal data, the inference of personal information, or the potential risks. We are pleased to report that our call for ethical statements was met with an overwhelmingly positive response from the authors.

The ECML PKDD 2023 Organizing Committee supported Diversity and Inclusion by awarding some grants that enable early career researchers to attend the conference, present their research activities, and become part of the ECML PKDD community. A total of 8 grants covering all or part of the registration fee (4 free registrations and 4 with 50% discount) were awarded to individuals who belong to underrepresented communities, based on gender and role/position, to attend the conference and present their research activities. The goal of the grants was to provide financial support to early-career (women) scientists and Master and Ph.D. students from developing countries. The Diversity and Inclusion action also includes the SoBigData Award, fully sponsored by the SoBigData++ Horizon2020 project, which aims to encourage more diverse participation in computer science and machine learning events. The award is intended to cover expenses for transportation and accommodation.

The papers presented during the three main conference days were organized in four different tracks:

- Research Track: research or methodology papers from all areas in machine learning, knowledge discovery, and data mining;
- Applied Data Science Track: papers on novel applications of machine learning, data mining, and knowledge discovery to solve real-world use cases, thereby bridging the gap between practice and current theory;
- Journal Track: papers published in special issues of the journals Machine Learning and Data Mining and Knowledge Discovery;
- Demo Track: short papers introducing new prototypes or fully operational systems that exploit data science techniques and are presented via working demonstrations.

We received 829 submissions for the Research track and 239 for the Applied Data Science Track.

We accepted 196 papers (24%) in the Research Track and 58 (24%) in the Applied Data Science Track. In addition, there were 44 papers from the Journal Track and 16 demo papers (out of 28 submissions).

We want to thank all participants, authors, all chairs, all Program Committee members, area chairs, session chairs, volunteers, co-organizers, and organizers of workshops and tutorials for making ECML PKDD 2023 an outstanding success. Thanks to Springer for their continuous support and Microsoft for allowing us to use their CMT software for conference management and providing support throughout. Special thanks to our sponsors and the ECML PKDD Steering Committee for their support. Finally, we thank the organizing institutions: CENTAI (Italy) and Politecnico di Torino (Italy).

September 2023

Elena Baralis
Francesco Bonchi
Manuel Gomez Rodriguez
Danai Koutra
Claudia Plant
Gianmarco De Francisci Morales
Claudia Perlich

Organization

General Chairs

Elena Baralis	Politecnico di Torino, Italy
Francesco Bonchi	CENTAI, Italy and Eurecat, Spain

Research Track Program Chairs

Manuel Gomez Rodriguez	Max Planck Institute for Software Systems, Germany
Danai Koutra	University of Michigan, USA
Claudia Plant	University of Vienna, Austria

Applied Data Science Track Program Chairs

Gianmarco De Francisci Morales	CENTAI, Italy
Claudia Perlich	NYU and TwoSigma, USA

Journal Track Chairs

Tania Cerquitelli	Politecnico di Torino, Italy
Marcello Restelli	Politecnico di Milano, Italy
Charalampos E. Tsourakakis	Boston University, USA and ISI Foundation, Italy
Fabio Vitale	CENTAI, Italy

Workshop and Tutorial Chairs

Rosa Meo	University of Turin, Italy
Fabrizio Silvestri	Sapienza University of Rome, Italy

Demo Chairs

Nicolas Kourtellis Telefonica, Spain
Natali Ruchansky Netflix, USA

Local Chairs

Daniele Apiletti Politecnico di Torino, Italy
Paolo Bajardi CENTAI, Italy
Eliana Pastor Politecnico di Torino, Italy

Discovery Challenge Chairs

Danilo Giordano Politecnico di Torino, Italy
André Panisson CENTAI, Italy

PhD Forum Chairs

Yllka Velaj University of Vienna, Austria
Matteo Riondato Amherst College, USA

Diversity and Inclusion Chair

Tania Cerquitelli Politecnico di Torino, Italy

Proceedings Chairs

Eliana Pastor Politecnico di Torino, Italy
Giulia Preti CENTAI, Italy

Sponsorship Chairs

Daniele Apiletti Politecnico di Torino, Italy
Paolo Bajardi CENTAI, Italy

Web Chair

Alessandro Fiori	Flowygo, Italy

Social Media and Publicity Chair

Flavio Giobergia	Politecnico di Torino, Italy

Online Chairs

Alkis Koudounas	Politecnico di Torino, Italy
Simone Monaco	Politecnico di Torino, Italy

Best Paper Awards Chairs

Peter Flach	University of Bristol, UK
Katharina Morik	TU Dortmund, Germany
Arno Siebes	Utrecht University, The Netherlands

ECML PKDD Steering Committee

Massih-Reza Amini	Université Grenoble Alpes, France
Annalisa Appice	University of Bari, Aldo Moro, Italy
Ira Assent	Aarhus University, Denmark
Tania Cerquitelli	Politecnico di Torino, Italy
Albert Bifet	University of Waikato, New Zealand
Francesco Bonchi	CENTAI, Italy and Eurecat, Spain
Peggy Cellier	INSA Rennes, France
Saso Dzeroski	Jožef Stefan Institute, Slovenia
Tias Guns	KU Leuven, Belgium
Alípio M. G. Jorge	University of Porto, Portugal
Kristian Kersting	TU Darmstadt, Germany
Jefrey Lijffijt	Ghent University, Belgium
Luís Moreira-Matias	Sennder GmbH, Germany
Katharina Morik	TU Dortmund, Germany
Siegfried Nijssen	Université catholique de Louvain, Belgium
Andrea Passerini	University of Trento, Italy

Fernando Perez-Cruz	ETH Zurich, Switzerland
Alessandra Sala	Shutterstock, Ireland
Arno Siebes	Utrecht University, The Netherlands
Grigorios Tsoumakas	Aristotle University of Thessaloniki, Greece
Isabel Valera	Universität des Saarlandes, Germany

Program Committee

Guest Editorial Board, Journal Track

Richard Allmendinger	University of Manchester, UK
Marie Anastacio	RWTH Aachen University, Germany
Giuseppina Andresini	University of Bari, Aldo Moro, Italy
Annalisa Appice	University of Bari, Aldo Moro, Italy
Ira Assent	Aarhus University, Denmark
Martin Atzmueller	Osnabrück University, Germany
Jaume Bacardit	Newcastle University, UK
Anthony Bagnall	University of East Anglia, UK
Mitra Baratchi	Leiden University, The Netherlands
Nicola Basilico	University of Milan, Italy
Franka Bause	University of Vienna, Austria
Viktor Bengs	LMU Munich, Germany
Anna Bernasconi	Politecnico di Milano, Italy
Lorenzo Bisi	ML cube, Italy
Veronica Bolon-Canedo	University of A Coruña, Spain
Paolo Bonetti	Politecnico di Milano, Italy
Ilaria Bordino	UniCredit, Italy
Claudio Borile	CENTAI, Italy
Luca Cagliero	Politecnico di Torino, Italy
Ricardo Campello	University of Newcastle, Australia
Barbara Catania	University of Genoa, Italy
Michelangelo Ceci	University of Bari, Aldo Moro, Italy
Loïc Cerf	Universidade Federal de Minas Gerais, Brazil
Julen Cestero	Politecnico di Milano, Italy
Sudhanshu Chanpuriya	University of Massachusetts, Amherst, USA
Tianyi Chen	Boston University, USA
Federico Cinus	Sapienza University of Rome, Italy
Gabriele Ciravegna	Politecnico di Torino, Italy
Luca Colomba	Politecnico di Torino, Italy
Silvia Corchs	University of Milan, Italy

Marco Cotogni	University of Pavia, Italy
Gabriele D'Acunto	Sapienza University of Rome, Italy
Cassio Fraga Dantas	TETIS, Université Montpellier, INRAE, France
Jérôme Darmont	Université Lumière Lyon 2, France
George Dasoulas	Harvard University, USA
Sébastien Destercke	Université de Technologie de Compiègne, France
Shridhar Devamane	Global Academy of Technology, India
Claudia Diamantini	Università Politecnica delle Marche, Italy
Gianluca Drappo	Politecnico di Milano, Italy
Pedro Ferreira	University of Lisbon, Portugal
Cèsar Ferri	Universitat Politècnica de València, Spain
M. Julia Flores	Universidad de Castilla-La Mancha, Spain
Germain Forestier	University of Haute-Alsace, France
Elisa Fromont	Université de Rennes 1, France
Emanuele Frontoni	University of Macerata, Italy
Esther Galbrun	University of Eastern Finland, Finland
Joao Gama	University of Porto, Portugal
Jose A. Gamez	Universidad de Castilla-La Mancha, Spain
David García Soriano	ISI Foundation, Italy
Paolo Garza	Politecnico di Torino, Italy
Salvatore Greco	Politecnico di Torino, Italy
Riccardo Guidotti	University of Pisa, Italy
Francesco Gullo	UniCredit, Italy
Shahrzad Haddadan	Rutgers Business School, USA
Martin Holena	Czech Academy of Sciences, Czech Republic
Jaakko Hollmén	Stockholm University, Sweden
Dino Ienco	INRAE, France
Georgiana Ifrim	University College Dublin, Ireland
Felix Iglesias	TU Vienna, Austria
Angelo Impedovo	Niuma, Italy
Manfred Jaeger	Aalborg University, Denmark
Szymon Jaroszewicz	Warsaw University of Technology, Poland
Panagiotis Karras	Aarhus University, Denmark
George Katsimpras	National Center for Scientific Research Demokritos, Greece
Mehdi Kaytoue	Infologic R&D, France
Dragi Kocev	Jožef Stefan Institute, Slovenia
Yun Sing Koh	University of Auckland, New Zealand
Sotiropoulos Konstantinos	Boston University, USA
Lars Kotthoff	University of Wyoming, USA
Alkis Koudounas	Politecnico di Torino, Italy
Tommaso Lanciano	Sapienza University of Rome, Italy

Helge Langseth	Norwegian University of Science and Technology, Norway
Thien Le	MIT, USA
Hsuan-Tien Lin	National Taiwan University, Taiwan
Marco Lippi	University of Modena and Reggio Emilia, Italy
Corrado Loglisci	University of Bari, Aldo Moro, Italy
Manuel López-ibáñez	University of Manchester, UK
Nuno Lourenço	CISUC, Portugal
Claudio Lucchese	Ca' Foscari University of Venice, Italy
Brian Mac Namee	University College Dublin, Ireland
Gjorgji Madjarov	Ss. Cyril and Methodius University in Skopje, North Macedonia
Luigi Malagò	Transylvanian Institute of Neuroscience, Romania
Sagar Malhotra	Fondazione Bruno Kessler, Italy
Fragkiskos Malliaros	CentraleSupélec, Université Paris-Saclay, France
Giuseppe Manco	ICAR-CNR, Italy
Basarab Matei	Sorbonne Université Paris Nord, France
Michael Mathioudakis	University of Helsinki, Finland
Rosa Meo	University of Turin, Italy
Mohamed-Lamine Messai	Université Lumière Lyon 2, France
Sara Migliorini	University of Verona, Italy
Alex Mircoli	Università Politecnica delle Marche, Italy
Atsushi Miyauchi	University of Tokyo, Japan
Simone Monaco	Politecnico di Torino, Italy
Anna Monreale	University of Pisa, Italy
Corrado Monti	CENTAI, Italy
Katharina Morik	TU Dortmund, Germany
Lia Morra	Politecnico di Torino, Italy
Arsenii Mustafin	Boston University, USA
Mirco Mutti	Politecnico di Milano/University of Bologna, Italy
Amedeo Napoli	University of Lorraine, CNRS, LORIA, France
Kleber Oliveira	CENTAI, Italy
Gabriella Olmo	Politecnico di Torino, Italy
Marios Papachristou	Cornell University, USA
Panagiotis Papapetrou	Stockholm University, Sweden
Matteo Papini	Universitat Pompeu Fabra, Spain
Vincenzo Pasquadibisceglie	University of Bari, Aldo Moro, Italy
Eliana Pastor	Politecnico di Torino, Italy
Andrea Paudice	University of Milan, Italy
Charlotte Pelletier	IRISA - Université Bretagne-Sud, France
Ruggero G. Pensa	University of Turin, Italy
Simone Piaggesi	University of Bologna/ISI Foundation, Italy

Matteo Pirotta	Meta, France
Marc Plantevit	EPITA, France
Konstantinos Pliakos	KU Leuven, Belgium
Kai Puolamäki	University of Helsinki, Finland
Jan Ramon	Inria, France
Rita P. Ribeiro	INESC TEC/University of Porto, Portugal
Matteo Riondato	Amherst College, USA
Antonio Riva	Politecnico di Milano, Italy
Shota Saito	University College London, UK
Flora Salim	University of New South Wales, Australia
Roberto Santana	University of the Basque Country, Spain
Lars Schmidt-Thieme	University of Hildesheim, Germany
Thomas Seidl	LMU Munich, Germany
Kijung Shin	KAIST, South Korea
Shinichi Shirakawa	Yokohama National University, Japan
Konstantinos Sotiropoulos	Boston University, USA
Fabian Spaeh	Boston University, USA
Gerasimos Spanakis	Maastricht University, The Netherlands
Myra Spiliopoulou	Otto-von-Guericke-University Magdeburg, Germany
Jerzy Stefanowski	Poznan University of Technology, Poland
Mahito Sugiyama	National Institute of Informatics, Japan
Nikolaj Tatti	University of Helsinki, Finland
Maximilian Thiessen	TU Vienna, Austria
Josephine Thomas	University of Kassel, Germany
Kiran Tomlinson	Cornell University, USA
Leonardo Trujillo	Tecnológico Nacional de México, Mexico
Grigorios Tsoumakas	Aristotle University of Thessaloniki, Greece
Genoveva Vargas-Solar	CNRS, LIRIS Lab, France
Edoardo Vittori	Politecnico di Milano/Intesa Sanpaolo, Italy
Christel Vrain	University of Orléans, France
Willem Waegeman	Ghent University, Belgium
Yanbang Wang	Cornell University, USA
Pascal Welke	University of Bonn, Germany
Marcel Wever	LMU Munich, Germany
Stefan Wrobel	University of Bonn/Fraunhofer IAIS, Germany
Guoxian Yu	Shandong University, China
Ilias Zavitsanos	National Center for Scientific Research Demokritos, Greece
Ye Zhu	Deakin University, Australia
Albrecht Zimmermann	Université de Caen Normandie, France

Area Chairs, Research Track

Fabrizio Angiulli	University of Calabria, Italy
Annalisa Appice	University of Bari, Aldo Moro, Italy
Antonio Artés	Universidad Carlos III de Madrid, Spain
Martin Atzmueller	Osnabrück University, Germany
Christian Böhm	University of Vienna, Austria
Michael R. Berthold	KNIME, Switzerland
Albert Bifet	Université Paris-Saclay, France
Hendrik Blockeel	KU Leuven, Belgium
Ulf Brefeld	Leuphana University, Germany
Paula Brito	INESC TEC - LIAAD/University of Porto, Portugal
Wolfram Burgard	University of Technology Nuremberg, Germany
Seshadhri C.	UCSC, USA
Michelangelo Ceci	University of Bari, Aldo Moro, Italy
Peggy Cellier	IRISA - INSA Rennes, France
Duen Horng Chau	Georgia Institute of Technology, USA
Nicolas Courty	IRISA - Université Bretagne-Sud, France
Bruno Cremilleux	Université de Caen Normandie, France
Jesse Davis	KU Leuven, Belgium
Abir De	IIT Bombay, India
Tom Diethe	AstraZeneca, UK
Yuxiao Dong	Tsinghua University, China
Kurt Driessens	Maastricht University, The Netherlands
Tapio Elomaa	Tampere University, Finland
Johannes Fürnkranz	JKU Linz, Austria
Sophie Fellenz	RPTU Kaiserslautern-Landau, Germany
Elisa Fromont	IRISA/Inria rba - Université de Rennes 1, France
Thomas Gärtner	TU Vienna, Austria
Patrick Gallinari	Criteo AI Lab - Sorbonne Université, France
Joao Gama	INESC TEC - LIAAD, Portugal
Rayid Ghani	Carnegie Mellon University, USA
Aristides Gionis	KTH Royal Institute of Technology, Sweden
Chen Gong	Nanjing University of Science and Technology, China
Francesco Gullo	UniCredit, Italy
Eyke Hüllermeier	LMU Munich, Germany
Junheng Hao	University of California, Los Angeles, USA
José Hernández-Orallo	Universitat Politècnica de Valencia, Spain
Daniel Hernández-Lobato	Universidad Autonoma de Madrid, Spain
Sibylle Hess	TU Eindhoven, The Netherlands

Jaakko Hollmén	Aalto University, Finland
Andreas Hotho	University of Würzburg, Germany
Georgiana Ifrim	University College Dublin, Ireland
Jayaraman J. Thiagarajan	Lawrence Livermore, USA
Alipio M. G. Jorge	INESC TEC/University of Porto, Portugal
Ross King	Chalmers University of Technology, Sweden
Yun Sing Koh	University of Auckland, New Zealand
Lars Kotthoff	University of Wyoming, USA
Peer Kröger	Christian-Albrechst University of Kiel, Germany
Stefan Kramer	JGU Mainz, Germany
Jörg Lücke	University of Oldenburg, Germany
Niklas Lavesson	Blekinge Institute of Technology, Sweden
Bruno Lepri	Fondazione Bruno Kessler, Italy
Jefrey Lijffijt	Ghent University, Belgium
Marius Lindauer	Leibniz University Hannover, Germany
Patrick Loiseau	Inria, France
Jose A. Lozano	UPV/EHU, Spain
Emmanuel Müller	TU Dortmund, Germany
Donato Malerba	University of Bari, Aldo Moro, Italy
Fragkiskos Malliaros	CentraleSupelec, France
Giuseppe Manco	ICAR-CNR, Italy
Pauli Miettinen	University of Eastern Finland, Finland
Dunja Mladenic	Jožef Stefan Institute, Slovenia
Anna Monreale	University of Pisa, Italy
Luis Moreira-Matias	Sennder GmbH, Germany
Katharina J. Morik	TU Dortmund, Germany
Siegfried Nijssen	Université catholique de Louvain, Belgium
Evangelos Papalexakis	UC, Riverside, USA
Panagiotis Papapetrou	Stockholm University, Sweden
Andrea Passerini	University of Trento, Italy
Mykola Pechenizkiy	TU Eindhoven, The Netherlands
Jaakko Peltonen	Tampere University, Finland
Franz Pernkopf	TU Graz, Austria
Bernhard Pfahringer	University of Waikato, New Zealand
Fabio Pinelli	IMT Lucca, Italy
Goran Radanovic	Max Planck Institute for Software Systems, Germany
Jesse Read	École Polytechnique, France
Matthias Renz	Christian-Albrechst University of Kiel, Germany
Marian-Andrei Rizoiu	University of Technology, Sydney, Australia
Celine Robardet	INSA Lyon, France
Juho Rousu	Aalto University, Finland

Sriparna Saha	IIT Patna, India
Ute Schmid	University of Bamberg, Germany
Lars Schmidt-Thieme	University of Hildesheim, Germany
Michele Sebag	LISN CNRS, France
Thomas Seidl	LMU Munich, Germany
Junming Shao	University of Electronic Science and Technology of China, China
Arno Siebes	Utrecht University, The Netherlands
Fabrizio Silvestri	Sapienza University of Rome, Italy
Carlos Soares	University of Porto, Portugal
Christian Sohler	University of Cologne, Germany
Myra Spiliopoulou	Otto-von-Guericke-University Magdeburg, Germany
Jie Tang	Tsinghua University, China
Nikolaj Tatti	University of Helsinki, Finland
Evimaria Terzi	Boston University, USA
Marc Tommasi	Lille University, France
Heike Trautmann	University of Münster, Germany
Herke van Hoof	University of Amsterdam, The Netherlands
Celine Vens	KU Leuven, Belgium
Christel Vrain	University of Orleans, France
Jilles Vreeken	CISPA Helmholtz Center for Information Security, Germany
Wei Ye	Tongji University, China
Jing Zhang	Renmin University of China, China
Min-Ling Zhang	Southeast University, China

Area Chairs, Applied Data Science Track

Annalisa Appice	University of Bari, Aldo Moro, Italy
Ira Assent	Aarhus University, Denmark
Martin Atzmueller	Osnabrück University, Germany
Michael R. Berthold	KNIME, Switzerland
Hendrik Blockeel	KU Leuven, Belgium
Michelangelo Ceci	University of Bari, Aldo Moro, Italy
Peggy Cellier	IRISA - INSA Rennes, France
Yi Chang	Jilin University, China
Nicolas Courty	IRISA - UBS, France
Bruno Cremilleux	Université de Caen Normandie, France
Peng Cui	Tsinghua University, China
Anirban Dasgupta	IIT Gandhinagar, India

Tom Diethe	AstraZeneca, UK
Carlotta Domeniconi	George Mason University, USA
Dejing Dou	BCG, USA
Kurt Driessens	Maastricht University, The Netherlands
Johannes Fürnkranz	JKU Linz, Austria
Faisal Farooq	Qatar Computing Research Institute, Qatar
Paolo Frasconi	University of Florence, Italy
Elisa Fromont	IRISA/Inria rba - Université de Rennes 1, France
Glenn Fung	Liberty Mutual, USA
Joao Gama	INESC TEC - LIAAD, Portugal
Jose A. Gamez	Universidad de Castilla-La Mancha, Spain
Rayid Ghani	Carnegie Mellon University, USA
Aristides Gionis	KTH Royal Institute of Technology, Sweden
Sreenivas Gollapudi	Google, USA
Francesco Gullo	UniCredit, Italy
Eyke Hüllermeier	LMU Munich, Germany
Jingrui He	University of Illinois at Urbana-Champaign, USA
Jaakko Hollmén	Aalto University, Finland
Andreas Hotho	University of Würzburg, Germany
Daxin Jiang	Microsoft, Beijing, China
Alipio M. G. Jorge	INESC TEC/University of Porto, Portugal
George Karypis	University of Minnesota, USA
Eamonn Keogh	UC, Riverside, USA
Yun Sing Koh	University of Auckland, New Zealand
Parisa Kordjamshidi	Michigan State University, USA
Lars Kotthoff	University of Wyoming, USA
Nicolas Kourtellis	Telefonica Research, Spain
Stefan Kramer	JGU Mainz, Germany
Balaji Krishnapuram	Pinterest, USA
Niklas Lavesson	Blekinge Institute of Technology, Sweden
Chuan Lei	Amazon Web Services, USA
Marius Lindauer	Leibniz University Hannover, Germany
Patrick Loiseau	Inria, France
Giuseppe Manco	ICAR-CNR, Italy
Gabor Melli	PredictionWorks, USA
Anna Monreale	University of Pisa, Italy
Luis Moreira-Matias	Sennder GmbH, Germany
Nuria Oliver	ELLIS Alicante, Spain
Panagiotis Papapetrou	Stockholm University, Sweden
Mykola Pechenizkiy	TU Eindhoven, The Netherlands
Jian Pei	Simon Fraser University, Canada
Julien Perez	Naver Labs Europe, France

Fabio Pinelli	IMT Lucca, Italy
Zhiwei (Tony) Qin	Lyft, USA
Visvanathan Ramesh	Goethe University, Germany
Zhaochun Ren	Shandong University, China
Sriparna Saha	IIT Patna, India
Ute Schmid	University of Bamberg, Germany
Lars Schmidt-Thieme	University of Hildesheim, Germany
Thomas Seidl	LMU Munich, Germany
Fabrizio Silvestri	Sapienza University of Rome, Italy
Myra Spiliopoulou	Otto-von-Guericke-University Magdeburg, Germany
Karthik Subbian	Amazon, USA
Liang Sun	Alibaba Group, China
Jie Tang	Tsinghua University, China
Jiliang Tang	Michigan State University, USA
Sandeep Tata	Google, USA
Nikolaj Tatti	University of Helsinki, Finland
Marc Tommasi	Lille University, France
Yongxin Tong	Beihang University, China
Vincent S. Tseng	National Yang Ming Chiao Tung University, Taiwan
Antti Ukkonen	University of Helsinki, Finland
Willem Waegeman	Ghent University, Belgium
Fei Wang	Cornell University, USA
Jie Wang	University of Science and Technology of China, China
Sinong Wang	Meta AI, USA
Zheng Wang	Alibaba DAMO Academy, China
Lingfei Wu	Pinterest, USA
Yinglong Xia	Meta, USA
Hui Xiong	Rutgers University, USA
Hongxia Yang	Alibaba Group, China
Min-Ling Zhang	Southeast University, China
Jiayu Zhou	Michigan State University, USA
Xingquan Zhu	Florida Atlantic University, USA
Fuzhen Zhuang	Institute of Artificial Intelligence, China
Albrecht Zimmermann	Université de Caen Normandie, France

Program Committee, Research Track

Matthias Aßenmacher	LMU Munich, Germany
Sara Abdali	Microsoft, USA
Evrim Acar	Simula Metropolitan Center for Digital Engineering, Norway
Homayun Afrabandpey	Nokia Technologies, Finland
Reza Akbarinia	Inria, France
Cuneyt G. Akcora	University of Manitoba, Canada
Ranya Almohsen	West Virginia University, USA
Thiago Andrade	INESC TEC/University of Porto, Portugal
Jean-Marc Andreoli	Naverlabs Europe, France
Giuseppina Andresini	University of Bari, Aldo Moro, Italy
Alessandro Antonucci	IDSIA, Switzerland
Xiang Ao	Institute of Computing Technology, CAS, China
Héber H. Arcolezi	Inria/École Polytechnique, France
Jerónimo Arenas-García	Universidad Carlos III de Madrid, Spain
Yusuf Arslan	University of Luxembourg, Luxemburg
Ali Ayadi	University of Strasbourg, France
Steve Azzolin	University of Trento, Italy
Pierre-Luc Bacon	Mila, Canada
Bunil K. Balabantaray	NIT Meghalaya, India
Mitra Baratchi	LIACS/Leiden University, The Netherlands
Christian Bauckhage	Fraunhofer IAIS, Germany
Anna Beer	Aarhus University, Denmark
Michael Beigl	Karlsruhe Institute of Technology, Germany
Khalid Benabdeslem	Université de Lyon, Lyon 1, France
Idir Benouaret	Epita Research Laboratory, France
Paul Berg	IRISA, France
Christoph Bergmeir	Monash University, Australia
Gilberto Bernardes	INESC TEC/University of Porto, Portugal
Eva Besada-Portas	Universidad Complutense de Madrid, Spain
Jalaj Bhandari	Columbia University, USA
Asmita Bhat	TU Kaiserslautern, Germany
Monowar Bhuyan	Umeå University, Sweden
Adrien Bibal	University of Colorado Anschutz Medical Campus, USA
Manuele Bicego	University of Verona, Italy
Przemyslaw Biecek	Warsaw University of Technology, Poland
Alexander Binder	University of Oslo, Norway
Livio Bioglio	University of Turin, Italy
Patrick Blöbaum	Amazon Web Services, USA

Thomas Bonald	Télécom Paris, France
Ludovico Boratto	University of Cagliari, Italy
Stefano Bortoli	Huawei Research Center, Germany
Tassadit Bouadi	Université de Rennes 1, France
Ahcène Boubekki	UiT, Arctic University of Norway, Norway
Luc Brogat-Motte	Télécom Paris, France
Jannis Brugger	TU Darmstadt, Germany
Nhat-Tan Bui	University of Science - VNUHCM, Vietnam
Mirko Bunse	TU Dortmund, Germany
John Burden	University of Cambridge, UK
Wolfram Burgard	University of Technology, Germany
Julian Busch	Siemens Technology, Germany
Sebastian Buschjäger	TU Dortmund, Germany
Oswald C.	NIT Trichy, India
Seshadhri C.	UCSC, USA
Xin-Qiang Cai	University of Tokyo, Japan
Zekun Cai	University of Tokyo, Japan
Xiaofeng Cao	University of Technology, Sydney, Australia
Giuseppe Casalicchio	LMU Munich, Germany
Guilherme Cassales	University of Waikato, New Zealand
Oded Cats	TU Delft, The Netherlands
Remy Cazabet	Université de Lyon, Lyon 1, France
Mattia Cerrato	JGU Mainz, Germany
Ricardo Cerri	Federal University of Sao Carlos, Brazil
Prithwish Chakraborty	IBM Research, USA
Harry Kai-Ho Chan	University of Sheffield, UK
Joydeep Chandra	IIT Patna, India
Vaggos Chatziafratis	Stanford University, USA
Zaineb Chelly Dagdia	UVSQ - Université Paris-Saclay, France
Hongyang Chen	Zhejiang Lab, China
Huaming Chen	University of Sydney, Australia
Hung-Hsuan Chen	National Central University, Taiwan
Jin Chen	University of Electronic Science and Technology of China, China
Kuan-Hsun Chen	University of Twente, The Netherlands
Ling Chen	University of Technology, Australia
Lingwei Chen	Wright State University, USA
Minyu Chen	Shanghai Jiaotong University, China
Xi Chen	Ghent University, Belgium
Xiaojun Chen	Institute of Information Engineering, CAS, China
Xuefeng Chen	Chongqing University, China
Ying Chen	RMIT University, Australia

Yueguo Chen	Renmin University of China, China
Yuzhou Chen	Temple University, USA
Zheng Chen	Osaka University, Japan
Ziheng Chen	Walmart, USA
Lu Cheng	University of Illinois, Chicago, USA
Xu Cheng	Shanghai Jiao Tong University, China
Zhiyong Cheng	Shandong Academy of Sciences, China
Yann Chevaleyre	Université Paris Dauphine, France
Chun Wai Chiu	Keele University, UK
Silvia Chiusano	Politecnico di Torino, Italy
Satyendra Singh Chouhan	MNIT Jaipur, India
Hua Chu	Xidian University, China
Sarel Cohen	Academic College of Tel Aviv-Yaffo, Israel
J. Alberto Conejero	Universitat Politècnica de València, Spain
Lidia Contreras-Ochando	Universitat Politècnica de València, Spain
Giorgio Corani	IDSIA, Switzerland
Luca Corbucci	University of Pisa, Italy
Roberto Corizzo	American University, USA
Baris Coskunuzer	University of Texas at Dallas, USA
Fabrizio Costa	Exeter University, UK
Gustavo de Assis Costa	Instituto Federal de Goiás, Brazil
Evan Crothers	University of Ottawa, Canada
Pádraig Cunningham	University College Dublin, Ireland
Jacek Cyranka	University of Warsaw, Poland
Tianxiang Dai	Huawei European Research Institute, Germany
Xuan-Hong Dang	IBM T.J. Watson Research Center, USA
Thi-Bich-Hanh Dao	University of Orleans, France
Debasis Das	Indian Institute of Technology Jodhpur, India
Paul Davidsson	Malmö University, Sweden
Marcilio de Souto	LIFO, University of Orleans, France
Klest Dedja	KU Leuven, Belgium
Elena Demidova	University of Bonn, Germany
Caglar Demir	Paderborn University, Germany
Difan Deng	Leibniz University Hannover, Germany
Laurens Devos	KU Leuven, Belgium
Nicola Di Mauro	University of Bari, Aldo Moro, Italy
Jingtao Ding	Tsinghua University, China
Yao-Xiang Ding	Nanjing University, China
Lamine Diop	EPITA, France
Gillian Dobbie	University of Auckland, New Zealand
Stephan Doerfel	Kiel University of Applied Sciences, Germany
Carola Doerr	Sorbonne Université, France

Nanqing Dong	University of Oxford, UK
Haizhou Du	Shanghai University of Electric Power, China
Qihan Du	Renmin University of China, China
Songlin Du	Southeast University, China
Xin Du	University of Edinburgh, UK
Wouter Duivesteijn	TU Eindhoven, The Netherlands
Inês Dutra	University of Porto, Portugal
Sourav Dutta	Huawei Research Centre, Ireland
Saso Dzeroski	Jožef Stefan Institute, Slovenia
Nabil El Malki	IRIT, France
Mohab Elkaref	IBM Research Europe, UK
Tapio Elomaa	Tampere University, Finland
Dominik M. Endres	University of Marburg, Germany
Georgios Exarchakis	University of Bath, UK
Lukas Faber	ETH Zurich, Switzerland
Samuel G. Fadel	Leuphana University, Germany
Haoyi Fan	Zhengzhou University, China
Zipei Fan	University of Tokyo, Japan
Hadi Fanaee-T	Halmstad University, Sweden
Elaine Ribeiro Faria	UFU, Brazil
Fabio Fassetti	University of Calabria, Italy
Anthony Faustine	ITI/LARSyS - Técnico Lisboa, Portugal
Sophie Fellenz	RPTU Kaiserslautern-Landau, Germany
Wenjie Feng	National University of Singapore, Singapore
Zunlei Feng	Zhejiang University, China
Daniel Fernández-Sánchez	Universidad Autónoma de Madrid, Spain
Luca Ferragina	University of Calabria, Italy
Emilio Ferrara	USC ISI, USA
Cèsar Ferri	Universitat Politècnica València, Spain
Flavio Figueiredo	Universidade Federal de Minas Gerais, Brazil
Lucie Flek	University of Marburg, Germany
Michele Fontana	University of Pisa, Italy
Germain Forestier	University of Haute-Alsace, France
Raphaël Fournier-S'niehotta	CNAM, France
Benoît Frénay	University of Namur, Belgium
Kary Främling	Umeå University, Sweden
Holger Froening	University of Heidelberg, Germany
Fabio Fumarola	Prometeia, Italy
María José Gómez-Silva	Universidad Complutense de Madrid, Spain
Vanessa Gómez-Verdejo	Universidad Carlos III de Madrid, Spain
Pratik Gajane	TU Eindhoven, The Netherlands
Esther Galbrun	University of Eastern Finland, Finland

Claudio Gallicchio	University of Pisa, Italy
Chen Gao	Tsinghua University, China
Shengxiang Gao	Kunming University of Science and Technology, China
Yifeng Gao	University of Texas Rio Grande Valley, USA
Luis Garcia	University of Brasilia, Brazil
Dominique Gay	Université de La Réunion, France
Suyu Ge	University of Illinois at Urbana-Champaign, USA
Zhaocheng Ge	Huazhong University of Science and Technology, China
Alborz Geramifard	Facebook AI, USA
Ahana Ghosh	Max Planck Institute for Software Systems, Germany
Shreya Ghosh	Penn State University, USA
Flavio Giobergia	Politecnico di Torino, Italy
Sarunas Girdzijauskas	KTH Royal Institute of Technology, Sweden
Heitor Murilo Gomes	University of Waikato, Sweden
Wenwen Gong	Tsinghua University, China
Bedartha Goswami	University of Tübingen, Germany
Anastasios Gounaris	Aristotle University of Thessaloniki, Greece
Michael Granitzer	University of Passau, Germany
Derek Greene	University College Dublin, Ireland
Moritz Grosse-Wentrup	University of Vienna, Austria
Marek Grzes	University of Kent, UK
Xinyu Guan	Xian Jiaotong University, China
Massimo Guarascio	ICAR-CNR, Italy
Riccardo Guidotti	University of Pisa, Italy
Lan-Zhe Guo	Nanjing University, China
Lingbing Guo	Zhejiang University, China
Shanqing Guo	Shandong University, China
Karthik S. Gurumoorthy	Walmart, USA
Thomas Guyet	Inria, France
Huong Ha	RMIT University, Australia
Benjamin Halstead	University of Auckland, New Zealand
Massinissa Hamidi	LIPN-UMR CNRS 7030, France
Donghong Han	Northeastern University, USA
Marwan Hassani	TU Eindhoven, The Netherlands
Rima Hazra	Indian Institute of Technology, Kharagpur, India
Mark Heimann	Lawrence Livermore, USA
Cesar Hidalgo	University of Toulouse, France
Martin Holena	Institute of Computer Science, Czech Republic
Mike Holenderski	TU Eindhoven, The Netherlands

Adrian Horzyk	AGH University of Science and Technology, Poland
Shifu Hou	Case Western Reserve University, USA
Hongsheng Hu	CSIRO, Australia
Yaowei Hu	University of Arkansas, USA
Yang Hua	Queen's University Belfast, UK
Chao Huang	University of Hong Kong, China
Guanjie Huang	Penn State University, USA
Hong Huang	Huazhong University of Science and Technology, China
Nina C. Hubig	Clemson University, USA
Dino Ienco	Irstea Institute, France
Angelo Impedovo	Niuma, Italy
Roberto Interdonato	CIRAD, France
Stratis Ioannidis	Northeastern University, USA
Nevo Itzhak	Ben-Gurion University, Israel
Raghav Jain	IIT Patna, India
Kuk Jin Jang	University of Pennsylvania, USA
Szymon Jaroszewicz	Polish Academy of Sciences, Poland
Shaoxiong Ji	University of Helsinki, Finland
Bin-Bin Jia	Lanzhou University of Technology, China
Caiyan Jia	School of Computer and Information Technology, China
Xiuyi Jia	Nanjing University of Science and Technology, China
Nan Jiang	Purdue University, USA
Renhe Jiang	University of Tokyo, Japan
Song Jiang	University of California, Los Angeles, USA
Pengfei Jiao	Hangzhou Dianzi University, China
Di Jin	Amazon, USA
Guangyin Jin	National University of Defense Technology, China
Jiahui Jin	Southeast University, China
Ruoming Jin	Kent State University, USA
Yilun Jin	The Hong Kong University of Science and Technology, Hong Kong
Hugo Jonker	Open University of the Netherlands, The Netherlands
Adan Jose-Garcia	Lille University, France
Marius Köppel	JGU Mainz, Germany
Vana Kalogeraki	Athens University of Economics and Business, Greece
Konstantinos Kalpakis	University of Maryland Baltimore County, USA

Andreas Kaltenbrunner	ISI Foundation, Italy
Shivaram Kalyanakrishnan	IIT Bombay, India
Toshihiro Kamishima	National Institute of Advanced Industrial Science and Technology, Japan
Bo Kang	Ghent University, Belgium
Murat Kantarcioglu	UT Dallas
Thommen Karimpanal George	Deakin University, Australia
Saurav Karmakar	University of Galway, Ireland
Panagiotis Karras	Aarhus University, Denmark
Dimitrios Katsaros	University of Thessaly, Greece
Eamonn Keogh	UC, Riverside, USA
Jaleed Khan	University of Galway, Ireland
Irwin King	Chinese University of Hong Kong, China
Mauritius Klein	LMU Munich, Germany
Tomas Kliegr	Prague University of Economics and Business, Czech Republic
Dmitry Kobak	University of Tübingen, Germany
Dragi Kocev	Jožef Stefan Institute, Slovenia
Lars Kotthoff	University of Wyoming, USA
Anna Krause	University of Würzburg, Germany
Amer Krivosija	TU Dortmund, Germany
Daniel Kudenko	L3S Research Center, Germany
Meelis Kull	University of Tartu, Estonia
Sergey O. Kuznetsov	HSE, Russia
Beatriz López	University of Girona, Spain
Jörg Lücke	University of Oldenburg, Germany
Firas Laakom	Tampere University, Finland
Mateusz Lango	Poznan University of Technology, Poland
Hady Lauw	Singapore Management University, Singapore
Tuan Le	New Mexico State University, USA
Erwan Le Merrer	Inria, France
Thach Le Nguyen	Insight Centre, Ireland
Tai Le Quy	L3S Research Center, Germany
Mustapha Lebbah	UVSQ - Université Paris-Saclay, France
Dongman Lee	KAIST, South Korea
Yeon-Chang Lee	Georgia Institute of Technology, USA
Zed Lee	Stockholm University, Sweden
Mathieu Lefort	Université de Lyon, France
Yunwen Lei	University of Birmingham, UK
Vincent Lemaire	Orange Innovation, France
Daniel Lemire	TÉLUQ University, Canada
Florian Lemmerich	RWTH Aachen University, Germany

Youfang Leng	Renmin University of China, China
Carson K. Leung	University of Manitoba, Canada
Dan Li	Sun Yat-Sen University, China
Gang Li	Deakin University, Australia
Jiaming Li	Huazhong University of Science and Technology, China
Mark Junjie Li	Shenzhen University, China
Nian Li	Tsinghua University, China
Shuai Li	University of Cambridge, UK
Tong Li	Hong Kong University of Science and Technology, China
Xiang Li	East China Normal University, China
Yang Li	University of North Carolina at Chapel Hill, USA
Yingming Li	Zhejiang University, China
Yinsheng Li	Fudan University, China
Yong Li	Huawei European Research Center, Germany
Zhihui Li	University of New South Wales, Australia
Zhixin Li	Guangxi Normal University, China
Defu Lian	University of Science and Technology of China, China
Yuxuan Liang	National University of Singapore, Singapore
Angelica Liguori	University of Calabria, Italy
Nick Lim	University of Waikato, Sweden
Baijiong Lin	The Hong Kong University of Science and Technology, Hong Kong
Piotr Lipinski	University of Wrocław, Poland
Marco Lippi	University of Modena and Reggio Emilia, Italy
Bowen Liu	Stanford University, USA
Chien-Liang Liu	National Chiao Tung University, Taiwan
Fenglin Liu	University of Oxford, UK
Junze Liu	University of California, Irvine, USA
Li Liu	Chongqing University, China
Ninghao Liu	University of Georgia, USA
Shenghua Liu	Institute of Computing Technology, CAS, China
Xiao Fan Liu	City University of Hong Kong, Hong Kong
Xu Liu	National University of Singapore, Singapore
Yang Liu	Institute of Computing Technology, CAS, China
Zihan Liu	Zhejiang University/Westlake University, China
Robert Loftin	TU Delft, The Netherlands
Corrado Loglisci	University of Bari, Aldo Moro, Italy
Mingsheng Long	Tsinghua University, China
Antonio Longa	Fondazione Bruno Kessler, Italy

Grigorios Loukides	King's College London, UK
Tsai-Ching Lu	HRL Laboratories, USA
Zhiwu Lu	Renmin University of China, China
Pedro Henrique Luz de Araujo	University of Vienna, Austria
Marcos M. Raimundo	University of Campinas, Brazil
Maximilian Münch	University of Applied Sciences Würzburg-Schweinfurt, Germany
Fenglong Ma	Pennsylvania State University, USA
Pingchuan Ma	The Hong Kong University of Science and Technology, Hong Kong
Yao Ma	New Jersey Institute of Technology, USA
Brian Mac Namee	University College Dublin, Ireland
Henryk Maciejewski	Wrocław University of Science and Technology, Poland
Ayush Maheshwari	IIT Bombay, India
Ajay A. Mahimkar	AT&T, USA
Ayan Majumdar	Max Planck Institute for Software Systems, Germany
Donato Malerba	University of Bari, Aldo Moro, Italy
Aakarsh Malhotra	IIIT-Delhi, India
Fragkiskos Malliaros	CentraleSupelec, France
Pekka Malo	Aalto University, Finland
Hiroshi Mamitsuka	Kyoto University, Japan/Aalto University, Finland
Domenico Mandaglio	University of Calabria, Italy
Robin Manhaeve	KU Leuven, Belgium
Silviu Maniu	Université Paris-Saclay, France
Cinmayii G. Manliguez	National Sun Yat-Sen University, Taiwan
Naresh Manwani	IIIT Hyderabad, India
Giovanni Luca Marchetti	KTH Royal Institute of Technology, Sweden
Koji Maruhashi	Fujitsu Research, Fujitsu Limited, Japan
Florent Masseglia	Inria, France
Sarah Masud	IIIT-Delhi, India
Timothée Mathieu	Inria, France
Amir Mehrpanah	KTH Royal Institute of Technology, Sweden
Wagner Meira Jr.	Universidade Federal de Minas Gerais, Brazil
Joao Mendes-Moreira	INESC TEC, Portugal
Rui Meng	BNU-HKBU United International College, China
Fabio Mercorio	University of Milan-Bicocca, Italy
Alberto Maria Metelli	Politecnico di Milano, Italy
Carlo Metta	CNR-ISTI, Italy
Paolo Mignone	University of Bari, Aldo Moro, Italy
Tsunenori Mine	Kyushu University, Japan

Nuno Moniz	INESC TEC, Portugal
Pierre Monnin	Université Côte d'Azur, Inria, CNRS, I3S, France
Carlos Monserrat-Aranda	Universitat Politècnica de València, Spain
Raha Moraffah	Arizona State University, USA
Davide Mottin	Aarhus University, Denmark
Hamid Mousavi	University of Oldenburg, Germany
Abdullah Mueen	University of New Mexico, USA
Shamsuddeen Hassan Muhamamd	University of Porto, Portugal
Koyel Mukherjee	Adobe Research, India
Yusuke Mukuta	University of Tokyo, Japan
Pranava Mummoju	University of Vienna, Austria
Taichi Murayama	NAIST, Japan
Ankur Nahar	IIT Jodhpur, India
Felipe Kenji Nakano	KU Leuven, Belgium
Hideki Nakayama	University of Tokyo, Japan
Géraldin Nanfack	University of Namur, Belgium
Mirco Nanni	CNR-ISTI, Italy
Franco Maria Nardini	CNR-ISTI, Italy
Usman Naseem	University of Sydney, Australia
Reza Nasirigerdeh	TU Munich, Germany
Rajashree Nayak	MIT ADT University, India
Benjamin Negrevergne	Université Paris Dauphine, France
Stefan Neumann	KTH Royal Institute of Technology, Sweden
Anna Nguyen	IBM, USA
Shiwen Ni	SIAT, CAS, China
Siegfried Nijssen	Université catholique de Louvain, Belgium
Iasonas Nikolaou	Boston University, USA
Simona Nisticò	University of Calabria, Italy
Hao Niu	KDDI Research, Japan
Mehdi Nourelahi	University of Wyoming, USA
Slawomir Nowaczyk	Halmstad University, Sweden
Eirini Ntoutsi	Bundeswehr University Munich, Germany
Barry O'Sullivan	University College Cork, Ireland
Nastaran Okati	Max Planck Institute for Software Systems, Germany
Tsuyoshi Okita	Kyushu Institute of Technology, Japan
Pablo Olmos	Universidad Carlos III de Madrid, Spain
Luis Antonio Ortega Andrés	Autonomous University of Madrid, Spain
Abdelkader Ouali	Université de Caen Normandie, France
Latifa Oukhellou	IFSTTAR, France
Chun Ouyang	Queensland University of Technology, Australia
Andrei Paleyes	University of Cambridge, UK

Menghai Pan	Visa Research, USA
Shirui Pan	Griffith University, Australia
Apostolos N. Papadopoulos	Aristotle University of Thessaloniki, Greece
Chanyoung Park	KAIST, South Korea
Emilio Parrado-Hernandez	Universidad Carlos III de Madrid, Spain
Vincenzo Pasquadibisceglie	University of Bari, Aldo Moro, Italy
Eliana Pastor	Politecnico di Torino, Italy
Anand Paul	Kyungpook National University, South Korea
Shichao Pei	University of Notre Dame, USA
Yulong Pei	TU Eindhoven, The Netherlands
Leonardo Pellegrina	University of Padua, Italy
Ruggero Pensa	University of Turin, Italy
Fabiola Pereira	UFU, Brazil
Lucas Pereira	ITI/LARSyS - Técnico Lisboa, Portugal
Miquel Perello-Nieto	University of Bristol, UK
Lorenzo Perini	KU Leuven, Belgium
Matej Petkovifá	University of Ljubljana, Slovenia
Lukas Pfahler	TU Dortmund, Germany
Ninh Pham	University of Auckland, New Zealand
Guangyuan Piao	Maynooth University, Ireland
Francesco Piccialli	University of Naples Federico II, Italy
Martin Pilát	Charles University, Czech Republic
Gianvito Pio	University of Bari, Aldo Moro, Italy
Giuseppe Pirrò	Sapienza University of Rome, Italy
Francesco S. Pisani	ICAR-CNR, Italy
Srijith P. K.	IIIT Hyderabad, India
Marc Plantevit	EPITA, France
Mirko Polato	University of Turin, Italy
Axel Polleres	Vienna University of Economics and Business, Austria
Giovanni Ponti	ENEA, Italy
Paul Prasse	University of Potsdam, Germany
Mahardhika Pratama	University of South Australia, Australia
Philippe Preux	Inria, France
Ricardo B. Prudencio	Universidade Federal de Pernambuco, Brazil
Chiara Pugliese	CNR-ISTI, Italy
Erasmo Purificato	Otto-von-Guericke-University Magdeburg, Germany
Abdulhakim Qahtan	Utrecht University, The Netherlands
Lianyong Qi	China University of Petroleum, China
Kun Qian	Amazon Web Services, USA
Tieyun Qian	Wuhan University, China

Chuan Qin	BOSS Zhipin, China
Yumou Qiu	Iowa State University, USA
Dimitrios Rafailidis	University of Thessaly, Greece
Edward Raff	Booz Allen Hamilton, USA
Chang Rajani	University of Helsinki, Finland
Herilalaina Rakotoarison	Inria, France
M. José Ramírez-Quintana	Universitat Politècnica de Valencia, Spain
Jan Ramon	Inria, France
Rajeev Rastogi	Amazon, India
Domenico Redavid	University of Bari, Aldo Moro, Italy
Qianqian Ren	Heilongjiang University, China
Salvatore Rinzivillo	CNR-ISTI, Italy
Matteo Riondato	Amherst College, USA
Giuseppe Rizzo	Niuma, Italy
Marko Robnik-Sikonja	University of Ljubljana, Slovenia
Christophe Rodrigues	Pôle Universitaire Léonard de Vinci, France
Federica Rollo	University of Modena and Reggio Emilia, Italy
Luca Romeo	University of Macerata, Italy
Benjamin Roth	University of Vienna, Austria
Céline Rouveirol	LIPN - Université Sorbonne Paris Nord, France
Salvatore Ruggieri	University of Pisa, Italy
Pietro Sabatino	ICAR-CNR, Italy
Luca Sabbioni	Politecnico di Milano, Italy
Tulika Saha	University of Manchester, UK
Pablo Sanchez Martin	Max Planck Institute for Intelligent Systems, Germany
Parinya Sanguansat	Panyapiwat Institute of Management, Thailand
Shreya Saxena	Quantiphi, India
Yücel Saygin	Sabanci Universitesi, Turkey
Patrick Schäfer	Humboldt-Universität zu Berlin, Germany
Kevin Schewior	University of Southern Denmark, Denmark
Rainer Schlosser	Hasso Plattner Institute, Germany
Johannes Schneider	University of Liechtenstein, Liechtenstein
Matthias Schubert	LMU Munich, Germany
Alexander Schulz	CITEC - Bielefeld University, Germany
Andreas Schwung	Fachhoschschule Südwestfalen, Germany
Raquel Sebastião	IEETA/DETI-UA, Portugal
Pierre Senellart	ENS, PSL University, France
Edoardo Serra	Boise State University, USA
Mattia Setzu	University of Pisa, Italy
Ammar Shaker	NEC Laboratories Europe, Germany
Shubhranshu Shekhar	Carnegie Mellon University, USA

Jiaming Shen	Google Research, USA
Qiang Sheng	Institute of Computing Technology, CAS, China
Bin Shi	Xi'an Jiaotong University, China
Jimeng Shi	Florida International University, USA
Laixi Shi	Carnegie Mellon University, USA
Rongye Shi	Columbia University, USA
Harsh Shrivastava	Microsoft Research, USA
Jonathan A. Silva	Universidade Federal de Mato Grosso do Sul, Brazil
Esther-Lydia Silva-Ramírez	Universidad de Cádiz, Spain
Kuldeep Singh	Cerence, Germany
Moshe Sipper	Ben-Gurion University of the Negev, Israel
Andrzej Skowron	University of Warsaw, Poland
Krzysztof Slot	Lodz University of Technology, Poland
Marek Smieja	Jagiellonian University, Poland
Gavin Smith	University of Nottingham, UK
Carlos Soares	University of Porto, Portugal
Cláudia Soares	NOVA LINCS, Portugal
Andy Song	RMIT University, Australia
Dongjin Song	University of Connecticut, USA
Hao Song	Seldon, UK
Jie Song	Zhejiang University, China
Linxin Song	Waseda University, Japan
Liyan Song	Southern University of Science and Technology, China
Zixing Song	Chinese University of Hong Kong, China
Arnaud Soulet	University of Tours, France
Sucheta Soundarajan	Syracuse University, USA
Francesca Spezzano	Boise State University, USA
Myra Spiliopoulou	Otto-von-Guericke-University Magdeburg, Germany
Janusz Starzyk	WSIZ, Poland
Jerzy Stefanowski	Poznan University of Technology, Poland
Julian Stier	University of Passau, Germany
Michiel Stock	Ghent University, Belgium
Eleni Straitouri	Max Planck Institute for Software Systems, Germany
Łukasz Struski	Jagiellonian University, Poland
Jinyan Su	University of Electronic Science and Technology of China, China
David Q. Sun	Apple, USA
Guangzhong Sun	University of Science and Technology of China, China

Mingxuan Sun	Louisiana State University, USA
Peijie Sun	Tsinghua University, China
Weiwei Sun	Shandong University, China
Xin Sun	TU Munich, Germany
Maryam Tabar	Pennsylvania State University, USA
Anika Tabassum	Virginia Tech, USA
Shazia Tabassum	INESC TEC, Portugal
Andrea Tagarelli	University of Calabria, Italy
Acar Tamersoy	NortonLifeLock Research Group, USA
Chang Wei Tan	Monash University, Australia
Cheng Tan	Zhejiang University/Westlake University, China
Garth Tarr	University of Sydney, Australia
Romain Tavenard	LETG-Rennes/IRISA, France
Maguelonne Teisseire	INRAE - UMR Tetis, France
Evimaria Terzi	Boston University, USA
Stefano Teso	University of Trento, Italy
Surendrabikram Thapa	Virginia Tech, USA
Maximilian Thiessen	TU Vienna, Austria
Steffen Thoma	FZI Research Center for Information Technology, Germany
Simon Tihon	Euranova, Belgium
Kai Ming Ting	Nanjing University, China
Abhisek Tiwari	IIT Patna, India
Gabriele Tolomei	Sapienza University of Rome, Italy
Guangmo Tong	University of Delaware, USA
Sunna Torge	TU Dresden, Germany
Giovanni Trappolini	Sapienza University of Rome, Italy
Volker Tresp	Siemens AG/LMU Munich, Germany
Sofia Triantafillou	University of Crete, Greece
Sebastian Trimpe	RWTH Aachen University, Germany
Sebastian Tschiatschek	University of Vienna, Austria
Athena Vakal	Aristotle University of Thessaloniki, Greece
Peter van der Putten	Leiden University, The Netherlands
Fabio Vandin	University of Padua, Italy
Aparna S. Varde	Montclair State University, USA
Julien Velcin	Université Lumière Lyon 2, France
Bruno Veloso	INESC TEC/University of Porto, Portugal
Rosana Veroneze	LBiC, Brazil
Gennaro Vessio	University of Bari, Aldo Moro, Italy
Tiphaine Viard	Télécom Paris, France
Herna L. Viktor	University of Ottawa, Canada

Joao Vinagre	Joint Research Centre - European Commission, Belgium
Jordi Vitria	Universitat de Barcelona, Spain
Jean-Noël Vittaut	LIP6 - CNRS - Sorbonne Université, France
Marco Viviani	University of Milan-Bicocca, Italy
Paola Vocca	Tor Vergata University of Rome, Italy
Tomasz Walkowiak	Wrocław University of Science and Technology, Poland
Ziwen Wan	University of California, Irvine, USA
Beilun Wang	Southeast University, China
Chuan-Ju Wang	Academia Sinica, Taiwan
Deng-Bao Wang	Southeast University, China
Di Wang	KAUST, Saudi Arabia
Dianhui Wang	La Trobe University, Australia
Hongwei Wang	University of Illinois at Urbana-Champaign, USA
Huandong Wang	Tsinghua University, China
Hui (Wendy) Wang	Stevens Institute of Technology, USA
Jiaqi Wang	Penn State University, USA
Puyu Wang	City University of Hong Kong, China
Qing Wang	Australian National University, Australia
Ruijie Wang	University of Illinois at Urbana-Champaign, USA
Senzhang Wang	Central South University, China
Shuo Wang	University of Birmingham, UK
Suhang Wang	Pennsylvania State University, USA
Wei Wang	Fudan University, China
Wenjie Wang	Shanghai Tech University, China
Yanhao Wang	East China Normal University, China
Yimu Wang	University of Waterloo, Canada
Yue Wang	Microsoft Research, USA
Yue Wang	Waymo, USA
Zhaonan Wang	University of Tokyo, Japan
Zhi Wang	Southwest University, China
Zijie J. Wang	Georgia Tech, USA
Roger Wattenhofer	ETH Zurich, Switzerland
Pascal Weber	University of Vienna, Austria
Jörg Wicker	University of Auckland, New Zealand
Michael Wilbur	Vanderbilt University, USA
Weng-Fai Wong	National University of Singapore, Singapore
Bin Wu	Zhengzhou University, China
Chenwang Wu	University of Science and Technology of China, China

Di Wu	Chongqing Institute of Green and Intelligent Technology, CAS, China
Guoqiang Wu	Shandong University, China
Peng Wu	Shanghai Jiao Tong University, China
Xiaotong Wu	Nanjing Normal University, China
Yongkai Wu	Clemson University, USA
Danyang Xiao	Sun Yat-Sen University, China
Zhiwen Xiao	Southwest Jiaotong University, China
Cheng Xie	Yunnan University, China
Hong Xie	Chongqing Institute of Green and Intelligent Technology, CAS, China
Yaqi Xie	Carnegie Mellon University, USA
Huanlai Xing	Southwest Jiaotong University, China
Ning Xu	Southeast University, China
Xiaolong Xu	Nanjing University of Information Science and Technology, China
Hao Xue	University of New South Wales, Australia
Yexiang Xue	Purdue University, USA
Sangeeta Yadav	Indian Institute of Science, India
Qiao Yan	Shenzhen University, China
Yan Yan	Carleton University, Canada
Yu Yan	People's Public Security University of China, China
Yujun Yan	Dartmouth College, USA
Jie Yang	University of Wollongong, Australia
Shaofu Yang	Southeast University, China
Yang Yang	Nanjing University of Science and Technology, China
Liang Yao	Tencent, China
Muchao Ye	Pennsylvania State University, USA
Michael Yeh	Visa Research, USA
Kalidas Yeturu	Indian Institute of Technology Tirupati, India
Hang Yin	University of Copenhagen, Denmark
Hongwei Yong	Hong Kong Polytechnic University, China
Jaemin Yoo	KAIST, South Korea
Mengbo You	Iwate University, Japan
Hang Yu	Shanghai University, China
Weiren Yu	University of Warwick, UK
Wenjian Yu	Tsinghua University, China
Jidong Yuan	Beijing Jiaotong University, China
Aras Yurtman	KU Leuven, Belgium
Claudius Zelenka	Christian-Albrechts University of Kiel, Germany

Akka Zemmari	University of Bordeaux, France
Bonan Zhang	Princeton University, USA
Chao Zhang	Zhejiang University, China
Chuang Zhang	Nanjing University of Science and Technology, China
Danqing Zhang	Amazon, USA
Guoqiang Zhang	University of Technology, Sydney, Australia
Guoxi Zhang	Kyoto University, Japan
Hao Zhang	Fudan University, China
Junbo Zhang	JD Intelligent Cities Research, China
Le Zhang	Baidu Research, China
Ming Zhang	National Key Laboratory of Science and Technology on Information System Security, China
Qiannan Zhang	KAUST, Saudi Arabia
Tianlin Zhang	University of Manchester, UK
Wenbin Zhang	Michigan Tech, USA
Xiang Zhang	National University of Defense Technology, China
Xiao Zhang	Shandong University, China
Xiaoming Zhang	Beihang University, China
Xinyang Zhang	University of Illinois at Urbana-Champaign, USA
Yaying Zhang	Tongji University, China
Yin Zhang	University of Electronic Science and Technology of China, China
Yongqi Zhang	4Paradigm, China
Zhiwen Zhang	University of Tokyo, Japan
Mia Zhao	Airbnb, USA
Sichen Zhao	RMIT University, Australia
Xiaoting Zhao	Etsy, USA
Tongya Zheng	Zhejiang University, China
Wenhao Zheng	Shopee, Singapore
Yu Zheng	Tsinghua University, China
Yujia Zheng	Carnegie Mellon University, USA
Jiang Zhong	Chongqing University, China
Wei Zhou	School of Cyber Security, CAS, China
Zhengyang Zhou	University of Science and Technology of China, China
Chuang Zhu	Beijing University of Posts and Telecommunications, China
Jing Zhu	University of Michigan, USA
Jinjing Zhu	Hong Kong University of Science and Technology, China

Program Committee, Applied Data Science Track

Jingtao Ding	Tsinghua University, China
Kaize Ding	Arizona State University, USA
Manqing Dong	eBay, Australia
Yushun Dong	University of Virginia, USA
Yingtong Dou	University of Illinois, Chicago, USA
Yixiang Fang	Chinese University of Hong Kong, China
Kaiyu Feng	Beijing Institute of Technology, China
Dayne Freitag	SRI International, USA
Yanjie Fu	University of Central Florida, USA
Matteo Gabburo	University of Trento, Italy
Sabrina Gaito	University of Milan, Italy
Chen Gao	Tsinghua University, China
Liangcai Gao	Peking University, China
Yunjun Gao	Zhejiang University, China
Lluis Garcia-Pueyo	Meta, USA
Mariana-Iuliana Georgescu	University of Bucharest, Romania
Aakash Goel	Amazon, USA
Marcos Goncalves	Universidade Federal de Minas Gerais, Brazil
Francesco Guerra	University of Modena e Reggio Emilia, Italy
Huifeng Guo	Huawei Noah's Ark Lab, China
Ruocheng Guo	ByteDance, China
Zhen Hai	Alibaba DAMO Academy, China
Eui-Hong (Sam) Han	The Washington Post, USA
Jinyoung Han	Sungkyunkwan University, South Korea
Shuchu Han	Stellar Cyber, USA
Dongxiao He	Tianjin University, China
Junyuan Hong	Michigan State University, USA
Yupeng Hou	UC San Diego, USA
Binbin Hu	Ant Group, China
Jun Hu	National University of Singapore, Singapore
Hong Huang	Huazhong University of Science and Technology, China
Xin Huang	Hong Kong Baptist University, China
Yizheng Huang	York University, Canada
Yu Huang	University of Florida, USA
Stratis Ioannidis	Northeastern University, USA
Radu Tudor Ionescu	University of Bucharest, Romania
Murium Iqbal	Etsy, USA
Shoaib Jameel	University of Southampton, UK
Jian Kang	University of Rochester, USA
Pinar Karagoz	METU, Turkey
Praveen C. Kolli	Carnegie Mellon University, USA

Deguang Kong	Yahoo Research, USA
Adit Krishnan	University of Illinois at Urbana-Champaign, USA
Mayank Kulkarni	Amazon, USA
Susana Ladra	University of A Coruña, Spain
Renaud Lambiotte	University of Oxford, UK
Tommaso Lanciano	KTH Royal Institute of Technology, Sweden
Md Tahmid Rahman Laskar	Dialpad, Canada
Matthieu Latapy	CNRS, France
Noah Lee	Meta, USA
Wang-Chien Lee	Pennsylvania State University, USA
Chang Li	Apple, USA
Chaozhuo Li	Microsoft Research Asia, China
Daifeng Li	Sun Yat-Sen University, China
Lei Li	Hong Kong University of Science and Technology, China
Shuai Li	University of Cambridge, UK
Xiang Lian	Kent State University, USA
Zhaohui Liang	National Library of Medicine, NIH, USA
Bang Liu	University of Montreal, Canada
Ji Liu	Baidu Research, China
Jingjing Liu	MD Anderson Cancer Center, USA
Tingwen Liu	Institute of Information Engineering, CAS, China
Weiwen Liu	Huawei Noah's Ark Lab, China
Andreas Lommatzsch	TU Berlin, Germany
Jiyun Luo	Pinterest, USA
Ping Luo	CAS, China
Xin Luo	Shandong University, China
Jing Ma	University of Virginia, USA
Xian-Ling Mao	Beijing Institute of Technology, China
Mirko Marras	University of Cagliari, Italy
Zoltan Miklos	Université de Rennes 1, France
Ahmed K. Mohamed	Meta, USA
Mukesh Mohania	IIIT Delhi, India
Corrado Monti	CENTAI, Italy
Sushant More	Amazon, USA
Jose G. Moreno	University of Toulouse, France
Aayush Mudgal	Pinterest, USA
Sepideh Nahali	York University, Canada
Wolfgang Nejdl	L3S Research Center, Germany
Yifan Nie	University of Montreal, Canada
Di Niu	University of Alberta, Canada
Symeon Papadopoulos	CERTH/ITI, Greece

Manos Papagelis	York University, Canada
Leonardo Pellegrina	University of Padua, Italy
Claudia Perlich	TwoSigma, USA
Fabio Pinelli	IMT Lucca, Italy
Giulia Preti	CENTAI, Italy
Buyue Qian	Xi'an Jiaotong University, China
Chuan Qin	BOSS Zhipin, China
Xiao Qin	Amazon Web Services AI/ML, USA
Yanghui Rao	Sun Yat-Sen University, China
Yusuf Sale	LMU Munich, Germany
Eric Sanjuan	Avignon University, France
Maria Luisa Sapino	University of Turin, Italy
Emmanouil Schinas	CERTH/ITI, Greece
Nasrullah Sheikh	IBM Research, USA
Yue Shi	Meta, USA
Gianmaria Silvello	University of Padua, Italy
Yang Song	Apple, USA
Francesca Spezzano	Boise State University, USA
Efstathios Stamatatos	University of the Aegean, Greece
Kostas Stefanidis	Tampere University, Finland
Ting Su	Imperial College London, UK
Munira Syed	Procter & Gamble, USA
Liang Tang	Google, USA
Ruiming Tang	Huawei Noah's Ark Lab, China
Junichi Tatemura	Google, USA
Mingfei Teng	Amazon, USA
Sofia Tolmach	Amazon, Israel
Ismail Hakki Toroslu	METU, Turkey
Kazutoshi Umemoto	University of Tokyo, Japan
Yao Wan	Huazhong University of Science and Technology, China
Chang-Dong Wang	Sun Yat-Sen University, China
Chong Wang	Amazon, USA
Chuan-Ju Wang	Academia Sinica, Taiwan
Hongzhi Wang	Harbin Institute of Technology, China
Kai Wang	Shanghai Jiao Tong University, China
Ning Wang	Beijing Jiaotong University, China
Pengyuan Wang	University of Georgia, USA
Senzhang Wang	Central South University, China
Sheng Wang	Wuhan University, China
Shoujin Wang	Macquarie University, Australia
Wentao Wang	Michigan State University, USA

Yang Wang	University of Science and Technology of China, China
Zhihong Wang	Tsinghua University, China
Zihan Wang	Shandong University, China
Shi-ting Wen	Ningbo Tech University, China
Song Wen	Rutgers University, USA
Zeyi Wen	Hong Kong University of Science and Technology, China
Fangzhao Wu	Microsoft Research Asia, China
Jun Wu	University of Illinois at Urbana-Champaign, USA
Wentao Wu	Microsoft Research, USA
Yanghua Xiao	Fudan University, China
Haoyi Xiong	Baidu, China
Dongkuan Xu	North Carolina State University, USA
Guandong Xu	University of Technology, Sydney, Australia
Shan Xue	Macquarie University, Australia
Le Yan	Google, USA
De-Nian Yang	Academia Sinica, Taiwan
Fan Yang	Rice University, USA
Yu Yang	City University of Hong Kong, China
Fanghua Ye	University College London, UK
Jianhua Yin	Shandong University, China
Yifang Yin	A*STAR-I2R, Singapore
Changlong Yu	Hong Kong University of Science and Technology, China
Dongxiao Yu	Shandong University, China
Ye Yuan	Beijing Institute of Technology, China
Daochen Zha	Rice University, USA
Feng Zhang	Renmin University of China, China
Mengxuan Zhang	University of North Texas, USA
Xianli Zhang	Xi’an Jiaotong University, China
Xuyun Zhang	Macquarie University, Australia
Chen Zhao	Baylor University, USA
Di Zhao	University of Auckland, New Zealand
Yanchang Zhao	CSIRO, Australia
Kaiping Zheng	National University of Singapore, Singapore
Yong Zheng	Illinois Institute of Technology, USA
Jingbo Zhou	Baidu, China
Ming Zhou	University of Technology, Sydney, Australia
Qinghai Zhou	University of Illinois at Urbana-Champaign, USA
Tian Zhou	Alibaba DAMO Academy, China
Xinyi Zhou	University of Washington, USA

Yucheng Zhou	University of Macau, China
Jiangang Zhu	ByteDance, China
Yongchun Zhu	CAS, China
Ziwei Zhu	George Mason University, USA
Jia Zou	Arizona State University, USA

Program Committee, Demo Track

Ferran Diego	Telefonica Research, Spain
Jan Florjanczyk	Netflix, USA
Mikko Heikkila	Telefonica Research, Spain
Jesus Omaña Iglesias	Telefonica Research, Spain
Nicolas Kourtellis	Telefonica Research, Spain
Eduard Marin	Telefonica Research, Spain
Souneil Park	Telefonica Research, Spain
Aravindh Raman	Telefonica Research, Spain
Ashish Rastogi	Netflix, USA
Natali Ruchansky	Netflix, USA
David Solans	Telefonica Research, Spain

Sponsors

Platinum

VOLKSWAGEN GROUP

Gold

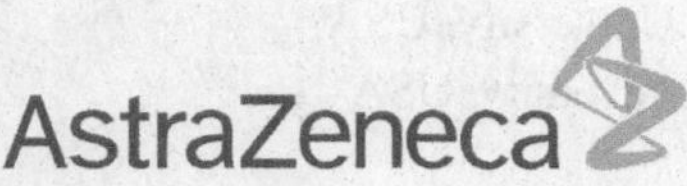

CRITEO

Silver

Google

mercari

Bronze

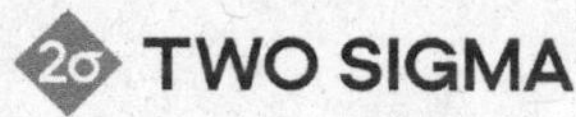

PhD Forum Sponsor

Publishing Partner

Invited Talks Abstracts

Neural Wave Representations

Max Welling

University of Amsterdam, The Netherlands

Abstract. Good neural architectures are rooted in good inductive biases (a.k.a. priors). Equivariance under symmetries is a prime example of a successful physics-inspired prior which sometimes dramatically reduces the number of examples needed to learn predictive models. In this work, we tried to extend this thinking to more flexible priors in the hidden variables of a neural network. In particular, we imposed wavelike dynamics in hidden variables under transformations of the inputs, which relaxes the stricter notion of equivariance. We find that under certain conditions, wavelike dynamics naturally arises in these hidden representations. We formalize this idea in a VAE-over-time architecture where the hidden dynamics is described by a Fokker-Planck (a.k.a. drift-diffusion) equation. This in turn leads to a new definition of a disentangled hidden representation of input states that can easily be manipulated to undergo transformations. I also discussed very preliminary work on how the Schrödinger equation can also be used to move information in the hidden representations.

Biography. Prof. Dr. Max Welling is a research chair in Machine Learning at the University of Amsterdam and a Distinguished Scientist at MSR. He is a fellow at the Canadian Institute for Advanced Research (CIFAR) and the European Lab for Learning and Intelligent Systems (ELLIS) where he also serves on the founding board. His previous appointments include VP at Qualcomm Technologies, professor at UC Irvine, postdoc at the University of Toronto and UCL under the supervision of Prof. Geoffrey Hinton, and postdoc at Caltech under the supervision of Prof. Pietro Perona. He finished his PhD in theoretical high energy physics under the supervision of Nobel laureate Prof. Gerard 't Hooft. Max Welling served as associate editor-in-chief of IEEE TPAMI from 2011–2015, he has served on the advisory board of the NeurIPS Foundation since 2015 and was program chair and general chair of NeurIPS in 2013 and 2014 respectively. He was also program chair of AISTATS in 2009 and ECCV in 2016 and general chair of MIDL in 2018. Max Welling was a recipient of the ECCV Koenderink Prize in 2010 and the ICML Test of Time Award in 2021. He directs the Amsterdam Machine Learning Lab (AMLAB) and co-directs the Qualcomm-UvA deep learning lab (QUVA) and the Bosch-UvA Deep Learning lab (DELTA).

Physics-Inspired Graph Neural Networks

Michael Bronstein

University of Oxford, UK

Abstract. The message-passing paradigm has been the "battle horse" of deep learning on graphs for several years, making graph neural networks a big success in a wide range of applications, from particle physics to protein design. From a theoretical viewpoint, it established the link to the Weisfeiler-Lehman hierarchy, allowing us to analyse the expressive power of GNNs. We argue that the very "node-and-edge"-centric mindset of current graph deep learning schemes may hinder future progress in the field. As an alternative, we propose physics-inspired "continuous" learning models that open up a new trove of tools from the fields of differential geometry, algebraic topology, and differential equations so far largely unexplored in graph ML.

Biography. Michael Bronstein is the DeepMind Professor of AI at the University of Oxford. He was previously a professor at Imperial College London and held visiting appointments at Stanford, MIT, and Harvard, and has also been affiliated with three Institutes for Advanced Study (at TUM as a Rudolf Diesel Fellow (2017–2019), at Harvard as a Radcliffe fellow (2017–2018), and at Princeton as a short-time scholar (2020)). Michael received his PhD from the Technion in 2007. He is the recipient of the Royal Society Wolfson Research Merit Award, Royal Academy of Engineering Silver Medal, five ERC grants, two Google Faculty Research Awards, and two Amazon AWS ML Research Awards. He is a Member of the Academia Europaea, Fellow of the IEEE, IAPR, BCS, and ELLIS, ACM Distinguished Speaker, and World Economic Forum Young Scientist. In addition to his academic career, Michael is a serial entrepreneur and founder of multiple startup companies, including Novafora, Invision (acquired by Intel in 2012), Videocites, and Fabula AI (acquired by Twitter in 2019).

Physics-Informed Graph Neural Networks

Michael Bronstein

Mapping Generative AI

Kate Crawford

USC Annenberg, USA

Abstract. Training data is foundational to generative AI systems. From Common Crawl's 3.1 billion web pages to LAION-5B's corpus of almost 6 billion image-text pairs, these vast collections – scraped from the internet and treated as "ground truth" – play a critical role in shaping the epistemic boundaries that govern generative AI models. Yet training data is beset with complex social, political, and epistemological challenges. What happens when data is stripped of context, meaning, and provenance? How does training data limit what and how machine learning systems interpret the world? What are the copyright implications of these datasets? And most importantly, what forms of power do these approaches enhance and enable? This keynote is an invitation to reflect on the epistemic foundations of generative AI, and to consider the wide-ranging impacts of the current generative turn.

Biography. Professor Kate Crawford is a leading international scholar of the social implications of artificial intelligence. She is a Research Professor at USC Annenberg in Los Angeles, a Senior Principal Researcher at MSR in New York, an Honorary Professor at the University of Sydney, and the inaugural Visiting Chair for AI and Justice at the École Normale Supérieure in Paris. Her latest book, *Atlas of AI* (Yale, 2021) won the Sally Hacker Prize from the Society for the History of Technology, the ASIS&T Best Information Science Book Award, and was named one of the best books in 2021 by *New Scientist* and the *Financial Times*. Over her twenty-year research career, she has also produced groundbreaking creative collaborations and visual investigations. Her project *Anatomy of an AI System* with Vladan Joler is in the permanent collection of the Museum of Modern Art in New York and the V&A in London, and was awarded with the Design of the Year Award in 2019 and included in the Design of the Decades by the Design Museum of London. Her collaboration with the artist Trevor Paglen, *Excavating AI*, won the Ayrton Prize from the British Society for the History of Science. She has advised policymakers in the United Nations, the White House, and the European Parliament, and she currently leads the Knowing Machines Project, an international research collaboration that investigates the foundations of machine learning.

Contents – Part V

Robustness

Time Series

Robustness

MMA: Multi-Metric-Autoencoder for Analyzing High-Dimensional and Incomplete Data

Cheng Liang[1], Di Wu[2(✉)], Yi He[3], Teng Huang[1], Zhong Chen[4], and Xin Luo[2]

[1] Institute of Artificial Intelligence and Blockchain, Guangzhou University, Guangzhou 510006, China
c_liang@e.gzhu.edu.cn,huangteng1220@gzhu.edu.cn

[2] College of Computer and Information Science, Southwest University, Chongqing 400715, China
wudi.cigit@gmail.com

[3] Department of Computer Science, Old Dominion University, Norfolk, VA 23529, USA
yihe@cs.odu.edu

[4] Department of Computer Science, Xavier University of Louisiana, New Orleans, LA 70125, USA
zchen@xula.edu

Abstract. High-dimensional and incomplete (HDI) data usually arise in various complex applications, e.g., bioinformatics and recommender systems, making them commonly heterogeneous and inclusive. Deep neural networks (DNNs)-based approaches have provided state-of-the-art representation learning performance on HDI data. However, most prior studies adopt fixed and exclusive L_2-norm-oriented *loss* and *regularization* terms. Such a single-metric-oriented model yields limited performance on heterogeneous and inclusive HDI data. Motivated by this, we propose a Multi-Metric-Autoencoder (MMA) whose main ideas are two-fold: 1) employing different L_p-norms to build four variant Autoencoders, each of which resides in a unique metric representation space with different *loss* and *regularization* terms, and 2) aggregating these Autoencoders with a tailored, self-adaptive weighting strategy. Theoretical analysis guarantees that our MMA could attain a better representation from a set of dispersed metric spaces. Extensive experiments on four real-world datasets demonstrate that our MMA significantly outperforms seven state-of-the-art models. Our code is available at the link https://github.com/wudi1989/MMA/

Keywords: Data Science · High-dimensional and Sparse Matrices · Deep Neural Network-based Representation · Matrix Representation · Multi-Metric Modeling

This work is supported by the National Natural Science Foundation of China under grant 62176070.

D. Koutra et al. (Eds.): ECML PKDD 2023, LNAI 14173, pp. 3–19, 2023.
https://doi.org/10.1007/978-3-031-43424-2_1

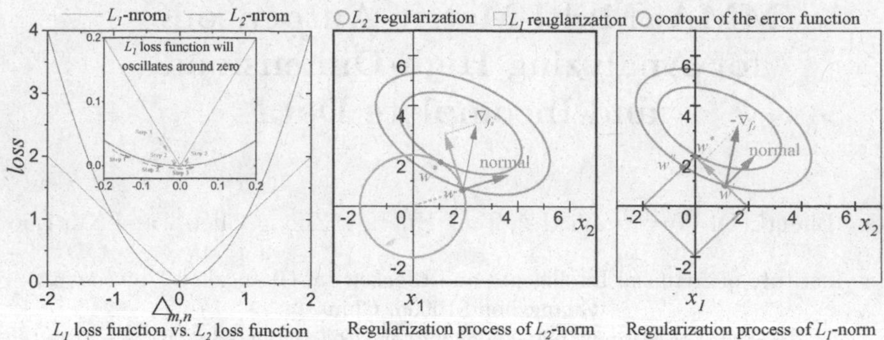

Fig. 1. An example of L_p-norms as *loss* function and *regularization*. The orange/blue/green arrow represents the *regularization*'s normal/gradient/real update direction at the current parameter position w', and w^* is the optimal parameter.

1 Introduction

Matrices are commonly adopted to describe pairwise relationships between entities with a wide range of application scenarios, such as bioinformatics [15], industrial manufacturing [1], and recommendation system (RS) [8,14,32] to mention a few. For instance, the user-item matrix is usually used to record users' behaviors interacting with different items in online shopping systems [35]. Typically, the rows/columns of the user-item matrix represent users/items, and the entries record the results of their interactions.

The core of analyzing and representing these data matrices lies in handling their high-dimensional and incomplete (HDI) characteristics [20,22,47] that conceptually and basically exist in real application scenarios. For example, an RS usually has a large number of items that a user cannot fully access, leaving the user behavior data to be highly incomplete [13,31]. Moreover, the different types of interactions and systems mold the diversity of data matrices. Hence, well-designed methods are desired to represent HDI matrices for excavating hidden patterns and knowledge [3,21,43].

With the rapid development of deep learning, deep neural network (DNNs) has been widely adopted for analyzing HDI matrix [32] and provided state-of-the-art representation performance. Despite their success, they share the same essence: their *loss* and *regularization* terms are exclusive and fixed, i.e., they are a single-metric-oriented model. However, the real-world HDI data are heterogeneous and diversified with various underlying properties [2,33], manifesting the limitations of such single-metric-oriented model [19,42]. A brief example is provided in Fig 1 to discuss the differences of L_p-norms as *loss* function and *regularization*, respectively.

- **Difference between L_p-norms as *loss* function.** Let $\triangle_{j,k} = x_{j,k} - \hat{x}_{j,k}$ denotes the distance between the ground truth and the prediction, L_1-norm-oriented *loss* is $l(\triangle_{j,k}) = \|\triangle_{j,k}\|_{L_1}$, and L_2-norm-oriented *loss* is $l(\triangle_{j,k}) =$

$\|\triangle_{j,k}\|_{L_2}^2$ (left panel of Fig 1). The significant differences between them are three-fold: 1) Robustness. L_2-norm-oriented *loss* is more sensitive to errors, making it less robust than L_1-norm-oriented *loss* to the outliers; 2) Stability. Since L_1-norm-oriented *loss* has vertices causing the gradient of L_1-norm-oriented *loss* oscillates around zero, while L_2-norm-oriented is smooth, so the *loss* is stable; 3) Uniqueness of solution. There are multi-solution of L_1-norm-oriented *loss* in high dimensional space, while L_2-norm-oriented *loss* has a unique solution.

- **Difference between L_p-norms as *regularization*.** Regularization is used to prevent overfitting. Let L_1-norm regularization be $r(w_i) = \|w_i\|_{L_1}$, and L_2-norm regularization be $r(w_i) = \|w_i\|_{L_2}^2$, as shown in the middle and right panels of Fig. 1. Their major difference is their contour shape, i.e., L_1-norm regularization's contour shape is a rectangle, while L_2-norm regularization is a circle. Then, they have two-fold different consequences: 1) Sparse parameters. The updating process of L_1-norm regularization is mostly stopped at its vertices, resulting in the regularized parameters being mostly zero, providing a feature selection effect. 2) Fine representation. The parameters regularized by L_2-norm are mostly non-zero, which can fine-tune the value of parameters for a better representation.

We offer an affirmative answer by proposing a Multi-Metric-Autoencoder (MMA) with a two-fold main idea: 1) employing different L_p-norms to build four variant Autoencoders, each of which resides in a unique metric space with distinct *loss* and *regularization* terms, and 2) aggregating these Autoencoders with a tailored, self-adaptive weighting strategy. By doing so, the proposed MMA enjoys a better multi-metric-based learning ability, achieving non-biased and comprehensive representations of HDI data. This paper has the following contributions:

- It first proposes to exploit a multi-metric strategy to boost a DNNs-based model's representation learning ability on the HDI matrix.
- It proposes a Multi-Metric-Autoencoder (MMA) that can accurately represent an HDI matrix by ensembling four variant Autoencoders built with different L_p-norms.
- Empirical studies verify that the proposed MMA can aggregate the merits from disparate metric spaces with different L_p-norms.
- Algorithm design and comprehensive analyses are provided for the proposed MMA.

Experimental results on four real-world benchmark datasets demonstrate that the proposed MMA significantly outperforms both non-DNN-based and DNN-based single-metric state-of-the-art models.

2 Related Work

2.1 LFA-Based Model

Latent factor analysis-based (LFA-based) models are widely used to represent HDI matrices [10,44]. However, prior works have mainly used only one fixed *loss* function or *regularization* to train their models. Examples include matrix factorization based [37], generalized non-negative with momentum-based [24], linked open data-based [26], dual regularization based [29], mapreduce-based [11], and generalized nesterov-based [23] to name a few. Although the L_2 *loss* function has been shown to be more sensitive to outliers but stable during training [34], the L_1 *loss* function is more robust to outliers but unstable during training [18], and L_1 *regularization* contains the built-in feature selection characterize [18]. Hence, LFA-based representation methods trained under different L_p-norms have been proposed, including elastic-net regression regularize-based [28], and smooth L_1-norm-oriented [40]. However, these studies are built on the linear MF model, and they only discuss different metrics on *loss* function while ignoring the *regularization*. Thus, there is currently a lack of discussion on multi-metric DNN-based HDI matrix representation methods built on different L_p-norms.

2.2 Deep Learning-Based Model

The recent development of deep learning has led to the widespread use of deep learning-based models for representing HDI data, owing to their ability to learn highly non-linear representations [38,41,47]. Comprehensive reviews of recent DNN-based HDI matrix representation methods have been conducted by some researchers [47]. Among these methods, one of the representative methods is autoencoder-based [30], which has inspired the development of variational autoencoder-based methods [6], kernelized synaptic-based autoencoder [25] and global and Local Kernels-based autoencoder [9]. Other notable research includes neural rating regression-based [17], unsupervised disentangle representation [39], unsupervised hyperbolic representation [27], and dual metric learning-based [36]. In addition, GNN-based representation methods [7,12] have also been proposed for representing HDI data, such as inductive matrix completion-based methods [45].

Compared to the aforementioned methods, MMA holds the following significance: 1) DNN-based models possess greater data representation capabilities owing to their nonlinear features compared to LFA-based models; 2) DNN-based models do not require complex graph data in contrast to GNN-based models, resulting in lower computational resource consumption; 3) To the best of our knowledge, MMA is the first work to investigate the performance of multi-metrics-oriented DNN-based models regarding representing HDI data. Section 3 of the paper presents numerical experiments and comparisons with state-of-the-art models, demonstrating the superior performance of the proposed MMA.

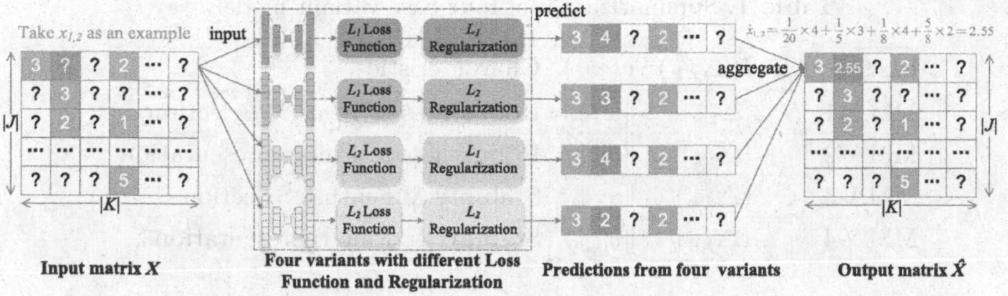

Fig. 2. The architecture and predicting process of the proposed MMA

3 Methodology

To aggregate the advantages of different L_p-norm, we propose the MMA model. Figure 2 demonstrates the architecture and predicting process of MMA, which can be divided into two parts: 1) Utilization of the observed entries of X to train four variant models with independent parameters and predict the unobserved entries; 2) Ensemble these predictions with a tailored self-adaptive weighting strategy to obtain the final output. The establishment of the variant, the self-adaptively weighting strategy, and the theoretical analysis are depicted in the following contents.

3.1 Establishment of Base Model

We choose the representative I-AutoRec [30] to be the basic model in this paper. Formally, given a vector $\mathbf{x}^{(k)} \in X$, I-AutoRec completes the unknown entities by excavating the hidden pattern from known entries. Its error function $\mathcal{L}(\cdot)$ is:

$$\mathcal{L}(f) = \sum_{\mathbf{x}^{(k)} \in X} \left\| \left(\mathbf{x}^{(k)} - f\left(\mathbf{x}^{(k)}; \theta\right)\right) \odot \mathbf{m}^{(k)} \right\|_{L_2}^2 + \frac{\lambda}{2} \cdot \sum_{i \in I} \|w_i\|_{L_2}^2, \qquad (1)$$

where $\lambda > 0$ is the *regularization* factor, $\theta = \{w_i, b_i\}(i \in (1, 2, \cdots, I)$ denotes the weighted term and bias term of i_{th} hidden layer, $\|\cdot\|_{L_2}^2$ is the square of L_2-norm, $\odot$ represents the Hadamard product, and vector $\mathbf{x}^{(k)} = \{x_{1,k}, \cdots, x_{|J|,k}\}$ of k column of X, $\mathbf{m}^{(k)}$ is the k_{th} column of index matrix M for I-AutoRec in which $m_{j,k}$ records whether $x_{j,k}$ is observed, $m_{j,k} = 1$ if there is, $m_{j,k} = 0$ otherwise.

We employ different L_p-norms in *loss* function $l(\cdot)$ and *regularization* $r(\cdot)$ to establish four base variant models summarized in Table 1.

MMA-1 (L_1 *loss* function and L_1 *Regularization*). The objective function for MMA-1 to minimize is as follows:

$$\mathcal{L}^1(f) = \sum_{\mathbf{x}^{(k)} \in X} \left\| \left(\mathbf{x}^{(k)} - f^1\left(\mathbf{x}^{(k)}; \theta\right)\right) \odot \mathbf{m}^{(k)} \right\|_{L_1} + \frac{\lambda}{2} \cdot \sum_{i \in I} \|w_i\|_{L_1}. \qquad (2)$$

Table 1. Summarization of four base variant models

base models	$l(\triangle_{j,k})$	$r(w_i)$	Characteristic
MMA-1	$\|\triangle_{j,k}\|$	$\|w_i\|_1$	Robustness & Feature Selection
MMA-2	$\|\triangle_{j,k}\|$	$\|w_i\|_2^2$	Robustness & Fine representation
MMA-3	$(\triangle_{j,k})^2$	$\|w_i\|_1$	Stability & Feature Selection
MMA-4	$(\triangle_{j,k})^2$	$\|w_i\|_2^2$	Stability & Fine representation

MMA-2 (L_1 *loss* function and L_2 *Regularization*). The objective function for MMA-2 to minimize is as follows:

$$\mathcal{L}^2(f) = \sum_{\mathbf{x}^{(k)} \in X} \left\| \left(\mathbf{x}^{(k)} - f^2\left(\mathbf{x}^{(k)}; \theta\right)\right) \odot \mathbf{m}^{(k)} \right\|_{L_1} + \frac{\lambda}{2} \cdot \sum_{i \in I} \|w_i\|_{L_2}^2. \tag{3}$$

MMA-3 (L_2 *loss* function and L_1 *Regularization*). The objective function for MMA-3 to minimize is as follows:

$$\mathcal{L}^3(f) = \sum_{\mathbf{x}^{(k)} \in X} \left\| \left(\mathbf{x}^{(k)} - f^3\left(\mathbf{x}^{(k)}; \theta\right)\right) \odot \mathbf{m}^{(k)} \right\|_{L_2}^2 + \frac{\lambda}{2} \cdot \sum_{i \in I} \|w_1\|_{L_1}. \tag{4}$$

MMA-4 (L_2 *loss* function and L_2 *Regularization*). The objective function for MMA-4 to minimize is as follows:

$$\mathcal{L}^4(f) = \sum_{\mathbf{x}^{(k)} \in X} \left\| \left(\mathbf{x}^{(k)} - f^4\left(\mathbf{x}^{(k)}; \theta\right)\right) \odot \mathbf{m}^{(k)} \right\|_{L_2}^2 + \frac{\lambda}{2} \cdot \sum_{i \in I} \|w_1\|_{L_2}^2. \tag{5}$$

3.2 Self-Adaptively Aggregation

Ensemble learning is an excellent method for aggregating multi-models. It requires the base model to be diversified and accurate. The usage of different L_p-norm guarantees diversity. And the representative I-AutoRec guarantees accuracy. Thus, the base models satisfy the two requirements of the ensemble. We adopt the self-adaptively aggregation method in the validation set according to their *loss*. The principle of this idea is to increase the weight of the t_{th} base model if its *loss* decreases in the n_{th} training iteration or reduce its weight otherwise. We present the related definitions to explain the theoretical analysis better.

Definition 1 (Separate *Loss* of Base Models). We use $Sl^t(n)$ to denote the separate *loss* of the t_{th} base model at n_{th} iteration, which can be computed as follows:

$$Sl^t(n) = \sqrt{\sum_{j \in J, k \in K, (J,K \in \Gamma)} \left(\left(x_{j,k} - \hat{x}_{j,k}^t\right) \times m_{j,k}\right)^2 / \|\Gamma\|_0}$$
$$\hat{x}_{j,k}^t = f^t(j,k;\theta) \qquad \text{s.t.} \;\; t = 1,2,3,4, \tag{6}$$

where $\|\cdot\|_0$ represents the L_0-norm of a matrix which indicates the number of non-zero elements in it, and Γ denotes the validation subset of X.

Definition 2 (Accumulative *Loss* of Base Models). The accumulative *loss* $Al^t(n)$ of Sl^t until n_{th} training iteration can be computed as follows:

$$Al^t(n) = \sum_{h=1}^{n} Sl^t(h). \tag{7}$$

Definition 3 (Ensemble Weight of Base Models). The ensemble weight ε^t of the t_{th} base model can be calculated as follows:

$$\varepsilon^t(n) = \frac{e^{-\delta Al^t(n)}}{\sum_{t=1}^{4} e^{-\delta Al^t(n)}}, \tag{8}$$

where δ is the equilibrium factor that controls the ensemble aggregation weights during the training process. Based on Definitions 1–3, the final prediction of MMA in n_{th} training iteration can be represented as follows:

$$\hat{x}_{j,k} = \sum_{t=1}^{4} \varepsilon^t(n)\hat{x}^t_{j,k}. \tag{9}$$

3.3 Theoretical Analysis

Definition 4 (Separate *Loss* of MMA). We use $Sl(n)$ to represent the *loss* of MMA at n_{th} training iteration, which is computed as follows:

$$Sl(n) = \sqrt{\sum_{j\in J,k\in K,(J,K\in\Gamma)} ((x_{j,k} - \hat{x}_{j,k}) \times m_{j,k})^2 / \|\Gamma\|_0}. \tag{10}$$

where $\hat{x}_{j,k}$ is calculated by align (9).

Definition 5 (Accumulative *Loss* of MMA). The accumulative *loss* of MMA can be represented as follows:

$$Al(n) = \sum_{h=1}^{n} Sl(h). \tag{11}$$

Theorem 1. *Given an MMA model, supposing the $Al^t(n)$ of base models lies between [0,1]. If $\varepsilon^t(n)$ sets as align (8) during the training, then the following align holds:*

$$Al(N) \leq \min\{Al^t(N) \mid t = 1,2,3,4\} + \frac{\ln 4}{\delta} + \frac{\delta N}{8}, \tag{12}$$

where N is the maximum iteration.

By setting $\delta = \sqrt{1/\ln N}$ of *Theorem* 1, the upper bound becomes:

$$Al(N) \leq \min\{Al^t(N) \mid t = 1,2,3,4\} + \ln 4\sqrt{\ln N} + \frac{N}{8\sqrt{\ln N}}, \tag{13}$$

where $\ln 4\sqrt{\ln N} + \frac{N}{8\sqrt{\ln N}}$ is bound by N linearly. Then we have the following proposition.

Proposition 1. *Gvien* $\delta = \frac{1}{\sqrt{\ln N}}$ *the inequality holds:*

$$Al(N) \leq \min\{Al^t(N) \mid t = 1,2,3,4\} + const, \tag{14}$$

where $\lim_{N\to\infty} const = 19.45$.

Remark 1. **Proposition** 1 indicates that $Al(N)$ is constrained by $\min\{Al^t(N) \mid t = 1,2,3,4\} + const$ with $\delta = \sqrt{1/\ln N}$. Remarkably, each base variant with different L_p-norms as *loss* function and *regularization* leave them to enjoy separate metric space. The ensemble weight in align (8) guarantees that the MMA's *loss* is always lesser than that of the base models, empowering it to have multi-metric orientation from different L_p-norms. In addition, **Proposition** 1 is not intended to demonstrate the accuracy improvement of MMA on the test set, but rather to establish that the model possesses the advantages of the basic models. By showing that the proposed model achieves a smaller loss compared to each individual basic model used separately, it indicates that the model retains the respective strengths of the basic models without compromising its ability to fit the data.

4 Experiments

In this session, the subsequent experiments are aimed at answering the following research questions (RQs):

- RQ. 1. Does the proposed MMA outperform state-of-the-art models in representing the original and outlier-added HDI matrix?
- RQ. 2. How does the MMA self-adaptively control the ensemble weights of its based models during the training process to guarantee performance?
- RQ. 3. Are the base models of MMA diversified in representing the identical HDI matrix to ensure better performance of MMA?

4.1 General Settings

Datasets. Four commonly used real-world HDI datasets are collected to conduct the subsequent experiments. The details of these datasets are summarized in Table 2. These HDI matrix datasets include MovieLens_1M (D1), MovieLens_100k (D2), MovieLens_HetRec (D3), and Yahoo (D4). We adopt a 70%-10%-20% train-validate-test division ratio for all datasets in all experiments involved.

Table 2. Properties of all the datasets.

No.	Name	|M|	|N|	H_o	Density*
D1	MovieLens_1M	6040	3952	1 000 209	4.19%
D2	MovieLens_100k	943	1682	100 000	6.30%
D3	MovieLens_HetRec	2113	10 109	855 598	4.01%
D4	Yahoo	15 400	1000	365 704	2.37%

* Density denotes the percentage of observed entries in the user-item matrix.

Evaluation Metrics. The primary purpose of representing the HDI matrix is to predict its missing entries. To evaluate the representation's accuracy of the tested model, we adopt the root mean square error (RMSE) and mean absolute error (MAE) as the evaluation metrics according to [40,42]. In addition, we have adopted commonly used metrics in recommendation systems, namely Normalized Discounted Cumulative Gain (NDCG) and Hit Ratio to evaluate the performance of our proposed model in the specific task of ranking prediction. To calculate NDCG and Hit Ratio, We select k items that users like (with ratings greater than or equal to 4) as positive samples and pair them with 100 negative samples (with ratings lower than 4). If a positive sample ranks within the top k in the recommendation list, it is considered a hit. The NDCG calculation formula is $NDCG_{u,i} = 1/(log2(rank_{u,i} + 1))$. By calculating the average metric values of positive samples for each user, we obtain the NDCG and Hit Ratio results.

Baselines. The proposed MMA model is compared with seven state-of-the-art HDI data representation models, including one original model AutoRec [30], two Latent factor analysis-based (LFA-based) models MF [16] and FML [46], and four DNN-based models NRR [17], SparseFC [25], IGMC [45], and GLocal-K [9]. Table 3 briefly describes these competitors.

Implementation Details. The hyper-parameters of all the models involved are fine-tuned to achieve optimal performance. Expressly, we set the regularization coefficient of MMA-1 and MMA-2 to 0.01 and that of MMA-3 and MMA-4 to 30 to get a comprehensive high-performance MMA to all datasets. And the learning rate of all variants is set to 0.001 for a better representation performance. The final testing result is output by the optimal model that reaches the lowest prediction error in the validation set during the training process. The training procedure of a model will terminate if its training iterations reach the preset threshold, and all the experiments are conducted on a GPU server with two 2.4 GHz Xeon Gold 6240R with 24 cores, 376.40 GB RAM, and 4 T V100 GPU.

4.2 Performance Comparison (RQ.1)

Comparison of Missing Entries Prediction. Table 4 records the prediction accuracy of all models involved in D1 to D4. The statistical analysis of the loss/tie/win, the Wilcoxon signed-ranks test [4], and the Friedman test [4] are

Table 3. Descriptions of all the contrasting models.

Model	Description
MF [16]	The representative LFA-based model factorizes the HDI matrix for data representation. *Computer 2009.*
AutoRec [30]	The representative autoencoder-based model encodes HDI data into low-dimension representation and decodes them to finish the prediction. *WWW 2015.*
NRR [17]	It is a DNN-based multi-task learning framework for HDI data representation. *SIGIR 2017.*
SparceFC [25]	A DNN-based model parametrizes the weighted matrices into low-dimensional vectors to capture essential features of the HDI matrices. *ICML 2018.*
IGMC [45]	It is a GNN-based model which can excavate hidden patterns from graphs built from a HDI matrix without using side information. *ICLR 2020.*
FML [46]	An LFA-based model combines metric learning (distance space) with collaborative filtering. *IEEE TII 2020.*
GLocal-K [9]	A DNN-based model generalizes and represents user behavior data into a low-dimensional space with the fine-tuned global kernel. *CIKM 2021*

Table 4. The comparison of the prediction accuracy of MMA and its competitors, including the loss/tie/win counts, Wilcoxon signed-ranks test, and Friedman test.

Dataset	Metric	MF	AutoRec	NRR	SparseFC	IGMC	FML	Glocal-K	MMA (ours)
D1	RMSE	0.857•	0.847•	0.881•	0.839∘	0.867•	0.849•	0.839∘	0.840
	MAE	0.673•	0.667•	0.691•	0.656	0.681•	0.667•	0.655∘	0.656
D2	RMSE	0.913•	0.897•	0.923•	0.899•	0.915•	0.904•	0.892•	0.889
	MAE	0.719•	0.706•	0.725•	0.706•	0.722•	0.718•	0.697•	0.695
D3	RMSE	0.757•	0.752•	0.774•	0.749•	0.769•	0.754•	0.756•	0.744
	MAE	0.572•	0.569•	0.583•	0.567•	0.582•	0.573•	0.573•	0.561
D4	RMSE	1.206•	1.172•	1.227•	1.203•	1.133∘	1.176•	1.204•	1.163
	MAE	0.937•	0.900•	0.949•	0.915•	0.848∘	0.937•	0.905•	0.879
Statistic	loss/tie/win	0/0/8	0/0/8	0/0/8	1/1/6	2/0/6	0/0/8	2/0/6	**5/1/50***
	p-value	0.006	0.006	0.005	0.014	0.018	0.006	0.018	-
	F-rank	5.938	3.375	8.0	3.188	5.5	4.938	3.375	**1.688**

*The total loss/tie/win cases of MMA. • The cases that MMA wins the other models in comparison. ∘ The cases that MMA loses the comparison.

made to analyze these results better. These results are presented in the third-to-last, second-to-last, and last row of Table 4. From Table 4, we observe that MMA achieves the lowest RMSE/MAE in most cases, and the total loss/tie/win cases are 5/1/50. Its p-value is lower than the significance level of 0.05 and achieves the lowest F-rank among all the participants. These observations reveal that MMA achieves a better representation accuracy for the HDI matrix than other models.

Comparison of Ranking Prediction. We have also conducted statistical analysis on the results of NDCG and Hit Ratio and recorded them in Table 5.

Table 5. The NDCG and Hit Ratio of MMA and its competitors.

Dataset	Metric	MF	AutoRec	NRR	SparseFC	IGMC	FML	Glocal-K	MMA (ours)
D1	NDCG@5	0.550•	0.551•	0.520•	0.565○	0.532•	0.563•	0.567○	0.564
	Hit@5	0.746•	0.749•	0.717•	0.758	0.728•	0.755•	0.758	0.758
	NDCG@10	0.599•	0.602•	0.568•	0.608	0.571•	0.606•	0.608	0.608
	Hit@10	0.883•	0.887•	0.866•	0.892○	0.875•	0.887•	0.891○	0.890
D2	NDCG@5	0.529•	0.542•	0.509•	0.541•	0.519•	0.541•	0.548•	0.559
	Hit@5	0.738•	0.742•	0.717•	0.750•	0.730•	0.744•	0.761•	0.761
	NDCG@10	0.579•	0.593•	0.564•	0.592•	0.568•	0.592•	0.595•	0.608
	Hit@10	0.892•	0.897•	0.886•	0.904•	0.889•	0.899•	0.904•	0.911
D3	NDCG@5	0.479•	0.483•	0.455•	0.491•	0.461•	0.486•	0.473•	0.493
	Hit@5	0.645•	0.648•	0.623•	0.660•	0.631•	0.651•	0.644•	0.662
	NDCG@10	0.526•	0.529•	0.504•	0.540•	0.511•	0.532•	0.520•	0.542
	Hit@10	0.789•	0.791•	0.773•	0.800•	0.779•	0.794•	0.790•	0.802
D4	NDCG@5	0.526•	0.574•	0.520•	0.558•	0.612○	0.580•	0.552•	0.603
	Hit@5	0.789•	0.802•	0.764•	0.794•	0.835○	0.807•	0.795•	0.828
	NDCG@10	0.549•	0.628•	0.578•	0.612•	0.659○	0.631•	0.608•	0.651
	Hit@10	0.784•	0.960•	0.942•	0.958•	0.979○	0.961•	0.966•	0.973
Statistic	loss/tie/win	0/0/16	0/0/16	0/0/16	2/2/12	4/0/12	0/0/16	2/2/12	**8/4/100***
	p-value	0.002	0.0002	0.0002	0.0014	0.0013	0.0278	0.0015	-
	F-rank	5.938	3.969	7.563	3.094	5.438	4.844	3.375	**1.781**

* The total loss/tie/win cases of MMA. • The cases that MMA wins the other models in comparison. ○ The cases that MMA loses the comparison.

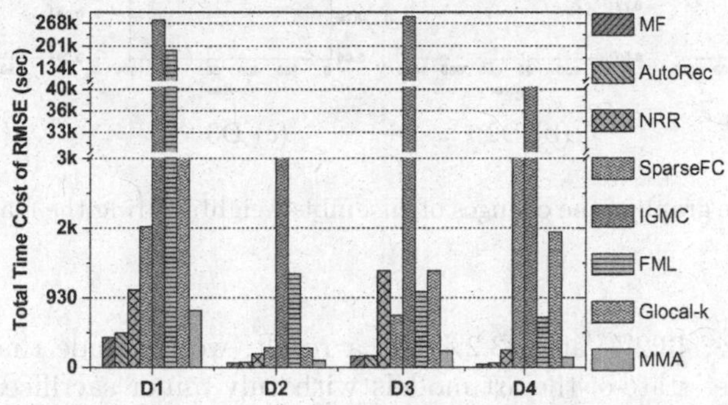

Fig. 3. The histogram graph of the total time cost to reach the optimal accuracy of all the participating models.

From the results in Table 5, we can observe that our proposed model outperforms other comparison methods in most cases, with a final score of 8/4/100 in terms of loss/tie/win. Moreover, the p-values are below the significant value of 0.05, and MMA also reaches the lowest F-rank.

Comparison of Computational Efficiency. Figure 3 displays the total time all models require to reach the optimal RMSE on the validation set. As shown in Fig. 3, LFA-based models are more efficient than DNN-based models as they only train on observed data. Additionally, due to its complex data form and architecture, the GNN-based model consumes significant computational resources and time. Our proposed MMA is with acceptable time consumption, which lands between the LFA-based and GNN-based models. Compared to the original model, MMA's growth time mainly focuses on calculating ensemble weights since its basic model is trained in parallel. The time ratios for D1 to D4 growth

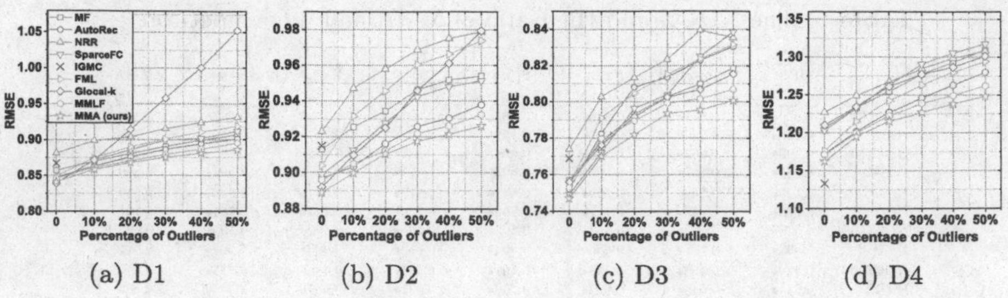

Fig. 4. The robustness testing results under the RMSE metric of MMA and its competitors.

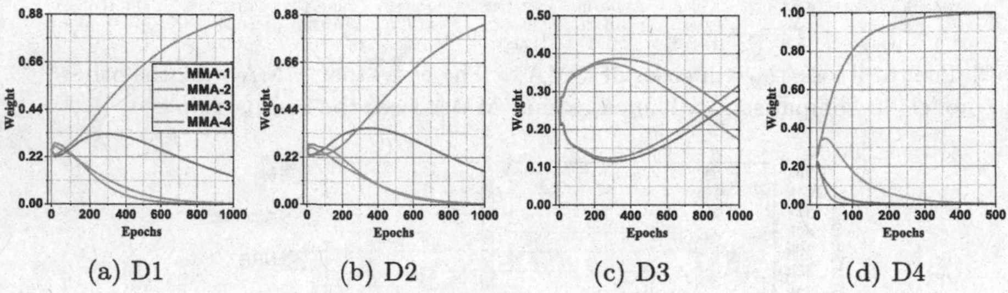

Fig. 5. The curve graph of the changes of ensemble weights during the training process.

are: 64%, 37.5%, 43.2%, and 43.2%. As a result, we conclude that MMA can outperform other state-of-the-art models with only minor sacrifices in terms of computational resources and time.

Robustness of MMA to Outlier Data. As previously discussed, the L_1 *loss* function has been shown to be more robust to outlier data. To investigate if MMA can inherit this robustness from the ensemble, we compare its accuracy on datasets with 10% to 50% outliers added, which includes two steps: 1) Select 10% to 50% of the known entries from the original dataset, and 2) randomly assign maximum or minimum known value to these entries. In reality, HDI matrices often contain various outliers that can impair the accuracy of the representation, making robustness an important evaluation indicator for HDI data representation.

Figure 4 records the accuracy of different models' RMSE on D1 to D4 and Fig. IGMC's computational efficiency is limited due to its time-consuming graph construction and operations, as evidenced by the over 70 h running the original data set (Fig. 3). With increasing noise and data set size, its performance further deteriorates. We omit its results after a five-day failed run. Figure 4 and Fig. S2 show that MMA outperforms its competitors in all cases, e.g., on D1 with 50% outliers, MMA's RMSE/MAE is 0.886/0.691, while most other models are above 0.9/0.7, indicating that it benefits from different metrics to obtain robustness.

Table 6. The comparison of the prediction accuracy of MMA and its base models with statistical analysis.

Dataset	Metric	MMA-1	MMA-2	MMA-3	MMA-4	MMA
D1	RMSE	0.867•	0.859•	0.849•	0.847•	0.840
	MAE	0.663•	0.660•	0.668•	0.667•	0.656
D2	RMSE	0.909•	0.906•	0.898•	0.897•	0.889
	MAE	0.700•	0.698•	0.706•	0.706•	0.695
D3	RMSE	0.755•	0.755•	0.752•	0.751•	0.744
	MAE	0.563•	0.563•	0.571•	0.569•	0.561
D4	RMSE	1.198•	1.194•	1.185•	1.173•	1.161
	MAE	0.870○	0.887•	0.900•	0.900•	0.879
Statistic	loss/tie/win	1/0/7	0/0/8	0/0/8	0/0/8	**1/0/32***
	p-value	0.025	0.006	0.006	0.006	-
	F-rank	3.625	3.250	3.875	3.125	1.125

* The MMA's total loss/tie/win cases. • The cases that MMA wins the base models in comparison. ○ The cases that MMA loses the comparison.

4.3 The Self-ensembling of MMA (RQ.2)

We further record the ensemble weights during the training process and compare the accuracy between MMA and its base models to discuss how MMA achieves self-adaptively control empirically.

Monitoring the Variations of Ensemble Weights. Figure5 demonstrates the ensemble weight variations of D1 to D4. In Fig 5, we find that all the weights self-adaptively change across the training process. We note that the ensemble weights of MMA-3 and MMA-4, calculated according to Equation (8) on the validation set, gradually increase and surpass MMA-1 and MMA-2 until the base models are fitted. The reason may be that this dataset has fewer outliers, making the L_2-norm *loss* function dominant during the training process to achieve better predictions.

Accuracy Comparison between MMA and its Base Models. The prediction accuracy of MMA and the base variant models are recorded in Table6. In like manner, we also conduct the loss/tie/win count, the Wilcoxon singed-rank test, and the Friedman test. Table 6 demonstrates that the MAE of MMA-1 and MMA-2 are generally lower than MMA-3 and MMA-4, but RMSE is the opposite.

Summary. We can conclude that MMA does take advantage of different metric spaces. MMA outperforms other state-of-the-art models with minor computational resource sacrifice by ensembling different metric spaces in the aggregation stage.

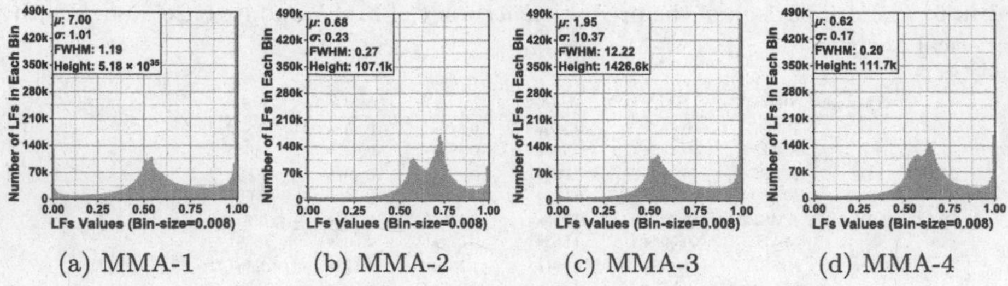

(a) MMA-1 (b) MMA-2 (c) MMA-3 (d) MMA-4

Fig. 6. The distribution histogram of latent factors (LFs) of the base models on D3..

4.4 Base Models' Latent Factors Distribution (RQ. 3)

To verify if the base models of MMA are diversified in representing the HDI matrix, we visualize the encoder output of these base models, which we regard as its latent factors. We adopt the Gaussian Function for better analysis. Figure 6 depicts the LF's distribution of the base models on D3. The figure shows that MMA-1 and MMA-3 distribute around 0 and 1 because parameters regularized by L_1-norm are sparse due to their feature selection characteristic.

These observations prove the base models are diversified in representing the HDI matrix. According to the principle of the ensemble theory [5], such variation is beneficial for boosting a base model, guaranteeing the representation accuracy of MMA on HDI data.

5 Conclusion

This paper proposes a multi-metric-Autoencoder to represent HDI data matrices more accurately. Its essential idea is two-fold: 1) deploy different L_p-norms as *loss* function and *regularization* to develop four variant Autoencoders with unique metric spaces, and 2) aggregate these Autoencoders with self-adaptively weighting ensemble strategy. Extensive theoretical and empirical studies verify that the proposed MMA model is benefited from the multi-metrics of basic models. Experiments on four real-world datasets prove that 1) MMA has remarkably higher accuracy and better robustness in representing HDI data, and 2) its computational efficiency is higher than most DNN-based models. In addition, the loss functions of the four different basic models can also be integrated into a single loss function and applied to other types of models, such as latent factor analysis models. We hope to expand the work of MMA in these aspects in the future.

References

1. Alhayani, B.S., et al.: Visual sensor intelligent module based image transmission in industrial manufacturing for monitoring and manipulation problems. J. Intell. Manuf. **32**(2), 597–610 (2021)
2. Cai, D., Qian, S., Fang, Q., Xu, C.: Heterogeneous hierarchical feature aggregation network for personalized micro-video recommendation. IEEE Trans. Multimedia **24**, 805–818 (2021)
3. Chen, J., Luo, X., Zhou, M.: Hierarchical particle swarm optimization-incorporated latent factor analysis for large-scale incomplete matrices. IEEE Trans. Big Data **8**(6), 1524–1536 (2021)
4. Demšar, J.: Statistical comparisons of classifiers over multiple data sets. J. Mach. Learn. Res. **7**, 1–30 (2006)
5. Dong, X., Yu, Z., Cao, W., Shi, Y., Ma, Q.: A survey on ensemble learning. Front. Comp. Sci. **14**(2), 241–258 (2020)
6. Fang, L., Du, B., Wu, C.: Differentially private recommender system with variational autoencoders. Knowl.-Based Syst. **250**, 109044 (2022)
7. Gao, C., et al.: A survey of graph neural networks for recommender systems: Challenges, methods, and directions. ACM Trans. Recommender Syst. (2023). https://doi.org/10.1145/3568022
8. Gharahighehi, A., Vens, C., Pliakos, K.: Multi-stakeholder news recommendation using hypergraph learning. In: Koprinska, I., et al. (eds.) ECML PKDD 2020. CCIS, vol. 1323, pp. 531–535. Springer, Cham (2020). https://doi.org/10.1007/978-3-030-65965-3_36
9. Han, S.C., Lim, T., Long, S., Burgstaller, B., Poon, J.: Glocal-k: global and local kernels for recommender systems. In: Proceedings of the 30th ACM International Conference on Information & Knowledge Management, pp. 3063–3067 (2021)
10. Hu, L., Pan, X., Tang, Z., Luo, X.: A fast fuzzy clustering algorithm for complex networks via a generalized momentum method. IEEE Trans. Fuzzy Syst. **30**(9), 3473–3485 (2021)
11. Hu, L., Yang, S., Luo, X., Yuan, H., Sedraoui, K., Zhou, M.: A distributed framework for large-scale protein-protein interaction data analysis and prediction using mapreduce. IEEE/CAA J. Automatica Sinica **9**(1), 160–172 (2021)
12. Hu, L., Yang, S., Luo, X., Zhou, M.: An algorithm of inductively identifying clusters from attributed graphs. IEEE Trans. Big Data **8**(2), 523–534 (2020)
13. Hu, L., Zhang, J., Pan, X., Luo, X., Yuan, H.: An effective link-based clustering algorithm for detecting overlapping protein complexes in protein-protein interaction networks. IEEE Trans. Netw. Sci. Eng. **8**(4), 3275–3289 (2021)
14. Islek, I., Oguducu, S.G.: A hybrid recommendation system based on bidirectional encoder representations. In: Koprinska, I., et al. (eds.) ECML PKDD 2020. CCIS, vol. 1323, pp. 225–236. Springer, Cham (2020). https://doi.org/10.1007/978-3-030-65965-3_14
15. Khan, S., Huh, J., Ye, J.C.: Adaptive and compressive beamforming using deep learning for medical ultrasound. IEEE Trans. Ultrason. Ferroelectr. Freq. Control **67**(8), 1558–1572 (2020). https://doi.org/10.1109/TUFFC.2020.2977202
16. Koren, Y., Bell, R., Volinsky, C.: Matrix factorization techniques for recommender systems. Computer **42**(8), 30–37 (2009)
17. Li, P., Wang, Z., Ren, Z., Bing, L., Lam, W.: Neural rating regression with abstractive tips generation for recommendation. In: Proceedings of the 40th International ACM SIGIR conference on Research and Development in Information Retrieval, pp. 345–354 (2017)

18. Li, Y., Sun, H., Yan, W., Cui, Q.: R-CTSVM+: robust capped L1-norm twin support vector machine with privileged information. Inf. Sci. **574**, 12–32 (2021)
19. Li, Z., Li, S., Bamasag, O.O., Alhothali, A., Luo, X.: Diversified regularization enhanced training for effective manipulator calibration. IEEE Transactions on Neural Networks and Learning Systems, pp. 1–13 (2022). https://doi.org/10.1109/TNNLS.2022.3153039
20. Liu, Z., Luo, X., Wang, Z.: Convergence analysis of single latent factor-dependent, nonnegative, and multiplicative update-based nonnegative latent factor models. IEEE Trans. Neural Netw. Learn. Syst. **32**(4), 1737–1749 (2020)
21. Luo, X., Chen, M., Wu, H., Liu, Z., Yuan, H., Zhou, M.: Adjusting learning depth in nonnegative latent factorization of tensors for accurately modeling temporal patterns in dynamic QoS data. IEEE Trans. Autom. Sci. Eng. **18**(4), 2142–2155 (2021)
22. Luo, X., Wu, H., Li, Z.: NeuLFT: a novel approach to nonlinear canonical polyadic decomposition on high-dimensional incomplete tensors. IEEE Trans. Knowl. Data Eng. **35**(6), 6148–6166 (2023)
23. Luo, X., Zhou, Y., Liu, Z., Hu, L., Zhou, M.: Generalized Nesterov's acceleration-incorporated, non-negative and adaptive latent factor analysis. IEEE Trans. Serv. Comput. **15**(5), 2809–2823 (2021)
24. Luo, X., Zhou, Y., Liu, Z., Zhou, M.: Fast and accurate non-negative latent factor analysis on high-dimensional and sparse matrices in recommender systems. IEEE Trans. Know. Data Eng. 35, 3897–3911 (2021). https://doi.org/10.1109/TKDE.2021.3125252
25. Muller, L., Martel, J., Indiveri, G.: Kernelized synaptic weight matrices. In: International Conference on Machine Learning, pp. 3654–3663. PMLR (2018)
26. Natarajan, S., Vairavasundaram, S., Natarajan, S., Gandomi, A.H.: Resolving data sparsity and cold start problem in collaborative filtering recommender system using linked open data. Expert Syst. Appl. **149**, 113248 (2020)
27. Park, J., Cho, J., Chang, H.J., Choi, J.Y.: Unsupervised hyperbolic representation learning via message passing auto-encoders. In: Proceedings of the IEEE/CVF Conference on Computer Vision and Pattern Recognition, pp. 5516–5526 (2021)
28. Raza, S., Ding, C.: A regularized model to trade-off between accuracy and diversity in a news recommender system. In: 2020 IEEE International Conference on Big Data (Big Data), pp. 551–560. IEEE (2020)
29. Saberi-Movahed, F., et al.: Dual regularized unsupervised feature selection based on matrix factorization and minimum redundancy with application in gene selection. Knowl.-Based Syst. **256**, 109884 (2022)
30. Sedhain, S., Menon, A.K., Sanner, S., Xie, L.: AutoRec: autoencoders meet collaborative filtering. In: Proceedings of the 24th International Conference on World Wide Web, pp. 111–112 (2015)
31. Shang, M., Yuan, Y., Luo, X., Zhou, M.: An α-β-divergence-generalized recommender for highly accurate predictions of missing user preferences. IEEE Trans. Cybern. **52**(8), 8006–8018 (2021)
32. Shao, B., Li, X., Bian, G.: A survey of research hotspots and frontier trends of recommendation systems from the perspective of knowledge graph. Expert Syst. Appl. **165**, 113764 (2021)
33. Shi, Q., Liu, M., Li, S., Liu, X., Wang, F., Zhang, L.: A deeply supervised attention metric-based network and an open aerial image dataset for remote sensing change detection. IEEE Trans. Geosci. Remote Sens. **60**, 1–16 (2022). https://doi.org/10.1109/TGRS.2021.3085870

34. Shi, X., Kang, Q., An, J., Zhou, M.: Novel L1 regularized extreme learning machine for soft-sensing of an industrial process. IEEE Trans. Ind. Inf. **18**(2), 1009–1017 (2021)
35. Song, Y., Zhu, Z., Li, M., Yang, G., Luo, X.: Non-negative latent factor analysis-incorporated and feature-weighted fuzzy double c-means clustering for incomplete data. IEEE Trans. Fuzzy Syst. **30**(10), 4165–4176 (2022)
36. Tay, Y., Anh Tuan, L., Hui, S.C.: Latent relational metric learning via memory-based attention for collaborative ranking. In: Proceedings of the 2018 World Wide Web Conference, pp. 729–739 (2018)
37. Wang, H., Hong, Z., Hong, M.: Research on product recommendation based on matrix factorization models fusing user reviews. Appl. Soft Comput. (2022). https://doi.org/10.1016/j.asoc.2022.108971
38. Wang, S., Cao, J., Yu, P.S.: Deep learning for spatio-temporal data mining: a survey. IEEE Trans. Knowl. Data Eng. **34**(8), 3681–3700 (2022). https://doi.org/10.1109/TKDE.2020.3025580
39. Wang, X., Chen, H., Zhou, Y., Ma, J., Zhu, W.: Disentangled representation learning for recommendation. IEEE Trans. Pattern Anal. Mach. Intell. **45**(1), 408–424 (2022)
40. Wu, D., Luo, X.: Robust latent factor analysis for precise representation of high-dimensional and sparse data. IEEE/CAA J. Automatica Sinica **8**(4), 796–805 (2021)
41. Wu, D., Luo, X., He, Y., Zhou, M.: A prediction-sampling-based multilayer-structured latent factor model for accurate representation to high-dimensional and sparse data. IEEE Trans. Neural Netw. Learn. Syst. 1–14 (2022). https://doi.org/10.1109/TNNLS.2022.3200009
42. Wu, D., Zhang, P., He, Y., Luo, X.: A double-space and double-norm ensembled latent factor model for highly accurate web service QoS prediction. IEEE Trans. Serv. Comput. (2022). https://doi.org/10.1109/TSC.2022.3178543
43. Wu, H., Luo, X., Zhou, M., Rawa, M.J., Sedraoui, K., Albeshri, A.: A PID-incorporated latent factorization of tensors approach to dynamically weighted directed network analysis. IEEE/CAA J. Automatica Sinica **9**(3), 533–546 (2021)
44. Yuan, Y., He, Q., Luo, X., Shang, M.: A multilayered-and-randomized latent factor model for high-dimensional and sparse matrices. IEEE Trans. Big Data **8**(3), 784–794 (2020)
45. Zhang, M., Chen, Y.: Inductive matrix completion based on graph neural networks. In: International Conference on Learning Representations (2020). https://openreview.net/forum?id=ByxxgCEYDS
46. Zhang, S., Yao, L., Wu, B., Xu, X., Zhang, X., Zhu, L.: Unraveling metric vector spaces with factorization for recommendation. IEEE Trans. Ind. Inf. **16**(2), 732–742 (2019)
47. Zheng, Y., Wang, D.X.: A survey of recommender systems with multi-objective optimization. Neurocomputing **474**, 141–153 (2022)

Exploring and Exploiting Data-Free Model Stealing

Chi Hong[1], Jiyue Huang[1], Robert Birke[2], and Lydia Y. Chen[1](✉)

[1] Delft University of Technology, Delft, Netherlands
{c.hong,j.huang-4,Y.Chen-10}@tudelft.nl
[2] University of Torino, Turin, Italy
robert.birke@unito.it

Abstract. Deep machine learning models, e.g., image classifier, are increasingly deployed in the wild to provide services to users. Adversaries are shown capable of stealing the knowledge of these models by sending inference queries and then training substitute models based on query results. The availability and quality of adversarial query inputs are undoubtedly crucial in the stealing process. The recent prior art demonstrates the feasibility of replacing real data by exploring the synthetic adversarial queries, so called data-free attacks, under strong adversarial assumptions, i.e., the deployed classier returns not only class labels but also class probabilities. In this paper, we consider a general adversarial model and propose an effective data-free stealing algorithm, TandemGAN, which not only explores synthetic queries but also explicitly exploits the high quality ones. The core of TandemGAN is composed of (i) substitute model which imitates the target model through synthetic queries and their inferred labels; and (ii) a tandem generator consisting of two networks, $\mathcal{G}_x$ and $\mathcal{G}_e$, which first explores the synthetic data space via $\mathcal{G}_x$ and then exploits high-quality examples via $\mathcal{G}_e$ to maximize the knowledge transfer from the target to the substitute model. Our results on four datasets show that the accuracy of our trained substitute model ranges between 96–67% of the target model and outperforms the existing state-of-the-art data-free model stealing approach by up to 2.5X.

Keywords: model stealing · data-free · generative adversarial networks

1 Introduction

Emerging intelligent services, such as Google translate and optical character recognition [8], are increasingly powered by deep models. Users can access these services by sending queries via APIs to get outputs, for instance, the class labels of queried images. While an open access to deployed models greatly eases users' experience, it opens up vulnerability issues related to model stealing [10,26, 29]. Adversaries may use such an access to steal the knowledge of the deployed model and create a copy of it, named substitute model, which can then be used to do malicious actions, e.g., adversarial attacks [4,6,14,26,27] or membership

D. Koutra et al. (Eds.): ECML PKDD 2023, LNAI 14173, pp. 20–35, 2023.
https://doi.org/10.1007/978-3-031-43424-2_2

attacks [28]. Several studies design defenses against model stealing [11,12,21], but [2] provides theoretical evidence that model extraction is inevitable.

To launch a model stealing attack, the adversary first needs to query the target model and get the corresponding inference results. For instance, to steal an image classifier, the adversary sends query images to the deployed classifier and then receives the predicted class labels. Recognizing the issue of limited availability of real data, recent studies [10,26] introduce data-free model stealing methods, i.e., only using synthetic query images. Generative adversarial networks (GANs), composed of generator and substitute models, are key to synthesize queries. Synthetic query quality is paramount to extract knowledge from the target model. Low quality queries provide little information to train the substitute model, e.g. low confidence results from the target model leading to small feedback losses.

Though the existing studies demonstrate the feasibility to steal models in a (real) data-free way, they are limited in the adversarial assumptions and quality of synthesised queries. The common adversarial assumption of the prior art [10, 26] is that both predicted class labels and confidence are provided by the target model. The additional information beyond class labels is crucial for existing methods to carry out GANs training which can not backpropagate the gradients simply from the class labels.

Furthermore, the competition between generator and substitute models pushes the two networks to continuously **explore** the synthetic data space, but the classic min-max loss used in training GANs eschews to **exploit** synthetic examples [3]. As a result the average quality of synthetic queries is low, i.e., target model has low confidence in classifying synthetic data, and further limits the knowledge extraction performance in model stealing. Fig. 1 illustrates the average prediction confidence of the target model on real and synthetic data generated by the state of the art data-free stealing methods, namely DFME [26], DaST [29] and MAZE [10]. In this example, the target model is ResNet34 trained on CIFAR 10 and the settings of adversaries can be found in the evaluation section. Shown in the figure, the existing methods can only generate synthetic queries reaching an average confidence level of 80% that is 20% lower than the real data and limits its capacity to extract knowledge.

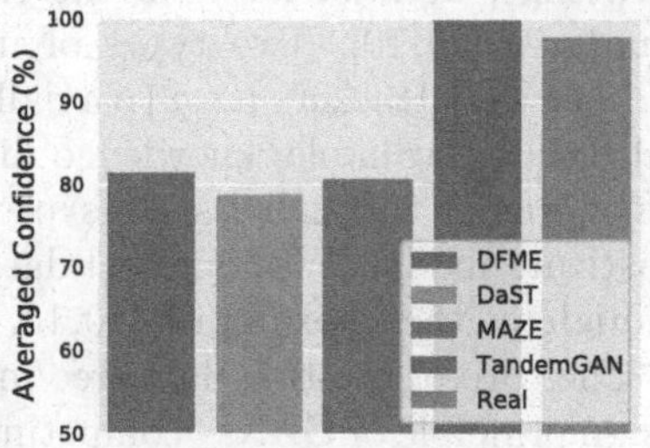

Fig. 1. Average target model confidence on 1K real data and 1K synthetic data generated by DFME, DaST, MAZE and TandemGAN respectively.

In this paper, we propose an effective data-free model stealing framework, TandemGAN, which does not require any real data and considers general adversarial assumptions where queries return label predictions, termed *label-only*, or label probabilities, termed *probability-only*. The core components of TandemGAN are (i) the substitute model and (ii) the tandem generator consisting of two networks to explore and exploit the synthesizing space. The substitute model minimizes the distance loss between its and the target model's predictions while the two tandem generator networks jointly synthesize diverse and high confidence query examples which maximize the stealing potential. The first network, $\mathcal{G}_x$, explores the synthetic data space, whereas the second network $\mathcal{G}_e$ exploits and refines the synthesizing space to produce high-quality synthetic examples with high target model confidence. In the example of Fig. 4, we demonstrate more systematically the effectiveness of incorporating exploitation evaluating the performance of TandemGAN on stealing four deployed classifiers under both scenarios of label-only and probability-only against SOTA prior art.

The contributions of this paper are: (i) an effective data-free model stealing framework, TandemGAN, which uniquely features joint exploration and exploitation of synthetic data space and examples; (ii) more general adversarial scenarios: only class labels are available to the adversary; (iii) extensive evaluation and comparison against existing SOTA data-free model stealing approaches; and (iv) remarkable accuracy of the trained substitute models, i.e., reaching 67% up to 96% accuracy of the target classifiers.

2 Related Work

Model stealing aims to distill the knowledge from a deployed (target) model, specifically, to train a highly similar substitute model [2,9,13,20,24,26,29]. A successful substitute model is able to obtain the implicit mapping function (or knowledge, at high level) of the target model via different (simpler) network structures [10,20]. Two types of model stealing methods exist depending on whether the attackers have (partially) access to real training data or not. When real data is available, knowledge distilling [7,19] extracts the knowledge of the target model through its class probabilities and transfers it to a lightweight substitute model. Without real data attackers can only query the target model through synthetic examples [10,13,18,29] –a data-free approach.

The core of existing data-free model stealing methods [10,26,29] follows the design principle of GANs –competing generator-substitute networks. A generator produces synthetic examples to query the target model, $\mathcal{T}$, whereas the substitute model, $\mathcal{S}$, tries to imitate/steal $\mathcal{T}$ via the synthetic query results. The target model parameters and architecture are unknown. MAZE [10] and DFME [26] rely on a gradient approximation [22] to train their generator. DFME and MAZE can not be applied to scenarios where the target model provides only inference labels, Furthermore, DaST [29] regards the output of the target model as a constant vector forgoing the need for gradient approximation. Aforementioned studies explore the general synthesizing space, overlooking the option of exploitation. The features of different data-free model stealing methods are summarized in Table 1.

Table 1. Existing data-free model stealing methods.

Method	Probability-only	Label-only	Exploration	Exploitation
MAZE [10]	✓	✗	✓	✗
DFME [26]	✓	✗	✓	✗
DaST [29]	✓	✓	✓	✗
TANDEMGAN (ours)	✓	✓	✓	✓

3 Methodology

In this section, we introduce TANDEMGAN, a data-free model stealing framework that explores and exploits synthetic queries. Prior to introducing the design of TANDEMGAN, we first introduce the adversarial assumptions.

Adversarial Assumptions. We consider a realistic deployment setting where a target classifier[1] $\mathcal{T}$ is deployed and its parameters and architecture of $\mathcal{T}$ are unknown. The only way to interact with the target model is by sending queries, e.g., images, and getting the inferred results, for both benign and malicious adversaries. Furthermore, due to the limitation and difficulty of obtaining real data, we further assume adversaries have no access to the real data. According to the format of the inference results, we consider two types of adversarial scenarios: (i) *label-only* scenario: $\mathcal{T}$ only provides a label prediction for each query without any additional information, and (ii) *probability-only* scenario: $\mathcal{T}$ returns the class probabilities instead.

3.1 TandemGAN Framework

We propose TANDEMGAN to steal the knowledge from $\mathcal{T}$ and train an accurate substitute model $\mathcal{S}$, shown in Fig. 2. $\mathcal{S}$ can be regarded as a clone of $\mathcal{T}$ but

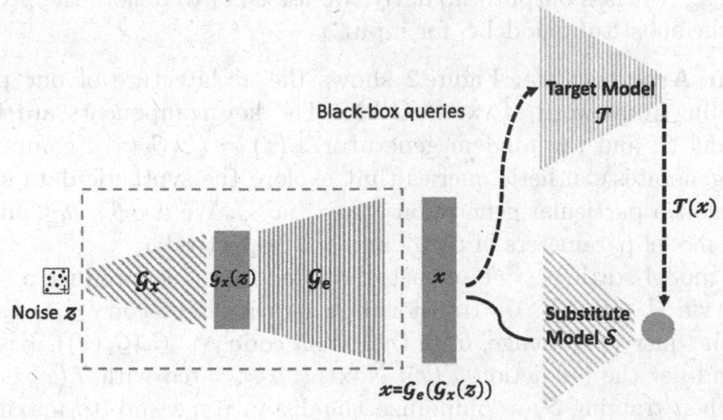

Fig. 2. TANDEMGAN framework: data-free model stealing process.

[1] TANDEMGAN can be extended to other model types but here we only discuss classification tasks.

with a different network architecture. Different from related work TandemGAN leverages a tandem generator which generates synthetic queries[2] with high classification confidence. Specifically, the generating process includes two networks, one network for exploring the new areas of the synthetic data space and one network for exploiting a particular space to generate high-quality synthetic queries. In Fig. 3, we illustrate the projected synthesizing space of TandemGAN on CIFAR10, the exploration points randomly scatter, whereas the exploitation points center around some exploration points. Note that we apply UMAP [16] to reduce the data dimension for visualization.

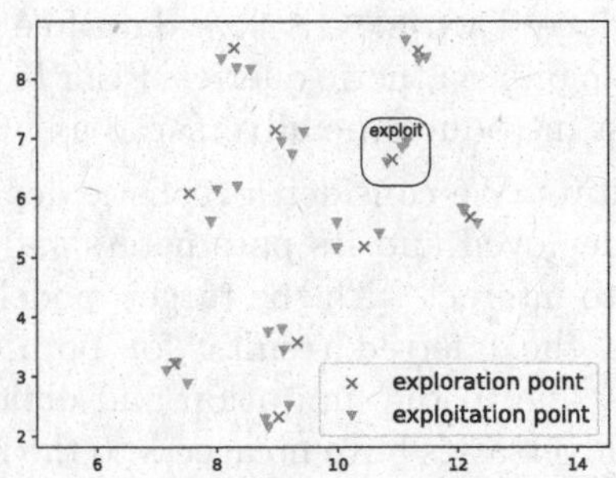

Fig. 3. Exploration and exploitation of TandemGAN in projected 2D space.

Preliminary. In the data-free model stealing, a generator $\mathcal{G}$ is fed a noise vector z as seed to generate a synthetic example $x = \mathcal{G}(z)$ to query $\mathcal{T}$ and obtain $\mathcal{T}(x)$. We assume $\mathcal{T}$ to be a model for classification task with N classes. Depending on the context, $\mathcal{T}(x)$ is either the predicted probability vector (*probability-only*) or predicted one-hot encoded label (*label-only*) for input x and $\mathcal{T}_i(x)$ denotes the i-th ($i = 1, ..., N$) class output. Similarly, we use $\mathcal{S}(x)$ to denote the probability output of the substitute model $\mathcal{S}$ for input x.

Algorithm Architecture. Figure 2 shows the architecture of our proposed model stealing framework, TandemGAN. The key components are the substitute model $\mathcal{S}$, and the tandem generator, $\mathcal{G}(z) = \mathcal{G}_e(\mathcal{G}_x(z))$, comprising $\mathcal{G}_x$ and $\mathcal{G}_e$. $\mathcal{G}$ generates synthetic queries that explore the synthetic data space via $\mathcal{G}_x$ and exploit a particular generation space via $\mathcal{G}_e$. We use $\theta_\mathcal{S}$, $\theta_{\mathcal{G}_x}$ and $\theta_{\mathcal{G}_e}$ to denote the model parameters of $\mathcal{S}$, $\mathcal{G}_x$ and $\mathcal{G}_e$, respectively.

During model stealing, a noise vector z is fed into $\mathcal{G}$ to produce a synthetic example x via $\mathcal{G}_x$ and $\mathcal{G}_e$. $\mathcal{G}_x$ transforms z into a latent code $\mathcal{G}_x(z)$ while $\mathcal{G}_e$ generates the query, e.g. image, from the latent code $x = \mathcal{G}_e(\mathcal{G}_x(z))$. x is used to query $\mathcal{T}$ and get the prediction $\mathcal{T}(x)$. Next, x associated with $\mathcal{T}(x)$ is used to train $\mathcal{S}$. When training $\mathcal{S}$, we minimize the distance measure to maximize the agreement between $\mathcal{S}$ and $\mathcal{T}$. Besides training $\mathcal{S}$, we separately train $\mathcal{G}_x$ and $\mathcal{G}_e$

[2] We refer the data sample sent to the target model as a query. In case of querying via synthetic data sample, we abbreviate it as a synthetic query.

according to the outputs $\mathcal{T}(x)$ and $\mathcal{S}(x)$. Since $\mathcal{G}_x$ is designed to explore new areas of the data generating space which can provide new knowledge to train $\mathcal{S}$, we employ the design idea of GANs – a minmax optimization to train $\mathcal{G}_x$ and $\mathcal{S}$ jointly.

Hence to train $\mathcal{G}_x$, we optimize the model parameters $\theta_{\mathcal{G}_x}$ to maximize the distance measure between $\mathcal{T}(x)$ and $\mathcal{S}(x)$. $\mathcal{G}_e$ is responsible to refine the new area searched by $\mathcal{G}_x$ to generate high-quality synthetic queries. The objective of $\mathcal{G}_e$ thus needs to be aligned with the definition of query quality. Following the risk analysis of knowledge distillation [17], we define the optimization objective of $\mathcal{G}_e$ according to effectiveness of knowledge extraction, i.e., maximizing the confidence of the target model in predicting synthetic queries. Other possible definitions by active learning [1] are discussed in Sect. 5. As a result $\mathcal{G}$ simultaneously explores and exploits the synthetic data space to find diverse and highly informative examples which maximize the knowledge transfer to $\mathcal{S}$. The optimization objectives of $\mathcal{S}$, $\mathcal{G}_x$ and $\mathcal{G}_e$ are detailed in the following.

3.2 Optimization Objectives and Training Procedure

Optimization Objective of $\mathcal{S}$. Since $\mathcal{S}$ is a substitute of $\mathcal{T}$, their outputs are expected to be as similar as possible. Inspired by knowledge distillation [7], $\mathcal{S}$ imitates the outputs of $\mathcal{T}$ through the loss of distance measure. The loss function of $\mathcal{S}$ over a query example x is as follows:

$$\mathcal{L}_{\mathcal{S}} = \mathrm{D}(\mathcal{T}(x), \mathcal{S}(x)), \tag{1}$$

where $\mathrm{D}(\cdot)$ denotes the distance measure for loss, e.g., L1-Norm or cross-entropy. L1-Norm provides a stronger feedback than cross-entropy. This fits well the *probability-only* scenario where the loss inputs are the class probabilities. When working with the more limited scenario of *label-only*, the L1-Norm would require the output of the two models to be identical which is an aggressive condition given that only a one-hot output is provided rather than the full distribution on all classes. Thus, cross-entropy is applied for *label-only*. After training $\mathcal{S}$, we can steal the knowledge of $\mathcal{T}$ because $\mathcal{S}$ learns the mapping of $\mathcal{T}$.

Optimization objective of $\mathcal{G}_x$. We incorporate $\mathcal{G}_x$ to diversify the latent codes fed to $\mathcal{G}_e$ and generate queries in new areas of the data space. $\mathcal{G}_x$ aims at making $\mathcal{S}(x)$ as different as possible from $\mathcal{T}(x)$. This is the opposite training objective of $\mathcal{S}$. Thus, we formulate the loss of $\mathcal{G}_x$ as:

$$\mathcal{L}_{\mathcal{G}_x} = -\mathcal{L}_{\mathcal{S}} = -\mathrm{D}(\mathcal{T}(x), \mathcal{S}(x)), \quad where\ x = \mathcal{G}_e(\mathcal{G}_x(z)). \tag{2}$$

By this means, $\mathcal{G}_x$ ensures that $\mathcal{S}$ is trained by a broad spectrum of diverse synthetic queries in data space to prevent model collapse or degenerated cases. It should be noted that although $\mathcal{T}(x)$ can not be differentiated directly via backpropagation (since its network parameters are unavailable), it is possible to apply gradient approximation (details below) under *probability-only* scenario.

On the other hand, under *label-only* scenario, the output of the target model is the class label and it is a non-differentiable constant.

Optimization Objective of $\mathcal{G}_e$. We incorporate $\mathcal{G}_e$ to generate high quality queries around a latent space explored by $\mathcal{G}_x$. We derive the loss function of $\mathcal{G}_e$ inspired by the risk analysis of knowledge distillation [17]. We aim to achieve high quality $\mathcal{T}$ so as to better teach $\mathcal{S}$. Specifically, the quality of the probability estimate of $\mathcal{T}$ can be measured by log-loss and calibration error [5], the lower the better. Inspired by this observation, for minimizing the log-loss (or calibration error) on the outputs $\mathcal{T}(x)$, in our model stealing process, the inference confidence of x, i.e., the biggest element of $\mathcal{T}(x)$, is expected to be high. Consequently, the objective of $\mathcal{G}_e$ is to generate a synthetic query x that maximizes the confidence over model $\mathcal{T}$. We thus define high-quality queries as ones with high inference confidence on $\mathcal{T}$. Then, we define the loss function of $\mathcal{G}_e$ as:

$$\mathcal{L}_{\mathcal{G}_e} = -\left\{\log \mathcal{T}_k(x) \mid \forall_j : \mathcal{T}_j(x) \leq \mathcal{T}_k(x)\right\}, \qquad \text{where } x = \mathcal{G}_e(\mathcal{G}_x(z)). \tag{3}$$

With this loss, for an input example $x = \mathcal{G}_e(\mathcal{G}_x(z))$, we maximize the value of the k-th element of $\mathcal{T}(x)$ where k is the index of the biggest element. For *probability-only*, calculating Eq. (3) relies on gradient approximation (details below). For *label-only*, $\mathcal{T}(x)$ is a constant (one-hot label) and gradient approximation is not applicable because one can not obtain its directional derivative. Thus, we use $\mathcal{S}(x)$ to approximate $\mathcal{T}(x)$ since $\mathcal{S}(x)$ gradually approaches $\mathcal{T}(x)$ during training. Hence, updating $\mathcal{G}_e$ only needs the gradient of $\mathcal{S}$ which fits the *label-only* scenario.

Gradient Approximation. Training the generator $\mathcal{G}$ requires the gradient $\nabla_{\theta_g}\mathcal{L}$ where $\mathcal{L}$ has two arguments $\mathcal{T}(x)$ and $\mathcal{S}(x)$. However, $\mathcal{T}$ is not differentiable in our black-box setting as its model parameters are unknown. Therefore we cannot obtain $\nabla_{\theta_g}\mathcal{L}$ without $\nabla_{\theta_g}\mathcal{T}(\mathcal{G}(z))$. To address this challenge, we apply gradient approximation [26] to approximate $\nabla_{\theta_g}\mathcal{L}$. Given

$$\nabla_{\theta_g}\mathcal{L} = \frac{\partial \mathcal{L}}{\partial \theta_g} = \frac{\partial \mathcal{L}}{\partial x} \times \frac{\partial x}{\partial \theta_g},$$

the second term can be computed because $\mathcal{G}$ is differentiable with known parameters. Thus, we only need to approximate $\frac{\partial \mathcal{L}}{\partial x}$. This can be done by the forward differences method [22]. It approximates the gradient of a function at a point by computing directional derivatives along some random directions. For a synthetic example $x \in \mathbb{R}^d$, the approximate gradient is:

$$\hat{\nabla}_x \mathcal{L}(x) = \frac{1}{M}\sum_{j=1}^{M} \frac{\mathcal{L}(x + \epsilon u_j) - \mathcal{L}(x)}{\epsilon} u_j$$

where u_j is a random direction (a d-dimensional unit vector) and M is the number of directions used for the approximation. ϵ is a small step size in the direction of u_j. The approximate value becomes more precise when M increases. For TandemGAN, gradient approximation is used to optimize both $\mathcal{G}_x$ and $\mathcal{G}_e$ under *probability-only* scenario.

Algorithm 1. TandemGAN

Input: n_x, n_e, n_s, μ_x, μ_e and μ_s
In the following, $z \sim \mathcal{N}(0, 1)$
for *number of rounds* **do**
  for $i = 1, \ldots, n_x$ **do** // explore the data space
1   Get $\mathcal{T}(x)$ and $\mathcal{S}(x)$, $x = \mathcal{G}_e(\mathcal{G}_x(z))$
    if *probability-only* **then**
2     $\mathcal{L}_{\mathcal{G}_x}(x) = -\|\mathcal{T}(x) - \mathcal{S}(x)\|_1$
3   **else**
4     $\mathcal{L}_{\mathcal{G}_x}(x) = -CE(\mathcal{T}(x), \mathcal{S}(x))$
5   $\theta_{\mathcal{G}_x} \leftarrow \theta_{\mathcal{G}_x} - \mu_x \nabla_{\theta_{\mathcal{G}_x}} \mathcal{L}_{\mathcal{G}_x}(x)$
6 **for** $j = 1, \ldots, n_e$ **do** // exploit the data space
7   Get $\mathcal{T}(x)$ and $\mathcal{S}(x)$, $x = \mathcal{G}_e(\mathcal{G}_x(z))$
    Compute $\mathcal{L}_{\mathcal{G}_e}(x)$ // see Eq. (3) for the loss calculation
    $\theta_{\mathcal{G}_e} \leftarrow \theta_{\mathcal{G}_e} - \mu_e \nabla_{\theta_{\mathcal{G}_e}} \mathcal{L}_{\mathcal{G}_e}(x)$
8 **for** $j = 1, \ldots, n_s$ **do**
9   Get $\mathcal{T}(x)$ and $\mathcal{S}(x)$, $x = \mathcal{G}_e(\mathcal{G}_x(z))$
    if *probability-only* **then**
10    $\mathcal{L}_{\mathcal{S}}(x) = \|\mathcal{T}(x) - \mathcal{S}(x)\|_1$
11 **else**
12    $\mathcal{L}_{\mathcal{S}}(x) = CE(\mathcal{T}(x), \mathcal{S}(x))$
13 $\theta_{\mathcal{S}} \leftarrow \theta_{\mathcal{S}} - \mu_s \nabla_{\theta_{\mathcal{S}}} \mathcal{L}_{\mathcal{S}}(x)$
Result: The trained $\mathcal{S}$

Stealing Algorithm. Algorithm 1 shows the training process. In each round, there are two stages, exploration (line 1–5) and exploitation (line 6–7). In exploration, $\mathcal{G}$ and $\mathcal{S}$ are playing a min-max game just like GANs. By the game, $\mathcal{G}_x$ is updated to explore a new area in the latent space of $\mathcal{G}_e$. In exploitation, $\mathcal{G}_e$ exploits the area and produces synthetic examples to train $\mathcal{S}$. After the exploitation, we sample multiple examples for updating the substitute model $\mathcal{S}$ (line 8–13).

To fine-tune the balance between exploration and exploitation in each round, each training stage of the tandem generator is repeated n_x and n_e times, respectively. The optimization goal of $\mathcal{G}_x$ is opposite to $\mathcal{S}$. If the exploration is too aggressive, the training of $\mathcal{S}$ diverges. If the exploration is too conservative, $\mathcal{S}$ can collapse to a bad local optima because of the limited area searched in the latent space during training. After training $\mathcal{G}_e$, $\mathcal{S}$ needs enough updates to extract knowledge from $\mathcal{T}$.

4 Evaluation

In this section, we comprehensively evaluate the model stealing performance via the accuracy of the substitute model. We compare TandemGAN with state-of-the-art data-free model stealing approaches and conduct an ablation study to verify the effectiveness of exploration and exploitation, and the impact of different substitute model architectures.

Table 2. Comparison of the $\mathcal{S}$ubstitute model Acc(uracy) under DaST, MAZE, DFME, and TANDEMGAN. Arch. stands for model architecture.

Dataset	$\mathcal{T}$arget		$\mathcal{S}$	Label-only		Probability-only			
	Acc	Arch	Arch	DaST	TANDEMGAN	MAZE	DFME	DaST	TANDEMGAN
MNIST	99.51	VGG16	VGG11	83.98	91.30	95.13	90.22	90.16	95.95
F-MNIST	93.09	VGG16	VGG11	43.00	72.15	41.63	48.43	44.43	79.96
SVHN	94.96	ResNet34	VGG11	58.39	62.41	52.60	50.62	55.69	68.80
CIFAR10	90.71	ResNet34	VGG11	21.28	29.58	58.67	54.79	29.81	75.81

Datasets and Model Structures. We evaluate our proposed method on four benchmark datasets: MNIST, Fashion-MNIST (F-MNIST), SVHN and CIFAR10. For MNIST and F-MNIST, we use VGG16 for the target model and ResNet34 for SVHN and CIFAR10. For the substitute model, we apply VGG11 for every dataset so that comparisons on the same/different network architecture(s) family between $\mathcal{S}$ and $\mathcal{T}$ are possible. However, for each baseline approach and TANDEMGAN, we use the same target and substitute models to guarantee a fair comparison. Finally, TANDEMGAN uses a two convolutional layers network for $\mathcal{G}_x$ and a one convolutional layer network for $\mathcal{G}_e$.

Evaluation Criteria. The goal of our data-free model stealing is to achieve high classification **accuracy** on substitute model. We also compare the convergence process of TANDEMGAN with the baseline models to show the learning performance. For evaluating the attack efficiency, we also show the accuracy of the substitute model on different **number of queries** during model stealing.

Experiment Settings. The networks $\mathcal{S}$, $\mathcal{G}_x$ and $\mathcal{G}_e$ are trained with a batch size of 256. We apply RMSprop as the optimizer for all the networks. The recommended learning rates for $\mathcal{S}$, $\mathcal{G}_x$ and $\mathcal{G}_e$ are 0.001, 10^{-5} and 10^{-6} respectively. $\mathcal{G}_x$ has two convolutional layers and $\mathcal{G}_e$ has one convolutional layer. We apply batch normalization after each convolutional layer on the generator. For gradient approximation, we set the number of random directions M to be 1 and choose the step size $\epsilon = 0.001$. To balance the training of $\mathcal{S}$, $\mathcal{G}_x$ and $\mathcal{G}_e$, we let $n_s = 5$, $n_x \in \{1, 3, 5\}$ and $n_e \in \{1, 3, 5\}$ for all experiments. We implement our method using pytorch. Intel Xeon E3-1200 CPUs and Nvidia GeForce RTX 2080 Ti GPUs are utilized to run the experiments. The code of our method will be released should the paper be accepted.

4.1 Model Stealing Performance

Model Stealing Accuracy. We evaluate the accuracy of model stealing results compared to the DaST, MAZE and DFME, for both *label-only* and *probability-only* scenarios, and the original target model. Table 2 and Fig. 4 summarize the results. Here we use VGG11 as substitute model. This is more challenging for SVHN and CIFAR10 since the target model is ResNet34, differing significantly in neural network architecture family. The accuracy of the target model represents the upper bound accuracy for the substitute model. It should be noted that MAZE and DFME are only used on *probability-only* scenario since they require the additional information on class probabilities. We further note that DaST, MAZE, DFME and TANDEMGAN generate synthetic data per training iteration for generator or substitute model in different ways and different order. For a fair comparison, we report the accuracy under same number of queries.

Table 2 shows that TANDEMGAN achieves the highest accuracy among all datasets and inference scenarios. The accuracy of TANDEMGAN's substitute models trails behind the target models by margins of 4 to 32%, except for CIFAR10 under the label-only case. In other words, TANDEMGAN can achieve roughly 96 to 67% of the accuracy of the target model for a given dataset and inference scenario. The substitute model accuracy of TANDEMGAN is consistently and significantly higher than DaST, MAZE and DFME, showing an accuracy improvement up to 67% for the challenging label-only scenario, and up to 250% for the probability-only scenario.

Comparing probability-only to label-only, the accuracy of substitute models is higher for any given stealing method that is applicable to both scenarios. This is due to the fact that probability-only provides more inference information about the target model and we do not need to use $\mathcal{S}$ to approximate $\mathcal{T}$. For label-only scenarios, the accuracy of the substitute model trained by TANDEMGAN on MNIST surpasses 90% with a less than 10This strongly demonstrates the effectiveness of TANDEMGAN. Owing to the increasing task difficulty, for F-MNIST, SVHN and CIFAR10, the stealing performance of TANDEMGAN drops. Even so the accuracy of the trained substitute models is still more than half of the target models (except CIFAR10), and 1.67×, 1.06× and 1.39× the accuracy achieved by DaST. For probability-only scenarios, the additional information provided by the class probabilities improves the accuracy of the substitute models. DFME outperforms MAZE and DaST on F-MNIST. MAZE outperforms DFME and DaST on MNIST and CIFAR10. DaST is better on SVHN. However, TANDEMGAN outperforms all. More impressive, TANDEMGAN achieves results close to the target model. The gap is limited from 3 to 26

Model Stealing Convergence. Figure 4 shows the evolution of the substitute model accuracy across the number of queries to the target model. For DaST, we can see that for all cases the accuracy fluctuates and does not converge at a good local optima during the entire training. Sometimes the accuracy does not even show an increasing trend, for instance Fig. 4b, 4f and 4h. Due to the unstable convergence, another issue with DaST is to choose an appropriate stopping criteria for training. Further, DaST saves the substitute model at each iteration, and chooses the one with the highest accuracy to be the final result. We argue that this is normally infeasible because attackers do not have real data to evaluate their saved substitute models. It also requires additional resources and efforts to store and select the best substitute model once the model stealing process ends. This further leads to the unstable training process of DaST. For MAZE and DFME, the convergence has no significant oscillation. The convergence of TANDEMGAN is almost monotonic. The accuracy increases smoothly

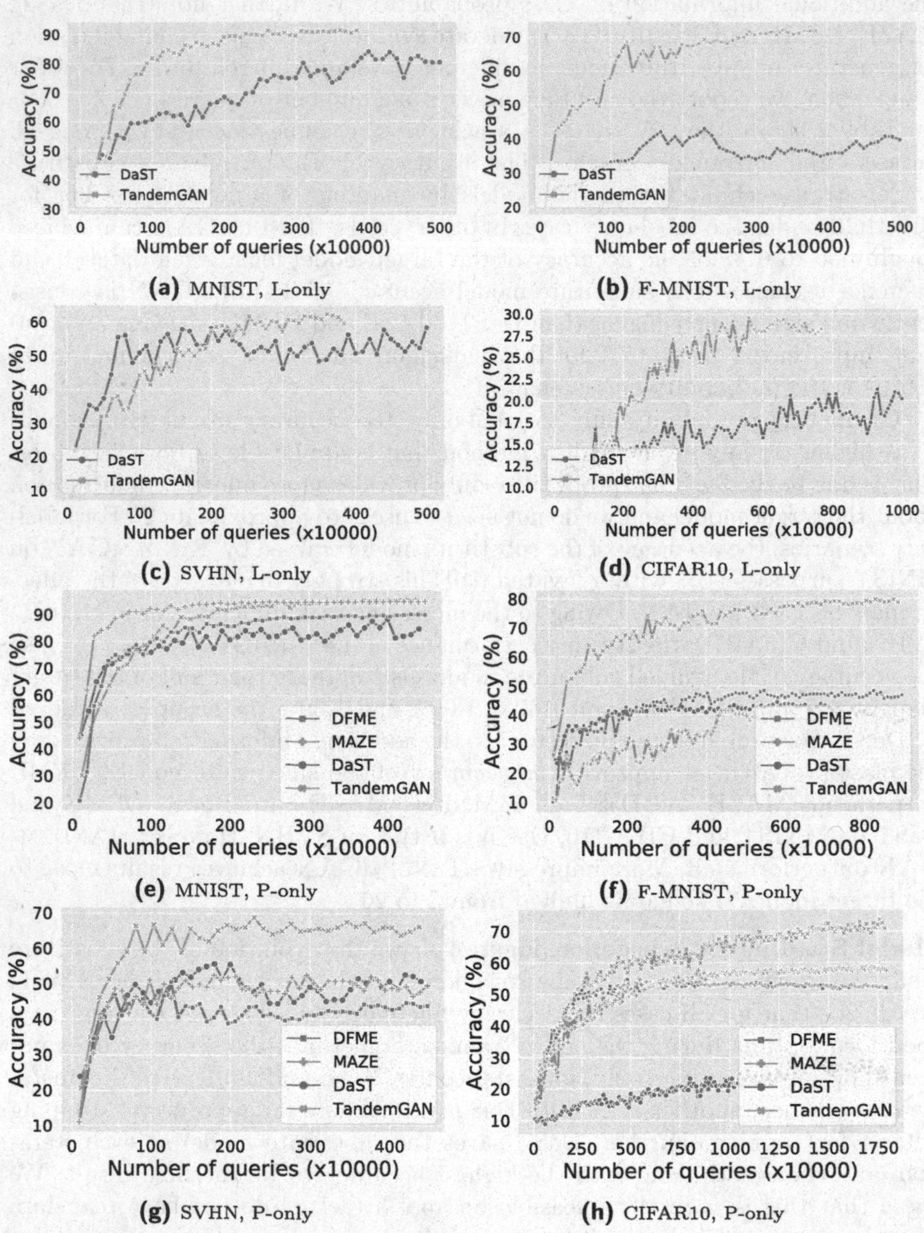

(a) MNIST, L-only
(b) F-MNIST, L-only
(c) SVHN, L-only
(d) CIFAR10, L-only
(e) MNIST, P-only
(f) F-MNIST, P-only
(g) SVHN, P-only
(h) CIFAR10, P-only

Fig. 4. The convergence of accuracy of substitute models during training.

during the whole training, and converges to local optima at around 2M queries for MNIST and SVHN, and 4M for F-MNIST respectively. For CIFAR10, label-only scenario requires 6M queries while it takes around 13M for probability-only scenario. The reason behind the different number of queries is that label-only scenario provides limited information which cannot improve the accuracy even with increased queries for this relatively difficult task. This observation also implies that less information provided by the target model may serve as the short board for challenging tasks to apply model stealing attack.

Inherited from GANs, the generator design of DaST, MAZE and DFME only contains exploration to train the generator and substitute model in a min-max game. In TandemGAN, besides $\mathcal{G}_x$ to search for new space areas which generate diverse data examples, the tandem generator also contains $\mathcal{G}_e$ to exploit the latent code generated by $\mathcal{G}_x$, fine-tuning the task-specific data properties to train $\mathcal{S}$ for model stealing. Benefiting from both exploration and exploitation, our synthetic data captures the real data training scenarios better, resulting in stable convergence towards a good local optima.

4.2 Ablation Study

Table 3. Ablation study for exploration and exploitation.

Ablation	TandemGAN
main results	75.81
w/o exploration	60.74
w/o exploitation	67.23

Table 4. Analysis for different substitute model architectures.

Architecture	TandemGAN
VGG11	75.81
ResNet18	84.70
AlexNet	23.25

Importance of Both Exploring and Exploiting. In previous sections we highlight the advantages to additionally exploit, and not only explore, the synthetic examples. To quantify the benefits of either phase, we present an ablation study using VGG11 as $\mathcal{S}$ for CIFAR10 where TandemGAN forgoes either $\mathcal{G}_x$ (w/o exploration) or $\mathcal{G}_e$ (w/o exploitation). This is achieved by skipping the corresponding training phase, i.e. keeping either $\theta_{\mathcal{G}_x}$ or $\theta_{\mathcal{G}_e}$ fixed. Table 3 shows the results. One clearly sees that both exploring the synthetic data space and exploiting known examples holds the best results. Without exploitation the accuracy drops by 8

Impact of Architecture Choice. As the neural network architecture is unknown by the attacker, we evaluate the impact of choosing different architectures for $\mathcal{S}$ Besides VGG11, we try ResNet-18, which is of the same neural network family of the target model (using ResNet34), as well as AlexNet which is a simpler CNN [15,25]. The accuracy of the substitute AlexNet is low, i.e., 23.25% (see Table 4). The reason is that AlexNet contains 5 convolutional layers

Table 5. Comparison of the $\mathcal{S}$ubstitute model Acc(uracy) under DaST, MAZE, DFME, and TANDEMGAN. Arch. stands for model architecture.

Dataset	$\mathcal{T}$arget		$\mathcal{S}$	Label-only		Probability-only	
	Acc	Arch	Arch	Public Samples	TANDEMGAN	Public Samples	TANDEMGAN
F-MNIST	93.09	VGG16	VGG11	37.08	72.15	32.06	79.96
CIFAR10	90.71	ResNet34	VGG11	15.45	29.58	14.01	75.81

and 3 fully connected layers which is too shallow to train on CIFAR10. Choosing a suitable task-specific substitute model architecture is crucial. ResNet18 achieves the highest accuracy. While ResNet18 is able to achieve slightly better accuracy than VGG11 on CIFAR10, i.e. 92.36% against 91.6% , we impute the performance gap of 9Since the exact architecture of $\mathcal{T}$ is unknown to attackers we choose VGG11 for our main results. Using VGG11 we can better verify broadly the effectiveness and generality of TANDEMGAN.

Stealing the Target Using Publicly Available Data Samples. It is possible to query a target model and steal it using publicly available data samples (E.g., MNIST samples etc), when the real training dataset of the target model is unknown. To study the effectiveness of directly using publicly available data samples for model stealing, in the following, we apply MNIST samples to steal a F-MNIST target model and use SVHN samples to steal a CIFAR10 target model. The results are shown in Table 5. We can see that TANDEMGAN significantly outperforms the baseline which directly uses public samples for querying. Besides, comparing to Table 2, DaST, MAZE and DFME also outperform the baseline. Directly using public data samples to query cannot effectively and efficiently search the input data space of the target model, especially when the model and the task are complicated e.g., the CIFAR10 target. It also cannot utilize the inference feedback from the target to adjust the stealing process. That's why it is much worse than DaST, MAZE, DFME and TANDEMGAN which apply data sample generators for data space searching. In a data-free scenario, it is important to design a good data space searching strategy to perform model stealing attacks.

5 Possible Extension

In this section, we discuss the possible extension of the proposed algorithm. In the following, we show some other perspectives of exploitation.

In the methodology part, we derive the optimization objective of $\mathcal{G}_e$ from a statistical observation [17] that the quality of a target (or a teacher) $\mathcal{T}$ can be measured by log-loss and calibration error (the lower the better). Since we regard the predictions from $\mathcal{T}$ as the ground truth labels in model stealing, in order to minimize the log-loss (or calibration error) on $\mathcal{T}$ we aim to increase the inference confidence of each data example x. Then we define the loss (see Eq. (3)) according to this motivation. From the statistical perspective, the high-quality examples produced by exploitation are defined as examples with high inference confidence on $\mathcal{T}$. Actually, it is possible to extend TandemGAN by designing the optimization objective of $\mathcal{G}_e$ from other perspectives.

From active learning [23] perspectives, $\mathcal{T}$ can be seen as an oracle or a expert who can provide ground truth labels for unlabeled examples. In order to train $\mathcal{S}$, we need examples to query $\mathcal{T}$ and get the predictions. For efficiently and effectively querying $\mathcal{T}$, we need query strategies to select informative examples (high-quality examples). Therefore the query strategies, e.g., variance reduction, entropy sampling and margin sampling etc., of active learning can be utilized to define high-quality examples and design the optimization objective of $\mathcal{G}_e$.

If attackers know some prior information about the training data space of $\mathcal{T}$, e.g., data distribution, we can also consider the information when designing the loss of $\mathcal{G}_e$. In this case, $\mathcal{G}_e$ can be utilized to ensure that the data examples are sampled from the prior distribution. A special case is to consider the class balance of the generated examples when training $\mathcal{G}_e$.

6 Conclusion

It is challenging to design adversarial attacks without knowing the target model parameters nor having access to real-world data. In this paper, we propose a novel and effective data-free model stealing framework, TandemGAN, consisting of substitute model and a tandem generator networks, which aims to steal the knowledge of the target model by synthetic queries. Beyond the state of the art, we not only consider a general adversarial scenario with only the availability of predicted class labels only but also design a steal optimization algorithm to explore and exploit synthetic queries generation. We empirically demonstrate that TandemGAN effectively steals the target model using a small number of queries for four datasets. Under various adversarial scenarios, we show that the model stolen through TandemGAN achieves up to 2.5 times higher accuracy than state-of-the-art data-free model stealing attacks, and its accuracy is as high as the 96 − 67% of target model.

Acknowledgements. This work has been supported by the Spoke "FutureHPC & BigData" of the ICSC-Centro Nazionale di Ricerca in "High Performance Computing, Big Data and Quantum Computing", funded by European Union - NextGenerationEU and the EuPilot project funded by EuroHPC JU under G.A. n. 101034126.

References

1. Aggarwal, C.C., Kong, X., Gu, Q., Han, J., Yu, P.S.: Active learning: a survey, pp. 571–606 (2014)
2. Chandrasekaran, V., Chaudhuri, K., Giacomelli, I., Jha, S., Yan, S.: Exploring connections between active learning and model extraction. In: USENIX Security, pp. 1309–1326 (2020)
3. Goodfellow, I.J., et al.: Generative adversarial nets. In: NIPS (2014)

4. Granese, F., Picot, M., Romanelli, M., Messina, F., Piantanida, P.: MEAD: a multi-armed approach for evaluation of adversarial examples detectors. In: Amini, M.R., Canu, S., Fischer, A., Guns, T., Kralj Novak, P., Tsoumakas, G. (eds.) ECML PKDD 2022. LNCS, vol. 13715, pp. 286–303. Springer, Cham (2023). https://doi.org/10.1007/978-3-031-26409-2_18
5. Guo, C., Pleiss, G., Sun, Y., Weinberger, K.Q.: On calibration of modern neural networks. In: PMLR (2017)
6. Gupta, V., Chakraborty, T.: VIKING: adversarial attack on network embeddings via supervised network poisoning. In: Karlapalem, K., et al. (eds.) PAKDD 2021. LNCS (LNAI), vol. 12714, pp. 103–115. Springer, Cham (2021). https://doi.org/10.1007/978-3-030-75768-7_9
7. Hinton, G.E., Vinyals, O., Dean, J.: Distilling the knowledge in a neural network. CoRR abs/1503.02531 (2015)
8. ur Rehman, S., Huang, Y., Tu, S., Ahmad, B.: Learning a semantic space for modeling images, tags and feelings in cross-media search. In: U., L.H., Lauw, H.W. (eds.) PAKDD 2019. LNCS (LNAI), vol. 11607, pp. 65–76. Springer, Cham (2019). https://doi.org/10.1007/978-3-030-26142-9_7
9. Juuti, M., Szyller, S., Marchal, S., Asokan, N.: PRADA: protecting against DNN model stealing attacks. In: IEEE EuroS&P, pp. 512–527 (2019)
10. Kariyappa, S., Prakash, A., Qureshi, M.K.: MAZE: data-free model stealing attack using zeroth-order gradient estimation. In: IEEE/CVF CVPR (2021)
11. Kariyappa, S., Prakash, A., Qureshi, M.K.: Protecting DNNs from theft using an ensemble of diverse models. In: ICLR (2021)
12. Kariyappa, S., Qureshi, M.K.: Defending against model stealing attacks with adaptive misinformation. In: 2020 IEEE/CVF CVPR, pp. 767–775 (2020)
13. Krishna, K., Tomar, G.S., Parikh, A.P., Papernot, N., Iyyer, M.: Thieves on sesame street! model extraction of BERT-based APIs. In: ICLR (2020)
14. Lin, Z., Shi, Y., Xue, Z.: IDSGAN: generative adversarial networks for attack generation against intrusion detection. In: Gama, J., Li, T., Yu, Y., Chen, E., Zheng, Y., Teng, F. (eds.) PAKDD 2022. LNCS, vol. 13282, pp. 79–91. Springer, Cham (2022). https://doi.org/10.1007/978-3-031-05981-0_7
15. Lu, S., Lu, Z., Zhang, Y.D.: Pathological brain detection based on AlexNet and transfer learning. J. Comput. Sci. **30**, 41–47 (2019)
16. McInnes, L., Healy, J.: UMAP: uniform manifold approximation and projection for dimension reduction. CoRR abs/1802.03426 (2018)
17. Menon, A.K., Rawat, A.S., Reddi, S.J., Kim, S., Kumar, S.: A statistical perspective on distillation. In: ICML. vol. 139, pp. 7632–7642 (2021)
18. Micaelli, P., Storkey, A.J.: Zero-shot knowledge transfer via adversarial belief matching. In: NeurIPS, pp. 9547–9557 (2019)
19. Nguyen, D., et al.: Knowledge distillation with distribution mismatch. In: Oliver, N., Pérez-Cruz, F., Kramer, S., Read, J., Lozano, J.A. (eds.) ECML PKDD 2021. LNCS (LNAI), vol. 12976, pp. 250–265. Springer, Cham (2021). https://doi.org/10.1007/978-3-030-86520-7_16
20. Orekondy, T., Schiele, B., Fritz, M.: Knockoff nets: stealing functionality of black-box models. In: IEEE CVPR, pp. 4954–4963 (2019)
21. Orekondy, T., Schiele, B., Fritz, M.: Prediction poisoning: towards defenses against DNN model stealing attacks. In: ICLR (2020)
22. Polyak, B.T.: Introduction to optimization. Optimization software. Inc., Publications Division, New York **1**, 32 (1987)
23. Ren, P., et al.: A survey of deep active learning. ACM Comput. Surv. (CSUR) **54**(9), 1–40 (2021)

24. Sanyal, S., Addepalli, S., Babu, R.V.: Towards data-free model stealing in a hard label setting. In: IEEE/CVF CVPR, pp. 15284–15293 (2022)
25. Şeker, A.: Evaluation of fabric defect detection based on transfer learning with pre-trained AlexNet. In: IDAP, pp. 1–4. IEEE (2018)
26. Truong, J., Maini, P., Walls, R.J., Papernot, N.: Data-free model extraction. In: IEEE/CVF CVPR 2021, pp. 4771–4780 (2021)
27. Vijayaraghavan, P., Roy, D.: Generating black-box adversarial examples for text classifiers using a deep reinforced model. In: Brefeld, U., Fromont, E., Hotho, A., Knobbe, A., Maathuis, M., Robardet, C. (eds.) ECML PKDD 2019. LNCS (LNAI), vol. 11907, pp. 711–726. Springer, Cham (2020). https://doi.org/10.1007/978-3-030-46147-8_43
28. Yeom, S., Giacomelli, I., Fredrikson, M., Jha, S.: Privacy risk in machine learning: analyzing the connection to overfitting. In: IEEE CSF, pp. 268–282 (2018)
29. Zhou, M., Wu, J., Liu, Y., Liu, S., Zhu, C.: DaST: data-free substitute training for adversarial attacks. In: 2020 IEEE/CVF CVPR, pp. 231–240 (2020)

Exploring the Training Robustness of Distributional Reinforcement Learning Against Noisy State Observations

Ke Sun[1], Yingnan Zhao[2], Shangling Jui[3], and Linglong Kong[1](✉)

[1] University of Alberta, Edmonton, AB, Canada
{ksun6,lkong}@ualberta.ca
[2] Harbin Engineering University, Harbin, China
zhaoyingnan@hrbeu.edu.cn
[3] Huawei Kirin Solution, Shanghai, China
jui.shangling@huawei.com

Abstract. In real scenarios, state observations that an agent observes may contain measurement errors or adversarial noises, misleading the agent to take suboptimal actions or even collapse while training. In this paper, we study the training robustness of distributional Reinforcement Learning (RL), a class of state-of-the-art methods that estimate the whole distribution, as opposed to only the expectation, of the total return. Firstly, we validate the contraction of distributional Bellman operators in the State-Noisy Markov Decision Process (SN-MDP), a typical tabular case that incorporates both random and adversarial state observation noises. In the noisy setting with function approximation, we then analyze the vulnerability of least squared loss in expectation-based RL with either linear or nonlinear function approximation. By contrast, we theoretically characterize the bounded gradient norm of distributional RL loss based on the categorical parameterization equipped with the Kullback-Leibler (KL) divergence. The resulting stable gradients while the optimization in distributional RL accounts for its better training robustness against state observation noises. Finally, extensive experiments on the suite of environments verified that distributional RL is less vulnerable against both random and adversarial noisy state observations compared with its expectation-based counterpar (Code is available in https://github.com/datake/RobustDistRL. The extended version of the paper is in https://arxiv.org/abs/2109.08776.).

Keywords: Distributional Reinforcement Learning · State Observation Noise · Robustness

1 Introduction

Learning robust and high-performance policies for continuous state-action reinforcement learning (RL) domains is crucial to enable the successful adoption of

D. Koutra et al. (Eds.): ECML PKDD 2023, LNAI 14173, pp. 36–51, 2023.
https://doi.org/10.1007/978-3-031-43424-2_3

deep RL in robotics, autonomy, and control problems. However, recent works have demonstrated that deep RL algorithms are vulnerable either to model uncertainties or external disturbances [3,7,9,10,17–19,21]. Particularly, model uncertainties normally occur in a noisy reinforcement learning environment where the agent often encounters systematic or stochastic measurement errors on state observations, such as the inexact locations and velocity obtained from the equipped sensors of a robot. Moreover, external disturbances are normally adversarial in nature. For instance, the adversary can construct adversarial perturbations on state observations to degrade the performance of deep RL algorithms. These two factors lead to noisy state observations that influence the performance of algorithms, precluding the success of RL algorithms in real-world applications.

Existing works mainly focus on improving the robustness of algorithms in the *test environment* with noisy state observations. Smooth Regularized Reinforcement Learning [18] introduced a regularization to enforce smoothness in the learned policy, and thus improved its robustness against measurement errors in the test environment. Similarly, the State-Adversarial Markov Decision Process (SA-MDP) [21] was proposed and the resulting principled policy regularization enhances the adversarial robustness of various kinds of RL algorithms against adversarial noisy state observations. However, both of these works assumed that the agent can access *clean* state observations *during the training*, which is normally not feasible when the environment is inherently noisy, such as unavoidable measurement errors. Hence, the maintenance and formal analysis of policies robust to noisy state observations *during the training* is a worthwhile area of research.

Recent distributional RL algorithms, e.g., C51 [2], Quantile-Regression DQN (QRDQN) [5], Implicit Quantile Networks (IQN) [4] and Moment-Matching DQN (MMD) [16], constantly set new records in Atari games, gaining huge attention in the research community. Existing literature mainly focuses on the performance of distributional RL algorithms, but *other benefits, including the robustness in the noisy environment, of distributional RL algorithms are less studied.* As distributional RL can leverage additional information about the return distribution that captures the uncertainty of the environment more accurately, it is natural to expect that distributional RL with this better representation capability can be less vulnerable to the noisy environment while training, which motivates our research. In this paper, we probe the robustness superiority of distributional RL against various kinds of state observation noises during the training process. Our contributions can be summarized as follows:

- **Tabular setting**. We firstly analyze a systematical noisy setting, i.e., State-Noisy Markov Decision Process (SN-MDP), incorporating both random and adversarial state observation noises. Theoretically, we derive the convergence of distributional Bellman operator in SN-MDP.
- **Function approximation setting**. We elaborate the additional convergence requirement of linear Temporal difference (TD) when exposed to noisy state observations. To clearly compare with distributional RL, we attribute its robustness advantage to the bounded gradients norms regarding state

features based on the categorical parameterization of return distributions. This stable optimization behavior is in contrast to the potentially unbounded gradient norms of expectation-based RL.

- **Experiments**. We demonstrate that distributional RL algorithms potentially enjoy better robustness under various types of noisy state observations across a wide range of classical and continual control environments as well as Atari games. Our conclusion facilitates the deployment of distributional RL algorithms in more practical noisy settings.

2 Background: Distributional RL

In the tabular setting without noisy states, the interaction of an agent with its environment can be naturally modeled as a standard Markov Decision Process (MDP), a 5-tuple $(\mathcal{S}, \mathcal{A}, R, P, \gamma)$. $\mathcal{S}$ and $\mathcal{A}$ are the state and action spaces, $P : \mathcal{S} \times \mathcal{A} \times \mathcal{S} \rightarrow [0, 1]$ is the environment transition dynamics, $R : \mathcal{S} \times \mathcal{A} \times \mathcal{S} \rightarrow \mathbb{R}$ is the reward function and $\gamma \in (0, 1)$ is the discount factor.

Value Function vs Return Distribution. Firstly, we denote the *return* as $Z^\pi(s) = \sum_{k=0}^{\infty} \gamma^k r_{t+k+1}$, where $s_t = s$, representing the cumulative rewards following a policy π, and r_{t+k+1} is reward scalar obtained in the step $t + k + 1$. In the algorithm design, classical expectation-based RL normally focuses on *value function* $V^\pi(s)$, the expectation of the random variable $Z^\pi(s)$:

$$V^\pi(s) := \mathbb{E}\left[Z^\pi(s)\right] = \mathbb{E}\left[\sum_{k=0}^{\infty} \gamma^k r_{t+k+1} \mid s_t = s\right]. \tag{1}$$

In distributional RL we focus on the *return distribution*, the full distribution of $Z^\pi(s)$, and the *state-action return distribution* $Z^\pi(s, a)$ in the control case where $s_t = s, a_t = a$. Both of these distributions can better capture the uncertainty of returns in the MDP beyond just its expectation [4,14].

Distributional Bellman Operator. In expectation-based RL, we update the value function via the Bellman operator $\mathcal{T}^\pi$, while in distributional RL, the updating is applied on the return distribution via the *distributional Bellman operator* $\mathfrak{T}^\pi$. To derive $\mathfrak{T}^\pi$, we firstly define the transition operator $P^\pi : \mathcal{Z} \rightarrow \mathcal{Z}$:

$$\mathcal{P}^\pi Z(s, a) :\stackrel{D}{=} Z\left(S', A'\right), S' \sim P(\cdot|s, a), A' \sim \pi\left(\cdot|S'\right), \tag{2}$$

where we use capital letters S' and A' to emphasize the random nature of both, and $:\stackrel{D}{=}$ indicates convergence in distribution. For simplicity, we denote $Z^\pi(s, a)$ by $Z(s, a)$. Thus, the distributional Bellman operator $\mathfrak{T}^\pi$ is defined as:

$$\mathfrak{T}^\pi Z(s, a) :\stackrel{D}{=} R(s, a, S') + \gamma \mathcal{P}^\pi Z(s, a). \tag{3}$$

$\mathfrak{T}^\pi$ is still a contraction for policy evaluation under the maximal form of either Wasserstein metric d_p (Quantile Regression distributional RL) [2,5] or the categorical parameterization equipped with Kullback-Leibler (KL) divergence (Categorical distributional RL) [2] over the target and current return distributions.

3 Tabular Case: State-Noisy MDP

In this section, we extend State-Adversarial Markov Decision Process (SA-MDP) [21] to a more general State-Noisy Markov Decision Process (SN-MDP) by incorporating both random and adversarial state noises, and particularly provide a proof of the convergence and contraction of distributional Bellman operators in this setting.

Definitions. SN-MDP is a 6-tuple $(\mathcal{S}, \mathcal{A}, R, P, \gamma, N)$, as exhibited in Fig. 1, where the noise generating mechanism $N(\cdot|s)$ maps the state from s to $v(s)$ using either random or adversarial noise with the Markovian and stationary probability $N(v(s)|s)$. It is worthwhile to note that the explicit definition of the noise mechanism N here is based on discrete state transitions, but the analysis can be naturally extended to the continuous case if we let the state space go to infinity. Moreover, let $\mathcal{B}(s)$ be the set that contains the allowed noise space for the noise generating mechanism N, i.e., $v(s) \in \mathcal{B}(s)$.

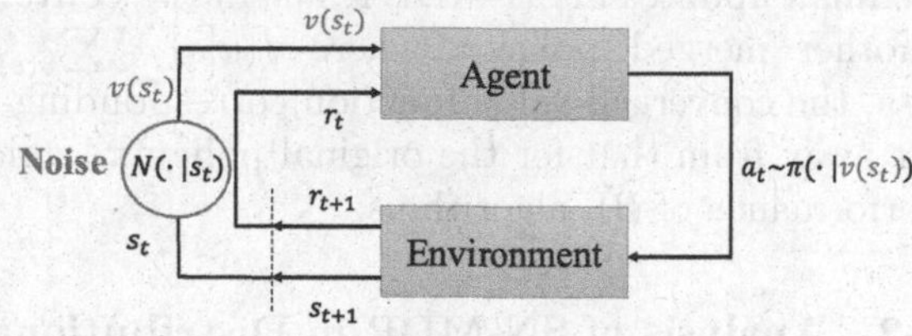

Fig. 1. State-Noisy Markov Decision Process. $v(s_t)$ is perturbed by the noise mechanism N.

Following the setting in [21], we only manipulate state observations but do not change the underlying environment transition dynamics based on s or the agent's actions directly. As such, our SN-MDP is more suitable to model the random measurement error, e.g., sensor errors and equipment inaccuracies, and adversarial state observation perturbations in safety-critical scenarios. This setting is also aligned with many adversarial attacks on state observations [9,12]. The following contractivity analysis regarding value function or distribution is directly based the state s rather than $v(s)$ as it is more natural and convenient to capture the uncertainty of MDP.

3.1 Analysis of SN-MDP for Expectation-Based RL

We define the value function $\tilde{V}_{\pi \circ N}$ given π in SN-MDP. The Bellman Equations regarding the new value function $\tilde{V}_{\pi \circ N}$ are given by:

$$\tilde{V}_{\pi \circ N}(s) = \sum_{a} \sum_{v(s)} N(v(s)|s)\pi(a|v(s)) \sum_{s'} p(s'|s,a) \left[R(s,a,s') + \gamma \tilde{V}_{\pi \circ N}(s') \right], \tag{4}$$

where the random noise transits s into $v(s)$ with a certain probability and the adversarial noise is the special case of $N(v(s)|s)$ where $N(v^*(s)|s) = 1$ if $v^*(s)$ is the optimal adversarial noisy state given s, and $N(v(s)|s) = 0$ otherwise. We denote Bellman operators under random noise mechanism $N^r(\cdot|s)$ and adversarial noise mechanism $N^*(\cdot|s)$ as $\mathcal{T}_r^\pi$ and $\mathcal{T}_a^\pi$, respectively. This implies that $\mathcal{T}_r^\pi \tilde{V}_{\pi \circ N} = \tilde{V}_{\pi \circ N^r}$ and $\mathcal{T}_a^\pi \tilde{V}_{\pi \circ N} = \tilde{V}_{\pi \circ N^*}$. We extend Theorem 1 in [21] to both random and adversarial noise scenarios, and immediately obtain that both $\mathcal{T}_r^\pi$ and $\mathcal{T}_a^\pi$ are contraction operators in SN-MDP. We provide a rigorous description in Theorem 3 with the proof in Appendix A.

The insightful and pivotal conclusion from Theorem 3 is $\mathcal{T}_a^\pi \tilde{V}_{\pi \circ N} = \min_N \tilde{V}_{\pi \circ N}$. This implies that the adversary attempts to minimize the value function, forcing the agent to select the worse-case action among the allowed transition probability space $N(\cdot|s)$ for each state s. The crux of the proof is that Bellman updates in SN-MDP result in the convergence to the value function for another "merged" policy π' where $\pi'(a|s) = \sum_{v(s)} N(v(s)|s)\pi(a|v(s))$. Nevertheless, the converged value function corresponding to the merged policy might be far away from that for the original policy π, which is more likely to worsen the performance of RL algorithms.

3.2 Analysis of SN-MDP in Distributional RL

In the SN-MDP setting for distributional RL, the new distributional Bellman equations use new transition operators in place of $\mathcal{P}^\pi$ in Eq. 2. The new transition operators $\mathcal{P}_r^\pi$ and $\mathcal{P}_a^\pi$, for the random and adversarial settings, are defined as:

$$\begin{aligned} \mathcal{P}_r^\pi Z_N(s,a) &: \overset{D}{=} Z_{N^r}(S', A'), A' \sim \pi(\cdot|V(S')), \text{and} \\ \mathcal{P}_a^\pi Z_N(s,a) &: \overset{D}{=} Z_{N^*}(S', A'), A' \sim \pi(\cdot|V^*(S')), \end{aligned} \tag{5}$$

where $V(S') \sim N^r(\cdot|S')$ is the state random variable after the transition, and $V^*(S')$ is attained from $N^*(\cdot|S')$ under the optimal adversary. Besides, $S' \sim P(\cdot|s,a)$. Therefore, the corresponding new distributional Bellman operators $\mathfrak{T}_r^\pi$ and $\mathfrak{T}_a^\pi$ are formulated as:

$$\begin{aligned} \mathfrak{T}_r^\pi Z_N(s,a) &: \overset{D}{=} R(s,a,S') + \gamma \mathcal{P}_r^\pi Z_N(s,a), \text{and} \\ \mathfrak{T}_a^\pi Z_N(s,a) &: \overset{D}{=} R(s,a,S') + \gamma \mathcal{P}_a^\pi Z_N(s,a). \end{aligned} \tag{6}$$

In this sense, four sources of randomness define the new compound distribution in the SN-MDP: (1) randomness of reward, (2) randomness in the new environment transition dynamics $\mathcal{P}_r^\pi$ or $\mathcal{P}_a^\pi$ that additionally includes (3) the stochasticity of the noisy transition N, and (4) the random next-state return distribution $Z(S', A')$. As our first theoretical contribution, we now show that the new derived distribution Bellman Operators defined in Eq. 6 in SN-MDP setting are convergent and contractive for policy evaluation in Theorem 1.

Theorem 1. *(Convergence and Contraction of Distributional Bellman operators in the SN-MDP) Given a policy π, we define the distributional Bellman operators $\mathfrak{T}_r^\pi$ and $\mathfrak{T}_a^\pi$ in Eq. 6, and consider the Wasserstein metric d_p, the following results hold.*

(1) $\mathfrak{T}_r^\pi$ is a contraction under the maximal form of d_p.
(2) $\mathfrak{T}_a^\pi$ is also a contraction under the maximal form of d_p when $p = 1$, following the greedy adversarial rule, i.e., $N^*(\cdot|s') = \arg\min_{N(\cdot|s')} \mathbb{E}\left[Z(s', a')\right]$ where $a' \sim \pi(\cdot|V(s'))$ and $V(s') \sim N(\cdot|s')$.

We provide the proof in Appendix B. Similar to the convergence conclusions in classical RL, Theorem 1 justified that distributional RL is also capable of converging in this SN-MDP setting. The contraction and convergence of distributional Bellman operators in the SN-MDP is one of our main contributions. This result allows us to deploy distributional RL algorithms comfortably in the tabular setting even with noisy state observations.

4 Function Approximation Case

In the tabular case, both expectation-based and distributional RL have convergence properties. However, in the function approximation case, we firstly show linear TD requires more conditions for the convergence, and point out the vulnerability of expectation-based RL against noisy states even under the bounded rewards assumption. In contrast, we analyze that distributional RL with the categorical representation for the return distributions, is more robust against noisy state observations due to its bounded gradient norms.

4.1 Convergence of Linear TD Under Noisy States

In classical RL with function approximation, the value estimator $\hat{v} : \mathcal{S} \times \mathbb{R}^d \to \mathbb{R}$ parameterized by $\mathbf{w}$ is expressed as $\hat{v}(s, \mathbf{w})$. The objective function is *Mean Squared Value Error* [20] denoted as $\overline{\mathrm{VE}}$:

$$\overline{\mathrm{VE}}(\mathbf{w}) \doteq \sum_{s \in \mathcal{S}} \mu(s) \left[v_\pi(s) - \hat{v}(s, \mathbf{w})\right]^2, \tag{7}$$

where μ is the state distribution. In linear TD, the value estimate is formed simply as the inner product between state features $\mathbf{x}(s)$ and weights $\mathbf{w} \in \mathbb{R}^d$, given by $\hat{v}(s, \mathbf{w}) \stackrel{\text{def}}{=} \mathbf{w}^\top \mathbf{x}(s)$. At each step, the state feature can be rewritten as $\mathbf{x}_t \stackrel{\text{def}}{=} \mathbf{x}(S_t) \in \mathbb{R}^d$. Thus, the TD update at step t is:

$$\mathbf{w}_{t+1} \leftarrow \mathbf{w}_t + \alpha_t (R_{t+1} + \gamma \mathbf{w}_t^\top \mathbf{x}_{t+1} - \mathbf{w}_t^\top \mathbf{x}_t) \mathbf{x}_t \tag{8}$$

where α_t is the step size at time t. Once the system has reached the steady state for any $\mathbf{w}_t$, then the expected next weight vector can be written as $\mathbb{E}[\mathbf{w}_{t+1}|\mathbf{w}_t] = \mathbf{w}_t + \alpha_t(\mathbf{b} - \mathbf{A}\mathbf{w}_t)$, where $\mathbf{b} = \mathbb{E}(R_{t+1}\mathbf{x}_t) \in \mathbb{R}^d$ and $\mathbf{A} \doteq \mathbb{E}\left[\mathbf{x}_t d_t^\top\right] \in \mathbb{R}^{d \times d}$. The TD fixed point $\mathbf{w}_{\mathrm{TD}}$ to the system satisfies $\mathbf{A}\mathbf{w}_{\mathrm{TD}} = \mathbf{b}$. From [20], we know that the matrix $\mathbf{A}$ determines the convergence in the linear TD setting. In particular, $\mathbf{w}_t$ converges with probability one to the TD fixed point if $\mathbf{A}$ is positive definite. However, if we add state noises η on $\mathbf{x}_t$ in Eq. 8, the convergence condition will be different. As shown in Theorem 2 (a more formal version with the proof is given in Appendix D), linear TD under noisy state observations requires additional positive definiteness condition.

Theorem 2. *(Covergence Conditions for Linear TD under Noisy State Observations) Define* $\mathbf{P}$ *as the* $|\mathcal{S}| \times |\mathcal{S}|$ *matrix forming from the state transition probability* $p(s'|s)$, $\mathbf{D}$ *as the* $|\mathcal{S}| \times |\mathcal{S}|$ *diagonal matrix with* $\mu(s)$ *on its diagonal, and*

$\mathbf{X}$ as the $|\mathcal{S}| \times d$ matrix with $\mathbf{x}(s)$ as its rows, and $\mathbf{E}$ is the $|\mathcal{S}| \times d$ perturbation matrix with each perturbation vector $\mathbf{e}(s)$ as its rows. $\mathbf{w}_t$ converges to TD fixed point **when both A and $(\mathbf{X}+\mathbf{E})^\top\mathbf{DPE}$ are positive definite.**

However, directly analyzing the convergence conditions of distributional linear TD and then comparing with them in Theorem 2 for classical linear TD is tricky in theory. As such, we additionally provide a sensitivity comparison of both expectation-based and distributional RL through the lens of their gradients regarding state features as follows.

4.2 Vulnerability of Expectation-Based RL

We reveal that the vulnerability of expectation-based RL can be attributed to its unbounded gradient characteristics in both linear and nonlinear approximation settings.

Linear Approximation Setting. To solve the *weighted* least squared minimization in Eq. 7, we leverage Stochastic Gradient Descent (SGD) on the empirical version of $\overline{\text{VE}}$, which we denote as $g_{\overline{\text{VE}}}$. *We focus on the gradient norm of $g_{\overline{\text{VE}}}$ regarding the state features $\mathbf{x}(s)$ (or $\mathbf{x}_t$) as the gradient of loss w.r.t state observations is highly correlated with the sensitivity or robustness of algorithms against the noisy state observations.* For a fair comparison with distributional RL in next section, we additionally bound the norm of $\mathbf{w}$, i.e., $\|\mathbf{w}\| \leq l$, which can also be easily satisfied by imposing ℓ_1 or ℓ_2 regularization. Therefore, we derive the upper bound of gradient norm of $g_{\overline{\text{VE}}}$ as

$$\|\frac{\partial g_{\overline{\text{VE}}(\mathbf{w})}}{\partial \mathbf{x}_t}\| = |U_t - \mathbf{w}_t^\top \mathbf{x}_t| \|\mathbf{w}_t\| \leq |U_t - \mathbf{w}_t^\top \mathbf{x}_t| l, \tag{9}$$

where the target U_t can be either an unbiased estimate via Monte Carlo method with $U_t = \sum_{k=0}^{\infty} \gamma^k r_{t+k+1}$, or a biased estimate via TD learning with $U_t = r_{t+1} + \gamma \mathbf{w}_t^\top \mathbf{x}_{t+1}$. However, this upper bound $|U_t - \mathbf{w}_t^\top \mathbf{x}_t| l$ heavily depends on the perturbation size or noise strength. Even under the bounded rewards assumption, i.e., $r \in [R_{\min}, R_{\max}]$, we can bound U_t as $U_t = \sum_{k=0}^{\infty} \gamma^k r_{t+k+1} \in [\frac{R_{\min}}{1-\gamma}, \frac{R_{\max}}{1-\gamma}]$. However, this upper bound can be arbitrarily large if we have no restriction on the noise size, leading to a potentially huge vulnerability against state observation noises.

Nonlinear Approximation Setting. The potentially unbounded gradient norm issue of expectation-based RL in the linear case still remains in the nonlinear approximation setting. We express the value estimate $\hat{v}$ as $\hat{v}(s; \mathbf{w}, \theta) = \phi_{\mathbf{w}}(\mathbf{x}(s))^\top \theta$, where $\phi_{\mathbf{w}}(\mathbf{x}(s))$ is the representation vector of the state feature $\mathbf{x}(s)$ in the penultimate layer of neural network-based value function approximator. Correspondingly, θ would be the parameters in the last layer of this value neural network. We simplify $\phi_{\mathbf{w}}(\mathbf{x}(s))_t$ as $\phi_{\mathbf{w},t}$ in the step t update. As such, akin to the linear case, we derive the upper bound of gradient norm of $g_{\overline{\text{VE}}}$ as

$$\|\frac{\partial g_{\overline{\text{VE}}(\mathbf{w},\theta)}}{\partial \mathbf{x}_t}\| = |U_t - \phi_{\mathbf{w},t}^\top \theta_t| \|\nabla_{\mathbf{x}_t} \phi_{\mathbf{w},t}^\top \theta_t\| \leq |U_t - \phi_{\mathbf{w},t}^\top \theta_t| lL, \tag{10}$$

where we assume the function $\phi_{\mathbf{w}}(\cdot)$ is L-Lipschitz continuous regarding its input state feature $\mathbf{x}(s)$, and $\|\theta\| \leq l$ as well for a fair comparison with distributional RL. It turns out that $|U_t - \phi_{\mathbf{w},t}^{\top}\theta_t|$ still depends on the perturbation size, and can be still arbitrarily large if there is no restriction on the noise size. In contrast, we further show that gradient norms in distributional RL can be upper bounded **regardless of the perturbation size or noise strength.**

4.3 Robustness Advantage of Distributional RL

We analyze the distributional loss in distributional RL can potentially lead to bounded gradient norms regarding state features regardless of the perturbation size or noise strength, yielding its training robustness against state noises. In distributional RL our goal is to minimize a distribution loss $\mathcal{L}\left(Z_{\mathbf{w}}, \mathfrak{T}Z_{\mathbf{w}}\right)$ between the current return distribution of $Z_{\mathbf{w}}$ and its target return distribution of $\mathfrak{T}Z_{\mathbf{w}}$.

Our robustness analysis is based on the categorical parameterization [11] on the return distribution with the KL divergence, a typical choice also used in the first distributional RL branch, i.e., C51 [2]. Specifically, we uniformly partition the support of $Z_{\mathbf{w}}(s)$ into k bins, and let the histogram function $f : \mathcal{X} \rightarrow [0,1]^k$ provide k-dimensional vector $f(\mathbf{x}(s))$ of the coefficients indicating the probability the target is in that bin given $\mathbf{x}(s)$. We use *softmax* to output the k probabilities of $f(\mathbf{x}(s))$. Therefore, the categorical distributional RL loss $\mathcal{L}(Z_{\mathbf{w}}(s), \mathfrak{T}Z_{\mathbf{w}}(s))$, denoted as $\mathcal{L}_{\mathbf{w}}$, equipped with KL divergence between $Z_{\mathbf{w}}$ and $\mathfrak{T}Z_{\mathbf{w}}$ can be simplified as

$$\mathcal{L}(Z_{\mathbf{w}}(s), \mathfrak{T}Z_{\mathbf{w}}(s)) \propto -\sum_{i=1}^{k} p_i \log f_i^{\mathbf{w}}(\mathbf{x}(s)), \tag{11}$$

where we use $\mathbf{w}$ to parameterize the function f in the distributional loss $\mathcal{L}_{\mathbf{w}}$, and the target probability p_i is the cumulative probability increment of target distribution $\mathfrak{T}Z_{\mathbf{w}}$ within the i-th bin. Detailed derivation about the simplification of categorical distributional loss is in Appendix C.

Linear Approximation Setting. We leverage $\mathbf{x}(s)^{\top}\mathbf{w}_i$ to express the i-th output of f, i.e., $f_i(\mathbf{x}(s)) = \exp\left(\mathbf{x}(s)^{\top}\mathbf{w}_i\right) / \sum_{j=1}^{k} \exp\left(\mathbf{x}(s)^{\top}\mathbf{w}_j\right)$, where all parameters are $\mathbf{w} = \{\mathbf{w}_1, ..., \mathbf{w}_k\}$. Based on this categorical distributional RL loss, we obtain Proposition 1 (proof in Appendix C), revealing that value-based categorical distributional RL loss can result in bounded gradient norms regarding state features $\mathbf{x}(s)$.

Proposition 1. *(Gradient Property of distributional RL in Linear Approximation) Consider the categorical distributional RL loss $\mathcal{L}_{\mathbf{w}}$ in Eq. 11 with the linear approximation. Assume $\|\mathbf{w}_i\| \leq l$ for $\forall i = 1, .., k$, then $\left\| \frac{\partial \mathcal{L}_{\mathbf{w}}}{\partial \mathbf{x}(s)} \right\| \leq kl$.*

In contrast with the unbounded gradient norm in Eq. 9 of classical RL, we have a restricted upper bound in distributional RL loss with a linear approximator, i.e., kl, which is independent of the perturbation size or noise strength.

Nonlinear Approximation Setting. Similar to the nonlinear form in classical expectation-based RL as analyzed in Sect. 4.2, we express the i-th output probabilities of $f(\mathbf{x}(s))$ as $f_i^{\mathbf{w},\theta}(\mathbf{x}(s)) = \exp\left(\phi_{\mathbf{w}}(\mathbf{x}(s))^\top \theta_i\right) / \sum_{j=1}^{k} \exp\left(\phi_{\mathbf{w}}(\mathbf{x}(s))^\top \theta_j\right)$ in distributional RL, where the last layer parameter $\theta = \{\theta_1, ..., \theta_k\}$ and $\phi_{\mathbf{w}}(\mathbf{x}(s))$ is still the representation vector of $\mathbf{x}(s)$. In Proposition 2, we can still attain a bounded gradient norm of distributional RL loss in the nonlinear case.

Proposition 2. *(Gradient Property of distributional RL in Nonlinear Approximation) Consider the categorical distributional RL loss $\mathcal{L}_{\mathbf{w},\theta}$ in Eq. 11 with the nonlinear approximation. Assume $\|\theta_i\| \leq l$ for $\forall i = 1, .., k$ and $\phi_{\mathbf{w}}(\cdot)$ is L-Lipschitz continuous, then $\left\|\frac{\partial \mathcal{L}_{\mathbf{w},\theta}}{\partial \mathbf{x}(s)}\right\| \leq klL$.*

Please refer to Appendix C for the proof. For a fair comparison with nonlinear approximation in classical RL, we still assume the function $\phi_{\mathbf{w}}(\cdot)$ to be L-Lipschitz continuous and $\|\theta_i\| \leq l$. *Interestingly, the bounded gradient norm of the distributional RL loss is independent of the noise size, which is in stark contrast to the potentially unrestricted gradients in classical RL in Eq.* 10 *that heavily depends on the noise size.* Based on Theorems 1 and 2, we conclude that the bounded gradient behaviors of distributional RL could reduce its sensitivity to state noises, and thus mitigate the interference of the state observation noises compared with expectation-based RL, potentially leading to better training robustness.

Extension of TD Convergence and Sensitivity Analysis. As supplementary, we also conduct the analysis on different TD convergence conditions under the unbalanced perturbations on either the current or next state observations. Please refer to Theorem 4 with the detailed explanation in Appendix D. In addition, we also conduct a sensitivity analysis from the perspective of the *influence function* to characterize the impact of state noises on an estimator. We provide the details in Theorem 5 of Appendix E.

5 Experiments

We make a comparison between expectation-based and distributional RL algorithms against various noisy state observations across **classical and continuous control environments as well as Atari games, including Cartpole and MountainCar (classical control), Ant, Humanoidstandup and Halfcheetah (continuous control), Breakout and Qbert (Atari games)**. For the continuous control environment, we use Soft Actor Critic [8] and Distributional Soft Actor Critic [13] with C51 as the critic loss and thus we denote them as SAC and DAC (C51), respectively. For the classical control and Atari games, we utilize DQN [15] as the baseline, and C51 [2], QRDQN [5] as its distributional counterparts. The training robustness of C51 could be consistent with our theoretical analysis, while QRDQN, the more commonly-used one, is also applied to demonstrate that our robustness analysis can also be empirically applicable to broader distributional RL algorithms.

Implementation and Experimental Setup. For the continuous control environment, we modified our algorithm based on released implementation of [13]. For classical control and Atari games, we followed the procedure in [6,23]. All the experimental settings, including parameters, are identical to the distributional RL baselines implemented by [5,22]. We perform 200 runs on both Cart Pole and Mountain Car and 3 runs on Breakout and Qbert. Reported results are averaged with shading indicating the standard error. The learning curve is smoothed over a window of size 10 before averaging across runs. Please refer to Appendix F for more details about the experimental setup.

Evaluation of Training Robustness. Due to final performance difference between expectation-based and distributional RL, for a fair comparison we calculate *the ratio between final average returns under random or adversarial state noises with different noise strengths and the original level without any state noises.* This ratio can be used to measure the robustness maintenance after the agent gets exposed to noisy state observations.

Random and Adversarial State Noises. We use Gaussian noise with different standard deviations to simulate random state noises, while for the adversarial state noise, we apply the most typical adversarial state perturbations proposed in [9,17]. For the choice of perturbation size, we followed [21], where the set of noises $B(s)$ is defined as an ℓ_∞ norm ball around s with a radius ϵ, given

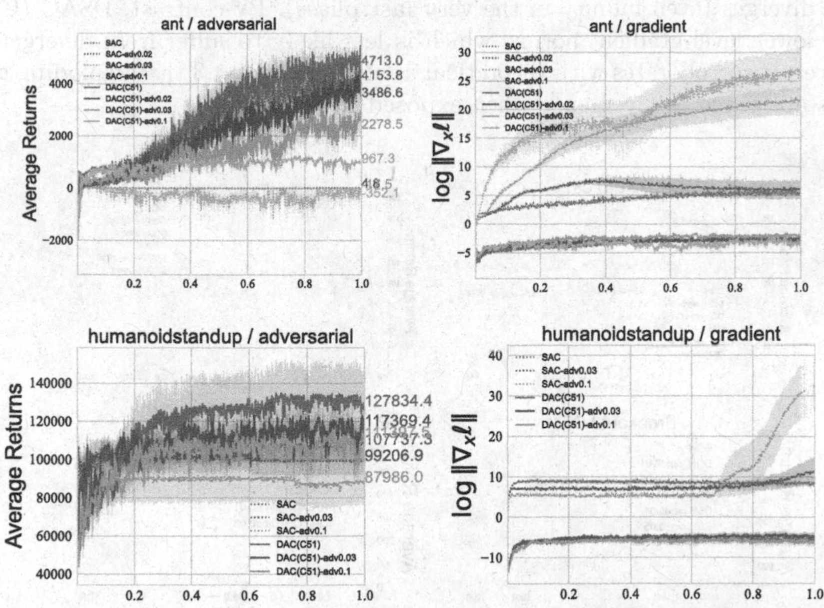

Fig. 2. Average returns of SAC and DAC (C51) against **adversarial** state observation noises in the training on Ant and Humanoidstandup under 5 runs. Gradient norms in the logarithm scale of AC and DAC (C51) in the adversarial setting. **advX** in the legend indicates random state observations with the perturbation size ϵ **X**.

by $\ell_\infty B(s) := \{\hat{s} : \|s - \hat{s}\|_\infty \leq \epsilon\}$. We apply Projected Gradient Descent (PGD) version in [17], with 3 fixed iterations while adjusting ϵ to control the perturbation strength. Due to the page limit, we defer similar results under more advanced MAD attack [21] in Appendix H.

5.1 Results on Continuous Control Environments

We compare SAC with DAC (C51) on Ant and Humanoidstandup. Due to the space limit, we mainly present the algorithm performance in the **adversarial** setting. Figure 2 suggests that distributional RL algorithms, i.e., DAC (C51), are less sensitive to their expectation-based counterparts, i.e., SAC, according to learning curves of average returns on Ant and Humanoidstandup. More importantly, Fig. 2 demonstrates that DAC (C51) enjoys smaller gradient norms compared with SAC, and SAC with a larger perturbation size is prone to unstable training with much larger gradient magnitudes. In particular, On Humanoidstandup, SAC converges undesirably with adv0.01 (green line), but its gradient norm diverges (even infinity in the very last phase). By contrast, DSAC (C51) has a lower level gradient norms, which is less likely to suffer from divergence. This result corroborates with theoretical analysis in Sect. 4.3 that exploding gradients are prone to divergence when exposed to state noises.

Table 1. Robustness ratio of algorithms under **adversarial** state observations with different ϵ on Ant and Humanoidstandup.

Robustness(%)	Adversarial	$\epsilon = 0.02$	$\epsilon = 0.03$	$\epsilon = 0.1$
Ant	SAC	≈ 0	≈ 0	≈ 0
	DAC (C51)	**74.0**	**48.3**	**20.5**
Robustness(%)	Adversarial	$\epsilon = 0.03$	$\epsilon = 0.1$	
Humanoidstandup	SAC	**92.1**	81.7	
	DAC (C51)	91.8	**87.1**	

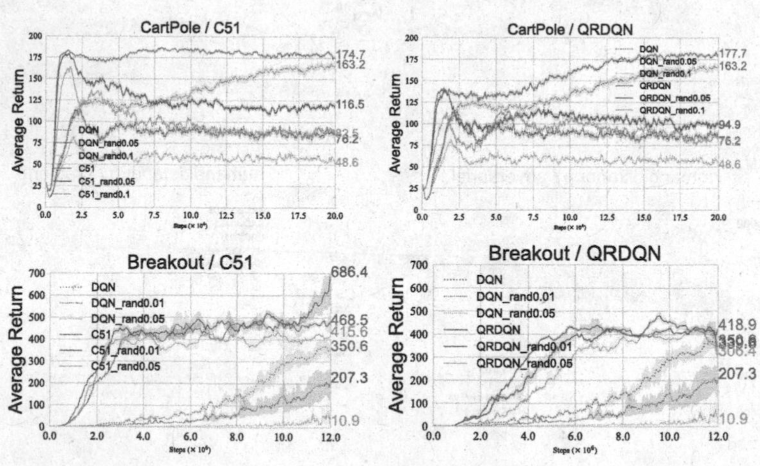

Fig. 3. Average returns of DQN, C51 and QRDQN against **random** state observation noises on CartPole and Breakout. **randX** in the legend indicates random state observations with the standard deviation **X**.

A quantitative result is also shown in Table 1, where distributional RL algorithms tend to maintain a higher robustness ratio as opposed to their expectation-based RL versions. We also note that the training robustness of distributional RL algorithms may not be significant if the perturbation size is slightly small, e.g., on Humanoidstandup. However, if we carefully vary perturbation sizes in a proper range, we can easily observe the robustness advantage of distributional RL against adversarial noises, e.g., on Ant. We also investigate the training robustness of more distributional RL algorithms over more games. Thus, we evaluate the sensitivity of D4PG [1] against adversarial noises on Halfcheetah, which can be viewed as the distributional version of DDPG. As suggested in Fig. 12 in Appendix I, the distributional RL algorithm D4PG is much less vulnerable than it expectation-based RL counterpart DDPG against adversarial noises.

5.2 Results on Classical Control and Atari Games

Results under Random State Noises. We investigate the training robustness of DQN, C51 and QRDQN on classical control environments and typical Atari games, against the random noisy state observations. Gaussian state noises are continuously injected in the while training process of RL algorithms, while the agent encounters noisy current state observations while conducting the TD learning. Due to the space limit, here we mainly present learning curves of algorithms on CartPole and Breakout. As shown in Fig. 3, both C51 and QRDQN achieve similar performance to DQN after the training *without any random state noises.* However, when we start to inject random state noises with different noise sizes during the training process, their learning curves show different sensitivity and robustness. Both C51 and QRDQN are more robust against the random state noises than DQN, with the less interference for the training under the same random noises. Remarkably, in Breakout the performance of both C51 and QRDQN (solid lines) only slightly decreases, while DQN (dashed lines) degrades dramatically and even diverges when the standard deviation is 0.05. This significant difference provides a strong empirical evidence to verify the robustness advantage of distributional RL algorithms.

Table 2. Robustness ratio of three algorithms under **random** state observations with different standard deviations (std) on CartPole and Breakout.

Robustness(%)	Random	std = 0.05	std = 0.1
CartPole	DQN	44.2	28.6
	QRDQN	54.5	43.4
	C51	**67.0**	**47.3**
Robustness(%)	Random	std = 0.01	std = 0.05
Breakout	DQN	59.1	≈ 0
	QRDQN	81.1	73.1
	C51	**146.5**	**88.7**

A detailed comparison is summarized in Table 2. It turns out that the training robustness of both QRDQN and C51 surpass DQN significantly. Note that the robustness ratio for C51 under std = 0.01 noises is 146.5%, which is above 100%. This can be explained as a proper randomness added in the training might be beneficial to exploration, yielding better generalization of algorithms.

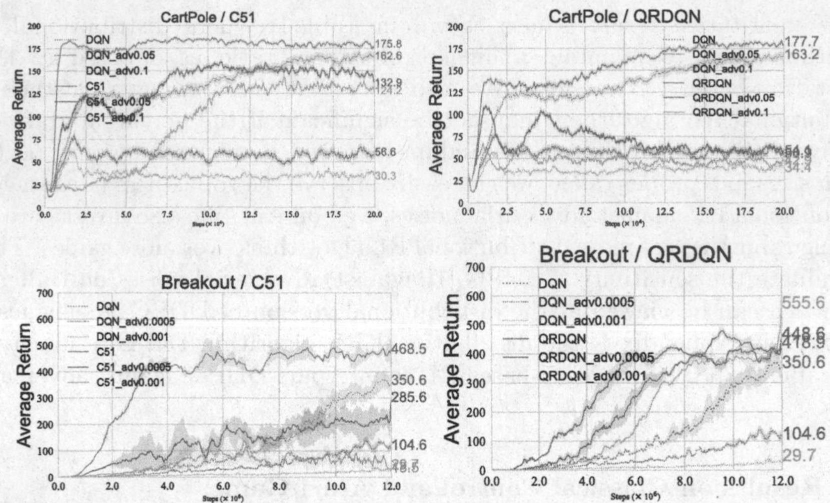

Fig. 4. Average returns of DQN, C51 and QRDQN against **adversarial** state observation noises across four games. **advX** in the legend indicates random state observations with the perturbation size ϵ **X**.

Results under Adversarial State Noises. Next, we probe the training robustness of DQN, QRDQN and C51 in the setting where the agent encounters the *adversarial* state observations in the current state in the function approximation case. Figure 4 presents the learning curves of algorithms on CartPole and Breakout against noisy states under different adversarial perturbation sizes ϵ.

Table 3. Robustness ratio of three algorithms under **adversarial** state observations with different perturbation sizes ϵ on CartPole and Breakout.

Robustness(%)	Adversarial	$\epsilon = 0.05$	$\epsilon = 0.1$
CartPole	DQN	34.8	18.6
	QRDQN	26.0	24.8
	C51	**75.6**	**70.6**
Robustness(%)	Adversarial	$\epsilon = 0.0005$	$\epsilon = 0.001$
Breakout	DQN	29.8	≈ 0
	QRDQN	**107.1**	**132.6**
	C51	61.0	6.3

It turns out that results under the adversarial state observations are similar to those in the random noises case. Specifically, all algorithms tend to degrade when getting exposed to adversarial state observations, and even are more likely to diverge. However, a key observation is that *distributional RL algorithms, especially QRDQN, are capable of obtaining desirable performance even when DQN diverges.* For instance, in Breakout DQN (dotted green line) in Fig. 4 under the adversarial perturbation with $\epsilon = 0.001$ leads to divergence, while QRDQN (solid green lines) still maintains a desirable performance. The quantitative robustness ratio comparison is also provided in Table 3. It suggests that the adversarial robustness of C51 is superior to DQN and QRDQN in CartPole, while QRDQN is remarkably less sensitive to adversarial noises than both DQN and C51 in Breakout.

Results on MountainCar and Qbert. Due to the space limit, we mainly summarize the robustness ratio of algorithms on MountainCar and Qbert in Table 4. It turns out that the training robustness of QRDQN is significantly advantageous over DQN on both MountainCar and Qbert environments across two types of state noises, which also corroborates the robustness advantage of distributional RL algorithms over their expectation-based RL counterpart.

Table 4. Robustness ratio of DQN and QRDQN under random and adversarial state noises on MountainCar and Qbert.

Robustness(%)	Algorithms	std = 0.0125	$\epsilon = 0.1$
MountainCar	DQN	32.4	32.5
	QRDQN	**79.0**	**44.7**
Robustness(%)	Algorithms	std = 0.05	$\epsilon = 0.005$
Qbert	DQN	10.8	6.3
	QRDQN	**34.5**	**32.9**

Sensitivity Analysis of Different Perturbed States and Influence Function Analysis. We also conduct experiments to verify the sensitivity analysis results (Theorems 4 and 5) in Appendix D about more TD convergence conditions and influence function in Appendix E. These empirical evidence also coincides with our theoretical results.

6 Discussion and Conclusion

Our analysis is mainly based on categorical distributional RL, and it would be more convincing if we can still have an analytical conclusion under Wasserstein distance. Moreover, we attribute the robustness advantage of distributional RL algorithms into the unbounded gradient norms regarding state features, but other factors, e.g., representation ability, may also contribute to the training robustness. We leave the exploration towards this direction as future works.

In this paper, we explore the training robustness of distributional RL against both random and adversarial noisy state observations. Based on the convergence proof of distributional RL in the SN-MDP, we further reveal the stable gradient behavior of distributional RL loss as opposed to classical RL, accounting for its less vulnerability. Empirical observations coincides with our theoretical results.

Acknowledgements. We would like to thank the anonymous reviewers for great feedback on the paper. Dr. Kong was supported by the Natural Sciences and Engineering Research Council of Canada (NSERC), the University of Alberta/Huawei Joint Innovation Collaboration, Huawei Technologies Canada Co., Ltd., and Canada Research Chair in Statistical Learning, the Alberta Machine Intelligence Institute (Amii), and Canada CIFAR AI Chair (CCAI). Yingnan Zhao and Ke Sun were supported by the State Scholarship Fund from China Scholarship Council (No: 202006120405 and No: 202006010082).

References

1. Barth-Maron, G., et al.: Distributed distributional deterministic policy gradients. In: International Conference on Learning Representations (ICLR) (2018)
2. Bellemare, M.G., Dabney, W., Munos, R.: A distributional perspective on reinforcement learning. In: International Conference on Machine Learning (ICML) (2017)
3. Chen, T., Liu, J., Xiang, Y., Niu, W., Tong, E., Han, Z.: Adversarial attack and defense in reinforcement learning-from AI security view. Cybersecurity **2**(1), 11 (2019)
4. Dabney, W., Ostrovski, G., Silver, D., Munos, R.: Implicit quantile networks for distributional reinforcement learning. In: International Conference on Machine Learning (ICML) (2018)
5. Dabney, W., Rowland, M., Bellemare, M.G., Munos, R.: Distributional reinforcement learning with quantile regression. In: Association for the Advancement of Artificial Intelligence (AAAI) (2018)
6. Ghiassian, S., Patterson, A., Garg, S., Gupta, D., White, A., White, M.: Gradient temporal-difference learning with regularized corrections. In: International Conference on Machine Learning, pp. 3524–3534. PMLR (2020)
7. Guan, Z., et al.: Robust stochastic bandit algorithms under probabilistic unbounded adversarial attack. In: AAAI, pp. 4036–4043 (2020)
8. Haarnoja, T., Zhou, A., Abbeel, P., Levine, S.: Soft actor-critic: off-policy maximum entropy deep reinforcement learning with a stochastic actor. In: International Conference on Machine Learning, pp. 1861–1870. PMLR (2018)
9. Huang, S., Papernot, N., Goodfellow, I., Duan, Y., Abbeel, P.: Adversarial attacks on neural network policies. In: International Conference on Learning Representations (ICLR) workshop (2017)
10. Ilahi, I., et al.: Challenges and countermeasures for adversarial attacks on deep reinforcement learning. arXiv preprint arXiv:2001.09684 (2020)
11. Imani, E., White, M.: Improving regression performance with distributional losses. In: International Conference on Machine Learning, pp. 2157–2166. PMLR (2018)
12. Lin, Y.C., et al.: Tactics of adversarial attack on deep reinforcement learning agents. arXiv preprint arXiv:1703.06748 (2017)
13. Ma, X., Xia, L., Zhou, Z., Yang, J., Zhao, Q.: DSAC: distributional soft actor critic for risk-sensitive reinforcement learning. arXiv preprint arXiv:2004.14547 (2020)
14. Mavrin, B., Zhang, S., Yao, H., Kong, L., Wu, K., Yu, Y.: Distributional reinforcement learning for efficient exploration. In: International Conference on Machine Learning (ICML) (2019)
15. Mnih, V., et al.: Human-level control through deep reinforcement learning. Nature **518**(7540), 529–533 (2015)
16. Nguyen, T.T., Gupta, S., Venkatesh, S.: Distributional reinforcement learning with maximum mean discrepancy. In: Association for the Advancement of Artificial Intelligence (AAAI) (2020)
17. Pattanaik, A., Tang, Z., Liu, S., Bommannan, G., Chowdhary, G.: Robust deep reinforcement learning with adversarial attacks. In: AAMAS (2018)
18. Shen, Q., Li, Y., Jiang, H., Wang, Z., Zhao, T.: Deep reinforcement learning with robust and smooth policy. In: International Conference on Machine Learning, pp. 8707–8718. PMLR (2020)
19. Singh, R., Zhang, Q., Chen, Y.: Improving robustness via risk averse distributional reinforcement learning. arXiv preprint arXiv:2005.00585 (2020)

20. Sutton, R.S., Barto, A.G.: Reinforcement Learning: An Introduction. MIT Press, Cambridge (2018)
21. Zhang, H., Chen, H., Xiao, C., Li, B., Boning, D., Hsieh, C.J.: Robust deep reinforcement learning against adversarial perturbations on observations. In: Advances in Neural Information Processing Systems (2020)
22. Zhang, S.: Modularized implementation of deep RL algorithms in PyTorch (2018). https://github.com/ShangtongZhang/DeepRL
23. Zhang, S., Yao, H.: Quota: The quantile option architecture for reinforcement learning. In: Proceedings of the AAAI Conference on Artificial Intelligence, vol. 33, pp. 5797–5804 (2019)

Overcoming the Limitations of Localization Uncertainty: Efficient and Exact Non-linear Post-processing and Calibration

Moussa Kassem Sbeyti[1,2(✉)], Michelle Karg[1], Christian Wirth[1], Azarm Nowzad[1], and Sahin Albayrak[2]

[1] Continental AG, Hanover, Germany
{moussa.kassem.sbeyti,michelle.karg,christian.2.wirth, azarm.nowzad}@continental-corporation.com
[2] DAI-Labor, Technische Universität Berlin, Berlin, Germany
sahin.albayrak@dai-labor.de

Abstract. Robustly and accurately localizing objects in real-world environments can be challenging due to noisy data, hardware limitations, and the inherent randomness of physical systems. To account for these factors, existing works estimate the aleatoric uncertainty of object detectors by modeling their localization output as a Gaussian distribution $\mathcal{N}(\mu, \sigma^2)$, and training with loss attenuation. We identify three aspects that are unaddressed in the state of the art, but warrant further exploration: (1) the efficient and mathematically sound propagation of $\mathcal{N}(\mu, \sigma^2)$ through non-linear post-processing, (2) the calibration of the predicted uncertainty, and (3) its interpretation. We overcome these limitations by: (1) implementing loss attenuation in EfficientDet, and proposing two deterministic methods for the exact and fast propagation of the output distribution, (2) demonstrating on the KITTI and BDD100K datasets that the predicted uncertainty is miscalibrated, and adapting two calibration methods to the localization task, and (3) investigating the correlation between aleatoric uncertainty and task-relevant error sources. Our contributions are: (1) up to five times faster propagation while increasing localization performance by up to 1%, (2) up to fifteen times smaller expected calibration error, and (3) the predicted uncertainty is found to correlate with occlusion, object distance, detection accuracy, and image quality.

Keywords: Aleatoric Localization Uncertainty · Object Detection · Loss Attenuation · Uncertainty Calibration

1 Introduction

Object detectors in safety-critical systems face multiple challenges, including limited sensor resolution, difficult weather conditions, and ambiguous situations [8,16,20]. These challenges decrease performance regardless of the training frequency, as they induce an inevitable uncertainty called aleatoric uncertainty [17].

D. Koutra et al. (Eds.): ECML PKDD 2023, LNAI 14173, pp. 52–68, 2023.
https://doi.org/10.1007/978-3-031-43424-2_4

Therefore, existing works explicitly integrated aleatoric uncertainty into object detectors via loss attenuation [17] for varying applications, such as enhancing safety, robustness, and performance [5,20,24]. This paper prioritizes localization due to the absence of confidence information from the localization head in object detectors, when compared to the scores provided by the classification head.

EfficientDet [31], a one-stage anchor-based detector, demonstrates state-of-the-art performance in terms of both accuracy and speed on various benchmark datasets, making it an ideal use-case for this paper. An anchor-based detector predicts anchor-relative offsets, which are subjected to non-linear transformations during post-processing to compute the final object coordinates. These offsets are modeled as distributions to account for uncertainty, which raises the crucial question: **How is the output distribution propagated through non-linear functions?** Le et al. [24] is the only work known to us that considers the propagation, and addresses it via sampling. Sampling from a distribution involves drawing samples, transforming them, then recalculating the distribution parameters. It has the downside of either a high computation time for a large sample size or a reduced accuracy for a small one. We therefore develop two novel, fast and exact approaches. The first method is based on normalizing flows, with the advantage of universal applicability to many non-linear, arbitrarily complex functions and output distributions. The second method is tailored for a normal distribution and an exponential transformation. It utilizes the properties of the log-normal distribution, and its advantage is efficiency.

Once the uncertainty is propagated, the focus shifts to assessing its quality: **Is the predicted localization uncertainty calibrated?** Other research on localization uncertainty estimation typically overlooks its calibration [5,15,16,20,24]. Hence, we introduce different approaches inspired by calibration for general classification and regression tasks. We select two established methods: calibrating via an auxiliary model, e.g. isotonic regression [3,21,33], and factor scaling [14,22]. We extend the first method to coordinate- and class-specific calibration. For the second calibration method, we establish and evaluate loss functions during the optimization of the scaling factor, which directly adjusts the predicted uncertainty based on its proximity to the residuals. Both methods are further improved by incorporating the object size, where each object's uncertainty is normalized by its width and height, resulting in a balanced calibration of objects of all sizes and aspect ratios. Furthermore, we provide a data selection process for calibration, which allocates all predictions to their ground-truth based on proximity, in contrast to, e.g. thresholding detections based on the classification score.

After the localization uncertainty is estimated, propagated and calibrated, its interpretability is required to define potential applications (see Fig. 1): **What correlations exist between the data and the uncertainty?** Related works discover that aleatoric uncertainty correlates with occlusion [5,8,10,20] and object distance due to sparsity in point clouds [8], but not with detection accuracy [8,10]. We investigate the latter and discover the contrary. We verify and show to which extent aleatoric uncertainty correlates with occlusion and detection performance, and extend the analysis to object distance and image quality.

In summary, the contributions of our work are:

- Development of two novel, exact and fast methods for uncertainty propagation through non-linear functions, enabling accurate uncertainty estimation without additional drawbacks.
- Development and extension of two calibration methods and a data selection approach for accurate calibration in the context of object localization.
- A comprehensive experimental overview of the quality and correlation between aleatoric uncertainty and traceable metrics, which further advances the understanding of aleatoric uncertainty.

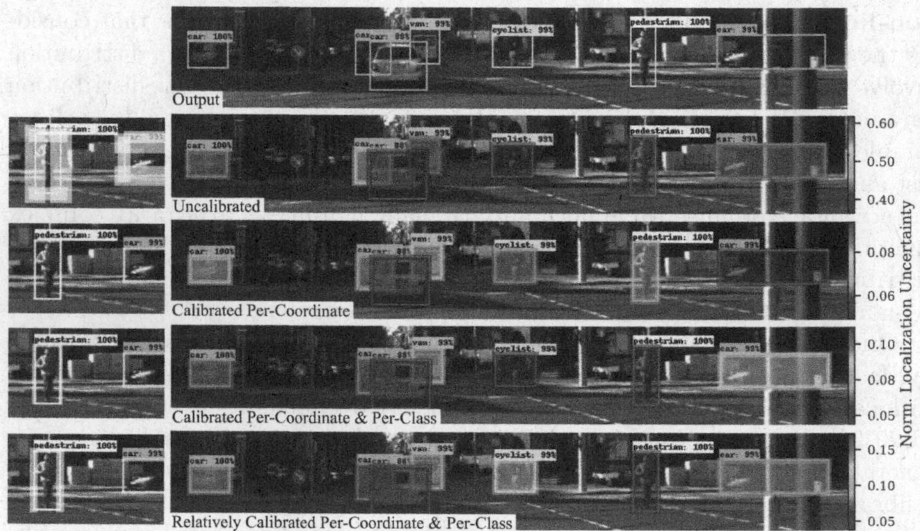

Fig. 1. Aleatoric localization uncertainty σ **per object** normalized by its width and height (right), and an example crop with $\mu \pm 10\sigma$ **per coordinate** (left). Uncertainty correlates with occlusion, distance and localization accuracy. Calibration reduces uncertainty. Per-coordinate calibration strengthens the correlation with accuracy. Per-class calibration shifts the uncertainty towards classes with lower accuracy. Relative calibration considers object area and aspect ratio.

2 Background and Related Work

This section presents a concise overview of existing works on aleatoric uncertainty estimation, decoding in object detectors, and calibration for regression.

Loss Attenuation. A widely adopted approach for estimating aleatoric uncertainty is the sampling-free loss attenuation, which assumes that observation noise depends on the input [17]. By extending the network output to include both the mean μ and variance σ^2, i.e. modeling it as a Gaussian distribution, and training the network on the negative log-likelihood (NLL), the uncertainty can be learned as a function of the data. Choi et al. [5], Kraus and Dietmayer [20] and Feng, Rosenbaum and Dietmayer [8, 10] show that loss attenuation enhances the performance of 2D and 3D object detectors. They find that the estimated uncertainty correlates with occlusion [8,10,20] and object distance based on LiDAR data [8,10], but it does not correlate with detection accuracy, measured via the intersection over union (IoU) [8,10]. These works focus primarily on the performance enhancement of object detectors, as they place less emphasis on the reliability and interpretability of the uncertainty estimates.

Anchor-Relative Localization. Choi et al. [5] and Kraus and Dietmayer [20] implement loss attenuation in YOLOv3 [30]. Anchor-based object detectors such as YOLOv3 [30], single-shot detector (SSD) [26], and EfficientDet [31] divide their final feature maps into a grid. Whereby each grid cell contains a pre-defined set of static bounding boxes known as anchors. During training, the detector learns the offsets for the center, width and height between the pre-defined anchors and the ground truth. In the post-processing, the predicted offsets are decoded based on their corresponding anchors, usually via non-linear functions, such as exponential and sigmoid [26, 29–31]. This transforms them into bounding box coordinates, which are then scaled to the original image size. As introduced in Sect. 1, Le et al. [24] is the only work that considers the non-linearity in the decoding process. They implement loss attenuation in SSD [26]. To decode the anchor-relative coordinates along their corresponding variances, they draw samples from the predicted multivariate normal distribution $\mathcal{N}(\mu, \sigma^2)$, decode the samples, then calculate the mean and variance of the decoded values. Other works do not explicitly address the non-linearity in the decoding process, i.a. decode the predicted variance by reversing the encoding equation of the mean [5,15,16,20]. Therefore, there is currently no deterministic and exact method available for decoding the values of both μ and σ^2.

Regression Uncertainty Calibration. Calibration is crucial after estimating and propagating the uncertainty. Approximate Bayesian approaches such as loss attenuation produce miscalibrated uncertainties [7]. Laves et al. [22] and Feng et al. [9] argue that minimizing the NLL should result in the estimation of σ^2 matching the squared error. However, they and Phan et al. [28] find that the prediction of σ^2 is in reality biased, since it is predicted relative to the estimated mean. Kuleshov, Fenner and Ermon [21] propose a calibration method, which is guaranteed to calibrate the regression uncertainty given sufficient data. Calibration via an *(1) auxiliary model* implies training a model, e.g. isotonic regression, on top of a network so that its predicted distribution is calibrated. Its main disadvantage is that it is not suitable for fitting heavy-tailed distributions, and is prone to over-fitting [4]. Laves et al. [22,23] propose *(2) factor scaling*, another approach that consists of scaling the predicted uncertainty using a single scalar value s. The latter is optimized using gradient descent with respect to the NLL on the validation dataset. Method *(2)* is more suitable for embedded applications and requires less data than *(1)*, but it has less calibration potential since one value is equally applied to all the uncertainties. Phan et al. [28] adapt method *(1)* for the localization of single objects, and show that it results in more reliable uncertainty estimates. Part of their future work and Kraus et al.'s [20] is to extend it to multiple-object detection; as addressed in this work.

3 Method

This section presents our approach to loss attenuation in EfficientDet [31] and outlines its decoding process. Furthermore, it introduces our uncertainty propagation methods, and explains our extensions for uncertainty calibration in localization tasks. The proposed methods are model agnostic, i.e. they are identically applicable to any other object detector.

3.1 Uncertainty Estimation

The loss attenuation introduced by Kendall and Gal [17] is defined as follows:

$$\mathcal{L}_{\text{NN}} = \frac{1}{2N} \sum_{i=1}^{N} \frac{\|\mathbf{y}_i^* - \mathbf{f}(\mathbf{x}_i)\|^2}{\sigma(\mathbf{x}_i)^2} + \log \sigma(\mathbf{x}_i)^2 \tag{1}$$

with N samples, ground truth $\mathbf{y}^*$, variance $\sigma(\mathbf{x})^2$ and output $\mathbf{f}(\mathbf{x})$ for input $\mathbf{x}$.

The output of the localization head in anchor-based object detectors consists of four variables: the anchor-relative object center coordinates $(\hat{\mathbf{x}}, \hat{\mathbf{y}})$, width $\hat{\mathbf{w}}$, and height $\hat{\mathbf{h}}$. For the estimation of the aleatoric uncertainty, the four variables are modeled via a multivariate Gaussian distribution $\mathcal{N}(\mu, \sigma^2)$ with a diagonal covariance approximation. Hence, we extend Eq. (1) for object detection:

$$\mathcal{L}_{\text{NN}} = \frac{1}{8N_{pos}} \sum_{i=1}^{N} \sum_{j=1}^{4} \left(\frac{\|y_{ij}^* - \hat{\mu_j}(\mathbf{x}_i)\|^2}{\hat{\sigma_j}(\mathbf{x}_i)^2} + \log \hat{\sigma_j}(\mathbf{x}_i)^2 \right) \odot m_i \tag{2}$$

with N_{pos} as the number of anchors with assigned ground truth in each batch of input images, and the mask $\mathbf{m}$ consisting of foreground ground truth boxes $\mathbf{m} = [\mathbf{y}^* \neq 0]$. These features are specific for the EfficientDet baseline loss.

3.2 Uncertainty Propagation

The default decoding process of the localization output in EfficientDet is similar to other anchor-based object detectors such as SSD [26] and YOLO [29]. The final coordinates ($\mathbf{y}, \mathbf{x}, \mathbf{h}$ and $\mathbf{w}$) are computed via two post-processing steps. The first step consists of transforming the anchor-relative center coordinates $\hat{\mathbf{x}}, \hat{\mathbf{y}}$, width $\hat{\mathbf{w}}$ and height $\hat{\mathbf{h}}$ based on the center coordinates $\mathbf{x_a}, \mathbf{y_a}$, width $\mathbf{w_a}$, and height $\mathbf{h_a}$ of the corresponding anchor:

$$\begin{aligned} \mathbf{y} &= \hat{\mathbf{y}} \odot \mathbf{h_a} + \mathbf{y_a} \qquad & \mathbf{h} &= \exp(\hat{\mathbf{h}}) \odot \mathbf{h_a} \\ \mathbf{x} &= \hat{\mathbf{x}} \odot \mathbf{w_a} + \mathbf{x_a} \qquad & \mathbf{w} &= \exp(\hat{\mathbf{w}}) \odot \mathbf{w_a} \end{aligned} \tag{3}$$

Equation (3) is calculated for each prediction in the five feature maps, resulting in $A_{cell} \cdot (\frac{I_H \cdot I_W}{128^2} + \frac{I_H \cdot I_W}{64^2} + \frac{I_H \cdot I_W}{32^2} + \frac{I_H \cdot I_W}{16^2} + \frac{I_H \cdot I_W}{8^2})$ iterations, with A_{cell} as the number of anchors per grid cell, I_H as the height of the input image and I_W as its width. The decoding process yields coordinates that are relative to the scaled input image rather than the corresponding anchors. As a result, the second step consists of linearly rescaling the decoded coordinates to the original image size.

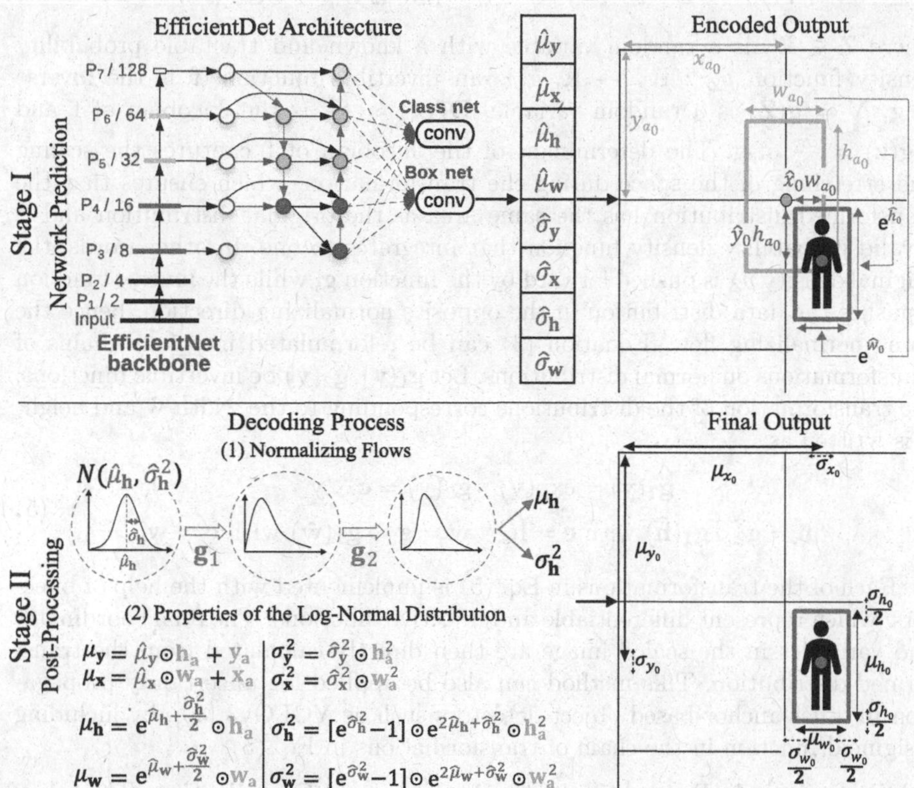

Fig. 2. Illustration of our uncertainty propagation methods in the decoding process of EfficientDet [31]. The output of the localization head is adjusted to predict an output distribution for each coordinate (in red). These distributions are relative to the pre-defined anchor coordinates (in orange). During post-processing, the distributions undergo non-linear transformations to obtain coordinates that are relative to the image. Both our methods provide a fast and exact propagation, with (1) allowing universality and (2) being computationally efficient.

Sampling is the only approach in existing works that enables the transformation of a distribution via a non-linear function such as the exponential in Eq. (3). It however either increases computation time or reduces accuracy. We therefor present two novel, exact and fast methods for decoding, via *(1) normalizing flows* and via *(2) properties of the log-normal distribution.*

(1) Decoding via Normalizing Flows. As explained by Kobyzev, Prince and Brubaker [18], a normalizing flow is a transformation of a probability distribution via a sequence of invertible and differentiable mappings. The density of a sample in the transformed distribution can be evaluated by computing the original density of the inverse-transformed sample, multiplied by the absolute values of the determinants of the Jacobians for each transformation:

$$p_{\mathbf{Y}}(\mathbf{y}) = p_{\mathbf{Z}}(\mathbf{f}(\mathbf{y}))|\det \mathbf{Df}(\mathbf{y})| = p_{\mathbf{Z}}(\mathbf{f}(\mathbf{y}))|\det \mathbf{Dg}(\mathbf{f}(\mathbf{y}))|^{-1} \tag{4}$$

where $\mathbf{Z} \in \mathbb{R}^{\mathbb{D}}$ is a random variable with a known and tractable probability density function $p_{\mathbf{Z}} : \mathbb{R}^{\mathbb{D}} \rightarrow \mathbb{R}$, $\mathbf{g}$ is an invertible function, $\mathbf{f}$ is the inverse of $\mathbf{g}$, $\mathbf{Y} = \mathbf{g}(\mathbf{Z})$ is a random variable, $\mathbf{Df}(\mathbf{y}) = \frac{\partial \mathbf{f}}{\partial \mathbf{y}}$ is the Jacobian of $\mathbf{f}$ and $\mathbf{Dg}(\mathbf{z}) = \frac{\partial \mathbf{g}}{\partial \mathbf{z}}$ of $\mathbf{g}$. The determinant of the Jacobian of $\mathbf{f}$ captures the scaling and stretching of the space during the transformation, which ensures that the transformed distribution has the same area as the original distribution and is a valid probability density function that integrates to one. In other words, the original density $p_{\mathbf{Z}}$ is pushed forward by the function $\mathbf{g}$, while the inverse function $\mathbf{f}$ pushes the data distribution in the opposite normalizing direction, hence the name normalizing flow. Equation (3) can be reformulated into four chains of transformations on normal distributions. Let $\mathbf{g}_1(\mathbf{y}), \mathbf{g}_2(\mathbf{y})$ be invertible functions; the transformation of the distributions corresponding to the width $\hat{\mathbf{w}}$ and height $\hat{\mathbf{h}}$ is written as:

$$\begin{gathered} \mathbf{g}_1(\mathbf{y}) = \exp(\mathbf{y}) \quad \mathbf{g}_2(\mathbf{y}) = \mathbf{c} \odot \mathbf{y} \\ \mathbf{h} = \mathbf{g}_2 \circ \mathbf{g}_1(\hat{\mathbf{h}}) \text{ with } \mathbf{c} = \mathbf{h_a} \quad \mathbf{w} = \mathbf{g}_2 \circ \mathbf{g}_1(\hat{\mathbf{w}}) \text{ with } \mathbf{c} = \mathbf{w_a} \end{gathered} \tag{5}$$

Each of the transformations in Eq. (5) is implemented with the help of bijectors, which represent differentiable and injective functions. The final coordinates and variances in the scaled image are then directly calculated from the transformed distribution. This method can also be applied for uncertainty propagation in other anchor-based object detectors such as YOLOv3 [30], by including a sigmoid function in the chain of transformations in Eq. (5).

(2) Decoding via Properties of the Log-Normal Distribution. The calculation of the Jacobi matrix and inverse functions is computationally expensive. We therefore introduce a different method that directly calculates the transformed mean and variance for the specific case of a normal distribution and exponential or sigmoid transformation. If $\mathbf{Z}$ follows a normal distribution with mean μ and variance σ^2, then $\mathbf{Y} = \exp(\mathbf{Z})$ follows a log-normal distribution. The density function, mean and standard deviation of a log-normal distribution are calculated as follows [2]:

$$\begin{aligned} f(y;\mu,\sigma^2) &= \frac{1}{y\sigma\sqrt{2\pi}} \exp\Big(\frac{-[\log(y) - \mu]^2}{2\sigma^2}\Big) \\ Mean(\mathbf{Y}) &= \exp(\mu)\sqrt{\exp(\sigma^2)} = \exp\Big(\mu + \frac{\sigma^2}{2}\Big) \\ SD(\mathbf{Y}) &= \exp(\mu)\sqrt{\exp(\sigma^2)(\exp(\sigma^2) - 1)} \end{aligned} \tag{6}$$

Combining Eq. (6) with Eq. (3) results in the transformed mean and variance for the width and height, as shown in Fig. 2. Due to the preservation of linearity for Gaussian distributions, Eq. (3) remains unchanged for the mean of the center coordinates. For the variance, the equations undergo modification in compliance with the applicable transformation rules.

Log-Normal During Training. Figure 2 and $Mean(\mathbf{Y})$ in Eq. (6) show that a factor $\frac{\sigma^2}{2}$ is added to the mean of the width and height during the decoding. This always results in an enlargement of the bounding boxes ($\sigma^2 > 0$, $\exp(\sigma^2) > 1$). However, the model fits the offsets during training based solely on the mean, with no regard to the uncertainty (see Eqs. (1) and (2)). We propose incorporating the same factor during training, thereby accounting for the exponential transformation in the decoding equations of $\mu_{\mathbf{h}}$ and $\mu_{\mathbf{w}}$. This results in $\|y^*_{ij} - [\hat{\mu_j}(\mathbf{x}_i) + \frac{\hat{\sigma_j}(\mathbf{x}_i)^2}{2}]\|^2$ for $j = 3, 4$ in Eq. (2).

3.3 Uncertainty Calibration

The main idea behind post-hoc calibration on the validation set is to map the uncertainty to the residuals via a model $\mathbf{r}$ or a scaling factor s.

Extensions to Caliration by a Model. Since the model predicts a multivariate Gaussian distribution with a diagonal covariance matrix (see Sect. 3.1), all four coordinates are predicted independently. Furthermore, the performance of the object detector varies from one class to the other due to heavy class imbalance, potentially leading to a bias towards one class during calibration while neglecting the other. Therefore, we extend calibration via an auxiliary model [3] from calibrating all four uncertainties simultaneously with one isotonic regression model $\mathbf{r}$ to the calibration of the uncertainty for each coordinate c with a separate model $\mathbf{r}_c$ for $c \in [1, 4]$, each ground truth class k with $\mathbf{r}_k$ for $k \in [1, n_{classes}]$, and each coordinate i plus each ground truth class k with $\mathbf{r}_{c,k}$. For an input $\mathbf{x}$, a ground truth $\mathbf{y}$ and predicted output $\mathbf{p} = \mathbf{r}(\mathbf{x})$, an isotonic regression model minimizes $\sum_{i=0}^{N} w_i(y_i - p_i)^2$ on N predictions [3], with $\mathbf{w} \geq 0$ as the observation weight and $p_i \leq p_j$ for all $i, j \in \mathbb{E}$, where $\mathbb{E} = \{(i, j) : x_i \leq x_j\}$.

Extensions to Calibration by a Factor. Laves et al. [22] optimize the factor s by minimizing the NLL with gradient descent. However, the log-likelihood objective is highly sensitive towards outliers and mislabeled variables, which is particularly relevant for real-world datasets [11,19]. Since their method only adjusts the predicted uncertainty σ in $\mathcal{N}(\mu, (s \cdot \sigma)^2)$, we propose to directly optimize the scaling factor s based on a distance metric between the predicted uncertainty and the true intervals, similar to the isotonic regression optimization goal. Therefore, two different loss functions are introduced, the root-mean-square uncertainty error (RMSUE) and the mean absolute uncertainty error (MAUE):

$$\text{RMSUE}(s) = \sqrt{\frac{1}{N}\sum_{i=1}^{N}(\Delta_i - s \cdot \sigma_i)^2} \quad \text{MAUE}(s) = \frac{1}{N}\sum_{i=1}^{N}|\Delta_i - s \cdot \sigma_i| \tag{7}$$

with N detections, σ as the predicted uncertainty, and $\mathbf{\Delta} = |\mathbf{y}^* - \mu|$ as the residual.

Relative Uncertainty. Existing methods are not attuned to localization tasks as they do not account for varying aspect ratios and sizes of bounding boxes. We introduce relative calibration, which consists of calibrating σ after normalizing σ and Δ with the width w and height h of their corresponding object, defined by its four coordinates $(x_{min}, x_{max}, y_{min}, y_{max})$. Specifically, $\sigma_{x_{min}}$, $\sigma_{x_{max}}$, $\Delta_{x_{min}}$, $\Delta_{x_{max}}$ are divided by w and $\sigma_{y_{min}}$, $\sigma_{y_{max}}$, $\Delta_{y_{min}}$, $\Delta_{y_{max}}$ by h. This prevents large objects from negatively influencing the calibration of smaller objects. Contextualizing the uncertainty with respect to its object also helps mitigate the effect of missing depth information in 2D images, which is crucial for comprehending a detector's confidence in real-world detections.

Proximity-Based Data Sorting. Post-hoc calibration is performed on the validation set. The output of non-maximum suppression (NMS) in object detectors typically involves selecting top n detections based on their classification score using a manually specified threshold, resulting in the exclusion of specific detections. Such exclusions, in turn, could correspond to actual ground truths and therefore can impede the calibration of the localization uncertainty. EfficientDet employs soft-NMS, which entails the adjustment and subsequent sorting of its output based on the classification score. Nevertheless, a higher score does not necessarily imply a more accurate detection. We propose resorting the NMS output based on the nearest neighbor to the ground truth via a distance metric, such as mean squared error (MSE), hence retaining and correctly allocating all samples in the validation set.

4 Experiments

The datasets used in this work are common in autonomous driving research: KITTI [12] (all 7 classes, 20% split for validation), and BDD100K [32] (all 10 classes, 12.5% official split). The baseline is EfficientDet-D0 [31] pre-trained on COCO [25] and fine-tuned on the two datasets respectively for 500 epochs with 8 batches and an input image resolution of 1024×512 pixels. The default hyperparameters for EfficientDet-D0 are maintained. To prevent the classification results from affecting the localization output, we use ground truth classes for the per-class calibration and reorder the detections based on MSE (the distance measure used during training, see Eq. (2)) for both calibration and evaluation.

4.1 Decoding Methods

To showcase the effectiveness of the presented methods, eight metrics are selected. For localization: Average Precision (AP), root-mean-square error (RMSE), mean intersection over union (mIoU) and average time: model exporting time (ET) in seconds (s) and inference time (IT) in milliseconds (ms) per image. For uncertainty: RMSUE, expected calibration error (ECE) [21], negative log-likelihood (NLL) and sharpness (Sharp). Sharpness is the average of the variance, i.e. it relates to the concentration of the predictive distribution [13]. Each model is trained three times. The results of sampling and IT are averaged over three trials on the validation set. ET is calculated as the average of three exporting iterations. Time measurements are performed on one GPU (RTX 3090). We compare our normalizing flows (N-FLOW) and log-normal (L-NORM) approaches to the baseline without uncertainty, and to the sampling method (SAMP) with 30, 100 and 1000 samples, inspired by Le et al. [24]. We also add false decoding (FALSEDEC), where both μ and σ are decoded via Eq. (3), as an ablation study to analyze the effect of correct propagation and including the uncertainty in the decoding process of the mean (see Eq. (6)). The N-FLOW method is implemented using the library TensorFlow Probability [6].

Table 1. KITTI (top) and BDD100K (bottom): Comparison between EfficientDet-D0 baseline and model with uncertainty. Our propagation methods are faster and more accurate than sampling. Uncertainty estimation increases localization performance and reduces computation time.

Method	AP↑	RMSE↓	mIoU↑	NLL↓	ET↓ (s)	IT↓ (ms)
Baseline	72.8 ± 0.1	**5.07 ± 0.1**	90.1 ± 0.1	–	**115.6 ± 3**	34.8 ± 4
FalseDec	73.1 ± 0.5	5.27 ± 0.1	90.3 ± 0.1	4.27 ± 0.1	116.0 ± 3	31.1 ± 3
L-norm	**73.3** ± 0.5	5.17 ± 0.2	90.3 ± 0.0	3.22 ± 0.0	**115.6 ± 2**	**31.0 ± 3**
N-flow	**73.3** ± 0.5	5.17 ± 0.2	90.3 ± 0.0	3.22 ± 0.0	116.6 ± 1	31.6 ± 3
Samp30	68.6 ± 0.4	5.43 ± 0.1	88.7 ± 0.1	**3.19 ± 0.0**	118.8 ± 2	34.5 ± 3
Samp100	71.8 ± 0.5	5.23 ± 0.1	90.1 ± 0.0	3.20 ± 0.0	117.4 ± 4	47.0 ± 3
Samp1000	73.1 ± 0.5	5.18 ± 0.2	**90.4 ± 0.0**	3.21 ± 0.0	117.9 ± 4	187.4 ± 4
Baseline	**24.7 ± 0.1**	8.96 ± 0.2	66.6 ± 1.6	–	115.7 ± 3	33.0 ± 4
FalseDec	23.9 ± 0.2	8.81 ± 0.2	67.3 ± 0.0	4.40 ± 0.1	115.9 ± 2	**30.4 ± 4**
L-norm	24.4 ± 0.1	**8.53 ± 0.2**	**67.7 ± 0.0**	**3.69 ± 0.0**	**115.3 ± 1**	30.6 ± 4
N-flow	24.4 ± 0.1	**8.53 ± 0.2**	**67.7 ± 0.0**	**3.69 ± 0.0**	116.4 ± 1	31.0 ± 3
Samp30	21.0 ± 0.1	9.02 ± 0.2	64.7 ± 0.0	3.70 ± 0.0	118.0 ± 3	33.6 ± 4
Samp100	23.2 ± 0.1	8.68 ± 0.2	66.7 ± 0.0	**3.69 ± 0.0**	117.0 ± 3	45.4 ± 4
Samp1000	24.2 ± 0.1	8.55 ± 0.2	67.6 ± 0.1	**3.69 ± 0.0**	118.4 ± 3	187.3 ± 4

Baseline vs Uncertainty. Predicting the localization aleatoric uncertainty increases the original 3,876,321 parameters by only 2,327 (0.06%). It reduces the required inference time per image, due to the Tensor Cores in the GPU utilizing the extension of the model output to eight values (mean and variance) [1]. The exporting time varies by decoding function. Direct calculation functions (Baseline, FALSEDEC, L-NORM) are faster than distribution-based (N-FLOW, SAMPL) functions, due to lower complexity of operations in the graph. Estimating the uncertainty improves the baseline AP and mIoU by 0.5% on KITTI. On BDD100K, it reduces the AP by 0.3%, but improves both the mIoU and RMSE, as seen in Table 1. Therefore, on both datasets, the localization performance increases. The COCO-style AP is affected by the classification performance, since it is calculated per class and detections are sorted based on their classification score to determine the cumulative true and false positives. This is amplified in the case of BDD100K, due to the larger number of images and their lower fidelity, and by extension, the overall decrease in performance and higher misclassification rate (see Fig. 4) in comparison to KITTI.

Our Methods vs Sampling. The only difference between N-FLOW and L-NORM is the processing time, due to different mathematical complexity (see Sect. 3.2). The main advantage of the N-FLOW approach is the flexibility in changing the distribution or the transformations without manually recalculating the posterior distribution. The latter is especially beneficial when the transformations render the posterior distribution intractable. Table 1 shows that incorrectly propagating the mean and variance (FALSEDEC) reduces performance, and the precision of the uncertainty. Compared to our methods, sampling shows on both datasets either a substantial reduction in performance (up to 3% AP and mIoU) or a longer inference time per image (up to 5 times slower). However, sampling with 30 samples does offer slightly sharper uncertainties on KITTI, which results in a lower NLL. The opposite is true for BDD100K. This can be retraced to the overestimation of the uncertainty by the model. Therefore, any reduction in the uncertainty leads to an enhancement of its precision. Sampling with a mere 30 samples can result in substantial deviation in both directions, hence the fluctuation between the datasets. Based on the results in Table 1, we select the L-NORM decoding method for the calibration evaluation.

4.2 Calibration Evaluation

Calibration improves the reliability and interpretability of predicted uncertainties by reducing misalignment between the error distribution and the standard Gaussian distribution. This is highly relevant for safety-critical applications, where uncertainty should reflect the true outcome likelihood.

Uncertainty Behavior. We notice that EfficientDet predicts a lower σ on the validation set, despite the higher NLL and RMSE compared to the training set, in accordance with Laves et al. [22]. We also found that σ^2 is predicted higher than the MSE, hence being miscalibrated. Reasons therefor can be found in the optimization of multiple losses and uneven data distribution. For both datasets, the model overestimates the uncertainty, with the interval $\mu \pm \sigma$ containing 99% of the true values instead of the expected 68.27%.

Calibration Methods. For factor scaling (FS), gradient descent is applied for 100 optimization epochs with a learning rate of 0.1 on the validation dataset. Optimizing the factor s based on MAUE and RMSUE (see Sect. 3.3 and Eq. (7)) results in a lower ECE and sharper uncertainties, but a higher NLL (see Table 2). We discover a trade-off between the ECE and NLL, since optimizing s based on the NLL instead results in a higher ECE. For the auxiliary isotonic regression (IR) model, we compare its extensions to per-coordinate (PCo) and per-class (CL) calibration. An illustrative example is featured in Fig. 1. Table 2 shows that per-coordinate calibration outperforms the calibration on all coordinates as expected, since all four normal distributions are assumed to be independent. Per-class calibration further reduces the ECE, RMSUE and NLL, since both datasets contain heavily unbalanced classes with different aspect ratios and localization accuracy. IR outperforms FS for both datasets, because the size of the calibration dataset is large enough for the auxiliary model to train on, as also observed by Feng et al. [9]. Relative calibration results in further improvement for IR in both NLL and ECE. Our hypothesis in Sect. 3.3 is that relative calibration mitigates bias towards larger objects. We empirically demonstrate that it effectively achieves this objective by conducting a comparative analysis on small, medium and large objects based on their area as defined by the COCO API [25]. Our findings reveal that relative calibration causes a more substantial reduction in ECE on small objects with a 6-fold further decrease compared to absolute calibration, whereas it is 2-fold on medium objects and 3-fold on large objects. Accordingly, relative isotonic regression per-coordinate and per-class (Rel. IR PCo CL) is selected for further investigations.

Table 2. KITTI (left) and BDD100K (right): Comparison between different calibration methods. Our factor scaling (FS) losses outperform NLL. Isotonic regression (IR) per-coordinate (PCo) and per-class (CL) outperforms classic one-model IR and all FS approaches. Relativity increases calibration performance.

Method	RMSUE↓	ECE↓	NLL↓	Sharp↓	RMSUE↓	ECE↓	NLL↓	Sharp↓
Uncalibrated	13.0 ± 0.0	0.384 ± 0.000	3.22 ± 0.0	14.9 ± 0.0	15.1 ± 0.1	0.323 ± 0.000	3.69 ± 0.0	17.22 ± 0.0
FS MAUE	4.6 ± 0.2	0.047 ± 0.001	3.14 ± 0.4	**2.5 ± 0.0**	7.5 ± 0.3	0.026 ± 0.001	4.72 ± 0.2	4.28 ± 0.0
FS RMSUE	4.6 ± 0.2	0.088 ± 0.003	2.79 ± 0.2	3.0 ± 0.0	7.6 ± 0.3	0.074 ± 0.000	6.43 ± 0.3	**3.21 ± 0.0**
FS NLL	5.0 ± 0.3	0.194 ± 0.021	**2.51 ± 0.1**	4.7 ± 0.5	9.4 ± 0.4	0.217 ± 0.008	**3.46 ± 0.0**	9.72 ± 0.4
Rel. FS RMSUE	7.2 ± 0.1	0.306 ± 0.002	2.74 ± 0.0	8.3 ± 0.1	8.5 ± 0.3	0.175 ± 0.003	3.50 ± 0.1	8.06 ± 0.1
Abs. IR	4.5 ± 0.2	0.032 ± 0.001	3.15 ± 0.3	**2.5 ± 0.0**	7.5 ± 0.3	0.027 ± 0.001	4.60 ± 0.1	4.09 ± 0.0
Abs. IR CL	4.4 ± 0.2	0.029 ± 0.001	2.86 ± 0.2	2.7 ± 0.0	7.4 ± 0.3	0.026 ± 0.001	4.39 ± 0.1	4.23 ± 0.0
Abs. IR PCo	4.5 ± 0.2	0.032 ± 0.001	3.03 ± 0.2	2.6 ± 0.0	7.5 ± 0.3	0.027 ± 0.001	4.57 ± 0.2	4.11 ± 0.0
Abs. IR PCo CL	**4.3 ± 0.2**	0.028 ± 0.000	2.70 ± 0.1	2.9 ± 0.0	7.4 ± 0.3	0.025 ± 0.001	4.36 ± 0.1	4.33 ± 0.0
Rel. IR	4.5 ± 0.2	0.027 ± 0.001	3.06 ± 0.3	**2.5 ± 0.0**	7.4 ± 0.3	0.018 ± 0.001	4.52 ± 0.1	4.07 ± 0.0
Rel. IR CL	4.4 ± 0.2	0.026 ± 0.001	2.78 ± 0.2	3.1 ± 0.4	**7.3 ± 0.3**	**0.017 ± 0.000**	4.29 ± 0.1	4.24 ± 0.0
Rel. IR PCo	4.5 ± 0.2	0.027 ± 0.001	3.03 ± 0.2	**2.5 ± 0.1**	7.4 ± 0.3	0.018 ± 0.000	4.49 ± 0.1	4.08 ± 0.0
Rel. IR PCo CL	4.4 ± 0.3	**0.025 ± 0.000**	2.69 ± 0.2	3.2 ± 0.5	**7.3 ± 0.3**	**0.017 ± 0.000**	4.23 ± 0.1	4.27 ± 0.0

4.3 Uncertainty Correlation

We investigate the correlation between the localization aleatoric uncertainty and performance, object area, i.e. distance in the real world, occlusion level and the Blind/Referenceless Image Spatial Quality Evaluator (BRISQUE) [27]. In the following, $\sigma_{obj} = \frac{1}{4}\sum_{i=1}^{4} \sigma_i$ is the average of all four uncertainties per object.

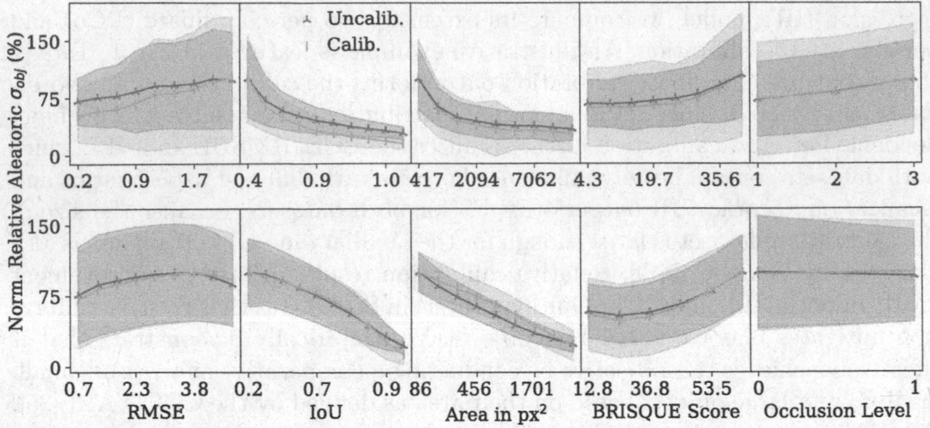

Fig. 3. KITTI (top) and BDD100K (bottom): Correlation between aleatoric uncertainty ($\mu_{\sigma_{obj}} \pm \sigma_{\sigma_{obj}}$) and performance metrics, object area, BRISQSUE score and occlusion level. Uncalibrated and calibrated via Rel. IR PCo CL, binned based on quantiles and normalized with the highest $\mu_{\sigma_{obj}}$ post-binning.

Uncertainty vs Real-World Metrics. We assume that the distance of an object in the real world is connected to its area in an image in pixels^2 (px^2). For both datasets, Fig. 3 demonstrates that the smaller the object in the image, or the farther away it is, the higher its aleatoric uncertainty. As mentioned in Sect. 2, aleatoric uncertainty correlates with occlusion. Figure 3 visualizes the results based on the annotations for occlusion in both datasets. KITTI has three occlusion levels: 0 is fully visible, 1 is occluded less than 50% and 2 is occluded more than 50%. BDD100K has only two: 0 is visible and 1 is occluded. The correlation is present in both datasets, but less for BDD100K. We trace this back to the model predicting double the uncertainty on average for the traffic light and sign classes, as compared to other classes. While 56568 instances of these classes were labeled as visible, only 5040 were labeled as occluded (8%). This, combined with the high uncertainty, negatively impacts the correlation. However, when excluding these two classes, the average uncertainty of visible objects is 34% lower than occluded objects pre-calibration and 40% lower post-calibration.

Uncertainty vs Image Quality. The assumption that aleatoric uncertainty correlates with inherent noise in the data is investigated based on the BRISQUE score. For every detection, the score is calculated on the standardized crop around its bounding box in the corresponding image. Standardizing crops involves mean subtraction and division by the standard deviation of pixel values. As Fig. 3 shows, the BRISQUE score positively correlates with the uncertainty, indicating a higher uncertainty for lower image quality.

Uncertainty vs Detection Performance. Aleatoric uncertainty estimated via loss attenuation should ideally correlate with localization accuracy given that the uncertainty is fitted during training with respect to the MSE distance metric (see Eq. (2)). The comparison with IoU and RMSE for both datasets in Fig. 3 shows this correlation. Overall, calibration via Rel. IR PCo CL strengthens the correlation with all metrics. The calibrated uncertainty can be used as a threshold between misdetections (IoU <= threshold) and correct detections (IoU > threshold) for both datasets. As shown in Fig. 4, this also extends to classification and the resulting false and true positives. Therefore, the localization aleatoric uncertainty allows for the detection of the model prediction errors.

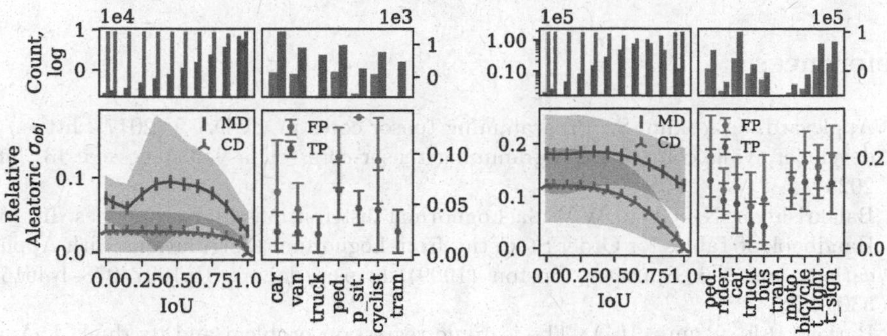

Fig. 4. KITTI (left) and BDD100K (right): Calibrated aleatoric uncertainty ($\mu_{\sigma_{obj}} \pm \sigma_{\sigma_{obj}}$) for misdetections (MD, IoU <= threshold) and correct detections (CD, IoU > threshold) at each IoU threshold, and true positives (TP) and false positives (FP) for the classification of each class. The uncertainty of MDs and FPs is on average higher than CDs and TPs.

5 Conclusion

We provide an object detection pipeline with reliable and interpretable localization uncertainty, by covering the estimation, propagation, calibration, and explanation of aleatoric uncertainty. Our methods enhance the safety and reliability of object detectors without introducing drawbacks. We propose two approaches to propagation, which allow an exact and fast propagation of distributions, along the corresponding uncertainty, through non-linear functions such as exponential, sigmoid and softmax. We demonstrate the efficacy of our techniques through their implementation in the post-processing of EfficientDet as a use-case. Our propagation methods improve the localization performance of the baseline detector on both datasets KITTI and BDD100K, and decrease the inference time. They generalize to any model with a tractable output distribution requiring its transformation via invertible and differentiable functions. They particularly alleviate the disadvantages of sampling, namely either low accuracy and reproducibility or high computation time. Furthermore, we extend regression calibration to localization, by considering the relativity of the uncertainty to its bounding box, as well as per-class and per-coordinate calibration with different optimization functions. We also investigate the data selection process for calibration and propose an approach for the allocation of predictions to their corresponding ground truth, which alleviates the disadvantages of manual thresholding. We find a correlation between aleatoric uncertainty and detection accuracy, image quality, object occlusion, and object distance in the real world. We hope the methods and results presented in this paper will encourage wider adoption of uncertainty estimation in different industrial and safety-critical applications, e.g. for safer decision making via more reliable detection monitoring, and more efficient use of labeled data in active learning.

References

1. Appleyard, J., Yokim, S.: Programming tensor cores in CUDA 9 (2017). https://developer.nvidia.com/blog/programming-tensor-cores-cuda-9/. Accessed 13 Jan 2023
2. Balakrishnan, N., Chen, W.W.S.: Lognormal distributions and properties. In: In: Handbook of Tables for Order Statistics from Lognormal Distributions with Applications, pp. 5–6. Springer, Boston (1999). https://doi.org/10.1007/978-1-4615-5309-0_2
3. Barlow, R.E., Brunk, H.D.: The isotonic regression problem and its dual. J. Am. Stat. Assoc. **67**(337), 140–147 (1972)
4. Chatterjee, S., Sen, S.: Regret minimization in isotonic, heavy-tailed contextual bandits via adaptive confidence bands. arXiv preprint arXiv:2110.10245 (2021)
5. Choi, J., Chun, D., Kim, H., Lee, H.J.: Gaussian YOLOv3: an accurate and fast object detector using localization uncertainty for autonomous driving. In: 2019 IEEE/CVF International Conference on Computer Vision (ICCV), pp. 502–511. IEEE (2019)
6. Dillon, J.V., et al.: Tensorflow distributions. arXiv preprint arXiv:1711.10604 (2017)
7. Feng, D., Harakeh, A., Waslander, S.L., Dietmayer, K.: A review and comparative study on probabilistic object detection in autonomous driving. IEEE Trans. Intell. Transp. Syst. **23**(8), 9961–9980 (2022)
8. Feng, D., Rosenbaum, L., Dietmayer, K.: Towards safe autonomous driving: capture uncertainty in the deep neural network for lidar 3D vehicle detection. arXiv preprint arXiv:1804.05132 (2018)
9. Feng, D., Rosenbaum, L., Glaeser, C., Timm, F., Dietmayer, K.: Can we trust you? on calibration of a probabilistic object detector for autonomous driving. arXiv preprint arXiv:1909.12358 (2019)
10. Feng, D., Rosenbaum, L., Timm, F., Dietmayer, K.: Leveraging heteroscedastic aleatoric uncertainties for robust real-time lidar 3D object detection. In: 2019 IEEE Intelligent Vehicles Symposium (IV), pp. 1280–1287. IEEE (2019)
11. Futami, F., Sato, I., Sugiyama, M.: Variational inference based on robust divergences. In: Proceedings of the 21st International Conference on Artificial Intelligence and Statistics, pp. 813–822. PMLR (2018)
12. Geiger, A., Lenz, P., Urtasun, R.: Are we ready for autonomous driving? The KITTI vision benchmark suite. In: 2012 IEEE Conference on Computer Vision and Pattern Recognition, pp. 3354–3361. IEEE (2012)

13. Gneiting, T., Raftery, A.E.: Strictly proper scoring rules, prediction, and estimation. J. Am. Stat. Assoc. **102**(477), 359–378 (2007)
14. Guo, C., Pleiss, G., Sun, Y., Weinberger, K.Q.: On calibration of modern neural networks. In: Proceedings of the 34th International Conference on Machine Learning, pp. 1321–1330. PMLR (2017)
15. Harakeh, A., Smart, M., Waslander, S.L.: Bayesod: A Bayesian approach for uncertainty estimation in deep object detectors. In: 2020 IEEE International Conference on Robotics and Automation (ICRA), pp. 87–93. IEEE (2020)
16. He, Y., Zhu, C., Wang, J., Savvides, M., Zhang, X.: Bounding box regression with uncertainty for accurate object detection. In: 2019 IEEE/CVF Conference on Computer Vision and Pattern Recognition (CVPR), pp. 2883–2892. IEEE (2019)
17. Kendall, A., Gal, Y.: What uncertainties do we need in Bayesian deep learning for computer vision? In: Advances in Neural Information Processing Systems, vol. 30 (2017)
18. Kobyzev, I., Prince, S.J., Brubaker, M.A.: Normalizing flows: an introduction and review of current methods. IEEE Trans. Pattern Anal. Mach. Intell. **43**(11), 3964–3979 (2021)
19. Krähenbühl, P., Koltun, V.: Parameter learning and convergent inference for dense random fields. In: Proceedings of the 30th International Conference on Machine Learning, pp. 513–521. PMLR (2013)
20. Kraus, F., Dietmayer, K.: Uncertainty estimation in one-stage object detection. In: 2019 IEEE Intelligent Transportation Systems Conference (ITSC), pp. 53–60. IEEE (2019)
21. Kuleshov, V., Fenner, N., Ermon, S.: Accurate uncertainties for deep learning using calibrated regression. In: Proceedings of the 35th International Conference on Machine Learning, pp. 2796–2804. PMLR (2018)
22. Laves, M.H., Ihler, S., Fast, J.F., Kahrs, L.A., Ortmaier, T.: Recalibration of aleatoric and epistemic regression uncertainty in medical imaging. arXiv preprint arXiv:2104.12376 (2021)
23. Laves, M.H., Ihler, S., Kortmann, K.P., Ortmaier, T.: Well-calibrated model uncertainty with temperature scaling for dropout variational inference. arXiv preprint arXiv:1909.13550 (2019)
24. Le, M.T., Diehl, F., Brunner, T., Knoll, A.: Uncertainty estimation for deep neural object detectors in safety-critical applications. In: 2018 21st International Conference on Intelligent Transportation Systems (ITSC), pp. 3873–3878. IEEE (2018)
25. Lin, T.-Y., et al.: Microsoft COCO: common objects in context. In: Fleet, D., Pajdla, T., Schiele, B., Tuytelaars, T. (eds.) ECCV 2014. LNCS, vol. 8693, pp. 740–755. Springer, Cham (2014). https://doi.org/10.1007/978-3-319-10602-1_48
26. Liu, W., et al.: SSD: single shot multibox detector. arXiv preprint arXiv:1512.02325 (2016)
27. Mittal, A., Moorthy, A.K., Bovik, A.C.: Blind/referenceless image spatial quality evaluator. In: 2011 Conference Record of the Forty Fifth Asilomar Conference on Signals, Systems and Computers (ASILOMAR), pp. 723–727. IEEE (2011)
28. Phan, B., Salay, R., Czarnecki, K., Abdelzad, V., Denouden, T., Vernekar, S.: Calibrating uncertainties in object localization task. arXiv preprint arXiv:1811.11210 (2018)
29. Redmon, J., Divvala, S., Girshick, R., Farhadi, A.: You only look once: Unified, real-time object detection. In: 2016 IEEE Conference on Computer Vision and Pattern Recognition (CVPR), pp. 779–788. IEEE (2016)
30. Redmon, J., Farhadi, A.: YOLOv3: an incremental improvement. arXiv preprint arXiv:1804.02767 (2018)

31. Tan, M., Pang, R., Le, Q.V.: EfficientDet: scalable and efficient object detection. In: 2020 IEEE/CVF Conference on Computer Vision and Pattern Recognition (CVPR), pp. 10778–10787. IEEE (2020)
32. Yu, F., et al.: Bdd100k: a diverse driving dataset for heterogeneous multitask learning. In: 2020 IEEE/CVF Conference on Computer Vision and Pattern Recognition (CVPR), pp. 2633–2642. IEEE (2020)
33. Zadrozny, B., Elkan, C.: Transforming classifier scores into accurate multiclass probability estimates. In: Proceedings of the Eighth ACM SIGKDD International Conference on Knowledge Discovery and Data Mining, pp. 694–699. ACM (2002)

Label Shift Quantification with Robustness Guarantees via Distribution Feature Matching

Bastien Dussap[1(✉)], Gilles Blanchard[1], and Badr-Eddine Chérief-Abdellatif[2]

[1] Université Paris-Saclay, CNRS, Inria, Laboratoire de mathématiques d'Orsay, Orsay, France
{bastien.dussap,gilles.blanchard}@univerite-paris-saclay.fr

[2] CNRS, LPSM, Sorbonne Université, Université Paris Cité, Paris, France
badr-eddine.cherief-abdellatif@cnrs.fr

Abstract. Quantification learning deals with the task of estimating the target label distribution under label shift. In this paper, we first present a unifying framework, distribution feature matching (DFM), that recovers as particular instances various estimators introduced in previous literature. We derive a general performance bound for DFM procedures, improving in several key aspects upon previous bounds derived in particular cases. We then extend this analysis to study robustness of DFM procedures in the misspecified setting under departure from the exact label shift hypothesis, in particular in the case of contamination of the target by an unknown distribution. These theoretical findings are confirmed by a detailed numerical study on simulated and real-world datasets. We also introduce an efficient, scalable and robust version of kernel-based DFM using Random Fourier Features.

Keywords: Learning Theory · Quantification · Kernel Mean Embedding · Label Shift · Class ratio estimation

1 Introduction

The success of supervised learning over the last decades is mainly based on the belief that the training and test samples follow the same data generation process. However, in real-world applications, this assumption is often violated and classical learning methods are challenged. Unsupervised domain adaptation, a field of transfer learning, specifically addresses this problem by transferring knowledge from the different but related *training* or *source* domain to the *test* or *target* domain of interest [30,31].

From a formal point of view, consider a covariate space $\mathcal{X}$, typically a subset of $\mathbb{R}^d$, and a label space $\mathcal{Y} = [c] := \{1, \dots, c\}$. We define the two *source* and *target* domains as different probability distributions over the covariate-label space pair $\mathcal{X} \times \mathcal{Y}$. The target label distribution is denoted $\alpha^* = (\alpha_i^*)_{i=1}^c$ while each class-i conditional target distribution is denoted $\mathbb{Q}_i$. Similarly, the source

D. Koutra et al. (Eds.): ECML PKDD 2023, LNAI 14173, pp. 69–85, 2023.
https://doi.org/10.1007/978-3-031-43424-2_5

label distribution is denoted $\beta^* = (\beta_i^*)_{i=1}^c$ while each class-i conditional source distribution is denoted $\mathbb{P}_i$. We will consider the classical label shift hypothesis:

$$\forall i = 1, \dots, c\,, \quad \mathbb{P}_i = \mathbb{Q}_i. \qquad (\mathcal{LS})$$

Another setting we will consider involves contamination of the target by a new class. In this *contaminated label shift* setting, we assume that the target domain is $\mathcal{X} \times \tilde{\mathcal{Y}}$, with $\tilde{\mathcal{Y}} = \{0, \dots, c\}$ and that the label shift hypothesis is still verified for the class $\{1, \dots, c\}$:

$$\mathbb{Q} = \sum_{i=1}^{c} \alpha_i^* \mathbb{P}_i + \alpha_0^* \mathbb{Q}_0 \qquad (\mathcal{CLS})$$
$$\forall i = 1, \dots, c\,, \quad \mathbb{P}_i = \mathbb{Q}_i.$$

The distribution $\mathbb{Q}_0$ is seen as a noise or a contamination, for which we have no prior knowledge nor sample. Therefore, our objective in this contaminated scenario is to be robust to a large class of noise distributions. In Sect. 3.2, we will give insight on the kind of contamination we can be robust to.

In both settings, we suppose a source dataset $\{(x_j, y_j)\}_{j \in [n]} \in (\mathcal{X} \times \mathcal{Y})^n$ and a target dataset $\{x_{n+j}\}_{j \in [m]} \in \mathcal{X}^m$ are given. All data points from the source (respectively the target) dataset are independently sampled from the source (resp. the target) domain. We have access to the source labels y_j but not to the target labels which are not observed. We denote by $\hat{\mathbb{P}}_i := \sum_{j \in [n] : y_j = i} \delta_{x_j}(\cdot)/n_i$ the empirical source class-i conditional distribution, where δ_{x_j} denotes the Dirac measure at point x_j and n_i the number of instances labeled i in the source dataset. Note that $n_1 + \ldots + n_c = n$. We finally denote by $\tilde{\beta}$ the empirical proportions of each class in the source dataset, i.e. $\tilde{\beta}_i := n_i/n$.

Several different objectives have been addressed under the label shift assumption in the literature, and can be summarised in three points: (i) *detection*, i.e. determining whether distribution shift has occurred; (ii) *correction*, i.e. fitting a classifier with high accuracy on the target distribution; and (iii) *quantification*, i.e. estimating the target label distribution [2,15,18,19,26,35]. We focus here on the last challenge, and develop a general analysis unifying several existing techniques with estimation guarantees for the target proportions α^*, as well as dealing with the contaminated label shift setting.

1.1 Related Literature

The research area of quantification learning has a somewhat fragmented nature. Quantifying the target label distribution and learning a classifier are actually very closely related objectives. The most classical approach for the construction of efficient classifiers on the target domain is based on weighted empirical risk minimisation, which itself requires the estimation of the shift between the source and target distributions. Thus, while we are here interested in estimating the target proportions α_i^*, many related works are interested in estimating the weights $w_i = \alpha_i^*/\beta_i^*$. Obtaining an estimator of those weights from an estimator of the target proportions α_i^* is straightforward: simply use the labels in the source data to form a direct estimate of the source proportions and then consider the ratio. Conversely, starting from the weights estimator, it is possible to obtain an estimate of the weights α_i^*/β_i^* by multiplying it by an estimate of the source proportions. For this reason, there have been two different literature threads that address closely related problems but apparently grew independently: the Quantification Learning literature [13,19] and the Label Shift literature [18].

Most methods dealing with label shift are expressed as variants of the so-called *Classify & Count (CC)* technique proposed in the seminal works of Forman [15–17]. The idea is to fit a classifier on the source dataset, e.g. a random forest [28], an SVM [3], or a Nearest-Neighbour [4], and to estimate the target class distribution using the distribution of predictions. To account for the misclassification that the underlying classifier suffers on the target set due to the label shift, Forman [17] proposed the *Adjusted Classify & Count (ACC)* method, a modification to the standard Classify & Count which simply adjusts the estimate after computing the quantifier. This approach is also popular in the label shift correction literature. Based on the same principle, more recently the *Black-Box Shift Estimation (BBSE)* algorithm introduced by [26] used the confusion matrix of the classifier to adjust the predicted label distribution, while Azizzadenesheli et al. [2] proposed to regularise the re-weighting vector in BBSE in order to make the final estimated target distribution less sensitive to the quality of the estimated confusion matrix. Another technique, using an off-the-shelf classifier, is based on the maximum likelihood principle. The most popular version of this approach is probably the *Maximum Likelihood Label Shift (MLLS)* [1] strategy which is widely used in the label shift correction community. This technique is actually a variation of the original work of Saerens et al. [35] that uses an Expectation-Maximisation (EM) algorithm to efficiently correct for the shift in class proportions between source and target distributions given estimates from a predictive model, alternately updating the target class-prior and class-posterior probabilities from some initial estimates until convergence. In fact, [18] argues that only the choice of the calibration method differs between MLLS and BBSE and that both procedures actually solve the same optimisation objective, thus explaining that the empirical advantage of MLLS over BBSE is only due to coarse calibration of the latter.

Another completely different approach consists in viewing quantification as a statistical mixture problem. Since both source and target covariates marginal distributions can be written as mixtures $\mathbb{P} = \sum_{i=1}^{c} \beta_i^* \mathbb{P}_i$ and $\mathbb{Q} = \sum_{i=1}^{c} \alpha_i^* \mathbb{Q}_i$ respectively. Under the label shift assumption, the conditional distribution of the covariates given the label is the same for both source and target data ($\mathbb{P}_i = \mathbb{Q}_i$), and can be estimated using the empirical conditional distribution $\hat{\mathbb{P}}_i := \sum_{j/y_j=i} \delta_{\{x_j\}}(\cdot)/n_i$ based on the labeled source sample. Thus, the marginal covariates distribution $\mathbb{Q}$ can be approximated by $\sum_{i=1}^{c} \alpha_i^* \hat{\mathbb{P}}_i$, and the goal of quantification can be seen as finding the mixture weights $(\alpha_i)_{i=1}^{c}$ such that the mixture $\sum_{i=1}^{c} \alpha_i \hat{\mathbb{P}}_i$ resembles the most the empirical target covariates marginal distribution $\hat{\mathbb{Q}} := \sum_{j=1}^{m} \delta_{\{x_{j+n}\}}(\cdot)/m$ based on the target dataset, with respect to some metric. Many different statistical divergences have been considered in the literature, such as the Hellinger distance [20], the Wasserstein distance [5], the Pearson divergence [10], the Energy distance [25] or the Maximum Mean Discrepancy (MMD) [24,38]. The last two distances operate in a Reproducing Kernel Hilbert Space (RKHS) and adapt to the label shift problem the Kernel Mean Matching (KMM) approach [22], that minimises the RKHS distance between the kernel mean embeddings of the distributions. The use of kernel methods enables here to operate in an implicit high-dimensional space without requiring computing the coordinates of the data in that space, but rather by simply computing the inner products between the images of all pairs of data in the space. However, the applicability of these methods on a larger scale still remains an important limitation due to the computation of the kernel matrix. Consequently, distribution matching has sometimes been performed on a low-dimensional function of the covariates instead of a high-dimensional kernel embedding. For instance, the Distribution y-Similarity framework (DyS) [27] exploits the histogram of a decision function obtained by a trained binary classifier and then minimises the Topsøe distance between the two histograms, while the HDx algorithm [20] uses the Hellinger distance between histograms of the Source and Target directly. *The general formulation we will adopt in this paper is in line with this approach of minimising some distance in a feature space between feature mappings of the distributions.*

1.2 Contributions of the Paper

We introduce a general framework for label shift quantification, *Distribution Feature Matching* (DFM), that generalises existing methods such as Black-Box Shift Estimation (BBSE) [26], Kernel Mean Matching (KMM) [24,38] and its variant Energy Distance Matching [25].

The contributions of the paper are the following:

1. In Sect. 2, we propose a general framework of Label-shift quantification based on the minimisation of the distance between representations of distributions (in a Euclidean or Hilbert space) obtained by taking expectations of a feature mapping. We show that existing methods in the literature such as KMM or BBSE are particular instances of this general framework.
2. In Sect. 3, we provide a general statistical analysis of DFM under label shift. In particular, we show that our bound on the estimation error significantly improves the previous ones derived in the literature for both KMM and BBSE.
3. We also derive a novel analysis of DFM methods under departures of the label shift hypothesis, using a geometric decomposition of the problem and we show the implication of this analysis when we are in the contamination setting presented earlier. We thus show that certain DFM methods can exhibit robustness against particular types of perturbations or contaminations.
4. In Sect. 4, we support our theoretical results regarding the robustness of the different methods, with experiments on synthetic Gaussian mixtures and real cytometric datasets.

5. Finally, we implement the KMM procedure in Python, using fast GPU-compatible code, using Random Fourier Features (RFF) to significantly reduce the computation burden while keeping the same type of theoretical guarantees. This implementation can still be used on GPU with limited memory.

2 Distribution Feature Matching

Let $\Phi : \mathcal{X} \to \mathcal{F}$ be a fixed feature mapping from $\mathcal{X}$ into a Hilbert space $\mathcal{F}$ (possibly $\mathcal{F} = \mathbb{R}^D$). We extend the mapping Φ to probability distributions on $\mathcal{X}$ via taking expectation, i.e. $\Phi\colon \mathbb{P} \mapsto \Phi(\mathbb{P}) := \mathbb{E}_{X\sim\mathbb{P}}[\Phi(X)] \in \mathcal{F}$. Thus, it holds $\Phi(\hat{\mathbb{P}}_i) = n_i^{-1}\sum_{j\in[n]:y_j=i}\Phi(x_j)$, and similarly $\Phi(\hat{\mathbb{Q}}) = m^{-1}\sum_{j=n+1}^{n+m}\Phi(x_j)$.

We call *Distribution Feature Matching* (DFM) any estimation procedure that can be formulated as the minimiser of the following problem:

$$\hat{\alpha} = \arg\min_{\alpha\in\Delta^c}\left\|\sum_{i=1}^{c}\alpha_i\Phi(\hat{\mathbb{P}}_i) - \Phi(\hat{\mathbb{Q}})\right\|_{\mathcal{F}}^2 \qquad (\mathcal{P})$$

where Δ^c is the $(c-1)$-dimensional simplex.

In the contamination setting, we aim at finding the proportions of the non-noise classes of the target. As these proportions don't sum to one, the "hard" condition $\sum_i \alpha_i = 1$ is no longer needed. One way to overcome this is to introduce a fictitious "dummy" class in the source that formally has a vectorisation equal to 0 (note that adding a dummy class is a computational and theoretical convenience; we don't require to have a real distribution $\mathbb{P}_0$ that maps to 0 in the feature space for the results to hold). If we write $\Phi(\hat{\mathbb{P}}_0) := 0$ one can see that:

$$\arg\min_{\alpha\in\Delta^{c+1}}\left\|\sum_{i=0}^{c}\alpha_i\Phi(\hat{\mathbb{P}}_i) - \Phi(\hat{\mathbb{Q}})\right\|_{\mathcal{F}}^2 = \arg\min_{\alpha\in\mathrm{int}(\Delta^c)}\left\|\sum_{i=1}^{c}\alpha_i\Phi(\hat{\mathbb{P}}_i) - \Phi(\hat{\mathbb{Q}})\right\|_{\mathcal{F}}^2, \qquad (\mathcal{P}_2)$$

where $\mathrm{int}(\Delta^c) := \{x \in \mathbb{R}^c\colon x \geq 0,\ \sum x_i \leq 1\}$. A procedure that solves $\mathcal{P}_2$ will be called *soft*-DFM. In Sect. 3, we will present theoretical results, in the classical Label Shift hypothesis ($\mathcal{LS}$), for DFM methods of the form ($\mathcal{P}$) under an identifiability and boundedness assumption.

In Sect. 3.2, we will show a general result for ("hard") DFM methods when the label shift hypothesis is not verified. As a corollary of these bounds we will directly obtain corresponding guarantees for the *soft*-DFM methods as well through the representation ($\mathcal{P}_2$) and formal inclusion of the dummy class.

In the remainder of this section, we will show the link between DFM and other classical Label Shift Quantification algorithms. However, any black-box feature mapping will be suitable for the results of Sect. 3.

2.1 Kernel Mean Matching

Iyer et al. [24] used Kernel Mean embedding (KME) as their mapping. We refer the reader to [29] for a survey on KME. We briefly recall that for any symmetric and semi-definite positive kernel k defined on $\mathcal{X}$, one can associate a Hilbert space denoted $\mathcal{H}_k$, or simply $\mathcal{H}$ when there is no ambiguity, and a "feature" mapping $\Phi : \mathcal{X} \to \mathcal{H}$ such that $\langle \Phi(x), \Phi(y) \rangle = k(x, y)$.

This mapping can be extended to the space of distributions by taking expectations as described above, which constitutes the principle of KME. We can compute scalar products between mappings using the formula $\langle \Phi(\mathbb{P}), \Phi(\mathbb{Q}) \rangle_{\mathcal{H}} = \mathbb{E}_{(X,Y)\sim\mathbb{P}\otimes\mathbb{Q}}[k(X, Y)]$, which provides a way to find an explict solution of $(\mathcal{P})$ in practice. Then $D_\Phi(\mathbb{P}, \mathbb{Q}) = \|\Phi(\mathbb{P}) - \Phi(\mathbb{Q})\|_{\mathcal{H}}$ is a pseudo-distance on the space of measures on $\mathcal{X}$, called *Maximum Mean Discrepancy* (MMD) [21]. The specific use of a kernel feature mapping for class proportion estimation via $(\mathcal{P})$ has been called Kernel Mean Matching (KMM) by [24].

If $\mathcal{X} = \mathbb{R}^d$ with the usual Euclidean norm, Kawakubo et al. [25] proposed a particular case of KMM using the Energy kernel: $k(x, y) = \|x\| + \|y\| - \|x - y\|$, which is indeed a reproducing kernel [36].

2.2 BBSE as Distribution Feature Matching

Black-Box Shift Estimation is a method using the output of a black-box classifier to estimate the proportions in the target. To take into account the bias of the training data (i.e. the source) [26] used the confusion matrix.

To understand how Black-Box Shift Estimation can be cast as a Distribution Feature Matching procedure, we start from its original formulation as seeking the vector of proportions α that satisfies $Y = M\alpha$, where M is the estimated conditional confusion matrix defined as $M_{ij} = \frac{1}{n_i} \sum 1\{f(x_l) = i \text{ and } y_l = j\}$ and Y is the empirical mean of the observed outputs of the black-box classifier f on the target data, $Y_i = \frac{1}{n} \sum_l 1\{f(x_l) = i\}$. The BBSE estimate is then $\hat{\alpha} = M^{-1}Y$ (M is explicitly assumed invertible by [26]).

Proposition 1. *The BBSE estimator based on the black-box classifier f is the same as the solution of the DFM problem $(\mathcal{P})$ using the feature mapping $\Phi(x) = (1\{f(x) = i\})_{i=1,\dots,c} \in \mathbb{R}^c$, where the positivity constraint on α is dropped.*

In the experiments to come, we will use BBSE+, our modified version of BBSE including the positivity constraint. The experimental results are slightly better for BBSE+. The reason is that in many cases, due to the presence of small classes in the source and in the target, BBSE returns negative proportions. When it does not output negative values, the two algorithms are the same.

This version of BBSE already existed in the literature, it has been used for text content analysis [23] and as a building block for classification, in a domain adaptation setting, more general than Label Shift [9].

3 Theoretical Guarantees

We now provide statistical guarantees for DFM quantification procedures, All proofs can be found in the ArXiv version of the paper [12].

We make the following identifiability hypothesis on the mapping Φ:

$$\sum_{i=1}^{c} \beta_i \Phi(\mathbb{P}_i) = 0 \iff \beta_i = 0 \; \forall i = 1, \ldots, c, \tag{$\mathcal{A}_1$}$$

and

$$\exists C > 0 : \qquad \|\Phi(x)\| \leq C \text{ for all } x. \tag{$\mathcal{A}_2$}$$

If we use KMM, the boundedness property is satisfied as soon as the kernel is bounded (e.g. Gaussian kernel, or any continuous kernel on a compact space). For BBSE, the boundedness is verified with $C = 1$.

Concerning Condition $\mathcal{A}_1$, it is satisfied in the KMM case as long as the kernel is characteristic (e.g. Gaussian kernel) and the distributions $\mathbb{P}_i$ are linearly independent (which is the minimal assumption for the class proportions to be identifiable). These assumption have been previously used by [24] for KMM. Similarly, for BBSE, [26] also assumed identifiability and required that the expected classifier outputs for each class be linearly independent.

We introduce the following notation and state our main theorem:

Definition 1. *We denote $\hat{\boldsymbol{G}}$ the Gram matrix, resp. $\hat{\boldsymbol{M}}$ the centered Gram matrix of $\{\Phi(\hat{\mathbb{P}}_1), \cdots, \Phi(\hat{\mathbb{P}}_c)\}$. That is, $\hat{\boldsymbol{G}}_{ij} = \langle \Phi(\hat{\mathbb{P}}_i), \Phi(\hat{\mathbb{P}}_j) \rangle$ and $\hat{\boldsymbol{M}}_{ij} = \langle \Phi(\hat{\mathbb{P}}_i) - \overline{\Phi}, \Phi(\hat{\mathbb{P}}_j) - \overline{\Phi} \rangle$ with $\overline{\Phi} = c^{-1} \sum_{k=1}^{c} \Phi(\hat{\mathbb{P}}_k)$. Furthermore, let Δ_{min} be the second smallest eivenvalue of $\hat{\boldsymbol{M}}$ and λ_{min} the smallest eigenvalue of $\hat{\boldsymbol{G}}$. In particular, it holds $\Delta_{min} \geq \lambda_{min}$.*

Theorem 1. *If the Label Shift hypothesis ($\mathcal{LS}$) holds, and if the mapping Φ verifies Assumptions ($\mathcal{A}_1$) and ($\mathcal{A}_2$), then for any $\delta \in (0, 1)$, with probability greater than $1 - \delta$, the solution $\hat{\alpha}$ of ($\mathcal{P}$) satisfies:*

$$\|\hat{\alpha} - \alpha^*\|_2 \leq \frac{2CR_{\delta/c}}{\sqrt{\Delta_{min}}} \left(\frac{\|w\|_2}{\sqrt{n}} + \frac{1}{\sqrt{m}} \right) \tag{1}$$

$$\leq \frac{2CR_{\delta/c}}{\sqrt{\Delta_{min}}} \left(\frac{1}{\sqrt{\min_i n_i}} + \frac{1}{\sqrt{m}} \right), \tag{2}$$

where $R_x = 2 + \sqrt{2 \log(2/x)}$, $w_i = \frac{\alpha_i^*}{\beta_i}$.

The same result holds when replacing α^* by the (unobserved) vector of empirical proportions $\tilde{\alpha}$ in the target sample, both on the left-hand side and in the definition of w.

Under the same assumptions, the solution $\hat{\alpha}_{\text{soft}}$ of ($\mathcal{P}_2$) satisfies the same bounds with Δ_{min} replaced by λ_{min}.

3.1 Comparison to Related Literature

We compare our result to Theorem 1 of [24] and Theorem 3 of [26], which as we have mentioned earlier hold under the same assumptions as we make here.

Concerning KMM, a comparison between our inequality (2) and Theorem 1 in [24] shows that our bound is tighter than theirs, which is of leading order

$$\frac{c}{\sqrt{m}} + \sum_i \frac{1}{\sqrt{n_i}} \quad \text{vs ours in} \quad \frac{1}{\sqrt{m}} + \max_i \frac{1}{\sqrt{n_i}}$$

up to logarithmic factors. Thus, Theorem 1 improves upon the previous upper bound by a factor of c with respect to the term in m, and reduces the sum into a maximum regarding the number of instances per class n_i, which may also decrease the order of by factor c when the classes are evenly distributed in the source dataset. Furthermore, Inequality (1) even significantly improves over both Inequality (2) and Theorem 1 in [24]. Indeed, in situations where one of the classes i on the source domain is rare, then the rate $\max_i n_i^{-1/2}$ in Inequality (2) explodes, which is not the case of the rate $\|w\|_2/\sqrt{n}$ in Inequality (1) when the source and target proportions are similar, as the weight vector w reflects the similarity between the source and target distributions. Note that we use the theoretical proportions α^* for the target in the definition of w as the empirical ones are unknown here. Hence, our theorem significantly improves the existing bound for KMM established by [24]. Similarly, our bound (1) applied to BBSE also improves Theorem 3 in [26]. In particular, when both inequalities are formulated with the same probability level (e.g. $1-\delta$), our bound for BBSE is tighter by a factor $\sqrt{c}$ w.r.t. the term in m than the guarantee provided by [26]. Note however that contrary to our result and to Theorem 1 in [24], the bound of [26] does not involve any empirical quantity that can be computed using the source dataset.

Another key component of the bounds is the second smallest eigenvalue $\Delta_{\min}$ of the centered Gram matrix, which replaces the minimum singular value of the Gram matrix in the case of KMM (see Theorem 1 in [24]) and the smallest eigenvalue of the confusion matrix divided by the infinite norm of the source proportions in the case of BBSE (see Inequality (3) of Theorem 3 in [26]), and improves upon both of them.

This improvement is particularly important when the two source classes are unbalanced. For instance, in a two-class setting with a black-box classifier feature map and $\beta^* = (p, 1-p)$, the theoretical version of $\Delta_{\min}$ is equal to 1 when the classifier is perfect and replaces the factor that would be $\min\left(\frac{p}{1-p}, \frac{1-p}{p}\right) < 1$ in the bound of [26]. When the classifier is not perfect but both classes share the same classification accuracy $a \in (1/2, 1)$, then $\Delta_{\min} = 2a - 1$, which strictly improves the factor of [26] except when both classes are equally balanced, in which case both quantities are equal.

To fully understand the nature of $\Delta_{\min}$, we can interpret DFM as the projection of the target feature mapping onto the convex hull of the source feature mappings. Our estimation is then simply the barycentric coordinate of the projection, as formalised in (QP), and $\Delta_{\min}$ is a geometric property of that convex hull. It represents the ease with which our mapping can distinguish between one class and any mixture of the other classes. For instance, for two classes and two embeddings (Φ_1, Φ_2), one can show that $\Delta_{\min} = \frac{1}{2}\|\Phi_1 - \Phi_2\|_{\mathcal{F}}^2$. From a geometric point of view, it is clear that the larger the convex hull (i.e. the line connecting the two features in situations where there are two classes), the less the barycentric coordinate will be affected by a small perturbation of the weights. From a statistical point of view, if our mixture is composed of two very different distributions, it will be intuitively easier to distinguish them in a new sample. The quantity $\Delta_{\min}$ (which we recall is empirical) also provides a natural criterion for the choice of the feature map hyperparameter (i.e. choice of the kernel in KMM), as the dependence in our bound only appears in $\Delta_{\min}$ which can then be maximised.

3.2 Robustness to Contamination

We now introduce a novel theoretical analysis of the robustness of the method with respect to the contamined label shift model (assumption $\mathcal{CLS}$). First, let us obtain a general result when Label Shift is not verified.

A naive approach would simply include the bias term $\|\Phi(\mathbb{P}_i) - \Phi(\mathbb{Q}_i)\|_{\mathcal{F}}$ in the bound. We put into light the robustness of the procedure with respect to certain types of perturbation.

Theorem 2. *Denote V the affine span of the vectors $\Phi(\mathbb{P}_i)$ and $\mathcal{C}$ the convex hull of those same vectors. Denote Π_V and $\Pi_{\mathcal{C}}$ the orthogonal resp. convex projection onto V and $\mathcal{C}$.*

Suppose the same assumptions as in Theorem 1 hold, except for the exact label shift assumption $\mathcal{LS}$. Then, with probability greater than $1-\delta$:

$$\|\hat{\alpha} - \alpha^*\|_2 \leq \frac{1}{\sqrt{\Delta_{min}}}\left(3\epsilon_n + \varepsilon_m + \sqrt{2\epsilon_n}B^{\perp} + B^{\parallel}\right), \tag{3}$$

with:

$$\epsilon_n = C\frac{R_{\delta/c}}{\sqrt{\min_i n_i}}; \quad \varepsilon_m = C\frac{R_\delta}{\sqrt{m}}; \tag{4}$$

$$B^{\perp} = B^{\perp}(\mathbb{P}, \mathbb{Q}) = \sqrt{\|\Phi(\mathbb{Q}) - \Pi_{\mathcal{C}}(\Phi(\mathbb{Q}))\|_{\mathcal{F}}};$$
$$B^{\parallel} = B^{\parallel}(\mathbb{P}, \mathbb{Q}) = \max_i \|\Phi(\mathbb{P}_i) - \Pi_V(\Phi(\mathbb{Q}_i))\|_{\mathcal{F}}.$$

Observe that the bound (3) shows robustness of a DFM procedure against perturbations $B^{\perp}$ that are "orthogonal" to the source space V in feature space. In particular, *consistency* (i.e. convergence of the bound to 0 as the sample sizes grow to infinity) is still granted if $\mathbb{Q}_i \neq \mathbb{P}_i$ but $\Pi_V(\mathbb{Q}_i) = \mathbb{P}_i$. Which type of perturbation of the distributions will result in (close to) orthogonal shifts in feature space very much depends on the feature mapping used. For BBSE, the feature space is of the same dimension as the number of sources, thus under condition $(\mathcal{A}_1)$, V will coincide with E_1, the affine space of vectors summing to one. Since any distribution will be also mapped to E_1, the orthogonal component will always be 0. Thus, we expect no particular robustness property for BBSE methods. For more general feature maps, such as kernel methods or any other vectorisations, this orthogonality property remains to be investigated in general, but we will exhibit below a favorable scenario for KMM in the *contaminated label shift* setting $\mathcal{CLS}$.

We first state a corollary in the $\mathcal{CLS}$ scenario. To do so, we recall that, in this case, we use the *soft*-DFM procedure $\mathcal{P}_2$. We are now in a particular case, where the only difference between source and target is that the unknown noise class $\mathbb{Q}_0$ is formally replaced by the dummy class having feature map equal to 0 in the source. Introduce $\bar{V} := \mathrm{Span}\{\Phi(\mathbb{P}_i), i \in [c]\}$ (i.e. vector span rather than affine span for V previously) and let $\Pi_{\bar{V}}$ be the orthogonal projection on $\bar{V}$.

Corollary 1. *Denote by $\hat{\alpha}_{\mathrm{soft}}$ the minimiser of the soft-DFM problem $\mathcal{P}_2$. Assume the contaminated Label Shift hypothesis ($\mathcal{CLS}$) holds, and if the mapping Φ verifies Assumptions ($\mathcal{A}_1$) and ($\mathcal{A}_2$). Then, with probability greater than $1-\delta$:*

$$\|\hat{\alpha}_{\mathrm{soft}} - \alpha^*\|_2 \leq \frac{1}{\sqrt{\lambda_{min}}}\Big(3\epsilon_n + \varepsilon_m + \sqrt{2\alpha_0\ \epsilon_n\ \|\Phi(\mathbb{Q}_0)\|} + \|\Pi_{\bar{V}}(\Phi(\mathbb{Q}_0))\|_{\mathcal{F}}\Big),$$

with $\epsilon_n, \varepsilon_m$ defined as in (4).

In the particular case of KMM with a translation-invariant kernel $k(x,y) = \varphi(x-y)$, for any distributions $\mathbb{P}, \mathbb{P}'$ it holds $\langle \Phi(\mathbb{P}), \Phi(\mathbb{P}')\rangle = \mathbb{E}_{(X,Y)\sim\mathbb{P}\otimes\mathbb{P}'}[\varphi(X - Y)]$. Thus, if φ is rapidly decaying with distance (e.g. Gaussian kernel), the feature mappings $\Phi(\mathbb{P})$ and $\Phi(\mathbb{P}')$ will be close to orthogonal (have a scalar product close to 0) whenever the distributions $\mathbb{P}, \mathbb{P}'$ are well-separated. From this analysis, we anticipate that KMM with a Gaussian kernel will be robust against contaminations distributions $\mathbb{Q}_0$ whose main mass is far away from the source distributions, since its representation $\Phi(\mathbb{Q}_0)$ will then be close to orthogonal to $\bar{V}$ in feature space.

4 Algorithm and Applications

In this section, we will apply four methods on both synthetic and real datasets.

We choose to test three soft-DFM methods: KMM using the Energy Kernel [25], our modified version of BBSE [26] and KMM using the Gaussian kernel [24] enhanced with Random Fourier Features, that we present in the next section. To show the benefit of the soft version, we also compare with one *hard*-DFM method: KMM enhanced with Random Fourier Features.

The main objective of the experiments is, in view of our theoretical results of Sect. 3.2 and particularly Corollary 1, to test robustness properties of several DFM methods against contamination of the the target dataset by different types of noise. Moreover, we want to check if the *soft* version presented in Sect. 2 leads to improved results in some cases, and will not hurt the results in the others.

All the code and datasets are publicly available [11]. All the computations were done on a computer equipped with a NVIDIA RTX A2000 Laptop.

4.1 Optimisation Problem

Whatever the chosen mapping, solving ($\mathcal{P}$) amounts to solving a Quadratic Programming (QP) in dimension c. Indeed, we can rewrite the problem as:

$$\begin{aligned} &\text{minimise } \frac{1}{2}\alpha^T \hat{\boldsymbol{G}} \alpha + q^T \alpha \\ &\text{subject to } \alpha \succeq 0_c \text{ and } \mathbf{1}_c^T \alpha = 1, \end{aligned} \tag{QP}$$

with $q = \left(\langle \Phi(\mathbb{P}_i), \Phi(\hat{\mathbb{Q}}) \rangle \right)_{i=1}^{c}$. This is a c-dimensional QP problem, which can be solved efficiently.

The computational bottleneck is the computation of the Gram matrix $\hat{\boldsymbol{G}}$ and the vector q. Using KMM directly leads to a complexity of $O(n(n+m))$, as computing q requires evaluating the kernel for every pair of points from the source and the target and computing $\hat{\boldsymbol{G}}$ requires evaluating the kernel for every pair of points between the source classes. Moreover, one needs to have permanent access to the source distributions, as computing q requires both the source and target raw dataset.

Due to such issues, kernel matrix approximations are often used in order to reduce the computational cost of kernel methods [7,33]. In our case we use the well-established principle of Random Fourier Features (RFF) approximation [32]. RFF allows to obtain an approximation of a translation invariant kernel k, i.e. $k(x,y) = \varphi(x-y)$, of the form: $\tilde{k}(x,y) = \tilde{\Phi}(x)^T \tilde{\Phi}(y)$, with $\tilde{\Phi}(x) \in \mathbb{R}^D$, which is itself a positive semi-definite kernel. For a theoretical analysis of the uniform approximation quality of k by $\tilde{k}$, see e.g. [34,37].

Relying on RFF with D Fourier features induces a complexity of $O(D(n+m))$ since we only have to compute $\tilde{\Phi}(\mathbb{P}_i)$ and $\tilde{\Phi}(\hat{\mathbb{Q}})$. Computing $\tilde{\Phi}(\mathbb{P})$ reduces to a matrix multiplication, for which GPU are well suited. To deal with memory overflow on GPU, we rely on the Python package *PyKeops* [8]. With this implementation can solve ($\mathcal{P}$) for high-dimensional data with a very large number of points in sub-second times. For example, for two datasets containing 5×10^6 points in dimension 5, ($\mathcal{P}$) is solved in less than a second, while almost 2 min are needed when we use the exact KMM.

In the experiments, we will design by Random Fourier Features Matching (RFFM) the DFM method that uses $\tilde{\Phi}$ as a feature mapping. RFFM can be used with any translation invariant kernel, but we choose to stick to the classical Gaussian kernel: $k(x,y) = \exp\left(-\|x-y\|^2/(2\sigma^2)\right)$ where the parameter σ is optimised using the criterion derived from (1). Note that RFFM is only used as a way to speed up the computation, and hence we would obtain similar results with a classical KMM using the Gaussian kernel.

4.2 Experiments

We want to test the robustness of the DFM methods in the contaminated scenario $\mathcal{CLS}$. We will compare 4 methods: RFFM, softRFFM, softEnergy and softBBSE+. RFFM is the method introduced in the previous section while softRFFM is RFFM when we use the soft procedure introduced in Sect. 2. SoftEnergy is the kernel mean matching method when we used the Energy kernel [25] and softBBSE+ is our version of BBSE [26].

We will test the methods on both synthetic data and real datasets.

Gaussian Mixture

In this setting, the source is a list of c Gaussian distributions: $\mathbb{P}_1, \cdots, \mathbb{P}_c$. Our objective is to estimate α^* for different values of the contamination level $\epsilon = \alpha_0^*$ ranging from 0 to 0.3 and different kinds of noise distributions $\mathbb{Q}_0$. We will test three kinds of noise:

1. $\mathbb{Q}_0$ is uniformly distributed over the data range ("Background noise").
2. $\mathbb{Q}_0$ is Gaussian with a mean distant from the other means.
3. $\mathbb{Q}_0$ is Gaussian with a similar mean to the others.

Throughout the experiments, we fix the number of classes in the source to $c = 5$ and the number of non-contaminated points to 10000. The dimension varies from 2 to 10. For each contamination level ϵ and each possible dimension, we perform 20 repetitions with different Gaussian distributions. Results for the three experiments can be found in Fig. 1.

In the absence of noise contamination in the target, all methods give excellent results because the source distributions are easy to distinguish. Obviously, the results deteriorate as the contamination level increases. All methods still perform well against background noise (the loss is around 0.1 in the worst case), with softRFFM being significantly better than the others. In the same fashion, when we add a Gaussian far away from the other distributions, softRFFM significantly outperforms the others. As discussed following Corollary 1, this is because when contamination puts mostly mass far from the other classes, the Gaussian KME of the noise distribution will be close to orthogonal to the source KMEs. This property does not hold when a class is added close to the others and thus can be more easily confounded. Thus, the results align well with our theoretical analysis.

While Theorem 2 and Corollary 1 hold for the Energy kernel as well (assuming bounded data) or BBSE+, we don't observe robustness against noise. Again, this is in line with the theoretical study for BBSE+ for which we expected no robustness. Concerning the Energy kernel, we surmise that the lack of robustness comes from the fact that $k(x, y)$ can take large values even if $\|x - y\|$ is large, hence near-orthogonality of the noise distribution to the source does not hold in the corresponding feature space, in contrast to the Gaussian kernel.

Cytometry Dataset

We test the robustness of our methods on the T-cell panel of the Human Immunology Project Consortium (HIPC) [6,14]. HIPC is composed of 63 samples. Seven laboratories analysed 3 replicates from 3 different patients. The number of measurements in the samples range from 10^4 to 10^5. The samples were manually separated into 10 categories using 7 markers.

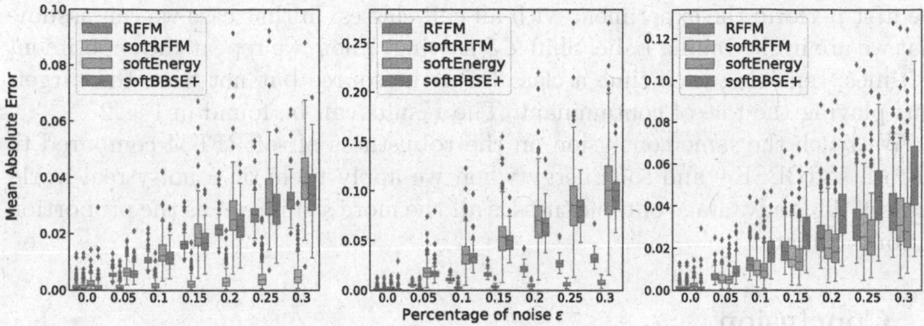

Fig. 1. Robustness of the algorithms to three types of noise. (Lower is better.) Left: background noise; middle: noise is a new class far from the others; right: noise is a new class in the middle of the others.

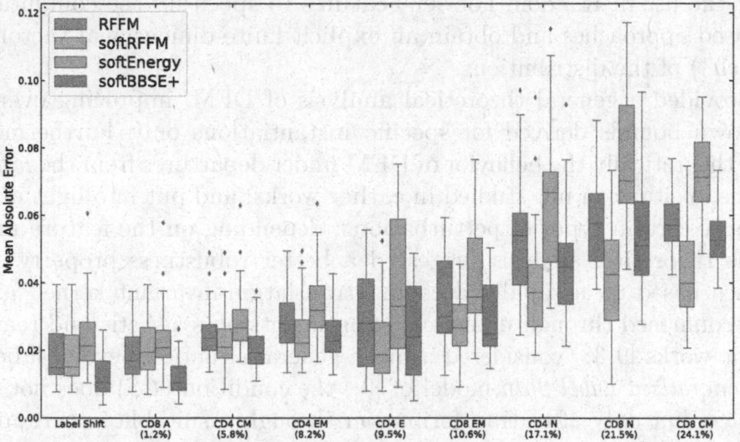

Fig. 2. Each column represents the error - computed using the ℓ_2 norm between the true proportions and the estimated proportions - obtained when some class is absent from the source but present in the target distribution. The first column gives the results when no class is discarded. The class are sorted according to the average proportions they represent in the samples (x labels mention class held out from the source and its proportion)

To put ourselves in the $\mathcal{CLS}$ setting, we choose to remove one of the class of the source, so that this class becomes the noise in the target. In detail, each of the patient replicates are joined into a single patient sample, resulting in 3 patient joined samples for each of the seven laboratories. We take each sample successively as source, and patients samples of the same laboratory as target.[1]

[1] There can be large variability between samples coming from different laboratories, while there is homogeneity within each lab. The label shift hypothesis is therefore reasonable when keeping source and target from the same lab.

We first perform the experiment with all cell classes: in that case we can assume that we are in the vanilla Label Shift $\mathcal{LS}$ setting. Then, we repeat the experiment 10 times, removing each time a class from the source but not from the target, thus playing the role of contaminant. The results can be found in Fig. 2

We reach the same conclusion on the robustness of softRFFM compared to RFFM, softBBSE+ and softEnergy when we apply them on a noisy real-world dataset. This advantage of robustness is all the more significant as the proportion of noise is high.

5 Conclusion

We introduced Distribution Feature Matching (DFM) as a general approach for class proportion estimation (also known at label shift estimation or quantification learning), recovering methods from previous literature as special cases. We also proposed the use of Random Fourier Features to speed up the computation of kernel-based approaches and obtain an explicit finite-dimensional vectorization (or "sketch") of the distributions.

We provided a general theoretical analysis of DFM, improving over previously known bounds derived for specific instantiations only. Furthermore, we analysed theoretically the behavior of DFM under departures from the label shift hypothesis, a situation not studied in earlier works, and put into light a robustness against certain types of perturbations, depending on the feature mapping used. The theoretical analysis suggested a better robustness property of RFF approaches based on a rapidly decaying translation-invariant kernel, and this could be confirmed through numerical experiments on synthetic and real data.

Recent works [9,38] considered a more general situation beyond label shift. In the *Generalized Label Shift* model of [9], the condition ($\mathcal{LS}$) does not hold in input space, but only after transformation through a suitable feature mapping Φ, and these authors proposed an algorithm alternating between class proportion estimation using BBSE+ and feature learning (using a separate domain adaptation algorithm, suitably adapted to handle label proportion shift). We believe that using one of the proposed methods in the present paper could be used fruitfully in such a framework to replace the BBSE+ module.

Acknowledgements. B. Dussap was supported by the program Paris Region Ph.D. of DIM Mathinnov. G. Blanchard acknowledges support of the ANR under ANR-19-CHIA-0021-01 "BiSCottE", IDEX REC-2019-044, and of the DFG under SFB1294 - 318763901.

Ethical Statement. Label shift quantification has uses in a number of application domains; the results in this paper are chiefly oriented towards theory and general methodology so that we don't discuss an application in particular. We only mention that the flow cytometry data used for proof-of-concept experiments is publicly available from a reputable scientific consortium and has been up to our knowledge collected following all established ethical standards.

The original *Classify & Count* [15] method for label shift quantification is known to inherit the potential biases of the classification method it is based on (i.e. the misclassification errors can be very unevenly distributed across classes and "favor" majority classes). The *Adjusted Classify & Count (ACC)* approach and related methods [17,26] aim at rectifying this bias. In the present paper, we aim at going one step further and analyze certain robustness properties of the proposed label shift quantification methods, and introduce the contaminated label shift ($\mathcal{CLS}$) setting with the goal of investigating trustworthiness of such methods under mild violations of the standard Label Shift model. Certainly the robustness property is desirable for improved reliability in practice, but does not mean immunity against biases; additionally, the user should always be wary of stronger model violations between reference and test data, in particular class-conditional distribution shifts. We therefore recommend established good practice of regularly checking on control data possible biases or drifts from the model, in particular for sensitive applications.

References

1. Alexandari, A., Kundaje, A., Shrikumar, A.: Maximum likelihood with bias-corrected calibration is hard-to-beat at label shift adaptation. In: International Conference on Machine Learning, pp. 222–232. PMLR (2020)
2. Azizzadenesheli, K., Liu, A., Yang, F., Anandkumar, A.: Regularized learning for domain adaptation under label shifts. arXiv preprint arXiv:1903.09734 (2019)
3. Barranquero, J., Díez, J., del Coz, J.J.: Quantification-oriented learning based on reliable classifiers. Pattern Recogn. **48**(2), 591–604 (2015)
4. Barranquero, J., González, P., Díez, J., Del Coz, J.J.: On the study of nearest neighbor algorithms for prevalence estimation in binary problems. Pattern Recogn. **46**(2), 472–482 (2013)
5. Bigot, J., Freulon, P., Hejblum, B.P., Leclaire, A.: On the potential benefits of entropic regularization for smoothing Wasserstein estimators. arXiv preprint arXiv:2210.06934 (2022)
6. Brusic, V., Gottardo, R., Kleinstein, S.H., Davis, M.M.: Computational resources for high-dimensional immune analysis from the human immunology project consortium. Nat. Biotechnol. **32**, 146–148 (2014)
7. Camoriano, R., Angles, T., Rudi, A., Rosasco, L.: Nytro: when subsampling meets early stopping. In: Artificial Intelligence and Statistics, pp. 1403–1411. PMLR (2016)
8. Charlier, B., Feydy, J., Glaunès, J.A., Collin, F.D., Durif, G.: Kernel operations on the GPU, with autodiff, without memory overflows. J. Mach. Learn. Res. **22**(74), 1–6 (2021). https://www.kernel-operations.io/keops/index.html
9. Tachet des Combes, R., Zhao, H., Wang, Y.X., Gordon, G.J.: Domain adaptation with conditional distribution matching and generalized label shift. In: Advances in Neural Information Processing Systems, vol. 33, pp. 19276–19289 (2020)
10. Du Plessis, M.C., Sugiyama, M.: Semi-supervised learning of class balance under class-prior change by distribution matching. Neural Netw. **50**, 110–119 (2014)
11. Dussap, B.: Distribution Feature Matching for Label Shift (2023). https://plmlab.math.cnrs.fr/dussap/Label-shift-DFM
12. Dussap, B., Blanchard, G., Chérief-Abdellatif, B.E.: Label shift quantification with robustness guarantees via distribution feature matching. arXiv preprint arXiv:2306.04376 (2023)

13. Esuli, A., Fabris, A., Moreo, A., Sebastiani, F.: Learning to quantify (2023)
14. Finak, G., et al.: Standardizing flow cytometry immunophenotyping analysis from the human immunophenotyping consortium. Sci. Rep. **6**(1), 1–11 (2016)
15. Forman, G.: Counting positives accurately despite inaccurate classification. In: Gama, J., Camacho, R., Brazdil, P.B., Jorge, A.M., Torgo, L. (eds.) ECML 2005. LNCS (LNAI), vol. 3720, pp. 564–575. Springer, Heidelberg (2005). https://doi.org/10.1007/11564096_55
16. Forman, G.: Quantifying trends accurately despite classifier error and class imbalance. In: Proceedings of the 12th ACM SIGKDD International Conference on Knowledge Discovery and Data Mining, pp. 157–166 (2006)
17. Forman, G.: Quantifying counts and costs via classification. Data Min. Knowl. Disc. **17**(2), 164–206 (2008)
18. Garg, S., Wu, Y., Balakrishnan, S., Lipton, Z.C.: A unified view of label shift estimation. arXiv preprint arXiv:2003.07554 (2020)
19. González, P., Castaño, A., Chawla, N.V., Coz, J.J.D.: A review on quantification learning. ACM Comput. Surv. (CSUR) **50**(5), 1–40 (2017)
20. González-Castro, V., Alaiz-Rodríguez, R., Alegre, E.: Class distribution estimation based on the hellinger distance. Inf. Sci. **218**, 146–164 (2013)
21. Gretton, A., Borgwardt, K.M., Rasch, M.J., Schölkopf, B., Smola, A.: A kernel two-sample test. J. Mach. Learn. Res. **13**(1), 723–773 (2012)
22. Gretton, A., Smola, A., Huang, J., Schmittfull, M., Borgwardt, K., Schölkopf, B.: Covariate shift by kernel mean matching. Dataset Shift Mach. Learn. **3**(4), 5 (2009)
23. Hopkins, D.J., King, G.: A method of automated nonparametric content analysis for social science. Am. J. Political Sci. **54**(1), 229–247 (2010)
24. Iyer, A., Nath, S., Sarawagi, S.: Maximum mean discrepancy for class ratio estimation: convergence bounds and kernel selection. In: International Conference on Machine Learning, pp. 530–538. PMLR (2014)
25. Kawakubo, H., Du Plessis, M.C., Sugiyama, M.: Computationally efficient class-prior estimation under class balance change using energy distance. IEICE Trans. Inf. Syst. **99**(1), 176–186 (2016)
26. Lipton, Z., Wang, Y.X., Smola, A.: Detecting and correcting for label shift with black box predictors. In: International Conference on Machine Learning, pp. 3122–3130. PMLR (2018)
27. Maletzke, A., dos Reis, D., Cherman, E., Batista, G.: DyS: a framework for mixture models in quantification. In: Proceedings of the AAAI Conference on Artificial Intelligence, vol. 33, pp. 4552–4560 (2019)
28. Milli, L., Monreale, A., Rossetti, G., Giannotti, F., Pedreschi, D., Sebastiani, F.: Quantification trees. In: 2013 IEEE 13th International Conference on Data Mining, pp. 528–536. IEEE (2013)
29. Muandet, K., Fukumizu, K., Sriperumbudur, B., Schölkopf, B., et al.: Kernel mean embedding of distributions: a review and beyond. Found. Trends® Mach. Learn. **10**(1–2), 1–141 (2017)
30. Patel, V.M., Gopalan, R., Li, R., Chellappa, R.: Visual domain adaptation: a survey of recent advances. IEEE Signal Process. Mag. **32**(3), 53–69 (2015)
31. Quinonero-Candela, J., Sugiyama, M., Schwaighofer, A., Lawrence, N.D.: Dataset Shift in Machine Learning. MIT Press, Cambridge (2008)
32. Rahimi, A., Recht, B.: Random features for large-scale kernel machines. In: Advances in Neural Information Processing Systems, vol. 20 (2007)
33. Rudi, A., Camoriano, R., Rosasco, L.: Less is more: Nyström computational regularization. In: Advances in Neural Information Processing Systems, vol. 28 (2015)

34. Rudi, A., Rosasco, L.: Generalization properties of learning with random features. In: Advances in Neural Information Processing Systems, vol. 30 (2017)
35. Saerens, M., Latinne, P., Decaestecker, C.: Adjusting the outputs of a classifier to new a priori probabilities: a simple procedure. Neural Comput. **14**(1), 21–41 (2002)
36. Sejdinovic, D., Sriperumbudur, B., Gretton, A., Fukumizu, K.: Equivalence of distance-based and RKHS-based statistics in hypothesis testing. Ann. Stat. 2263–2291 (2013)
37. Sutherland, D.J., Schneider, J.: On the error of random Fourier features. In: Proceedings of the Thirty-First Conference on Uncertainty in Artificial Intelligence, pp. 862–871 (2015)
38. Zhang, K., Schölkopf, B., Muandet, K., Wang, Z.: Domain adaptation under target and conditional shift. In: International Conference on Machine Learning, pp. 819–827. PMLR (2013)

Robust Classification of High-Dimensional Data Using Data-Adaptive Energy Distance

Jyotishka Ray Choudhury[1(✉)], Aytijhya Saha[1], Sarbojit Roy[2], and Subhajit Dutta[3]

[1] Indian Statistical Institute, Kolkata, India
{mb2203,bs2002}@isical.ac.in
[2] King Abdullah University of Science and Technology, Thuwal, Saudi Arabia
sarbojit.roy@kaust.edu.sa
[3] Indian Institute of Technology Kanpur, Kanpur, India
duttas@iitk.ac.in

Abstract. Classification of high-dimensional low sample size (HDLSS) data poses a challenge in a variety of real-world situations, such as gene expression studies, cancer research, and medical imaging. This article presents the development and analysis of some classifiers that are specifically designed for HDLSS data. These classifiers are free of tuning parameters and are robust, in the sense that they are devoid of any moment conditions of the underlying data distributions. It is shown that they yield perfect classification in the HDLSS asymptotic regime, under some fairly general conditions. The comparative performance of the proposed classifiers is also investigated. Our theoretical results are supported by extensive simulation studies and real data analysis, which demonstrate promising advantages of the proposed classification techniques over several widely recognized methods.

Keywords: Classification · Data Mining · Generalized Energy · High-Dimensional Asymptotics

1 Introduction

High-dimensional low sample size data is characterized by having a large number of features or variables, but only a few samples or observations. The problem of HDLSS classification has been an important problem in the statistics and machine learning communities. In today's world, high-dimensional low sample size problems are frequently encountered in scientific areas including microarray gene expression studies, medical image analysis, and spectral measurements in chemometrics to name a few.

Traditional classification techniques such as logistic regression, support vector machines, and k-nearest neighbors [9,12] often fail on this type of data [20] when

J. Ray Choudhury and A. Saha—Both authors contributed equally to this research.

D. Koutra et al. (Eds.): ECML PKDD 2023, LNAI 14173, pp. 86–101, 2023.
https://doi.org/10.1007/978-3-031-43424-2_6

certain regularity conditions on the underlying distributions are not met. In case of k-nearest neighbors, for example, when the dimension of the data is far greater than the number of observations, the concept of neighbors becomes loose and ill-defined. Consequently, the k-nearest neighbor classifier exhibits erratic behavior [4]. Due to distance concentration, Euclidean distance (ED)-based classifiers suffer certain limitations in HDLSS situations [2, 13]. Some recent work has studied the effect of distance concentration on some widely used classifiers based on Euclidean distances, such as 1-nearest neighbor (1-NN) classifier [15], support vector machines (SVM) [8], etc. They derived conditions under which these classifiers yield perfect classification in the HDLSS setup [14]. Moreover, ED-based classifiers lack robustness to outliers, since ED is sensitive to outliers.

For the HDLSS setup, numerous studies adopt dimension reduction approach as a pre-processing step before performing the classification. These work include modern classifiers and learning techniques centered mainly on feature selection (e.g., correlation-based, information theory-based, feature clustering [27], etc.), projection based on transformation [1, 17], regularization (ridge, LASSO, SCAD, and Elastic-net [32]), deep learning (autoencoders [16, 30]), etc. However, this is not optimal when the dimension reduction step is conducted independently of the goals of finding reduced features that maximize the separation between classes of signals. In fact, it is inevitable that some information is lost via dimension reduction if a large number of features turn out to be relevant and weakly dependent upon each other. A few studies have conducted classification of HDLSS data without employing dimension reduction (see, e.g., [23, 26, 31]).

Energy distance was introduced in [3, 28] as a statistical measure of distance between two probability distributions on $\mathbb{R}^d$. It was primarily designed with a goal of testing for equality of two or more multivariate distributions, and worked particularly well with high-dimensional data. Recently, energy distances have been utilized in the context of classification (see, e.g., [22–24]) as well. In this article, we develop classifiers based on a more general version of energy distance that yield asymptotically perfect classification (i.e., zero misclassification rate) under fairly general assumptions in an HDLSS setting, without maneuvering dimension reduction.

Suppose $\mathbf{X}$ and $\mathbf{Y}$ are two d-variate random vectors following the distribution functions $\mathbf{F}$ and $\mathbf{G}$, respectively. In the context of testing for equality of the two distributions, a constant multiple of the following was introduced in [18] as squared multivariate Cramér-von Mises (CvM) distance between $\mathbf{F}$ and $\mathbf{G}$. It is a special case of the generalized energy distance [25]:

$$\mathcal{W}^*_{\mathbf{FG}} = 2\int\int \left(\mathbf{F}_{\boldsymbol{\beta}}(t) - \mathbf{G}_{\boldsymbol{\beta}}(t)\right)^2 d\mathbf{H}(\boldsymbol{\beta}, t)\ , \tag{1}$$

where $\boldsymbol{\beta} \in \mathbb{R}^d$, and $\mathbf{F}_{\boldsymbol{\beta}}(t) = \mathbb{P}\left[\boldsymbol{\beta}^\top \mathbf{X} \le t\right]$ and $\mathbf{G}_{\boldsymbol{\beta}}(t) = \mathbb{P}\left[\boldsymbol{\beta}^\top \mathbf{Y} \le t\right]$, for $t \in \mathbb{R}$, are the cumulative distribution functions of $\boldsymbol{\beta}^\top\mathbf{X}$ and $\boldsymbol{\beta}^\top\mathbf{Y}$ respectively, evaluated at t, $d\mathbf{H}(\boldsymbol{\beta}, t) = d\mathbf{H}_{\boldsymbol{\beta}}(t)\, d\lambda(\boldsymbol{\beta})$ with $\lambda(\boldsymbol{\beta})$ being the uniform probability measure on d-dimensional unit sphere $\mathbb{S}^{d-1} = \{\mathbf{x} \in \mathbb{R}^d : \mathbf{x}^\top\mathbf{x} = 1\}$, and $\mathbf{H}_{\boldsymbol{\beta}}(t) = \alpha\mathbf{F}_{\boldsymbol{\beta}}(t) + (1-\alpha)\mathbf{G}_{\boldsymbol{\beta}}(t)$. Here, α is a fixed value in $(0, 1)$. In the same context of hypothesis testing, [19] considered a constant multiple of (1), with

$\mathbf{H}(\boldsymbol{\beta}, t)$ as the distribution function of a $(d+1)$-dimensional normal random vector with mean $\mathbf{0}_{d+1}$, the $(d+1)$-dimensional zero vector, and covariance matrix I_{d+1}, the identity matrix of order $(d+1)$. However, considering such a fixed distribution which is not data-dependent may not be useful in general. On the other hand, the weight function $\mathbf{H}_{\beta}$ considered in [18] is more flexible, since it adapts according to the underlying class distributions. In that sense, $\mathcal{W}^*_{\mathbf{FG}}$ is referred to as a data-adaptive energy distance between $\mathbf{F}$ and $\mathbf{G}$. It was shown in [18] that $\mathcal{W}^*_{\mathbf{FG}} = 0$ if and only if $\mathbf{F} = \mathbf{G}$. This property of $\mathcal{W}^*_{\mathbf{FG}}$ says that it has the capability of discriminating between two different distributions. This motivates us to utilize $\mathcal{W}^*_{\mathbf{FG}}$ in the context of binary classification problems.

1.1 Our Contribution

In this article, we start off by developing a classifier based on $\mathcal{W}^*_{\mathbf{FG}}$. However, it suffers certain limitations in the HDLSS setting. We investigate and address those issues by modifying $\mathcal{W}^*_{\mathbf{FG}}$ in different ways, and based on the new measures of distance, we develop classifiers that are robust in the sense that their performance does not depend on the existence of the moments of the underlying class distributions. Moreover, the proposed classifiers are free from tuning parameters and admit strong theoretical guarantees under fairly general assumptions, in an HDLSS setup.

The rest of the paper is organized as follows. In Sect. 2, we develop a classifier based on $\mathcal{W}^*_{\mathbf{FG}}$, discuss its limitations and modify it to obtain three robust classifiers to achieve asymptotically perfect classification under milder conditions. Section 3 provides an analysis of the asymptotic behaviors and a relative comparison of the proposed classifiers. Section 4 demonstrates convincing advantages of the proposed classifiers using numerical simulations and real data analysis. Proofs of the theoretical results are included in Section A of Supplementary Material. Lastly, Section B of the Supplementary Material contains some additional details on the simulation studies and real data analysis. The supplementary material and the relevant R codes for simulation studies and real data analysis are available at: https://github.com/jyotishkarc/sub-834-ecml-2023.

2 Methodology

Consider two mutually independent samples

$$\mathbf{X}_1^{(d)}, \mathbf{X}_2^{(d)}, \ldots, \mathbf{X}_m^{(d)} \overset{\text{i.i.d.}}{\sim} \mathbf{F}_d \text{ and } \mathbf{Y}_1^{(d)}, \mathbf{Y}_2^{(d)}, \ldots, \mathbf{Y}_n^{(d)} \overset{\text{i.i.d.}}{\sim} \mathbf{G}_d$$

where $\mathbf{X}_i^{(d)} = (X_{i1}, X_{i2}, \ldots, X_{id})^\top$ for $i = 1, 2, \ldots, m$, and $\mathbf{Y}_j^{(d)} = (Y_{j1}, Y_{j2}, \ldots, Y_{jd})^\top$ for $j = 1, \ldots, n$ are d-dimensional random vectors arising from two different population distributions $\mathbf{F}_d$ and $\mathbf{G}_d$. For the sake of convenience, we shall drop d from notations where dependence on d is obvious. As mentioned in Sect. 1.1, we shall keep the sample sizes m and n fixed throughout our analysis.

The angular distance between any $\mathbf{u}, \mathbf{v} \in \mathbb{R}^d$ was defined in [18] as follows:

$$\rho(\mathbf{u}, \mathbf{v}) = \mathbb{E}\left[\rho_0(\mathbf{u}, \mathbf{v}; \mathbf{Q})\right] \text{ with } \mathbf{Q} \sim \alpha \mathbf{F} + (1-\alpha)\mathbf{G}. \quad (2)$$

$$\rho_0(\mathbf{u}, \mathbf{v}; \mathbf{w}) = \begin{cases} \frac{1}{\pi}\angle(\mathbf{u}-\mathbf{w}, \mathbf{v}-\mathbf{w}) & \text{if } \mathbf{u} \neq \mathbf{w} \text{ and } \mathbf{v} \neq \mathbf{w}, \\ 0 & \text{otherwise,} \end{cases} \quad (3)$$

with $\alpha = \frac{m}{m+n}$, and $\angle(\mathbf{a}, \mathbf{b}) = \cos^{-1}\left(\frac{\mathbf{a}^\top \mathbf{b}}{\|\mathbf{a}\|_2 \|\mathbf{b}\|_2}\right)$ with $\|\mathbf{v}\|_2$ as the l_2 norm of $\mathbf{v}$. Note that $\rho \in [0,1]$ since ρ_0 takes values in $[0,1]$. It was shown in [18] that $\mathcal{W}^*_{\mathbf{FG}}$, defined in (1), has the following closed-form expression:

$$\mathcal{W}^*_{\mathbf{FG}} = \mathbb{E}\left[2\rho(\mathbf{X}_1, \mathbf{Y}_1) - \rho(\mathbf{X}_1, \mathbf{X}_2) - \rho(\mathbf{Y}_1, \mathbf{Y}_2)\right]. \quad (4)$$

2.1 A Classifier Based on $\mathcal{W}^*_{\mathbf{FG}}$

Let us consider the unknown expectations $t_{\mathbf{FF}} = \mathbb{E}\left[\rho(\mathbf{X}_1, \mathbf{X}_2)\right]$ and $t_{\mathbf{GG}} = \mathbb{E}\left[\rho(\mathbf{Y}_1, \mathbf{Y}_2)\right]$. We start off by defining estimators of $t_{\mathbf{FF}}$ and $t_{\mathbf{GG}}$ as follows.

$$\hat{t}_{\mathbf{FF}} = \frac{1}{m(m-1)} \sum_{i \neq j} \hat{\rho}(\mathbf{X}_i, \mathbf{X}_j) \text{ and } \hat{t}_{\mathbf{GG}} = \frac{1}{n(n-1)} \sum_{i \neq j} \hat{\rho}(\mathbf{Y}_i, \mathbf{Y}_j),$$

where $\hat{\rho}$ is defined as a sample version of ρ in the following manner:

$$\hat{\rho}(\mathbf{u}, \mathbf{v}) = \frac{1}{m+n}\Big(\sum_{i=1}^{m} \rho_0(\mathbf{u}, \mathbf{v}, \mathbf{X}_i) + \sum_{j=1}^{n} \rho_0(\mathbf{u}, \mathbf{v}, \mathbf{Y}_j)\Big). \quad (5)$$

Similarly, for $\mathbf{z} \in \mathbb{R}^d$, we define

$$\begin{aligned} \hat{t}_{\mathbf{F}}(\mathbf{z}) &= \tfrac{1}{m}\textstyle\sum_i \hat{\rho}(\mathbf{X}_i, \mathbf{z}), \ \hat{t}_{\mathbf{G}}(\mathbf{z}) = \tfrac{1}{n}\textstyle\sum_j \hat{\rho}(\mathbf{Y}_j, \mathbf{z}), \\ l_{\mathbf{F}}(\mathbf{z}) &= \hat{t}_{\mathbf{F}}(\mathbf{z}) - \tfrac{1}{2}\hat{t}_{\mathbf{FF}}, \ l_{\mathbf{G}}(\mathbf{z}) = \hat{t}_{\mathbf{G}}(\mathbf{z}) - \tfrac{1}{2}\hat{t}_{\mathbf{GG}}. \end{aligned} \quad (6)$$

Finally, the classifier δ_0 is defined as follows:

$$\delta_0(\mathbf{z}) = \begin{cases} 1 & \text{if } l_{\mathbf{G}}(\mathbf{z}) - l_{\mathbf{F}}(\mathbf{z}) > 0, \\ 2 & \text{otherwise,} \end{cases} \quad (7)$$

where $\delta_0(\mathbf{z}) = 1$ or $\delta_0(\mathbf{z}) = 2$ correspond to assigning $\mathbf{z}$ to class 1 or class 2 having data distribution $\mathbf{F}$ or $\mathbf{G}$, respectively. Let $\boldsymbol{\mu}_{\mathbf{F}}$ and $\boldsymbol{\mu}_{\mathbf{G}}$ denote the mean vectors for $\mathbf{F}$ and $\mathbf{G}$, respectively, and $\boldsymbol{\Sigma}_{\mathbf{F}}$ and $\boldsymbol{\Sigma}_{\mathbf{G}}$ denote the covariance matrices for $\mathbf{F}$ and $\mathbf{G}$, respectively. In order to analyze the behavior of the δ_0 in HDLSS setup, consider the following assumptions:

Assumption 1. *There exists a constant $c < \infty$ such that $E[|U_k|^4] < c$ for all $1 \leq k \leq d$, where $\mathbf{U} = (U_1, \cdots, U_d)^\top$ follows either $\mathbf{F}$ or $\mathbf{G}$.*

Assumption 2. $\lambda_{\mathbf{FG}} = \lim_{d \to \infty}\left\{\frac{1}{d}\|\boldsymbol{\mu}_{\mathbf{F}} - \boldsymbol{\mu}_{\mathbf{G}}\|^2\right\}$ *and* $\sigma_I^2 = \lim_{d \to \infty}\left\{\frac{1}{d}\operatorname{trace}(\boldsymbol{\Sigma}_I)\right\}$ *exist for $I \in \{\mathbf{F}, \mathbf{G}\}$.*

Assumption 3. *Let* $\mathbf{U}$, $\mathbf{V}$ *and* $\mathbf{Z}$ *be three independent random vectors such that each of them follows either* $\mathbf{F}$ *or* $\mathbf{G}$. *Then,*

$$\sum_{i<j} \operatorname{cov}((U_i - Z_i)(V_i - Z_i), (U_j - Z_j)(V_j - Z_j)) = o(d^2).$$

Assumption 1 requires finiteness of the fourth moments of all marginals of $\mathbf{F}$ and $\mathbf{G}$. Assumption 2 demands the existence of the limiting values of the average of the squared mean difference between the marginals of two distributions and the variances of the marginals to exist. Assumption 3 is trivially satisfied when the component variables of the underlying populations are independent. It also holds with certain additional constraints on their dependence structure, e.g., when the sequence $\{(U_k - Z_k)(V_k - Z_k)\}_{k\geq 1}$ has ρ-mixing property. In fact, if the sequences $\{U_k\}_{k\geq 1}$, $\{V_k\}_{k\geq 1}$ and $\{Z_k\}_{k\geq 1}$ all have ρ-mixing property, then the sequence $\{h(U_k, V_k, Z_k)\}_{k\geq 1}$ also has ρ-mixing property, for any Borel measurable function h (see [7] for more details).

Theorem 1. *Suppose Assumptions 1 to 3 are satisfied. Then,* $\theta^*_{\mathbf{FG}} = \lim_{d\to\infty} \mathcal{W}^*_{\mathbf{FG}}$ *is finite, and for a test observation* $\mathbf{Z}$,

(a) if $\mathbf{Z} \sim \mathbf{F}$, *then* $l_{\mathbf{G}}(\mathbf{Z}) - l_{\mathbf{F}}(\mathbf{Z}) \xrightarrow{\mathbb{P}} \frac{1}{2}\theta^*_{\mathbf{FG}}$ *as* $d \to \infty$;
(b) if $\mathbf{Z} \sim \mathbf{G}$, *then* $l_{\mathbf{G}}(\mathbf{Z}) - l_{\mathbf{F}}(\mathbf{Z}) \xrightarrow{\mathbb{P}} -\frac{1}{2}\theta^*_{\mathbf{FG}}$ *as* $d \to \infty$.

As $d \to \infty$, $l_{\mathbf{G}}(\mathbf{Z}) - l_{\mathbf{F}}(\mathbf{Z})$ converges in probability to the limit of $\frac{1}{2}\mathcal{W}^*_{\mathbf{FG}}$ if $\mathbf{Z} \sim \mathbf{F}$, and to the negative of it, if $\mathbf{Z} \sim \mathbf{G}$. This justifies the construction of the classifier δ_0 in (7). The probability of misclassification of a classifier δ is defined as $\Delta = \alpha P[\delta(\mathbf{Z}) = 2|\mathbf{Z} \sim \mathbf{F}] + (1-\alpha)P[\delta(\mathbf{Z}) = 1|\mathbf{Z} \sim \mathbf{G}]$. Now, we state a result on the convergence of the misclassification probabilities of the classifier δ_0 (denoted by Δ_0), under the set of assumptions stated above.

Theorem 2. *Suppose that Assumptions 1 to 3 are satisfied, and either* $\lambda_{\mathbf{FG}} \neq 0$ *or* $\sigma^2_{\mathbf{F}} \neq \sigma^2_{\mathbf{G}}$ *holds. Then,* $\Delta_0 \to 0$ *as* $d \to \infty$.

It follows from Theorem 2 that if $\mathbf{F}$ and $\mathbf{G}$ differ in their locations and/or scales, then Δ_0 converges to 0 as the dimension grows. Clearly, the asymptotic properties of the classifier δ_0 are governed by the limiting constants, $\lambda_{\mathbf{FG}}, \sigma_{\mathbf{F}}$, and $\sigma_{\mathbf{G}}$. Similar issues regarding assumptions on the existence of moments of class distributions were also present in the two-sample test based on $\mathcal{W}^*_{\mathbf{FG}}$ in [18]. Let us now consider the following two examples:

Example 1: $X_{1k} \overset{\text{i.i.d.}}{\sim} N(1,1)$ and $Y_{1k} \overset{\text{i.i.d.}}{\sim} N(1,2)$
Example 2: $X_{1k} \overset{\text{i.i.d.}}{\sim} N(0,3)$ and $Y_{1k} \overset{\text{i.i.d.}}{\sim} t_3$

for $1 \leq k \leq d$. Here, $N(\mu, \sigma^2)$ refers to a Gaussian distribution with mean μ and variance σ^2, and t_s denotes the Student's t-distribution with s degrees of freedom.

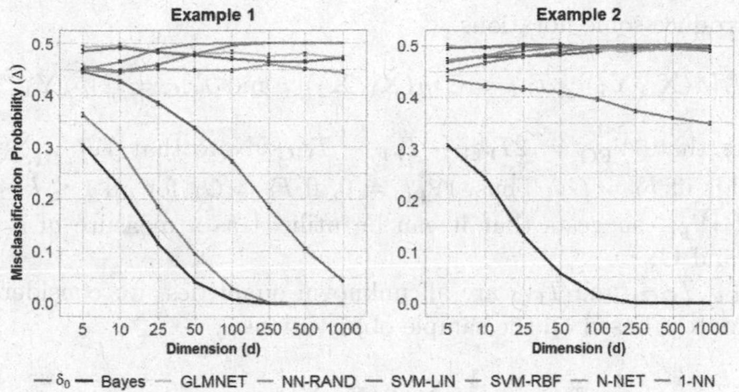

Fig. 1. Average misclassification rates with errorbars for δ_0, along with some popular classifiers for increasing dimensions. Bayes classifier is treated as a benchmark.

In **Example 1**, $\|\boldsymbol{\mu}_{\mathbf{F}} - \boldsymbol{\mu}_{\mathbf{G}}\|^2 = 0$ but $\sigma^2_{\mathbf{F}} = 1, \sigma^2_{\mathbf{G}} = 2$. It can be observed from Fig. 1 that δ_0 identifies this difference in scale and its performance improves as d increases, whereas most of the popular classifiers misclassify nearly 45% of the observations.

In **Example 2**, $\|\boldsymbol{\mu}_{\mathbf{F}} - \boldsymbol{\mu}_{\mathbf{G}}\|^2 = 0$ and $\sigma^2_{\mathbf{F}} = \sigma^2_{\mathbf{G}} = 3$, i.e., there is no difference between either location parameters or scale parameters. Consequently, δ_0 (as well as the popular classifiers) fails to classify the test observations correctly since the assumptions in Theorem 2 are not met.

These simulations support Theorem 2 (see Fig. 1) and illustrate the limitations of the classifier δ_0 when there is no difference in either location parameters or scale parameters. In the next subsection, we refine δ_0 to develop some classifiers whose asymptotic properties are free of any moment conditions, as well as the limiting constants $\lambda_{\mathbf{FG}}, \sigma^2_{\mathbf{F}}$, and $\sigma^2_{\mathbf{G}}$, mentioned in Assumptions 1 and 2.

2.2 Refinements of δ_0

A New Measure of Distance: We modify $\mathcal{W}^*_{\mathbf{FG}}$ by taking the average of the distances between each F_k and G_k, the k-th marginals of $\mathbf{F}$ and $\mathbf{G}$, respectively. Define $\overline{\mathcal{W}}^*_{\mathbf{FG}} = \frac{1}{d}\sum_{k=1}^{d} \mathcal{W}^*_{F_k G_k}$. For each $1 \leq k \leq d$, it follows from (4) the quantity $\mathcal{W}^*_{F_k G_k}$ has the following closed-form expression:

$$\mathcal{W}^*_{F_k G_k} = \mathbb{E}\left[2\rho\left(X_{1k}, Y_{1k}\right) - \rho\left(X_{1k}, X_{2k}\right) - \rho\left(Y_{1k}, Y_{2k}\right)\right], \tag{8}$$

where $\mathbf{X}_1, \mathbf{X}_2 \overset{i.i.d.}{\sim} \mathbf{F}$ and $\mathbf{Y}_1, \mathbf{Y}_2 \overset{i.i.d.}{\sim} \mathbf{G}$.

Recall the definition of ρ in (2). For any two d-dimensional random variables $\mathbf{u} = (u_1, u_2, \ldots, u_d)^\top$ and $\mathbf{v} = (v_1, v_2, \ldots, v_d)^\top$, we define

$$\bar{\rho}(\mathbf{u}, \mathbf{v}) = \frac{1}{d}\sum_{k=1}^{d} \rho\left(u_k, v_k\right). \tag{9}$$

We now introduce some notations:

$$T_{\mathbf{FG}} = \mathbb{E}\left[\bar{\rho}\left(\mathbf{X}_1, \mathbf{Y}_1\right)\right], \ T_{\mathbf{FF}} = \mathbb{E}\left[\bar{\rho}\left(\mathbf{X}_1, \mathbf{X}_2\right)\right], \text{ and } T_{\mathbf{GG}} = \mathbb{E}\left[\bar{\rho}\left(\mathbf{Y}_1, \mathbf{Y}_2\right)\right].$$

This implies that $\overline{\mathcal{W}}^*_{\mathbf{FG}} = 2T_{\mathbf{FG}} - T_{\mathbf{FF}} - T_{\mathbf{GG}}$. Note that $\mathcal{W}^*_{F_k G_k} \geq 0$, and equality holds iff $F_k = G_k$. Thus, $\overline{\mathcal{W}}^*_{\mathbf{FG}} = 0$ iff $F_k = G_k$ for all $1 \leq k \leq d$. This property of $\overline{\mathcal{W}}^*_{\mathbf{FG}}$ suggests that it can be utilized as a measure of separation between $\mathbf{F}$ and $\mathbf{G}$.

Since $T_{\mathbf{FF}}, T_{\mathbf{GG}}$, and $T_{\mathbf{FG}}$ are all unknown quantities, we consider the following estimators based on the sample observations:

$$\hat{T}_{\mathbf{FG}} = \frac{1}{mn}\sum_{i,j} \hat{\bar{\rho}}\left(\mathbf{X}_i, \mathbf{Y}_j\right),$$

$$\hat{T}_{\mathbf{FF}} = \frac{1}{m(m-1)}\sum_{i \neq j} \hat{\bar{\rho}}\left(\mathbf{X}_i, \mathbf{X}_j\right),$$

$$\hat{T}_{\mathbf{GG}} = \frac{1}{n(n-1)}\sum_{i \neq j} \hat{\bar{\rho}}\left(\mathbf{Y}_i, \mathbf{Y}_j\right).$$

where $\hat{\bar{\rho}}(\mathbf{u}, \mathbf{v})$ is a natural estimator of $\bar{\rho}(\mathbf{u}, \mathbf{v})$, defined as follows:

$$\hat{\bar{\rho}}(\mathbf{u}, \mathbf{v}) = \frac{1}{d}\sum_{k=1}^{d} \hat{\rho}\left(u_k, v_k\right). \tag{10}$$

This leads to an empirical version of $\overline{\mathcal{W}}^*_{\mathbf{FG}}$ defined as

$$\hat{\overline{\mathcal{W}}}^*_{\mathbf{FG}} = 2\hat{T}_{\mathbf{FG}} - \hat{T}_{\mathbf{FF}} - \hat{T}_{\mathbf{GG}}. \tag{11}$$

For $\mathbf{z} = (z_1, z_2, \ldots, z_d)^\top \in \mathbb{R}^d$, we define:

$$\begin{aligned} \hat{T}_{\mathbf{F}}(\mathbf{z}) &= \tfrac{1}{m}\textstyle\sum_i \hat{\bar{\rho}}\left(\mathbf{X}_i, z_i\right), \ \hat{T}_{\mathbf{G}}(\mathbf{z}) = \tfrac{1}{n}\textstyle\sum_j \hat{\bar{\rho}}\left(\mathbf{Y}_j, z_j\right), \\ L_{\mathbf{F}}(\mathbf{z}) &= \hat{T}_{\mathbf{F}}(\mathbf{z}) - \tfrac{1}{2}\hat{T}_{\mathbf{FF}}, \ L_{\mathbf{G}}(\mathbf{z}) = \hat{T}_{\mathbf{G}}(\mathbf{z}) - \tfrac{1}{2}\hat{T}_{\mathbf{GG}}, \\ S(\mathbf{z}) &= \hat{T}_{\mathbf{F}}(\mathbf{z}) + \hat{T}_{\mathbf{G}}(\mathbf{z}) - \tfrac{1}{2}\left(\hat{T}_{\mathbf{FF}} + \hat{T}_{\mathbf{GG}}\right) - \hat{T}_{\mathbf{FG}}. \end{aligned}$$

Classifier Based on $\overline{\mathcal{W}}^*_{\mathbf{FG}}$: Define $\mathscr{D}_1(\mathbf{z}) = L_{\mathbf{G}}(\mathbf{z}) - L_{\mathbf{F}}(\mathbf{z})$. We prove that $\mathscr{D}_1(\mathbf{Z})$ converges in probability to $\frac{1}{2}\overline{\mathcal{W}}^*_{\mathbf{FG}}$, if $\mathbf{Z} \sim \mathbf{F}$ and to $-\frac{1}{2}\overline{\mathcal{W}}^*_{\mathbf{FG}}$, if $\mathbf{Z} \sim \mathbf{G}$, as $d \to \infty$ (see Theorem 3). This, along with the fact that the average energy distance, $\overline{\mathcal{W}}^*_{\mathbf{FG}}$ is non-negative, motivates us to consider the following classifier:

$$\delta_1(\mathbf{z}) = \begin{cases} 1 & \text{if } \mathscr{D}_1(\mathbf{z}) > 0, \\ 2 & \text{otherwise.} \end{cases} \tag{12}$$

Recall that $(T_{\mathbf{FG}} - T_{\mathbf{FF}})$ and $(T_{\mathbf{FG}} - T_{\mathbf{GG}})$ sum up to $\overline{\mathcal{W}}^*_{\mathbf{FG}}$. So, in case $T_{\mathbf{FG}}$ lies between $T_{\mathbf{FF}}$ and $T_{\mathbf{GG}}$, adding them up might nearly cancel each other out, resulting in a very small value of $\overline{\mathcal{W}}^*_{\mathbf{FG}}$. Consequently, it may not fully capture the actual dissimilarity between $\mathbf{F}$ and $\mathbf{G}$. A natural way to address this problem is to square the two quantities before adding them. We define

$$\bar{\tau}_{\mathbf{FG}} = (T_{\mathbf{FG}} - T_{\mathbf{FF}})^2 + (T_{\mathbf{FG}} - T_{\mathbf{GG}})^2 .$$

It follows from simple calculations that one may write $\bar{\tau}_{\mathbf{FG}}$ in the following form:

$$\bar{\tau}_{\mathbf{FG}} = \frac{1}{2}\overline{\mathcal{W}}^{*2}_{\mathbf{FG}} + \frac{1}{2}\left(T_{\mathbf{FF}} - T_{\mathbf{GG}}\right)^2 . \tag{13}$$

Note that $\bar{\tau}_{\mathbf{FG}}$ being a convex combination of squares of $\overline{\mathcal{W}}^*_{\mathbf{FG}} = 2T_{\mathbf{FG}} - T_{\mathbf{FF}} - T_{\mathbf{GG}}$ and $T_{\mathbf{FF}} - T_{\mathbf{GG}}$, both of which are measures of disparity between $\mathbf{F}$ and $\mathbf{G}$, can be considered as a new measure of disparity between the two distributions. The modification approach proposed in (13) is similar to what had been suggested in the literature of two-sample hypothesis tests to improve the power of some two-sample tests for HDLSS data in [6].

Classifier Based on $\bar{\tau}_{\mathbf{FG}}$: We now develop a classifier that utilizes $\bar{\tau}_{\mathbf{FG}}$. Recall the definitions of $\mathscr{D}_1(\mathbf{z})$ and $S(\mathbf{z})$. For $\mathbf{z} \in \mathbb{R}^d$, define

$$\mathscr{D}_2(\mathbf{z}) = \frac{1}{2}\hat{\overline{\mathcal{W}}}^*_{\mathbf{FG}} \cdot \mathscr{D}_1(\mathbf{z}) + \frac{1}{2}\left(\hat{T}_{\mathbf{FF}} - \hat{T}_{\mathbf{GG}}\right) \cdot S(\mathbf{z}).$$

We show that as $d \to \infty$, $\mathscr{D}_2(\mathbf{Z})$ converges in probability to $\bar{\tau}_{\mathbf{FG}}$ (> 0) if $\mathbf{Z} \sim \mathbf{F}$, and to $-\bar{\tau}_{\mathbf{FG}}$ (< 0) if $\mathbf{Z} \sim \mathbf{G}$ (see Theorem 3 in Sect. 3 below). This motivates us to consider the following classifier:

$$\delta_2(\mathbf{z}) = \begin{cases} 1 & \text{if } \mathscr{D}_2(\mathbf{z}) > 0, \\ 2 & \text{otherwise.} \end{cases} \tag{14}$$

We consider another measure of disparity between $\mathbf{F}$ and $\mathbf{G}$ (say, $\bar{\psi}_{\mathbf{FG}}$), by simply replacing the squares of $\overline{\mathcal{W}}_{\mathbf{FG}}$ and $S_{\mathbf{FG}}$ by their absolute values in the expression for $\bar{\tau}_{\mathbf{FG}}$. A similar modification has already been considered, in the context of two-sample testing (see, e.g., [29]). Based on this, we define yet another measure of separation:

$$\bar{\psi}_{\mathbf{FG}} = \frac{1}{2}\overline{\mathcal{W}}^*_{\mathbf{FG}} + \frac{1}{2}\left|T_{\mathbf{FF}} - T_{\mathbf{GG}}\right| .$$

Classifier Based on $\bar{\psi}_{\mathbf{FG}}$: For $\mathbf{z} \in \mathbb{R}^d$, we define

$$\mathscr{D}_3(\mathbf{z}) = \frac{1}{2}\hat{\overline{\mathcal{W}}}^*_{\mathbf{FG}} \operatorname{sign}\left(\mathscr{D}_1(\mathbf{z})\right) + \frac{1}{2}\left(\hat{T}_{\mathbf{FF}} - \hat{T}_{\mathbf{GG}}\right) \cdot \operatorname{sign}\left(S(\mathbf{z})\right)$$

where $\operatorname{sign}(\cdot)$ is defined as $\operatorname{sign}(x) = \frac{x}{|x|}$ for $x \neq 0$, and 0 for $x = 0$.

We prove that as $d \to \infty$, $\mathscr{D}_3(\mathbf{Z})$ converges in probability to $\bar{\psi}_{\mathbf{FG}}$, a positive quantity if $\mathbf{Z} \sim \mathbf{F}$, and to $-\bar{\psi}_{\mathbf{FG}}$, a negative quantity if $\mathbf{Z} \sim \mathbf{G}$ (see Theorem 4 in Sect. 3 below). This motivates us to construct the following classifier:

$$\delta_3(\mathbf{z}) = \begin{cases} 1 & \text{if } \mathscr{D}_3(\mathbf{z}) > 0, \\ 2 & \text{otherwise.} \end{cases} \tag{15}$$

3 Asymptotics Under HDLSS Regime

Suppose $\mathbf{U} = (U_1, U_2, \ldots, U_d)^\top$ and $\mathbf{V} = (V_1, V_2, \ldots, V_d)^\top$ are drawn independently from $\mathbf{F}$ or $\mathbf{G}$. We assume that the component variables are weakly dependent. In particular, we assume the following.

Assumption 4. *For any four d-dimensional random vectors* $\mathbf{U}, \mathbf{V}, \mathbf{Q}, \mathbf{Q}^*$ *having distribution* $\mathbf{F}$ *or* $\mathbf{G}$, *such that they are mutually independent,*

i. $\sum_{1 \le k_1 < k_2 \le d} \mathrm{cov}(\rho_0(U_{k_1}, V_{k_1}; Q_{k_1}), \rho_0(U_{k_2}, V_{k_2}; Q_{k_2})) = o(d^2)$;
ii. $\sum_{1 \le k_1 < k_2 \le d} \mathrm{cov}(\rho_0(U_{k_1}, V_{k_1}; Q_{k_1}), \rho_0(U_{k_2}, V_{k_2}; Q^*_{k_2})) = o(d^2)$.

Assumption 4 is trivially satisfied if the component variables of the underlying distributions are independently distributed, and it continues to hold when the components have ρ-mixing property.

Theorem 3. *Suppose Assumption 4 is satisfied. For a test observation* $\mathbf{Z}$,

(a) if $\mathbf{Z} \sim \mathbf{F}$, *then* $\left|\mathscr{D}_1(\mathbf{Z}) - \frac{1}{2}\overline{\mathcal{W}}^*_{\mathbf{FG}}\right| \xrightarrow{\mathbb{P}} 0$ *and* $|\mathscr{D}_2(\mathbf{Z}) - \bar{\tau}_{\mathbf{FG}}| \xrightarrow{\mathbb{P}} 0$ *as* $d \to \infty$;
(b) if $\mathbf{Z} \sim \mathbf{G}$, *then* $\left|\mathscr{D}_1(\mathbf{Z}) + \frac{1}{2}\overline{\mathcal{W}}^*_{\mathbf{FG}}\right| \xrightarrow{\mathbb{P}} 0$ *and* $|\mathscr{D}_2(\mathbf{Z}) + \bar{\tau}_{\mathbf{FG}}| \xrightarrow{\mathbb{P}} 0$ *as* $d \to \infty$.

Theorem 3 states that if $\mathbf{Z} \sim \mathbf{F}$ (respectively, $\mathbf{Z} \sim \mathbf{G}$), the discriminants corresponding to δ_1 and δ_2 converge in probability to a positive (respectively, negative) quantity as $d \to \infty$. This justifies our construction of the classifiers δ_1 and δ_2 in (12) and (14), respectively.

Now, we expect δ_1 to yield an optimal performance if $\overline{\mathcal{W}}^*_{\mathbf{FG}}$ does not vanish with increasing dimensions. Hence, it is reasonable to assume the following:

Assumption 5.

$$\liminf_{d \to \infty} \overline{\mathcal{W}}^*_{\mathbf{FG}} > 0.$$

Assumption 5 implies that the separation between $\mathbf{F}$ and $\mathbf{G}$ is asymptotically non-negligible. Observe that this assumption is satisfied if the component variables of $\mathbf{F}$ and $\mathbf{G}$ are identically distributed. We also need the following assumption for the asymptotic analysis of δ_3.

Assumption 6.

$$\liminf_{d \to \infty} |T_{\mathbf{FF}} - T_{\mathbf{GG}}| > 0.$$

Theorem 4. *Suppose Assumptions 4 to 6 hold true. For a test observation* $\mathbf{Z}$,

(a) if $\mathbf{Z} \sim \mathbf{F}$, *then* $|\mathscr{D}_3(\mathbf{Z}) - \bar{\psi}_{\mathbf{FG}}| \xrightarrow{\mathbb{P}} 0$ *as* $d \to \infty$;
(b) if $\mathbf{Z} \sim \mathbf{G}$, *then* $|\mathscr{D}_3(\mathbf{Z}) + \bar{\psi}_{\mathbf{FG}}| \xrightarrow{\mathbb{P}} 0$ *as* $d \to \infty$.

Theorem 4 states that if $\mathbf{Z} \sim \mathbf{F}$ (respectively, $\mathbf{Z} \sim \mathbf{G}$), the discriminant $\mathscr{D}_3$ corresponding to δ_3 converges in probability to a positive (respectively, negative) quantity as $d \to \infty$, which justifies our construction of the classifier δ_3 in (15).

3.1 Misclassification Probabilities of δ_1, δ_2, and δ_3 in the HDLSS Asymptotic Regime

We now show the convergence of the misclassification probabilities of our classifiers δ_i (denoted as Δ_i), under some fairly general assumptions for $i = 1, 2, 3$.

Theorem 5. *Suppose Assumptions 4 and 5 hold. Then, $\Delta_1 \to 0$ and $\Delta_2 \to 0$ as $d \to \infty$. If, in addition, Assumption 6 holds, then $\Delta_3 \to 0$ as $d \to \infty$.*

Observe that the asymptotic behaviors of the classifiers δ_1, δ_2, and δ_3 are no longer governed by the constants $\lambda_{\mathbf{FG}}, \sigma_{\mathbf{F}}$ and $\sigma_{\mathbf{G}}$. In fact, they are robust in terms of moment conditions since their behavior does not depend on the existence of any moments of **F** and **G** altogether.

3.2 Comparison of the Classifiers

Although the proposed classifiers yield perfect classification with increasing dimensions, they have some ordering among their misclassification rates under appropriate conditions. The following result describes the same.

Theorem 6. *Suppose Assumptions 4 and 5 hold. Then,*

(a) if $\liminf_{d\to\infty} (\max\{T_{\mathbf{FF}}, T_{\mathbf{GG}}\} - T_{\mathbf{FG}}) > 0$, there exists $d_0' \in \mathbb{N}$ such that $\Delta_2 \leq \Delta_3 \leq \Delta_1$ for all $d \geq d_0'$,

(b) if $\liminf_{d\to\infty} (T_{\mathbf{FG}} - \max\{T_{\mathbf{FF}}, T_{\mathbf{GG}}\}) > 0$ and Assumption 6 holds, there exists $d_0' \in \mathbb{N}$, such that $\Delta_2 \geq \Delta_3 \geq \Delta_1$ for all $d \geq d_0'$.

Remark. If Assumption 6 is dropped from Theorem 6(b), it can still be concluded that if $\liminf_{d\to\infty} (T_{\mathbf{FG}} - \max\{T_{\mathbf{FF}}, T_{\mathbf{GG}}\}) > 0$, under Assumptions 4 and 5, there exists $d_0' \in \mathbb{N}$ such that $\Delta_2 \geq \Delta_1$ for all $d \geq d_0'$ (see Lemma A.8(b) of the Supplementary Material).

We observe that δ_3 always works 'moderately' among the proposed classifiers, in the sense that its misclassification probability is neither the largest nor the smallest in both the aforementioned situations. It might be difficult to verify the conditions in Theorem 6 in practice. Under such circumstances, it is more reasonable to use δ_3 since it is the most 'stable' among the proposed classifiers.

4 Empirical Performance and Results

We examine the performance of our classifiers on a variety of simulated and real datasets, compared to several widely recognized classifiers such as GLMNET [15], Nearest Neighbor Random Projection (NN-RP) [11], Support Vector Machine with Linear (SVM-LIN) as well as Radial Basis Function (SVM-RBF) kernels [8], Neural Networks (N-NET) [5], and k-Nearest Neighbor [9,12] with $k = 1$ (i.e., 1-NN). Additionally, the Bayes classifier is treated as a benchmark classifier in all the aforementioned simulated examples to assess the performances of the proposed classifiers, since it performs optimally when the true data distributions are known. All numerical exercises were executed on an Intel Xeon Gold 6140 CPU (2.30 GHz, 2295 Mhz) using the R programming language [21]. Details about the packages used to implement the popular classifiers are provided in Section B of Supplementary Material.

4.1 Simulation Studies

We perform our comparative study on five different simulated examples concerning different location problems as well as scale problems. In each example, we consider a binary classification problem with data simulated from two different d-variate distributions. Fixing the training sample size, we increase d to mimic an HDLSS setting. In such situations, our proposed classifiers are expected to achieve perfect classification at higher values of d. We carry out our analysis for eight different values of d, namely, $5, 10, 25$, 50, 100, 250, 500, and 1000.

Examples 1 and **2** were already introduced in Sect. 2. We consider three more simulated examples as follows:

Example 3: $X_{1k} \overset{\text{i.i.d}}{\sim} C(0,1)$ and $Y_{1k} \overset{\text{i.i.d}}{\sim} C(1,1)$,
Example 4: $X_{1k} \overset{\text{i.i.d}}{\sim} C(1,1)$ and $Y_{1k} \overset{\text{i.i.d}}{\sim} C(1,2)$,
Example 5: $X_{1k} \overset{\text{i.i.d}}{\sim} \frac{9}{10}N(1,1) + \frac{1}{10}C(4,1)$ and $Y_{1k} \overset{\text{i.i.d}}{\sim} \frac{9}{10}N(1,2) + \frac{1}{10}C(4,1)$,

for $1 \leq k \leq d$. Here, $C(\mu, \sigma^2)$ refers to Cauchy distribution with location μ and scale σ. **Example 3** and **Example 4** are location and scale problems, respectively. In **Example 5**, we consider the competing distributions to be $N(1,1)$ and $N(1,2)$ but with 10% contamination from a $C(4,1)$ distribution.

For all the examples, a training dataset was formed with a random sample of 20 observations from each class, and a randomly generated test dataset of size 200 (100 from each class) is used. The same process was repeated 100 times independently, and all individual misclassification rates were averaged to estimate the probability of misclassification of δ_1, δ_2, and δ_3 as well as the popular classifiers, which are reported in Sect. 2 of the Supplementary Material.

In **Examples 2, 3,** and **4**, the competing distributions have identical first and second moments. Consequently, δ_0 performs poorly in such situations. For this reason, we have dropped δ_0 from further analysis. Plots of estimated misclassification probabilities of δ_1, δ_2, and δ_3 along with those of the aforementioned popular classifiers are given in Fig. 2. In each example, since the component variables are i.i.d., Assumptions 4 and 5 hold. Conseqently, $\hat{T}_{IJ}$ is a consistent estimator of T_{IJ} as $d \to \infty$ (see Lemma A.7(b) of the Supplementary Material) for $I, J \in \{\mathbf{F}, \mathbf{G}\}$. Hence, we estimate T_{IJ} by $\hat{T}_{IJ}$ to explain Fig. 2. Figure 2 shows that Δ_1, Δ_2 and Δ_3 approach zero as d increases for all the examples.

For **Examples 1, 2,** and **4**, we observe $\max\{\hat{T}_{\mathbf{FF}}, \hat{T}_{\mathbf{GG}}\} > \hat{T}_{\mathbf{FG}}$. For these three examples, Fig. 2 shows that $\Delta_2 \leq \Delta_3 \leq \Delta_1$. For **Example 3**, we observe that $\max\{\hat{T}_{\mathbf{FF}}, \hat{T}_{\mathbf{GG}}\} < \hat{T}_{\mathbf{FG}}$ (see Table 1, Section B of the Supplementary Material). For this example, Fig. 2 shows that $\Delta_2 \geq \Delta_3 \geq \Delta_1$. Thus, the numerical findings are consistent with Theorems 5 and 6 (see Sects. 3.1 and 3.2).

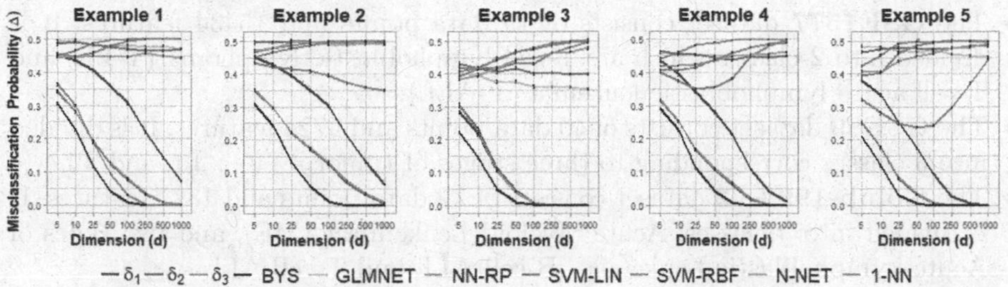

Fig. 2. Average misclassification rates with errorbars for δ_1, δ_2, and δ_3, along with some popular classifiers for different dimensions. Bayes classifier is treated as a benchmark.

Example 5 was specially curated to validate the effectiveness of our classifiers in terms of robustness to outliers. In this example, we have considered two competing mixture distributions with contamination arising from the $C(4, 1)$ distribution. All of δ_1, δ_2, and δ_3 outperform the popular classifiers as d increases. Even in the presence of contamination, all of our proposed classifiers tend to achieve perfect classification as d increases.

4.2 Implementation on Real Data

Alongside the simulation studies, we implement our methods on several HDLSS datasets for a comprehensive performance evaluation. For each dataset, 50% of the observations were selected at random to create a training set, while keeping the proportions of observations from each class consistent with those of all original datasets. The remaining observations were used to create the test set. To obtain stable estimates of the misclassification probabilities, this procedure was repeated 100 times independently, and individual misclassification rates were averaged out to estimate the probability of misclassification of δ_1, δ_2, and δ_3, as well as the popular classifiers.

Although our methods are primarily designed for binary classification, we implement a majority voting ensemble in the case of J-class problems with $J \geq 3$. So, for a dataset with J different classes, we consider all $\binom{J}{2} = \frac{J(J-1)}{2}$ many unordered pairs of classes and treat them as separate binary classification problems. For each test observation, we perform classification for all of those $\binom{J}{2}$ many problems and classify the test observation to the class to which it gets assigned the maximum number of times. Ties are broken at random.

We conduct a case study on six real HDLSS datasets, namely, GSE1577 and GSE89 from the Microarray database[1], Golub-1999-v2 and Gordon-2002 from the CompCancer database[2], and Computers and DodgerLoopDay from the UCR Time Series Classification Archive[3] [10]. A brief description follows.

[1] Available at https://file.biolab.si/biolab/supp/bi-cancer/projections/.
[2] Available at https://schlieplab.org/Static/Supplements/CompCancer/datasets.htm.
[3] Available at https://www.cs.ucr.edu/~eamonn/time_series_data_2018/.

- The **GSE1577** dataset consists of 19 data points and 15434 features. It is divided into 2 classes which are T-cell lymphoblastic lymphoma (T-LL) and T-cell acute lymphoblastic leukemia (T-ALL).
- The **GSE89** dataset consists of 40 data points and 5724 features. It is divided into 3 classes corresponding to three stages of tumor - T2+, Ta, and T1.
- The **Golub-1999-v2** dataset consists of 72 data points and 1877 features. It is divided into 3 classes: Acute Myeloid Leukemia (AML), and two types of Acute Lymphoblastic Leukemia - B-cell ALL and T-cell ALL.
- The **Gordon-2002** dataset consists of 181 data points and 1626 features, divided into 2 classes about the pathological distinction between malignant pleural mesothelioma (MPM) and adenocarcinoma (AD) of the lung.
- The **Computers** dataset contains readings on electricity consumption from 500 households in the UK, sampled in two-minute intervals over a month. Each observation has 720 features. The data points are categorized into two classes: 'Desktop' and 'Laptop'.
- The **DodgerLoopDay** dataset consists of 158 data points and 288 features, divided into 7 classes corresponding to the 7 days of a week.

The estimated misclassification probabilities of δ_1, δ_2, and δ_3, and the popular classifiers for these datasets are reported in Table 1. The number of classes, data points, and features are denoted by class, N, and d, respectively.

Table 1. Estimated misclassification probabilities (in %) with standard errors (in parentheses) for δ_1, δ_2, and δ_3, and popular classifiers for real datasets. For each dataset, the entries corresponding to the minimum misclassification rates are **boldfaced**.

Dataset	Description			Popular Classifiers						Proposed Classifiers		
	class	N	d	GLM-NET	NN-RP	SVM-LIN	SVM-RBF	N-NET	1-NN	δ_1	δ_2	δ_3
GSE1577	2	19	15434	6.51 (0.66)	11.59 (0.44)	6.38 (0.35)	30.06 (0.36)	33.87 (0.98)	11.12 (0.39)	**6.06** (0.84)	7.33 (1.04)	**6.06** (0.84)
GSE89	3	40	5724	25.67 (0.47)	25.15 (0.49)	20.18 (1.05)	41.12 (0.46)	43.03 (1.92)	17.54 (0.28)	**15.21** (0.80)	24.26 (0.97)	16.53 (0.96)
Golub-1999-v2	3	72	1877	8.78 (0.62)	15.28 (0.44)	10.55 (0.43)	33.05 (0.39)	75.26 (0.67)	8.98 (0.39)	**6.89** (0.41)	9.40 (0.43)	7.49 (0.44)
Gordon-2002	2	181	1626	2.58 (0.47)	4.11 (0.12)	1.26 (0.09)	1.84 (0.09)	11.28 (2.83)	2.69 (0.10)	**0.53** (0.01)	0.54 (0.01)	**0.53** (0.01)
Computers	2	500	720	39.99 (0.69)	42.53 (0.62)	47.06 (0.39)	40.76 (0.27)	46.92 (0.41)	41.33 (0.57)	38.65 (0.28)	**36.38** (0.21)	36.50 (0.22)
DodgerLoopDay	7	158	288	55.45 (0.32)	48.72 (0.79)	39.42 (0.44)	47.03 (0.36)	71.32 (1.08)	47.38 (0.68)	**37.68** (0.39)	44.73 (0.44)	42.23 (0.52)

For the datasets GSE1577, GSE89, Golub-1999-v2, Gordon-2002, and DodgerLoopDay, the estimated misclassification probabilities of our proposed classifiers are in the order $\Delta_1 \leq \Delta_3 \leq \Delta_2$, i.e., the performance of δ_1 is the best for these examples and the misclassification probability of δ_3 lies in between that of δ_1 and δ_2. To understand the relative performance of these classifiers, we computed $\hat{T}_{\mathbf{FF}}$, $\hat{T}_{\mathbf{FG}}$ and $\hat{T}_{\mathbf{GG}}$, and they satisfy $(\hat{T}_{\mathbf{FG}} - \max\{\hat{T}_{\mathbf{FF}}, \hat{T}_{\mathbf{GG}}\}) > 0$.

As discussed in Theorem 6, this ordering among the empirical versions of $T_{\mathbf{FF}}$, $T_{\mathbf{FG}}$ and $T_{\mathbf{GG}}$ is consistent with the relative ordering of the performances of δ_1, δ_2 and δ_3. Furthermore, δ_1 and δ_3 performed better than all the popular classifiers. Although δ_2 performed relatively worse than δ_1 and δ_3, it outperformed NN-RP, SVM-RBF, N-NET, and 1-NN.

For the dataset Computers, the estimated misclassification probabilities of our proposed classifiers are in the order $\Delta_2 \leq \Delta_3 \leq \Delta_1$, i.e., δ_2 showed the best performance with a misclassification probability close to 36%. The misclassification probability of δ_3 lies between that of δ_1 and δ_2. It turns out that $\hat{T}_{\mathbf{FF}}$, $\hat{T}_{\mathbf{FG}}$ and $\hat{T}_{\mathbf{GG}}$ satisfy $(\max\{\hat{T}_{\mathbf{FF}}, \hat{T}_{\mathbf{GG}}\} - \hat{T}_{\mathbf{FG}}) > 0$. This ordering among the empirical versions of $T_{\mathbf{FF}}$, $T_{\mathbf{FG}}$ and $T_{\mathbf{GG}}$ is consistent with the relative ordering of the performances of δ_1, δ_2 and δ_3 (see Theorem 6 of Sect. 3.2). All of δ_1, δ_2, and δ_3 performed better than every popular classifier mentioned earlier.

Table 1 shows that δ_1, δ_2 and δ_3 outperform widely recognized classifiers in a majority of the reported datasets, which establishes the merit of our proposed methods over the widely recognized ones. In addition, for all the reported datasets, the ordering among $\hat{T}_{\mathbf{FF}}$, $\hat{T}_{\mathbf{FG}}$ and $\hat{T}_{\mathbf{GG}}$ were found out to be consistent with the results stated in Theorem 6.

5 Concluding Remarks

In this paper, we developed some classification methods that draw good intuition from both classical and recent developments. We proved that under some general conditions, the misclassification probabilities of these classifiers steadily approach 0 in the HDLSS asymptotic regime. The major advantages of our proposed methods are that they are free of tuning parameters, robust in terms of moment conditions, and easy to implement. Theoretical justification and comprehensive empirical studies against other well-established classification methods establish the advantages of our approach.

Nevertheless, when the competing distributions have at most $o(d)$ many different marginals, and the rest are identically distributed, Assumptions 5 and 6 will no longer hold. The theoretical guarantees for the optimal performance of the proposed classifiers will break down in such situations. Developing classifiers that avoid these assumptions is a fruitful avenue for further research.

Acknowledgements. We express our sincere gratitude to Professor Hernando Ombao (KAUST) for his generous support and insightful comments. We also thank the anonymous reviewers for their comments on improving our manuscript.

References

1. Abdi, H., Williams, L.J.: Principal component analysis. Wiley Interdiscip. Rev. Comput. Stat. **2**(4), 433–459 (2010)
2. Aggarwal, C.C., Hinneburg, A., Keim, D.A.: On the surprising behavior of distance metrics in high dimensional space. In: Van den Bussche, J., Vianu, V. (eds.) Database Theory, pp. 420–434. Springer, Heidelberg (2001). https://doi.org/10.1007/3-540-44503-X_27
3. Baringhaus, L., Franz, C.: On a new multivariate two-sample test. J. Multivar. Anal. **88**(1), 190–206 (2004)
4. Beyer, K., Goldstein, J., Ramakrishnan, R., Shaft, U.: When is "nearest neighbor" meaningful? In: Beeri, C., Buneman, P. (eds.) ICDT 1999. LNCS, vol. 1540, pp. 217–235. Springer, Heidelberg (1999). https://doi.org/10.1007/3-540-49257-7_15
5. Bishop, C.M., et al.: Neural Networks for Pattern Recognition. Oxford University Press, Oxford (1995)
6. Biswas, M., Ghosh, A.K.: A nonparametric two-sample test applicable to high dimensional data. J. Multivar. Anal. **123**, 160–171 (2014)
7. Bradley, R.C.: Introduction to Strong Mixing Conditions. Kendrick Press, Heber City (2007)
8. Cortes, C., Vapnik, V.: Support-vector networks. Mach. Learn. **20**(3), 273–297 (1995)
9. Cover, T., Hart, P.: Nearest neighbor pattern classification. IEEE Trans. Inf. Theory **13**(1), 21–27 (1967)
10. Dau, H.A., et al.: Hexagon-ML: The UCR Time Series Classification Archive (2018)
11. Deegalla, S., Bostrom, H.: Reducing high-dimensional data by principal component analysis vs. random projection for nearest neighbor classification. In: 2006 5th International Conference on Machine Learning and Applications (ICMLA 2006), pp. 245–250. IEEE (2006)
12. Fix, E., Hodges, J.L.: Discriminatory analysis. Nonparametric discrimination: consistency properties. Int. Stat. Rev./Revue Internationale de Statistique **57**(3), 238–247 (1989)
13. Francois, D., Wertz, V., Verleysen, M.: The concentration of fractional distances. IEEE Trans. Knowl. Data Eng. **19**(7), 873–886 (2007)
14. Hall, P., Marron, J.S., Neeman, A.: Geometric representation of high dimension, low sample size data. J. Roy. Stat. Soc. Ser. B (Stat. Methodol.) **67**(3), 427–444 (2005)
15. Hastie, T., Tibshirani, R., Friedman, J.H., Friedman, J.H.: The Elements of Statistical Learning: Data Mining, Inference, and Prediction, vol. 2. Springer, New York (2009). https://doi.org/10.1007/978-0-387-84858-7
16. Hinton, G.E., Salakhutdinov, R.R.: Reducing the dimensionality of data with neural networks. Science **313**(5786), 504–507 (2006)
17. Hyvärinen, A., Oja, E.: Independent component analysis: algorithms and applications. Neural Netw. **13**(4–5), 411–430 (2000)
18. Kim, I., Balakrishnan, S., Wasserman, L.: Robust multivariate nonparametric tests via projection averaging. Ann. Stat. **48**(6), 3417–3441 (2020)
19. Li, Z., Zhang, Y.: On a projective ensemble approach to two sample test for equality of distributions. In: Proceedings of the 37th International Conference on Machine Learning. Proceedings of Machine Learning Research, vol. 119, pp. 6020–6027. PMLR (2020)

20. Pestov, V.: Is the k-NN classifier in high dimensions affected by the curse of dimensionality? Comput. Math. Appl. **65**(10), 1427–1437 (2013)
21. R Core Team: R: A Language and Environment for Statistical Computing. R Foundation for Statistical Computing, Vienna, Austria (2022)
22. Roy, S., Ray Choudhury, J., Dutta, S.: On some fast and robust classifiers for high dimension, low sample size data. In: Proceedings of The 25th International Conference on Artificial Intelligence and Statistics. Proceedings of Machine Learning Research, vol. 151, pp. 9943–9968. PMLR (2022)
23. Roy, S., Sarkar, S., Dutta, S., Ghosh, A.K.: On generalizations of some distance based classifiers for HDLSS data. J. Mach. Learn. Res. **23**(14), 1–41 (2022)
24. Roy, S., Sarkar, S., Dutta, S., Ghosh, A.K.: On exact feature screening in ultrahigh-dimensional binary classification (2023)
25. Sejdinovic, D., Sriperumbudur, B., Gretton, A., Fukumizu, K.: Equivalence of distance-based and RKHS-based statistics in hypothesis testing. Ann. Stat. **41**(5), 2263–2291 (2013)
26. Shen, L., Er, M.J., Yin, Q.: Classification for high-dimension low-sample size data. Pattern Recogn. **130**, 108828 (2022)
27. Song, Q., Ni, J., Wang, G.: A fast clustering-based feature subset selection algorithm for high-dimensional data. IEEE Trans. Knowl. Data Eng. **25**(1), 1–14 (2011)
28. Szekely, G., Rizzo, M.: Testing for equal distributions in high dimension. InterStat **5**, 1249–1272 (2004)
29. Tsukada, S.I.: High dimensional two-sample test based on the inter-point distance. Comput. Stat. **34**(2), 599–615 (2019)
30. Wang, W., Huang, Y., Wang, Y., Wang, L.: Generalized autoencoder: a neural network framework for dimensionality reduction. In: Proceedings of the IEEE Conference on Computer Vision and Pattern Recognition Workshops, pp. 490–497 (2014)
31. Yin, Q., Adeli, E., Shen, L., Shen, D.: Population-guided large margin classifier for high-dimension low-sample-size problems. Pattern Recogn. **97**, 107030 (2020)
32. Zou, H., Hastie, T.: Regularization and variable selection via the elastic net. J. Roy. Stat. Soc. Ser. B (Stat. Methodol.) **67**(2), 301–320 (2005)

DualMatch: Robust Semi-supervised Learning with Dual-Level Interaction

Cong Wang[1], Xiaofeng Cao[1(✉)], Lanzhe Guo[2], and Zenglin Shi[3]

[1] School of Artificial Intelligence, Jilin University, Changchun 130012, China
cwang21@mails.jlu.edu.cn, xiaofengcao@jlu.edu.cn

[2] National Key Laboratory for Novel Software Technology, Nanjing University, Nanjing 210023, China
guolz@lamda.nju.edu.cn

[3] I2R, Agency for Science, Technology and Research (A*STAR), Singapore, Singapore
shizl@i2r.a-star.edu.sg

Abstract. Semi-supervised learning provides an expressive framework for exploiting unlabeled data when labels are insufficient. Previous semi-supervised learning methods typically match model predictions of different data-augmented views in a single-level interaction manner, which highly relies on the quality of pseudo-labels and results in semi-supervised learning not robust. In this paper, we propose a novel SSL method called DualMatch, in which the class prediction jointly invokes feature embedding in a dual-level interaction manner. DualMatch requires consistent regularizations for data augmentation, specifically, 1) ensuring that different augmented views are regulated with consistent class predictions, and 2) ensuring that different data of one class are regulated with similar feature embeddings. Extensive experiments demonstrate the effectiveness of DualMatch. In the standard SSL setting, the proposal achieves 9% error reduction compared with SOTA methods, even in a more challenging class-imbalanced setting, the proposal can still achieve 6% error reduction. Code is available at https://github.com/CWangAI/DualMatch.

Keywords: Semi-supervised learning · Dual-Level interaction · Data augmentation · Feature embeddings

1 Introduction

Machine learning, especially deep learning [12], has achieved great success in various tasks. These tasks, however, crucially rely on the availability of an enormous amount of labeled training data. In many real-world applications, the acquisition of labeled data is expensive and inefficient. On the contrary, there are usually massive amounts of unlabeled data. Therefore, how to exploit unlabeled data to improve learning performance is a hot topic in the machine learning community [18].

Semi-supervised learning (SSL) provides an expressive framework for leveraging unlabeled data when labels are insufficient. Existing SSL methods can be

C. Wang and X. Cao—Equal contribution.

D. Koutra et al. (Eds.): ECML PKDD 2023, LNAI 14173, pp. 102–119, 2023.
https://doi.org/10.1007/978-3-031-43424-2_7

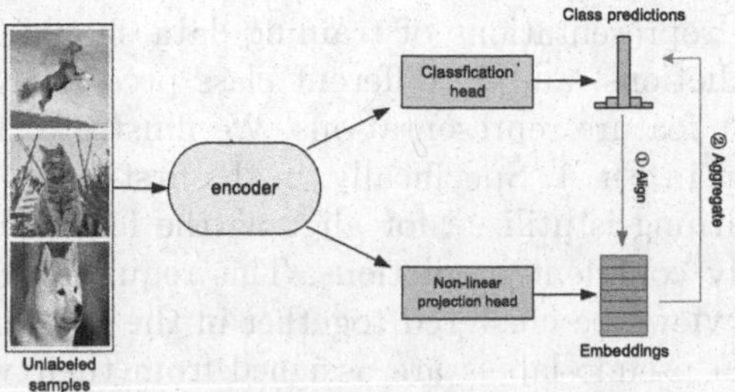

Fig. 1. An illustration of DualMatch with dual-level head interaction. Aligning the predictions of augmented data into their ground-truth labels is a single-level interaction manner (①) in semi-supervised learning, while the class predictions in such a manner may lack a stability guarantee for pseudo-labeling, even not robust. DualMatch reconsiders ① by aligning the feature embedding of one class and then considers a new interaction ② by aggregating class distribution with consistent feature embeddings.

categorized into several main classes in terms of the use of unlabeled data, such as pseudo-labeling methods [13], which assign pseudo-labels to unlabeled data based on the model prediction and train the model with labels and pseudo-labels in a supervised manner, and consistency regularization methods, which require that the output of the model should be the same when the model or data is perturbed. In much recent work, it has been reported that holistic SSL methods, e.g., MixMatch [3], ReMixMatch [2], and FixMatch [21], which consider the pseudo-labeling and consistency strategies simultaneously, have reached state-of-the-art (SOTA) performance. For example, in the image classification task, holistic SSL methods can achieve the performance of fully supervised learning even when a substantial portion of the labels in a given dataset have been discarded [21].

Although the holistic SSL methods have been reported to achieve positive results, they mainly adopt a single-level interaction manner between class prediction and the feature embedding, resulting in low quality of the pseudo-labels and weak SSL robustness performance. Take the SOTA FixMatch method as an example: FixMatch generates both weakly and strongly augmented views for unlabeled data, assigns high-confidence pseudo-labels predicted on the weakly augmented data to the strongly augmented one, and then optimizes the model by minimizing the cross-entropy loss between the prediction of the strongly augmented views and the corresponding pseudo-labels. This process is a single-level interaction since only different data augmentations are regulated by consistent class predictions. This results in the SSL performance being highly related to the correctness of the pseudo-label, and wrong pseudo-labels can lead to the confirmation bias of the model with error accumulation [1]. How to improve the robustness of SSL methods for pseudo-labels has emerged as a critical issue in SSL research.

In this paper, we propose a novel SSL algorithm called DualMatch. Compared with previous SSL methods that only consider the consistency between predictions for different augmentations, two consistency regularization factors are proposed in DualMatch, which derives more robust learning performance: 1) different augmented representations of training data should be regulated with consistent class predictions, and 2) different class predictions should be regulated with consistent feature representations. We illustrate the new manner of dual-level interaction in Fig. 1. Specifically, in the first-level interaction, supervised contrastive learning is utilized for aligning the feature representations of one class with highly confident predictions. This requires that the features of strongly augmented views be clustered together in the low-dimensional embedding space, and then pseudo-labels are assigned from their weakly augmented views. In the second-level interaction, class distributions with consistent feature embeddings are aggregated to generate pseudo-labels for class prediction fine-tuning. Under this dual-level learning manner, the consistency of the same data represented in two heads is enhanced, and more reliable pseudo-labels are generated for matching strongly augmented class prediction. Compared with the FixMatch algorithm, the DualMatch achieves 9% error reduction in the CIFAR-10 dataset; even on a more challenging class-imbalanced semi-supervised learning task, the DualMatch can still achieve 6% error reduction compared with the FixMatch algorithm.

Our contributions can be summarized as follows:

- We point out that the single-level interaction that existing SSL methods commonly adopted will result in weak SSL robustness performance.
- We first propose the dual-level interaction between classification and feature embeddings and a novel DualMatch algorithm to improve the robustness of SSL.
- We rigorously evaluate the efficacy of our proposed approach by conducting experiments on standard SSL benchmarks and class-imbalanced semi-supervised learning. Our results demonstrate significant performance improvement.

2 Related Work

2.1 Semi-supervised Learning

A prerequisite for SSL is that the data distribution should be based on a few assumptions, including smoothness, cluster, and manifold [4]. Technically, the smoothing assumption denotes that the nearby data are likely to share the same class label, and the manifold assumption denotes that the data located inner on low-dimensional streaming clusters are more likely to share the same labels. Recently, consistency regularization methods [3,26] have been widely applied and achieved outstanding results in SSL. An inherent observation is that the consistency regularization could be founded on the manifold or smoothness assumption, and requires that different perturbation methods for the same data hold consistent predictions against their employed diverse models.

From the perspective of consistency, there are two classical branches: model-level [11,20] and data-level consistency. As an early branch, [20] denotes the addition of random perturbation techniques (such as dropout [22] and random max-pooling methods) to the model should have consistent prediction results. To improve its robustness, [11] further aggregates the previous results of the model. Considering the pseudo-label cannot vary in iterative epochs, [24] then replace the aggregation with the exponential moving average (EMA) method. Data-level consistency is established by virtual adversarial training (VAT) [17] and unsupervised data augmentation (UDA) [26]. As an expressive consistency method, VAT produces optimally augmented views by adding random noise to the data and using an adversarial attack method. Differently, UDA utilizes the random augmentation (RA) [7] technique to produce strongly augmented views and minimizes the prediction disagreement between those views and their associated original data. Considering different levels of perturbations to the original input data, aligning different models' feedback to their early slightly perturbed inputs, i.e., anchoring, has been proven to be more effective. A series of strategies are then presented by taking this augmentation anchoring idea. In detail, MixMatch [3] adopts the mixup [28] trick to generate more augmented data by randomly pairing samples with each other and sharpening the average of multiple augmented data prediction distributions to generate pseudo-labels. Remixmatch [2] further improves the MixMatch approach by proposing a distribution alignment method (DA), which encourages the prediction of the marginal distribution of mixed data to be consistent with the true data distribution. FixMatch [21] simply considers weakly augmented view predictions with high confidence in unlabeled data as pseudo-labels for strongly augmented views and achieves SOTA performance.

2.2 Supervised Contrastive Learning

Self-supervised contrastive learning has been widely noticeable for its excellent performance by training models using unlabeled data and fine-tuning them for downstream tasks. MoCo [8] and SimCLR [5] establish the classical framework of self-supervised contrastive learning, which distinguishes the representations of each sample from the others. The contrastive learning frameworks consider different augmented views of the same sample as positive sample pairs and other samples as negative samples, by minimizing the info Noise Contrastive Estimation (InfoNCE) loss to pull the positive samples together and to push the negative samples away in the low-dimensional embedding space. For semi-supervised tasks, SimCLR v2 [6] indicates that a big self-supervised pre-trained model is a strong semi-supervised learner and simply fine-tunes the pre-trained model by using labeled samples to train a semi-supervised model. However, self-supervised contrastive learning only considers data features without focusing on class information and causes class conflicts by pushing far away samples, resulting in the inability to be directly combined with SSL. Supervised contrastive learning [9] extends the self-supervised contrastive learning methods by leveraging labeled data information to pull the samples of one class closer and push apart clusters of samples from different classes in a low-dimensional embedding space. Therefore, supervised contrastive learning mitigates the class collision phenomenon and it can be considered for application in SSL tasks.

3 Method

In this section, we introduce the preliminaries and present the two levels of interaction of DualMatch. Consisting of the new manner, the final objective is constructed.

3.1 Preliminaries

The semi-supervised classification setting is described as follows. For an C-class classification problem, given a batch of B labeled samples $\mathcal{X} = \{(x_b, y_b) : b \in (1, \ldots, B)\}$, where x_b denotes the training samples and y_b denotes its one-hot label, and a batch of unlabeled samples are denoted by $\mathcal{U} = \{u_b : b \in (1, \ldots, \mu B)\}$, where μ determines the relative sizes of $\mathcal{X}$ and $\mathcal{U}$. Given those settings, the next is to learn a convolutional encoder $f(\cdot)$ with labeled and unlabeled samples, a fully connected classification head $g(\cdot)$, and a non-linear projection head $h(\cdot)$. In particular, the labeled samples are randomly weakly augmented $\mathrm{Aug_w}(\cdot)$ predicted by the classifier head $p_b = g(f(\mathrm{Aug_w}(x_b)))$. Then the labeled samples can be optimized with cross-entropy loss which evaluates the ground-truth labels and the class predictions:

$$\mathcal{L}_x = \frac{1}{B} \sum_{b=1}^{B} \mathrm{H}(y_b, p_b), \tag{1}$$

where $\mathrm{H}(\cdot, \cdot)$ denotes the cross-entropy between two distributions.

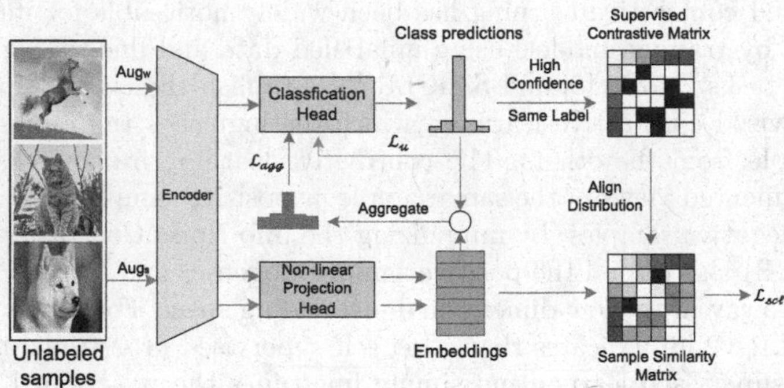

Fig. 2. The framework of the proposed DualMatch. Given a batch of unlabeled images, a class prediction of weakly augmented views is generated by the classifier head. The first-level interaction aligning distribution: pseudo-labels with high confidence are used to generate the supervised contrastive matrix and the sample similarity matrix is constructed by computing the similarity between strongly augmented embeddings to match the supervised contrastive matrix. The second-level interaction aggregating pseudo-labeling: the low-dimensional embedding similarity features of the weakly augmented view are combined with predictions to aggregate the class distribution of samples. (The red and green lines indicate the process lines of the weakly and strongly augmented views, respectively.) (Color figure online)

Following FixMatch, [21] apply the weak augmentation operation and the Random Augmentation method as strong augmentation operation $\text{Aug}_\text{s}(\cdot)$ to the unlabeled samples to obtain weakly and strongly augmented views respectively. The unsupervised classification loss can be defined as the cross-entropy loss of the predictions of the two views:

$$\mathcal{L}_u = \frac{1}{\mu B}\sum_{b=1}^{\mu B} \mathbb{1}\left(\max(\text{DA}\left(p_b^w\right)) \geq \tau\right) \text{H}\left(\hat{y_b}, p_b^s\right), \tag{2}$$

where $p_b^w = g\left(f\left(\text{Aug}_\text{w}\left(u_b\right)\right)\right)$ and $p_b^s = g\left(f\left(\text{Aug}_\text{s}\left(u_b\right)\right)\right)$ refer to the prediction distributions of the weakly augmented and strongly augmented classifications of unlabeled samples. $\hat{y_b} = \text{argmax}\left(\text{DA}\left(p_b^w\right)\right)$ is the pseudo-label of the predicted weakly augmented view. τ is the pseudo-label confidence threshold. We only consider data pseudo-labels with maximum class probability greater than the threshold τ. By following [2], $\text{DA}(\cdot)$ denotes the distribution alignment (DA) trick that is applied to the model's class prediction for unlabeled samples. DA maintains the predicted marginal distribution of the data consistent with the true data distribution. We compute $\tilde{p}^w$ as the moving average of the model's predictions for unlabeled samples over the last 32 steps as the marginal distribution and adjust p_b^w with $\text{Normalize}\left(p_b^w/\tilde{p}^w\right)$.

3.2 The DualMatch Structure

Motivation of DualMatch. In DualMatch, we adopts dual-level interaction between class prediction p of classification head and feature embedding $z = h\left(f\left(x\right)\right)$ of non-linear projection head. Following the augmentation anchoring method [2], there are two augmented views used to represent the feature embedding, i.e., weakly augmented embedding z_b^w and strongly augmented embedding z_b^s. However, some strategies use multiple augmented views to capture the feature embedding and also obtain promised performance. To provide a fair comparison with classical SSL methods [21], we generate a weakly augmented view for labeled samples and also solicit another strongly augmented view for unlabeled samples.

Framework of DualMatch. Figure 2 illustrates the DualMatch framework with dual-level interaction. In the first-level interaction, we introduce the aligning distribution algorithm, which utilizes supervised contrastive learning to cluster the feature embedding with consistent predictions. Then, we show the aggregated pseudo-labeling method in the second-level interaction, which fine-tunes the class prediction by aggregating pseudo-labels of similar feature embeddings. We below explain the two interactions of DualMatch in detail.

3.3 First-Level Interaction: Align

The first-level interaction aligning distribution aims to align the underlying distribution of the class prediction and feature embedding, where its inherent assumption is that different data of one class should have similar feature embedding. Theoretically, strongly augmented views of unlabeled samples should be clustered together in the low-dimensional embedding space, while their weakly augmented views should have the same confidence level on pseudo-labeling.

Protocol of Aligning. Our protocol of aligning the class prediction and feature embedding is generalized into their matrix match. Specifically, we construct a supervised contrastive matrix to solicit those predictions with high confidence from the weakly augmented views, which are required to match its associated embeddings of the sample similarity matrix from the strongly augmented views.

In short, we construct the set $\mathcal{Z} = \mathcal{Z}_x \cup \mathcal{Z}_u$ of the feature embeddings, including all labeled feature embeddings and partial unlabeled feature embeddings, where $\mathcal{Z}_x = \{(z_b^x, y_b) : b \in (1, \ldots, B)\}$ and $\mathcal{Z}_u = \{(z_b^s, \hat{y_b}) : \max(p_b^w) \geq \tau, b \in (1, \ldots, \mu B)\}$. Note that τ denotes the confidence level threshold.

Supervised Contrastive Matrix aims to obtain associations between samples from the class prediction information of the weakly augmented views. Inspired by the positive and negative sample pairs proposed by self-supervised contrastive learning [8], we consider the samples of one class as positive samples and samples of different classes as negative samples. In this way, we construct a supervised contrastive matrix $\mathbf{W}_{scl}$ to represent the category relationship between different samples, where the element located at the i-th row and j-th column is defined as follows:

$$w_{ij}^{scl} = \begin{cases} 0 & \text{if } i = j, \\ 1 & \text{if } y_i = y_j \text{ and } i \neq j, \\ 0 & \text{otherwise.} \end{cases} \tag{3}$$

Remark 1. Following contrastive learning, each sample is used as an anchor for the other samples, not as a positive sample. We thus set the samples with the same indices (i.e., elements on the diagonal) as 0 and the samples with the same labels as 1.

Sample Similarity Matrix aims to obtain the similarity between the low-dimensional feature embeddings of the samples. The sample similarity matrix $\mathbf{S}$ is constructed by computing the similarity between embeddings in the set $\mathcal{Z}$. For each element $s_{ij} \in \mathbf{S}$, it is characterized by the cosine similarity, i.e.,

$$\text{sim}(z_i, z_j) = \frac{z_i^T z_j}{\|z_i\| \, \|z_j\|}. \tag{4}$$

where z_i and z_j are feature embeddings of $\mathcal{Z}$.

Recalling the protocol of aligning, improving the consistency between the class predictions and feature embeddings can be achieved by matching two matrices $\mathbf{W}_{scl}$ and $\mathbf{S}$. Due to the disagreement of metrics in the two matrices, we employ the InfoNCE loss of supervised contrastive learning [9] to align their elements:

$$\begin{aligned}\mathcal{L}_{scl} &= \sum_{i\in I} \mathcal{L}_i(z_i) \\ &= \sum_{i\in I} \frac{-1}{|\mathcal{J}(i)|} \sum_{j\in\mathcal{J}(i)} \log \frac{\exp(z_i \cdot z_j/t)}{\sum_{a\in A(i)} \exp(z_i \cdot z_a/t)},\end{aligned} \tag{5}$$

where $i \in I$ denotes the indices of the embedding in Z, $A(i) = I \setminus \{i\}$ denotes the set of indices without i, $\mathcal{J}(i) = \{j \in A(i) : y_j = y_i\}$ is the indices of the set of positive instances of the same label as i, and t is a temperature parameter. Let $\mathbf{W}_i$ denote the i-th row of the matrix $\mathbf{W}_{scl}$. To facilitate computer calculations, the Eq. (5) can be simplified by the elements in matrix $\mathbf{W}_{scl}$ and $\mathbf{S}$ as follows:

$$\mathcal{L}_{scl} = -\sum_{i\in I} \frac{1}{\|\mathbf{W}_i\|} \sum_{j\in I} \log \frac{w_{ij}^{scl} \cdot \exp(s_{ij}/t)}{\sum_{a\in A(i)} \exp(s_{ia}/t)} \tag{6}$$

3.4 Second-Level Interaction: Aggregate

The second-level interaction aggregating pseudo-labeling aims to aggregate class distributions with consistent feature embeddings to generate pseudo-labels for class prediction fine-tuning. Intuitively, samples with similar features embeddings in the low-dimensional embedding space should have the same labels, so that, for a batch of unlabeled samples, we can generate aggregated pseudo-labels by aggregating the class predictions of each sample's neighbors in the embedding space to improve pseudo-labeling robustness. To avoid the cumulative error caused by the class predictions of dissimilar samples, we select K neighbor samples with the most similar feature embeddings. Then the aggregated pseudo-label q_b^w of u_b in a batch of unlabeled samples can be defined as follows:

$$q_b^w = \frac{1}{K} \sum_{k=1}^{K} \mathrm{sim}(z_b^w, z_k^w) \cdot p_k^w, \tag{7}$$

where p_k^w and z_k^w denote the class prediction and feature embedding of weakly augmented unlabeled views, respectively. In particular, the class distribution is weighted by the similarity $\mathrm{sim}(z_b^w, z_k^w)$ of the samples to their neighbors. Since the weighted class distribution cannot directly represent the classification probabilities, we adjust $q_b^w = \mathrm{Normalize}(q_b^w)$. Like the unsupervised classification loss, we only consider the samples with high confidence aggregated pseudo-labels. The difference is that aggregated pseudo-label is soft (a vector of probabilities) because we aim to adjust the class predictions. The aggregation loss can be optimized by cross-entropy as follows:

$$\mathcal{L}_{agg} = \frac{1}{\mu B} \sum_{b=1}^{\mu B} \mathbb{1}\left(\max(q_b^w) \geq \tau_1\right) \mathrm{H}(q_b^w, p_b^s), \tag{8}$$

where τ_1 is the confidence threshold of the aggregated label.

3.5 Final Objective

The overall loss of the semi-supervised DualMatch method consists of the supervised loss $\mathcal{L}_x$ (w.r.t. Eq. (1)) and unsupervised loss $\mathcal{L}_u$ (w.r.t. Eq. (2)). Meanwhile, to achieve the consistency of the classification prediction and feature embedding, we add the supervised contrastive loss $\mathcal{L}_{scl}$ (w.r.t. Eq. (6)), and aggregation loss $\mathcal{L}_{agg}$ (w.r.t. Eq. (8)). In such settings, our optimization objective is to minimize the overall loss:

$$\mathcal{L}_{overall} = \mathcal{L}_x + \lambda_u \mathcal{L}_u + \lambda_{scl} \mathcal{L}_{scl} + \lambda_{agg} \mathcal{L}_{agg}, \tag{9}$$

where λ_u, λ_{scl}, and λ_{agg} are hyperparameters used to control the weights of loss. DualMatch can be summarized as Algorithm 1.

Algorithm 1: DualMatch algorithm.

Input: Labeled batch $\mathcal{X} = \{(x_b, y_b) : b \in (1, \ldots, B)\}$, unlabeled batch $\mathcal{U} = \{u_b : b \in (1, \ldots, \mu B)\}$, encoder $f(\cdot)$, classification head $g(\cdot)$, non-linear projection head $h(\cdot)$.

for *step=1 to total-step* **do**

- $p_b = g\left(f\left(\text{Aug}_\text{w}\left(x_b\right)\right)\right) \quad z_b^x = h\left(f\left(\text{Aug}_\text{w}\left(x_b\right)\right)\right)$
- $p_b^w = g\left(f\left(\text{Aug}_\text{w}\left(u_b\right)\right)\right) \quad z_b^w = h\left(f\left(\text{Aug}_\text{w}\left(x_b\right)\right)\right)$
- $p_b^s = g\left(f\left(\text{Aug}_\text{s}\left(u_b\right)\right)\right) \quad z_b^s = h\left(f\left(\text{Aug}_\text{s}\left(x_b\right)\right)\right)$
- $\hat{y}_b = \text{argmax}\left(\text{DA}\left(p_b^w\right)\right)$
- Construct feature embedding set $\mathcal{Z} = \mathcal{Z}_x \cup \mathcal{Z}_u$
- $\mathcal{Z}_x = \{(z_b^x, y_b) : b \in (1, \ldots, B)\}$
- $\mathcal{Z}_u = \{(z_b^s, \hat{y}_b) : \max(p_b^w) > \tau, b \in (1, \ldots, \mu B)\}$
- **for** $i \in \{1, ..., \mu B\}$ *and* $j \in \{1, ..., \mu B\}$ **do**
  - $w_{ij}^{scl} = \in \mathbf{W}_{scl}$ is constructed by Eq.(3)
  - $s_{ij} \in \mathbf{S}$ is constructed by Eq. (4)
- **end**
- $q_b^w = \frac{1}{K} \sum_{k=1}^{K} \text{sim}(z_b^w, z_k^w) \cdot p_k^w$
- $q_b^w = \text{Normalize}\left(q_b^w\right)$
- $\mathcal{L}_x = \frac{1}{B} \sum_{b=1}^{B} \text{H}\left(y_b, p_b\right),$
- $\mathcal{L}_u = \frac{1}{\mu B} \sum_{b=1}^{\mu B} \mathbb{1}\left(\max(\text{DA}\left(p_b^w\right)) \geq \tau\right) \text{H}\left(\hat{y}_b, p_b^s\right)$
- $\mathcal{L}_{scl} = -\sum_{i \in I} \frac{1}{\|\mathbf{W}_i\|} \sum_{j \in I} \log \frac{w_{ij}^{scl} \cdot \exp(s_{ij}/t)}{\sum_{a \in A(i)} \exp(s_{ia}/t)}$
- $\mathcal{L}_{agg} = \frac{1}{\mu B} \sum_{b=1}^{\mu B} \mathbb{1}\left(\max\left(q_b^w\right) \geq \tau_1\right) \text{H}\left(q_b^w, p_b^s\right)$
- $\mathcal{L}_{overall} = \mathcal{L}_x + \lambda_u \mathcal{L}_u + \lambda_{scl} \mathcal{L}_{scl} + \lambda_{agg} \mathcal{L}_{agg}$
- Optimize $f(\cdot)$, $g(\cdot)$,and $h(\cdot)$ by minimizing $\mathcal{L}_{overall}$

end

Output: Trained model.

Exponential Moving Average. From the perspective of consistent model regularization, we employ the Exponential Moving Average (EMA) strategy [24] to smooth the model parameters with an expectation of lower variation. Technically, the parameters of EMA are usually weighted by previously associated model parameters in the iterative updates:

$$\overline{\theta} = m\overline{\theta} + (1 - m)\,\theta, \tag{10}$$

where $\overline{\theta}$ denotes the parameters of the EMA model, θ denotes the parameters of the training model, and m denotes the EMA decay rate. Note that the experiments also employ the EMA model for testing.

4 Experiment

In this section, we evaluate DualMatch on several semi-supervised tasks including semi-supervised classification and class-imbalanced semi-supervised classification. Our ablation studies the effect of dual-level interaction and hyperparameters on the framework.

4.1 Semi-supervised Classification

First, we evaluate DualMatch on the semi-supervised classification using the CIFAR-10, CIFAR-100 and STL-10 datasets. CIFAR-10 consists of 60,000 32×32 images divided into 10 classes, with 6,000 images in each class. There are 50,000 training images and 10,000 test images. Following the widely adopted setting in SSL studies Fixmatch [21], we randomly select 4, 25, and 400 samples per class from the training set as labeled data and then use the rest of the training set as unlabeled data, respectively. In this setting, CIFAR-100 has the same number of training set and test set images as CIFAR-10, while CIFAR-100 is divided into 100 classes with 600 images in each class. We thus randomly select 25, 100 samples per class as labeled data. STL-10 has 5,000 labeled and 100,000 unlabeled 96×96 images in 10 classes for training, and 8,000 images for testing. We randomly select 100 samples per class from labeled images as labeled data. Please note that we evaluate the experiment with different random seeds for 5 runs.

Implementation Details. We use the Wide ResNet-28-2 [27] with a weight decay of 0.0005 for the CIFAR-10, Wide ResNet-28-8 with a weight decay of 0.001 for the CIFAR-100, and Wide ResNet-37-2 with a weight decay of 0.0005 for the STL-10. The classification head is a softmax layer and the non-linear projection head is set as a two-layer MLP. Following the implementation of [21], the model uses the SGD optimizer with the Nesterov momentum [23] of 0.9. For the learning rate, we use the cosine learning rate decay and set the learning rate to $0.03 \cdot \cos\left(\frac{7\pi n}{16N}\right)$, where n denotes the current training steps and N denotes the number of the total training steps. For the rest of the hyperparameters, we set $\lambda_u = 1$, $\lambda_{scl} = 1$, $\lambda_{agg} = 0.5$, $\mu = 7$, $B = 64$, $\tau = 0.95$, $\tau_1 = 0.9$, and $t = 0.5$, $m = 0.999$. For the training steps, we set $N = 2^{20}$ for CIFAR-10, STL-10 and $N = 2^{19}$ for CIFAR-100. Moreover, we utilize the warm-up trick

Table 1. Error rate (mean ± std %) of semi-supervised classification of DualMatch vs. baseline methods over varying numbers of labeled samples (5 runs).

Method	CIFAR-10			CIFAR-100		STL-10
	40 labels	250 labels	4000 labels	2500 labels	10000 labels	1000 labels
Π-Model	74.34 ± 1.76	54.26 ± 3.97	41.01 ± 0.38	57.25 ± 0.48	37.88 ± 0.11	32.78 ± 0.40
Pseudo-Labeling	74.61 ± 0.26	49.78 ± 0.43	16.09 ± 0.28	57.38 ± 0.46	36.21 ± 0.19	32.64 ± 0.71
Mean Teacher	70.09 ± 1.60	32.32 ± 2.30	9.19 ± 0.19	53.91 ± 0.57	35.83 ± 0.24	33.90 ± 1.37
MixMatch	47.54 ± 11.50	11.05 ± 0.86	6.42 ± 0.10	39.94 ± 0.37	28.31 ± 0.33	21.70 ± 0.68
UDA	29.05 ± 5.93	8.82 ± 1.08	4.88 ± 0.18	33.13 ± 0.22	24.50 ± 0.25	6.64 ± 0.17
ReMixMatch	19.10 ± 9.64	5.44 ± 0.05	4.72 ± 0.13	27.43 ± 0.31	23.03 ± 0.56	6.74 ± 0.14
FixMatch	13.81 ± 3.37	5.07 ± 0.65	4.26 ± 0.05	28.29 ± 0.11	22.60 ± 0.12	6.25 ± 0.33
CoMatch	6.91 ± 1.39	4.91 ± 0.33	4.06 ± 0.03	27.18 ± 0.21	21.83 ± 0.23	8.66 ± 0.41
CR	**5.69** ± 0.90	5.04 ± 0.30	4.16 ± 0.13	27.58 ± 0.37	21.03 ± 0.23	6.96 ± 0.42
DualMatch(Ours)	5.75 ± 1.01	**4.89** ± 0.52	**3.88** ± 0.10	**27.08** ± 0.23	**20.78** ± 0.15	**5.94** ± 0.08

to train aggregation loss after the first 30×2^{10} training steps. For the neighbor settings, we set $K = 10$ for CIFAR-10, STL-10 and $K = 2$ for CIFAR-100. For data augmentation, we follow the implementation details of the weak and strong augmentation of FixMatch [21].

Compared Methods. We compare with the following baseline methods: 1) Model-level consistency methods including the Π-Model [19], Pseudo-labeling [13], and Mean Teacher [24], 2) Data-level methods including the UDA [26], MixMatch [3], ReMixMatch [2], FixMatch [21], CoMatch [15], CR [14].

Results. The SSL results are presented in Table 1, where DualMatch achieves SOTA performance at different number settings of labeled samples. For model-level consistency, we observe that the Π-model, Pseudo-Labeling, and Mean Teacher perform poorly with extremely few numbers of labeled samples, but the improvement in error rate becomes more significant after adding more labeled samples. It is thus the model-level consistency semi-supervised methods that are highly dependent on the number of labeled samples. For data-level consistency, we observed that the performance of UDA, MixMatch, ReMixMatch, and FixMatch with the help of data augmentation methods improved significantly in extremely few labeled samples. Moreover, the performance of the semi-supervised methods using strong augmentation (e.g., Randaugment [7]) tricks exceeds that of simple that of the simple tricks for data augmentation, e.g., mixup. Therefore, the data-level consistency semi-supervised methods utilize various data augmentation tricks to overcome the shortcoming of insufficient labeled data volume. Compared to the above methods, CoMatch and DualMatch introduce feature embedding to further exploit the underlying distribution of classes, and the error rate reduction of training on 40 labeled samples of CIFAR-10 is much better than that of the data-level and model-level consistency methods. Furthermore, training on 250 and 4000 labeled samples of CIFAR-10 also achieves attractive results, but not so significantly as 40 labeled samples. Additionally, compared with FixMatch, DualMatch achieves a 9% error reduction in CIFAR-10. The

Table 2. Error rate (mean ± std %) for CIFAR-10 with the labeled ratio $\beta = 10\%$ and imbalance ratio $\gamma = \{50, 100, 200\}$ (5 runs).

Method	$\gamma = 50$	$\gamma = 100$	$\gamma = 200$
Pseudo-Labeling	47.5 ± 0.74	53.5 ± 1.29	58.0 ± 1.39
Mean Teacher	42.9 ± 3.00	51.9 ± 0.71	54.9 ± 1.28
MixMatch	30.9 ± 1.18	39.6 ± 2.24	45.5 ± 1.87
FixMatch	20.6 ± 0.65	33.7 ± 1.74	40.3 ± 0.74
FixMatch w/ DA	19.8 ± 0.45	30.3 ± 1.27	38.0 ± 0.84
CoMatch	19.7 ± 0.68	28.6 ± 1.85	40.0 ± 1.56
DualMatch(Ours)	**19.0** ± 0.82	**28.3** ± 1.38	**37.3** ± 0.39

potential result is that such a semi-supervised training manner with efficient feature embeddings performs closely to fully supervised training in CIFAR-10.

4.2 Class-Imbalanced Semi-supervised Classification

Standard SSL assumes the class distribution is balanced, however, in real-world tasks, the data distribution is often class-imbalanced [16]. How to guarantee the performance robustness of SSL algorithms under class-imbalanced settings is an important problem that has attracted the great attention of SSL researchers [10, 25]. Therefore, we also conduct experiments to evaluate the effectiveness of our proposal on class-imbalanced semi-supervised learning problems. DARP [10] denotes that class-imbalanced data biases SSL methods in generating pseudo-labels for the majority classes. To evaluate the effectiveness of the semi-supervised model in the class-imbalance task, we compare the results of Dualmatch and major semi-supervised methods under imbalanced data distribution.

Problem Setup. By following [25], for an C-class classification problem, given a labeled set $\mathcal{X} = (x_m, y_m) : m \in (1, \ldots, M)$, where x_m are the training samples and y_m are one-hot labels. The number of class c in $\mathcal{X}$ is denoted as M_c and $\sum_{c=1}^{C} M_c = M$. [25] assume that the marginal class distribution of $\mathcal{X}$is skewed and the classes are ordered by decreasing order, i.e. $M_1 \geq M_2 \geq \cdots \geq M_C$. Class imbalance can be measured by the imbalance ratio $\gamma = \frac{M_1}{M_C}$. And given a unlabeled set $\mathcal{U} = (u_l : l \in (1, \ldots, L)$ with the same class distribution as $\mathcal{X}$. The labeled ratio $\beta = \frac{M}{M+L}$ denotes the percentage of labeled data to the training data. Specifically, the CIFAR-10 dataset consists of 5000 images in each class, and the imbalanced majority class employs 5000 images. The setting of our evaluation experiment is on CIFAR-10 with the labeled ratio β of 10%, i.e. 500 labeled images and 4500 unlabeled images in the majority class and the imbalance ratio γ of 50, 100, and 200, respectively. For the evaluation criterion of the experiment, the data of the test set is class-balanced.

Implementation Details. We use mostly the same parameter settings as for the semi-supervised classification task, except that the number of neighbor samples K is set to 2. For each experimental setting, the training steps are set to 2^{17} for MixMatch and 2^{16} for FixMatch and CoMatch. For a fair comparison, we set the total training steps to 2^{16} for DualMatch. For each experiment, we evaluate 5 times with different random seeds and report the mean and std of the test error rate. We report the performance using the EMA model.

Results. The results of class-imbalanced semi-supervised classification are presented in Table 2. Overall, the DualMatch achieves better performance than the typical semi-supervised baselines using different imbalance ratios. Moreover, all semi-supervised baselines are affected by class-imbalanced data, and their error rate increases with the increase of the imbalance ratio. For this ratio, we also observe that the data-level consistency baselines achieve the best performance if the imbalance ratio is set as 100, at least better than the setting of 50 and 200. The potential reasons are as follows. For the imbalance ratio of 200, there is only 1 labeled sample for the minority class, which leads difficult to learn the features of the minority class during model training. For the imbalance ratio of 50, the effect of imbalanced data is not significant in causing class bias, but rather in the increase in error rate due to the reduction of training samples. For the imbalance ratio of 100, the class bias caused by class-imbalanced data leads to instability of the model and increases the std of error rate. The results show that CoMatch is more affected by the imbalance ratio and performs poorly at the imbalance ratio of 200, and the improvement of DualMatch is effective. We can conclude that DualMatch aligns the feature embeddings of one class during the training period, which can separate the features of different classes and make the classification boundary clearer. It also adjusts the bias of class prediction by aggregating feature embeddings to enhance the robustness of the classification boundary and mitigate the influence of class with few samples from others. Additionally, DualMatch achieves a 6% error reduction at the imbalance rate of 100 compared to FixMatch, and a 6.5% error reduction at the imbalance rate of 200 compared to CoMatch.

4.3 Ablation Study

We study the unlabeled data error rate of FixMatch and DualMatch on the setting of training CIFAR-100 with 10000 labeled samples. This helps us to reveal the potential influence of pseudo-labeling on semi-supervised training. Then, we analyze the head interaction and parameter perturbation of each level of DualMatch on the setting of training CIFAR-10 with 250 labeled samples.

Unlabeled Samples Error Rate. In Fig. 3, we study the training process of FixMatch, FixMatch with DA, and DualMatch on the setting of training CIFAR-100 with 10000 labeled samples. The potential observation factors are 1) the unlabeled sample error rate, and 2) the sample ratio of high-confidence pseudo-labels. From the presented curves of Figs. 3b and 3a, as the number of training

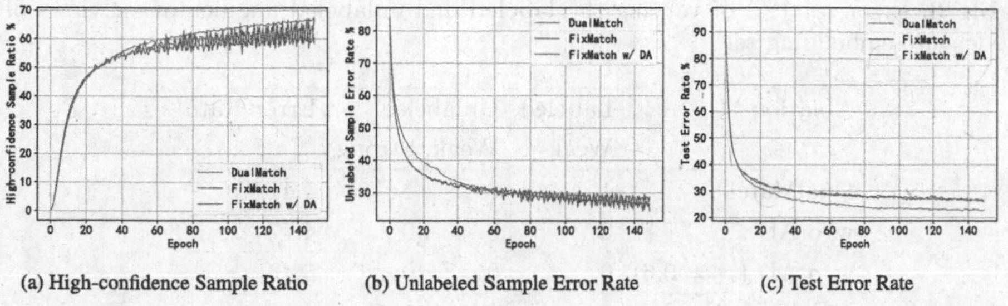

Fig. 3. The training process of FixMatch and DualMatch on CIFAR-100 with 10000 labeled samples. (a) Ratio of samples with high-confidence pseudo-labels. (b) Error rate of all unlabeled sample. (c) Error rate of test samples.

epochs increases, both the unlabeled sample error rate and high-confidence sample ratio of FixMatch fluctuate dramatically and become increasingly unstable. It is worth noting that the DualMatch starts with a high unlabeled sample error rate in the first few epochs, however, as the number of training epochs increases, the unlabeled sample error rate decreases more smoothly to the FixMatch level. The DualMatch achieves a lower test error rate than FixMatch and FixMatch with DA throughout the training process. The results show that the pseudo-labels of the unlabeled samples of FixMatch vary continuously, which makes the learning model's poor stability even worse and affects the classification results. In contrast, DualMatch provides more robust and high-quality pseudo-labeling during training, which significantly improves the performance of the semi-supervised learning model.

Align Distribution. We vary the labeled and unlabeled augmentation views of the feature embedding set to perform the ablation study of Align Distribution (AD). The results are presented in Table 3. Note that when the feature embeddings are not used, the experiments fall back to DualMatch without AD. Furthermore, we also observe that simultaneously employing both labeled and unlabeled feature embeddings can effectively improve the model performance.

Number of Neighbors. Figure 4a illustrates the effect of different numbers of neighbors K of Eq. (7) on the aggregating pseudo-labeling. Note that $K = 0$ means that DualMatch only uses Aligning Distribution. We observe that aggregating neighbor information improves model performance, but the number of neighbors within a scope has less influence on the model with a high confidence threshold.

Table 3. Error rate(%) of varying the labeled and unlabeled augmentation views of the feature embedding set.

Ablation	Labeled	Unlabeled		Error Rate
	Weak	Weak	Strong	
DualMatch	1	0	1	4.41
w/o AD	0	0	0	4.77
w/o AD ($\tau_1 = 0.6$)	0	0	0	5.49
w/o labeled	0	0	1	4.68
w/o unlabeled	1	0	0	4.93
w/ multi	2	1	1	4.48

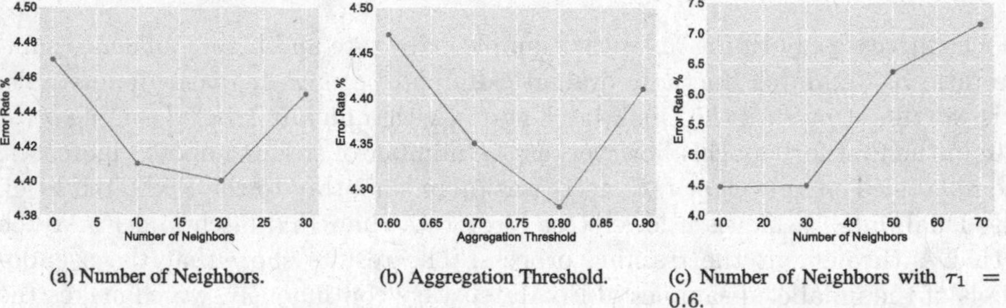

(a) Number of Neighbors. (b) Aggregation Threshold. (c) Number of Neighbors with $\tau_1 = 0.6$.

Fig. 4. Ablation study of the Second-level Interaction: (a) Error rate of the varying number of neighbors. (b) Error rate of the varying threshold of aggregated pseudo-labeling. (c) Error rate of the varying number of neighbors with $\tau_1 = 0.6$.

Aggregation Threshold. We vary the threshold τ_1 of Eq. (8) to control the confident level of aggregated labels. Figure 4b shows the effect on aggregation threshold. When $\tau_1 > 0.6$, the aggregated labels are less affected by the unreliable pseudo-labels.

We also investigate the effect of different aggregation thresholds combined with different numbers of neighbors on model performance. Figure 4c illustrates the effect of the number of neighbors K with the aggregation threshold $\tau_1 = 0.6$. We observe that performance decreases as the number of neighbors increases with a low confidence threshold. The number of neighbors interacts with the aggregation threshold to ensure the reliability of aggregated pseudo-labeling.

5 Conclusion

Our paper introduces a novel dual-interaction method for SSL that regulates diverse augmented representations with consistent class predictions and different class predictions with coherent feature representations. Leveraging this new perspective, we present a new SSL technique named DualMatch. DualMatch could learn more data-efficient representation and provide more robust pseudo-labels than the previous single-interaction-based SSL methods. Experimental results on both standard semi-supervised settings and more challenging class-imbalanced semi-supervised settings clearly demonstrate that DualMatch can achieve significant performance improvement.

Ethical Statement

The purpose of this research paper is to explore a picture classification task under semi-supervised learning. In our study, we strictly adhere to ethical practice standards.

A number of ethical considerations were taken into account in conducting this study:

- We ensure that no private data with others is directly involved in the study.
- We ensure that no indirect leakage of researcher or participant privacy occurs or privacy can be inferred in the course of the study.
- The data were collected from publicly available datasets. The data was analyzed using open source models. We ensure that the data is reliable and public, and that our analysis methods are widely accepted by the open source community and do not contain any bias or undue influence.

We also considered potential ethical issues that may arise in the course of the study. Semi-supervised learning has been widely used in various real-world scenarios, and this study explores the potential feature of data in semi-supervised scenarios, which is uninterpretable, and uses this feature to improve the performance and robustness of the model. With the development of deep learning, the potential features provided by the encoder may be interpreted, which may lead to the leakage of data privacy when improperly handled in the application of realistic scenarios.

We can conclude that our study is based on the open source community's code, models and public datasets. At this stage it does not cause privacy issues such as personal data leakage. Moreover, our study is currently not applied in real-world scenarios and there is no conflict of interest.

Acknowledgements. This work was supported in part by National Natural Science Foundation of China, Grant Number: 62206108 and Natural Science Foundation of Jilin Province, Grant Number: 20220101107JC.

References

1. Arazo, E., Ortego, D., Albert, P., O'Connor, N.E., McGuinness, K.: Pseudo-labeling and confirmation bias in deep semi-supervised learning. In: 2020 International Joint Conference on Neural Networks (IJCNN), pp. 1–8 (2020)
2. Berthelot, D., et al.: Remixmatch: semi-supervised learning with distribution matching and augmentation anchoring. In: International Conference on Learning Representations (2019)

3. Berthelot, D., Carlini, N., Goodfellow, I., Papernot, N., Oliver, A., Raffel, C.A.: Mixmatch: a holistic approach to semi-supervised learning. In: Advances in Neural Information Processing Systems, vol. 32 (2019)
4. Chapelle, O., Scholkopf, B., Zien, A.: Semi-supervised Learning. MIT Press, Cambridge (2006)
5. Chen, T., Kornblith, S., Norouzi, M., Hinton, G.: A simple framework for contrastive learning of visual representations. In: International Conference on Machine Learning, pp. 1597–1607 (2020)
6. Chen, T., Kornblith, S., Swersky, K., Norouzi, M., Hinton, G.E.: Big self-supervised models are strong semi-supervised learners. In: Advances in Neural Information Processing Systems, vol. 33 (2020)
7. Cubuk, E.D., Zoph, B., Shlens, J., Le, Q.V.: Randaugment: practical automated data augmentation with a reduced search space. In: Proceedings of the IEEE/CVF Conference on Computer Vision and Pattern Recognition Workshops, pp. 702–703 (2020)
8. He, K., Fan, H., Wu, Y., Xie, S., Girshick, R.: Momentum contrast for unsupervised visual representation learning. In: Proceedings of the IEEE/CVF Conference on Computer Vision and Pattern Recognition, pp. 9729–9738 (2020)
9. Khosla, P., et al.: Supervised contrastive learning. In: Advances in Neural Information Processing Systems, vol. 33 (2020)
10. Kim, J., Hur, Y., Park, S., Yang, E., Hwang, S.J., Shin, J.: Distribution aligning refinery of pseudo-label for imbalanced semi-supervised learning. In: Advances in Neural Information Processing Systems, vol. 33 (2020)
11. Laine, S., Aila, T.: Temporal ensembling for semi-supervised learning. In: International Conference on Learning Representations (2016)
12. LeCun, Y., Bengio, Y., Hinton, G.: Deep learning. Nature **521**, 436–444 (2015)
13. Lee, D.H., et al.: Pseudo-label: the simple and efficient semi-supervised learning method for deep neural networks. In: Workshop on Challenges in Representation Learning, ICML, p. 896 (2013)
14. Lee, D., Kim, S., Kim, I., Cheon, Y., Cho, M., Han, W.S.: Contrastive regularization for semi-supervised learning. In: Proceedings of the IEEE/CVF Conference on Computer Vision and Pattern Recognition, pp. 3911–3920 (2022)
15. Li, J., Xiong, C., Hoi, S.C.: Comatch: semi-supervised learning with contrastive graph regularization. In: Proceedings of the IEEE/CVF International Conference on Computer Vision, pp. 9475–9484 (2021)
16. Mahajan, D., et al.: Exploring the limits of weakly supervised pretraining. In: Proceedings of the European Conference on Computer Vision (ECCV), pp. 181–196 (2018)
17. Miyato, T., Maeda, S.I., Koyama, M., Ishii, S.: Virtual adversarial training: a regularization method for supervised and semi-supervised learning. IEEE Trans. Pattern Anal. Mach. Intell. **41**, 1979–1993 (2018)
18. Oliver, A., Odena, A., Raffel, C.A., Cubuk, E.D., Goodfellow, I.: Realistic evaluation of deep semi-supervised learning algorithms. In: Advances in Neural Information Processing Systems, vol. 31 (2018)
19. Rasmus, A., Berglund, M., Honkala, M., Valpola, H., Raiko, T.: Semi-supervised learning with ladder networks. In: Advances in Neural Information Processing Systems, vol. 28 (2015)
20. Sajjadi, M., Javanmardi, M., Tasdizen, T.: Regularization with stochastic transformations and perturbations for deep semi-supervised learning. In: Advances in Neural Information Processing Systems, vol. 29 (2016)

21. Sohn, K., et al.: Fixmatch: simplifying semi-supervised learning with consistency and confidence. In: Advances in Neural Information Processing Systems, vol. 33 (2020)
22. Srivastava, N., Hinton, G., Krizhevsky, A., Sutskever, I., Salakhutdinov, R.: Dropout: a simple way to prevent neural networks from overfitting. J. Mach. Learn. Res. **15**, 1929–1958 (2014)
23. Sutskever, I., Martens, J., Dahl, G., Hinton, G.: On the importance of initialization and momentum in deep learning. In: International Conference on Machine Learning, pp. 1139–1147 (2013)
24. Tarvainen, A., Valpola, H.: Mean teachers are better role models: weight-averaged consistency targets improve semi-supervised deep learning results. In: Advances in Neural Information Processing Systems, vol. 30 (2017)
25. Wei, C., Sohn, K., Mellina, C., Yuille, A., Yang, F.: Crest: a class-rebalancing self-training framework for imbalanced semi-supervised learning. In: Proceedings of the IEEE/CVF Conference on Computer Vision and Pattern Recognition, pp. 10857–10866 (2021)
26. Xie, Q., Dai, Z., Hovy, E., Luong, T., Le, Q.: Unsupervised data augmentation for consistency training. In: Advances in Neural Information Processing Systems, vol. 33 (2020)
27. Zagoruyko, S., Komodakis, N.: Wide residual networks. In: British Machine Vision Conference 2016 (2016)
28. Zhang, H., Cisse, M., Dauphin, Y.N., Lopez-Paz, D.: Mixup: beyond empirical risk minimization. In: International Conference on Learning Representations (2018)

Detecting Evasion Attacks in Deployed Tree Ensembles

Laurens Devos(✉), Lorenzo Perini, Wannes Meert, and Jesse Davis

KU Leuven, Leuven, Belgium
{laurens.devos,lorenzo.perini,wannes.meert,jesse.davis}@kuleuven.be

Abstract. Tree ensembles are powerful models that are widely used. However, they are susceptible to evasion attacks where an adversary purposely constructs an adversarial example in order to elicit a misprediction from the model. This can degrade performance and erode a user's trust in the model. Typically, approaches try to alleviate this problem by verifying how robust a learned ensemble is or robustifying the learning process. We take an alternative approach and attempt to detect adversarial examples in a post-deployment setting. We present a novel method for this task that works by analyzing an unseen example's output configuration, which is the set of leaves activated by the example in the ensemble's constituent trees. Our approach works with any additive tree ensemble and does not require training a separate model. We evaluate our approach on three different tree ensemble learners. We empirically show that our method is currently the best adversarial detection method for tree ensembles.

Keywords: Evasion attack detection · Tree ensembles

1 Introduction

Tree ensembles such as (gradient) boosted trees and random forests are a popular class of models. However, like many other model families, such as neural networks [2,18,40], they are susceptible to **evasion attacks** [9,12,14,23,47,50]. In this attack setting, a previously trained model is deployed and, while operating in the wild, is exposed to **adversarial examples** that an adversary purposely constructed to elicit a misprediction from the model. Such examples are undesirable because they degrade a model's performance and erode a user's trust in the model. For tree ensembles, the literature attempts to deal with evasion attacks in one of two ways. First, verification techniques attempt to ascertain how robust a learned ensemble is to adversarial examples [9,12,34] by empirically determining how much an example would have to be perturbed (according to some norm) for its predicted label to change. Second, the problem can be addressed at training time by trying to learn a more robust model by adding adversarial examples to the training set [23], pruning the training data [49], changing aspects of the learner such as the splitting criteria [1,7,8,44] or the objective [21], relabeling

D. Koutra et al. (Eds.): ECML PKDD 2023, LNAI 14173, pp. 120–136, 2023.
https://doi.org/10.1007/978-3-031-43424-2_8

the values in the leaves [45], using constraint solvers to learn optimal trees [46], or interleaving learning and verification [35].

This paper explores an alternative approach to mitigating the effect of an evasion attack. Given a current example for which a prediction is required, we attempt to ascertain if this current example is adversarial or not. If the example is identified as being adversarial, then the deployed model could refrain from making a prediction similar to a learning with rejection setting [11]. While this question has been extensively explored for neural networks, this is not the case for tree ensembles. Unfortunately, most existing methods for neural networks are not applicable to tree ensembles because they use properties unique to neural networks [51]. For example, some modify the model [17,19,30], learn other models (e.g., nearest neighbors) on top of the network's intermediate representations [16,24,27,39], or learn other models on top of the gradients [37]. Moreover, nearly all methods focus only on detecting evasion attacks for image classification.

Tree ensembles are powerful because they combine the predictions made by many trees. Hence, the prediction procedure involves sorting the given example to a leaf node in each tree. The ordered set of the reached leaf nodes is an *output configuration* of the ensemble and fully determines the ensemble's resulting prediction. However, there are many more possible output configurations than there are examples in the data used to train the model. For example, the California housing dataset [31] only has eight attributes, but training an XGBoost ensemble containing 6, 7, or 8 trees each of at most depth 5 yields 62 248, 173 826, and 385 214 output configurations respectively.[1] These numbers (far) exceed the 20,600 examples in the dataset. The situation will be worse for the larger ensembles sizes that are used in practice. Our hypothesis is that in an evasion attack

> adversarial examples exploit **unusual output configurations**, that is, ones that are very different to those observed in the data used to train the model.

That is, small, but carefully selected perturbations can yield an example that is quite similar to another example observed during training, but yields an output configuration that is far away from those covered by the training data.

Based on this intuition, we present a novel method to detect an evasion attack based on assessing whether an example encountered post deployment has an unusual output configuration. When a new example is encountered, our approach encodes it by its output configuration and then measures the distance between the encoded example and its nearest (encoded) neighbor in a reference set. If this distance is sufficiently high, the example is flagged as being an adversarial one and the model can abstain from making a prediction. Our approach has several benefits. First, it is general: it works with any additive tree ensemble. Second, it is integrated: it does not require training a separate model to identify adversarial examples, one simply has to set a threshold on the distance. Finally, it is surprisingly fast as the considered distance metric can be efficiently computed by exploiting instruction level parallelism (SIMD).

[1] Computed using Veritas [12].

Empirically, we evaluate and compare our approach on three ensemble methods: gradient boosted trees (XGBoost [10]), random forests [4], and GROOT [44], which is an approach for training robust tree ensembles. We empirically show that our method outperforms multiple competing approaches for detecting adversarial examples post deployment for all three considered tree ensembles. Moreover, it can detect adversarial examples with a comparable computational effort.

2 Preliminaries

We assume a d-dimensional input space $\mathcal{X} = \mathbb{R}^d$ and a target space $\mathcal{Y} = \{0, 1\}$. Though we evaluate our algorithm on binary classification problems, the method generalizes to multi-classification and regression. The random variable X with distribution $p(X)$ represents a d dimensional feature vector, and the random variable Y with distribution $p(Y)$ represents the target variable. The instances $(x, y) \in D$ are sampled from the joint distribution $p(X, Y)$, written $(x, y) \sim p(X, Y)$. We use A_k to denote the kth attribute in the data, $k = 1, \ldots, d$.

Additive Tree Ensembles. This paper proposes a method that works with *additive tree ensembles of decision trees.* These are a frequently used family of machine learning models encompassing both random forests and (gradient) boosted trees. Excellent open-source packages are available such as XGBoost [10], LightGBM [25], Scikit-learn [32] and many others. The models are learned from a dataset $D \subseteq \mathcal{X} \times \mathcal{Y}$ and define a mapping from $\mathcal{X}$ to $\mathcal{Y}$.

A binary decision tree T is a recursive data structure consisting of nodes. It starts at a root node that is not a descendant of any other node. Every node is either a leaf node storing an output value, or an internal node storing a test (e.g., *is attribute A_k less than 5?*) and two child nodes. A tree is evaluated for an example $x \in \mathcal{X}$ starting at the root node. If the node is an internal node, the test is executed for the node and, if successful, x moves down to the left child node, or if unsuccessful, moves down to the right child node, and the procedure recurs. If the node is a leaf, the output value of the leaf is the prediction for x.

An additive ensemble of trees $\boldsymbol{T}$ is a sum of M trees. The prediction is the sum of the predictions of the trees: $\boldsymbol{T}(x) = \sigma(\sum_{m=1}^{M} T_m(x))$. The transformation σ depends on the ensemble type and the learning task. Figure 1 shows an example of a tree ensemble.

Output Configuration (OC). The output configuration of an example x in an ensemble $\boldsymbol{T}$ is the ordered set of leaves $(l^{(1)}, \ldots, l^{(M)})$ visited by x in each tree of the ensemble. Each leaf is reached by exactly one root-to-leaf path. The split conditions in the internal nodes along the root-to-leaf paths of all leaves in an OC define the *box* in the input space of the OC. That is, for an OC $o \in \mathcal{O}$, $\text{box}(o) = \prod_{k \leq d}[u_k, v_k)$, where each $[u_k, v_k)$ is an interval constraining the kth attribute. Note that a valid OC has a non-empty box. This also means that the *OC-space* is not just the Cartesian product of all leaves because some leaf

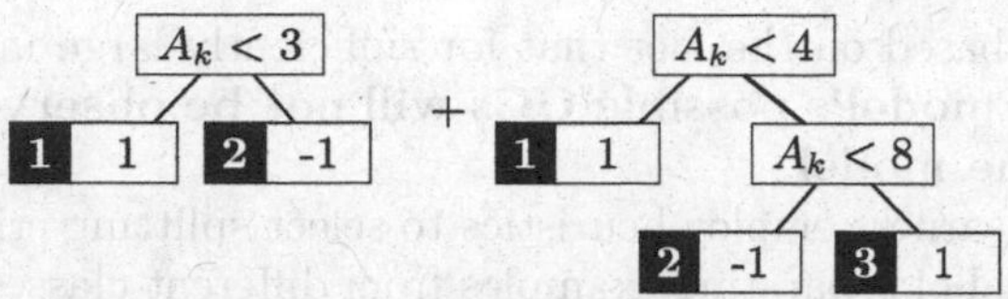

Fig. 1. A simple tree ensemble. Each leaf has an identifier in black, and leaf class predictions.

combinations are impossible. For example, in Fig. 1, (1, 2) and (1, 3) are invalid OCs because A_k cannot be both less than 3 and greater than 4 at the same time.

We define an operator OC : $x \mapsto (l^{(1)}, \ldots, l^{(M)})$ mapping an example x to its output configuration, where $l^{(m)}$ are leaf identifiers. This naturally defines the **OC-space** $\mathcal{O} = \{\mathrm{OC}(x) \mid x \in \mathcal{X}\}$ as the discrete space of all OCs. There is a one-to-one map between the boxes and the *OC-space* and the set of all boxes is a partition of the input space. Moreover, if two examples have the same OC, they belong to the same box and the ensemble $\boldsymbol{T}$ produces the same output for both examples.

Evasion Attacks and Adversarial Examples. Adversaries can attack machine learning models at training time (*poisoning*), or at deployment time (*evasion*) [3]. We focus on detecting *evasion attacks.* An evasion attack consists of constructing an example $\tilde{x}$ close to a real correctly labeled example x such that $\tilde{x}$ elicits a misprediction, i.e., $\boldsymbol{T}(x) \neq \boldsymbol{T}(\tilde{x})$ and $\|\tilde{x} - x\| < \varepsilon$ for some norm $\|\cdot\|$ and some $\varepsilon > 0$. We call such an $\tilde{x}$ an **adversarial example**. The same definition of an adversarial example is also used in previous work on tree ensembles [9,12,23], and corresponds to the *prediction-change* setting of [13].

Evasion attacks can vary on two important dimensions: (1) black-box vs. white-box, and (2) low-confidence vs. high-confidence. A white-box method has full access to the structure of the model, while a black-box method only uses the model's predictions. Low- and high-confidence refers to how the attacker tries to manipulate the confidence that the ensemble assigns to the incorrect label. For example, a low-confidence adversarial example in binary classification problem has a predicted probability close to 0.5.

3 Detecting Evasion Attacks with *OC-score*

We assume a post-deployment setting where a tree ensemble $\boldsymbol{T}$ is operating in the wild. The OC-score method then solves the following task:

Given: a deployed tree ensemble $\boldsymbol{T}$ and an unseen example $x \in \mathcal{X}$ for which a prediction is required,

Do: assign a score OC-score(x) to x indicating whether x is an adversarial example generated by an evasion attack.

Our algorithm is based on the fact that for sufficiently large models, **the vast majority of the model's possible OCs will not be observed in the data used to train the model.**

Decision tree learners employ heuristics to select splitting criteria in internal nodes with the goal of separating examples from different classes. Consequently, most leaf nodes tend to be (strongly) predictive of one class. Correctly classified examples will tend to have OCs consisting largely of leaves that are predictive of the correct class. An evasion attack constructs an adversarial example using carefully selected perturbations to a small number of attribute values so that enough leaves in the original example's OC are replaced by leaves that are predictive of the opposing class, yielding *unusual OCs* with an incorrect output label. This suggests that measuring how unusual an OC is, i.e., measuring how similar a newly encountered example's OC is to those that appear in the training set, is an effective strategy to detect adversarial examples.

3.1 The *OC-score* Metric

Our approach requires a learned ensemble $\boldsymbol{T}$ and a reference set $D_R \subseteq D$ of correctly classified examples. It constructs two reference sets $R_{\hat{y}} = \{\mathrm{OC}(x) \mid (x, y) \in D_R, y = \hat{y}\}$, one for each class, by encoding the examples in D_R into the *OC-space* by finding each one's output configuration.

Given a newly encountered example $x \in \mathcal{X}$, the ensemble is used to obtain its predicted label $\hat{y} = \boldsymbol{T}(x)$ and output configuration $o = \mathrm{OC}(x)$. Then it receives an *OC-score* by computing the Hamming distance to the closest OC in $R_{\hat{y}}$:

$$\text{OC-score}(x) = \min_{o' \in R_{\hat{y}}} h(o, o'), \tag{1}$$

with $h(o, o') = \sum_{m=1}^{M} \mathbb{1}[l^{(m)} \neq l'^{(m)}]$ the number of leaves that differ between the OCs and $l^{(m)}$ and $l'^{(m)}$ the mth leaf in o and o' respectively. Higher *OC-scores* correspond to a higher chance of being an adversarial example. Operationally, a threshold can be set on the *OC-scores* to flag potential adversarial examples: when the threshold is exceeded, the model abstains from making a prediction.

The *OC-score* algorithm can be implemented very efficiently by exploiting instruction-level parallelism using SIMD. The reference set's OCs can be compactly represented as a matrix of small integers (e.g., 8-bit integers), with in the ith row the identifiers of the leaves in the OC of the ith example in R. To compute OC-score(x), we slide the vector OC(x) over the rows of this matrix and compute the Hamming distance. This can be done on x86 using the 256-bit `AVX*` SIMD extensions. The full details are in the supplement and the source code is available at https://github.com/laudv/ocscore.

3.2 Theoretical Analysis

Our approach flags adversarial examples generated as part of an evasion attack by setting a threshold on the *OC-score*. It will only be accurate if, on average, the expected *OC-score* of an adversarial example is larger than the expected *OC-score* of a normal example. We prove that with two reasonable assumptions that this is indeed the case.

The first is the split-uniqueness assumption, which requires that no two splits in the ensemble are identical. The second assumption requires that adversarial examples produce OCs that are unlikely to be observed in the data used to train the model. Therefore, we first need to formally define how likely an OC is and what constitutes an unlikely OC.

Definition 1 (Probability of an OC). *Let X be a random variable denoting the feature vector, the probability $\mathbb{P}_X(o)$ of an OC $o \in \mathcal{O}$ is the probability of finding a normal example $x \sim p(X)$ in the box of o:*

$$\mathbb{P}_X(o) = \mathbb{P}_X(\text{box}(o)) = \mathbb{P}(X \in \text{box}(o)). \tag{2}$$

We can then restrict ourselves to low probability OCs:

Definition 2 (Unlikely OC). *Given an $\varepsilon > 0$, an OC $o \in \mathcal{O}$ is unlikely if $\mathbb{P}_X(o) < \varepsilon$.*

The supplement shows that there always exists an ε such that unlikely OCs exist.

We want the *OC-score* to be high for adversarial examples, and low for normal ones. This leads to the definition of an unusual OC. The *OC-score* measures the distance to the closest reference set example in *OC-space*. For the *OC-score* to be large with high probability, the likelihood of finding a reference set example in the *OC-space* neighborhood must be low. Specifically, given an unlikely OC o_ε and its *OC-space* neighbors o', $h(o_\varepsilon, o') \leq w$ for some distance $w \leq M$, the likelihood of finding a reference set example $x \sim p(X)$ in the a box of any neighbor must be low.

Definition 3 (Unusual OCs). *Choose ε such that unlikely OCs exist. Then, for any distance $w \leq M$, an unlikely OC o_ε is unusual if its OC-space neighborhood is less likely to contain a reference set example than the neighborhood of a non-unlikely OC o:*

$$\mathbb{P}_X\Big(\bigcup\{\text{box}(o') \,|\, h(o', o_\varepsilon) \leq w, o' \in \mathcal{O}\}\Big) \leq \mathbb{P}_X\Big(\bigcup\{\text{box}(o') \,|\, h(o', o) \leq w, o' \in \mathcal{O}\}\Big) \tag{3}$$

If we assume that adversarial examples use unusual OCs, then we prove that adversarial examples must have larger expected *OC-scores* on average than normal examples:

Theorem 1. *Let $\varepsilon > 0$. Let $\mathcal{O}_{<\epsilon} = \{o \in \mathcal{O} \mid \mathbb{P}_X(o) < \epsilon\}$ the set of unlikely OCs and $\mathcal{O}_{\geq \epsilon} = \mathcal{O} \setminus \mathcal{O}_{<\epsilon}$. Let $x_\varepsilon \sim p(X|\mathcal{O}_{<\epsilon})$, with $p(X|\mathcal{O}_{<\epsilon})$ the distribution of instances with unlikely OCs, i.e., $x_\varepsilon \sim p(X)$ such that $x_\varepsilon \in \text{box}(o_\varepsilon)$ and $o_\varepsilon \in \mathcal{O}_{<\epsilon}$. Similarly, let $x \sim p(X|\mathcal{O}_{\geq \epsilon})$, where $p(X|\mathcal{O}_{\geq \epsilon})$ is the distribution of instances with non-unlikely OCs. Then,*

$$\mathbb{E}_{x \sim p(X|\mathcal{O}_{\geq \epsilon})}\left[\mathbb{E}_R[\text{OC-score}(x)]\right] < \mathbb{E}_{x_\varepsilon \sim p(X|\mathcal{O}_{<\epsilon})}\left[\mathbb{E}_R[\text{OC-score}(x_\varepsilon)]\right] \tag{4}$$

The proof is in the supplement.

4 Related Work

Beyond the approaches mentioned in the introduction for detecting adversarial examples in neural networks, there are methods that look at the behavior of the decision boundary in an example's neighborhood [15,36,42]. Unfortunately, these methods do not work well with tree ensembles because the use of binary axis-parallel splits make them step functions, which makes exploring the neighborhood difficult. Also, the work investigating the relation between model uncertainty and adversarial examples [20,29] is relevant to this paper.

Certification methods [26,33] try to guarantee that, given an example, no adversarial examples exist within an l_∞ ball. In practice, this is achieved by (1) certifying the training data where labels are known, or (2) sampling in the neighborhood around an unseen instance and certifying that the unseen example and the sampled instances have the same predicted label. These methods achieve tractability by relaxing and approximating the (neural) model (e.g., bounding the activation function).

Each example's *OC-score* can be viewed as a model's secondary output with the predicted class being its primary output. This fits into the larger task of machine learning with a reject option [11]. Rejection aims to identify test examples for which the model was not properly trained. For such examples, the model's predictions have an elevated risk of being incorrect, and hence may not be trustworthy. An example can be rejected due to ambiguity (i.e., how well the decision boundary is defined in a region) or novelty (i.e., how anomalous an example is with respect to the observed training data) [22]. The *OC-score* metric goes beyond measuring ambiguity in an ensemble (i.e., the model's confidence in a prediction). Therefore, it can detect adversarial examples even if they fall in a region of the input space where the model's decision boundary appears to be well defined given the training data.

The random forest manual [5] discusses defining distances between training examples in an analogous manner to *OC-score*. Typically, (variations on) this distance has been used for tasks such as clustering [38], feature transformations [43], or making tree ensembles more interpretable [41]. To our knowledge, it has not been used for detecting adversarial examples.

5 Experimental Evaluation

Our experimental evaluation addresses three questions:

Q1. Can *OC-score* more accurately detect adversarial examples than its competitors?
Q2. What is each approach's prediction time cost associated with detecting adversarial examples?
Q3. How does the size of the reference set affect the performance of our *OC-score* metric?

We compare our *OC-score* to four approaches:

Ambiguity (*ambig*). This approach uses the intuition that because adversarial examples are somehow different than the training ones, the model will be uncertain about an adversarial example's predicted label [20]. This entails deciding whether an example lies near a model's decision boundary. This can be done by ranking examples according to the uncertainty of the classifier: $\text{ambig}(x) = 1 - |2\, p_T(x) - 1|$, where p_T is the probability of the positive class as predicted by the ensemble $\boldsymbol{T}$ for an example x.

Local Outlier Factor (*lof*). [6] Another intuition to detect adversarial examples is to employ an anomaly detector under the assumption that adversarial examples are drawn from a different distribution than non-adversarial ones. *lof* is a state-of-the-art unsupervised anomaly detection method that assigns a score to each example denoting how anomalous it is. This approach entails learning a *lof* model which is applied to each example.

Isolation Forests (*iforest*). An isolation forest [28] is a state-of-the-art anomaly detector. It learns a tree ensemble that separates anomalous from normal data points by splitting on a randomly selected attribute using a randomly chosen split value between the minimum and maximum value of the attribute. Outliers tend to be split off earlier in the trees, so the depth of an example in the tree is indicative of how normal an example is. Again, this requires learning a separate model at training time.

ML-LOO (*mlloo*). This is an approach for detecting adversarial examples from the neural network literature [48]. Unlike most other approaches, it is model agnostic as it looks at statistics of the features. It uses the accumulated *feature attributions* to rank examples: $\text{std}_k \left\{ p_T(x) - p_T(x_{(k)}) \right\}$, where p_T is the probability prediction of ensemble $\boldsymbol{T}$, and $x_{(k)}$ is x with the kth attribute set to 0. The observation in [48] is that variation in the feature attributions is larger for adversarial examples.

5.1 Experimental Methodology

We mimic the post-deployment evasion attack setting using 5-fold cross validation. In each fold, an ensemble is trained on four folds of clean training data. Then, using random subsets (with replacement) of the remaining fold, we generate 4×500 adversarial examples using four different methods. The adversarial examples are then supplemented by 2000 randomly selected normal (i.e., unmodified) examples. The resulting test set has an equal number of adversarial examples (4×500) as normal examples (2000). The different detection methods are then evaluated on the test set by comparing their performance on the task of distinguishing the adversarial examples from the normal examples.

We test our approach on the eight benchmark datasets listed in Table 1. All datasets are min-max normalized to make perturbations of the same size to different attributes comparable. To demonstrate our approach's generality, we consider three types of additive tree ensembles: (1) XGBoost boosted trees

Table 1. Datasets' characteristics and learners' hyperparameter settings. #F and n are the number of features resp. examples. M is the number of trees. The learning rate and tree depth for XGBoost are η and d_T. *calhouse* is a regression dataset converted to binary classification by predicting when the target is greater than the median value.

	#F	n	η	M	d_T	class balance
calhouse	8	20.6k	0.5	100	5	50%
electricity	8	45.3k	0.4	80	8	58%
covtype	54	581.0k	0.5	80	6	51%
higgs	33	250.0k	0.1	100	8	66%
ijcnn1	22	141.7k	0.9	50	5	90%
mnist2v4	784	13.8k	0.7	50	5	51%
fmnist2v4	784	14.0k	0.1	100	4	50%
webspam	254	350.0k	0.9	50	5	39%

[10], (2) Scikit-learn random forests [32], and (3) GROOT robustified random forests [44], which modifies the criteria for selecting the split condition when learning a tree to make them more robust against adversarial examples. Due to space constraints, we only show plots for some of the datasets. The results for the remaining datasets are along the same lines and are provided in the supplement.

Experimental Settings. For a given dataset, each learner has the same number of trees in the ensemble. The XGBoost trees are depth-limited to the values in Table 1. The random forests are not depth limited, but are limited to have at most 255 leaves. GROOT ensembles are limited to depth 8. Table 1 reports other characteristics for the datasets. Except for Q3, the reference set contains all correctly classified training examples. We use the scikit-learn [32] implementation for *lof* and *iforest* and use the default hyper-parameters. The supplement reports the average accuracies of the learned models on each dataset and the attack model ε of the GROOT ensembles. All experiments ran on an Intel E3-1225 with 32GB of memory. Multi-threading was enabled for all methods.

Simulating the Evasion Attacks. We use four different evasion attack methods. Each of these generates a different set of 500 adversarial examples. All the methods use the l_∞-norm to measure the perturbation size. They are:

- **LT-attack** (abbreviated '*lt*', [50]) iteratively moves a random initial example $\tilde{x}$ with $\boldsymbol{T}(\tilde{x}) \neq \boldsymbol{T}(x)$ towards the attacked example x in steps within a neighborhood such that $\|x - \tilde{x}\|_\infty$ is minimized.
- **Kantchelian attack** (abbr. '*kan*', [23]) is an exact approach[2] that directly minimizes $\|x - \tilde{x}\|_\infty$.

[2] We use Veritas's binary-search approach to find the closest adversarial example because it is an order of magnitude faster than their mixed-integer linear programming solution.

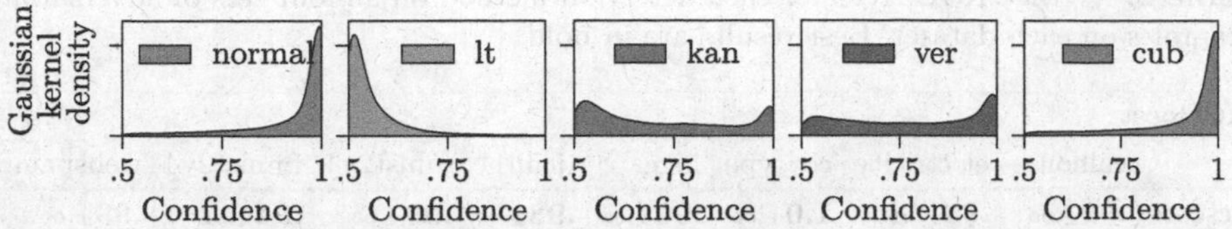

Fig. 2. The distribution of the confidence values $0.5 + |0.5 - p_T(x)|$ of the XGBoost ensembles for the test examples and the adversarial examples of all generation methods. The results are aggregated over all datasets and all folds.

- **Veritas attack** (abbr. '*ver*', [12]) is an approximate search-based approach that optimizes the ensemble's output in an l_∞ box of size δ centered around an original example x: $\max_{\tilde{x}} \boldsymbol{T}(\tilde{x})$ subject to $\|\tilde{x} - x\|_\infty < \delta$.
- **Cube attack** (abbr. '*cub*', [1]) is a model agnostic approach. Given an example x, it iteratively makes a random perturbation. If the perturbation moves the prediction towards the desired label it is accepted and otherwise it is rejected. The procedure is successful if the desired label is reached after a fixed number of iterations.

The Cube attack is the only *black box* approach. It does not use the ensemble's inner structure and uses only the ensemble's predictions.

5.2 Results Q1: Detecting Evasion Attacks

The task is to distinguish the adversarial from the normal examples. Each method generates a score, ranking the examples ideally from least adversarial (low score) to most adversarial (high score).

First, we evaluate the ranking performance using the area under the ROC (ROC AUC). This measures the quality of a ranking with respect to the classification task of separating adversarial and normal examples. Table 2 shows the mean AUC values for each method and the standard deviations over the five folds for XGBoost, random forests, and GROOT. Averaged over all adversarial sets, *OC-score* outperforms all other methods. An interesting observation is that XGBoost is less robust than random forests, and random forests are less robust than GROOT ensembles. The perturbations required to flip the label become larger as the models become more robust, and thus some adversarial examples become outliers in the traditional sense. Nonetheless, the results show that even robust GROOT ensembles benefit from detecting evasion attacks during deployment.

Second, we evaluate the performance of each detection method on one important characteristic of the evasion attack: model confidence. The confidence with which the ensemble predicts the incorrect class is computed as $0.5+|0.5-p_T(x)|$. The attack can simply try to elicit a misprediction or it can try to construct an adversarial example such that the model is highly confident in its misprediction. The LT- and Kantchelian attacks optimize the distance $\|x - \tilde{x}\|_\infty$ between the

Table 2. Average ROC AUC for each detection method on all four sets of adversarial examples on each dataset. Best results are in bold.

XGBoost								
	calhouse	electricity	covtype	higgs	ijcnn1	mnist2v4	fmnist2v4	webspam
ocscore	**.92**$\pm$.00	**.94**$\pm$.01	**1.0**$\pm$.00	**.90**$\pm$.01	**.98**$\pm$.00	**.99**$\pm$.00	**.94**$\pm$.01	**.99**$\pm$.00
ambig	.76$\pm$.01	.78$\pm$.01	.76$\pm$.01	.82$\pm$.01	.75$\pm$.02	.88$\pm$.02	.74$\pm$.04	.96$\pm$.01
iforest	.61$\pm$.02	.59$\pm$.02	.56$\pm$.01	.60$\pm$.02	.62$\pm$.01	.50$\pm$.00	.55$\pm$.01	.51$\pm$.02
lof	.67$\pm$.00	.53$\pm$.01	.65$\pm$.01	.54$\pm$.02	.73$\pm$.01	.61$\pm$.01	.60$\pm$.01	.53$\pm$.01
mlloo	.55$\pm$.01	.61$\pm$.02	.49$\pm$.01	.72$\pm$.01	.62$\pm$.02	.89$\pm$.02	.73$\pm$.03	.93$\pm$.01
Random forests								
	calhouse	electricity	covtype	higgs	ijcnn1	mnist2v4	fmnist2v4	webspam
ocscore	**.92**$\pm$.01	**.97**$\pm$.00	**1.0**$\pm$.00	**.91**$\pm$.00	**.99**$\pm$.00	**1.0**$\pm$.00	**.98**$\pm$.00	**.99**$\pm$.00
ambig	.87$\pm$.01	.82$\pm$.01	.88$\pm$.01	.82$\pm$.01	.97$\pm$.00	.95$\pm$.01	.77$\pm$.02	.96$\pm$.01
iforest	.61$\pm$.02	.63$\pm$.02	.60$\pm$.01	.61$\pm$.01	.56$\pm$.01	.46$\pm$.01	.61$\pm$.01	.51$\pm$.01
lof	.77$\pm$.00	.63$\pm$.01	.81$\pm$.00	.60$\pm$.01	.76$\pm$.00	.61$\pm$.00	.65$\pm$.01	.59$\pm$.01
mlloo	.37$\pm$.02	.48$\pm$.02	.39$\pm$.02	.58$\pm$.01	.37$\pm$.03	.93$\pm$.01	.51$\pm$.02	.36$\pm$.01
GROOT								
	calhouse	electricity	covtype	higgs	ijcnn1	mnist2v4	fmnist2v4	webspam
ocscore	**.87**$\pm$.02	**.96**$\pm$.00	**.85**$\pm$.01	**.96**$\pm$.01	**.99**$\pm$.00	**.94**$\pm$.01	**.94**$\pm$.00	**.99**$\pm$.00
ambig	.85$\pm$.01	.80$\pm$.01	.72$\pm$.04	.82$\pm$.02	**.99**$\pm$.00	.92$\pm$.02	.77$\pm$.03	.86$\pm$.01
iforest	.67$\pm$.01	.78$\pm$.02	.70$\pm$.03	.84$\pm$.01	.77$\pm$.03	.55$\pm$.01	.65$\pm$.01	.72$\pm$.01
lof	.83$\pm$.01	.73$\pm$.01	.84$\pm$.00	.81$\pm$.01	.89$\pm$.01	.69$\pm$.01	.71$\pm$.01	.90$\pm$.01
mlloo	.37$\pm$.01	.55$\pm$.01	.34$\pm$.02	.52$\pm$.02	.04$\pm$.01	.86$\pm$.01	.66$\pm$.03	.46$\pm$.04

original example x and the adversarial example $\tilde{x}$. Hence, the methods find the smallest perturbation such that $\tilde{x}$ just crosses the decision boundary, which often results in the misprediction having a low confidence. Veritas directly optimizes the model's output, so it specifically looks for the example with the maximally incorrect output within the l_∞-box. Cube uses a fixed number of iterations and attempts to improve the confidence at each step. Because of the random model-agnostic approach, many iterations are required, resulting in high-confidence adversarial examples.

Figure 2 shows the distribution of ensemble's confidences for each set of adversarial examples and the normal test set examples, averaged over all datasets for XGBoost. As expected, the LT- and Kantchelian attacks produce low-confidence adversarial examples, and the Veritas and Cube attacks produce high-confidence ones. Additionally, the figure shows that XGBoost has very confident predictions for normal examples. This has the immediate effect that low-confidence attacks are weaker attack vectors that are easily detectable by *ambiguity*. *OC-score* also performs extremely well on these (see Table 3). However, *ambiguity* performs poorly on the more challenging high-confidence adversarial examples. Only *OC-score* consistently works well for high-confidence adversarial examples.

Table 3. The average ROC AUC values for each detection method on *low-confidence* (*lt* and *kan*) and *high-confidence* (*ver* and *cub*) adversarial examples for XGBoost (XGB), random forests (RF), and GROOT (GRT). The best results are in bold.

	low confidence			high confidence		
	XGB	RF	GRT	XGB	RF	GRT
ocscore	$.94_{\pm.05}$	$.98_{\pm.02}$	$.93_{\pm.10}$	$\mathbf{.97}_{\pm.03}$	$\mathbf{.95}_{\pm.05}$	$\mathbf{.93}_{\pm.07}$
ambig	$\mathbf{.98}_{\pm.02}$	$\mathbf{.99}_{\pm.01}$	$\mathbf{.98}_{\pm.03}$	$.63_{\pm.21}$	$.76_{\pm.15}$	$.70_{\pm.16}$
iforest	$.53_{\pm.02}$	$.52_{\pm.05}$	$.64_{\pm.10}$	$.60_{\pm.11}$	$.63_{\pm.15}$	$.77_{\pm.13}$
lof	$.52_{\pm.04}$	$.57_{\pm.08}$	$.70_{\pm.12}$	$.69_{\pm.18}$	$.78_{\pm.18}$	$.90_{\pm.10}$
mlloo	$.80_{\pm.19}$	$.54_{\pm.18}$	$.52_{\pm.26}$	$.58_{\pm.21}$	$.45_{\pm.25}$	$.43_{\pm.26}$

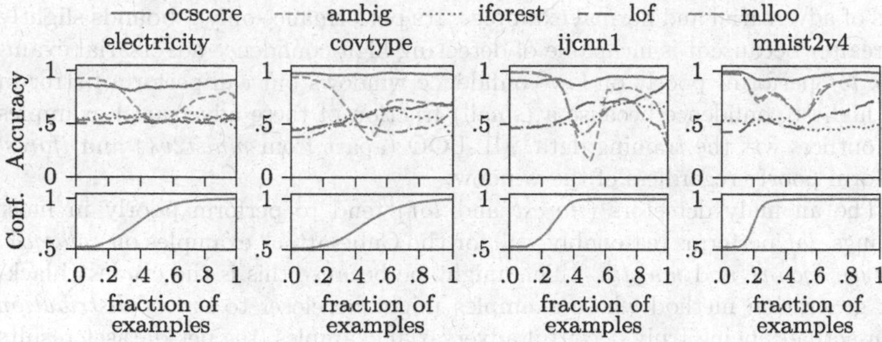

Fig. 3. Relation between detection performance and prediction confidence for XGBoost by sliding fixed-sized window over the full set of test examples (normal and the four sets of adversarial examples) sorted by model confidence. Top: Accuracy for each detection method in the window. Bottom: Average confidence in the window. The x-axis is the fraction of examples already considered by a window.

Next, we further investigate the effect of model confidence on detection performance for XGBoost. We order the examples by the ensemble's confidence and compute each method's detection accuracy within a window. Regardless of the window, a method's global median score over all examples is used to make a hard prediction. This is a sensible choice because the test set contains 50% normal and 50% adversarial examples. The top plots in Fig. 3 show the accuracy and the bottom plots show the model's average confidence for the examples in the considered window. The x-axis shows the fraction of examples processed as the window slides from left (low confidence) to right (high confidence). OC-score offers consistently strong performance across the full range of confidences and outperforms the other methods apart from *ambiguity* on the windows with the lowest average confidence. *ambiguity* offers good performance for low confidence examples. However, its detection performances declines dramatically when the x-axis approaches 0.5 because these windows start to contain roughly equal num-

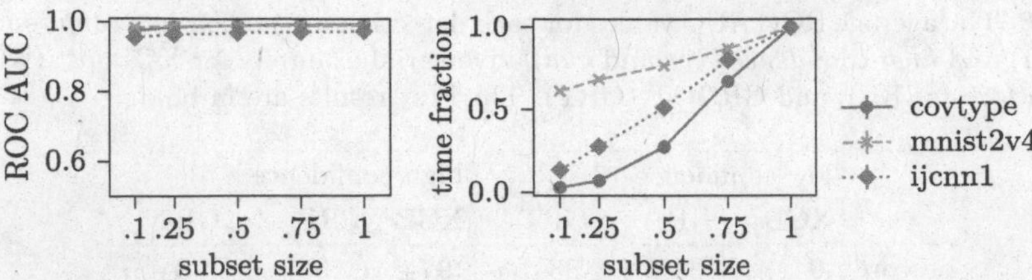

Fig. 4. Left: OC-score's ROC AUC values for detecting adversarial vs. non-adversarial test examples as a function of the reference set size. Right: fraction of time used to compute the OC-score relative to the case the full training set is used. Using a small reference set has a minimal impact on OC-score's performance.

bers of adversarial and normal examples. Its performance only rebounds slightly thereafter because it is incapable of detecting high-confidence adversarial examples. *lof* performs poorly on low confidence windows but can perform better in the highest confidence because a (small) fraction of these adversarial examples are outliers wrt the training data. ML-LOO (apart from *mnist2v4*) and *iforest* perform poorly regardless of the window.

The anomaly detectors (*iforest* and *lof*) tend to perform poorly in most settings. *lof* performs reasonably well for the Cube-attack examples on *calhouse*, *covtype*, *ijcnn1* and *mnist2v4*. This might be because this is the crudest black-box generation method whose examples might be closer to *out of distribution* than actually being truly deceitful adversarial examples (see per-dataset results in the supplement). ML-LOO has highly variable performance and is consistently worse than *OC-score*. It tends to work best on image data. However, it frequently performs worse than random on several other datasets (e.g., *calhouse*, *covtype*). For the XGBoost ensembles, ML-LOO is reasonably effective at detecting the low-confidence adversarial examples, but its performance is poor in general for high-confidence ones.

5.3 Results Q2: Prediction Time Cost

Regardless of the detection method, whether an example is adversarial can usually be computed in well under 1 millisecond (see timing results in the supplement). *ambiguity* consistently takes less than 0.01ms because it is a simple mathematical computation. *iforest* is also fast ($<$ 0.15 ms) because it only requires executing a tree ensemble. *OC-score* takes less than 0.2ms for 6 out of 8 datasets. Its prediction time scales with the number of trees and the reference set size, so higher prediction times are measure for the larger datasets. However, the results in Subsect. 5.4 indicate that it is possible to decrease the size of the reference set without degrading performance. ML-LOO's costs comes from computing an importance for each feature. Hence, it yields longer times for datasets with many features (1.4 ms for *mnist2v4*, 2.6 ms for *fmnist2v4*, $<$ 0.5 ms otherwise). The evaluation time of *lof* is similar for all larger datasets ($<$ 0.14 ms) because we limit the training set size to a random subset of at most 20 000 examples (affects *covtype*, *higgs*, *ijcnn1*, and *webspam*) because using the full training set takes hours.

5.4 Results Q3: Size of the Reference Set

Finally, we explore the effect of the reference set size on the detection performance. Reference set examples are randomly sampled from the set of correctly classified training examples (see model accuracies in supplement). Figure 4 shows the results for this experiment on three datasets using XGBoost. The plot on the left shows ROC AUC values for detecting adversarial vs. non-adversarial examples. These values are stable for all datasets. There is a small decline in performance for the smallest reference set proportion, where the number of examples in the reference set ranges from 1050 for *fmnist2v4* to 41 700 for *covtype*.

The plot on the right shows the time to compute the *OC-scores* as the reference set size is varied relative to using the full reference set. For *ijcnn1*, the relative time reduction follows the relative subset sizes almost exactly. The results for *covtype* are even better. With barely any effect on the detection performance using only 10% of the full reference set, the evaluation time drops by 97%. We expect that this is due to CPU cache performance (e.g. fewer cache misses). *mnist2v4* also sees a considerable reduction in time, but not as impressive as the previous two datasets. We suspect this is due to the smaller reference set, and the relatively higher constant overhead. *OC-score* already is really fast on *mnist2v4*, however, taking only 0.03 ms per example using the full reference set.

These experiments suggest that using a small reference set drastically improves the evaluation time without degrading performance. Note that changing the reference set does not require relearning the underlying ensemble used to make predictions, which is still learned using the full training set.

6 Conclusions and Discussion

This paper explored how to detect evasion attacks for tree ensembles. Our approach works with any additive tree ensemble and does not require training a separate model. If a newly encountered example's output configuration differs substantial from those in the reference set, then it is more likely to be adversarial. Empirically, our *OC-score* metric resulted in superior detection performance.

Acknowledgements. This research is supported by the Research Foundation – Flanders (LD: 1SB1322N; LP: 1166222N), the Flemish Government under the "Onderzoeksprogramma Artificiele Intelligentie (AI) Vlaanderen" program (JD), the European Union's Horizon Europe Research and Innovation program under the grant agreement TUPLES No. 101070149 (JD), and KU Leuven Research Fund (JD: iBOF/21/075; WM: IOF).

Ethical Statement. Machine learning is widely used in many different application areas. With the wide adoption, machine learned models, including tree ensembles, increasingly become high-stake targets for attackers who might employ evasion attacks to achieve their goal. This work proposes a defense method against evasion attacks for tree ensembles. Together with other approaches like robust tree ensembles, this work is a step forward in our ability to protect against evasion attacks. This could further improve the trust in machine learning, and further accelerate its adoption, especially in sensitive application areas.

Improved defenses will likely also result in the development of improved counter-attacks. We strongly feel that it is in the interest of the research community that (1) the research community stays on top of these developments so that machine learning libraries can adapt if necessary, and (2) all work done in this area is open-access. For that reason, all resources and codes are publicly available at https://github.com/laudv/ocscore.

References

1. Andriushchenko, M., Hein, M.: Provably robust boosted decision stumps and trees against adversarial attacks. In: Advances in Neural Information Processing Systems, vol. 32 (2019)
2. Biggio, B., et al.: Evasion attacks against machine learning at test time. In: Machine Learning and Knowledge Discovery in Databases, pp. 387–402 (2013)
3. Biggio, B., Roli, F.: Wild patterns: ten years after the rise of adversarial machine learning. Pattern Recogn. **84**, 317–331 (2018)
4. Breiman, L.: Random forests. Mach. Learn. **45**(1), 5–32 (2001)
5. Breiman, L., Cutler, A.: Random forests manual (2002). https://www.stat.berkeley.edu/~breiman/RandomForests
6. Breunig, M.M., Kriegel, H.P., Ng, R.T., Sander, J.: LOF: identifying density-based local outliers. In: Proceedings of the 2000 ACM SIGMOD International Conference on Management of Data, pp. 93–104 (2000)
7. Calzavara, S., Lucchese, C., Tolomei, G., Abebe, S.A., Orlando, S.: Treant: training evasion-aware decision trees. Data Min. Knowl. Disc. **34**(5), 1390–1420 (2020)
8. Chen, H., Zhang, H., Boning, D., Hsieh, C.J.: Robust decision trees against adversarial examples. In: Proceedings of the 36th International Conference on Machine Learning, pp. 1122–1131 (2019)
9. Chen, H., Zhang, H., Si, S., Li, Y., Boning, D., Hsieh, C.J.: Robustness verification of tree-based models. In: Advances in Neural Information Processing Systems, vol. 32, pp. 12317–12328 (2019)
10. Chen, T., Guestrin, C.: XGBoost: a scalable tree boosting system. In: Proceedings of the 22nd ACM SIGKDD International Conference on Knowledge Discovery and Data Mining, KDD 2016, pp. 785–794 (2016)
11. Cortes, C., DeSalvo, G., Mohri, M.: Learning with rejection. In: Proceedings of the 27th International Conference on Algorithmic Learning Theory (ALT 2016) (2016)
12. Devos, L., Meert, W., Davis, J.: Versatile verification of tree ensembles. In: Proceedings of the 38th International Conference on Machine Learning. Proceedings of Machine Learning Research, vol. 139, pp. 2654–2664 (2021)
13. Diochnos, D., Mahloujifar, S., Mahmoody, M.: Adversarial risk and robustness: general definitions and implications for the uniform distribution. In: Advances in Neural Information Processing Systems, vol. 31 (2018)
14. Einziger, G., Goldstein, M., Sa'ar, Y., Segall, I.: Verifying robustness of gradient boosted models. In: Proceedings of the AAAI Conference on Artificial Intelligence, vol. 33, pp. 2446–2453 (2019)

15. Fawzi, A., Fawzi, H., Fawzi, O.: Adversarial vulnerability for any classifier. In: Proceedings of the 32nd International Conference on Neural Information Processing Systems, pp. 1186–1195 (2018)
16. Feinman, R., Curtin, R.R., Shintre, S., Gardner, A.B.: Detecting adversarial samples from artifacts. arXiv preprint arXiv:1703.00410 (2017)
17. Gong, Z., Wang, W., Ku, W.S.: Adversarial and clean data are not twins. arXiv preprint arXiv:1704.04960 (2017)
18. Goodfellow, I.J., Shlens, J., Szegedy, C.: Explaining and harnessing adversarial examples. In: Proceedings of the 3rd International Conference on Learning Representations (2015)
19. Grosse, K., Manoharan, P., Papernot, N., Backes, M., McDaniel, P.: On the (statistical) detection of adversarial examples. arXiv preprint arXiv:1702.06280 (2017)
20. Grosse, K., Pfaff, D., Smith, M.T., Backes, M.: The limitations of model uncertainty in adversarial settings. In: 4th workshop on Bayesian Deep Learning (NeurIPS 2019) (2018)
21. Guo, J.Q., Teng, M.Z., Gao, W., Zhou, Z.H.: Fast provably robust decision trees and boosting. In: Proceedings of the 39th International Conference on Machine Learning. Proceedings of Machine Learning Research, vol. 162, pp. 8127–8144 (2022)
22. Hendrickx, K., Perini, L., der Plas, D.V., Meert, W., Davis, J.: Machine learning with a reject option: a survey. CoRR abs/2107.11277 (2021)
23. Kantchelian, A., Tygar, J.D., Joseph, A.: Evasion and hardening of tree ensemble classifiers. In: Proceedings of the 33rd International Conference on Machine Learning, pp. 2387–2396. PMLR (2016)
24. Katzir, Z., Elovici, Y.: Detecting adversarial perturbations through spatial behavior in activation spaces. In: 2019 International Joint Conference on Neural Networks, pp. 1–9 (2019)
25. Ke, G., et al.: LightGBM: a highly efficient gradient boosting decision tree. In: Advances in Neural Information Processing Systems, vol. 30, pp. 3146–3154 (2017)
26. Lecuyer, M., Atlidakis, V., Geambasu, R., Hsu, D., Jana, S.: Certified robustness to adversarial examples with differential privacy. In: 2019 IEEE Symposium on Security and Privacy (SP), pp. 656–672. IEEE (2019)
27. Lee, K., Lee, K., Lee, H., Shin, J.: A simple unified framework for detecting out-of-distribution samples and adversarial attacks. In: Advances in Neural Information Processing Systems, vol. 31 (2018)
28. Liu, F.T., Ting, K.M., Zhou, Z.H.: Isolation forest. In: Proceedings of the 8th IEEE International Conference on Data Mining, pp. 413–422. IEEE (2008)
29. Liu, X., Li, Y., Wu, C., Hsieh, C.J.: Adv-BNN: improved adversarial defense through robust Bayesian neural network. In: Proceedings of the 7th International Conference on Learning Representations (2019). https://openreview.net/forum?id=rk4Qso0cKm
30. Metzen, J.H., Genewein, T., Fischer, V., Bischoff, B.: On detecting adversarial perturbations. In: Proceedings of 5th International Conference on Learning Representations (2017)
31. Pace, R.K., Barry, R.: Sparse spatial autoregressions. Stat. Probab. Lett. **33**(3), 291–297 (1997)
32. Pedregosa, F., et al.: Scikit-learn: machine learning in Python. J. Mach. Learn. Res. **12**, 2825–2830 (2011)
33. Raghunathan, A., Steinhardt, J., Liang, P.: Certified defenses against adversarial examples. In: Proceedings of the 6th International Conference on Learning Representations (2018)

34. Ranzato, F., Zanella, M.: Abstract interpretation of decision tree ensemble classifiers. In: Proceedings of the AAAI Conference on Artificial Intelligence, vol. 34, pp. 5478–5486 (2020)
35. Ranzato, F., Zanella, M.: Genetic adversarial training of decision trees. In: Proceedings of the Genetic and Evolutionary Computation Conference, pp. 358–367 (2021)
36. Roth, K., Kilcher, Y., Hofmann, T.: The odds are odd: a statistical test for detecting adversarial examples. In: Proceedings of the 36th International Conference on Machine Learning, pp. 5498–5507. PMLR (2019)
37. Schulze, J.P., Sperl, P., Böttinger, K.: DA3G: detecting adversarial attacks by analysing gradients. In: European Symposium on Research in Computer Security, pp. 563–583 (2021)
38. Shi, T., Horvath, S.: Unsupervised learning with random forest predictors. J. Comput. Graph. Stat. **15**(1), 118–138 (2006)
39. Sperl, P., Kao, C.Y., Chen, P., Lei, X., Böttinger, K.: DLA: dense-layer-analysis for adversarial example detection. In: 2020 IEEE European Symposium on Security and Privacy (EuroS&P), pp. 198–215 (2020)
40. Szegedy, C., et al.: Intriguing properties of neural networks. In: Proceedings of the 2nd International Conference on Learning Representations (2014)
41. Tan, S., Soloviev, M., Hooker, G., Wells, M.T.: Tree space prototypes: another look at making tree ensembles interpretable. In: Proceedings of the 2020 ACM-IMS on Foundations of Data Science Conference, pp. 23–34 (2020)
42. Tian, J., Zhou, J., Li, Y., Duan, J.: Detecting adversarial examples from sensitivity inconsistency of spatial-transform domain. In: Proceedings of the AAAI Conference on Artificial Intelligence (2022)
43. Vens, C., Costa, F.: Random forest based feature induction. In: Proceedings of 11th IEEE International Conference on Data Mining, pp. 744–753 (2011)
44. Vos, D., Verwer, S.: Efficient training of robust decision trees against adversarial examples. In: Proceedings of the 38th International Conference on Machine Learning, pp. 10586–10595 (2021)
45. Vos, D., Verwer, S.: Adversarially robust decision tree relabeling. In: Joint European Conference on Machine Learning and Knowledge Discovery in Databases (2022)
46. Vos, D., Verwer, S.: Robust optimal classification trees against adversarial examples. In: Proceedings of the AAAI Conference on Artificial Intelligence (2022)
47. Wang, Y., Zhang, H., Chen, H., Boning, D., Hsieh, C.J.: On LP-norm robustness of ensemble decision stumps and trees. In: Proceedings of the 37th International Conference on Machine Learning, pp. 10104–10114 (2020)
48. Yang, P., Chen, J., Hsieh, C.J., Wang, J.L., Jordan, M.: ML-LOO: detecting adversarial examples with feature attribution. In: Proceedings of the AAAI Conference on Artificial Intelligence, vol. 34, no. 04, pp. 6639–6647 (2020)
49. Yang, Y.Y., Rashtchian, C., Wang, Y., Chaudhuri, K.: Robustness for nonparametric classification: a generic attack and defense. In: Proceedings of the Twenty Third International Conference on Artificial Intelligence and Statistics. Proceedings of Machine Learning Research, vol. 108, pp. 941–951 (2020)
50. Zhang, C., Zhang, H., Hsieh, C.J.: An efficient adversarial attack for tree ensembles. In: Advances in Neural Information Processing Systems, vol. 33, pp. 16165–16176 (2020)
51. Zhang, S., et al.: Detecting adversarial samples for deep learning models: a comparative study. IEEE Trans. Netw. Sci. Eng. **9**(1), 231–244 (2022)

Time Series

Deep Imbalanced Time-Series Forecasting via Local Discrepancy Density

Junwoo Park, Jungsoo Lee, Youngin Cho, Woncheol Shin, Dongmin Kim, Jaegul Choo, and Edward Choi(✉)

Kim Jaechul Graduate School of AI, Korea Advanced Institute of Science and Technology KAIST, Daejeon, South Korea
{junwoo.park,bebeto,choyi0521,swc1905,tommy.dm.kim, jchoo,edwardchoi}@kaist.ac.kr

Abstract. Time-series forecasting models often encounter abrupt changes in a given period of time which generally occur due to unexpected or unknown events. Despite their scarce occurrences in the training set (*i.e.*, data imbalance), abrupt changes incur loss that significantly contributes to the total loss (*i.e.*, heteroscedasticity). Therefore, they act as noisy training samples and prevent the model from learning generalizable patterns, namely the normal states. To resolve overfitting problem posed by heteroscedasticity and data imbalance, we propose a reweighting framework that down-weights the losses incurred by abrupt changes and up-weights those by normal states. For the reweighting framework, we first define a measurement termed *Local Discrepancy (LD)* which measures the degree of abruptness of a change in a given period of time. Since a training set is mostly composed of normal states, we then consider how frequently the temporal changes appear in the training set based on LD (*i.e.*, estimated LD density). Our reweighting framework is applicable to existing time-series forecasting models regardless of the architectures. Through extensive experiments on 12 time-series forecasting models over eight datasets with various in-output sequence lengths, we demonstrate that applying our reweighting framework reduces MSE by 10.1% on average and by up to 18.6% in the state-of-the-art model.

Keywords: Time-series forecasting · Data imbalance · Noisy samples

1 Introduction

As vast records are collected over time in diverse fields, the demand to predict the future based on the previous sequential data has led to efforts to solve the time-series forecasting problem in various applications such as energy [1], economics [7], traffic [24], weather [22], environment pollution [6] and mechanical system monitoring [30]. Previous studies focused on addressing the well-known challenges of time-series forecasting such as finding reliable dependencies from intricate and entangled temporal patterns [20,26] or extending the forecasting time (i.e., long-term forecasting) [18,26,30,31]. For example, recent studies

D. Koutra et al. (Eds.): ECML PKDD 2023, LNAI 14173, pp. 139–155, 2023.
https://doi.org/10.1007/978-3-031-43424-2_9

focused on improving the Transformer-based [23] models to address the long-term forecasting by taking the advantage of the long-term capacity of the self-attention mechanism and reducing quadratic computational costs [16,18,26,30].

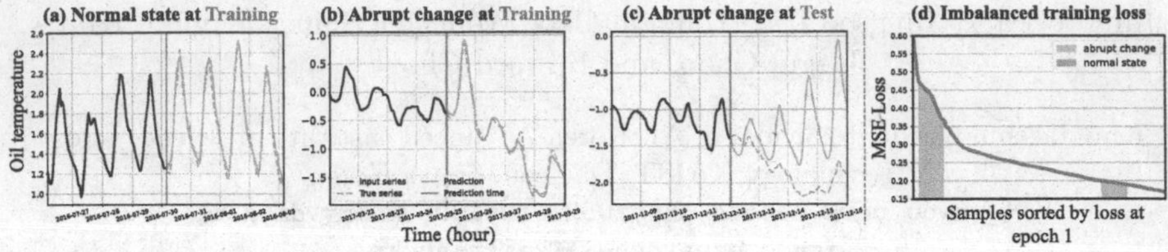

Fig. 1. We observe that the state-of-the-art forecaster correctly predicts the target values during the training phase over both (a) normal states and (b) abrupt changes, respectively. However, (c) illustrates that the model fails to correctly predict the abrupt change during the test phase. (d) shows imbalanced loss when the training samples are sorted by MSE loss of each sample in the early training phase. Our important finding is that the training samples with abrupt change (b) occupy the large portion of total loss. On the other hand, training samples within the normal states (a) have a relatively small loss. This leads the model to focus less on the normal states during training.

Despite the remarkable improvements of the previous studies, even the state-of-the-art models take little account of the *abrupt changes* in time-series data. Abrupt change refers to the drastic change of target values (either increase or decrease) beyond the extent of the changes observed in the recent past. These abrupt changes are challenging, if not impossible to predict based solely on previous observations of the target variable, as they are generally caused by unexpected and external events (*e.g.*, natural disaster and war). Such changes break the auto-correlation structures, the periodic relationships between target variables, which are essential for a time-series forecaster to predict futures. One straightforward remedy is to laboriously collect external variables (*e.g.*, annotations of external events) and enforce a model to learn the relationship between the collected variables and the target variables (*i.e.*, cross-correlation). However, utilizing additional variables without thorough verification causes the model to learn a spurious correlation between variables, which worsens the generalization ability. Moreover, some abrupt changes have unknown causes (*e.g.*, sensor malfunction), which cannot be addressed by simply collecting external variables.

While forecasting abrupt changes is known to be challenging [10,19], even worse, another significant issue of abrupt changes is that they limit the generalization performance of forecasting models during the test phase. Deep learning models are known to correctly predict all training samples regardless of the noisy labels by simply memorizing them (*i.e.*, overfitting) [28]. Our finding is that recent time-series forecasting models can easily memorize even abrupt changes in which the output sequence shows the different temporal characteristics (*e.g.*, mean, variance, and periodic structure) with the input sequence as shown in Fig. 1. To be more specific, Fig. 1(a) and (b) show that the model correctly predicts the target values during the training phase in both normal states (*i.e.*, trend or periodicity of input sequence maintained in the output sequence) and abrupt changes, respectively. However, Fig. 1(c) illustrates that the model fails to correctly predict the abrupt change during the test phase. The main reason is that the model is heavily overfitted to the abrupt changes since they take a significant portion of the total loss value compared to the ones in normal states (*i.e.*, heteroscedasticity problem as shown in Fig. 1(d)).

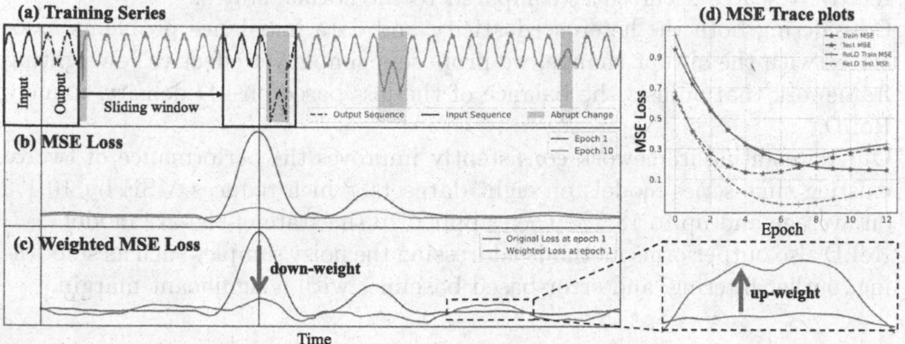

Fig. 2. (a) We trained a model with a training series including four abrupt changes (red-shaded regions). (b) While the losses caused by the abrupt changes are considerably high in the early training phase, they are reduced significantly after several epochs of training. (d) After the losses by abrupt changes are decreased, however, we observe that the test losses rather increase, implying the degraded generalization capability. (c) We mitigate such an issue by proposing a reweighting framework that down-weights the losses of samples containing the abrupt changes (blue arrow) and up-weights normal samples (red arrow). (d) The model trained with our proposed reweighting framework achieves lower test MSE compared to that of the model without our framework. (Color figure online)

Therefore, we propose a simple yet effective reweighting framework that encourages the model to balance the imbalanced loss between abrupt changes and normal states as shown in Fig. 2. Generally, time-series datasets do not provide explicit labels as to when the abrupt changes occur. Moreover, explicitly bisecting time stamps into abrupt changes and normal states is challenging since the definition of abrupt change may be vague depending on perspectives. Thus, we define a measure called *Local Discrepancy* (LD) which is used to determine how much a change in a given period of time is abrupt. By sliding a fixed-size window over the training time-series data, we compute the statistical difference between the in-output sequences as LD. Then, based on the observation that abrupt changes rarely appear in the training samples while normal states comprise the majority of the training set (*i.e.*, data imbalance problem), we count the frequency of temporal changes based on LD. We divide the LD values into a predefined number of bins which are smoothed by kernel density estimation (*i.e.*, estimated LD density). By obtaining low LD density for the abrupt changes and high ones for the normal states, we ***re***weight loss values proportional to the estimated ***LD*** ***D***ensity, which we term our method as *ReLD*. This enables to emphasize the normal states which are the ones a model should learn for enhancing the forecasting capability. In summary, the main contributions of our work are as follows:

- Our findings reveal that the time-series forecasting performance is significantly degraded by the losses resulting from the abrupt changes, despite their relatively scarce occurrences compared to the normal states.
- Considering both the heteroscedasticity and data imbalance problems associated with the abrupt change, we propose a simple yet effective reweighting framework that adjusts the balance of the loss based on LD density, namely ReLD.
- Our reweighting framework consistently improves the performance of twelve existing time-series models on eight datasets, which reduces MSE by 10.1% on average and up to 18.6% when applied to the state-of-the-art model.
- ReLD also outperforms methods addressing the noisy samples such as smoothing, outlier filtering, and error-based baselines with a significant margin.

2 Related Work

2.1 Deep Learning Models for Time-Series Forecasting

Deep learning-based models that have shown successful results in various domains have been actively applied to the time-series forecasting problem, which was originally dominated by classic statistical-based models [2]. Recent studies focused on extending forecasting time [18,26,30,31]. As the demand for long-term planning and early warning in the real-world applications has increased, long-term forecasting has become essential. Thus, transformer-based forecasting models, which are known to effectively learn global temporal patterns, have emerged. These studies proposed sparse attention mechanisms to reduce the computational cost of the canonical attention mechanism when processing long sequences. The previous studies have demonstrated their effectiveness on various time-series datasets across multiple domains. However, they do not deal with how the locally appearing anomalous patterns (*i.e.*, abrupt changes) of time series affect the generalization capability of models.

2.2 Robustness Against Noisy Samples and Data Imbalance

As aforementioned, deep learning models perfectly classify samples even with wrong annotations (*i.e.*, noisy samples) by simply memorizing them during the training phase [28], an issue explored widely in image classification [8,15,29]. Similarly, the abrupt changes in time-series forecasting are generally occurred by unexpected or unknown events, making them challenging to forecast correctly solely based on the previous time series. Due to this fact, perfectly forecasting them during the training phase indicates that the models simply memorized them which are in fact noisy samples in the time-series data.

Unlike studies addressing noisy samples in other fields, the number of abrupt changes is excessively scarce compared to that of normal states in time-series, so considering the data imbalance in addition to the noisy samples is important. The main intuition of addressing data imbalance is to emphasize the training of the minor samples based on the frequency of each class [17,27]. For example, Yang et al. [27] proposed the label distribution smoothing method that addresses the data imbalance in the image regression task. To tackle such data imbalance in time-series forecasting due to the scarce temporal patterns, few studies proposed an augmentation approach [19] or modified model architectures [10]. However, when addressing the data imbalance, they did not take account of models being overfitted to the scarce abrupt changes during the training phase. In this regard, we propose a reweighting framework that takes both issues into account: 1) abrupt changes work as noisy samples, and 2) they cause the data imbalance.

3 Method

We first describe the forecasting task in a rolling window setting [16,18,26,30], which covers all possible in-output sequence pairs of the entire time series $\mathcal{S} = \{\mathbf{s}_1, \ldots, \mathbf{s}_T \mid \mathbf{s}_t \in \mathbb{R}^m\}$, where T is the length of observed series and m denotes the number of variables at time t. Univariate and multivariate time-series forecasting addresses time-series data with $m = 1$ and $m > 1$, respectively. By sliding a fixed-size window on $\mathcal{S}$, we obtain the windows $\mathcal{D} = \{(\mathcal{X}_t, \mathcal{Y}_t)\}_{t=1}^{N}$, which are divided into two parts: input sequence $\mathcal{X}_t = \{\mathbf{s}_{t-I}, \ldots, \mathbf{s}_{t-1}\}$ with given length I and output sequence $\mathcal{Y}_t = \{\mathbf{s}_t, \ldots, \mathbf{s}_{t+O-1}\}$ with length O to predict. A forecaster f predicts the most probable length-O sequence in the future given the past length-I sequence by learning temporal dependencies in $\mathcal{S}$. We mainly address the loss imbalance caused by the in-output sequence pairs which include a large discrepancy between adjacent $\mathcal{X}_a$ and $\mathcal{Y}_a$ compared to other $\mathcal{X}_t$ and $\mathcal{Y}_t$ pairs where a is the time stamp with an abrupt change. However, since most time-series datasets do not provide a label for the abrupt change, we propose a training framework in an unsupervised setting.

3.1 Local Discrepancy

We propose the *Local Discrepancy* (LD) based on a statistical difference in order to measure how two adjacent in-output sequences, $\mathcal{X}_t$ and $\mathcal{Y}_t$, are different from each other. We define LD as follows:

$$\mathrm{LocalDis}(\mathcal{X}_t, \mathcal{Y}_t) = \frac{\bar{\mathcal{X}}_t - \bar{\mathcal{Y}}_t}{\sqrt{\frac{\mathrm{s}^2_{\bar{\mathcal{X}}_t}}{I} + \frac{\mathrm{s}^2_{\bar{\mathcal{Y}}_t}}{O} + \varepsilon}} := v_t, \quad (1)$$

where $\bar{\mathcal{X}}_t$ is the sample mean and $\mathrm{s}_{\bar{\mathcal{X}}_t}$ is the sample standard deviation of $\mathcal{X}_t$.

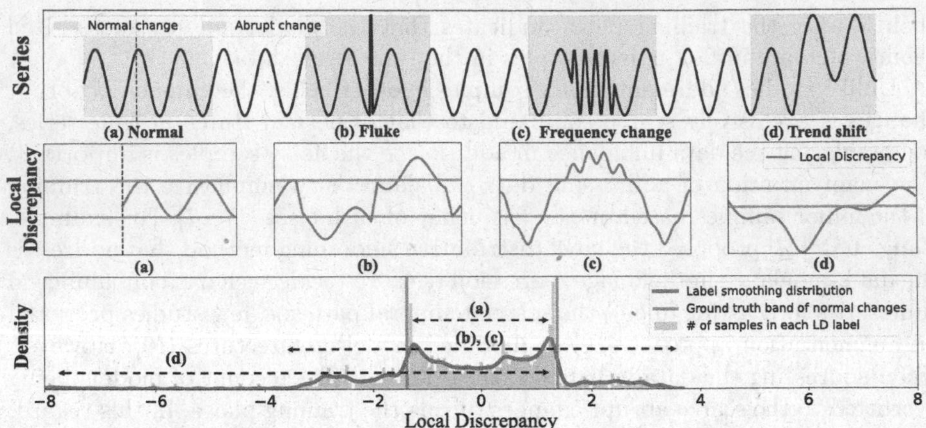

Fig. 3. The four examples of temporal changes locally seen in time series data: (a) normal, (b) fluke, (c) frequency change, and (d) trend shift. Local discrepancy computed by the sliding window captures the three abrupt changes beyond the bounds (red line) seen in normal states. In the estimated LD density distribution, training samples with abrupt changes are visibly fewer than training samples with normal state and are sparsely distributed with large absolute local discrepancy. (Color figure online)

Statistical tests are generally used to determine whether means of two samples (*i.e.*, groups of data points in a sequence) are identical or not [25]. In this regard, we leverage t-statistic[1], a scalar value, as normalized discrepancy to measure how much two adjacent groups of samples are distinct. Figure 3 describes how LD reflects the different types of local temporal changes in time-series data (e.g., (a) normal changes, (b) fluke point, (c) frequency change, and (d) trend shift). The LD values of normal states oscillate within a certain range (see (a) red line) since the LD also has periodicity as proven by Theorem 1, but the LD values of abrupt changes is beyond the range of normal LD. Additionally, the periodicity and boundedness of LD in normal periodic series are theoretically discussed in Supplementary with all proofs.

Theorem 1 (Periodicity of LD). *If f is a periodic function that satisfies $f(t) = f(t+p)$,*

$$LD(a, a+L) = \frac{m(a) - m(a+L)}{\sqrt{\frac{s(a)}{N} + \frac{s(a+L)}{N}}} \tag{2}$$

is also a periodic function with period p, where $m(a) = \frac{1}{N}\sum_{t\in I(a)} f(t)$, $s(a) = \frac{1}{N}\sum_{t\in I(a)}(f(t) - m(a))^2$, and $I(a) = \{a + \frac{L}{N}\cdot i\}_{i=0}^{N-1}$ for range $[a, a+L]$ and sampling interval L/N.

[1] Other statistics such as KPSS and t-squared can be used as LD. However, when we conduct a preliminary experiment, the t-statistic measures better than others. We further discuss the details in Sect. 4.

As aforementioned, the definition of abrupt change may be vague depending on perspectives. Thus, rather than bisecting the time stamps into abrupt changes and normal states, we utilize LD values as weights of reweighting framework to mitigate the impact of abrupt changes in training phase. In other words, losses of training samples which have large absolute v_t values will be down-weighed since we consider them to be close to the abrupt change. By computing LD over the training dataset $\mathcal{D}_{train}$ and each of m dimensions, we obtain the dataset $\mathcal{D}_{train} = \{(\mathcal{X}_t, \mathcal{Y}_t, v_t)\}_{t=1}^{N}$ containing local discrepancy $v_t \in \mathbb{R}^m$ for prediction time t and for each of m dimensions. We then assign the weight $w_t = \frac{c}{|v_t|+1} \propto \frac{1}{|v_t|+1} \in \mathbb{R}^m$ to each training sample inversely to LD value of sample in $\mathcal{D}_{train}$ with constant c as scaling factor. Finally, we calculate the reweighted MSE loss $\mathcal{L}_w$ as follows:

$$\mathcal{L}_w(\mathcal{Y}_t, \hat{\mathcal{Y}}_t) = \frac{1}{m \cdot O} \cdot \sum_{j=1}^{m} w_t^j \sum_{i=0}^{O-1} \cdot (\mathbf{s}_{t+i}^j - \hat{\mathbf{s}}_{t+i}^j)^2 \tag{3}$$

where $\hat{\mathcal{Y}}_t$ is forecasting results of f conditioned on $\mathcal{X}_t$. Through this simple reweighting framework which assigns weight inversely to LD values, namely *invLD*, we down-weight the loss of abrupt changes (large absolute LD) and up-weight the loss of normal states (small absolute LD), following the observation that the original MSE loss in the presence of abrupt changes is much larger than the loss at the normal state. Reweighting MSE only based on LD, however, does not take into account the property that normal states frequently appear while the abrupt changes are rarely included in the time-series data. We further improve our reweighting framework by considering such frequency differences between abrupt changes and normal states.

3.2 Density-Based Reweighting for Time-Series Forecasting

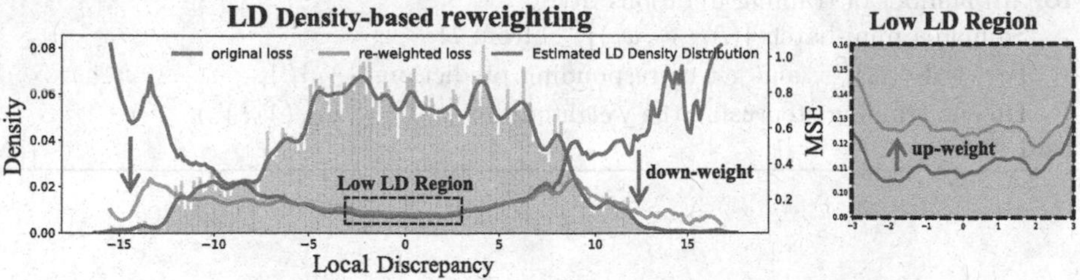

Fig. 4. For the real-world dataset (ETTh1), we visualize the estimated LD density distribution and the averaged MSE loss of samples in each LD bin after training a forecaster for one epoch. Our density-based re-weighting framework effectively down-weights (blue arrow) the losses on abrupt changes (low density and large LD) and up-weights (red arrow) those on normal states (high density and small LD). (Color figure online)

Time series often exhibit both short-term and long-term repeating patterns [14] by periodicity, and taking them into account is crucial for making accurate predictions. Suppose a time series which has large shifts in a short period, but repeated. We can assume such large shifts are part of the normal states considering their frequent occurrences. However, this temporal pattern is down-weighted because of their large LD values regardless of the number of occurrences. In other words, invLD based on the inverse of LD (*i.e.*, $w_t \propto \frac{1}{|v_t|}$) will not only down-weight the loss values of abrupt changes but also those of normal states, which the model should learn to properly forecast. Therefore, we improve the time-series forecasting by considering the frequency of temporal changes (*i.e.*, LD density) when reweighting loss values in time-series forecasting.

Inspired by deep imbalanced regression [27], we use the kernel density estimation to address the missing regions between continuous LD spaces. Through the estimated density of LD $\tilde{p}(v)$, we assign the weight $w_t = c \cdot \tilde{p}(v_t) \propto \tilde{p}(v_t)$ and use these weights to train a model as $\mathcal{L}_w$ described in Eq. 3. Figure 4 demonstrates that our final reweighting framework based on LD density, ReLD, mitigates the imbalanced loss problem in a real-world dataset. The procedure of our framework is described in Algorithm 1.

Algorithm 1 ReLD: **Re**weighting framework based on **L**ocal **D**iscrepancy Density

---

Require: Training set $\mathcal{D} = \{(\mathcal{X}_t, \mathcal{Y}_t)\}_{t=1}^{N}$, bin size Δb, symmetric kernel distribution $k(v, v')$

Compute Local Discrepancy LD $(\mathcal{X}_t, \mathcal{Y}_t) = \frac{\bar{\mathcal{X}}_t - \bar{\mathcal{Y}}_t}{\sqrt{\frac{s^2_{\mathcal{X}_t}}{I} + \frac{s^2_{\mathcal{Y}_t}}{O} + \varepsilon}} := v_t$

Compute the empirical label density distribution $p(v)$ based on Δb and $\mathcal{D}$

Compute the effective label density distribution $\tilde{p}(v') := \int_{\mathcal{V}} k(v, v') p(v) dv$

for all $(\mathcal{X}_t, \mathcal{Y}_t, v_t) \in \mathcal{D}$ **do**

  Assign weight for each sample as $w_t \propto c \cdot \tilde{p}(v_t)$ (constant c as scaling factor)

end for

for all number of training iterations **do**

  Sample a mini-batch $\{(\mathcal{X}_b, \mathcal{Y}_b, w_b)\}_{b=1}^{B}$ from $\mathcal{D}$

  Forward $\{\mathcal{X}_b\}_{b=1}^{B}$ and get corresponding predictions $\{\hat{\mathcal{Y}}_b\}_{b=1}^{B}$

  Do one training step using the weighted loss $\frac{1}{B} \sum_{b=1}^{B} \mathcal{L}_{w_b}(\hat{\mathcal{Y}}_b, \mathcal{Y}_b)$

end for

---

4 Experiments

This section demonstrates that our proposed framework consistently improves existing time-series forecasting models regardless of the architectures. We also provide other experiments in the Supplementary, which include results on synthetic series, hyperparameter sensitivity of the proposed method, qualitative results, and details for reproducibility. Our source code and Supplementary are available at GitHub[2].

4.1 Experiment Setting

Dataset Descriptions. As mainstream benchmarks, ETT are widely used to evaluate long-term forecasting methods [18,26,30,31] ETT contains the crucial indicators (e.g., oil temperature, load, etc.) collected from the electricity transformers over two years, and are categorized into four datasets depending on the location (ETT1 and ETT2) and interval (15 min and one hour). Electricity dataset contains the hourly electricity consumption of 321 customers from 2012 to 2014. Weather dataset is recorded every 10 min for a year, which contains 21 meteorological indicators (*e.g.*, air temperature, humidity, etc.). Pump dataset is collected from 52 sensors monitoring the water pump. AirQuality dataset [6], taken from the UCI repository, contains hourly averaged responses obtained from five metal oxide chemical sensors of an chemical multi-sensor. Traffic dataset compiles hourly data from the California Department of Transportation, detailing the occupancy rates of roads as measured by different sensors on freeways in the San Francisco Bay area. All dataset sources can be found in Supplementary.

Forecasting Models. To verify that our reweighting framework works consistently in existing forecasting models, we applied it to 12 forecasting models and reported the reduced forecasting errors by applying ReLD. The baselines are roughly categorized into three groups: Transformer-based [12,16,18,23,26,30, 31], CNN-based [4], and RNN-based [3,14] models. We also include two univariate forecasting models: DeepAR [21] and N-BEATS [20]. We applied our ReLD to the baselines without additional external data indicating abrupt changes or modifications of architectures.

Experiment Details. The forecasting performance is measured using the mean square error (MSE). Note that we follow the evaluation protocol proposed by previous work [26,30], including normalization through the mean and standard deviation of the train dataset. We conducted experiments on five different lengths of time series. All reported values are averaged MSE from five independent experiments with different random initializations. Due to the space limit, the main paper only reports the averaged MSE while the Supplementary includes the full benchmarks along with the confidence intervals.

[2] https://github.com/junwoopark92/ECMLPKDD2023-ReLD.

Table 1. Multivariate results with different input length I and prediction lengths O. A lower MSE indicates a better prediction and the best results in each row are bolded. Imp. means averaged MSE reduction rate for a given model and dataset. Total denotes the averaged MSE reduction rate of a given dataset across all baselines models. The full results, including other ETT datasets and univariate results, are available in Supplementary with their corresponding confidence intervals.

Models		FEDformer		Pyraformer		Autoformer		Informer		Reformer		LSTNet		LSTMa		TCN		Total
I/O		base	ReLD	base	ReLD	base	ReLD	base	ReLD	base	ReLD	base	ReLD	base	ReLD	base	ReLD	
ETTm1	96/96	0.359	**0.357**	0.536	0.471	0.524	0.455	0.640	0.543	0.777	0.641	0.548	0.536	0.705	0.592	0.676	0.594	**−12.91%**
	336/168	0.385	**0.379**	0.563	0.506	0.534	0.500	1.224	0.751	0.840	0.689	0.632	0.577	0.871	0.648	0.938	0.913	
	336/336	0.403	**0.396**	0.697	0.573	0.561	0.514	1.390	1.008	0.987	0.895	0.798	0.686	1.125	0.681	1.148	1.126	
	336/720	0.501	**0.480**	0.904	0.682	0.560	0.528	1.333	1.078	1.122	1.003	0.925	0.817	0.978	0.828	1.277	1.238	
	Imp.	−1.99%		−16.17%		−8.42%		−25.11%		−13.88%		−9.16%		−24.14%		−4.95%		
ETTm2	96/96	0.189	**0.184**	0.371	0.248	0.293	0.221	0.445	0.286	0.743	0.449	0.443	0.343	0.381	0.280	0.554	0.384	**−21.42%**
	336/168	0.343	**0.275**	0.566	0.551	0.309	0.283	2.283	1.453	1.208	0.836	0.950	0.830	1.178	0.601	1.868	1.956	
	336/336	0.338	**0.315**	1.601	1.330	0.508	0.331	2.479	1.764	2.239	1.425	1.610	1.019	1.479	0.745	2.769	2.773	
	336/720	0.432	**0.393**	5.476	5.037	0.502	0.413	6.580	5.777	3.068	2.827	6.130	4.449	3.083	2.381	3.204	3.187	
	Imp.	−9.47%		−15.15%		−21.39%		−28.29%		−28.65%		−24.85%		−36.96%		−6.57		
Weather-h	48/48	0.338	0.336	0.292	**0.279**	0.344	0.343	0.345	0.294	0.343	0.313	0.318	0.310	0.346	0.325	0.348	0.327	**−4.41%**
	48/96	0.403	0.400	0.393	**0.358**	0.464	0.446	0.453	0.443	0.526	0.416	0.414	0.386	0.409	0.387	0.450	0.424	
	96/192	0.458	0.447	0.421	**0.398**	0.516	0.491	0.530	0.498	0.659	0.673	0.464	0.461	0.420	0.416	1.018	1.005	
	168/336	0.510	0.516	0.454	**0.440**	0.612	0.566	0.592	0.568	0.841	0.782	0.490	0.473	0.473	0.452	1.147	1.209	
	Imp.	−0.65%		−5.55%		−4.21%		−6.79%		−8.66%		−3.41%		−4.17%		−1.88%		
AirQuality	96/96	0.825	**0.817**	1.121	1.112	0.992	0.986	1.353	1.193	1.210	1.196	1.146	1.141	1.145	1.081	1.026	0.992	**−3.97%**
	336/168	0.811	**0.808**	1.193	1.115	0.911	0.922	1.796	1.595	1.473	1.345	1.231	1.156	1.644	1.376	1.246	1.163	
	336/336	0.892	**0.872**	1.224	1.214	0.962	0.933	1.758	1.706	1.473	1.396	1.399	1.388	1.352	1.206	1.301	1.284	
	336/720	0.997	**0.953**	2.196	1.982	1.129	1.079	2.914	2.985	1.723	1.671	1.826	1.921	2.475	2.333	1.442	1.426	
	Imp.	−2.01%		−4.47%		−1.72%		−5.87%		−4.51%		−0.52%		−9.63%		−3.09%		
Pump	96/96	0.520	**0.513**	0.848	0.796	0.558	0.538	0.831	0.870	0.826	0.760	1.016	1.007	0.813	0.766	1.037	0.970	**−7.74%**
	336/168	0.550	**0.536**	0.851	0.843	0.597	0.581	1.705	1.527	1.094	0.856	1.327	1.202	0.909	0.816	1.109	1.077	
	336/336	0.593	**0.564**	0.922	0.951	0.661	0.621	1.676	1.492	0.966	0.918	1.654	1.292	0.934	0.859	1.521	1.208	
	336/720	0.723	**0.580**	1.370	1.283	0.707	0.619	1.704	1.699	1.328	1.218	1.608	1.642	1.464	1.244	2.075	1.546	
	Imp.	−7.10%		−2.61%		−6.17%		−4.28%		−10.73%		−7.49%		−9.77%		−13.85%		

4.2 Main Results

As shown in Table 1, applying our reweighting framework reduces the MSE consistently in all existing time-series forecasting models across different datasets and varying length-averaged settings. In addition, the lowest MSE in each setting was generally achieved by the models which applied ReLD. We also observe that the performance improvements vary depending on the datasets. For example, applying ReLD to the baselines achieves an average of 21.14% lower MSE compared to the average of original errors on ETTm2. On the other hand, applying ReLD achieves only 3.97% lower MSE on average with AirQuality dataset. We analyze such an issue in Sect. 4.5.

4.3 Comparisons with Other Methods

Smoothing and Outlier Filtering Methods. Table 2(a) compares our ReLD with two smoothing and outlier filtering methods. Moving average (MA) and exponential MA (EMA) are widely used smoothing techniques that remove noisiness and reduce values of outliers, allowing meaningful temporal patterns to stand out. Similarly, outlier filtering also mitigates the influence of outliers on learning the normal patterns. However, we observe that adopting such methods

Table 2. Comparison with other methods which can deal with abrupt changes. We conduct experiments using ETTm2 dataset on two recent state-of-the-art time-forecasting models. '↔' indicates adopting the method in replace of the original L2 loss and '+' indicates adding the method to the original L2 loss.

Group	Models	FEDformer						Autoformer						Imp.
	Methods I→O	336 → 168		336 → 336		336 → 720		336 → 168		336 → 336		336 → 720		
		MSE	MAE	MSE	MAE	MSE	MAE	MSE	MAE	MSE	MAE	MSE	MAE	
	Vanilla (L2)	0.343	0.406	0.338	0.387	0.432	0.461	0.309	0.371	0.508	0.490	0.502	0.478	-
(a)	+ MA	0.355	0.411	0.343	0.388	0.418	0.443	0.313	0.374	0.431	0.447	0.542	0.500	−0.85%
	+ EMA	0.364	0.419	0.343	0.389	0.404	0.432	0.319	0.377	0.516	0.473	0.549	0.506	1.33%
	+ Outlier	0.292	0.364	0.330	0.380	0.405	0.429	0.384	0.422	0.420	0.444	0.468	0.475	−3.26%
(b)	↔ L1	0.282	0.345	0.321	0.366	0.402	0.416	0.308	0.368	0.349	0.391	0.434	0.439	−11.24%
	↔ Huber	0.285	0.353	0.322	0.369	0.418	0.432	0.307	0.369	0.398	0.424	0.452	0.456	−8.32%
	↔ IRLS	0.281	0.345	0.322	0.368	0.398	0.416	0.292	0.356	0.350	0.387	0.435	0.433	−12.12%
	↔ Focal-R	0.403	0.451	0.377	0.423	0.504	0.523	0.315	0.379	0.445	0.463	0.520	0.497	6.02%
	↔ flip Focal-R	0.284	0.344	0.322	0.367	0.405	0.417	0.307	0.366	0.371	0.405	0.470	0.453	−9.70%
(c)	+ invLD	0.282	0.343	0.326	0.374	0.402	0.414	0.288	0.353	0.343	0.385	**0.411**	**0.421**	−12.82%
	+ ReLD	**0.275**	**0.339**	**0.315**	**0.361**	**0.393**	**0.409**	**0.283**	**0.348**	**0.331**	**0.377**	0.413	0.422	**−14.34%**

either shows insignificant performance improvement or rather aggravates the time-series forecasting performance.

Error-Aware Loss. We also compare our method with error-based reweighting approaches for robust regression, which aims at mitigating heteroscedasticity problem, (L1, Huber [11], and IRLS [5]) and data imbalance problem (Focal-R [17,27] and flip Focal-R). Focal-R, the regression version of focal loss, allows a model to focus on samples with relatively large loss while down-weighting loss on samples with small errors. It works in a way that is contrary to our findings. We modified such an approach by putting negation on the input of Focal-R, termed as flip Focal-R (Details in Supplementary). Table 2(b) shows that the performance of Focal-R is rather degraded while that of flip Focal-R improved. Such a result well demonstrates that our intuition, de-emphasizing the samples with high loss, is valid. Also, we observe that utilizing other error-based approaches fails to outperform our proposed method. We conjecture such superior performance of ReLD is mainly due to reflecting the temporal changes and periodicity.

Ablation Study of Our Reweighting Framework. We conduct the ablation study of our proposed method by comparing our full framework ReLD and an approach which considers the LD values only (invLD). Table 2(c) shows that our full framework is superior to invLD. Additionally, we observe that both approaches outperform the methods in (a) and (b).

4.4 Variants for Local Discrepancy

We propose the *Local Discrepancy* (LD) based on the statistics formulated by a statistical test, Welch's t-test [25], in order to measure how two adjacent in-output sequences, $\mathcal{X}_t$ and $\mathcal{Y}_t$, are different from each other. There may exist other

Table 3. Ablation study on variants of local discrepancy used in our reweighting framework. We compare models which uses 1) KPSS, 2) t-squared, and 3) t-statistic. The t-statistic shows more consistent and superior results compared to other statistics in the multivariate setting.

Model	Dataset	ETTh1			ETTh2			ETTm1			Imp.
	Predict-O	96	168	336	96	168	336	96	168	336	
Pyraformer		0.645	0.864	0.933	1.609	5.014	4.356	0.536	0.563	0.697	-
Pyraformer + KPSS		0.554	0.782	0.909	1.482	4.590	5.327	0.470	0.527	0.604	−5.84%
Pyraformer + t-squared		0.640	0.809	0.898	1.440	3.112	3.912	0.490	0.557	0.632	−9.84%
Pyraformer + t-statistic		0.534	0.742	0.889	1.173	3.976	3.281	0.471	0.506	0.573	**−16.51%**
Autoformer		0.442	0.504	0.569	0.386	0.439	0.494	0.524	0.534	0.561	-
Autoformer + KPSS		0.446	0.528	0.486	0.358	0.436	0.516	0.456	0.538	0.513	−3.68%
Autoformer + t-squared		0.454	0.521	0.515	0.357	0.403	0.436	0.503	0.548	0.512	−4.60%
Autoformer + t-statistic		0.444	0.491	0.511	0.351	0.413	0.424	0.455	0.500	0.514	**−7.74%**
Informer		0.908	1.372	1.343	3.400	5.796	3.901	0.640	1.224	1.390	-
Informer + KPSS		0.850	1.215	1.215	3.050	5.593	4.202	0.535	0.844	1.087	−11.41%
Informer + t-squared		0.871	1.262	1.234	2.796	4.393	3.419	0.594	0.992	1.195	−12.76%
Informer + t-statistic		0.856	1.113	1.151	2.462	4.723	3.788	0.543	0.751	1.008	**−18.81%**

metrics to measure the local discrepancy such as multivariate t-statistic [9] (i.e., Hotelling's t-squared statistic) and stationarity tests (*e.g.*, Kwiatkowski-Phillips-Schmidt-Shin (KPSS) tests [13]). We also report the performance of our reweighting framework using a different metric other than t-statistics for measuring the local discrepancy in Table 3. Hotelling's t-squared statistic is a generalization of Student's t-statistic that is used in multivariate hypothesis testing. We can naturally utilize t-squared statistic as LD for multivariate forecasting (*i.e.*, $\mathbf{s} \in \mathbb{R}^m$ and $m > 1$) as follows:

$$\text{LocalDis}(\mathcal{X}_t, \mathcal{Y}_t) = \frac{I \cdot O}{I + O}(\bar{\mathcal{X}}_t - \bar{\mathcal{Y}}_t)' \hat{\boldsymbol{\Sigma}}^{-1} (\bar{\mathcal{X}}_t - \bar{\mathcal{Y}}_t) := v_t^2 \tag{4}$$

where the mean and covariance are defined as follows:

$$\bar{\mathcal{X}}_t = \frac{1}{I}\sum_{i=1}^{I} \mathbf{s}_{t-i}, \quad \bar{\mathcal{Y}}_t = \frac{1}{O}\sum_{i=0}^{O-1} \mathbf{s}_{t+i}, \quad \hat{\boldsymbol{\Sigma}} = \frac{(I-1)\,\hat{\boldsymbol{\Sigma}}_{\bar{\mathcal{X}}} + (O-1)\,\hat{\boldsymbol{\Sigma}}_{\bar{\mathcal{Y}}}}{I + O - 2},$$

$$\hat{\boldsymbol{\Sigma}}_{\bar{\mathcal{X}}} = \frac{1}{I-1}\sum_{i=1}^{I} (\mathbf{s}_{t-i} - \bar{\mathcal{X}}_t)(\mathbf{s}_{t-i} - \bar{\mathcal{X}}_t)', \quad \hat{\boldsymbol{\Sigma}}_{\bar{\mathcal{Y}}} = \frac{1}{O-1}\sum_{i=1}^{O-1} (\mathbf{s}_{t+i} - \bar{\mathcal{Y}})(\mathbf{s}_{t+i} - \bar{\mathcal{Y}})'.$$

We can interpret the time-series data in terms of stochastic processes. KPSS tests are used for testing a null hypothesis that an observable time series is stationary around a deterministic trend (*i.e.*, trend-stationary) against the alternative of a unit root. When the given time series is trend stationary, the KPSS statistic has small value, which is close to zero. Thus, to measure the degree of abruptness of a change in a given period of time, we leverage the KPSS statistic as LD:

$$\text{LocalDis}(\text{concat}(\mathcal{X}_t, \mathcal{Y}_t)) = \frac{1}{(I+O)^2} \cdot \sum_{i=-I}^{O-1} \frac{\mathcal{E}_{t+i}^2}{\hat{\sigma}^2} := v_t \tag{5}$$

where $\mathcal{E}_t$ is partial sum of the residuals and $\hat{\sigma}^2$ is the estimate of the long-run variance of the residuals as follows:

$$\mathcal{E}_k = \sum_{k=1}^{t} e_i, \quad e = (e_{t-I}, e_{t-I+1}, \cdots, e_{O-1}),$$

where e means OLS residuals when regressing the concated in-output sequence (*i.e.*, concat$(\mathcal{X}_t, \mathcal{Y}_t)$).

We observe that our reweighting framework consistently outperforms the ones without our framework regardless of the statistics used for measuring the local discrepancy. While we empirically confirmed that using t-statistic is more suitable for LD compared to KPSS or t-Squared statistic, such result demonstrates that our framework can be used with any statistics measure the user deems appropriate.

4.5 Dataset Analysis

Preserving the Robustness on the Abrupt Changes. Since we impose less emphasis on the abrupt changes during the training phase, utilizing our framework may limit the model's ability to cope with the abrupt changes in the test phase. Table 4 reports the MSE of test samples by categorizing them into time series with abrupt changes and those without abrupt changes. For the experiment, we generated synthetic time-series dataset and injected abrupt changes into the series since the real-world dataset does not have labels for abrupt changes. As originally intended, applying our framework achieves larger MSE reduction rates (*i.e.*, MSE_N) compared to the ones without ReLD. As for the MSE of abrupt changes (*i.e.*, MSE_A), the MSE_A of three models decreased, and those of Pyraformer show competitive forecasting results. This result shows that our ReLD improves the forecasting performance on normal samples while preserving the robustness on the abrupt changes.

Different Performance Gains Across Datasets. From the multivariate results (Table 1) and univariate results, we found that the reduction rates of MSE vary depending on the datasets. For an in-depth analysis, we present the correlation between the average of reduction rate and the average of LD for each dataset using the scatter plot in Fig. 5. We observed a positive linear correlation between LD and the reduction rate, indicating that we obtain a higher reduction rate of MSE as the average of LD increases in a given dataset. To further demonstrate such a finding, we intentionally inject abrupt changes into the Traffic and ECL, the datasets which showed the marginal improvements in

Table 4. Forecasting results by categorizing time-series sequences into normal states and abrupt changes. We observe that our ReLD significantly reduces MSE on normal states (MSE_N) while also showing comparable MSE on abrupt changes (MSE_A).

Prediction length		48		96		168		336		720		Averaged Imp.	
Model	Metric	Base	ReLD	Base	ReLD	Base	ReLD	Base	ReLD	Base	ReLD		Total
Pyraformer	MSE_N	0.0702	**0.0305**	0.0580	**0.0232**	0.0547	**0.0221**	0.0449	**0.0326**	0.0379	**0.0247**	**−47.67%**	−27.38%
	MSE_A	0.4289	**0.4168**	**0.5525**	0.5905	0.6093	**0.5882**	**0.4300**	0.4350	**0.2555**	0.2665	1.21%	
Autoformer	MSE_N	0.2063	**0.1473**	0.2560	**0.1430**	0.2137	**0.1261**	0.3645	**0.1857**	0.5099	**0.3950**	**−37.06%**	−33.25%
	MSE_A	0.7385	**0.6946**	0.9878	**0.7312**	0.8152	**0.6541**	0.8185	**0.6224**	0.8230	**0.6776**	**−18.66%**	
N-BEATS	MSE_N	0.0472	**0.0345**	0.0592	**0.0401**	0.0469	**0.0355**	0.0646	**0.0411**	0.0517	**0.0394**	**−28.73%**	−17.84%
	MSE_A	**0.3331**	0.3794	0.6109	**0.5375**	0.5989	**0.5944**	0.4597	**0.4197**	**0.2853**	0.2909	**−1.12%**	
Informer	MSE_N	0.1350	**0.0538**	0.0819	**0.0341**	0.0762	**0.0344**	0.2954	**0.0492**	0.5564	**0.1775**	**−64.96%**	−51.84%
	MSE_A	0.5547	**0.4746**	**0.5625**	0.6031	0.6011	**0.5810**	0.7533	**0.4604**	0.7724	**0.3619**	**−20.28%**	

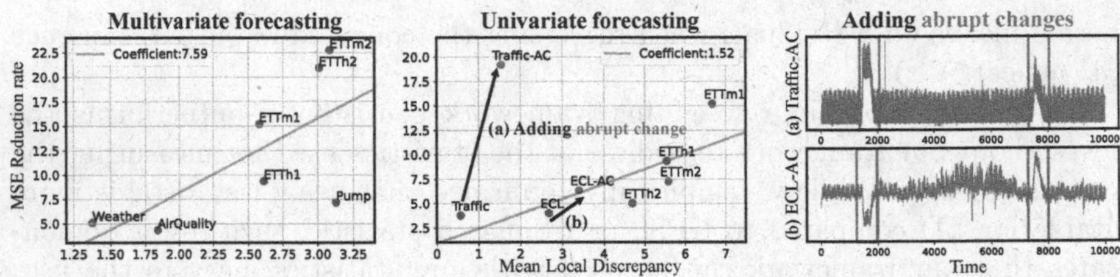

Fig. 5. Scatter plots showing the correlation between the averaged LD of each dataset and MSE reduction rates of experiments on the multivarite and univariate settings.

the univariate setting. We obtained a larger reduction rate of MSE with both Traffic and ECL including intentional abrupt changes compared to the original datasets. This demonstrates that the marginal performance gain in both Traffic and ECL is due to the few number of abrupt changes in the dataset. We emphasize that using ReLD does not degrade performance on such datasets, if not marginally improve it, due to a few number of abrupt changes inevitably included in time-series datasets.

4.6 Computational Cost of ReLD

Our reweighting framework requires a marginal amount of additional computational cost of calculating the weights for all input-output sequences before training. As shown in Table 5, the cost of calculating the weights on datasets with multiple settings is less than 1% of the time it takes to train with the dataset during one epoch. The absolute time was mostly less than 1 s.

Table 5. The processing time of ReLD and training time of Autoformer.

Dataset	# of Windows	Window size (I + O)	# of Series	ReLD time (a) (seconds)	Training time (b) (seconds per epoch)	Ratio (a)/(a) + (b)
ETTh1	8449	192 (96 + 96)	7	0.18	38.12	0.47%
ETTh2	8449	192 (96 + 96)	7	0.17	39.11	0.43%
ETTm1	34369	192 (96 + 96)	7	0.69	154.68	0.44%
ETTm2	34369	192 (96 + 96)	7	0.68	160.31	0.42%
Weather-hour	5093	1056 (336 + 720)	21	0.63	121.19	0.52%
Pump	9610	672 (336 + 336)	35	1.22	125.30	0.96%
ECL	17741	672 (336 + 336)	1	0.08	94.67	0.08%
Traffic	11225	1056 (336 + 720)	1	0.07	99.05	0.07%

5 Discussion and Limitation

In this paper, we reveal that abrupt changes between adjacent sequences deteriorate the generalization performance of time-series forecasting models by occupying most of the losses despite their scarce occurrence in the training set. To solve this problem, we propose a simple yet effective reweighting framework that down-weights loss values of abrupt changes and up-weights those of normal states based on LD density. Although our ReLD consistently enhances the performance on real-world datasets, there is a limitation we found. We assume that an abrupt change is caused by unobserved external variables. However, if we can have access to those variables, our framework may not show performance improvement from the down-weighted losses of the abrupt changes.

Acknowledgements. This work was supported by the National Research Foundation of Korea (NRF) grant funded by the Korea government (MSIT) (NRF-2020H1D3A2A03100945, NRF-2022R1A2B5B02001913) and the institute of Information & communications Technology Planning & Evaluation (IITP) grant funded by the Korea government (MSIT) (No. 2019-0-00075, No. 2022-0-00984).

References

1. Ahmad, A.S., et al.: A review on applications of ANN and SVM for building electrical energy consumption forecasting. Renew. Sustain. Energy Rev. **33**, 102–109 (2014)
2. Anderson, O.: Time-Series, 2nd edn (1976)
3. Bahdanau, D., Cho, K., Bengio, Y.: Neural machine translation by jointly learning to align and translate. arXiv preprint arXiv:1409.0473 (2014)
4. Bai, S., Kolter, J.Z., Koltun, V.: An empirical evaluation of generic convolutional and recurrent networks for sequence modeling. arXiv preprint arXiv:1803.01271 (2018)

5. Daubechies, I., DeVore, R., Fornasier, M., Güntürk, C.S.: Iteratively reweighted least squares minimization for sparse recovery. Commun. Pure Appl. Math. J. Issued Courant Inst. Math. Sci. **63**(1), 1–38 (2010)
6. De Vito, S., Massera, E., Piga, M., Martinotto, L., Di Francia, G.: On field calibration of an electronic nose for benzene estimation in an urban pollution monitoring scenario. Sens. Actuators B Chem. **129**(2), 750–757 (2008)
7. Granger, C.W.J., Newbold, P.: Forecasting Economic Time Series. Academic Press, Cambridge (2014)
8. Han, B., et al.: Co-teaching: robust training of deep neural networks with extremely noisy labels. In: Proceedings of the Advances in Neural Information Processing Systems (NeurIPS), pp. 8535–8545 (2018)
9. Hotelling, H.: The generalization of student's ratio. In: Kotz, S., Johnson, N.L. (eds.) Breakthroughs in Statistics, pp. 54–65. Springer, New York (1992). https://doi.org/10.1007/978-1-4612-0919-5_4
10. Hou, C., Wu, J., Cao, B., Fan, J.: A deep-learning prediction model for imbalanced time series data forecasting. Big Data Mining Anal. **4**(4), 266–278 (2021)
11. Huber, P.J.: Robust estimation of a location parameter. In: Kotz, S., Johnson, N.L. (eds.) Breakthroughs in Statistics, pp. 492–518. Springer, New York (1992). https://doi.org/10.1007/978-1-4612-4380-9_35
12. Kitaev, N., Kaiser, L., Levskaya, A.: Reformer: the efficient transformer. In: Proceedings of the International Conference on Learning Representations (ICLR) (2019)
13. Kwiatkowski, D., Phillips, P.C., Schmidt, P., Shin, Y.: Testing the null hypothesis of stationarity against the alternative of a unit root: how sure are we that economic time series have a unit root? J. Econom. **54**(1–3), 159–178 (1992)
14. Lai, G., Chang, W.C., Yang, Y., Liu, H.: Modeling long-and short-term temporal patterns with deep neural networks. In: The 41st International ACM SIGIR Conference on Research & Development in Information Retrieval, pp. 95–104 (2018)
15. Lee, J., Park, J., Kim, D., Lee, J., Choi, E., Choo, J.: Revisiting the importance of amplifying bias for debiasing. In: Proceedings of the AAAI Conference on Artificial Intelligence (AAAI) (2023)
16. Li, S., et al.: Enhancing the locality and breaking the memory bottleneck of transformer on time series forecasting. In: Proceedings of the Advances in Neural Information Processing Systems (NeurIPS) (2019)
17. Lin, T.Y., Goyal, P., Girshick, R.B., He, K., Dollár, P.: Focal loss for dense object detection. In: 2017 IEEE International Conference on Computer Vision (ICCV), pp. 2999–3007 (2017)
18. Liu, S., et al.: Pyraformer: low-complexity pyramidal attention for long-range time series modeling and forecasting. In: Proceedings of the International Conference on Learning Representations (ICLR) (2022)
19. Moniz, N., Branco, P., Torgo, L.: Resampling strategies for imbalanced time series forecasting. Int. J. Data Sci. Anal. **3**(3), 161–181 (2017). https://doi.org/10.1007/s41060-017-0044-3
20. Oreshkin, B.N., Carpov, D., Chapados, N., Bengio, Y.: N-beats: neural basis expansion analysis for interpretable time series forecasting. In: Proceedings of the International Conference on Learning Representations (ICLR) (2019)
21. Salinas, D., Flunkert, V., Gasthaus, J., Januschowski, T.: Deepar: probabilistic forecasting with autoregressive recurrent networks. Int. J. Forecast. **36**(3), 1181–1191 (2020)

22. Salman, A.G., Kanigoro, B., Heryadi, Y.: Weather forecasting using deep learning techniques. In: 2015 International Conference on Advanced Computer Science and Information Systems (ICACSIS), pp. 281–285. IEEE (2015)
23. Vaswani, A., et al.: Attention is all you need. In: Proceedings of the Advances in Neural Information Processing Systems (NeurIPS) (2017)
24. Vlahogianni, E.I., Karlaftis, M.G., Golias, J.C.: Short-term traffic forecasting: where we are and where we're going. Transp. Res. Part C Emerg. Technol. **43**, 3–19 (2014)
25. Welch, B.L.: The significance of the difference between two means when the population variances are unequal. Biometrika **29**(3/4), 350–362 (1938)
26. Wu, H., Xu, J., Wang, J., Long, M.: Autoformer: decomposition transformers with auto-correlation for long-term series forecasting. In: Proceedings of the Advances in Neural Information Processing Systems (NeurIPS) (2021)
27. Yang, Y., Zha, K., Chen, Y.C., Wang, H., Katabi, D.: Delving into deep imbalanced regression. In: Proceedings of the International Conference on Machine Learning (ICML) (2021)
28. Zhang, C., Bengio, S., Hardt, M., Recht, B., Vinyals, O.: Understanding deep learning requires rethinking generalization (2016). http://arxiv.org/abs/1611.03530
29. Zhang, Z., Sabuncu, M.: Generalized cross entropy loss for training deep neural networks with noisy labels. In: Proceedings of the Advances in Neural Information Processing Systems (NeurIPS) (2018)
30. Zhou, H., et al.: Informer: beyond efficient transformer for long sequence time-series forecasting. In: Proceedings of the AAAI Conference on Artificial Intelligence (AAAI) (2021)
31. Zhou, T., Ma, Z., Wen, Q., Wang, X., Sun, L., Jin, R.: Fedformer: frequency enhanced decomposed transformer for long-term series forecasting. In: Proceedings of the International Conference on Machine Learning (ICML) (2022)

Online Deep Hybrid Ensemble Learning for Time Series Forecasting

Amal Saadallah(✉) and Matthias Jakobs

Lamarr Institute for Machine Learning and Artificial Intelligence, TU Dortmund, Dortmund, Germany
{amal.saadallah,matthias.jakobs}@tu-dortmund.de

Abstract. The complex and changing nature of time series data renders forecasting one of the most challenging tasks in time series analysis. It is also commonly acknowledged that no single ML model can be perfectly appropriate for all applications. One solution to tackle this issue is to learn a heterogeneous ensemble by combining a diverse set of forecasters. In addition, ML models usually reveal a time-dependent performance. This can be explained by the fact that different models have varying regions of expertise or so-called Regions of Competence (RoCs) over the time series. In this paper, we propose a novel online deep hybrid ensemble architecture for time series forecasting. The architecture is composed of convolutional layers for learning new enriched time series representation connected to a pool of heterogeneous models composed of classical ML models and neural nets. The models are combined using a weighted average, where the weights are set in a timely adaptive manner using their pre-computed RoCs. The RoCs are computed using a gradient-based approach that maps the performance of these models to input regions in the time series and can therefore be exploited to generate saliency maps that provide suitable explanations for particular ensemble aggregation, i.e., weights setting at a particular time. The RoCs are updated in an informed manner following drift detection in the time series. An extensive empirical study on various real-world datasets demonstrates that our method achieves excellent or on-par results in comparison to the state-of-the-art approaches as well as several baselines.

Keywords: Ensemble Learning · Time Series Forecasting · Aggregation · Regions-of-Competence · Concept Drift · Explainability

This research has partly been funded by the Federal Ministry of Education and Research of Germany and the state of North-Rhine Westphalia as part of the Lamarr-Institute for Machine Learning and Artificial Intelligence.

Supplementary Information The online version contains supplementary material available at https://doi.org/10.1007/978-3-031-43424-2_10.

D. Koutra et al. (Eds.): ECML PKDD 2023, LNAI 14173, pp. 156–171, 2023.
https://doi.org/10.1007/978-3-031-43424-2_10

1 Introduction

Time series forecasting is considered one of the major steps in principled decision-making in a wide range of applications [11,13,19]. However, due to the complex and time-evolving nature of time series, forecasting has also been considered one of the most challenging tasks in time series analysis. Hence, time series may encompass sources of non-stationary variations and, as a result, be most often subject to the so-called concept drift phenomenon [9]. Several Machine Learning (ML) models have been effectively applied to address time series forecasting [4,17,18,21]. In particular, Deep Neural Networks (DNNs) have shown some improvements over previous shallow neural net architectures and have been successfully applied to time series forecasting [16]. Their success is mainly linked to their ability to address non-linearity and capture complex temporal patterns in time series data [16]. Recurrent-based NNs such as Long Short-Term Memory Networks (LSTMs), as well as Convolutional Neural Networks (CNNs), are considered State-of-the-Art (SoA) NN methods in the forecasting task [16]. More recently, particular attention has been given to CNNs due to their proven ability to automatically learn new enriched feature representations from raw input time series data [14]. Nevertheless, it has been proven that in many cases, classical ML models, such as linear autoregression models and exponential smoothing, can be effective in forecasting time series data, especially if the data is rather small and relatively simple [6]. These models are generally faster to train and require less data than deep learning models.

Even though some rules can guide the selection of an adequate family of ML models for forecasting, such as the complexity of the problem and the size of the data [6], it is widely agreed that none of the existing ML models is universally valid for all forecasting problems. This seems to be a direct consequence of the No Free Lunch theorem established by Wolpert [25], which implies that no learning algorithm can be optimal for all learning tasks. Furthermore, ML models can exhibit time-dependent behavior, even when used in the same forecasting application. This means that their accuracy may not remain consistent over time as a result of the aforementioned challenges in time series modeling [17,18]. Therefore, one reasonable solution would be to combine the forecasts of many experts, i.e., models, using an ensemble technique [4,21].

Ensemble learning can be divided into three main stages. The first consists of base model generation, where N multiple possible hypotheses are formulated to model a given time series. Second, ensemble pruning is performed, where only a subset of $M < N$ hypotheses is kept. Finally, ensemble aggregation or combination takes place to combine the predictions of the individual models into one single prediction. More recently, the concept of the so-called Regions of Competence (RoCs) of a forecasting model, i.e., time series parts in which the forecasting model outperforms other candidate models, is shown to be very useful for both online single model selection [17] and ensemble pruning [15,18] in the task of time series forecasting. The determination of the forecasting models' RoCs can be done in several ways. Some works have considered model-agnostic approaches [5,15], while others have focused on specific methods to

DNNs [17,18]. For ensemble aggregation, several approaches, ranging from averaging tactics [19] to applying meta-learning methods [8,24], have been proposed to learn how to combine individual models. Finding the optimal strategy for ensemble aggregation remains an open research question, particularly when the ensemble needs to be updated in real-time [20,22].

In this paper, we leverage both the power of CNNs as powerful feature extractors and ensemble learning to build an online deep hybrid ensemble model for time series forecasting. Hence, the ensemble is composed of many convolutional layers connected to a pool of heterogeneous models, including neural networks and classical ML models. The final prediction is output using a weighted average. We exploit the concept of models' RoCs to set up the weights in a timely adaptive manner. The RoCs of these models are determined using a gradient-based approach that establishes a mapping between the input time series and the performance of the models in the pool. At each time step, the weights are decided using the distance between the recent observed window of time series observations (i.e., lagged values used to compute the forecast) and the pre-computed RoCs. Additionally, the pre-computed RoCs are adaptively updated in an informed manner following concept drift detection in the time series. This adaptation aims at taking into account the probable presence of new concepts in the data when computing RoCs. These RoCs can also be exploited to provide suitable explanations for the reason behind opting for a given aggregation strategy, i.e., particular model weights setting, at a given time instant.

We further conduct an extensive empirical analysis to validate our method using 98 real-world time series datasets from various application domains. The obtained results demonstrate that our method achieves excellent results in comparison to the SoA approaches for online ensemble learning as well as several baselines for time series forecasting. The conducted experiments are fully reproducible, and both code and datasets are publicly available[1]. The main contributions of this paper are thus summarized as follows: We present a novel online deep hybrid ensemble for time series forecasting that combines CNN with a pool of heterogeneous ML models, including neural networks and classical ML models; Ensemble aggregation is performed using gradient-based pre-computed Regions of Competence (RoCs) in a timely adaptive manner following concept drift detection in time series; We exploit the gradient-based RoCs to generate saliency maps that provide suitable explanations for the reason behind opting for a specific aggregation strategy, i.e., weights setting, at a certain time instant. We provide a comparative empirical study with state-of-the-art methods and discuss their implications in terms of predictive performance and scalability.

2 Related Works

Several works in the literature highlighted the usefulness of using online heterogeneous ensembles, i.e., ensembles composed of individual models belonging to

[1] https://github.com/MatthiasJakobs/odh_ets.

different families of ML models [4,5,8,15,22] for time series forecasting, especially when these ensembles are designed to cope with the time-evolving nature of time series and the presence of concept drifts [19–21]. More recently, online ensembles of DNNs have also been successfully applied in the task of time series forecasting [18]. Many of these methods focus on optimizing one or many stages in ensemble learning, and amongst them, ensemble aggregation receives most of the interest [4,5,8,15]. Recent works focused restrictively on the online convex linear weighted combination of individual models [8,20–22]. These works apply different paradigms to estimate the weights of each model. Thus, learning the optimal combination strategy is an important research question [5,22]. In the first part of this section, we briefly describe the State-of-the-Art methods for online model combination in ensemble frameworks. Then, since our aggregation policy is based on the concept of RoCs, the second part of this section is dedicated to ensemble learning using the individual models' RoCs.

2.1 On Online Ensemble Aggregation for Time Series Forecasting

Aggregation strategies in an ensemble can be categorized into three main families [20]. The first family includes averaging approaches. Ensemble models often use simple averaging to combine the outputs of individual models in both forecasting and regression tasks [18]. Weighted averages can also be used with a time-sliding window and a forgetting mechanism to prioritize recent observations [19]. These approaches assume that the immediate future is more likely to resemble the most recent past. The second family relies on the Regret Minimization paradigm, where regret refers to the average error relative to the best possible outcome. Several online ensemble aggregation methods in the literature use regret minimization, including the exponentially and polynomially weighted averages [8], as well as the fixed share aggregation, which tracks the best expert in a time series. Additionally, Zinkevich et al. [26] proposed an approach based on online gradient descent that minimizes regret while guaranteeing theoretical loss bounds. The third family is based on meta-learning. Meta-learning is defined as a way of modeling the learning process of a given algorithm, and it can be exerted for ensemble aggregation to learn combination rules of individual models [4,8,20,22]. One popular approach for meta-learning-based online ensemble aggregation involves using multiple regression on the outcome of individual models. Gaillard and Goude [8] used ridge regression to adaptively estimate the ensemble weights. In [4], a meta-learning approach based on arbitrating, where the weights of individual models are combined based on their predicted loss, is proposed. In the same context, Saadallah et al. [21] introduced a meta-learning framework based on adaptive clustering. This method performs an online adaptive clustering of candidate models after selecting them using a drift-aware method. Finally, cluster representatives are integrated into a sliding-window weighted ensemble. More recently, Deep Reinforcement Learning (DRL) was leveraged as an online aggregation meta-learning procedure for learning linearly weighted ensembles [20,22]. In these works, the aggregation policy in ensembles is modeled as a sequential decision-making process and an actor-critic DRL-based approach that aims at learning the optimal weights of models in a continuous action space is used.

2.2 On Ensemble Learning Using RoCs

The concept of Regions of Competence (RoCs) has been used for ensemble learning, more precisely for ensemble pruning, i.e., the selection of individual models to take part in the ensemble [4,5,15], in the forecasting task. In [15], at test time, the most similar pattern to the current input (i.e., in our case, time series input sequence) is determined, and the model with the smallest error is selected for prediction. In [4,5], meta-learning is used to build models capable of modeling the competence of each ensemble member across the input space. The authors frame their ensemble learning as a ranking task, in which ensemble members are ranked sequentially by their decreasing weight (i.e., the one predicted to perform better is ranked first). Correlation among the output of the individual models is used to quantify their redundancy. A given individual model is penalized for its correlation to each individual model already ranked. If it is fully correlated with other individual models already ranked, its weight becomes zero. Opposingly, if it is completely uncorrelated with its ranked peers, it gets ranked with its original weight. In the above methods, the meta-models responsible for computing the RoCs are kept static over time. Only distances or error comparison is performed online in a blind manner at each time step, i.e., without taking into account the occurrence of significant changes in either the time series data or the performance of the candidate models. More recently, In [17], the authors use the most salient parts of the time series, called the models Region of Competence, to forecast new, unseen data points by comparing the new data to its historical record using an ensemble of DNNs. To extract these Regions of Competence, they use a variation of Grad-CAM [23], a gradient-based heat mapping method for highlighting important input regions in CNNs used for computer vision applications. Although the RoCs are updated following concept drift detection in time series, the proposed method is specific to a particular class of DNNs, namely Convolutional Neural Networks (CNNs). In this work, we exploit the gradient-based approach presented in [17] and generalize it to an ensemble of heterogeneous pool models connected to CNN layers devised to enable the extraction of meaningful time series representation and compute the RoCs of the models in the pool. These RoCs are used to attribute weights to the ensemble members in a timely manner and provide suitable explanations for these weights at a given time instant. The RoCs are updated in an informed manner following concept drift detection in time series.

3 Methodology

In this section, we present our method and its main stages. In the first stage, we design the hybrid network architecture that encompasses the pool of models. The second stage consists of determining the gradient-based RoCs of these models using time-sliding windows over a validation set. In the third stage, to generate a forecast at a given time t_f, the predictions of the individual models in the pool are combined using an RoC-based weighted average. The ensemble aggregation is also made in an adaptive, informed manner following concept drift detection in the time series. In addition, the RoCs can be used to provide suitable explanations for the reason for using particular weights at a particular point in time. Practical examples of explanations are presented in detail in Sect. 4. Our framework is referred to as **ODH-ETS**: Online Deep Hybrid Ensemble learning for Time Series forecasting in the rest of the paper.

3.1 Preliminaries

A time series X is a temporal sequence of values, where $X_{1:t} = \{x_1, x_2, \cdots, x_t\}$ is a sequence of X recorded until time t and x_i is the value of X at time i. Denote with $\mathbb{M} = \{M_1, M_2, \cdots, M_N\}$ a pool of N trained models. Let $\hat{x} = (\hat{x}_{t+f}^{M_1}, \hat{x}_{t+f}^{M_2}, \cdots, \hat{x}_{t+f}^{M_N})$ be the vector of forecast values of X at time instant $t+f, f \geq 1$ (i.e. x_{t+f}) by each of the models in $\mathbb{M}$. It is possible to formally write an ensemble of these N models for predicting x_{t+f} as a convex combination of their individual predictions at $t+f$.

$$\hat{x}_{t+f}^{E} = \sum_{j=1}^{N} w_{t+f}^{M_j} \hat{x}_{t+f}^{M_j}, \tag{1}$$

where $w_{t+f}^{M_j}, j \in \{1, \cdots, N\}$, determine the weights attributed to the model M_j. The weights are time-dependent as the optimal weight setting (i.e., aggregation strategy) should naturally be dependent on the dynamics of the time series data that change over time. In our work, the weights are adapted over time using timely computed distances between the current input time sequence of l-lagged values and the individual models' RoCs. We divide the time series X_t into $X_\omega^{train} = \{x_1, x_2, \cdots, x_{t-\omega}\}$ and $X_\omega^{val} = \{x_{t-\omega+1}, x_{t-\omega+2}, \cdots, x_t\}$, where ω is a provided window size. X_ω^{train} is used for training the ensemble, and X_ω^{val} is used to compute the RoCs since, to measure model performance, both true and predicted values of the time series are required. The RoCs are computed over many time windows in the validation. These windows are obtained by performing time-sliding window operations by one step of size $n_\omega, n_\omega < \omega$ over X_ω^{val}. These windows are denoted by $X_{n_\omega}^{val,i}$ with $i \in [1, Z]$ and Z is the total number of resulting windows.

3.2 Ensemble Architecture

ODH-ETS is composed of multiple convolutional layers connected to the pool $\mathbb{M}$ composed of N forecasting models belonging to different families of ML models. The architecture of **ODH-ETS** is shown in Fig. 1.

The introduction of the convolutional layers is motivated by their ability to learn new time series representations but also by the enriched spatial information

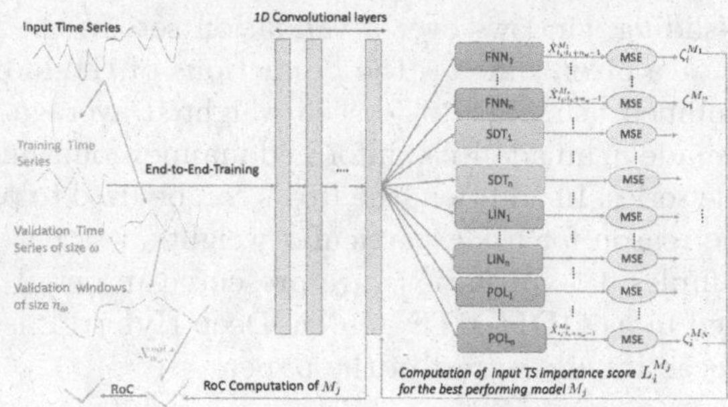

Fig. 1. ODH-ETS Architecture and Framework.

encompassed in the feature maps produced by the last convolutional layer that enables the computation of gradient-based saliency maps, which highlight important regions in the input time series. The importance can be defined with regard to the predicted output or to any other differentiable measure related to the predictive part linked to the convolutional layers. Performance Gradient-based Saliency Maps were introduced in [17] but restrictively used with CNNs. However, since only gradient information about the performance of each individual model given by its loss is required, PGSMs can be used with any ML model that can be trained with gradient descent. Therefore, we constructed a pool $\mathbb{M}$ composed of Feed Forward Neural Networks (FNNs), Soft Decision Trees (SDTs), Linear regression models (LINs), and Polynomial regression models (POLs), each with different hyperparameters. The candidate models are trained on X_ω^{train} in an end-to-end manner in conjunction with the feature extractor.

3.3 RoCs Computation

To compute the RoCs, the error of each model $M_j, j \in \{1, \cdots, N\}$ in $\mathbb{M}$ is evaluated using the Mean Squared Error, ζ_j^i on $X_{n_\omega}^{val,i}$, i.e., the ith time interval window of X_ω^{val} of size n_ω, $\zeta_i^{M_j} = MSE(X_{t_i:t_i+n_\omega-1}, \hat{X}_{t_i:t_i+n_\omega-1}^{M_j})$, where MSE is the Mean Square Error, $X_{t_i:t_i+n_\omega-1}$ $\hat{X}_{t_i:t_i+n_\omega-1}^{M_j}$ are the true and predicted values of X by the model M_j over $X_{n_\omega}^{val,i}$. The objective is to determine the significance of each time point in $X_{n_\omega}^{val,i}$ with respect to a specific performance of M_j This approach is similar to Grad-CAM, which utilizes spatial information preserved in convolutional layers to identify important regions of an input image for classification [23]. However, in this case, the focus is on the temporal information that explains certain behaviors of M_j. The last feature maps f_{maps} layer is utilized for this purpose. Importance weights α^ζ associated with $\zeta_i^{M_j}$ are computed for each activation unit u in each generic feature map A by calculating the gradient of $\zeta_i^{M_j}$ relative to A. Finally, a global average is computed over all units in A: $\alpha_i^{M_j} = \frac{1}{U} \sum_u \frac{\partial \zeta_i^{M_j}}{\partial A_u}$, where U is the total number of units in A. We use $\alpha_i^{M_j}$ to compute a weighted combination between all the feature maps for a given measured value of the error $\zeta_i^{M_j}$. Since we are mainly interested in highlighting temporal features contributing most to $\zeta_i^{M_j}$, ReLU is used to remove all the negative contributions by: $L_i^{M_j} = ReLU(\sum_{f_{maps}} \alpha_i^{M_j} A)$. To identify the regions in $X_{n_\omega}^{val,i}$ that primarily contributed to $\zeta_i^{M_j}$, $L_i^{M_j} \in \mathbb{R}^U$ is used. Note that U is chosen such that $U < n_\omega$. Multiple time windows of size n_ω are created from X_ω^{val} to evaluate the performance of the same model on different windows and increase the number of RoCs. An RoC buffer RoC^{M_j} is created for each model M_j. The models are ranked for each $X_{n_\omega}^{val,i}$, and only the RoC of the best model is computed. The models in $\mathbb{M}$ use the same l-lagged values of the time series as input. Therefore, we reject the smoothed RoCs with lengths different from l in order to constrain the RoCs lengths to l. The RoCs of a given model M_j in $\mathbb{M}$ are already collected in an RoC buffer $RoC^{M_j} = \{R_1^{M_j}, R_2^{M_j}, \cdots, R_{n_j}^{M_j}\}$, where n_j is the total number of regions of competence determined for M_j.

3.4 Ensemble Aggregation

At test time, in order to forecast the value of X at $t+f, f \geq 1$, one possible way is to use a weighted average to aggregate the individual predictions of the models in $\mathbb{M}$. The weights can be inferred from the pre-computed RoCs by measuring the distance/similarity between the input pattern $X_{t+f-l:t+f-1} = \{x_{t+f-l}, \cdots, x_{t+f-1}\}$ and the RoCs for each model in $\mathbb{M}$. The Euclidean Distance (ED) is used to measure the similarity between $X_{t+f-l:t+f-1}$ and each $R_z^{M_j}, \forall z \in [1, n_j]$ within each $RoC^{M_j}, \forall j \in \{1, \cdots, N\}$ buffer. For each model $M_j, \forall j \in \{1, \cdots, N\}$, the RoC $\mathcal{R}^{M_j}$ satisfying:

$$\mathcal{R}^{M_j} = \underset{R_z^{M_j} \in RoC^{M_j}}{\operatorname{argmin}} \; ED(R_z^{M_j}, X_{t+f-l:t+f-1}) \tag{2}$$

is selected to represent M_j for the ensemble aggregation for $t+f$. The weights are set such that the lower the distance between the models' representative RoCs $\mathcal{R}^{M_j}, \forall j \in \{1, \cdots, N\}$ and the current input pattern is, the higher the weight gets. This can be explained by the fact that the models' representative RoCs can be viewed as an approximation of the current input pattern. In other words, the prediction by M_j of the data points in $X_{t+f-l:t+f-1}$ are represented approximately by the data points $r_q^{M_j} \in \mathcal{R}^{M_j}, \forall q \in [1, l]$: $x_{t+f-1+q-l} \approx r_q^{M_j}, \forall q \in [1, l], t \geq l-1$. Therefore, the computed EDs between $X_{t+f-l:t+f-1}$ and $\mathcal{R}^{M_j}, \forall j \in \{1, \cdots, N\}$ can be considered as losses estimation of the models in $\mathbb{M}$ on the most recent pattern.

$$w_{t+f}^{M_j} = \sigma(\mathbf{w_{t+f}})^{M_j} = \frac{e^{-ED(\mathcal{R}^{M_j}, X_{t+f-l:t+f-1})}}{\sum_{M_j \in \mathbb{M}} e^{-ED(\mathcal{R}^{M_j}, X_{t+f-l:t+f-1})}} \tag{3}$$

where $\mathbf{w_{t+f}} = \{w_{t+f}^{M_1}, \cdots, w_{t+f}^{M_N}\}$ and σ is the softmax function to ensure that the combination is convex. The final prediction is the weighted average of the predictions given by Eq. 1.

3.5 Ensemble Adaptation

As previously stated, the ROCs are initially computed using the validation set X_{ω}^{val} offline. However, since time series exhibit dynamic behavior, streaming new values can lead to significant changes, such as concept drifts. Therefore, the ROCs need to be updated to account for these changes and to identify the most appropriate models to handle these new patterns. Note that the previously computed ROCs are preserved and enhanced with the new ones. When a concept drift is detected, an alarm is triggered to update the ROCs by sliding X_{ω}^{val} to include the new observations. To detect concept drifts, we monitor the deviation $\Delta\mathcal{M}_{X_{1:t_f}}$ in the mean of the time series recorded till time t_f [21]. Here, $\Delta\mathcal{M}_{X_{1:t_f}}$ is defined as $\mathbb{E}(\mathcal{M}_{X_{1:t_f}}) - \mu$, where μ is the initial computed mean of $X_{1:t}$ up to time t (i.e., $t \leq t_f$). A drift is assumed to have occurred at t_f if the true mean of $\Delta\mathcal{M}_{X_{1:t_f}}$ significantly diverges from 0. To determine this, we use the well-known Hoeffding-Bound [12], which states that after ω independent observations of a real-value random variable with range R, its true mean has not diverged if the sample mean is contained within $\pm\xi_{\mathcal{M}}$. Here, $\xi_{\mathcal{M}}$ is defined as: $\xi_{\mathcal{M}} = \sqrt{\frac{R^2 \ln(1/\delta)}{2\omega}}$ with a probability of $1-\delta$, a user-defined hyperparameter. Once $\left|\Delta\mathcal{M}_{t_f}\right|$ exceeds $\xi_{\mathcal{M}}$, an alarm is triggered, and the reference mean μ is reset by setting $t = t_f$. This procedure is continuously applied online during the forecasting time.

4 Experiments

We present the experiments carried out to validate **ODH-ETS** and to answer the following research questions: **Q1:** How does **ODH-ETS** perform compared to the state-of-the-art (SoA) and existing deep learning and online ensemble aggregation methods for time series forecasting?; **Q2:** What is the advantage of using the RoCs concept for the online ensemble aggregation?; **Q3:** What is the advantage of using a heterogeneous pool of models in **ODH-ETS**?; **Q4:** What is the advantage of updating the RoCs in an informed fashion (i.e., following drift detection)?; **Q5:** How scalable is **ODH-ETS** in terms of computational resources compared to the most competitive online ensemble aggregation methods? What is the computational advantage of the drift-aware adaption of the models' RoCs?; **Q6:** How can the RoCs be exploited to provide suitable explanations for the reason behind specific weights setting at a certain time interval or instant?

4.1 Experimental Set-Up

The methods used in the experiments were evaluated using the root mean squared error (RMSE). The time series data used in the experiments were split into three portions: 50% for training (X_{ω}^{train}), 25% for validation (X_{ω}^{val}), and 25% for testing. The results were compared using the non-parametric Wilcoxon Signed Rank test. A total of 98 real-world time series were utilized, originating from diverse application scenarios, including audio data, sensor readings, and financial forecasting. The code repository contains a comprehensive list of all the datasets used, accompanied by their descriptions[2]. The datasets are also included in the supplementary material.

4.2 ODH-ETS Setup and Baselines

We construct a pool $\mathbb{M}$ of heterogeneous ML models (Feed Forward Neural Networks (FNNs), Soft Decision Trees (SDTs), Linear regression models (LINs), and Polynomial regression models (POLs)). By varying the hyperparameters values of these models, we obtain a pool $\mathbb{M}$ of size 25. The pool $\mathbb{M}$ takes as input the time series representation created by the CNN-based feature extractor, which is composed of one 1-D Convolutional Layer with 64 filters and a size of 3, followed by a ReLU activation and a Dropout with $p = 0.3$. Afterward, we utilize a final 1-D Convolutional Layer with 32 filters to create the extracted features. **ODH-ETS** also has a number of hyper-parameters: l is the number of lagged values, i.e., size of the input to **ODH-ETS** $X_{t+f-l:t+f-1}$: 5; ω is the size of validation set: 25% of the dataset length; n_ω is the size of time windows within the validation set: 20; δ is the Hoeffding-Bound parameter: 0.05. We compare **ODH-ETS** against the following approaches, which include SoA methods for forecasting and ensemble aggregation methods devised in the context of forecasting. Some of them operate in an online fashion.

SoA Forecasting Models. We compare **ODH-ETS** against the AutoRegressive Integrated Moving Average **ARIMA** [1] and Exponential Smoothing **ETS** [1]. We also included ensemble-based regression models, precisely Random Forest **RF** [2]. We also add three popular SoA DNNs for forecasting, namely **LSTM** [10], **CNN** [16] and **CNN-LSTM** [16]. We also compare **ODH-ETS** against recent benchmarking DNN-based models for forecasting [11], namely **DeepAR**, **N-BEATS**, and the **Transformer**.

Online Ensemble Aggregation Methods. We feed the same pool $\mathbb{M}$ individual models of **ODH-ETS** to all the ensemble methods used for comparison: **SE** [7]: An ensemble model that averages the models in $\mathbb{M}$ using arithmetic mean; **SWE** [19]: A linear online combination of predictions of the models in $\mathbb{M}$, in which the weights are set based upon recent performance over a time sliding window; **EWA** [8]: An online ensemble combination using Exponential Weighted Average; **FS** [8]: The fixed share approach from Herbster and Warmuth is designed for the online tracking of the best expert across the time series; **OGD** [8]: An aggregation approach based on online gradient descent that provides theoretical loss-bound guarantees; **Top-Sel** [21]: A drift-aware method for selecting the Top-best performing models in $\mathbb{M}$ and combining them using **SWE**; **DEMSC** [21]: A drift-aware combination of **Top-Sel** for ensemble pruning and model clustering for diversity enhancement to construct the **SWE**-based ensemble model; **OEA-DRL** [20]: A drift-aware method that uses Deep RL for learning linearly

[2] https://github.com/MatthiasJakobs/odh_ets.

weighting combination policy. The policy is updated at test time following drift detection in the time series; **DETS** [5]: An advanced version of SWE, selecting a subset of members based on recent errors and using a smoothing function on the average of recent errors for weighting.

Online Ensemble RoCs-Based Methods. **KNN-RoC** [15]: computes static RoCs using a validation set as input and the rank of the individual candidates on each interval as labels for a *KNN* classifier, using DTW distance. At test time, the *KNN* predicts which candidate models from $\mathbb{M}$ should be selected; **ADE** [4,5]: is an online dynamic ensemble where a meta-learning strategy is used that specializes the models in $\mathbb{M}$ across the time series to determine their RoCs. In addition, model weighting is applied based on the estimated errors combined with a softmax. Weights are additionally adapted to take diversity between ensemble members into account; **OEP-RoC** [18]: is an online drift-aware ensemble of DNNs pruning method that uses gradient-based RoCs specifically for CNN-based single models. The final selected CNNs are combined using a simple average. Since our method is based on the same principle for computing the RoCs, we include the comparison to OEP-RoC to show the advantage of including a gradient-based trainable heterogeneous pool of models and exploiting the RoC for weighting which can implicitly solve the pruning stage.

***ODH-ETS** Variations.* We also compare **ODH-ETS** with some variants of itself. Note that **ODH-ETS** uses the Hoeffding-based drift detection mechanism to update the RoCs: **ODH-ETS-NoW**: Uses **ODH-ETS** architecture but no weighting is involved. The models in $\mathbb{M}$ are combined using a simple average; **ODH-ETS-St**: Same as our method, but the RoCs are not updated using the drift detection mechanism. The RoCs are computed and stored offline; only the selection takes place online; **ODH-ETS-Per**: Same as our method, but the RoCs are updated periodically in a blind manner (i.e., without taking into account the occurrence of concept drift) with periodicity each upcoming 10% data points.

4.3 Results

Table 1 presents the average ranks and their deviation for all methods. For the paired comparison, we compare our method **ODH-ETS** against each of the other methods. We counted wins and losses for each dataset using the RMSE scores. We use the non-parametric Wilcoxon Signed Rank test to compute significant wins and losses, which are presented in parenthesis (significance level 0.05).

The pairwise comparison results presented in Table 1 demonstrate that **ODH-ETS** performs better than the baseline methods. Online drift-aware ensemble approaches, including Top-Sel and DESCM, exhibit poorer performance than **ODH-ETS**, while online RoC-based ensemble models such as ADE, OEP-RoC, and KNN-RoC also fare worse. Although online aggregation methods that employ regret-minimization principles, namely EWA, FS, and OGD, perform better than these methods, they still lag behind **ODH-ETS**. ARIMA, ETS, CNN-LSTM, and CNN, which are state-of-the-art forecasting methods,

Table 1. Comparison between **ODH-ETS** and different SoA for 98 time series. The rank column presents the average rank achieved by each model, with a rank of 1 indicating the best performance across all datasets.

Method	ARIMA	ETS	RF	LSTM	CNN
Losses/Wins	0(0)/98(98)	0(0)/98(98)	0(0)/98(96)	25(19)/73(69)	16(13)/82(74)
Avg. Rank	20.04 ± 0.83	21.5 ± 0.87	15.16 ± 2.08	6.52 ± 6.51	9.46 ± 6.63
Method	CNN-LSTM	DeepAR	N-BEATS	Transformer	SE
Losses/Wins	22(18)/76(68)	23(18)/75(70)	20(15)/78(67)	24(17)/74(69)	18(15)/80(73)
Avg. Rank	7.76 ± 6.64	9.80 ± 8.17	7.12 ± 8.18	9.56 ± 7.82	10.4 ± 3.6
Method	SWE	ADE	DETS	DEMSC	KNN-RoC
Losses/Wins	12(8)/86(84)	13(4)/85(70)	16(3)/83(68))	32(13)/67(51)	34(19)/64(50)
Avg. Rank	13.8 ± 3.5	11.18 ± 3.80	10.81 ± 4.06	6.40 ± 4.23	6.35 ± 4.86
Method	OEP-RoC	Top-Sel	EWA	FS	OGD
Losses/Wins	18(10)/81(69)	41(7)/57(48)	44(24)/54(38)	41(20)/57(41)	43(24)/55(39)
Avg. Rank	12.01 ± 4.0	5.19 ± 3.20	4.39 ± 2.90	4.64 ± 4.07	4.50 ± 2.5
Method	OEA-DRL	**ODH-ETS**-NoW	**ODH-ETS**-St	**ODH-ETS**-Per	**ODH-ETS**
Losses/Wins	49(16)/49(33)	35(5)/63(39)	67(3)/32(24)	53(20)/45(29)	-/-
Avg. Rank	3.91 ± 3.31	4.04 ± 3.11	3.33 ± 4.11	3.37 ± 3.9	2.95 ± 3.52

have a considerably lower average rank than **ODH-ETS**. LSTM performs better than these individual baselines but is still significantly worse than **ODH-ETS**. Similarly, the latest DNNs used for forecasting, such as DeepAR, N-BEATS, and Transformer, are also inferior to **ODH-ETS**. The most competitive SoA approach to **ODH-ETS** is OEA-DRL, which is based on an online Deep Reinforcement procedure for aggregation, but it has a higher average rank and lower performance than all variants of our method that use the RoCs-based weighting. These findings demonstrate that our RoCs-based weighting scheme outperforms other ensemble aggregation methods, including simple and sliding-window averaging (SE, SWE, and DETS), regret-minimization (EWA, FS, and OGD), and meta-learning (ADE, Top-Sel, DESCM, and OEA-DRL). The performance of **ODH-ETS**-NoW, which is a variant of **ODH-ETS** that combines the outputs of models in the pool $\mathbb{M}$ using a simple average, also underscores the importance of RoCs-based weighting. In summary, these results address research questions **Q1** and **Q2**.

When comparing OEP-RoC, which uses gradient-based RoCs restrictively for an pruned ensemble of CNNs simply averages their predictions, there is a significant difference to **ODH-ETS** in the average rank. Specifically, OEP-RoC has an average rank that is almost four times higher than **ODH-ETS**. This highlights the advantage of not only using RoCs for the ensemble aggregation stage, which may implicitly solve the pruning stage by setting some of the weights to zero but also considering a heterogeneous pool of individual models. The benefits of this in the performance of **ODH-ETS** can be attributed to the fact that a heterogeneous pool of models enhances ensemble diversity, which affects the variance-type ensemble error [3,21]. In fact, diversity is reflected in the unique patterns of each model's inductive bias derived from the different hypotheses on which it is built to model the input time series data and its dependence structure. These findings address research question **Q3**.

ODH-ETS, which relies on an informed adaption of the RoCs using concept drift detection, is better than **ODH-ETS**-Per and **ODH-ETS**-St. This can be explained by the fact that the update of RoCs is only beneficial for datasets where concept drifts can be detected. Taking into account these newly appearing concepts is helpful for selecting models since knowledge of which models are more suitable to handle these patterns can be gained, and the old sets of RoCs are enriched. Additionally, we observe that **ODH-ETS**-St performs even better than **ODH-ETS**-Per, demonstrating that unnecessary updates are not always beneficial. This answers the research questions **Q4**.

The next experiment involves comparing the runtime of **ODH-ETS** and its variations with OEA-DRL, the most competitive SoA method, as shown in Table 1. Only the online operations are considered while reporting the runtime. **ODH-ETS** and **ODH-ETS**-Per consider possible new RoCs' computation after drift detection. OEA-DRL [20] also employs drift-aware updates of the aggregation policy with Deep Reinforcement Learning. The results in Table 2 show that **ODH-ETS** and its variations have a significantly lower average runtime than OEA-DRL. **ODH-ETS** exhibits lower runtime compared to **ODH-ETS**-Per due to the use of drift detection to update the RoCs only when required. This leads to faster predictions and fewer computational requirements. The wide range of runtime deviation for **ODH-ETS** is attributed to the varying number of drifts in each time series. This answers the research question **Q5**.

Table 2. Empirical runtime comparison between different methods in Seconds.

Method	OEA-DRL	**ODH-ETS**	**ODH-ETS**-St	**ODH-ETS**-Per
Avg. Runtime	33.06	6.12	2.60	12.42
±	16.40	4.00	0.30	2.15

Last but not least, we provide some insights into how the RoCs in **ODH-ETS** can be used to provide suitable explanations for the reason behind specific ensemble weights setting at a specific time instant.

We can see from the barplot on the left side of Fig. 2 the values of the weights attributed to the different models in $\mathbb{M}$. The right side shows a comparison between the current input pattern that will be fed to the models in the pool $\mathbb{M}$ composing **ODH-ETS** to forecast the next value and the pre-computed closest and furthest RoCs representative of two models in the pool $\mathbb{M}$ at the current time instant (See Eq. 2). We can see that the model with the furthest RoC from the current pattern gets the lowest weight. In fact, the visualization shows that this model is incompetent at predicting based on the current input pattern, as the closest pattern to the current one on which this model is the most competent (marked in red) is clearly very different from the current input pattern. This

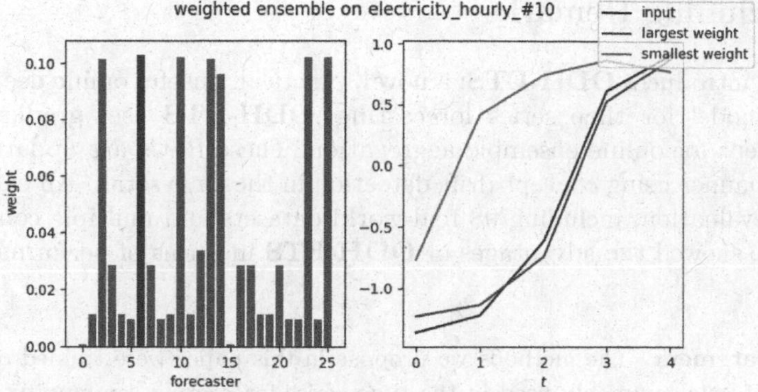

Fig. 2. A visualization of an example of aggregation on the Electricity data.

incompetence of the model explains why it gets the lowest weight, which is zero, and this is the case for another model in the pool. This also shows that our RoC-based aggregation can implicitly serve the pruning stage, resulting thus in an ensemble of smaller size by excluding incompetent models. Opposingly, the model with the closest RoC (marked in green) reveals a higher competence in handling such input pattern and gets, therefore, the highest weight, which confirms the coherence of the design of our aggregation method. This answers research question **Q6**.

4.4 Discussion

The empirical results indicate that **ODH-ETS** has performance advantages compared to popular forecasting methods and the most recent SoA approaches for online forecasting. We show that our method, using adaptive gradient-based RoCs of a heterogeneous pool of forecasters, is able to gain excellent and reliable empirical performance in our setting. The informed update of the RoCs following concept drift detection makes our method, in addition to better predictive performance, computationally cheaper than the most competitive SoA, namely OEA-DRL. **ODH-ETS** can also successfully be used for providing useful explanations behind ensemble aggregation, which can be used to explain the models' competence across different regions in the time series and optimize our framework further, e.g., by removing the models that always get weights equal to zero from the pool. In future work, we plan to enlarge the pool of candidate models. We also aim to investigate the impact of the length of the input pattern, i.e., the number of lags used for training the model pool, on the RoCs creation. In addition, the possible resulting large number of RoCs can be optimized further using a clustering inside each RoC^j for each model. Only cluster representatives are considered for distance computation to select the best model.

5 Concluding Remarks

This paper introduces **ODH-ETS**: a novel, practically useful online deep hybrid ensemble model for time series forecasting. **ODH-ETS** uses gradient-based RoCs concept for online ensemble aggregation. These RoCs are updated in an informed manner using concept drift detection in the time series. An exhaustive empirical evaluation, including 98 real-world datasets and multiple comparison algorithms, showed the advantages of **ODH-ETS** in terms of performance and scalability.

Ethical Statement. The methods we propose in this paper were trained on widely available datasets commonly used in the time-series forecasting community. They do not contain personal data. Additionally, we did not include any additional data that might contain personal information. Should our methods be applied to sensitive data by a third party, we caution the use of the explainability methods utilized in this work to draw quick conclusions that might impact people or institutions without an additional, rigorous evaluation of the results first. Our methods can be used in general for time-series forecasting and do not specifically target application scenarios where people's well-being is at stake. To summarize, to the best of our knowledge, our work does not have negative ethical implications.

References

1. Box, G.E., Jenkins, G.M., Reinsel, G.C., Ljung, G.M.: Time Series Analysis: Forecasting and Control. Wiley, Hoboken (2015)
2. Breiman, L.: Bagging predictors. Mach. Learn. **24**(2), 123–140 (1996)
3. Brown, G., Wyatt, J.L., Tiňo, P.: Managing diversity in regression ensembles. J. Mach. Learn. Res. **6**(Sep), 1621–1650 (2005)
4. Cerqueira, V., Torgo, L., Pinto, F., Soares, C.: Arbitrated ensemble for time series forecasting. In: Ceci, M., Hollmén, J., Todorovski, L., Vens, C., Džeroski, S. (eds.) ECML PKDD 2017. LNCS (LNAI), vol. 10535, pp. 478–494. Springer, Cham (2017). https://doi.org/10.1007/978-3-319-71246-8_29
5. Cerqueira, V., Torgo, L., Pinto, F., Soares, C.: Arbitrage of forecasting experts. Mach. Learn. **108**(6), 913–944 (2018). https://doi.org/10.1007/s10994-018-05774-y
6. Cerqueira, V., Torgo, L., Soares, C.: Machine learning vs statistical methods for time series forecasting: size matters. arXiv preprint arXiv:1909.13316 (2019)
7. Clemen, R.T., Winkler, R.L.: Combining economic forecasts. J. Bus. Econ. Stat. **4**(1), 39–46 (1986)
8. Gaillard, P., Goude, Y.: opera: Online Prediction by Expert Aggregation (2016). R package version 1.0. https://CRAN.R-project.org/package=opera
9. Gama, J., Žliobaitė, I., Bifet, A., Pechenizkiy, M., Bouchachia, A.: A survey on concept drift adaptation. ACM Comput. Surv. (CSUR) **46**(4), 1–37 (2014)
10. Gers, F.A., Eck, D., Schmidhuber, J.: Applying LSTM to time series predictable through time-window approaches. In: Tagliaferri, R., Marinaro, M. (eds.) Neural Nets, pp. 193–200. Springer, London (2002). https://doi.org/10.1007/978-1-4471-0219-9_20

11. Godahewa, R., Bergmeir, C., Webb, G.I., Hyndman, R.J., Montero-Manso, P.: Monash time series forecasting archive. In: Neural Information Processing Systems Track on Datasets and Benchmarks (2021, forthcoming)
12. Hoeffding, W.: Probability inequalities for sums of bounded random variables. In: Fisher, N.I., Sen, P.K. (eds.) The Collected Works of Wassily Hoeffding, pp. 409–426. Springer, New York (1994). https://doi.org/10.1007/978-1-4612-0865-5_26
13. Hyndman, R.J., Koehler, A.B., Snyder, R.D., Grose, S.: A state space framework for automatic forecasting using exponential smoothing methods. Int. J. Forecast. **18**(3), 439–454 (2002)
14. Ismail Fawaz, H., Forestier, G., Weber, J., Idoumghar, L., Muller, P.-A.: Deep learning for time series classification: a review. Data Min. Knowl. Disc. **33**(4), 917–963 (2019). https://doi.org/10.1007/s10618-019-00619-1
15. Priebe, F.: Dynamic model selection for automated machine learning in time series (2019)
16. Romeu, P., Zamora-Martínez, F., Botella-Rocamora, P., Pardo, J.: Time-series forecasting of indoor temperature using pre-trained deep neural networks. In: Mladenov, V., Koprinkova-Hristova, P., Palm, G., Villa, A.E.P., Appollini, B., Kasabov, N. (eds.) ICANN 2013. LNCS, vol. 8131, pp. 451–458. Springer, Heidelberg (2013). https://doi.org/10.1007/978-3-642-40728-4_57
17. Saadallah, A., Jakobs, M., Morik, K.: Explainable online deep neural network selection using adaptive saliency maps for time series forecasting. In: Oliver, N., Pérez-Cruz, F., Kramer, S., Read, J., Lozano, J.A. (eds.) ECML PKDD 2021. LNCS (LNAI), vol. 12975, pp. 404–420. Springer, Cham (2021). https://doi.org/10.1007/978-3-030-86486-6_25
18. Saadallah, A., Jakobs, M., Morik, K.: Explainable online ensemble of deep neural network pruning for time series forecasting. Mach. Learn. **111**(9), 3459–3487 (2022)
19. Saadallah, A., Moreira-Matias, L., Sousa, R., Khiari, J., Jenelius, E., Gama, J.: Bright-drift-aware demand predictions for taxi networks. IEEE Trans. Knowl. Data Eng. **32**(2), 234–245 (2018)
20. Saadallah, A., Morik, K.: Online ensemble aggregation using deep reinforcement learning for time series forecasting. In: 2021 IEEE 8th International Conference on Data Science and Advanced Analytics (DSAA). IEEE (2021)
21. Saadallah, A., Priebe, F., Morik, K.: A drift-based dynamic ensemble members selection using clustering for time series forecasting. In: Brefeld, U., Fromont, E., Hotho, A., Knobbe, A., Maathuis, M., Robardet, C. (eds.) ECML PKDD 2019. LNCS (LNAI), vol. 11906, pp. 678–694. Springer, Cham (2020). https://doi.org/10.1007/978-3-030-46150-8_40
22. Saadallah, A., Tavakol, M., Morik, K.: An actor-critic ensemble aggregation model for time-series forecasting. In: IEEE ICDE (2021)
23. Selvaraju, R.R., Cogswell, M., Das, A., Vedantam, R., Parikh, D., Batra, D.: Grad-cam: visual explanations from deep networks via gradient-based localization. In: Proceedings of the IEEE International Conference on Computer Vision (2017)
24. Wolpert, D.H.: Stacked generalization. Neural Netw. **5**(2), 241–259 (1992)
25. Wolpert, D.H.: The lack of a priori distinctions between learning algorithms. Neural Comput. **8**(7), 1341–1390 (1996)
26. Zinkevich, M.: Online convex programming and generalized infinitesimal gradient ascent. In: Proceedings of the 20th International Conference on Machine Learning (ICML 2003), pp. 928–936 (2003)

Sparse Transformer Hawkes Process for Long Event Sequences

Zhuoqun Li and Mingxuan Sun(✉)

Louisiana State University, Baton Rouge, LA 70803, USA
{zli82,msun11}@lsu.edu

Abstract. Large quantities of asynchronous event sequence data such as crime records, emergence call logs, and financial transactions are becoming increasingly available from various fields. These event sequences often exhibit both long-term and short-term temporal dependencies. Variations of neural network based temporal point processes have been widely used for modeling such asynchronous event sequences. However, many current architectures including attention based point processes struggle with long event sequences due to computational inefficiency. To tackle the challenge, we propose an efficient sparse transformer Hawkes process (STHP), which has two components. For the first component, a transformer with a novel temporal sparse self-attention mechanism is applied to event sequences with arbitrary intervals, mainly focusing on short-term dependencies. For the second component, a transformer is applied to the time series of aggregated event counts, primarily targeting the extraction of long-term periodic dependencies. Both components complement each other and are fused together to model the conditional intensity function of a point process for future event forecasting. Experiments on real-world datasets show that the proposed STHP outperforms baselines and achieves significant improvement in computational efficiency without sacrificing prediction performance for long sequences.

Keywords: Temporal point process · Long sequence forecasting · Sparse self-attention

1 Introduction

Event sequence data such as electronic patient diagnosis records, crime reports, disaster rescue events, and financial transactions are becoming increasingly available from various fields such as healthcare [22], predicted policing [16], and financial markets [1]. Different from traditional time series where observations are recorded at regular time intervals, the asynchronous event sequences contain events with arbitrary time stamps in continuous-time domain and the intervals between events are as crucial as the sequential order in modeling the dynamics [18]. Moreover, event sequences frequently demonstrate short-term and long-term dependencies on their history.

D. Koutra et al. (Eds.): ECML PKDD 2023, LNAI 14173, pp. 172–188, 2023.
https://doi.org/10.1007/978-3-031-43424-2_11

Temporal point processes (TPP) are popular tools in event sequence modeling. Classic statistical methods such as Hawkes Process and Poisson point process [10,11] make simple parametric assumptions of the conditional intensity function, which usually limits the model capacity of learning from arbitrary distributions. In contrast, emerging neural network based temporal point processes such as recurrent neural network (RNN) [7], continuous-time LSTM [15], and attention based Hawkes [27,29] have been increasingly powerful in modeling event sequences. Studies using the vanilla RNN [7] or its variations [15] demonstrate excellent ability to capture the historical dynamics of the sequence data and achieve significant improvements in likelihood event prediction accuracy.

It is important to capture both long-term and short-term dependencies for modeling event intensities of point processes. For example, in flood prediction, short-term dependency exists since a region that has been recently at risk may experience elevated risks in the near future. Long-term dependency also exists since flood events appear periodically in a specific season over a long period of time. In general, RNN based models [6,15] are less likely to capture long-term dependencies even with forget gates such as Gated Recurrent Gates (GRU). In contrast, attention based point processes [2,27,29] can model the influence among events by assigning attention scores and capture the influence of events that are at any temporal distance from the current event, which are better at capturing both long-term and short-term dependencies.

However, many current neural network based point processes struggle with long event sequences. For RNN-based models, events are fed into the model sequentially and future states are processed after the current state. Therefore, it is hard to process all events in parallel, which limits the ability to scale to long event sequences. For self-attention based models, it is also prohibitively expensive to scale to long sequences since the time and memory complexities are quadratic with respect to the sequence length.

To tackle the challenge, we propose a Sparse Transformer Hawkes Process (STHP), which is uniquely tailored to model long asynchronous event sequences. Our framework contains two closely coupled components to model temporal dynamics to capture both short-term and long-term dependencies.

The **contributions** of our paper are as follows:

- We propose a novel temporal sparse self-attention mechanism to substitute the classic self-attention in Transformer to focus more on short-term dependencies in modeling asynchronous long sequences. We remark that even though variations of sparse transformer have been proposed in natural language processing [3,12], such an architecture is not readily applicable to event sequences that are defined in a continuous-time domain. In particular, unlike regularly spaced tokens in natural languages, the time intervals between consecutive events can be arbitrary.
- To complement the first component, we introduce another transformer to model the time series of aggregated event counts in a fixed time window, which focuses more on capturing long-term periodical dependencies. Both components are fused together to model the conditional intensity function

of a point process for future event forecasting. By choosing an appropriate time bin size to aggregate counts, the integration of the two components can reduce computation complexity without sacrificing prediction performance.
- We provide extensive experimentation results on three real-world datasets with different sequence lengths and various event types, which shows the efficiency and state-of-art prediction accuracy of our model.

2 Related Work

Temporal Point Process. Point processes, such as the Hawkes process, have been widely used for modeling self- and mutual-excited event sequences and forecasting future events in various fields such as predictive policing [17,20] and online social activities [7,9,19,25]. In comparison with classic statistical methods such as Hawkes Process and Poisson point process, emerging neural network based temporal point processes such as RNN [7], continuous-time LSTM [15], and generative point process [24] have been increasingly powerful in modeling event sequences. Existing work [5] also considers the integration of GRU based point process with traditional time series analysis to capture both microscopic and macroscopic event dynamics.

Self-attention Mechanism. Self-attention has been shown to be a powerful mechanism for modeling temporal dependencies in a variety of sequential data domains such as natural language processing. Recently, several self-attention-based temporal point process models such as the self-attentive Hawkes process [27], the transformer Hawkes process [29], and the long-short evolution model [2] have been proposed to capture complex temporal dependencies among events. However, it is computational expensive to scale most of the current architectures to long sequences.

Sparse Attention Mechanism. Various efficient attention mechanisms have been proposed to reduce the quadratic computational and memory complexity of full attention in language and vision domains [4,26]. One category of methods is to construct a sparse attention matrix with predefined or learnable sparse patterns such as probabilistic-sparse attention [28] and sliding window attention mechanisms [3]. However, an efficient mechanism readily applicable to event sequences that are defined in a continuous-time domain is less explored. To the best of our knowledge, our proposed sparse Transformer Hawkes is the first of this type in point process literature.

3 Background

In this section, we briefly review Hawkes processes including traditional statistical methods [10] and neural network based Hawkes processes [6,15], as well as self-attention mechanism in Transformer [27,29].

3.1 Hawkes Process

A temporal point process (TPP) such as a Poisson process and a Hawkes process is a stochastic process, where its realization is a sequence of events in continuous time domain. Typically, a TPP is characterized by its intensity function denoted as $\lambda(t)$, which represents the expected instantaneous rate of occurrence for an event at time t. For example, a multivariate Hawkes process [10] is characterized by intensity functions $\lambda(t) = \{\lambda_k(t)\}_{k\in K, t\in[0,T)}$, where $\lambda_k(t)$ represents the intensity of type-k event at time t given all historical events, i.e., $\lambda_k(t) = \mu_k + \sum_{i:t_i<t} \phi_{k,k'}(t-t_i)$. Note μ_k is the base intensity of type-k event and $\phi_{k,k'}(\cdot)$ is a triggering kernel that captures the influence of a historical type-k' event at time t' on a subsequent type-k event [8]. The intensity function indicates that each historic event has a positive influence on the appearance of the current event and all influences are accumulated in an additive way.

Unlike traditional statistical methods that make simple parametric assumptions of intensity functions, a neural network based Hawkes process quantifies the influence of historical events in a more sophisticated way and its intensity function is parameterized by a neural network. Specifically,

$$\lambda_k(t) = f_k(\mathbf{w}_k^\top \mathbf{h}(t)), t \in [0, T), \tag{1}$$

where $\mathbf{h}(t)$ is the vectorized hidden state of the sequence, which can be obtained from a RNN [7], a continuous-time LSTM [15], or a self-attentive based network [27,29]. Also, f_k is a softplus function with parameter $\mathbf{w}_k$ that takes hidden state $\mathbf{h}(t)$ as input and output a positive intensity.

3.2 Self-attention

Self-attention [21] is a special attention mechanism that is commonly used in learning contextual relationships between elements in a sequence, which has been widely applied in machine translation [23], long-sequence time-series forecasting [28], and computer vision [14]. The self-attention mechanism operates by calculating a weighted sum of the input elements, where the weights are determined by a trained attention function defined as:

$$A[\mathbf{Q}, \mathbf{K}, \mathbf{V}] = Softmax(\frac{\mathbf{Q}\mathbf{K}^\top}{\sqrt{d}}) \cdot \mathbf{V}, \tag{2}$$

where $\mathbf{Q}, \mathbf{K}, \mathbf{V}$ represent the query, key, and value matrixes obtained from different transformations of the embedded input $\mathbf{X}$. One advantage of self-attention is its ability to capture long-range dependencies between elements in a sequence. Moreover, the self-attention mechanism exhibits faster convergence than RNNs.

In the transformer, the self-attention module always repeats the computation multiple times in parallel, which is also known as the multi-head attention mechanism. It allows the model to attend to different parts of the input sequence simultaneously, making it more effective at capturing various dependencies between events. The multi-head attention can be defined as:

$$\mathbf{A} = Concat(\mathbf{A_1}, \mathbf{A_2}, ..., \mathbf{A_h})W^O, \tag{3}$$

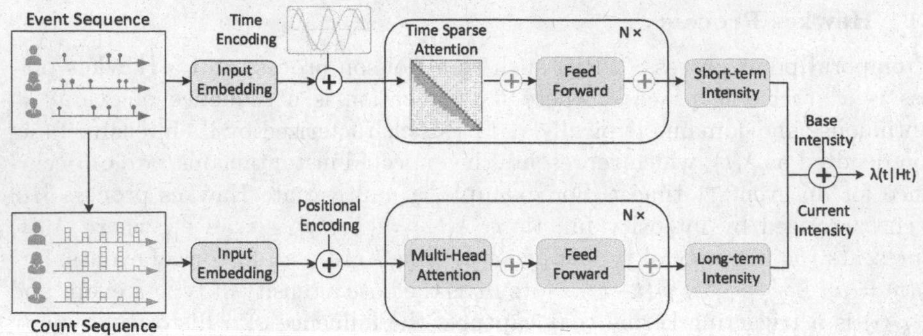

Fig. 1. The architecture of the Sparse Transformer Hawkes Process (STHP) consists of two components: event model and count model. For the event model, a transformer with a novel temporal sparse self-attention mechanism is applied to event sequences S, mainly focusing on short-term dependencies. For the count model, a transformer is applied to the time series of aggregated event counts C, primarily targeting the extraction of long-term periodic dependencies. The outputs (hidden representations) of both components are fused together to model the intensity function.

where $\mathbf{A_1}, \mathbf{A_2}, ..., \mathbf{A_h}$ are different attention outputs computed by different weights $\{W_h^Q, W_h^K, W_h^V\}_{h=1}^H$.

4 Proposed Model

In this section, we introduce our proposed STHP model. Formally, suppose we are given a sequence of N events $0 < t_1 < \cdots < t_n < T$ and $k_i \in \mathcal{K} = \{1, 2, .., K\}$ for $i = 1, ..., N$. The tuple (t_i, k_i) represents the i-th event in the sequence $\mathcal{S}$, t_i and k_i represent the event timestamp and type, respectively. Moreover, we create an auxiliary sequence to capture the aggregated event counts in fixed time intervals. Specifically, we partition the time into L equal-size bins and the bin size δ is a hyper-parameter of our model. Let $\mathbf{c}_j = [c_{j1}, c_{j2}, \ldots, c_{jK}]^\top$ be the event count vector of K types within the j-th interval $[(j-1)\delta, j\delta]$. The count sequence of L bins is essentially a multivariate time series, which can be represented as $\mathbf{C} = [\mathbf{c}_1, \mathbf{c}_2, \ldots, \mathbf{c}_L]^\top \in \mathbb{R}^{L \times K}$. Real-life examples of a sequence $\mathcal{S}$ include a sequence of crime events in a region or a sequence of stock transactions in a time period. A dataset (e.g., crime events in M regions or stock transactions in M time periods) is a collection of M event sequences $\mathcal{S}_1$, $\mathcal{S}_2 \ldots$, $\mathcal{S}_M$.

As shown in Fig. 1, our proposed model consists of two components: event model (Sect. 4.1) and count model (Sect. 4.2). The two components complement each other and the output of them are fused together in the intensity function (Sect. 4.3). Finally, the training objective is described in Sect. 4.4.

4.1 Event Model

Input Representation. In this component, temporal encoding is used to capture the time stamp information of input sequence $\mathcal{S}$. Different from positional encoding which is used to provide positional information about the order of the input, in temporal encoding, each event is encoded as a time difference relative to the previous event, and this information is added to the input data as an additional feature.

For the i-th event in the sequence $\mathcal{S} = \{(t_i, k_i)\}_{i=1}^N$, let $\mathbf{z}_i \in \mathbb{R}^D$ represent the temporal encoding vector of the i-th event occurring at time t_i, where D is the dimension of the encoding. The encoding procedure is defined using trigonometric functions [29] as:

$$\mathbf{z}_i^j = \begin{cases} cos(t_i/10000^{\frac{j-1}{D}}), \text{if } j \text{ is odd}, \\ sin(t_i/10000^{\frac{j}{D}}), \text{if } j \text{ is even}. \end{cases} \tag{4}$$

In addition to temporal encoding, in order to get the event type information of the sequence, we train an embedding matrix $W \in \mathbb{R}^{D \times K}$ for event types, where the k-th column of W is the embedding for type-k event. Denote $\mathbf{y}_i \in \mathbb{R}^K$ as the K-dimensional one-hot vector with value 1 for index k_i and value 0 otherwise. The final embedding of the event sequence $\mathcal{S}$ is defined by:

$$\mathbf{X} = (\mathbf{WY} + \mathbf{Z})^\top, \tag{5}$$

where $\mathbf{Y} = [\mathbf{y}_1, \mathbf{y}_2, ..., \mathbf{y}_N] \in \mathbb{R}^{K \times N}$ and $\mathbf{Z} = [\mathbf{z}_1, \mathbf{z}_2, \ldots, \mathbf{z}_N] \in \mathbb{R}^{D \times N}$ represent the collection of event type one-hot vectors and temporal encoding of the input sequence $\mathcal{S}$, respectively. Note that each row of $\mathbf{X} \in \mathbb{R}^{N \times D}$ is the embedding corresponding to a particular event in the sequence.

Temporal Sparse Self-attention. Following the initial encoding and embedding layers, we process the input $\mathbf{X}$ through a novel temporal sparse self-attention (TSSA) module for capturing short-term dependencies in a sequence. We first project $\mathbf{X}$ into query $\mathbf{Q}$, key $\mathbf{K}$, and value $\mathbf{V}$ matrices using linear transformations. Specifically,

$$\mathbf{Q} = \mathbf{X}W^Q, \mathbf{K} = \mathbf{X}W^K, \mathbf{V} = \mathbf{X}W^V, \tag{6}$$

where $W^Q, W^K \in \mathbb{R}^{D \times D_K}$, and $W^V \in \mathbb{R}^{D \times D_V}$ are learnable weight matrices. In particular, we calculate the time sparse attention output $\mathbf{A}$ by:

$$\mathbf{A}(i,:) = \sum_{j=t-\pi_i}^{i} Softmax(\frac{\mathbf{Q}(i,:) \cdot \mathbf{K}(j,:)^\top}{\sqrt{D_K}}) \cdot \mathbf{V}(j,:), \tag{7}$$

where $\mathbf{A}(i,:)$ denotes the i-th row of $\mathbf{A}$ (similar notation for $\mathbf{Q}(i,:)$, $\mathbf{K}(j,:)$, and $\mathbf{V}(j,:)$. Note that the attention mechanism employs a sliding window approach, where the window size π_i corresponding to the i-th event is the count of neighborhood events within time interval $[t_i - \delta, t_i]$.

Specifically, when calculating the attention output $\mathbf{A}(i,:)$, to prevent the attention algorithm from inadvertently "looking ahead" and incorporating information from future positions, we mask all subsequent positions by setting the values $Q(i,i+1),\ldots,Q(i,N)$ to infinity. This ensures that the softmax function does not assign any dependency to future events. In practice, we also use the multi-head mechanism to combine different self-attention results to increase model flexibility using the formula defined in Eq. 3 in Sect. 3.2.

The proposed TSSA mechanism has several advantages over traditional attention mechanisms for modeling asynchronous sequence. Firstly, the window size π_i changes dynamically according to the local temporal structure of the i-th event, allowing the model to dynamically focus on relevant local information. Secondly, the TSSA mechanism allows for more efficient computation. Specifically, the time interval δ is a hyper-parameter and is usually chosen to cover a few events; the computational and memory complexity of the attention matrix is reduced from $O(N^2)$ to $O(N)$.

After the attention sub-layer, the output $\mathbf{A}$ is subsequently passed through a position-wise feed-forward neural network:

$$\mathbf{H} = Relu(\mathbf{A}\mathbf{W}_1 + \mathbf{b}_1)\mathbf{W}_2 + \mathbf{b}_2, \tag{8}$$

where $\mathbf{W}_1 \in \mathbb{R}^{D\times D_k}$, $\mathbf{W}_2 \in \mathbb{R}^{D_k\times D}$, $\mathbf{b}_1 \in \mathbb{R}^{D_k}$, and $\mathbf{b}_2 \in \mathbb{R}^{D}$ are parameters of the neural network. The output matrix $\mathbf{H} \in \mathbb{R}^{N\times D}$ is the hidden representations of all the events in the input sequence, where each row corresponds to an event.

4.2 Count Model

Input Representation. In this component, a transformer is applied to a count sequence $\mathbf{C} = [\mathbf{c}_1, \mathbf{c}_2, \ldots, \mathbf{c}_L]^\top \in \mathbb{R}^{L\times K}$ to capture the long-term dependencies from the aggregated data. Since the temporal structure is inherently regular, we represent the relative positions of the element using a simpler positional encoding function. Specifically, let $\mathbf{e}_i$ represent the positional encoding vector of the i-th element in the sequence $\mathbf{C}$, we have:

$$\mathbf{e}_i^j = \begin{cases} cos(i/2L^{\frac{j-1}{D}}), \text{if } j \text{ is odd}, \\ sin(i/2L^{\frac{j}{D}}), \text{if } j \text{ is even}, \end{cases} \tag{9}$$

where $j \in \{1, ..., [D/2]\}$.

To get the count encoding, we project the K-dim vector $\mathbf{c}_i$ to a D-dim vector $\mathbf{u}_i$ using convolutional filters. Thus, we have the representations of the inputs:

$$\mathbf{X} = \mathbf{U} + \mathbf{E}, \tag{10}$$

where $\mathbf{U} = [\mathbf{u}_1, \mathbf{u}_2, ..., \mathbf{u}_L]$ is the positional encoding matrix and $\mathbf{E} = [\mathbf{e}_1, \mathbf{e}_2, ..., \mathbf{e}_L]$ is the count encoding matrix.

Self-attention. In order to capture the long-term dependencies from the count sequence, we use the traditional self-attention mechanism that can capture the long-dependencies efficiently. The formula is defined in Eq. 2 in Sect. 3.2. After that we use the multi-head attention mechanism defined in Eq. 3 in Sect. 3.2 to get the output $\mathbf{A}$, which is then passed to a position-wise feed-forward neural network defined by Eq. 8 in Sect. 4.1. The final output is $\mathbf{\Theta} \in \mathbb{R}^{L \times D}$, which is the hidden representation of all the elements in the count sequence.

4.3 Intensity

We present the continuous conditional intensity function that is used to describe the dynamics of temporal point processes. Note that the hidden representations ($\mathbf{H}$, $\mathbf{\Theta}$) are generated at discrete time stamps and thus a continuous intensity function is needed. The type-specific intensity function is formulated as follows:

$$\lambda_k(t) = f_k\left(\alpha_k \frac{t - t_i}{t_i} + \mathbf{w}_k^\top \mathbf{h}(t_i) + \rho_k^\top \theta(t_i) + b_k\right), t \in [0, T), \tag{11}$$

where f_k is a nonlinear activation function that maps the input to a non-negative output, ensuring that the intensity function remains non-negative for all input values. The intensity function consists of several components that contribute to the occurrence of events:

- $\alpha_k \frac{t-t_i}{t_i}$: The temporal decay term, which models the influence of the time elapsed since the last event t_i. The parameter α_k controls the rate of decay.
- $\mathbf{w}_k^\top \mathbf{h}(t_i)$: The short-term influence, which captures the effect of past few events on the current intensity. The vector $\mathbf{h}(t_i) = \mathbf{H}(\mathbf{i}, :)$ (obtained in Sect. 4.1) is a summary of the historical events in a time window $[t_i - \delta, t_i]$, and the weight vector $\mathbf{w}_k$ represents the importance of the short-term history.
- $\rho_k^\top \theta(t_i)$: The long-term trend, which models the influence of the underlying long-term patterns in the data. The vector $\theta(t_i) = \mathbf{\Theta}(\mathbf{j}, :)$, where $t_i \in [(j-1)\delta, j\delta]$ is obtained in Sect. 4.2. It captures the long-term dependencies at time t_i given the aggregated count history and the weight vector ρ_k represents the importance of the history.
- b_k: The base intensity term, which accounts for the intrinsic intensity of the event type k in the absence of any other influences.

By combining these components, the intensity function $\lambda_k(t)$ effectively captures the complex temporal dynamics in long sequences. The conditional intensity for the whole sequence is defined as:

$$\lambda(t) = \sum_{k=1}^{K} \lambda_k(t). \tag{12}$$

Given the conditional intensity function, we can predict the future event time and event type by:

$$p(t) = \lambda(t) \exp\left(-\int_{t_j}^{t} \lambda(\tau) d\tau\right), \tag{13}$$

$$t_{j+1} = \int_{t_j}^{\infty} t \cdot p(t) dt, \tag{14}$$

$$k_{j+1} = \arg\max_{k} \frac{\lambda_k(t_{j+1})}{\lambda(t_{j+1})}. \tag{15}$$

4.4 Training

Given an observed event sequence $\mathcal{S} = \{(t_i, k_i)\}_{i=1}^{N}$ with $0 < t_1 < \cdot < t_n < T$, the log-likelihood is:

$$l(\mathcal{S}) = \sum_{i=1}^{N} \log \lambda_{k_i}(t_i) - \int_0^T \lambda(t) dt. \tag{16}$$

The log-likelihood consists of two main components:

- $\sum_{i=1}^{N} \log \lambda_{k_i}(t_i)$: This term represents the sum of the log intensities of the observed events. By maximizing this term, we encourage the model to assign high intensity values to the observed events.
- $\int_0^T \lambda(t) dt$: This term represents the sum of the integrated intensities for all event types over the observation window $[0, T)$. By minimizing this term, we encourage the model to assign low intensity values to the unobserved events.

The goal of training is to maximize the final log-likelihood function given a collection of M sequences $\mathcal{S}_1$, $\mathcal{S}_2 \ldots$, $\mathcal{S}_M$. That is to solve $\max \sum_{i=1}^{M} l(\mathcal{S}_i)$, where $l(\mathcal{S}_i)$ is the log-likelihood of sequence $\mathcal{S}_i$. The optimization problem can be efficiently solved by stochastic gradient algorithms such as ADAM [13]. One challenge is to compute the integral in Eq. 16, for which we adopt the Monte Carlo approximation approach as described in [15].

5 Experiment

5.1 Data

We use three real-world datasets that contain diverse temporal dynamics in different domains. The statistics are shown in Table 1. **Boston** dataset, which is obtained from Kaggle[1], contains sequences of crime incidents of 65 different types such as burglary, street crime, and auto theft collected from the Boston Police Department during a 3-year period. Type "other" is not selected in our experiment. Each crime event is associated with a time stamp, region ID, and type. Crime events are partitioned into different sequences by region ID and

[1] https://www.kaggle.com/datasets/AnalyzeBoston/crimes-in-boston.

Table 1. Dataset Statistics.

Dataset	Type	Total Events	Avg. Length	Duration
Boston	65	282k	919	3 years
911 Call	3	301k	1709	3 years
Financial	2	415k	2074	1 day

we select about 307 region IDs with sufficiently long sequences. The average sequence length is 919. The **911Call** dataset[2] contains sequences of 3 types of emergency phone call records including EMS, fire, and traffic reported in Montgomery County, PA. We select a subset of data from Dec. 2015 to Dec. 2018 with no missing zip codes. The data is further divided into 177 sequences by their zip codes and the average sequence length is 1709. The **Financial** dataset contains transaction events for a stock in one day from NYSE. The dataset contains one long sequence of transaction events and each event is associated with a time stamp and a type in one of the two categories "buy" and "sell". The sequence is further divided into 200 sequences by time stamps. The average sequence length is 2074, which is the longest among all three datasets.

5.2 Baselines

We compare our proposed model with the following state-of-art temporal point process models on benchmark datasets.

Dual Temporal Point Process (Dual-TPP) [5]: This model is composed of two components: a GRU-based model to capture the microscopic event dynamics and a traditional count model to estimate the aggregated counts in a fixed time window. The two components are jointly optimized.

Transformer Hawkes (THP) [29]: This model uses a Transformer encoder to learn the history influence representation and proposes a temporal encoding for sequences with arbitrary time intervals.

Self-Attentive Hawkes Process (SAHP) [27]: This model uses the self-attention mechanism for learning the representation of influences from historical events. Also, time intervals are encoded by the time-shifted positional encoding.

Continuous Time LSTM Point Process (CTLSTM) [15]: This is a LSTM-based point process, which models sequences of discrete events in continuous time by using intensity decay. Also, it allows historical events to influence the future events in sophisticated ways.

5.3 Evaluation Metrics and Training Details

We adopt different metrics to evaluate the models. Firstly, we split the sequence to 80% training and 20% test and we evaluate the testset log-likelihood.

[2] https://www.kaggle.com/datasets/mchirico/montcoalert.

Table 2. Test-set Log-likelihood comparison.

Model	Boston	911Call	Financial
STHP (ours)	**−2.01**	**−2.81**	<u>−1.17</u>
SAHP	−2.15	−3.02	—
THP	<u>−2.12</u>	<u>−2.83</u>	**−1.12**
Dual-TPP	−2.19	−2.86	−1.51
CTLSTM	−3.13	−3.91	−2.71

Furthermore, we would like to evaluate the prediction accuracy of the type and time of future events based on training events as described in Eq. 13 in Sect. 4.3. In this setting, events before time t are in the training set and events after time t are in the testset. We use F1 score and RMSE to evaluate the results of event type prediction and time prediction, respectively.

The details of hyper-parameters used in training are the following. We set time bin size $\delta = 30$ days, 7 days, 60 s for Boston, 911Call, and Financial, respectively. In addition, for most of the datasets, we set learning rate = 0.0001, head number = 4, layer number = 4, and model dimension $D = 512$.

5.4 Results of Log-Likelihood

In this section, we use the log-likelihood as the evaluation method to compare the ability of models to fit event sequences. Table 2 shows the results of log-likelihood on different datasets. We can observe that our model STHP outperforms CTLSTM and Dual-TPP on all datasets. This is because the RNN-based model is not powerful enough to capture the long-term influence of the long sequence with complicated temporal dynamics. In addition, for our model, although the sparse attention mechanism at the event level focuses more on short-term dependency rather than long-term dependency, the second transformer applied to the aggregated event counts is capable of capturing long-term dependency and thus complements the first component. The results show that our model can achieve similar log-likelihood results with the best baseline model.

For all datasets, the overall performance of self-attention based models (STHP, THP, SHAP) are better than the RNN-based model. Also, for the Financial dataset with very long sequences, the SAHP model is not able to fit the data because of the extremely high memory cost per sequence. It shows that self-attentive based models with dense attention patterns struggle to deal with very long sequences.

5.5 Results of Event Type and Time Prediction

Tables 3 and 4 evaluate the performance of event type prediction using F1 score and time prediction using RMSE. For event type prediction, our STHP model demonstrates the highest F1 score on Boston and Financial datasets. Boston

Table 3. Event type prediction result comparison.

Model	Boston	911Call	Financial
STHP (ours)	**11.12**	57.23	**62.49**
SAHP	10.82	**57.32**	—
THP	11.08	57.16	62.42
Dual-TPP	10.76	57.11	61.67
CTLSTM	10.20	55.14	62.12

Table 4. Time prediction RMSE result comparison.

Model	Boston	911Call	Financial
STHP (ours)	2.74	40.11	1.09
SAHP	2.81	43.02	—
THP	2.79	40.27	1.12
Dual-TPP	**2.71**	**37.42**	**0.98**
CTLSTM	3.02	45.62	1.62

data has 65 event types, the biggest among the three. Financial data has the longest sequences among the three. It shows that our model performs well on both multi-type sequences and long sequences.

In terms of time prediction, the STHP model also performs relatively well on all three datasets. The Dual-TPP model achieves the best performance; this is because the Dual-TPP model uses a time-series component to model aggregated event counts and introduces an additional loss of event count, which can improve the accuracy of time prediction. Overall, the experiment results suggest that the STHP model performs well on both event type and time prediction tasks for all datasets, especially for datasets with many event types and long sequences.

5.6 Computational Efficiency

In event model, for a sequence of length N, the computational and memory complexity of the sparse attention matrix is reduced from $O(N^2)$ to $O(N)$. In count model, for a sequence of length L the computational and memory complexity of the attention matrix is $O(L^2)$. In practice, the number of time bins satisfies $L \ll N$ and thus the overall complexity is reduced from quadratic to linear.

We also compare in Fig. 2 the running time of all methods on the Boston dataset with a NVIDIA RTX A5000 GPU card. We use a mini-batch size 16 and the result running time is averaged by 15 epochs. In these bar plots, results are averaged across 5 distinct mini-batches and the error bars display the variance of these 5 experiments. We can see that CTLSTM and Dual-TPP are the least computationally efficient models; this is because the recurrent architectures process input sequences one step at a time and are harder to parallelize. Also, the

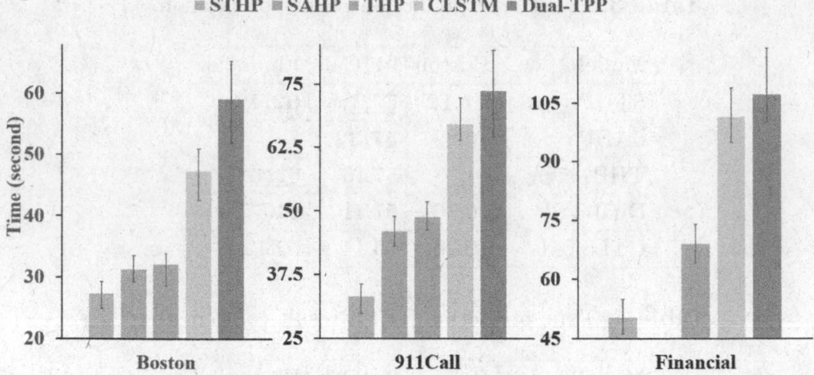

Fig. 2. Computational efficiency comparison.

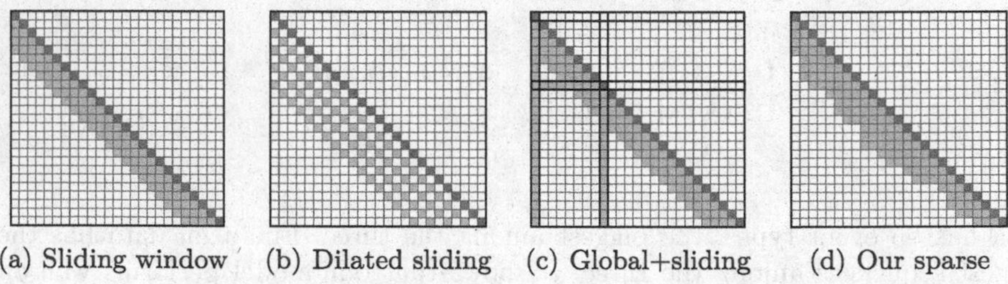

Fig. 3. Illustrations of different self-attention mechanisms.

DualTPP model has another layer for modeling the aggregated counts of events, which leads to more computational costs. Our proposed STHP model shows the best performance due to the sparse attention mechanism.

5.7 Sparse Attention Mechanism

We compare our proposed sparse attention mechanism with the following state-of-art mechanisms. Figure 3 illustrates the difference of those mechanisms graphically.

ProbSparse [28]: It introduces a sparse probability matrix $\mathbf{P} \in \mathbb{R}^{n \times n}$ for a sequence of length n. By selecting the top k token-pairs with the highest probabilities, the time and space complexity is reduced from $\mathcal{O}(n^2)$ to $\mathcal{O}(n \log n)$.

Sliding Window [3]: The mechanism restricts the attention computation to a local region defined by a sliding window of size w. The time and space complexity is reduced from $\mathcal{O}(n^2)$ to $\mathcal{O}(n \times w)$.

Dilated Sliding Window [3]: It builds upon the sliding window approach and incorporates dilated windows. The dilation factor d allows the mechanism to have a larger receptive field, enabling it to consider distant tokens.

Table 5. Comparison of different self-attention mechanisms on Financial.

Model	Log-likelihood	Type prediction	Time prediction
Sliding window	−2.01	59.12	1.75
Dilated sliding window	−1.92	60.93	2.01
Global and sliding window	<u>−1.42</u>	61.19	<u>1.39</u>
Prob-sparse	−1.64	<u>61.24</u>	1.42
Temporal sparse	**−1.17**	**62.19**	**1.09**

Table 6. Ablation study on Boston dataset.

Model	Log-likelihood	Type prediction	Time prediction	Run time
STHP	−2.01	11.12	2.74	27.38
STHP-without-sparse	−1.98	11.57	2.72	37.12
STHP-without-count	−2.32	10.12	3.14	20.07

Global and Sliding Window [3]: It integrates the sliding window mechanism and the full attention computation at selected tokens. The complexity is in between the full and sliding window mechanisms.

In Table 5, we compare our STHP using the proposed sparse attention mechanism with the others and evaluate the log-likelihood, event prediction (F1 score), and time prediction (RMSE) on the Financial dataset. In order to maintain similar computational complexity with TSSA, we set the window size $w = 10$ for sliding window, $w = 20$ for dilated sliding window, and $w = 10$ for global sliding window. In addition, for global sliding window approach, the global attention computation is added every 20 tokens. As shown in Table 5, the sliding window and dilated sliding window mechanisms are the least efficient. Fixed windows struggle to capture temporal structure for asynchronous events effectively since they do not consider time intervals between events. In contrast, our proposed STHP model uniquely considers the time interval between consecutive events and variable number of events will be included for each local attention computation. Therefore, it exhibits the best performance.

5.8 Ablation Study

We perform ablation study on Boston dataset and inspect the variants of STHP by removing sparse constraints in self-attention in the first component and the transformer for aggregated event counts in the second component. We evaluate model configurations in terms of log-likelihood, event prediction, time prediction, and run time. The results are shown in Table 6.

We can see that the sparse constraints in the attention mechanism in the first component improves computational efficiency. The second component (count model) may introduce additional computational cost. However, it significantly contributes to the performance of the model in both event and time prediction tasks. By choosing an appropriate time bin size to aggregate counts, the integration of the two components can largely improve computation efficiency without sacrificing model performance.

6 Conclusion

We proposed STHP model, an efficient Hawkes process to model long event sequence data with both long-term and short-term dependencies. The model leverages a Transformer with a novel temporal sparse self-attention mechanism to capture short-term influence, and utilizes a transformer to model the time series of aggregated event counts to capture the long-term periodical dependencies. To the best of our knowledge, our proposed sparse Transformer Hawkes is the first of this type in point process literature. Experiments on real-world datasets show that the proposed STHP outperforms baselines and achieves significant improvement in computational efficiency without sacrificing prediction performance for long sequences. Future work includes the investigation of more types of sparse attention mechanisms and over-parameterized models.

Acknowledgement. This work was supported in part by the NSF under Grant No. 1927513, No. 1943486, No. 2147253, and NSF EPSCoR-Louisiana program (No. 1946231).

Ethic Statement. In this ethical statement, we will discuss the ethical implications of our work in relation to machine learning and data mining. We recognize the importance of ethics in all aspects of our work and are committed to upholding ethical principles in our research and its application. In this statement, we will outline the potential ethical issues that arise from our work and the steps we have taken to mitigate these issues.

Collection and Processing of Personal Data. The datasets of our work are all public datasets. We have obtained all necessary permissions and have followed best practices for data download, processing, and storage to ensure that the privacy of individuals is protected.

Inference of Personal Information. Our work does not involve the inference of personal information from data.

Potential Use in Policing. Our work may have potential applications in policing contexts. We are aware of the potential ethical implications of this and are committed to ensuring that our work is not used in ways that violate human rights or result in harm to individuals. We will carefully consider the potential uses of our work and will take appropriate steps to prevent its misuse.

References

1. Bacry, E., Mastromatteo, I., Muzy, J.F.: Hawkes processes in finance. Market Microstruct. Liquidity **1**(01), 1550005 (2015)
2. Bai, T., et al.: CTRec: a long-short demands evolution model for continuous-time recommendation. In: Proceedings of the 42nd International ACM SIGIR Conference on Research and Development in Information Retrieval, pp. 675–684 (2019)
3. Beltagy, I., Peters, M.E., Cohan, A.: Longformer: the long-document transformer. arXiv preprint arXiv:2004.05150 (2020)
4. Child, R., Gray, S., Radford, A., Sutskever, I.: Generating long sequences with sparse transformers. arXiv preprint arXiv:1904.10509 (2019)
5. Deshpande, P., Marathe, K., De, A., Sarawagi, S.: Long horizon forecasting with temporal point processes. In: Proceedings of the 14th ACM International Conference on Web Search and Data Mining, pp. 571–579 (2021)
6. Du, N., Dai, H., Trivedi, R., Upadhyay, U., Rodriguez, M., Song, L.: Recurrent marked temporal point process. In: Proceedings of the ACM SIGKDD International Conference on Knowledge Discovery and Data Mining (KDD), pp. 447–456 (2016)
7. Du, N., Dai, H., Trivedi, R., Upadhyay, U., Gomez-Rodriguez, M., Song, L.: Recurrent marked temporal point processes: embedding event history to vector. In: Proceedings of the ACM SIGKDD International Conference on Knowledge Discovery and Data Mining (KDD), pp. 1555–1564 (2016)
8. Farajtabar, M., Du, N., Rodriguez, M.G., Valera, I., Zha, H., Song, L.: Shaping social activity by incentivizing users. In: Proceedings of the Annual Conference on Neural Information Processing Systems (NeurIPS), pp. 2474–2482 (2014)
9. Farajtabar, M., Wang, Y., Rodriguez, M.G., Li, S., Zha, H., Song, L.: Coevolve: a joint point process model for information diffusion and network co-evolution. In: Proceedings of the Annual Conference on Neural Information Processing Systems (NeurIPS), pp. 1954–1962 (2015)
10. Hawkes, A.G.: Spectra of some self-exciting and mutually exciting point processes. Biometrika **58**(1), 83–90 (1971)
11. Isham, V., Westcott, M.: A self-correcting point process. Stoch. Process. Their Appl. **8**(3), 335–347 (1979)
12. Jaszczur, S., et al.: Sparse is enough in scaling transformers. Adv. Neural. Inf. Process. Syst. **34**, 9895–9907 (2021)
13. Kingma, D.P., Ba, J.: Adam: a method for stochastic optimization. In: Proceedings International Conference on Learning Representations (ICLR) (2015)
14. Liu, Z., et al.: Swin transformer: hierarchical vision transformer using shifted windows. In: Proceedings of the IEEE/CVF International Conference on Computer Vision, pp. 10012–10022 (2021)
15. Mei, H., Eisner, J.M.: The neural Hawkes process: a neurally self-modulating multivariate point process. In: Proceedings of the Annual Conference on Neural Information Processing Systems (NeurIPS), pp. 6754–6764 (2017)
16. Mohler, G., Porter, M.D., Carter, J., LaFree, G.: Learning to rank spatio-temporal event hotspots. In: Proceedings of the 7th International Workshop on Urban Computing (2018)
17. Mohler, G., Raje, R., Carter, J., Valasik, M., Brantingham, J.: A penalized likelihood method for balancing accuracy and fairness in predictive policing. In: Proceedings of the IEEE International Conference on Systems, Man, and Cybernetics (SMC), pp. 2454–2459 (2018)
18. Ross, S.M., et al.: Stochastic Processes, vol. 2. Wiley, New York (1996)

19. Shang, J., Sun, M.: Geometric Hawkes processes with graph convolutional recurrent neural networks. In: Proceedings of the AAAI Conference on Artificial Intelligence, vol. 33, pp. 4878–4885 (2019)
20. Shelton, C.R., Qin, Z., Shetty, C.: Hawkes process inference with missing data. In: Proceedings of the AAAI Conference on Artificial Intelligence (2018)
21. Vaswani, A., et al.: Attention is all you need. In: Advances in Neural Information Processing Systems, vol. 30 (2017)
22. Wang, L., Zhang, W., He, X., Zha, H.: Supervised reinforcement learning with recurrent neural network for dynamic treatment recommendation. In: Proceedings of the 24th ACM SIGKDD International Conference on Knowledge Discovery & Data Mining, pp. 2447–2456 (2018)
23. Wang, Q., et al.: Learning deep transformer models for machine translation. arXiv preprint arXiv:1906.01787 (2019)
24. Xiao, S., Farajtabar, M., Ye, X., Yan, J., Song, L., Zha, H.: Wasserstein learning of deep generative point process models. In: Advances in Neural Information Processing Systems, vol. 30 (2017)
25. Xu, H., Farajtabar, M., Zha, H.: Learning granger causality for Hawkes processes. In: Proceedings of the International Conference on Machine Learning (ICML), pp. 1717–1726 (2016)
26. Yan, X., Lin, L., Mitra, N.J., Lischinski, D., Cohen-Or, D., Huang, H.: ShapeFormer: transformer-based shape completion via sparse representation. In: Proceedings of the IEEE/CVF Conference on Computer Vision and Pattern Recognition, pp. 6239–6249 (2022)
27. Zhang, Q., Lipani, A., Kirnap, O., Yilmaz, E.: Self-attentive Hawkes process. In: International Conference on Machine Learning, pp. 11183–11193. PMLR (2020)
28. Zhou, H., et al.: Informer: beyond efficient transformer for long sequence time-series forecasting. In: Proceedings of the AAAI Conference on Artificial Intelligence, vol. 35, pp. 11106–11115 (2021)
29. Zuo, S., Jiang, H., Li, Z., Zhao, T., Zha, H.: Transformer Hawkes process. In: International Conference on Machine Learning, pp. 11692–11702. PMLR (2020)

Adacket: ADAptive Convolutional KErnel Transform for Multivariate Time Series Classification

Junru Zhang[1], Lang Feng[1], Haowen Zhang[2], Yuhan Wu[1], and Yabo Dong[1(✉)]

[1] College of Computer Science and Technology, Zhejiang University, Hangzhou, China
{junruzhang,langfeng,wuyuhan,dongyb}@zju.edu.cn

[2] College of Computer Science and Technology, Zhejiang Sci-Tech University, Hangzhou, China
zhanghw@zstu.edu.cn

Abstract. While existing multivariate time series classification (MTSC) methods using massive convolutional kernels show promise, they are resource-intensive and also rely on the trial and error design of convolutional kernels, limiting comprehensive design space exploration. This hinders fully exploiting convolutional kernels for feature extraction from multivariate time series (MTS) data. To address this issue, we propose a novel method called Adaptive Convolutional Kernel Transform (Adacket) to automatically design efficient 1D dilated convolutional kernels for various MTSC scenarios. Adacket formulates the design problem as a multi-objective optimization problem, with a focus on performance and resource efficiency jointly. It introduces a reinforcement learning agent to adaptively determine convolutional kernels in a sequential decision-making manner, and creates multi-action spaces to support comprehensive search in both the channel and time dimensions. By exploring the maximum value of multi-objective rewards within continuous action spaces, Adacket achieves high granularity establishment of convolutional kernels. Empirical evaluations on public UEA archives demonstrate that Adacket outperforms other advanced MTSC baselines, while providing a deeper understanding of its design selections.

Keywords: Multivariate Time Series Classification · Model Automation · Convolutional Model

1 Introduction

Multivariate time series (MTS) datasets are commonly composed of multiple signals acquired from diverse sources or modalities. These signals are recorded as multi-channel data over time, such as triaxial acceleration collected in real-time from smartphones for human activity recognition (HAR) [2]. The analysis of cross-channel signals can provide valuable insights for decision making

D. Koutra et al. (Eds.): ECML PKDD 2023, LNAI 14173, pp. 189–204, 2023.
https://doi.org/10.1007/978-3-031-43424-2_12

by fully mining the temporal information hidden in these signals. Recently, 1D convolutional kernels show superiority in extracting temporal features from multi-channels, which highlights the potential of these convolutional kernels for multivariate time series classification (MTSC) tasks [16].

Despite the effectiveness of convolutional kernels in time series classification, existing methods rely on the empirical design of massive convolutional kernels to achieve high accuracy. As the complexity and number of MTS data increase, considerable resources are required to learn and store relevant parameters. For example, One Dimensional Convolutional Neural Networks (1D-CNNs) [12,16,25] require significant training time and computational resources when dealing with longer or higher-dimension time series. The Random Convolutional Kernel Transform (ROCKET) [6] has shown impressive performance on MTSC tasks, utilizing a random convolutional model, a feature extractor, and a linear classifier. Nevertheless, its random convolutional model employs plethora 1D dilated convolutional kernels, which will result in prohibitively high memory usage when storing the extracted features, particularly as the number of time series instances increases. This presents a formidable challenge for practical applications, especially for resource-limited devices. They may lack sufficient capacity to handle the significant memory overhead required by numerous kernels.

The problem has spawned extensive efforts to investigate various hyperparameters of the convolutional kernel to improve resource efficiency, with a focus on the channel [6,9,10,12] and temporal [6,12,21] dimensions. The channel dimension pertains to the input and output channels, which determine which channels of the time series are analyzed and the number of convolutional kernels generated. On the other hand, the temporal dimension concerns kernel size and dilation, which define the region that can be observed within the same channel dimension over time. However, some methods [6,12] rely on trial and error to optimize convolutional kernel hyperparameters, which can be computationally expensive due to the complexity of the hyperparameter space. Meanwhile, other studies [9,10,21] have only examined specific hyperparameters without comprehensively exploring their impact on model performance. As a result, the potential of convolutional kernels in extracting relevant features from MTS instances cannot be fully realized. Therefore, there is a need for a more efficient convolutional model that can automatically explore the comprehensive design space of convolutional hyperparameters and find out resource-efficient convolutional kernels.

To this end, we present a novel method, called ADAptive Convolutional KErnel Transform (Adacket), for the automatic design of efficient 1D dilated convolutional kernels in various MTSC scenarios. Our approach formulates the design problem as a multi-objective optimization problem that takes into account both the performance of the convolutional models and the convolutional resource efficiency. To search for optimal solutions to this multi-objective issue, Adacket introduces an effective Reinforcement Learning (RL) agent [18] that adaptively determines convolutional kernels in a sequential decision-making manner. Adacket supports comprehensive searches across the *channel and temporal* dimensions (i.e., input channel, output channel, kernel size and dilation) by designing multi-action spaces, which enables relevant channel-wise interaction. In addition, Adacket explores the maximum of our multi-objective reward within continuous action spaces, enabling the establishment of efficient convolutional kernels at a high granularity level. By replacing the random convolutional model of ROCKET with the model produced by Adacket, we create a new convolutional model that exhibits a more profound comprehension of the MTSC task. On the public UEA benchmark, we demonstrate that Adacket outperforms other advanced baselines, and we provide an in-depth analysis to understand its design selections.

To our best knowledge, Adacket is the first MTSC approach to incorporate RL for convolutional kernels adaptation. Our main contributions are summarized as follows: 1) We introduce a multi-objective convolutional kernel search method that jointly optimizes performance and resource efficiency. 2) We novelly model a multi-objective issue as a sequential decision-making problem using the RL paradigm, which enables the automatic design of convolutional kernels. 3) We propose a comprehensive search of the convolutional kernel design space through multiple action spaces. 4) Extensive experimental results demonstrate that Adacket exhibits excellent performance on both accuracy and resources.

2 Related Work

2.1 Multivariate Time Series Classification

According to a thorough review [16], convolution-based methods have emerged as the state-of-the-art approach, outperforming traditional distance-based and ensemble-based methods. 1D-CNNs, including TapNet [25], ResNet [16] and InceptionTime [12], have gained significant attention due to their ability to learn temporal features. InceptionTime, a high-accuracy model, employs convolutional layers with multiple parallel branches, which results in a large number of parameters and a long training time. Although InceptionTime attempted to discretely optimize its hyperparameters through a trial-and-error approach, this process could be time-consuming and impractical to comprehensively explore the design space due to the complex architecture. ROCKET [6], a non-deep learning method, used a convolutional model that includes massive non-trained random convolutional kernels to transform input time series, achieving state-of-the-art performance in MTSC. However, a large number of kernels require massive memory to store the transformed features, making its application to resource-limited scenarios seriously challenging. Moreover, ROCKET and its variates [7,19] were originally developed for univariate time series, and were optimized for specific hyperparameters within a limited design space, without involving MTSC. Although they can be technically extended to MTSC, the more intricate design space makes it impractical to perform a comprehensive design.

2.2 Reinforcement Learning

Reinforcement learning (RL) has emerged as a popular approach for dynamically adapting neural network architectures. In the field of computer vision, the neural architecture search (NAS) approach has been introduced to automate the design of state-of-the-art neural networks, utilizing RL agents to guide the construction of the model from a predefined design space with a vast number of candidate models. The accuracy of the resulting model serves as a reward signal to direct the decision-making process of the RL agent [15,20,26,27]. However, the RL agent needs to train numerous candidate models to determine the optimal one, which leads to expensive computational overhead. The memory requirement for storing and processing candidate models also quickly becomes prohibitive as the number of candidates increases. Although weight-sharing [17] is introduced to reduce the computational cost, memory bottlenecks still exist, limiting the size of the search space and the complexity of the models that can be explored.

In the context of time series classification, the utilization of the RL encounters similar challenges as those in image classification. To overcome these challenges, Adacket adopts a convolutional model without training and leverages a contrastive loss function [24] to create an alternative indicator without the need for time-consuming training. Moreover, instead of searching over a discrete space, Adacket designs multiple continuous action spaces for the RL agent to generate fine-grained convolutional hyperparameters. This also enables the convolutional model to comprehensively focus on temporal features and reduces the memory usage of storing candidate convolutional parameters.

3 Preliminaries

Multivariate Time Series. A multivariate time series (MTS) dataset can be represented as a matrix $\mathbf{X}$ containing N instances. Each instance, denoted as $\mathbf{X}_i = \{\mathbf{x}_{i,1}, \mathbf{x}_{i,2}, \ldots, \mathbf{x}_{i,F}\}$, is a sequence of events comprising F channels. Here, $\mathbf{x}_{i,j} \in \mathbb{R}^T$ represents the time series data of channel j with length T.

Candidate Convolutional Model. A candidate convolutional model denoted as $M = (\mathbf{V}, \mathbf{C})$ comprises a convolutional layer not requiring training. Specifically, $\mathbf{V} = \{\mathbf{v}_1, \mathbf{v}_2, ..., \mathbf{v}_S\}$ represents a set of 1D dilated convolutional kernel parameters, where each $\mathbf{v}_s$ corresponds to a group of convolutional kernel parameters. On the other hand, $\mathbf{C} = \{\mathbf{c}_1, \mathbf{c}_2, ..., \mathbf{c}_S\}$ denotes a set of input channel indexes, where each $\mathbf{c}_s$ corresponds to a group of indexes. Additionally, let p_s^{conv} and p_s^{out} respectively denote the total number of parameters and the total number of output channels of the subset $\{\mathbf{v}_1, \mathbf{v}_2, ..., \mathbf{v}_s\} \in \mathbf{V}$.

Kernel-Channel Pair. A kernel-channel pair $(\mathbf{v}_s, \mathbf{c}_s)$ associates a group of convolutional kernels $\mathbf{v}_s$ with a corresponding group of channel indexes $\mathbf{c}_s$ that indicates the input channels that the kernels operate on. Specifically, each convolutional kernel $\mathbf{v}_s$ consists of a set of weights $\mathbf{w}_s \in \mathbb{R}^{h_s^{in} \times h_s^{out} \times h_s^{ks}}$ and biases $\mathbf{b}_s \in \mathbb{R}^{h_s^{out}}$, with h_s^{in} as the input channel axis, h_s^{out} as the output channel axis, and h_s^{ks} as the kernel size axis. We also set the dilation of $\mathbf{v}_s$ to be h_s^{dil}. Following ROCKET, the weights are drawn from a Gaussian distribution, i.e., $\mathbf{w}_s \sim \mathcal{N}(0,1)$, and are mean centered after being set, i.e., $\mathbf{w}_s = \mathbf{w}_s - \bar{\mathbf{w}}_s$. The bias $\mathbf{b}_s$ are sampled from a uniform distribution $\mathcal{U}(-1,1)$. The stride is fixed at one, and standard zero padding is applied to ensure that the output size matches the input size. Consequently, 1D dilated convolutional kernels can be determined as a four-tuple $(h_s^{in}, h_s^{out}, h_s^{ks}, h_s^{dil})$, which reflects the convolutional hyperparameters of the convolutional kernel group $\mathbf{v}_s$.

Representations. The set of representations $\mathbf{R}_i$ is generated by applying the convolutional model M to the input instance $\mathbf{X}_i$. It consists of S representations, i.e., $\{\mathbf{r}_{i,1}, \mathbf{r}_{i,2}, ..., \mathbf{r}_{i,S}\}$, and each representation $\mathbf{r}_{i,s} \in \mathbb{R}^{h_s^{out} \times T}$ can be derived by

$$\mathbf{r}_{i,s} = \sum\nolimits_{m=1}^{h_s^{in}} \mathbf{w}_{s,m} \otimes \mathbf{X}_{i,c_{s,m}} + \mathbf{b}_s, \tag{1}$$

where $\otimes$ denotes the convolutional operation, $\mathbf{w}_{s,m}$ is the weights of the m-th input channel in $\mathbf{w}_s$, $c_{s,m}$ is the m-th channel index of the channel group $\mathbf{c}_s$ and $\mathbf{X}_{i,c_{s,m}}$ is the $c_{s,m}$-th channel of the i-th input instance.

Contrastive Loss. The contrastive loss [24] of the candidate model is used to evaluate their representations. For instance $\mathbf{X}_i$, we randomly sample two sub-series with overlapping time segments. A candidate model is then applied to transform these two sub-series from $\mathbf{X}_i$, generating corresponding representations $\mathbf{R}_i$ and $\mathbf{R}'_i$, respectively. Each representation is randomly masked along the time axis using a binary mask sequence. Then, for the representation $r_{i,s,k,t} \in \mathbf{r}_{i,s}$, where k is the output channel axis and t is the timestamp axis, the temporal contrastive loss $\mathcal{L}_1^{(i,s,k,t)}$ and instance-wise contrastive loss $\mathcal{L}_2^{(i,s,k,t)}$ are formulated as

$$\mathcal{L}_1^{(i,s,k,t)} = -\log \frac{\exp(r_{i,s,k,t} \cdot r'_{i,s,k,t})}{\sum_{t' \in \Omega} (\exp(r_{i,s,k,t} \cdot r'_{i,s,k,t'}) + \mathbb{1}_{[t \neq t']} \exp(r_{i,s,k,t} \cdot r_{i,s,k,t'}))}, \tag{2}$$

$$\mathcal{L}_2^{(i,s,k,t)} = -\log \frac{\exp(r_{i,s,k,t} \cdot r'_{i,s,k,t})}{\sum_{j=1}^{B} (\exp(r_{i,s,k,t} \cdot r'_{j,s,k,t}) + \mathbb{1}_{[i \neq j]} \exp(r_{i,s,k,t} \cdot r_{j,s,k,t}))}, \tag{3}$$

where Ω is the set of timestamps within the overlap of the two sub-series, $\mathbb{1}$ is the indicator function and batch size B is kept at its original setting of 8. The variables $r_{i,s,k,t}$, $r'_{i,s,k,t}$, and $r_{j,s,k,t}$ are representation vectors of the same timestamp s but from different augmentations or different instances of time series data. The overall contrastive loss can be expressed as

$$\mathcal{L}_{dual} = \frac{1}{S} \sum_{s=1}^{S} \frac{1}{NTh_s^{out}} \sum_{i=1}^{N} \sum_{t=1}^{T} \sum_{k=1}^{h_s^{out}} (\mathcal{L}_1^{(i,s,k,t)} + \mathcal{L}_2^{(i,s,k,t)}), \tag{4}$$

where N is the number of instances, while T and h_s^{out} are the number of timestamps and dimensions in each representation respectively. The loss function of the model M, denoted as $\ell(\cdot)$, can be obtained by the above steps.

Extracted Features and Classifier. Consistent with ROCKET, we extract two features from each representation sequence, feeding them into a linear classifier. Formally, for any representation sequence $\mathbf{r}_{i,s,k} \in \mathbb{R}^T$, we first compute its maximum value and the proportion of positive values (PPV), namely $Max(\mathbf{r}_{i,s,k})$ and $\frac{\sum_{t=0}^{T-1}[\mathbf{r}_{i,s,k,t}>0]}{T}$. Then, these extracted features from representations $\mathbf{R}_i$ are then incorporated into a corresponding feature set $\mathbf{E}_i$. Finally, a linear classifier (i.e., ridge regression classifier) with parameters φ is denoted as $\sigma_\varphi : \mathbf{E}_i \rightarrow y_i$. It is trained to accurately assign each instance $\mathbf{X}_i$ to its corresponding class y_i.

4 Method

In this section, we present our Adacket, a novel method for automatically designing convolutional modules. We first introduce the multi-objective optimization problem that integrates performance and resource efficiency. Then, we model this issue as a sequential decision-making problem using the RL paradigm, and design multiple action spaces to support comprehensive searches over the channel and temporal dimensions. Finally, we adapt the Deep Deterministic Policy Gradient (DDPG) algorithm [13] to explore efficient convolutional kernels within continuous action spaces.

4.1 Multi-objective Optimization: Performance and Resource

We formulate the design problem as a multi-objective issue over channel and temporal dimensions, aiming at finding a convolutional model with both a high score of performance and low redundancy on parameters. To intuitively assess the performance, we use the sigmoid function to transform the contrastive loss function $\ell(\cdot)$ into a score. By integrating this score with a parameter count metric, we can effectively balance the importance of model performance and resource efficiency in our design process.

For a given candidate convolutional model M, its performance is measured by the $Score(M)$, which is calculated using the sigmoid function as $Score(M) = \frac{1}{1+e^{-\ell(M)}}$. The resource efficiency metric $Resource(M)$ takes into account the parameters involved in the convolutional kernels and the linear classifier. Thus, the proposed multi-objective is defined by

$$Reward(M) = Score(M) \times \epsilon + \frac{Score(M)}{\log Resource(M)} \times (1 - \epsilon), \tag{5}$$

where $\epsilon \in [0, 1]$ is a hyperparameter that controls the weight of the two branches in the objective. $Score(M)$ emphasizes the importance of the model's performance, while $\frac{Score(M)}{\log Resource(M)}$ encourages the model to use fewer parameters without compromising its score. We use $Reward(M)$ to evaluate the value of the model M after considering performance and resources jointly. The multi-objective optimization goal is to maximize $Reward(M)$ w.r.t M. Inspired by the work [14,15,20,27], we next utilize the RL method to solve the multi-objective issue.

4.2 RL-Based Decision Model: Channel and Temporal Dimensions

Adacket utilizes an RL agent to explore the design space of 1D dilated convolutional kernels over channel and temporal dimensions. It does so by constructing a candidate convolutional model through a sequential decision-making process modeled as a Markov Decision Process (MDP), which comprises a 5-tuple $(\mathcal{S}, \mathcal{A}, \mathcal{T}, \mathcal{R}, \gamma)$. Concretely, $\mathcal{S}$ is a finite set of states, and $\mathcal{A}$ is a finite set of actions. $\mathcal{T} : \mathcal{S} \times \mathcal{A} \times \mathcal{S} \to [0, 1]$ is a state transition function, which defines the probability of transitioning from one state to another state after taking a specific action. $\mathcal{R}$ is the reward function, which assigns a real-valued reward signal to the agent after taking a specific action in a specific state. The discount factor $\gamma \in [0, 1]$ is used to discount future rewards. At each time step s, the agent observes the $c(s)$-th channel of instances $\mathbf{X}$ to encode a state $\mathbf{s}_s \in \mathcal{S}$, and perform an action $\mathbf{a}_s \in \mathcal{A}$ based on a policy function $\pi : \mathcal{S} \to \mathcal{A}$ to generate a group of kernels for this channel. The agent then receives a reward $r_s = \mathcal{R}(\mathbf{s}_s, \mathbf{a}_s)$ and moves to the next channel $c(s+1)$ to encode a new state $\mathbf{s}_{s+1}$ by the state transition function $\mathcal{T}$. In this sequential decision-making process, the goal of the agent is to learn a policy that maximizes the expected reward $\mathbb{E}_{\rho}[\sum_{s=1}^{S} \gamma^{s-1} \mathcal{R}(\mathbf{s}_s, \mathbf{a}_s)]$, where $\rho = \{(\mathbf{s}_1, \mathbf{a}_1), ..., (\mathbf{s}_S, \mathbf{a}_S)\} | \mathbf{a}_s = \pi(\mathbf{s}_s)\}$. We define $c(s) = (s \bmod F) + 1$ to ensure that the agent can cycle through each channel in a sequential manner. Next, we present $\mathcal{S}$, $\mathcal{A}$, and $\mathcal{R}$ in this RL environment as follows.

The State Space $\mathcal{S}$ is characterized by a state matrix $\mathbf{s}_s \in \mathbb{R}^{\alpha \times 15}$. It comprises $(\alpha - 1)$ historical observations and one current observation $\mathbf{z}_s$, which is a 15-dimension channel embedding. Thus, the expression for $\mathbf{s}_s$ is given by: $\mathbf{s}_s = [\mathbf{s}_{s-1,2}, \mathbf{s}_{s-1,3}, \cdots \mathbf{s}_{s-1,\alpha}, \mathbf{z}_s]$. By fusing historical observations into the state space, we help the agent adapt to dynamic environments and make more precise predictions about the current state. The composition of $\mathbf{z}_s$ is as follows.

- *The 1st-9th dimensions* correspond to *one* channel index $c(s)$ and *eight* distinctive attribute features. The eight features are extracted from the channel $c(s)$ of the time series using *two* 1D convolutional kernels of lengths 7 and 9. These lengths have proven effective in distinctively transforming time series in ROCKET. For each kernel, we extract *two* time-domain features (maximum value and PPV) [6] and *two* frequency-domain features (centroid frequency and peak factor) [1] from the output sequence. These features help the agent differentiate the current scanned channel from the others.
- *The 10th-15th dimensions* consist of *six* dynamics values returned by the environment, recorded as $[g_{s-1}, g'_{s-1}, a_{s-1,1}, a_{s-1,2}, a_{s-1,3}, a_{s-1,4}]$. Here, 1) g_{s-1} is the growth ratio of the parameter quantity of the convolutional kernels at time step $s-1$, calculated by $\frac{p_{s-1}^{conv} - p_{s-2}^{conv}}{p_{s-1}^{conv} + 1e-6}$, where a tiny value is used to avoid division by zero. 2) g'_{s-1} is the growth ratio of the output channels of the convolutional kernels at time step $s-1$, computed by $\frac{p_{s-1}^{out} - p_{s-2}^{out}}{p_{s-1}^{out} + 1e-6}$. These values are imperative in enabling the agent to adjust to variations in the candidate convolutional models. 3) The remaining four dynamics values are the four output action values in $\mathbf{a}_{s-1}$, which will be explained in the next paragraph.

They serve to provide information on the agent's prior decisions, aiding in the identification of patterns and trends in its behavior, and enhancing the performance.

The Action Space $\mathcal{A}$ determines each group of convolutional kernels in the multiple search spaces over channel and temporal dimensions. The agent takes four-dimension actions $\mathbf{a}_s = \{a_{s,1}, a_{s,2}, a_{s,3}, a_{s,4}\}$ from the continues action space, where each $a_{s,i}$ is a continues value between 0 and 1. Then, the agent maps them to a fine-grained four-tuple $(h_s^{in}, h_s^{out}, h_s^{ks}, h_s^{dil})$ and a corresponding channel group $\mathbf{c}_s$. They determine a kernel-channel pair $(\mathbf{v}_s, \mathbf{c}_s)$ for the candidate convolutional model. The mapping process at step s is described as follows.

- *Input channel* h_s^{in} is calculated by $\lfloor \frac{F-c(s)}{(F-c(s))\times a_{s,1}} \rfloor$, where $\lfloor \cdot \rfloor$ is the floor function. $F - c(s)$ means the remaining channels between the current channel $c(s)$ and the last one F. The term $(F - c(s)) \times a_{s,1}$ is defined as the interval of channel sampling from $c(s)$ to F. Subsequently, the indexes are grouped into a set $\mathbf{c}_s$, where a positive integer $c_{s,m} = c(s) + (m-1) \times \lfloor (F - c(s)) \times a_{s,1} \rfloor$. This approach enables a flexible and adaptive adjustment of the number of input channels based on the specific task and input data, thereby potentially improving model performance and optimizing resource utilization.
- *Output channel* h_s^{out} is formally derived by $\lfloor \beta * a_{s,2} \rfloor$, where β enforces an upper bound for the output channel number. This technique is effective in reducing the number of model parameters and computation required while preserving the model's capacity for complex representations.
- *Kernel size* h_s^{ks} is computed by $\lceil (a_{s,3} \times \kappa) \rceil$, where $\lceil \cdot \rceil$ is the ceil function and κ is the upper bound of the kernel size. It guarantees that the kernel size is significantly smaller than the input time series in most cases.
- *Dilation* h_s^{dil} is determined by h_s^{ks} and the receptive field size. Here, we define the receptive field size as a function w.r.t $a_{s,4}$, specifically $F_s = \lceil a_{s,4} \times T \rceil$. Hence, h_s^{dil} can be mathmatically calculated by $\lceil \frac{F_s - h_s^{ks}}{h_s^{ks} - 1 + 1e-6} \rceil$, according to the irrelationship across h_s^{dil}, h_s^{ks} and F_s [23]. This allows the convolutional kernels to capture features at a variable and adaptive receptive field.

If h_s^{out} is zero, no convolutional kernel will be added at step s. The above mapping process produces a four-tuple $(h_s^{in}, h_s^{out}, h_s^{ks}, h_s^{dil})$ and a corresponding channel group $\mathbf{c}_s$. Then, through initializing the convolutional kernel weights and biases according to the procedure outlined in Sect. 3, we create a kernel-channel pair $(\mathbf{v}_s, \mathbf{c}_s)$, and incorporate it into the candidate convolutional model. As such, the agent facilitates the association of the convolutional kernel with the input channel, enabling the fine-grained establishment of convolutional models and relevant channel-wise interaction. We describe the pseudocode of constructing the state space and action space in the Appendix.

The Reward $\mathcal{R}$ is set to *Reward*(M) at the final step S and 0 for all other steps. This delayed reward design encourages the agent to focus on the long-term outcome of the selection process [18]. Once the agent takes an action $\mathbf{a}_s$ at state $\mathbf{s}_s$, the environment returns the reward $r_s = \mathcal{R}(\mathbf{s}_s, \mathbf{a}_s)$ to the agent.

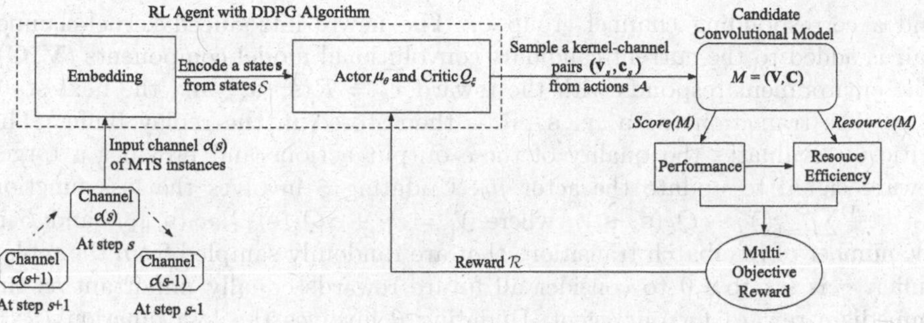

Fig. 1. Illustration of Adacket to introduce one kernel-channel pair. At each step s, the RL agent encodes the current state $\mathbf{s}_s$ using a channel embedding from channel $c(s)$, and samples a kernel-channel pair $(\mathbf{v}_s, \mathbf{c}_s)$ for the candidate convolutional model M. Then, the agent receives the reward $\mathcal{R}$ and moves to the next channel $c(s+1)$.

4.3 DDPG Adaptation: Efficient Kernel Exploration

By conceptualizing the establishment of a model M as an MDP, it becomes feasible to formulate the design of a series of convolutional kernels as an action sequence $\mathbf{a}_{1:S}$. This enables us to effectively train the Adacket's agent using an actor-critic method, i.e., the Deep Deterministic Policy Gradient (DDPG) algorithm.

The DDPG algorithm is a powerful method for exploring continuous action while balancing exploration and exploitation. This is accomplished through the actor-critic structure, which provides more stable training by reducing variance. Its core components are an actor $\mu_\theta : \mathcal{S} \to \mathcal{A}$, which utilizes a multi-layer perceptron (MLP) θ to process the current state and outputs a continuous action based on a learned policy, and a critic $Q_\xi : \mathcal{S} \times \mathcal{A} \to \mathbb{R}$, which employs another MLP ξ to assess the current state-action pair's reward. The primary objective is to maximize the expected reward $\mathbb{E}_{\mathbf{s}_s \sim \rho^\beta}[Q_\xi(\mathbf{s}_s, \mu_\theta(\mathbf{s}_s))]$, where ρ^β denotes the state visitation distribution for a different stochastic behavior policy β.

To train the Adacket's agent with DDPG, we begin by defining the neural architecture of the actor μ_θ as a two-layer MLP and four output heads with the sigmoid activation function. This architecture allows us to create a multi-dimensional continuous space, where each output can be mapped to a range (0, 1). That of critic Q_ξ is a two-layer MLP and one output head. Incorporating Fig. 1 and Algorithm 1, the main process can be described as follows.

We first initialize the best convolutional model, the best reward, and the actor-critic networks. During each episode, the candidate convolutional model $M = (\mathbf{V}, \mathbf{C})$ is initialized as empty and then created by sequentially adding convolutional kernels in S steps. At each step s, the actor takes the state space $\mathbf{s}_s$ as input and outputs the action $\mathbf{a}_s$, while adding exploration noise $\mathcal{N}_s$. This promotes better exploration of the environment and enables the agent to discover more optimal policies. We express this as $\mathbf{a}_s = \mu_\theta(\mathbf{s}_s) + \mathcal{N}_s$, where $\mathcal{N}_s$ is tailored to the specific environment. We then map $\mathbf{a}_s$ to a four-tuple $(h_s^{in}, h_s^{out}, h_s^{ks}, h_s^{dil})$

and a corresponding channel group $\mathbf{c}_s$. The newly introduced kernel-channel pair is added to the current candidate convolutional model components $(\mathbf{V}, \mathbf{C})$. The environment responds with the reward $r_s = \mathcal{R}(\mathbf{s}_s, \mathbf{a}_s)$ and the next state $\mathbf{s}_{s+1}$. The transition $(\mathbf{s}_s, \mathbf{a}_s, r_s, \mathbf{s}_{s+1})$ is then stored in the replay buffer. The critic Q_ξ evaluates the quality of these output actions and provides a target reward signal to update the actor μ_θ. Updating ξ involves the loss function $\mathcal{L}_\xi = \frac{1}{\mathcal{B}} \sum_{i=1}^{\mathcal{B}} (\mathcal{Y}_i - Q_\xi(\mathbf{s}_i, \mathbf{a}_i))$, where $\mathcal{Y}_i = r_i + \gamma Q_\xi(\mathbf{s}_{i+1}, \mu_\theta(\mathbf{s}_{i+1}))$ and $\mathcal{B}$ is the number of minibatch transitions that are randomly sampled from the replay buffer. γ is set to 1.0 to consider all future rewards equally important as the immediate reward for our agent. Updating θ involves the loss function $\mathcal{L}_\theta = -\frac{1}{\mathcal{B}} \sum_{i=1}^{\mathcal{B}} Q_\xi(\mathbf{s}_i, \mu_\theta(\mathbf{s}_i))$. If the reward at the last step is higher than the best reward, the agent updates the best model and best reward. Finally, we select the best model established in this sequential training process. Algorithm 1 outlines the above training process of the agent.

Algorithm 1: Adacket's agent updates with DDPG

Initialize the best model M^{best} and the best reward R^{best}
Create the actor μ_θ and the critic Q_ξ
for *episode = 0 to E* **do**
  Set $(\mathbf{V}, \mathbf{C})$ to empty sets
  for $s = \{1, 2, ..., S\}$ **do**
    Encode the state $\mathbf{s}_s$ by Algorithm A.1
    Select action $\mathbf{a}_s = \mu_\theta(\mathbf{s}_s) + \mathcal{N}_s$ according to the current policy and exploration noise
    Map action $\mathbf{a}_s$ to a kernel-channel pair $(\mathbf{v}_s, \mathbf{c}_s)$ by Algorithm A.2
    Add $(\mathbf{v}_s, \mathbf{c}_s)$ to candidate model components $(\mathbf{V}, \mathbf{C})$
    Observe reward $r_s = \mathcal{R}(\mathbf{s}_s, \mathbf{a}_s)$ and encode the next state $\mathbf{s}_{s+1}$
    Store transition $(\mathbf{s}_s, \mathbf{a}_s, r_s, \mathbf{s}_{s+1})$ in the replay buffer
    Sample a random minibatch of $\mathcal{B}$ transitions $(\mathbf{s}_i, \mathbf{a}_i, r_i, \mathbf{s}_{i+1})$ from replay buffer
    Update critic Q_ξ by minimizing the loss: $\mathcal{L}_\xi$
    Update actor μ_θ by minimizing the loss: $\mathcal{L}_\theta$
  end
  if $r_S \geq R^{best}$ **then**
    Update the best reward $R^{best} = r_S$
    Save the best model $M^{best} = (\mathbf{V}, \mathbf{C})$
  end
end
return M^{best}

After the Adacket agent is trained by Algorithm 1, the best model M^{best} is obtained, which is then used to replace the random convolutional model of ROCKET. Then, we perform the model M^{best} and provide the representations for feature extraction. A linear classifier is subsequently trained on these extracted features for classification.

5 Experiments

5.1 Experimental Settings

Datasets. Adacket's performance is evaluated on 30 MTSC sourced from the UEA archive [3]. They present an exceptional challenge due to their significant heterogeneity of properties, including channels, instances, and length. The processing of UEA datasets uses the `tslearn` package [22] with the default settings.

Details. Regarding the setting of parameters in the DDPG algorithm, we are consistent with its original paper (see the Appendix). Additionally, we set the value of ϵ to 0.99 in Eq. 5 to allow for a trade-off between model performance and resource. Additionally, we limit the upper bound of the output channel number $\beta = 16$ for each group of convolutional kernels, and set the upper bound of the kernel size κ to 10. We also investigate that ϵ can effectively control resource constraints, and β and κ have little effect on the accuracy, except when their values are too small (see the Appendix).

Baselines. Our proposed approach is compared against four benchmark methods, including ResNet, InceptionTime, TapNet, and ROCKET. These methods have demonstrated impressive performance on MTSC tasks [16] with ROCKET achieving the best rank among them.

Metrics. Adacket is evaluated on the following three different metrics.

- *Accuracy.* We conduct the pairwise posthoc analysis [4] to statistically rank the accuracy of different models over UEA archives and visualize the results by the Critical Difference (CD) Diagram [8] with Holm's α (5%) [11].
- *Computational Efficiency.* The training time and inference time of each method on all UEA datasets are used to measure computational efficiency.
- *Resource Efficiency.* Two metrics are used to compare the resource efficiency of Adacket. The first metric is the number of model parameters, which includes convolutional kernel parameters and classifier parameters and is a conventional metric for deep learning methods. The second metric is memory usage, as recommended by ROCKET, which is calculated by $O \times 8 \times n$ bytes, where O denotes the number of transformed features and n denotes the size of the training set. The default value of O in ROCKET is 20,000.

5.2 Classification Performance Evaluation

Accuracy. Figure 2 illustrates the CD diagrams of the five classifiers that completed all UEA datasets. The diagram demonstrates that our method outperforms all other compared baselines in terms of average accuracy rank, which indicates the superior performance of Adacket in MTSC tasks.

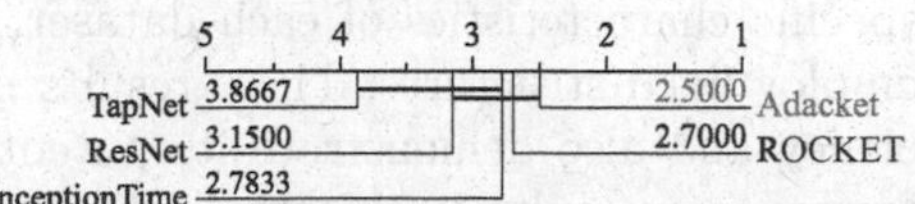

Fig. 2. CD diagrams for comparing different methods on all UEA datasets.

Computational Efficiency. To further compare Adacket with the two best baselines, i.e., InceptionTime and ROCKET, we present training and inference time comparisons in Table 1. The experiments are conducted on one GeForce RTX 3090 Ti GPU. In terms of train time, our results show that Adacket is nearly one order of magnitude faster than InceptionTime, requiring only 1.61 h to train all 30 UEA datasets, which is a comparable result to the performance of ROCKET. In terms of inference time, Adacket stands out as the fastest method thanks to its efficient design. These findings demonstrate the advantages of Adacket in terms of time overhead, highlighting the efficiency of our method.

Table 1. Train time (in hours) and inference time (in seconds) on all UEA datasets.

Method	Train Time	Inference Time
InceptionTime	48.55	1.61
ROCKET	**1.25**	1.58
Adacket	1.61	**0.68**

Resource Efficiency. We then present the accuracy, the number of parameters, and memory usage for three datasets with varying numbers of channels, including the dataset with the largest number of channels in the UEA benchmark. From Table 2, Adacket achieves better accuracy than InceptionTime and ROCKET while consuming fewer parameters and less memory. Interestingly, InceptionTime requires more parameters as the number of channels increases, whereas Adacket can control resources more efficiently to capture valuable features, even on datasets with a larger number of channels, such as the DuckDuckGeese dataset. This is due to Adacket's ability to adapt its components to suit the specific characteristics of each dataset, whereas InceptionTime and ROCKET employ fixed structures. These results underscore Adacket's flexibility and efficiency and also demonstrate its potential to achieve comprehensive high performance on multiple objectives. The complete results for all 30 UEA datasets, including accuracy, parameters, and memory cost, can be found at the provided link[1], along with the source code, datasets, and appendices. Crucially, the

Table 2. Comparison of accuracy (%), parameters (**MB**), and memory cost (**MB**) of three MTSC datasets, i.e., SelfRegulationSCP1 (SRS) with 7 channels, Heartbeat (HB) with 61 channels, and DuckDuckGeese (DDG) with 1345 channels, the most channels in the UEA archive.

Dataset	Method	Acc	Params	Mem
SRS	InceptionTime	86.55	4.685	-
	ROCKET	84.69	-	42.88
	Adacket	**89.42**	**0.021**	**3.34**
HB	InceptionTime	73.20	4.810	-
	ROCKET	71.76	-	32.64
	Adacket	**77.07**	**0.012**	**0.58**
DDG	InceptionTime	54.00	7.754	-
	ROCKET	46.13	-	8.00
	Adacket	**58.00**	**0.003**	**0.68**

[1] https://github.com/jrzhang33/Adacket.

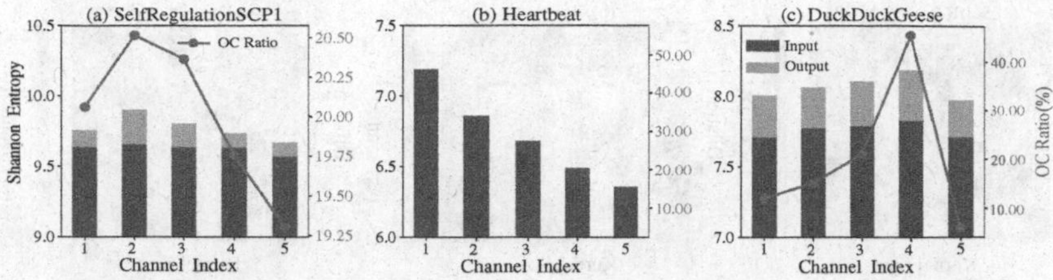

Fig. 3. Comparison of Shannon entropy in the first five channels of the initial test instance before (*Input*) and after (*Output*) passing through the convolutional model. We define the output channel ratio (*OC Ratio*) as the number of representations produced by each channel (normalized by the total number of representations).

complete results show that Adacket outperforms both ROCKET and InceptionTime in terms of resource efficiency across the entire set of 30 datasets.

5.3 Understanding Adacket's Design Selections

To further understand how Adacket determines the convolutional kernel across the channel and temporal dimensions, we conduct a series of empirical experiments to analyze the reasons behind its design selections.

Channel Dimension. Shannon entropy is a trusted measure of feature diversity [5], often quantifying information uncertainty in data. Increasing input channel uncertainty can yield more diverse and meaningful output representations. We compute Shannon entropy statistics for the first five channels of the three mentioned datasets before and after channel transformation. Figure 3 shows Adacket improves Shannon entropy for channels in both the SelfRegulationSCP1 and DuckDuckGeese datasets. Particularly, DuckDuckGeese channels with extremely low Shannon entropy exhibit a significant increase in information uncertainty after transformation, validating selected convolutional kernels' role in feature diversity enhancement in specific channels. Furthermore, as Fig. 3 illustrates, the trend of the output channel ratio is consistent with that of the output representation Shannon entropy. This confirms that Adacket tends to output more representations with higher Shannon entropy, thus providing more distinctive features for the classifier. We observe that in the Heartbeat dataset, the first five channels are discarded without assigned convolutional kernels, yet Adacket maintains high accuracy in Table 2. This could be due to the channels' structural attributes, exhibiting robust periodicity and local correlation, causing feature compression after convolution. Alternatively, other channels may be more suitable for feature extraction, yielding a valuable representation space. The results highlight Adacket's ability to increase feature diversity, reduce channel redundancy, and enable meaningful channel-wise interactions in convolutional models.

Temporal Dimension. To validate Adacket's kernel size and dilation choices, we employ grid search to find the optimal convolutional kernel. We search for the

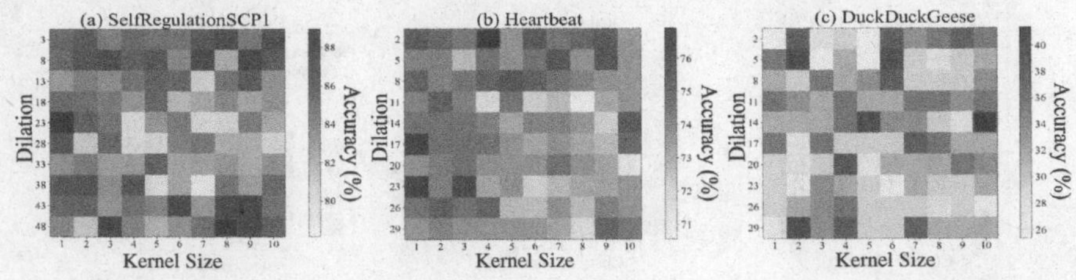

Fig. 4. The accuracy of the grid obtained by searching the combination of kernel size and dilation within that grid range. Darker colors represent higher accuracy and the red box represents the size-dilation combination selected by Adacket. The grid with darker colors indicates that there is a combination in it with higher accuracy. (Color figure online)

best kernel size and dilation coefficient combination, adopting Adacket's chosen input and output channels. By evaluating the extracted features from different convolutional kernel combinations, Fig. 4 displays the highest accuracy in each grid range. As we can see, the red box is located in the grid with the highest accuracy. This demonstrates Adacket's reliable convolutional kernel design search. Moreover, Fig. 4 demonstrates that the channels of different MTSC tasks exhibit distinct preferences for convolutional kernel design. For example, the DuckDuckGeese dataset achieves optimal performance with a kernel size of 10 and a dilation of 14, which is not the preference of the SelfRegulationSCP1 dataset. This confirms Adacket's effectiveness in designing optimal time-scale convolutional kernels, enabling the establishment of convolutional models at high-granularity levels. Overall, this comprehensive exploration enhances convolutional kernels' potential in MTSC tasks, leading to more accurate and meaningful results.

6 Conclusion

In this work, we introduce a novel method called Adacket to automatically design efficient convolutional models for various MTSC tasks. Adacket formulates the kernel design problem as a multi-objective optimization task, considering both performance and resource efficiency, and models this issue as a sequential decision-making problem using the RL paradigm. It achieves the adaptive design of the convolutional model, allowing for searches over channel and temporal dimensions. By training with DDPG, Adacket generates efficient convolutional kernels with high granularity. Our experimental evaluations on the UEA archive demonstrate that Adacket can achieve more competitive results on the accuracy, computational, and resource efficiency. Additionally, Adacket presents captivating avenues for future research, such as expanding termination conditions in each episode to accurately meet the budget constraints of end-users. In conclusion, Adacket is a promising method in MTSC scenarios and we hope that our work will inspire further investigation into the development of more meaningful convolutional models for time series analysis.

Acknowledgements. This work was supported by the Plan Project of Zhejiang Science and Technology (No. 2023C03183) and the Plan Project of Ningbo Municipal Science and Technology (No. 2022S172).

Ethical Statement. Adacket is a method designed to improve the prediction accuracy of multivariate time series classification problems. The data is adopted from public datasets, so it does not involve data stealing and adversarial attacks. Our work has several potential future applications, e.g. medical and architectural fields. Such applications hopefully have a positive societal impact. Additionally, we adhere to the principles of fairness, transparency, and interpretability when presenting the model's prediction results.

References

1. Ambikairajah, R., Phung, B.T., Ravishankar, J., Blackburn, T.: Spectral features for the classification of partial discharge signals from selected insulation defect models. IET Sci. Meas. Technol. **7**(2), 104–111 (2013)
2. Anguita, D., Ghio, A., Oneto, L., Parra Perez, X., Reyes Ortiz, J.L.: A public domain dataset for human activity recognition using smartphones. In: Proceedings of the 21th International European Symposium on Artificial Neural Networks, Computational Intelligence and Machine Learning, pp. 437–442 (2013)
3. Bagnall, A., et al.: The UEA multivariate time series classification archive, 2018. arXiv preprint arXiv:1811.00075 (2018)
4. Benavoli, A., Corani, G., Mangili, F.: Should we really use post-hoc tests based on mean-ranks? J. Mach. Learn. Res. **17**(1), 152–161 (2016)
5. Chu, J.L., Krzyżak, A.: Analysis of feature maps selection in supervised learning using convolutional neural networks. In: Sokolova, M., van Beek, P. (eds.) AI 2014. LNCS (LNAI), vol. 8436, pp. 59–70. Springer, Cham (2014). https://doi.org/10.1007/978-3-319-06483-3_6
6. Dempster, A., Petitjean, F., Webb, G.I.: ROCKET: exceptionally fast and accurate time series classification using random convolutional kernels. Data Min. Knowl. Disc. **34**(5), 1454–1495 (2020)
7. Dempster, A., Schmidt, D.F., Webb, G.I.: MiniRocket: a very fast (almost) deterministic transform for time series classification. In: Proceedings of the 27th ACM SIGKDD Conference on Knowledge Discovery & Data Mining, pp. 248–257 (2021)
8. Demšar, J.: Statistical comparisons of classifiers over multiple data sets. J. Mach. Learn. Res. **7**, 1–30 (2006)
9. Dhariyal, B., Nguyen, T.L., Ifrim, G.: Fast channel selection for scalable multivariate time series classification. In: Lemaire, V., Malinowski, S., Bagnall, A., Guyet, T., Tavenard, R., Ifrim, G. (eds.) AALTD 2021. LNCS (LNAI), vol. 13114, pp. 36–54. Springer, Cham (2021). https://doi.org/10.1007/978-3-030-91445-5_3
10. Han, S., Niculescu-Mizil, A.: Supervised feature subset selection and feature ranking for multivariate time series without feature extraction. arXiv preprint arXiv:2005.00259 (2020)
11. Holm, S.: A simple sequentially rejective multiple test procedure. Scand. J. Stat., 65–70 (1979)
12. Ismail Fawaz, H., et al.: InceptionTime: finding AlexNet for time series classification. Data Min. Knowl. Disc. **34**(6), 1936–1962 (2020)

13. Lillicrap, T.P., et al.: Continuous control with deep reinforcement learning. arXiv preprint arXiv:1509.02971 (2015)
14. Liu, C., et al.: Auto-DeepLab: hierarchical neural architecture search for semantic image segmentation. In: Proceedings of the IEEE/CVF Conference on Computer Vision and Pattern Recognition, pp. 82–92 (2019)
15. Pham, H., Guan, M., Zoph, B., Le, Q., Dean, J.: Efficient neural architecture search via parameters sharing. In: International Conference on Machine Learning, pp. 4095–4104. PMLR (2018)
16. Ruiz, A.P., Flynn, M., Large, J., Middlehurst, M., Bagnall, A.: The great multivariate time series classification bake off: a review and experimental evaluation of recent algorithmic advances. Data Min. Knowl. Disc. **35**(2), 401–449 (2021)
17. Stamoulis, D., et al.: Single-path NAS: device-aware efficient convnet design. arXiv preprint arXiv:1905.04159 (2019)
18. Sutton, R.S., Barto, A.G.: Reinforcement Learning: An Introduction. MIT Press, Cambridge (2018)
19. Tan, C.W., Dempster, A., Bergmeir, C., Webb, G.I.: MultiRocket: multiple pooling operators and transformations for fast and effective time series classification. Data Min. Knowl. Disc. **36**(5), 1623–1646 (2022)
20. Tan, M., et al.: MnasNet: platform-aware neural architecture search for mobile. In: Proceedings of the IEEE/CVF Conference on Computer Vision and Pattern Recognition, pp. 2820–2828 (2019)
21. Tang, W., Long, G., Liu, L., Zhou, T., Blumenstein, M., Jiang, J.: Omni-scale CNNs: a simple and effective kernel size configuration for time series classification. arXiv preprint arXiv:2002.10061 (2020)
22. Tavenard, R., et al.: Tslearn, a machine learning toolkit for time series data. J. Mach. Learn. Res. **21**(1), 4686–4691 (2020)
23. Wang, P., et al.: Understanding convolution for semantic segmentation. In: 2018 IEEE Winter Conference on Applications of Computer Vision (WACV), pp. 1451–1460. IEEE (2018)
24. Yue, Z., et al.: TS2Vec: towards universal representation of time series. In: Proceedings of the AAAI Conference on Artificial Intelligence, vol. 36, pp. 8980–8987 (2022)
25. Zhang, X., Gao, Y., Lin, J., Lu, C.T.: TapNet: multivariate time series classification with attentional prototypical network. In: Proceedings of the AAAI Conference on Artificial Intelligence, vol. 34, pp. 6845–6852 (2020)
26. Zoph, B., Le, Q.V.: Neural architecture search with reinforcement learning. arXiv preprint arXiv:1611.01578 (2016)
27. Zoph, B., Vasudevan, V., Shlens, J., Le, Q.V.: Learning transferable architectures for scalable image recognition. In: Proceedings of the IEEE Conference on Computer Vision and Pattern Recognition, pp. 8697–8710 (2018)

Efficient Adaptive Spatial-Temporal Attention Network for Traffic Flow Forecasting

Hongyang Su, Xiaolong Wang(✉), Qingcai Chen, and Yang Qin

Harbin Institute of Technology, Shenzhen, China
suhongyang@stu.hit.edu.cn, {xlwangsz,qingcai.chen,csyqin}@hit.edu.cn

Abstract. Urban traffic flow prediction is a challenging task in the field of intelligent transportation and spatio-temporal data analysis. Accurate prediction of traffic states by leveraging sophisticated spatio-temporal patterns is critical. However, existing methods ignore the local validity of dynamic spatio-temporal auto-correlations, resulting in bottlenecks in the performance and efficiency of the model. In this work, we investigate the effects of dominant as well as invalid spatio-temporal patterns and propose a spatio-temporal forecasting framework. Specifically, we propose a dominant spatial-temporal attention mechanism, which extends the empirical approximation of Kullback-Leibler divergence to the spatial-temporal domain to optimize the computational efficiency of the attention mechanism, and identifies locally valid associations through dominant query generation. Meanwhile, we theoretically demonstrate the validity of the extension. Furthermore, we design an adaptive spatial-temporal fusion embedding scheme to generate heterogeneous and synchronous traffic states without pre-defined graph structures. We further propose an Efficient Adaptive Spatial-Temporal Attention Network (EASTAN) to capture fine-grained spatio-temporal dependencies based on the above modules and perform sequential forecasting. Extensive experiments (Code and appendix available at: https://github.com/ecmlpkdd2023/EASTAN) on four real-world datasets show that the proposed framework improves the prediction accuracy by 3.31%–48.93%, and significantly reduces the training time as well as model parameters compared to state-of-the-arts.

Keywords: Traffic flow prediction · dominant spatio-temporal patterns · adaptive spatial-temporal fusion embedding · attention mechanism

1 Introduction

In the field of spatio-temporal data mining and intelligent transportation, traffic flow prediction has been an important problem. Accurate forecasting can provide essential indications for improving traffic conditions. Due to the connectivity of roads, traffic signals are potentially correlated in both temporal and spatial dimensions, which limits the performance of time series analysis models based on statistical analysis [1,23] or recurrent neural networks (RNNs) [13,15].

D. Koutra et al. (Eds.): ECML PKDD 2023, LNAI 14173, pp. 205–220, 2023.
https://doi.org/10.1007/978-3-031-43424-2_13

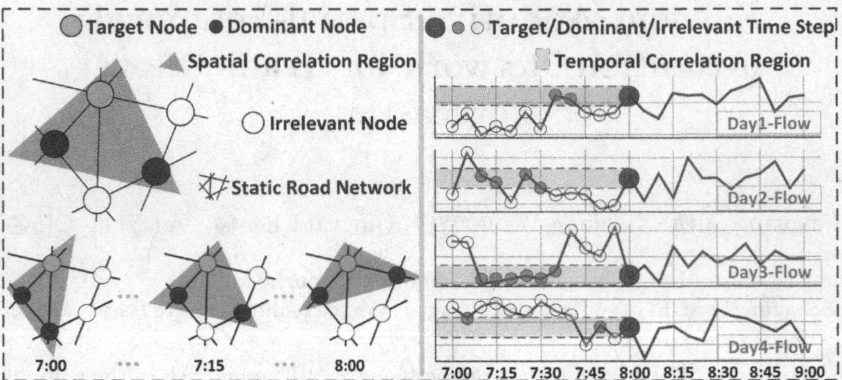

Fig. 1. The local validity of the dynamic spatio-temporal patterns. The effective spatio-temporal patterns exist mainly in the dominant nodes and time steps.

The road network is intuitively a graph structure based on location and can be further defined numerically as a Laplacian matrix to reflect spatial information. Therefore, previous studies employ graph convolutional neural networks (GCNs) to aggregate spatial associations from road network and combine variants of convolutional neural networks (CNNs) to explore spatio-temporal patterns [6,12,20]. Despite the desirable performance achieved by these models, several problems have been pointed out and extensively studied. **First**, the predefined graph reflecting the road network structure is static, which is not applicable in dynamic traffic environments. To address this issue, numerous adaptive methods have been proposed that replace the original predefined maps with data-driven learnable matrices as potential spatial information and achieve accurate predictions [2,18]. **Second**, the extraction of spatial and temporal correlations is separated, which ignores the heterogeneity of spatio-temporal patterns. Therefore, some spatio-temporal information fusion methods have been proposed recently to capture synchronous spatio-temporal information and achieve excellent performance [9,10,14,21]. However, there are still some issues and challenges that have not been fully considered:

(1) The contradiction between the heterogeneous and dynamic nature of spatio-temporal patterns. Fusing information from temporal and spatial dimensions is an effective way to capture heterogeneous spatio-temporal patterns. For example, STSGCN [14] as well as STFGNN [10] transform spatial-temporal embeddings into localized spatial-temporal sub-graphs and generate corresponding spatial-temporal representations by GCNs. GMAN [21] employs Node2Vec [5] to generate spatial embeddings and combine them with temporal features of sequences to form spatial-temporal embeddings. However, the above methods are all based on pre-defined graphs to describe spatial information, which weaken the dynamic characteristics of spatio-temporal patterns. **(2)** The local validity of the dynamic spatial and temporal associations. As shown in Fig. 1, the traffic flow of target node and time step is mainly influenced by the dominant nodes and time steps within the local validity correlation region rather than from the whole road network or historical time segments. The spatio-temporal patterns from the irrelevant nodes and time steps are redundant and even generate additional disturbances. **(3)** Efficiency bottlenecks. Existing methods have achieved noticeable improvements in performance, while ignoring the efficiency of the model, the non-negligible training time and the number of parameters weaken the practicality.

To solve the above issues, we propose an Efficient and Adaptive Spatial-Temporal Attention Network (EASTAN) for traffic flow forecasting, which has the following properties: **the adaptive spatial-temporal fusion embedding**, which adaptively learns heterogeneous spatio-temporal patterns and integrates local and global correlations in both temporal and spatial dimensions to enhance short-term and long-term forecasting capabilities; **the dominant spatial-temporal attention**, which extends Kullback-Leibler (KL) divergence [16] to the spatio-temporal domain to perform correlation calculations, and combines the long-tailed distribution properties of the self-attention to generate dominant spatio-temporal queries, efficiently filtering out the irrelevant spatio-temporal patterns; **the efficient spatial-temporal block (EST-Block)** integrates the dominant spatial-temporal attention and fusion gate to embed the dominant and heterogeneous spatio-temporal patterns into the historical sequence; **the EASTAN framework** consists of stackable EST-Blocks and a transform attention, and performs prediction through the generative interface. We summarize the contributions of this work as follows:

(1) We propose the dominant spatial-temporal attention to extract the relevant patterns precisely and efficiently by extending the long-tail distribution property of sequential correlations from the temporal domain to the spatio-temporal domain. Meanwhile, we theoretically prove the principle and stability of the computational process. **(2)** We propose the adaptive spatial-temporal fusion embedding, which consists of both adaptive spatial embedding and hierarchical temporal embedding to enrich the heterogeneous spatio-temporal information. It is completely data-driven and more lightweight. **(3)** Extensive experiments on 4 real-world datasets demonstrate the advantages of our well-designed framework in performance, efficiency, and interpretability. EASTAN outperforms 14 representative approaches with significant performance improvements of 3.31%–48.93%, reducing the training time by at least 82.78% and the number of parameters by at least 97.47% compared with state-of-the-arts.

2 Related Work

We classify the existing studies on traffic flow forecasting into 4 categories and present some representative papers in this field.

Sequential Methods. Traffic flow data can be easily modeled by time series prediction models based on statistical learning or machine learning [1,13,15,23]. However, these models cannot handle spatial information and their performance are restricted. **Pre-defined graph-based methods**. STGCN [20] proposes to use graph convolution to extract spatial associations based on location information and combine it with temporal convolution to perform serialized prediction. DCRNN [12] combines graph convolution and recurrent neural networks with an encoder-decoder framework to explore spatio-temporal correlations. ASTGCN [6] uses attention to explore spatio-temporal dependencies with dynamic properties. Besides, STGODE [4] explores dynamic spatial-temporal dependencies on road semantic adjacency matrices using tensor-based ordinary differential equations. Z-GCNETs [3] combine spatial topological information of adjacency matrices with time-aware graph convolution. Nevertheless, the prediction accuracy of these models is difficult to improve due to the static spatial information of the pre-defined graphs. **Adaptive graph-based methods**. Graph Wavenet [18] proposes an adaptive graph convolution that captures dynamic spatial-temporal dependencies in combination with a stacked dilated 1D convolution. AGCRN [2] proposes the node-level learnable parameters fused with GCN to model dynamic spatial associations. DSTAGNN [9] replaces the pre-defined graph with a dynamic spatial-temporal aware graph and uses a novel graph neural network combined with attention to explore dynamic spatial-temporal patterns. However, the above models ignore the heterogeneous properties of spatio-temporal patterns and the local validity of dynamic patterns. **Methods based on heterogeneous spatial-temporal patterns** maintain the synchronous properties of spatio-temporal patterns by fusing information in spatial and temporal dimensions and achieve desirable performance [10,14,19,21]. However, these methods still require pre-defined spatial information and cannot detect the effect of traffic flow on traffic states, such as anomalies triggered by unexpected traffic accidents.

In addition to the spatio-temporal prediction framework introduced above, recent studies have also achieved excellent breakthroughs in terms of efficiency with optimized attention mechanism [8,11,22]. However, all these models are limited by the inherent structure, which cannot directly explore the heterogeneous spatio-temporal information in traffic flow forecasting tasks. Inspired by these studies, in this work we intend to adopt the efficient calculation process to optimize the attention mechanism and extend it to the spatio-temporal domain.

3 Preliminaries

Referring to existing studies [7,10,14], we define the traffic data at time t as $\mathbf{X}_t \in \mathbb{R}^{N \times C}$, where N is the number of sensors, and C is the feature dimension. Therefore, the traffic data over a period of time is $\mathcal{X} = \{\mathbf{X}_1, \mathbf{X}_2, \cdots, \mathbf{X}_T\} \in \mathbb{R}^{T \times N \times C}$, where T is the length of the historical sequence. We define the traffic flow at time t as $\mathbf{Y}_t \in \mathbb{R}^{N \times 1}$ and consider the traffic flow forecasting task as learning the mapping function $f(\cdot)$, which satisfies: $\mathcal{Y} = f(\mathcal{X})$, where $\mathcal{Y} = \{\mathbf{Y}_{T+1}, \mathbf{Y}_{T+2}, \cdots, \mathbf{Y}_{T+H}\} \in \mathbb{R}^{H \times N \times 1}$, H is the prediction length. In this work, both T and H are set to 12 (1 h), which is the common setting for traffic flow forecasting tasks. We denote the fully connected layer with $RelU(\cdot)$ activation function as $FC(\cdot)$ for gradient back-propagation and dimension transformation[1].

[1] The critical symbols for this paper are given in Appendix D.

4 Methodology

4.1 Adaptive Spatial-Temporal Fusion Embedding

The challenge in exploring heterogeneous spatio-temporal information is how to integrate the features of both temporal and spatial dimensions rather than considering them separately and without contradicting the dynamic properties of spatio-temporal patterns. Therefore, we propose the adaptive spatial-temporal fusion embedding module, which inherits and optimizes the capability of adaptive graphs and generates heterogeneous spatial-temporal representations. Specifically, the proposed module can be considered from two dimensions:

In the spatial dimension, we design the adaptive spatial embedding (ASE). Specifically, ASE randomly initializes a node-level learnable embedding $\mathbf{E}_s \in \mathbb{R}^{N \times d_e}$, where N is the number of nodes and d_e is the embedding dimension. Here, we directly map the spatial information into a data-driven dense matrix where each row corresponds to a node embedding. Compared to adaptive adjacency matrix [2] or location-based spatial embedding [21], ASE is more simpler and lightweight, which has the linear complexity when N is determined. Besides, the learned $\mathbf{E}_s$ has better interpret-ability and can be directly integrated with temporal information. **In the temporal dimension**, we consider the impact of hierarchical temporal factors on traffic flow in terms of long-term and short-term effects, corresponding to the global and local levels, respectively.

At the global level, we encode different time slices of traffic flow such as time-of-day and day-of-week to reflect the intrinsic temporal properties. This is intuitive because the traffic state is influenced by a specific time such as the morning rush or the weekend. Specifically, we set the daily time slice to 5 min and the weekly time slice to 1 day, and employ one-hot encoding to describe the above time slices separately, and then concatenate them to obtain the global temporal embedding (GTE) $\mathbf{E}_t^g \in \mathbb{R}^{295}$. At the local level, we enhance the impact of different time steps in the sequence with positional information [17] to capture chronological information as well as short-term fluctuations in the traffic state. Further, we propose local temporal embedding (LTE) $\mathbf{E}_t^l$ as:

$$\mathbf{E}_t^l = \begin{cases} sin(pos/5000^{(p/D)}) & p = 2i \\ cos(pos/5000^{(p/D)}) & p = 2i+1, \end{cases} \tag{1}$$

where D is the model dimension, pos is the position of each time step, p is the index which distinguishes between odd and even positions and we set the maximum length of the marked position as 5000 to ensure that all positions of the temporal embedding are marked. Finally, We fuse the above embeddings into the adaptive spatial-temporal fusion embedding $\mathbf{E}_a \in \mathbb{R}^{(T+H) \times N \times D}$ by addition operation as:

$$\mathbf{E}_a = FC(\mathbf{E}_s) \oplus FC(\mathbf{E}_t^g) \oplus FC(\mathbf{E}_t^l), \tag{2}$$

4.2 Dominant Spatial-Temporal Attention

Efficient Spatial-Temporal Relations Calculation. The spatial-temporal self-attention [6] transforms the input in both spatial and temporal dimensions

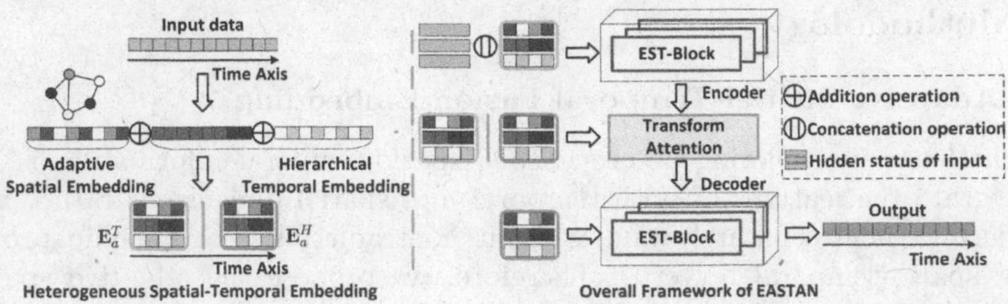

Fig. 2. The framework of EASTAN.

to extract the potential spatio-temporal patterns of the sequences. Given a target query $\mathbf{q}_i$, the spatial or temporal attention can be expressed as:

$$\mathcal{A}(\mathbf{q}_i, \mathbf{K}, \mathbf{V}) = \sum\nolimits_{j \in \mathcal{N}, j \in \mathcal{T}} \frac{p(\mathbf{q}_i, \mathbf{k}_j)}{\sum_{l \in \mathcal{N}, l \in \mathcal{T}} p(\mathbf{q}_i, \mathbf{k}_l)} \mathbf{v}_j, \tag{3}$$

where $\mathbf{q}_i \in \mathbf{Q}$, $\mathbf{k}_j, \mathbf{k}_l \in \mathbf{K}$, $\mathbf{v}_j \in \mathbf{V}$. $\mathbf{Q}$, $\mathbf{K}$ and $\mathbf{V}$ are the Query, Key, and Value matrices derived from the linear transformation of inputs. $\mathcal{N} \in \mathbb{R}^N$ is the nodes set, $\mathcal{T} \in \mathbb{R}^T$ is the time steps set. $p(\mathbf{q}_i, \mathbf{k}_j) = exp(\mathbf{q}_i \mathbf{k}_j^{\mathrm{T}} / \sqrt{d})$, d is the standardization factor. The computational complexity of the spatial-temporal attention is $O(N^2) + O(T^2)$ due to the repeated matrix multiplication and the requirement to traverse all query-key pairs, which greatly reduces the model efficiency. To solve this problem, recent studies [22] employ KL divergence instead of dot product to improve the efficiency of attention-based correlation computation and achieve promising performance. However, all these methods can only integrate information in the temporal dimension, and thus cannot handle spatial correlations of sequences. Inspired by the above insights, we adopt the empirical approximation of KL divergence to quantify the correlations within the attention mechanism and extend this approach in the spatio-temporal domain[2]. Specifically, we first define the target query as $\mathbf{q}_i^{st}$, which is similar to the target query in self-attention. Then we compute the spatial-temporal relations as:

$$\mathbf{R}_{st} = \overline{p}(\mathbf{q}_i^{st}, \mathbf{K}_{st}) = \max_j \{ \frac{\mathbf{q}_i^{st} (\mathbf{k}_j^{st})^{\mathrm{T}}}{\sqrt{d}} \} - \frac{1}{D_{st}} \sum\nolimits_{j=1}^{D_{st}} \frac{\mathbf{q}_i^{st} (\mathbf{k}_j^{st})^{\mathrm{T}}}{\sqrt{d}}, \tag{4}$$

where $\mathbf{q}_i^{st} \in \mathbf{Q}_{st}$, $\mathbf{k}_j^{st} \in \mathbf{K}_{st}$. Both $\mathbf{Q}_{st}$ and $\mathbf{K}_{st}$ are the linear transformations of the historical sequence in the spatial or temporal dimension. Our proposed computational method has two distinct advantages: **(i)** referring to [22], Eq. (4) can be considered as a max-mean operation, and its sorted computational results approximately match the long-tail distribution of the attention mechanism, which means that computing only a part of the query-key pairs during the training process is capable of representing the dominant attention scores. **(ii)** We define $D_{st} = dim_0(\mathbf{q}_i^{st})$ to extract the first dimension of the vector to perform the mean operation, which extends our method to the spatio-temporal domain. When the number of nodes is N and the input length is T, $D_{st} \in \{N, T\}$.

[2] Theoretical proofs are presented in Appendix A.

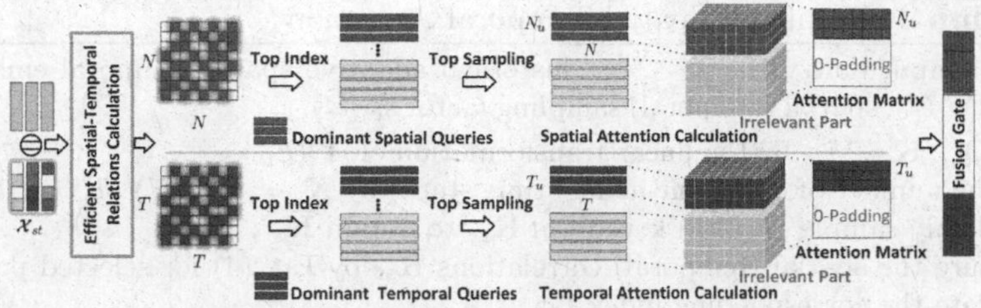

Fig. 3. Sketch of the workflow inside the EST-Block. Dominant spatial and temporal attention matrices are computed in parallel and aggregated by fusion gate.

Dominant Spatial-Temporal Query Generation. The key to capturing effective spatio-temporal patterns is to find the dominant sets of nodes and time steps. Thus, we propose an attention enhancement method to generate the dominant queries based on the long-tailed properties of numerical correlations[3].

To simplify the expressions, here we use $\mathbf{Q}_{st}$, $\mathbf{K}_{st}$ and $\mathbf{V}_{st}$ to uniformly represent the original spatial or temporal Query, Key and Value matrices. Specifically, we first propose the spatial sampling factor s_c and the temporal sampling factor t_c to control the number of dominant nodes N_u and the number of dominant time steps T_u, respectively. Inspired by [22], to ensure that the calculated correlations are non-long-tail distributed, we choose the log kernel function and set $N_u = s_c ln(N)$, $T_u = t_c ln(T)$. After that, we randomly sample N_u (T_u) keys from $\mathbf{K}_{st}$ to obtain $\overline{\mathbf{K}}_{st}$, which forms the dominant query-key pairs with all the target queries. Next, we compute the spatial-temporal associations using Eq. (4) and obtain the index $\mathbf{I}_d$ of the sorted dominant spatio-temporal patterns through the TopIndex operation. Finally, based on the $\mathbf{I}_d$, we sample the dominant queries from the $\mathbf{Q}_{st}$ by the TopSample operation and further form the dominant query matrix $\overline{\mathbf{Q}}_{st}$. The above generation process can be expressed as:

$$\begin{cases} \overline{\mathbf{K}}_{st} = RandomSample(\mathbf{K}_{st}, N_u, T_u) \\ \overline{\mathbf{R}}_{st} = \overline{p}(\mathbf{q}_i^{st}, \overline{\mathbf{K}}_{st}) \\ \mathbf{I}_d = TopIndex(\overline{\mathbf{R}}_{st}, N_u, T_u) \\ \overline{\mathbf{Q}}_{st} = TopSample(\mathbf{Q}_{st}, \mathbf{I}_d), \end{cases} \tag{5}$$

where the proposed Topindex operation sorts the associations by values and then extracts the indexes corresponding to the top N_u (T_u) results in $\mathbf{Q}_{st}$. The proposed TopSample operation extracts the query vectors from $\mathbf{Q}_{st}$ based on the above indexes and forms the dominant query matrix $\overline{\mathbf{Q}}_{st}$. We give the pseudo-code of the proposed dominant spatial-temporal attention in Algorithm 1.

Finally, we compute spatial-temporal correlations based on the dominant spatial and temporal query matrices as:

$$\mathcal{A}_{st}(\mathcal{X}) = Softmax(\overline{\mathbf{Q}}_{st}\mathbf{K}_{st}^{\mathrm{T}}/\sqrt{d})\mathbf{V}_{st}. \tag{6}$$

[3] Details of long-tail distribution of traffic states are presented in Appendix B.

Algorithm 1. Dominant Spatial-Temporal Attention

Require: Input data $\boldsymbol{\mathcal{X}} \in \mathbb{R}^{T\times N\times C}$, historical adaptive spatial-temporal embedding $E_a^T \in \mathbb{R}^{T\times N\times D}$, spatial (temporal) sampling factor s_c (t_c).

1: Get $\mathbf{Q}_{st}, \mathbf{K}_{st}, \mathbf{V}_{st}$ by the linear transformation of $\boldsymbol{\mathcal{X}}||E_a^T$;
2: Set the number of dominant nodes (time steps) by $N_u = s_c ln(N)$ ($T_u = t_c ln(T)$);
3: Randomly sample N_u (T_u) keys from $\mathbf{K}_{st}$ to obtain $\overline{\mathbf{K}}_{st}$;
4: Measure the spatial (temporal) correlations $\overline{\mathbf{R}}_{st}$ by Eq. (4) for selected pairs and generate the corresponding index $\mathbf{I}_d$;
5: Select queries from $\mathbf{Q}_{st}$ with $\mathbf{I}_d$ to form the dominant query matrix $\overline{\mathbf{Q}}_{st}$;
6: Get dominant spatial (temporal) attention results with $\overline{\mathbf{Q}}_{st}$ by Eq. (6);
7: **Return** dominant spatial (temporal) attention matrix.

Note that $\overline{\mathbf{Q}}_{st}$ is the sparse matrix containing only the dominant query vectors involved in information propagation, the other parts are filled with 0. Thus, the complexity of dominant spatial-temporal attention is $O(N\ln(N)) + O(T\ln(T))$. We show the workflow of the dominant spatial-temporal attention in Fig. 3.

4.3 Efficient Spatial-Temporal Block

We propose an efficient spatial-temporal block (EST-Block) which computes valid spatio-temporal patterns by dominant spatial-temporal attention mechanism, and then generates higher-order representations of the sequences through gating mechanism [12,21]. Inside EST-Block, both dominant spatial and temporal attention matrices are computed in parallel, which can be represented as:

$$\alpha_{n_i,n}^{(k)}, \beta_{t_j,t}^{(k)} = \mathcal{A}_{st}^{(k)}(FC(\mathcal{X}_{st}^L)), \tag{7}$$

where $\mathcal{X}_{st}^L$ is the inputs of the L_{th} EST-BLock, $\alpha_{n_i,n}^{(k)}$ and $\beta_{t_j,t}^{(k)}$ correspond to the dominant spatial and temporal correlations of the target node n_i at time step t_j, respectively. We adopt multi-head mechanism to enhance the adaptability, and k is the attention head. Further, we aggregate the hidden states of all target nodes and time steps, splice the information of each head, and obtain the final outputs of the dominant spatial-temporal attention in the L_{th} EST-Block as:

$$\mathbf{H}_S^L = ||_{k=1}^K\{\sum\nolimits_{n\in\mathcal{N}} \alpha_{n_i,n}^{(k)}\}; \mathbf{H}_T^L = ||_{k=1}^K\{\sum\nolimits_{t\in\mathcal{T}} \beta_{t_j,t}^{(k)}\}, \tag{8}$$

where K is the number of attention heads, $\mathbf{H}_S^L \in \mathbb{R}^{T\times N\times D}$ and $\mathbf{H}_T^L \in \mathbb{R}^{T\times N\times D}$ incorporate the spatial and temporal associations, respectively.

In order to aggregate potential correlations from both the spatial and temporal dimensions, we design a fusion gate as the output interface of each EST-Block, which can be expressed as:

$$\mathbf{H}^L = \lambda \cdot FC(\mathbf{H}_S^L) \oplus (1-\lambda) \cdot FC(\mathbf{H}_T^L), \tag{9}$$

where $\mathbf{H}^L \in \mathbb{R}^{T\times N\times D}$, $\lambda = \phi(FC(\mathbf{H}_S^L) \oplus FC(\mathbf{H}_T^L))$ is the gating parameter, $\phi(\cdot)$ is the Sigmoid activation function, and $\oplus$ is the addition operation.

Table 1. Dataset analysis and description.

Datasets	#Nodes	#Edges	#Time Steps (5mins)	#Time Range
PEMS03	358	547	26208	09/01/2018-11/30/2018
PEMS04	307	340	16992	01/01/2018-02/28/2018
PEMS07	883	866	28224	05/01/2017-08/31/2017
PEMS08	170	295	17856	07/01/2016-08/31/2016

4.4 Encoder-Decoder Architecture

As shown in Fig. 2, the proposed EASTAN is an encoder-decoder framework consisting of stacked EST-Blocks for encoder and decoder. **In the encoding phase**, we first generate heterogeneous spatial-temporal embedding $\mathbf{E}_a$ and then divide it chronologically into the historical part $\mathbf{E}_a^T$ and predictive part $\mathbf{E}_a^H$. Input data and $\mathbf{E}_a^T$ are concatenated and fed to the first EST-Block, and then each EST-Block receives the information from the previous one. **In the decoding phase**, we design a transform attention to establish the dynamic temporal connections between future and historical states. Specifically, we apply the multi-head attention to the adaptive spatial-temporal fusion embeddings and get the higher-order representations of predicted values as:

$$\gamma_t^{(k)} = Softmax\{FC(\mathbf{E}_a^T) \cdot FC(\mathbf{E}_a^H)/\sqrt{d}\} \cdot FC(\mathbf{H}^L), \quad (10)$$

$$\mathbf{H}_p = FC(||_{k=1}^K \sum_{l=1}^T \gamma_l^{(k)}), \quad (11)$$

where $\gamma_t^{(k)}$ is the attention score corresponding to the k_{th} head. $\mathbf{H}_p \in \mathbb{R}^{H \times N \times D}$ is the output of the proposed transform attention.

The inputs of the decoder includes the predicted part of the adaptive spatial-temporal fusion embedding and the output of the transform attention, which benefits from the information extraction capability of the designed EST-Block to jointly decode the fusion embedding and the prediction results. During the training phase, we adopt mean absolute error (MAE) as the loss function as:

$$\mathcal{L}_\theta = \frac{1}{H} \sum_{i=1}^H |\mathbf{Y}_{T+i} - \widehat{\mathbf{Y}}_{T+i}|, \quad (12)$$

where $\mathbf{Y}_{T+i}$ and $\widehat{\mathbf{Y}}_{T+i}$ are the predicted and true values at time step $T+i$.

5 Experiments

5.1 Experimental Setup

Datasets. As shown in Table 1, We use 4 real-world traffic datasets released by [10,14], which are sampled from different regions of California and provided by the Caltrans Performance Measurement System (PeMS). The data of each time step is aggregated by a 5-min window. The train/valid/test ratio of each dataset

Table 2. Prediction performance comparison results on 4 datasets. The best results are highlighted in bold, the second best results are highlighted with _, † marks the official reported results, ‡ marks the better results from fine-tuning the published source codes.

Model	PEMS03			PEMS04			PEMS07			PEMS08			Compare
	MAE	MAPE	RMSE	MAE	MAPE	RMSE	MAE	MAPE	RMSE	MAE	MAPE	RMSE	
HA	29.94	28.35	42.42	38.60	28.54	53.01	45.19	21.42	63.50	31.98	20.48	43.81	48.93%↑
VAR	24.39	28.34	41.59	29.03	19.96	44.13	33.27	16.82	49.89	25.40	18.85	40.37	38.60%↑
FC-LSTM	20.92	23.62	32.93	27.09	18.07	40.97	30.51	23.62	44.96	22.18	15.58	33.05	31.51%↑
STGCN	20.70	24.86	33.61	25.34	18.82	38.76	29.26	14.04	44.96	21.69	16.17	32.47	28.77%↑
ASTGCN	18.08	18.74	29.94	22.48	16.04	34.93	27.32	12.74	41.28	18.97	12.32	28.71	18.87%↑
DCRNN	16.11	16.26	27.62	21.30	14.05	33.58	22.70	9.90	35.46	16.64	10.70	26.14	8.80%↑
GraphWave	16.74	16.51	28.61	22.56	15.86	35.59	23.66	10.07	37.93	16.72	11.44	26.95	13.03%↑
AGCRN	15.92	16.58	28.33	19.76‡	12.92‡	31.82‡	21.20	8.89	35.01	15.95†	10.09†	25.22†	5.49%↑
GMAN	16.67	17.16	29.82	19.97	13.62	31.69	22.37	11.31	35.44	15.18	9.85	24.45	7.72%↑
STGODE	16.50†	16.69†	27.84†	20.84†	13.77†	32.82†	22.99†	10.14†	37.54†	16.81†	10.62†	25.97†	9.55%↑
STSGCN	17.54	16.75‡	29.00‡	21.22	13.80‡	33.58‡	24.22‡	10.19‡	38.87‡	17.13†	10.96†	26.80†	12.17%↑
STFGNN	16.83	16.29‡	28.44	19.84	12.94‡	31.80‡	22.07†	9.21†	35.80†	16.64†	10.60†	26.22†	7.41%↑
DSTAGNN-G	15.61†	14.79†	27.23†	19.41†	12.84†	31.63†	21.67†	9.06†	35.04†	15.90†	9.97†	25.24†	4.19%↑
DSTAGNN	15.57†	**14.68**†	27.21†	19.30†	12.70†	31.46†	21.42†	9.01†	34.51†	15.67†	9.94†	24.77†	3.31%↑
EASTAN	**15.37**	14.98	**26.11**	**18.88**	**12.66**	**30.44**	**20.56**	**8.55**	**33.77**	**14.15**	**9.40**	**23.54**	**0.00%↑**
Improvements	+1.28%	-2.04%	+4.04%	+2.18%	+0.31%	+3.24%	+3.02%	+3.82%	+2.14%	+6.79%	+4.57%	+3.72%	

is 6:2:2. We use Z-score standardization on the training set and apply the rules to the validation and test set.

Baselines. We select 14 baselines[4] and classify them into 4 categories: (1) Sequential methods without considering spatial correlations: **HA** [2], **VAR** [23] and **FC-LSTM** [15]. (2) Methods based on pre-defined graphs: **STGCN** [20], **ASTGCN** [6], **DCRNN** [12], **STGODE** [4], and **DSTAGNN-G** [9]. (3) Methods based on adaptive graphs: **GraphWave** [18], **AGCRN** [2] and **DSTAGNN** [9]. (4) Methods based on heterogeneous spatio-temporal patterns: **GMAN** [21], **STSGCN** [14] and **STFGNN** [10].

Parameters Setting. For EASTAN, we use the grid search strategy to determine the optimal encoder layer e_l is 1, decoder layer d_l is 1, the multi-heads of attention K is 4 and the model dimension D is 32. The dimensions of adaptive spatial embedding d_e are chosen from $\{16, 32, 64, 128, 256\}$. The spatial sampling factor s_c and temporal sampling factor t_c are chosen from $\{5, 10, 15, 20, 25\}$ and $\{1, 2, 3, 4, 5\}$, respectively. We use Adam optimizer and set the learning rate to 1e-3 and the batch size to 32. The maximum epoch is 1000 with the early-stop patience value of 20. All models are trained and tested independently for 5 times on one Tesla V100 32 GB GPU.

5.2 Overall Comparison

Performance Comparison. We choose three commonly used metrics for performance evaluation, including MAE, MAPE, and RMSE. Table 2 shows the performance comparison results on four datasets. **(1)** EASTAN outperforms all other

[4] Detailed descriptions of baselines are given in Appendix C.

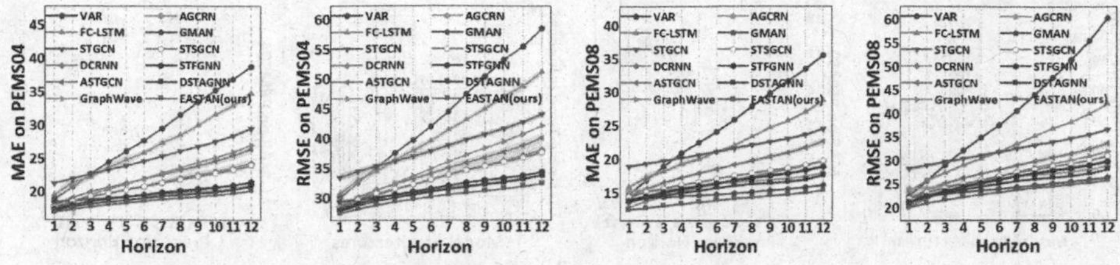

Fig. 4. Prediction performance at each horizon on PEMS04 and PEMS08 datasets.

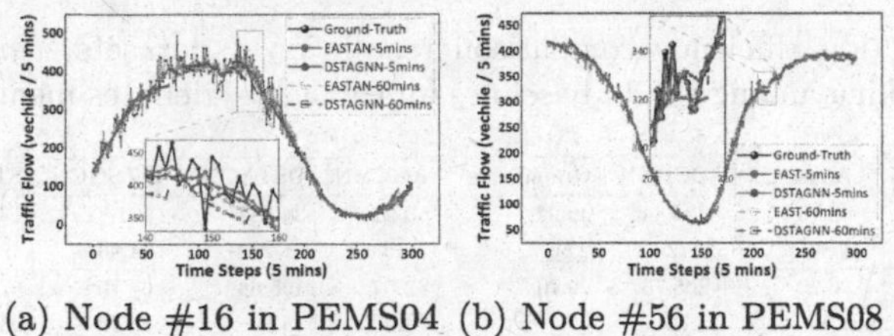

(a) Node #16 in PEMS04 (b) Node #56 in PEMS08

Fig. 5. Comparison of the ground-truth and prediction curves of EASTAN and DSTAGNN on PEMS04 and PEMS08. Please zoom in the plot area for a better view.

state-of-the-art baselines with the improvement of 3.31%–48.93% under all metrics on all datasets, which confirms the success of the proposed methods for traffic flow forecasting tasks. **(2)** We note that EASTAN's MAPE results on PEMS03 are slightly lower, but all other metrics are more favorable, such as the 4.04% decrease under RMSE metrics. **(3)** Compared with adaptive graph-based methods (Graph Wave, AGCRN and DSTAGNN), EASTAN significantly improves the inference performance with ratios 13.03%, 5.49% and 3.31%, because EASTAN is able to transform the adaptive spatial information into heterogeneous spatio-temporal information. Besides, EASTAN also outperforms existing methods based on heterogeneous spatio-temporal information, and the reason might be that the spatio-temporal patterns captured by these methods do not take into account the effect of noise generated by dynamic traffic states.

Figure 4 shows the performance of EASTAN compared with other models for each prediction horizon. It is obvious that as the number of prediction steps increases, the prediction error of EASTAN rises slowly and smoothly compared to all other methods. We also visualize the curves of ground-truth and predicted values for the second best model DSTAGNN and EASTAN in Fig. 5, and randomly select different sensors to compare their performance in short-term (5 min) and long-term (60 min) predictions. Clearly, the prediction curves of EASTAN are relatively close to the ground-truth under different prediction cases.

Efficiency Comparison. In Table 3, we measure the spatial complexity by the number of parameters $P_a(E+5)$ and the temporal complexity by the average training time of each epoch $T_t(s/epoch)$. **(1)** Comparing the DSTAGNN and our proposed EASTAN, the number of parameters of EASTAN on PEMS07 (PEMS08) is only 7.87 (97.47%) of DSTAGNN, and the average running time of

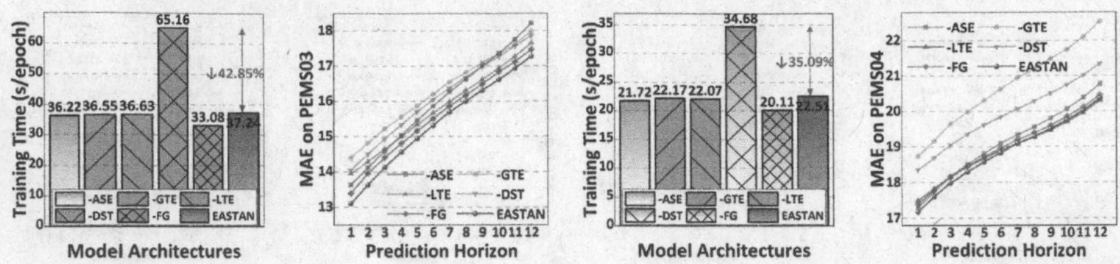

Fig. 6. Ablation experiments of performance and efficiency on PEMS03 and PEMS04.

Table 3. Prediction efficiency comparison results on 4 datasets. *rank* denotes the performance ranking among the 14 baselines in Table 2, '-' denotes memory bottleneck.

Model^{rank}		STGCN^{12}	ASTGCN^{11}	DCRNN^{7}	GraphWave^{10}	AGCRN^{4}	DSTAGNN^{2}	STSGCN^{9}	STFGNN^{5}	**EASTAN^{1}**
PEMS03	T_t	**15.07**	63.75	324.84	49.92	55.92	360.33	131.71	131.12	37.24
	P_a	2.75	5.89	3.72	2.56	7.49	41.72	34.96	49.69	**0.80**
PEMS04	T_t	**8.53**	36.20	205.76	29.70	32.67	195.68	68.70	67.13	22.51
	P_a	2.75	4.50	3.72	2.56	7.49	35.80	28.72	38.74	**0.98**
PEMS07	T_t	**35.40**	222.71	542.14	114.77	132.91	-	523.08	543.96	73.96
	P_a	2.77	32.30	3.72	2.56	7.55	143.54	153.58	259.18	**1.13**
PEMS08	T_t	**6.46**	24.77	201.33	21.56	36.39	111.24	38.30	37.04	19.16
	P_a	2.74	1.79	3.72	2.56	7.47	22.97	16.61	17.56	**0.58**

a single epoch on PEMS04 is only 11.5% of DSTAGNN. The non-negligible efficiency advantage highlights the contribution of our method, especially in the case of achieving comparable performance. **(2)** As the scale of the dataset increases, both temporal and spatial complexity of well-performing baselines increase noticeably, while our EASTAN still maintains stable efficiency advantages and avoids memory bottlenecks. **(3)** STGCN has a shorter training time, but is obviously limited by the rank of performance (12/14). Compared with other baselines, the training time of EASTAN is reduced by 11.13%-35.56%.

5.3 Ablation Study

We design 5 variants of EASTAN to better evaluate each component. **EASTAN-*wo*-ASE**, which replaces the adaptive spatial embedding with static spatial information from pre-defined graphs; **EASTAN-*wo*-GTE**, which removes the global spatial embedding; **EASTAN-*wo*-LTE**, which removes the local spatial embedding; **EASTAN-*wo*-DST**, which replaces dominant spatio-temporal attention with traditional spatio-temporal self-attention; **EASTAN-*wo*-FG**, which replaces fusion gate with linear layers.

We abbreviate the above variants as "-ASE", "-GTE", "-LTE", "-DST" and "-FG" in order and compare the performance as well as efficiency of all variants in Fig. 6. **(1)** The efficiency of the "-DST" model is reduced by 42.85% (PEMS03) and 35.09% (PEMS04), confirming the efficiency advantage of our proposed dominant spatial-temporal attention over traditional self-attention, while the corresponding performance improvement proves its ability to avoid the effect of invalid spatio-temporal patterns. **(2)** We could notice that the weak

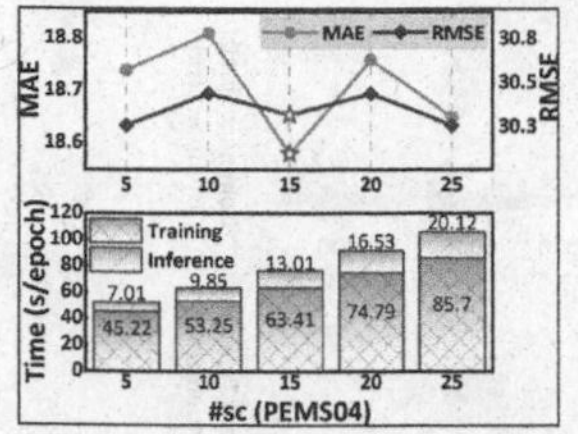

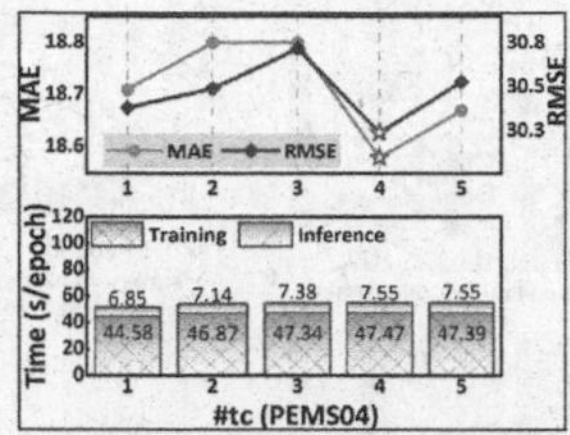

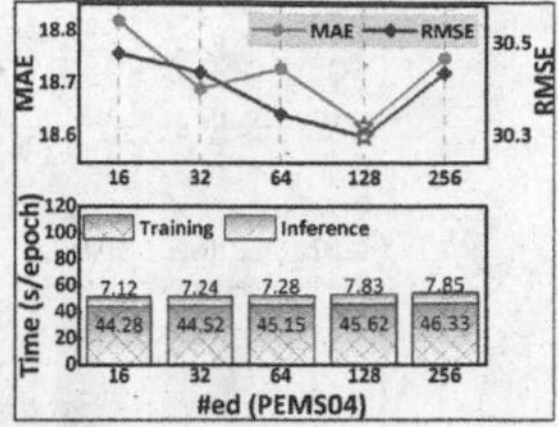

Fig. 7. Model analysis on s_c (left), t_c (middle) and d_e (right) for EASTAN ($e_l = 2$, $d_l = 3$) with respect to performance and efficiency on PEMS04.

performance of the "-GTE" model. The reason might be the periodic properties of traffic environments, such as the traffic states in the morning rush or weekend share similar patterns. **(3)** The performance of "-LTE" model decreases by 6.09% for Horizon = 1 on PEMS03. We consider that the addition of position information helps to reinforce the chronological properties of temporal embedding and therefore enables more fine-grained traffic states. **(4)** The performance of the "-ASE" and "-FG" models decrease significantly, indicating the effectiveness of dynamic heterogeneous spatio-temporal patterns captured by EASTAN.

5.4 Model Analysis

We expand the number of layers of EASTAN during the model analysis and find that the deeper EASTAN still offers the comprehensive efficiency and performance advantage. On this basis, we further analyze the sensitivity of several important parameters on PEMS04 and present the results in Fig. 7.

Sensitivity to s_c and t_c. As shown in Fig. 7 (left) and Fig. 7 (middle). **(1)** The spatio-temporal patterns sampled by s_c and t_c allow EASTAN to achieve the desired performance, indicating that the valid spatio-temporal patterns exist between the dominant nodes and time steps. **(2)** Both the excessively small and large s_c (t_c) will lead to weaker performance, a large number of samples will degrade the dominant attention to the traditional self-attention, which prevents EASTAN from filtering out irrelevant spatio-temporal patterns; while an insufficient number of samples will lead to the loss of important patterns.

Sensitivity to d_e. As shown in Fig. 7 (right), the optimal embedding dimension $d_e = 128$, we consider that too small d_e cannot fully reflect the complex spatio-temporal patterns, while too large d_e will lead to overfitting. Besides, the complexity of the adaptive spatial embedding is linear when the number of nodes is determined, thus d_e has little effect on the efficiency.

5.5 Interpretability of EASTAN

As shown in Fig. 8, we provide several case studies to give a more intuitive impression of the interpretability of our model. Specifically, we randomly choose 10 sensors (S_1–S_{10}) to study the spatial correlations in the 12 predicted horizons (H_1–H_{12}), and 1 sensor (S_1) to study the temporal correlations. Obviously,

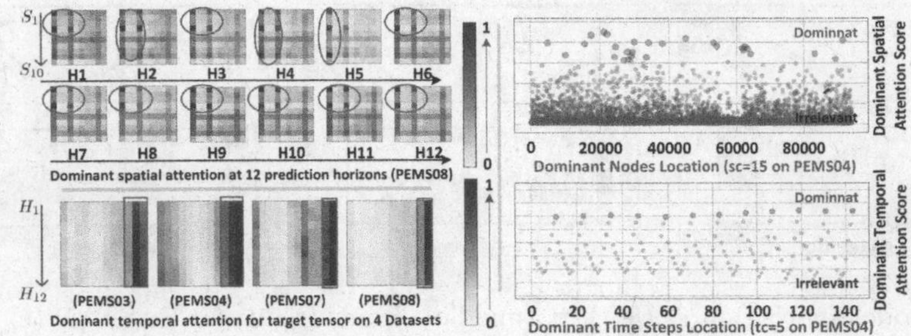

Fig. 8. (Left) Visualization for dominant spatial and temporal attention heatmap. (Right) Visualization for dominant correlations of node and time pairs from EASTAN.

(1) Both spatial and temporal associations are local valid, the red circled parts correspond to the dominant correlations captured by EASTAN. **(2)** The temporal correlations are clearly biased towards later time steps, which is practical because the latest traffic status in often decisive. Meanwhile, we flatten out the learned attention matrix and distinguish the dominant and irrelevant correlations based on the attention score. We find that both spatial and temporal correlations obtained from the attention-based mechanism are consistent with long-tailed distributions, while one of the main contributions of our EASTAN is to capture these dominant correlations that fall outside the long-tailed distribution region.

6 Conclusion

In this paper, we propose an efficient adaptive spatial-temporal attention network named EASTAN for traffic flow forecasting tasks. Specifically, we propose the adaptive spatial-temporal fusion embeddings to reflect heterogeneous spatio-temporal patterns. We propose the dominant spatial-temporal attention to dynamically filter the irrelevant patterns and avoid redundant computations from self-attention in the spatio-temporal domain. Also, the well-designed EST-Block aggregates the above modules and forms the encoder-decoder architecture to perform sequential prediction. Extensive experiments demonstrate that EASTAN has non-negligible efficiency advantages in achieving desirable performance.

This work can be further enhanced in the following two directions. First, the interpretability of the adaptive embedding dimension can be correlated with the traffic state and the complexity of the road network. Second, how to exploit the relatively stable geometric properties of the road structure (e.g., topological information) to reduce the influence of irrelevant patterns is an interesting extension work in the future.

Acknowledgements. This work is supported by the Science and Technology Planning Project of Shenzhen Municipality [No. JCYJ20190806112210067] and the National Natural Science Foundation of China [No. 62276075, 61872113].

Ethical Statement.. There are no ethical issues involved in this work, all data are publicly available and no personal information is involved. It is worth noting that accurate traffic flow forecasting might help related industries such as online traffic services to predict road congestion, which of course could also provide guidance for road construction.

References

1. Ahmed, M.S., Cook, A.R.: Analysis of freeway traffic time-series data by using Box-Jenkins techniques, No. 722 (1979)
2. BAI, L., Yao, L., Li, C., Wang, X., Wang, C.: Adaptive graph convolutional recurrent network for traffic forecasting. In: NeurIPS, vol. 33, pp. 17804–17815 (2020)
3. Chen, Y., Segovia, I., Gel, Y.R.: Z-GCNETs: time zigzags at graph convolutional networks for time series forecasting. In: ICML, vol. 139, pp. 1684–1694 (2021)
4. Fang, Z., Long, Q., Song, G., Xie, K.: Spatial-temporal graph ODE networks for traffic flow forecasting. In: SIGKDD, pp. 364–373 (2021)
5. Grover, A., Leskovec, J.: node2vec: scalable feature learning for networks. In: SIGKDD, pp. 855–864 (2016)
6. Guo, S., Lin, Y., Feng, N., Song, C., Wan, H.: Attention based spatial-temporal graph convolutional networks for traffic flow forecasting. In: AAAI, vol. 33, pp. 922–929 (2019)
7. Jiang, R., et al.: DL-Traff: survey and benchmark of deep learning models for urban traffic prediction. In: CIKM, pp. 4515–4525 (2021)
8. Kitaev, N., Kaiser, Ł., Levskaya, A.: Reformer: the efficient transformer. In: ICLR (2020)
9. Lan, S., Ma, Y., Huang, W., Wang, W., Yang, H., Li, P.: DSTAGNN: dynamic spatial-temporal aware graph neural network for traffic flow forecasting. In: ICML, vol. 162, pp. 11906–11917 (2022)
10. Li, M., Zhu, Z.: Spatial-temporal fusion graph neural networks for traffic flow forecasting. In: AAAI, vol. 35, pp. 4189–4196 (2021)
11. Li, S., et al.: Enhancing the locality and breaking the memory bottleneck of transformer on time series forecasting. In: NeurIPS, vol. 32, pp. 5243–5253 (2019)
12. Li, Y., Yu, R., Shahabi, C., Liu, Y.: Diffusion convolutional recurrent neural network: data-driven traffic forecasting. In: ICLR (2018)
13. Seo, Y., Defferrard, M., Vandergheynst, P., Bresson, X.: Structured sequence modeling with graph convolutional recurrent networks. In: NIPS, pp. 362–373 (2018)
14. Song, C., Lin, Y., Guo, S., Wan, H.: Spatial-temporal synchronous graph convolutional networks: a new framework for spatial-temporal network data forecasting. In: AAAI, vol. 34, pp. 914–921 (2020)
15. Sutskever, I., Vinyals, O., Le, Q.V.: Sequence to sequence learning with neural networks. In: NeurIPS, pp. 3104–3112 (2014)
16. Van Erven, T., Harremos, P.: Rényi divergence and Kullback-Leibler divergence. IEEE Trans. Inf. Theory **60**(7), 3797–3820 (2014)
17. Vaswani, A., et al.: Attention is all you need. In: NeurIPS, pp. 5998–6008 (2017)

18. Wu, Z., Pan, S., Long, G., Jiang, J., Zhang, C.: Graph WaveNet for deep spatial-temporal graph modeling. In: IJCAI, pp. 1907–1913 (2019)
19. Yang, S., Liu, J., Zhao, K.: Space meets time: local spacetime neural network for traffic flow forecasting. In: ICDM, pp. 817–826 (2021)
20. Yu, B., Yin, H., Zhu, Z.: Spatio-temporal graph convolutional networks: a deep learning framework for traffic forecasting. In: IJCAI, pp. 3634–3640 (2017)
21. Zheng, C., Fan, X., Wang, C., Qi, J.: GMAN: a graph multi-attention network for traffic prediction. In: AAAI, vol. 34, pp. 1234–1241 (2020)
22. Zhou, H., et al.: Informer: beyond efficient transformer for long sequence time-series forecasting. In: AAAI, pp. 11106–11115 (2021)
23. Zivot, E., Wang, J.: Vector autoregressive models for multivariate time series. In: Modeling Financial Time Series with S-Plus®, pp. 385–429. Springer, New York (2006). https://doi.org/10.1007/978-0-387-21763-5_11

Estimating Dynamic Time Warping Distance Between Time Series with Missing Data

Aras Yurtman[1,2](✉), Jonas Soenen[1,2], Wannes Meert[1,2], and Hendrik Blockeel[1,2]

[1] KU Leuven, Department of Computer Science, Celestijnenlaan 200A box 2402, 3001 Leuven, Belgium

{Aras.Yurtman,Jonas.Soenen,Wannes.Meert,Hendrik.Blockeel}@kuleuven.be

[2] Leuven.AI, Celestijnenlaan 200A box 2453, 3001 Leuven, Belgium

Abstract. Many techniques for analyzing time series rely on some notion of similarity between two time series, such as Dynamic Time Warping (DTW) distance. But DTW cannot handle missing values, and simple fixes (e.g., dropping missing values, or interpolating) fail when entire intervals are missing, as is often the case with, e.g., temporary sensor or communication failures. There is hardly any research on how to address this problem. In this paper, we propose two hyperparameter-free techniques to estimate the DTW distance between time series with missing values. The first technique, DTW-AROW, significantly decreases the impact of missing values on the DTW distance by modifying the optimization problem in the DTW algorithm. The second technique, DTW-CAI, can further improve upon DTW-AROW by exploiting additional contextual information when that is available (more specifically, more time series from the same population). We show that, on multiple datasets, the proposed techniques outperform existing techniques in estimating pairwise DTW distances as well as in classification and clustering tasks based on these distances. The proposed techniques can enable many machine learning algorithms to more accurately handle time series with missing values.

1 Introduction

Time series data arise in many problem domains. Often, these time series may contain intervals of missing data. Consider, for instance, sensors that send data over a wireless connection: a temporary failure of the sensor or the internet connectivity may lead to an entire interval of missing data. Application contexts where this can happen include wearables, smart electricity meters, and many more [15,29]. Despite the massive amount of research on analysis of time series, very little research seems to exist on how to handle such missing data.

Many methods for time series analysis rely on *pairwise distances* between time series. Examples are k-nearest neighbor (k-NN) and support vector machines for classification [1]; k-medoids for clustering [35]; and motif- and shapelet-based approaches for pattern discovery [14,18]. Making the computation of pairwise distances more robust to missing values would substantially

D. Koutra et al. (Eds.): ECML PKDD 2023, LNAI 14173, pp. 221–237, 2023.
https://doi.org/10.1007/978-3-031-43424-2_14

expand the usefulness of all these methods without requiring any modification to them.

For this reason, we study in this paper how to make the Dynamic Time Warping (DTW) distance, one of the most prevalent distance measures for time series [30], robust to missing intervals. DTW "warps" time series along the time axis to find an optimal match between them. A trivial extension of DTW that deals with missing values by optimally matching them with the other time series leads to pathological behavior, but by imposing restrictions on the warping, this can be countered. This idea leads to our first contribution: **DTW with Additional Restrictions On Warping (DTW-AROW)**, a method for estimating the DTW distance between time series with missing values.

DTW-AROW estimates the DTW distance by looking only at the time series, not at the context in which they occur. When more time series from the same population are available, one could in principle try to fill in the missing values analogously to the other time series, and then use standard DTW. Our second contribution is a method that does exactly that: **DTW with Clustering, Averaging, and Imputation (DTW-CAI)** clusters and then averages the other time series to construct prototypical time series, the most relevant of which is then warped onto the given time series to fill in the missing values. The clustering and averaging is done on the basis of DTW-AROW and a modified version of DTW Barycenter Averaging (DBA) that can handle missing values.

We experimentally evaluate DTW-AROW and DTW-CAI in two different ways: first, by evaluating how well they estimate the actual DTW distance; and second, how they affect the performance of classification and clustering methods that make use of them. In this context, it is relevant that DTW-AROW and DTW-CAI are instances of what is known in the literature as local, respectively global, approaches. A *local* approach exploits only the information in the pair of time series whose similarity is being computed; a *global* approach leverages the contextual information that other time series in the same dataset provide. Global approaches tend to outperform local approaches, but can obviously only be used when the required additional information is available. For example, in some motif discovery techniques such as [18], the DTW distance is computed only between actively selected pairs of time segments, where a global approach cannot be used. Our experiments show that DTW-AROW outperforms all local methods and performs at roughly the same level as global methods, while DTW-CAI outperforms all global methods.

The remainder of this paper is organized as follows: Sect. 2 formally introduces the notation and problem statement; Sect. 3, Sect. 4, and Sect. 5 explain DTW, DTW-AROW and DTW-CAI respectively; Sect. 6 discusses the related work; Sect. 7 contains the experiments; and Sect. 8 states conclusions and future work. Some details and additional results are provided in the Supplementary Material.

2 Notation and Problem Statement

A *time series dataset* $\mathcal{X} = \{\mathbf{x}^{(1)}, \ldots, \mathbf{x}^{(N)}\}$ is a collection of N time series $\mathbf{x}^{(i)} = \left[x_1^{(i)}, \ldots, x_{M_i}^{(i)}\right]$ that each contain M_i time samples $x_j^{(i)} \in \mathbb{R} \cup \{\text{NaN}\}$, where "NaN" indicates a missing value. We do not restrict the amount or location of missing values. $x_j^{(i)}$ is a scalar for univariate time series and a vector for multivariate time series. We use the representation of a scalar because the examples in this paper are based on univariate time series.

The objective of this paper is to enable the DTW method to operate on time series that contain missing values such that the resulting distance is as robust as possible to the missing values. In other words, if we consider that we are able to calculate the so-called *reference* DTW distance between the fully observed time series, then our aim is to estimate the reference distance as accurately as possible in the presence of missing values.

3 Background: Dynamic Time Warping (DTW)

DTW is a method to assess the dissimilarity between time series by allowing flexibility in time, i.e., by matching similar time samples in both time series with each other, as illustrated in Fig. 1a (top) [30]. DTW can be applied on time series with different lengths.

Mathematically, DTW distance[1] can be considered as an extension of Euclidean distance. For time series $\mathbf{x}$ and $\mathbf{x}'$ of lengths M and M', respectively, where $M = M'$, *Euclidean distance* is defined as $d_{\text{Euc.}}(\mathbf{x}, \mathbf{x}') = \sqrt{\sum_{j=1}^{M} \delta(x_j, x_j')}$ where $\delta(x_j, x_j') = \left(x_j - x_j'\right)^2$ is referred to as the *cost* function.[2] DTW distance is similar to Euclidean distance except that the time samples that are compared with each other are not necessarily at the same time instants.

To compute DTW, a *warping path* $\boldsymbol{\pi}$ is calculated, which optimally matches time samples from the two time series in order to minimize the dissimilarity, i.e. the total cost, between them. The warping path is defined as

$$\boldsymbol{\pi} = \{(j_1, j_1'), \ldots, (j_P, j_P')\} \tag{1}$$

where each pair (j_p, j_p') indicates that time sample x_{j_p} is matched with $x'_{j'_p}$.

The warping path is restricted by two conditions. First, the *boundary conditions* state that the first (and the last) time samples of the two time series need to be matched to each other:

$$(j_1, j_1') = (1, 1) \text{ and } (j_P, j_P') = (M, M'). \tag{2}$$

Second, the *step condition* restricts the progress of the warping path such that time monotonically increases along the path and each time sample is matched

[1] DTW is referred to as a distance, but this should not be interpreted as being a metric, as it does not satisfy the triangular inequality [22] .

[2] To apply DTW on multivariate time series, the cost function can be defined as the squared Euclidean distance between the two time samples [32].

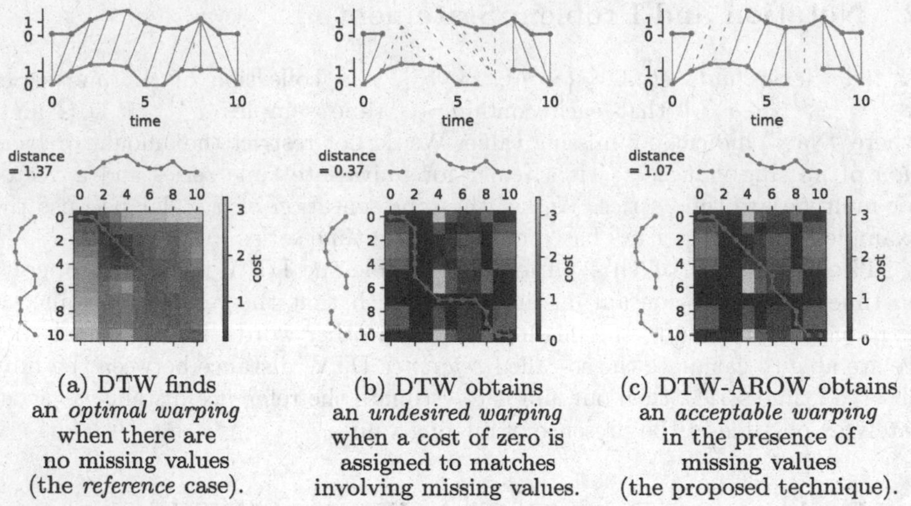

(a) DTW finds an *optimal warping* when there are no missing values (the *reference* case).

(b) DTW obtains an *undesired warping* when a cost of zero is assigned to matches involving missing values.

(c) DTW-AROW obtains an *acceptable warping* in the presence of missing values (the proposed technique).

Fig. 1. DTW and DTW-AROW for time series with or without missing data.

with at least one time sample of the other time series; that is, for $p = 2, ..., P$,

$$(j_p, j'_p) \in \left\{ \left(j_{p-1},\ j'_{p-1}+1\right), \left(j_{p-1}+1,\ j'_{p-1}+1\right), \left(j_{p-1}+1,\ j'_{p-1}\right) \right\}. \quad (3)$$

DTW distance is defined as the minimum total cost on a warping path that satisfies the boundary (2) and step (3) conditions:

$$d_{\mathrm{DTW}}(\mathbf{x}, \mathbf{x}') = \min_{\boldsymbol{\pi}} \sqrt{\sum_{(j,j')\in\boldsymbol{\pi}} \delta\left(x_j, x'_{j'}\right)} \quad \text{such that } \boldsymbol{\pi} \text{ satisfies (2) and (3).} \quad (4)$$

The *optimal warping path* $\boldsymbol{\pi}^*$ that solves this problem and the corresponding DTW distance can be calculated exactly with a computational complexity of $\mathcal{O}(MM')$ using a dynamic programming algorithm [22].

Figure 1a visually illustrates the DTW distance method. The costs of matching two time samples $\delta\left(x_j, x'_{j'}\right)$ are visualized as a color-coded cost matrix. Every path in the cost matrix from the top-left to bottom-right corner (boundary condition) where every step is to the right, bottom or bottom-right (step condition) is a valid warping path. The optimal warping path is indicated in red.

Despite its popularity, the DTW algorithm cannot handle missing values because the cost function δ is not defined for missing values, and simply defining it as zero for missing values has undesired consequences, as illustrated in Fig. 1b. The optimization problem of DTW tends to exploit these zero costs by matching some missing values in the first series to a long interval in the second, and vice versa, so that the reference distance (1.37 in Fig. 1a) is strongly underestimated (0.37 in Fig. 1b). Hence, we propose an extension of it, DTW-AROW, that can handle missing values.

4 DTW-AROW

DTW-AROW is a local approach that estimates the DTW distance in the presence of missing values in one or both of the time series, without using any contextual information obtained from (the other time series in) the dataset. To this end, we modify the cost function δ of DTW, impose an additional path restriction (6), and adjust the resulting distance by a correction factor (γ).

To assign a cost of zero to matches with missing time samples, we define an *extended cost function*:

$$\delta_{\text{ext}}(x_j, x'_{j'}) = \begin{cases} 0 & x_j = \text{NaN} \text{ or } x'_{j'} = \text{NaN} \\ \left(x_j - x'_{j'}\right)^2 & \text{otherwise.} \end{cases} \tag{5}$$

To avoid undesired warping paths, we impose an *additional restriction* to the warping path, which is, for $p = 2, \ldots, P$,

$$(j_p, j'_p) = (j_{p-1}+1,\ j'_{p-1}+1) \text{ if NaN} \in \left\{x_{j_p},\ x_{j_{p-1}},\ x'_{j'_p},\ x'_{j'_{p-1}}\right\}. \tag{6}$$

This restriction ensures that each missing interval is matched with an interval of the same length in the other time series. Equivalently, steps whose beginning or end points correspond to any missing values has to be diagonal (Fig. 1c). Hence, undesired warpings (Fig. 1b) are avoided.

Finally, because missing values are matched at no cost, the distance might be underestimated (Fig. 1a vs. 1b). To compensate for this, we adjust the resulting distance by the *correction factor* $\gamma = \frac{M+M'}{M_{\text{av}}+M'_{\text{av}}}$ where M_{av} and M'_{av} are the number of available (i.e., non-missing) time samples in $\mathbf{x}$ and $\mathbf{x}'$ of lengths M and M', respectively.

Hence, we define the **DTW-AROW distance** as

$$d_{\text{DTW-AROW}}(\mathbf{x}, \mathbf{x}') = \min_{\boldsymbol{\pi}} \sqrt{\gamma \sum_{(j,j')\in\boldsymbol{\pi}} \delta_{\text{ext}}\left(x_j, x'_{j'}\right)} \quad \text{such that } \boldsymbol{\pi} \text{ satisfies (2), (3), and (6).} \tag{7}$$

DTW-AROW provides the same result as DTW when there are no missing values. Figure 1c illustrates DTW-AROW on our running example, where the warping and the resulting distance are quite similar to those in Fig. 1a that are obtained using DTW from time series without missing values.

Algorithm 1 shows the exact computation of DTW-AROW with the same computational complexity $\mathcal{O}(MM')$ as DTW using dynamic programming. When computing the cumulative costs $c_{j,j'}$ (lines 1–7), the restriction (6) is enforced by prohibiting all possible horizontal and vertical steps whose beginning or end corresponds to a missing value in any of the time series. The element $c_{M,M'}$ is the total cost on the optimal warping path $\boldsymbol{\pi}^*$. The DTW-AROW distance is obtained by scaling $c_{M,M'}$ by the factor δ and taking the square root (line 9). Optionally, lines 10–13 obtain $\boldsymbol{\pi}^*$ by backtracking the previously saved step types $\phi_{j,j'}$ that store the direction of the step at every position (j, j').[3]

[3] Instead of saving $\phi_{j,j'}$, backtracking can also be performed by selecting the direction that minimizes the cumulative cost by complying with the restrictions in (6).

Algorithm 1: DTW-AROW

Input: $\mathbf{x}, \mathbf{x}'$: two time series of length M and M', respectively

Output: $d_{\text{DTW-AROW}}(\mathbf{x}, \mathbf{x}')$: DTW-AROW distance,

$\boldsymbol{\pi}^*$: optimal warping path — *if π^* is not needed, lines 7 and 10–13 can be skipped*

1 $c_{j,0} \leftarrow 0$ for $j = 0, \ldots, M$, $c_{0,j'} \leftarrow 0$ for $j' = 0, \ldots, M'$ — *initial cumulative costs*

2 **for** $j = 1, \ldots, M$ — *for every row*

3 **for** $j' = 1, \ldots, M'$ — *for every column*

4 $e_\text{h} \leftarrow \begin{cases} \infty & \text{if NaN} \in \left\{x_j,\ x'_{j'},\ x'_{j'-1}\right\} \\ 0 & \text{otherwise} \end{cases}$ — *when the horizontal step corresponds to missing values, its penalty is set to ∞*

5 $e_\text{v} \leftarrow \begin{cases} \infty & \text{if NaN} \in \left\{x_j,\ x_{j-1},\ x'_{j'}\right\} \\ 0 & \text{otherwise} \end{cases}$ — *when the vertical step corresponds to missing values, its penalty is set to ∞*

6 $c_{j,j'} \leftarrow \delta_\text{ext}\left(x_j, x'_{j'}\right) + \min\left\{c_{j-1,j'-1},\ c_{j,j'-1} + e_\text{h},\ c_{j-1,j'} + e_\text{v}\right\}$ — *cumulative cost*

7 $\phi_{j,j'} \leftarrow \arg\min\left\{c_{j-1,j'-1},\ c_{j,j'-1} + e_\text{h},\ c_{j-1,j'} + e_\text{v}\right\}$ — *step type*

8 $M_\text{av}, M'_\text{av} \leftarrow$ number of available (non-missing) time samples in $\mathbf{x}$ and $\mathbf{x}'$

9 $d_{\text{DTW-AROW}}(\mathbf{x}, \mathbf{x}') \leftarrow \sqrt{\gamma\, c_{M,M'}}$ where $\gamma = \frac{M+M'}{M_\text{av}+M'_\text{av}}$ — *DTW-AROW distance*

10 $\boldsymbol{\pi}^* \leftarrow \{(M, M')\}$, $j \leftarrow M$, $j' \leftarrow M'$ — *initialize path, row index, and column index*

11 **while** $j > 0$ and $j' > 0$

12 $\pi_\text{prev} \leftarrow \begin{cases} (j-1,\ j'-1) & \text{if } \phi_{j,j'} = 1 \\ (j,\ j'-1) & \text{if } \phi_{j,j'} = 2 \\ (j-1,\ j') & \text{if } \phi_{j,j'} = 3 \end{cases}$ — *previous step in the path*

13 $\boldsymbol{\pi}^* \leftarrow \{\pi_\text{prev}\} \cup \boldsymbol{\pi}^*$ — *append previous step to the left of the path*

5 DTW-CAI

DTW-AROW is a local approach; i.e., it compares two time series based on only the information in the time series themselves. When these two are part of a larger set, one could use a global approach that exploits the information in that set to obtain better results. Specifically, if the set contains many time series similar to the two being compared, these contain information about the likely shape of the missing intervals in the time series under consideration.

This idea leads to our second contribution: DTW-CAI. Given a dataset, DTW-CAI first finds clusters of time series, and computes representatives for these clusters. Next, when computing the similarity between two time series, it imputes the missing values in each series by mapping parts of the most similar representative series into it, and then calculates pairwise DTW-AROW distances. Because DTW-CAI needs to deal with missing values in all these steps, it uses DTW-AROW inside the clustering, averaging, and imputation steps.

The clustering algorithm in DTW-CAI is essentially a version of k-means in which the Euclidean distance is replaced by the DTW-AROW distance and the mean is replaced by DBA-Missing (DBAM), which is a method to find a representative of a set of time series. While DBA is a natural choice as it is commonly used to find representatives for sets of time series [27], it cannot handle missing values. Hence, we first extend DBA into DBAM, a version that can handle missing values.

Algorithm 2: DBAM

Input: $\mathcal{X}_s = \{\mathbf{x}^{(1)}, \ldots, \mathbf{x}^{(N_s)}\}$: a cluster of time series,
L_{DBAM}: maximum number of iterations *(optional, default: ∞)*,
E: threshold for stopping

Output: $\mathbf{z}$: the representative time series (i.e., DBA) of the cluster

$\mathbf{z} \leftarrow \arg\min_{\mathbf{x}^{(i)} \in \mathcal{X}_s} \sum_{i'=1}^{N_s} d_{\text{DTW-AROW}}(\mathbf{x}^{(i)}, \mathbf{x}^{(i')})$ — initialize the representative with medoid
$M_{\mathbf{z}} \leftarrow \text{length}(\mathbf{z})$, $l \leftarrow 0$
while $l \leq L_{\text{DBAM}}$
  $\mathbf{z}_{\text{prev}} \leftarrow \mathbf{z}$, $l \leftarrow l + 1$
  for $i = 1, \ldots, N_s$ — for every time series
    $\boldsymbol{\pi}_i^* \leftarrow$ optimal warping path of DTW-AROW($\mathbf{z}$, $\mathbf{x}^{(i)}$) — DTW-AROW in Algorithm 1
  for $j = 1, \ldots, M_{\mathbf{z}}$ — for every time instant
    $\mathcal{W}_j \leftarrow \bigcup_{i=1}^{N_s} \{x_{j'}^{(i)} : 1 \leq j' \leq \text{length}(\mathbf{x}_i),\ (j, j') \in \boldsymbol{\pi}_i^*,\ x_{j'}^{(i)} \neq \text{NaN}\}$
    $z_j \leftarrow \begin{cases} \text{NaN} & \text{if } \mathcal{W}_j = \emptyset \\ \text{mean}(\mathcal{W}_j) & \text{otherwise} \end{cases}$ — the average of the non-missing samples in $\mathcal{X}_s$ that are matched to z_j (or, NaN if all of them are missing)
  $\mathbf{z} \leftarrow [z_1, \ldots, z_{M_{\mathbf{z}}}]$ — update the DBA
  if $l > 1$ and $\|\mathbf{z} - \mathbf{z}_{\text{prev}}\|_1 / M_{\mathbf{z}} < E$ — if the change in $\mathbf{z}$ is too small
    break — terminate

5.1 DBAM

DBA is a prevalent method to compute a representative time series for a cluster (or a set) of time series such that the representative is as similar as possible to the time series in the cluster in terms of DTW distance. To handle missing values in the time series in the cluster, we extend DBA into DBAM (Algorithm 2) by computing warpings using DTW-AROW instead of DTW and by ignoring missing values in computing the average of time samples.

Convergence. Similarly to DBA [27], each iteration of DBAM decreases the *inertia*, which is the sum of the squared DTW-AROW distances between the instances and the representative; hence, its convergence is guaranteed.

5.2 DTW-CAI

DTW-CAI estimates pairwise DTW distances between time series that contain missing values by leveraging other similar time series in the dataset. DTW-CAI (Algorithm 3) first determines the number of clusters K through the *elbow method* [31] based on the inertia of k-medoids [6] applied on pairwise DTW-AROW distances (line 1). Then, it clusters the dataset using a modified K-means algorithm that uses DTW-AROW and DBAM to compute pairwise distances and cluster means, respectively (lines 2–10). Once the clustering is obtained, DTW-CAI calculates pairwise distances as follows: For each time series $\mathbf{x}^{(i)}$, it computes the optimal warping path between $\mathbf{x}^{(i)}$ and its cluster representative $\mathbf{z}^{(k)}$ using DTW-AROW (line 14). Then, it imputes each time sample $x_{j'}^{(i)}$ in $\mathbf{x}^{(i)}$ that contains a missing value by the time sample[4] in $\mathbf{z}^{(k)}$ that is matched

[4] There is only a single matched time sample because DTW-AROW matches each missing value with exactly one sample in the other time series (see Sect. 4).

Algorithm 3: DTW-CAI

Input: $\mathcal{X} = \{\mathbf{x}^{(1)}, \dots, \mathbf{x}^{(N)}\}$: a time series dataset,
$L_{\text{DTW-CAI}}$: maximum number of iterations *(optional, default: ∞)*

Output: $\mathbf{D} = \left[d_{\text{DTW-CAI}}(\mathbf{x}^{(i)}, \mathbf{x}^{(i')})\right]_{i,i' \in \{1,\dots,N\}}$: pairwise distance matrix

1 $K \leftarrow$ the number of clusters determined by the elbow method [31] based on pairwise DTW-AROW distances

2 $\mathcal{Z} = \{\mathbf{z}^{(1)}, \dots, \mathbf{z}^{(K)}\} \leftarrow K$ distinct time series randomly selected from $\mathcal{X}$ — initial cluster representatives

3 $l \leftarrow 0,\quad \mathcal{Y} \leftarrow \emptyset,\quad \hat{\mathcal{X}} \leftarrow \mathcal{X}$ — initialize the iteration number, cluster labels, and imputed data

4 **while** $l < L_{\text{DTW-CAI}}$

5 $\quad \mathcal{Y}_{\text{prev}} \leftarrow \mathcal{Y},\quad l \leftarrow l + 1$

6 $\quad \mathcal{Y} \leftarrow \left[\arg\min_k d_{\text{DTW-AROW}}(\mathbf{x}^{(i)}, \mathbf{z}^{(k)})\right]_{i=1,\dots N}$ — update cluster assignments based on DTW-AROW distances (Algorithm 1)

7 $\quad$ **for** $k = 1, \dots, K$ — for every cluster

8 $\quad\quad \mathbf{z}^{(k)} \leftarrow \texttt{DBAM}(\{\mathbf{x}^{(i)} \in \mathcal{X} :\ y_i = k\})$ — update the cluster representative

9 $\quad$ **if** $l > 1$ **and** $\mathcal{Y}_{\text{prev}} = \mathcal{Y}$ — no change in the cluster labels $\mathcal{Y}$

10 $\quad\quad$ **break**

11 **for** $k = 1, \dots, K$ — for every cluster

12 $\quad I_k \leftarrow \{i :\ i \in \{1, \dots, N\},\ y_i = k\}$ — indices of instances that are in cluster k

13 $\quad$ **for** $\forall i \in I_k$ — for every instance in the cluster

14 $\quad\quad \boldsymbol{\pi}_i^* \leftarrow$ optimal warping path of $\texttt{DTW-AROW}(\mathbf{z}^{(k)},\ \mathbf{x}^{(i)})$ — `DTW-AROW` in Algorithm 1

15 $\quad\quad$ **for** $j' \in \{j :\ x_j^{(i)} = \text{NaN},\ j \in \{1, \dots M_i\}\}$ — for every missing time sample

16 $\quad\quad\quad \hat{x}_{j'}^{(i)} \leftarrow \{z_j^{(k)} :\ j \in \{1, \dots, \text{length}(\mathbf{z}^{(k)})\},\ (j, j') \in \boldsymbol{\pi}_i^*\}$ — impute

17 $\mathbf{D} = \left[d_{\text{DTW-AROW}}(\hat{\mathbf{x}}^{(i)}, \hat{\mathbf{x}}^{(i')})\right]_{i,i' \in \{1,\dots,N\}}$ — compute pairwise distances

with $x_{j'}^{(i)}$ (line 16). Finally, the so-called pairwise *DTW-CAI distances* are calculated from the imputed time series using DTW-AROW (line 17).[5]

Convergence. DTW-CAI is guaranteed to converge because the inertia (defined in Sect. 5.1) decreases in every iteration (lines 4–10), similarly to k-means: The cluster assignment step (line 6) can only decrease the inertia. Updating the representatives (line 8), can only decrease the inertia for that cluster without changing the inertia for the remaining clusters.

6 Comparison to Related Work

Our work is the first to propose variants of DTW to compare time series that contain missing values. Until now, the predominant approach was to get rid of missing values in preprocessing by removing, interpolating, or imputing them [28].

In the *removal* approach, missing values are discarded and the rest is concatenated before applying DTW [19,34]. This causes the DTW distance to be overestimated when a certain pattern occurs in both time series $\mathbf{x}$ and $\mathbf{x}'$ but is not observed in $\mathbf{x}'$ due to missing values, because the pattern in $\mathbf{x}$ is forced to be matched with the observed values in $\mathbf{x}'$ that might be dissimilar, increasing

[5] The reason for using DTW-AROW instead of the original DTW is the fact that, on rare occasions, the representatives $\mathcal{Z}$ obtained by DBAM may still contain missing values (see line 8 of Algorithm 2), so as the imputed time series data $\hat{\mathcal{X}}$.

the distance. In this case, the proposed technique DTW-AROW can match the pattern in $\mathbf{x}$ with the missing part in $\mathbf{x}'$ at no cost, preventing the distance from being overestimated.

In the *interpolation* and *imputation* approaches, missing values are replaced by substituted values so that DTW or any other distance metric can be applied afterwards [5,21]. Interpolation is a local approach that fills in missing values by using neighboring samples. Some examples are *linear interpolation* that fits a straight line that passes through the preceding and following time samples of each missing interval, and polynomial interpolation that fits a higher-order function based on more than two neighboring time samples [9,13]. In contrast, imputation is a global approach that fills in missing values based on neighboring time series in the dataset [5]. A widely used technique is *k-NN imputation*, where, for each time series, k nearest neighbors are found based on the available time samples and each missing value is replaced by the average value over the neighbors at the same time index [5]. Imputation can also be performed using regression and deep learning techniques that exploit the patterns available in the data [2,5,16,37] Among them, *Clustering Representation Learning on Incomplete time-series data (CRLI)* is a state-of-the-art global approach that performs imputation with clustering [17]. In contrast to most of the existing techniques, CRLI jointly optimizes the imputation and clustering processes, and is shown to perform better than or on par with other techniques (such as [2]) in both tasks. CRLI learns representations for the time series, and obtains the final clustering based on pairwise distances between the representations. We evaluate CRLI based on the pairwise distances between time series it computes using these representations, because the objective of this paper is to obtain pairwise distances accurately in the presence of missing values, rather than focusing on a specific task such as classification, clustering, or imputation.

The literature also contains techniques to handle missing values in time series data that are tailored to a specific task or application. For example, [33] searches for a short time series (without any missing values) within a long time series that might contain missing values. Instead of comparing two individual time samples at a given time instant with each other, it considers the distribution of time samples in a window centered at that instant and ignore missing values in the distribution. Some other examples are clustering cancer gene expression data [4], classification of human activities using wearable sensors [36], and digit recognition from speech data [7]. We do not consider such specialized approaches in this paper, as they perform a certain ML task such as classification, and are highly customized for a dataset in a particular application. Instead, we focus on more generic and task-agnostic approaches.

7 Experimental Evaluation

We evaluate the proposed and existing techniques through three *Questions (Q)*:

- ***Q1***: How robust are pairwise distances (obtained by different techniques) to missing values?
- ***Q2 / Q3***: How accurately the dataset can be classified/clustered based on pairwise distances obtained by different techniques?

After explaining the datasets and implementation of the techniques (Sect. 7.1), we address *Q1*–*Q3* in Sects. 7.2–7.4.

7.1 Datasets and Implementation Details

We employ 47 publicly available time series datasets with at most 1000 instances of length less than 500 in the repository [3] by applying z-score normalization to each time series. We do *not* use the available class labels when computing distances between time series, as the techniques we propose are unsupervised. Details are provided in Sect. S.1 in Supplementary Material.

We introduce missing values under the *missing at random* assumption, where the probability that a time sample is missing, is independent of its value [23]. In each time series, we introduce a missing interval whose expected length is 0.1, 0.2, or 0.3 of the length of the time series, which correspond to three *contamination rates* (see Sect. S.2 in Supplementary Material for details).

We have implemented the proposed techniques DTW-AROW and DTW-CAI based on the Python library `DTAIdistance` [20], and made the codes publicly available[6]. In every DTW-CAI iteration, we execute only one iteration of DBAM by setting $E = 0$ in Algorithm 2. For comparison, we consider the existing techniques removal, linear interpolation, CRLI, and k-NN imputation (see Sect. 6). For removal, after removing missing values, we compute the DTW distance and adjust it by γ (see Sect. 4) to compensate for missing comparisons. We execute CRLI using its publicly available code with the hyperparameter values recommended by the authors [17] for the same repository of datasets as we use, and calculate Euclidean distances between the representations obtained by CRLI, as performed in clustering in [17]. We use the Python package *scikit-learn* [26] for k-NN imputation with $k = 10$, and then compute pairwise distances using DTW.

7.2 Evaluation of Pairwise Distances (*Q1*)

For each dataset, pairwise distances (between time series instances) that are obtained using a technique $\mathcal{T}$ (such as DTW-AROW) constitute a matrix $\mathbf{D}_{\mathcal{T}}$ with the (i, i')-th element being $d_{\mathcal{T},i,i'} = d_{\mathcal{T}}(\mathbf{x}^{(i)}, \mathbf{x}^{(i')})$ for $i, i' \in \{1, \ldots, N\}$. Since $\mathbf{D}_{\mathcal{T}}$ is symmetrical with the diagonal entries being zero, we only consider its upper- triangular entries for evaluation, and place them in a vector $\mathbf{d}_{\mathcal{T}}$ of

[6] https://github.com/aras-y/DTW_with_missing_values.

length $\frac{N(N-1)}{2}$. Then, the evaluation boils down to comparing $\mathbf{d}_{\mathcal{T}}$ (associated with each technique $\mathcal{T}$) with the *reference* vector $\mathbf{d}_{\text{ref}}$ that contains pairwise distances obtained by DTW from fully observed time series.

For every technique $\mathcal{T}$, we compare its pairwise distance matrix $\mathbf{D}_{\mathcal{T}}$ with $\mathbf{D}_{\text{ref}}$ by computing two types of correlation between their vector representations $\mathbf{d}_{\mathcal{T}}$ and $\mathbf{d}_{\text{ref}}$: *Pearson correlation coefficient (PCC)* [25] that measures the linear correlation between the distances and *Kendall rank correlation coefficient (KRCC)* [12] that measures the ordinal association between the two sets of distances. Both PCC and KRCC range from -1 to 1 (1: highest similarity), and are invariant to linear transformations. PCC considers the actual distances (albeit by ignoring the scale), whereas KRCC takes into account only their ranking. Hence, PCC is relevant for algorithms that use actual distances, such as k-medoids clustering, whereas KRCC is relevant for algorithms (such as k-NN classifier) that evaluate distances relatively to each other through comparison or ranking.

Since we have 47 datasets, we compare the correlations of the techniques in two different ways: (1) We plot the *distribution of correlation* over datasets using box plots that display the median, the first and third quantiles, and the minimum-maximum values. (2) We compute *average aligned rank (AAR)* where, for a given technique, the higher the (correlation) values are (relative to other techniques), the lower the AAR is [11] (see Sect. S3 in Supplementary Material).

Answer to *Q1*: Although the first proposed technique DTW-AROW is a local approach that does not leverage contextual information, it outperforms all of the existing local and global techniques according to the distributions (Fig. 2a) and AARs (Fig. 2b) of correlation coefficients over datasets. This is a striking result, given that global approaches leverage contextual information by processing the entire dataset to compute pairwise distances, and still outperformed by DTW-AROW. The second proposed technique DTW-CAI, which is a global approach, improves upon DTW-AROW, obtaining the highest performance. Correlation coefficients exhibit more variance (over datasets) for simpler techniques (removal and linear interpolation), indicating that their performance is more dataset-dependent. For an ablation study and results for individual datasets, refer to Sect. S.4 and S.5 of the Supplementary Material, respectively.

7.3 Evaluation Through Classification (*Q2*)

As a downstream task, we classify the datasets based on the pairwise distances obtained by different techniques to handle missing values. We use k-Nearest Neighbor (k-NN) classifier [1] with 10 neighbors by using precomputed pairwise distances and class labels available in the datasets. We evaluate the accuracy through 10-fold cross validation. For each dataset, we calculate (1) the *oracle accuracy* by using pairwise distances computed from fully observed time series ("reference" in Sect. 7.2), and then (2) the *reduction in accuracy due to missing values* relative to this oracle accuracy for each technique and for each contamination rate. We present the distribution of the reduction in accuracy over datasets

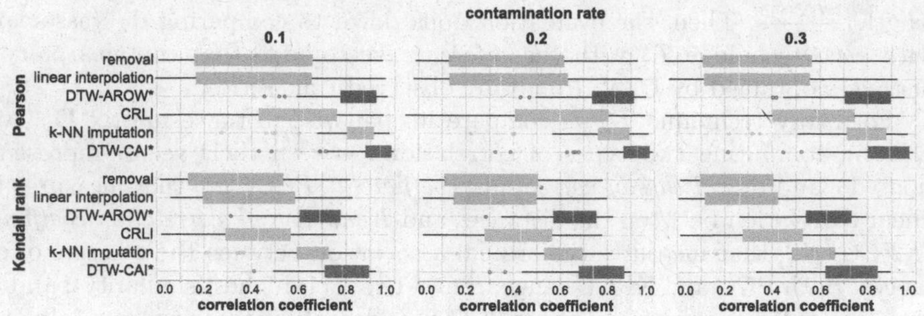

(a) Distribution of correlation coefficients over the datasets.

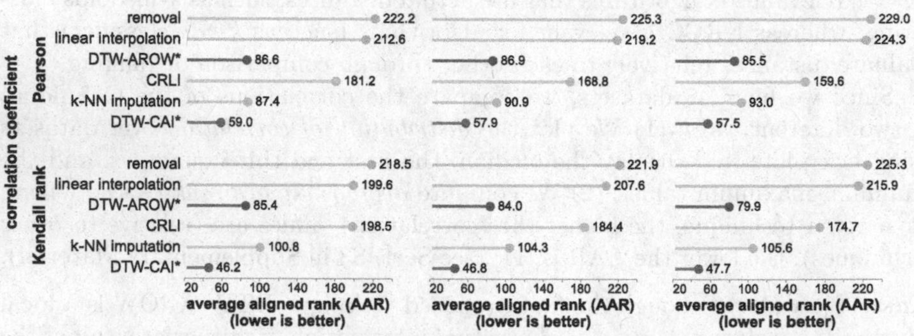

(b) Average aligned ranks (AAR) of the correlation coefficients for the techniques.

Fig. 2. Among both local (blue) and global (red) approaches, the proposed techniques (denoted by *) outperform existing techniques in terms of robustness of pairwise distances to missing values. (Color figure online)

for each technique and contamination rate, where lower reduction is better. We also calculate AAR of accuracy for each technique for each contamination rate, similarly to Sect. 7.2, where lower AAR is better.

Answer to ***Q2***: According to Fig. 3a,b, both proposed techniques, DTW-AROW and DTW-CAI, are the best approaches, where missing values cause the smallest reduction in classification accuracy. DTW-AROW, which is a local technique, surprisingly outperforms existing local and global techniques. The advantage of using global approaches over local approaches is less prominent in the classification task than the robustness of pairwise distances to missing values (Sect. 7.2). A possible reason is that classifiers might be tolerating deviations in pairwise distances by learning models based on labeled training data.

7.4 Evaluation Through Clustering (*Q3*)

As another downstream task, we perform clustering based on pairwise distances obtained by different techniques to handle missing values. We perform k-medoids clustering [24] where the number of clusters is selected as the number of classes in each dataset. To remove the effect of initialization, every time we cluster a dataset, we run k-medoids (with an initialization based on k-medoids++) 100 times [24], and select the clustering with the smallest inertia (see Sect. 5.1), which is an unsupervised method. We evaluate the quality of the selected clus-

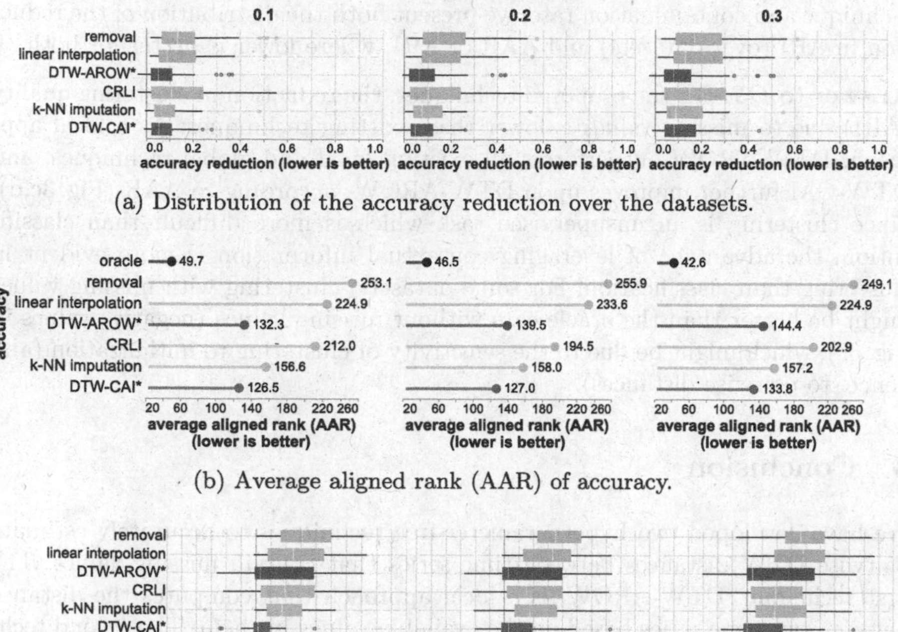

(a) Distribution of the accuracy reduction over the datasets.

(b) Average aligned rank (AAR) of accuracy.

(c) Distribution of ARI reduction over the datasets.

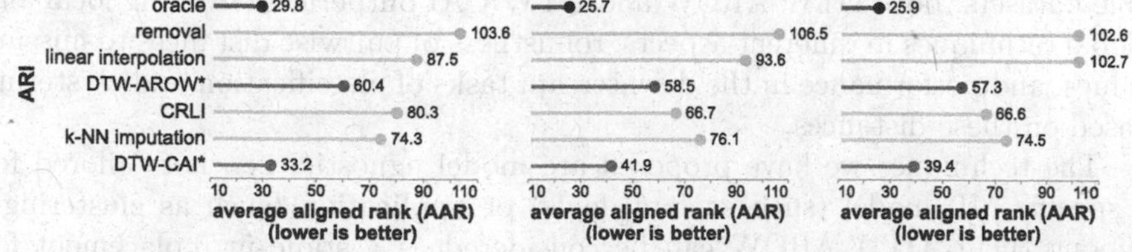

(d) Average aligned rank (AAR) of clustering quality (ARI).

Fig. 3. Among both local (blue) and global (red) approaches, proposed techniques (denoted by *) outperform existing techniques in terms of (a,b) classification accuracy and (c,d) clustering quality (ARI). (Color figure online)

tering by using Adjusted Rand Index (ARI), which ranges from −0.5 to 1 where −0.5 and 1 correspond to minimum and maximum agreement between cluster labels and class labels, whereas 0 corresponds to randomly selected cluster labels [8]. Similarly to calculating the reduction in accuracy for classification (Sect. 7.3), we calculate the *reduction in ARI due to missing values* relative to the oracle ARI that is obtained by using fully observed time series.

Since the datasets we use are labeled and mostly intended for classification, the clustering task fails for most of the datasets independent of the clustering technique used, as shown in [10]. Hence, for clustering, we select (19 of 47) datasets that have an ARI of at least 0.25 averaged over multiple clustering methods and distance metrics according to [10]. Similarly to Sect. 7.3, for each technique and contamination rate, we present both the distribution of the reduction in ARI (over datasets) and AAR of ARI, where lower is better for both.

Answer to *Q3*: For the proposed techniques, the reduction in clustering quality (ARI) due to missing values is lower than existing techniques: As a local approach, DTW-AROW outperforms all existing local and global techniques, and DTW-CAI further improves upon DTW-AROW, according to AAR (Fig. 3c,d). Since clustering is an unsupervised task which is more difficult than classification, the advantage of leveraging contextual information is more evident in clustering than classification. For some datasets, clustering with missing values might be better than the oracle case without missing values (negative values in Fig. 3c), which might be due to the sensitivity of clustering to initialization (and hence, to pairwise distances).

8 Conclusion

We have developed two hyperparameter-free techniques to accurately estimate pairwise DTW distances between time series that contain missing values. The first technique, DTW-AROW, is a local approach that computes the distance between two time series based on the available values in them. The second technique, DTW-CAI, is a global approach that improves DTW-AROW by additionally leveraging the contextual information contained in the dataset, provided that such a dataset is available. We have shown that, on multiple publicly available datasets, both DTW-AROW and DTW-CAI outperform existing local and global techniques in different aspects: robustness of pairwise distances to missing values, and performance in the downstream tasks of classification and clustering based on these distances.

The techniques we have proposed are model agnostic; i.e., not tailored for a specific ML model (such as k-medoids) or application (such as clustering). Among them, DTW-AROW can be considered as a stand-in replacement for DTW to handle missing values in existing ML models that operate on pairwise distances between time series. DTW-CAI, on the other hand, can be used as a more accurate replacement for DTW, provided that there is a time-series dataset available in which pairwise distances are to be computed.

Acknowledgement. This research received funding from the Flemish Government under the "Onderzoeksprogramma Artificiële Intelligentie (AI) Vlaanderen" programme.

References

1. Abanda, A., Mori, U., Lozano, J.A.: A review on distance based time series classification. Data Min. Knowl. Disc. **33**(2), 378–412 (2019)
2. Cao, W., Wang, D., Li, J., Zhou, H., Li, L., Li, Y.: Brits: bidirectional recurrent imputation for time series. In: Advances in Neural Information Processing Systems, vol. 31 (2018)
3. Dau, H.A., et al.: Hexagon-ML: the UCR time series classification archive, October 2018. https://www.cs.ucr.edu/~eamonn/time_series_data_2018/
4. deJong, J., et al.: Deep learning for clustering of multivariate clinical patient trajectories with missing values. GigaScience **8**(11), 134 (2019)
5. Fang, C., Wang, C.: Time series data imputation: a survey on deep learning approaches. arXiv preprint arXiv:2011.11347 (2020)
6. Fox, W.R.: Finding groups in data: an introduction to cluster analysis (1991)
7. Gemmeke, J.F., Virtanen, T., Hurmalainen, A.: Exemplar-based sparse representations for noise robust automatic speech recognition. IEEE Trans. Audio Speech Lang. Process. **19**(7), 2067–2080 (2011)
8. Hubert, L., Arabie, P.: Comparing partitions. J. Classif. **2**, 193–218 (1985)
9. Humpherys, J., Jarvis, T.: Foundations of Applied Mathematics, Volume 2: Algorithms, Approximation, Optimization. SIAM (2020)
10. Javed, A., Lee, B.S., Rizzo, D.M.: A benchmark study on time series clustering. Mach. Learn. App. **1**, 100001 (2020)
11. Jr., J.L.H., Lehmann, E.L.: rank methods for combination of independent experiments in analysis of variance. Ann. Math. Statist. **33**(2), 482–497 (1962)
12. Kendall, M.G.: A new measure of rank correlation. Biometrika. **30**(1–2), 81–93 (1938)
13. Lepot, M., Aubin, J.B., Clemens, F.: Interpolation in time series: an introductive overview of existing methods, their performance criteria and uncertainty assessment. Water. **9**(10), 796 (2017)
14. Li, G., Choi, B., Xu, J., Bhowmick, S.S., Chun, K.P., Wong, G.L.H.: Efficient Shapelet discovery for time series classification. IEEE Trans. Knowl. Data Eng. **34**(3), 1149–1163 (2022)
15. Lin, S., Wu, X., Martinez, G., Chawla, N.V.: Filling Missing Values on Wearable-Sensory Time Series Data, pp. 46–54 (2020). https://doi.org/10.1137/1.9781611976236.6
16. Luo, Y., Cai, X., Zhang, Y., Xu, J., et al.: Multivariate time series imputation with generative adversarial networks. In: Advances in Neural Information Processing Systems, vol. 31 (2018)
17. Ma, Q., Chen, C., Li, S., Cottrell, G.W.: Learning representations for incomplete time series clustering. In: Proceedings of the AAAI Conference on Artificial Intelligence, vol. 35, pp. 8837–8846 (2021)

18. Madrid, F., Imani, S., Mercer, R., Zimmerman, Z., Shakibay, N., Keogh, E.: Matrix Profile XX: finding and visualizing time series motifs of all lengths using the matrix profile. In: 2019 IEEE International Conference on Big Knowledge (ICBK), pp. 175–182. IEEE, Beijing, China, November 2019. https://doi.org/10.1109/ICBK.2019.00031, https://ieeexplore.ieee.org/document/8944710/
19. McKnight, P.E., McKnight, K.M., Sidani, S., Figueredo, A.J.: Missing data: a gentle introduction. Guilford Press (2007)
20. Meert, W., et al.: wannesm/dtaidistance: v2.3.5, January 2022. https://doi.org/10.5281/zenodo.5901139
21. Moritz, S., Bartz-Beielstein, T.: Imputets: time series missing value imputation in r. R J. **9**(1), 207 (2017)
22. Müller, M.: Information Retrieval for Music and Motion, vol. 2. Springer, Heidelberg (2007). https://doi.org/10.1007/978-3-540-74048-3
23. Oehmcke, S., Zielinski, O., Kramer, O.: KNN ensembles with penalized DTW for multivariate time series imputation. In: 2016 International Joint Conference on Neural Networks (IJCNN), pp. 2774–2781 (2016)
24. Park, H.S., Jun, C.H.: A simple and fast algorithm for k-medoids clustering. Expert Syst. App. **36**(2, Part 2), 3336–3341 (2009). https://doi.org/10.1016/j.eswa.2008.01.039, https://www.sciencedirect.com/science/article/pii/S095741740800081X
25. Pearson, K.: VII. mathematical contributions to the theory of evolution.–III. regression, heredity, and panmixia. Philos. Trans. R. Soc. London. Ser. A. **187**, 253–318 (1896)
26. Pedregosa, F., et al.: Scikit-learn: machine learning in Python. J. Mach. Learn. Res. **12**, 2825–2830 (2011)
27. Petitjean, F., Ketterlin, A., Gançarski, P.: A global averaging method for dynamic time warping, with applications to clustering. Pattern Recogn. **44**(3), 678–693 (2011)
28. Pratama, I., Permanasari, A.E., Ardiyanto, I., Indrayani, R.: A review of missing values handling methods on time-series data. In: 2016 International Conference on Information Technology Systems and Innovation (ICITSI), pp. 1–6 (2016). https://doi.org/10.1109/ICITSI.2016.7858189
29. Räsänen, T., Kolehmainen, M.: Feature-based clustering for electricity use time series data. In: Kolehmainen, M., Toivanen, P., Beliczynski, B. (eds.) ICANNGA 2009. LNCS, vol. 5495, pp. 401–412. Springer, Heidelberg (2009). https://doi.org/10.1007/978-3-642-04921-7_41
30. Sakoe, H., Chiba, S.: Dynamic programming algorithm optimization for spoken word recognition. IEEE Trans. Acoust. Speech Signal Process. **26**(1), 43–49 (1978)
31. Satopaa, V., Albrecht, J., Irwin, D., Raghavan, B.: Finding a "kneedle" in a haystack: Detecting knee points in system behavior. In: 2011 31st International Conference on Distributed Computing Systems Workshops, pp. 166–171 (2011)
32. Shokoohi-Yekta, M., Hu, B., Jin, H., Wang, J., Keogh, E.: Generalizing DTW to the multi-dimensional case requires an adaptive approach. Data Min. Knowl. Disc. **31**, 1–31 (2017)
33. Sitaram, D., Dalwani, A., Narang, A., Das, M., Auradkar, P.: A measure of similarity of time series containing missing data using the mahalanobis distance. In: 2015 Second International Conference on Advances in Computing and Communication Engineering, pp. 622–627 (2015). https://doi.org/10.1109/ICACCE.2015.14
34. Wothke, W.: Longitudinal and multigroup modeling with missing data. In: Modeling Longitudinal and Multilevel Data, pp. 205–224. Psychology Press (2000)
35. Xu, D., Tian, Y.: A comprehensive survey of clustering algorithms. Ann. Data Sci. **2**(2), 165–193 (2015)

36. Yazdanbakhsh, O., Dick, S.: Multivariate time series classification using dilated convolutional neural network. arXiv preprint arXiv:1905.01697 (2019)
37. Yoon, J., Jordon, J., van der Schaar, M.: GAIN: missing data imputation using generative adversarial nets. In: Dy, J., Krause, A. (eds.) Proceedings of the 35th International Conference on Machine Learning. Proceedings of Machine Learning Research, vol. 80, pp. 5689–5698. PMLR, 10–15 July 2018

Uncovering Multivariate Structural Dependency for Analyzing Irregularly Sampled Time Series

Zhen Wang[1], Ting Jiang[1], Zenghui Xu[1], Jianliang Gao[2], Ou Wu[3], Ke Yan[4], and Ji Zhang[5(✉)]

[1] Zhejiang Lab, Hangzhou, China
[2] Central South University, Changsha, China
[3] Tianjin University, Tianjin, China
[4] National University of Singapore, Singapore, Singapore
[5] University of Southern Queensland, Toowoomba, Australia
zhangji77@gmail.com

Abstract. Predictive analytics on Irregularly Sampled Multivariate Time Series (IS-MTS) presents a challenging problem in many real-world applications. Previous methods have primarily focused on incorporating temporal information into prediction while little effort is made to exploit the intrinsic structural information interchange among different IS-MTS at the same or across different timestamps. Recent developments in graph-based learning have shown promise in modeling spatial and structural dependencies of graph data. However, when applied to IS-MTS, they face significant challenges due to the complex data characteristics: 1) variable time intervals between observations; 2) asynchronous time points across dimensions resulting in missing values; 3) a lack of prior knowledge of connectivity structure for information propagation. To address these challenges, we propose a multivariate temporal graph network that coherently captures structural interactions, learns time-aware dependencies, and handles challenging characteristics of IS-MTS data. Specifically, we first develop a multivariate interaction module that handles the frequent missing values and adaptively extracts graph structural relations using a novel reinforcement learning module. Second, we design a correlation-aware neighborhood aggregation mechanism to capture within and across time dependencies and structural interactions. Third, we construct a novel masked time-aware self-attention to explicitly consider timestamp information and interval irregularity for determining optimal attention weights and distinguishing the influence of observation embeddings. Based on an extensive experimental evaluation, we demonstrate that our method outperforms a variety of competitors for the IS-MTS classification task.

Keywords: Irregularly sampled multivariate time series · graph structure learning · temporal attention · multivariate feature interaction

Z. Wang and T. Jiang—These authors contributed equally.

D. Koutra et al. (Eds.): ECML PKDD 2023, LNAI 14173, pp. 238–254, 2023.
https://doi.org/10.1007/978-3-031-43424-2_15

1 Introduction

Irregularly Sampled Multivariate Time Series (IS-MTS) are commonly found in various domains such as climate science, ecology, finance, and medicine [1,2,15,16].

IS-MTS data are characterized by a sequence of samples with irregular intervals between observation time points and asynchronous sampling rates between sequences. In an IS-MTS dataset, different sequences usually contain a varying number of observations recorded at different time points, as illustrated in Fig. 1. Such data can arise from multiple event-driven artificial sensors generating sparse, asynchronous streams of events, or from constrained observation processes that cannot receive regular and synchronous observation inputs. Accurate classification of IS-MTS is essential in many real-world applications as it can facilitate informed decision-making. For example, Electronic Health Records (EHR) are widely used in the healthcare industry and are typically systematic and structured collections of patients' in-hospital and demographic information. These datasets often contain numerous irregularly sampled medical time series. Based on historical EHR data, accurate prediction results of various tasks such as patient profiling [3], mortality risk prediction [4], and early disease detection [17] are vital for clinicians to provide precise diagnosis, personalized treatment, and medical management [18].

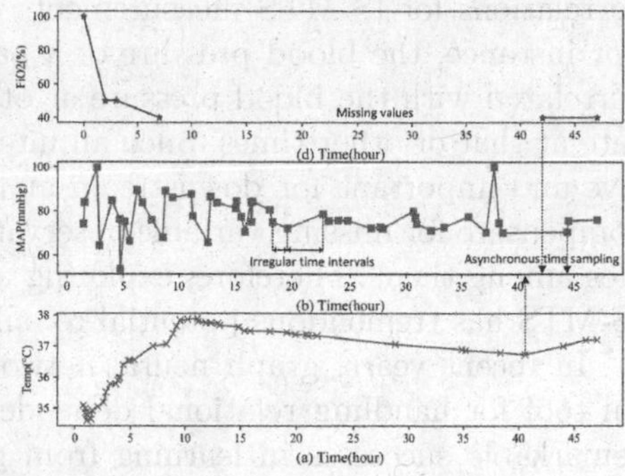

Fig. 1. An example of medical time series.

Classical machine learning methods face significant challenges in effectively processing IS-MTS since they require the data to be defined in a coherent, fixed-dimensional feature space with constant intervals between consecutive time steps. To address these challenges, specialized models and architectures have been developed over the past decade that are specifically designed for learning from IS-MTS data. For example, Che et al. [2] proposed GRU-D to incorporate irregular time intervals and address the problem of asynchronously sampled features from a missing data perspective. Zhang et al. [29] introduced an attention-based time-aware LSTM Network that models the time irregularity between events. Wang et al. [5] used a bidirectional RNN and multi-head attention network to explore both intra- and inter-time series value couplings for medical prediction. Shukla et al. [26] presented a continuous-time interpolation-based approach by constructing learnable temporal similarity functions. Horn et al. [6] employed a set function-based approach to handle irregular sampling and partial observations. Yin et al. [30] proposed a time gap embedding and time-aware attention to consider the irregular time intervals and variables' longitudinal information. Sun et al. [38] use a Hawkes-Process-based attention mechanism to handle the irregular intervals between visits. Other efforts based on ordinary differential equations (ODE) have also been dedicated to this problem [34,35,39].

Despite the progress made above, recent models have predominantly focused on incorporating time-aware dependencies, with little emphasis on exploiting the latent structural information that exists among variables for IS-MTS classification. This approach significantly limits the models' representation ability, as data correlations for IS-MTS measurements often exist across time series variables. For instance, the blood pressure of a patient at a given time point is not only correlated with the blood pressure at other time points but also with the heart rate at that or other times. Such an intertwined relationship is usually informative and important for downstream analytic tasks. The observed variables can compensate for missing variable observations by exploiting structural dependencies among them. Therefore, exploring and leveraging structural correlations in IS-MTS has tremendous potential to enhance classification performance.

In recent years, graph neural networks (GNNs) have emerged as a powerful tool for handling relational dependencies in data [8,9,19,20]. Despite their remarkable successes in learning from graph-structured data, standard GNNs face significant barriers when applied to the modeling of IS-MTS due to their unique data characteristics. Specifically, the variables of IS-MTS can be considered as nodes in a graph perspective, and learning time-aware dependencies using conventional dynamic network techniques is challenging because sequence nodes have asynchronous sampling rates and variable time intervals between observations. To confront the difficulties, Huang et al. [10] proposed a graph ODE generative model that can learn the coupled dynamics of nodes, enabling it to track the evolution of the underlying system from irregular observations. Oskarsson et al. [40] introduced a linear ODE that is defined by the output of a GRU. This ODE serves to model the latent states of an irregular time series variable, and they employ standard GNN layers to update its latent state. However, their methods are limited to scenarios where the spatial graph structure is known, typically built from the geographical locations of sensors. This reliance on a predefined graph structure renders them incapable of modeling IS-MTS when the structural dependencies within the data are unknown, such as in the case of irregular sampled medical time series.

Recurrently, Zhang et al. [14] proposed RainDrop, which considers IS-MTS as separate sensor graphs and models time-varying inter-sensor dependencies through neural message passing. However, their method has key drawbacks as RainDrop is built upon a highly customized dependency graph obtained by manually setting the filtering threshold. This manual intervention can substantially impede the learning of an optimal graph structure that is diverse in different types of datasets and tightly bound to specific tasks. Additionally, RainDrop only relies on the available observed values, limiting its ability to capture informative missingness patterns that are often correlated with the target label [30,33]. It also ignores within and across time structural dependencies between adjacent graph snapshots, which are essential for modeling the correlation of different time series variables and deriving a more comprehensive representation of IS-MTS for more accurate prediction results. Furthermore, IS-MTS data dynamically change with irregular time intervals, but RainDrop does not consider the irregular time span information when generating attention weights, leading to a failure to distinguish the influence of different time points on its final sequence-level representation.

To address the aforementioned challenges, we propose a novel graph-based learning model, called Multivariate Temporal Graph Networks. This model aims to overcome the limitations of existing methods in modeling IS-MTS and improve the performance of downstream classification tasks. The proposed model is designed to effectively capture time-aware dependencies, extract graph structural relations, and handle irregular sampling intervals and frequent missing values commonly encountered in IS-MTS. Specifically, our contributions are as follows:

- We propose a multivariate interaction module (MIM) to handle the asynchronous nature of observations between different sequences without the need for manually defining the connectivity structure. MIM embeds time series under a unified time set and automatically infers its graph structure by leveraging temporal attention between nodes in a data-driven fashion. To navigate the search for optimal vertex connectivity, we develop a reinforcement learning selector, which operates along with the GNN classifier training process.
- We build a novel graph propagation layer on top of MIM, with Markov property, aimed at enriching the representation of each node with the topological structure and features of its neighbors. This approach enables modeling both within and across time dependencies and structural interactions, thereby allowing for a more comprehensive representation of IS-MTS.
- To retain relevant information in varying data intervals, we introduce a novel masked time-aware self-attention module that explicitly incorporates temporal context and accounts for the impact of irregular intervals on attention weight generation between observation embeddings.
- We conducted comprehensive comparative experiments on real-world datasets to evaluate the proposed model. The results showed that our model significantly outperforms the state-of-the-art methods.

The remaining sections of this paper are structured as follows. In Sect. 2, we formulate the research problem of modeling and analyzing IS-MTS. In Sect. 3, we provide a detailed description of the proposed model. In Sect. 4, we present the experimental results and ablation study, which demonstrate the effectiveness of our approach. Finally, we conclude our work in Sect. 5.

2 Preliminaries

This section aims to introduce the essential notations required to formulate the classification of IS-MTS using graph-based learning modeling.

Irregularly Sampled Multivariate Time Series. Let $\mathcal{D} = \{(\boldsymbol{s}_k, y_k) \in (\mathcal{S}, \mathcal{Y}) \mid k = 1, ..., K\}$ represent K samples, where each sample comprises a d-dimensional IS-MTS $\boldsymbol{s}_k = \{\boldsymbol{s}_{k,i} \mid i = 1, ..., d\}$ and its associated label y_k. Each dimension of $\boldsymbol{s}_k$ is a univariate time series variable $\boldsymbol{s}_{k,i}$. The number of records in the kth sample at dimension i is denoted as

$N_{k,i}$. We represent each univariate time series as a list of observed tuples $\boldsymbol{s}_{k,i} = [(t_{k,i,1}, x_{k,i,1}), ..., (t_{k,i,m}, x_{k,i,m}), ..., (t_{k,i,N_{k,i}}, x_{k,i,N_{k,i}})]$, where $x_{k,i,m}$ is the observed value of the mth time step of ith dimension at time $t_{k,i,m} \in \mathbb{R}_0^+$ for the kth multivariate time series sample. We define $\boldsymbol{t}_{k,i} = [t_{k,i,1}, t_{k,i,2}, ..., t_{k,i,N_{k,i}}]$ as the list of timestamps and $\boldsymbol{x}_{k,i} = [x_{k,i,1}, x_{k,i,2}, ..., x_{k,i,N_{k,i}}]$ as the list of observations for the ith variable of the kth sample. It should be noted that for $i \neq j$, in general, $\boldsymbol{t}_{k,i} \neq \boldsymbol{t}_{k,j}$ and $N_{k,i} \neq N_{k,j}$.

Multivariate Temporal Graph Structure. We construct a sequence of time-ordered graphs $\mathcal{G}_k = \{\mathcal{G}_k^{t_1}, ..., \mathcal{G}_k^{t_{|\mathcal{T}_k|}}\}$ for every sample $\boldsymbol{s}_k$, where $\mathcal{G}_k^t = \{\mathcal{V}, \mathcal{E}_k, \mathcal{X}_k^t, \mathcal{A}_k^t\}$ refers to a snapshot of the graph at time t. The set $\mathcal{T}_k = \bigcup_{i=1}^{d} \bigcup_{m=1}^{N_{k,i}} \{t_{k,i,m}\}$ is defined as the union of observed timestamps across all variables for sample $\boldsymbol{s}_k$. Each node v_i in $\mathcal{V} = \{v_i\}_{i=1}^d$ corresponds to a univariate time series variable. $\mathcal{E}_k$ is a weighted adjacency matrix that describes interdependencies among variables in sample $\boldsymbol{s}_k$. Specifically, $e_{k,ij} > 0$ indicates that there exists an edge from v_i to v_j and $e_{k,ij}$ represents the strength of this edge. $\mathcal{X}_k^t = \{x_{k,i}^t \mid t \in \mathcal{T}_k\}_{i=1}^d$ represents observed values of MTS at time t, where each observation $x_{k,i}^t$ denotes the feature value affiliated with node v_i at time t. Here, we use $x_{k,i}^{t_{k,i,m}}$ to equivalently denote $x_{k,i,m}$ under the unified time set $\mathcal{T}_k$. The attention matrix $\mathcal{A}_k^t$ implies the time-dependent relationship between variables in sample $\boldsymbol{s}_k$, where each entry $\alpha_{k,ij}^t$ can be interpreted as a weighted coefficient characterizing the importance of the ith variable to the jth variable at time t.

Problem Formulation. We formulate the IS-MTS classification problem using multivariate temporal graph structure in the following way. Given observed values $\{\boldsymbol{x}_{k,i}\}_{i=1}^d$ and their corresponding creation times $\{\boldsymbol{t}_{k,i}\}_{i=1}^d$ for an IS-MTS $\boldsymbol{s}_k$, our goal is to extract the temporal and structural information from $\mathcal{T}_k$ graph snapshots inferred from data and use this information to train a model ($\mathscr{F} : \mathcal{S} \rightarrow \mathcal{Y}$) to predict the sequence-level label $\hat{y}_k \in \{0,1\}^C$, where C is the number of class labels. For simplicity, we will omit the sample index k hereinafter.

3 Our Proposed Model

In this section, we present the proposed Multivariate Temporal Graph Networks (MTGNet). Figure 2 illustrates the overall architecture of our model, and we will elaborate on the key modules of MTGNet in the following subsections.

3.1 Multivariate Interaction Module

To handle the inherent asynchrony of different sequences, we propose a relation embedding strategy that enables our model to learn latent correlations among time series and automatically infer the graph structure in a data-driven manner.

Time Series Data Encoding We represent an IS-MTS $\boldsymbol{s}$ as a graph $\mathcal{G}^t$ observed at timestamp $t = t_1, ..., t_{|\mathcal{T}|}$. The initial feature vector of each node v_i in $\mathcal{G}^t$ is

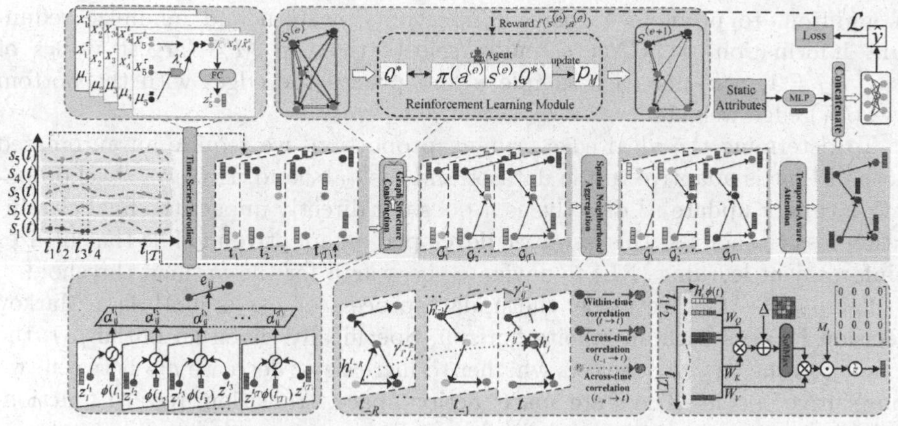

Fig. 2. The architecture of the proposed MTGNet for classifying ISMTS.

obtained by transforming the observed value x_i^t of the corresponding univariate time series variable $\boldsymbol{s}_i$ into a higher-level subspace for sufficient expressive power [21]. To accomplish this, we apply a node-specific Multi-layer Perceptron with ReLU activation, $\boldsymbol{z}_i^t = MLP(x_i^t; \boldsymbol{w}_i, \boldsymbol{b}_i)$, to every observation affiliated with the ith dimension of $\boldsymbol{s}$. For nodes that are not observed at timestamp t, we use a decayed imputation as the input, and the node-specific MLP learns trainable vectors for them. Specifically, for the unobserved node v_j at time t, its initial feature vector at time t can be generated through the following technique:

$$\boldsymbol{z}_j^t = MLP(\hat{x}_j^t; \boldsymbol{w}_j, \boldsymbol{b}_j); \quad \hat{x}_j^t = \lambda_\tau^t \hat{x}_j^\tau + (1 - \lambda_\tau^t)\mu_j \tag{1}$$

where $\hat{x}_j^\tau$ is the observed measurement of node v_j at the most recent time $\tau < t$, and $\mu_j = \frac{1}{\sum_k N_{k,j}} \sum_k \sum_{m=1}^{N_{k,j}} x_{k,j,m}$ is its empirical mean. The decay rate λ_τ^t is learned from the training data through $\lambda_\tau^t = exp\{-max(0, w_\lambda(t-\tau) + b_\lambda)\}$.

Graph Structure Construction After obtaining the initial node representation using data encoding, we calculate attention coefficients by matching the node embeddings while considering the influence of time interval irregularities.

$$\alpha_{ij}^t = \sigma\Big(\boldsymbol{c}^T \boldsymbol{W}_\alpha \big(\boldsymbol{z}_i^t || \boldsymbol{z}_j^t || \boldsymbol{\phi}(t)\big)\Big); \quad \boldsymbol{\phi}(t)[u] = \begin{cases} \omega_0 t + \varphi_0 & if\ u = 0 \\ sin(\omega_u t + \varphi_u) & if\ 1 \le u < d_t \end{cases} \tag{2}$$

where $\boldsymbol{\phi}(t) \in \mathbb{R}^{d_t}$ is the vector representation of timestamp encoding for time t. This encoding transforms the 1-dimensional time axis into a d_t-dimensional vector, where $\boldsymbol{\phi}(t)[u]$ is the uth dimension of the embedding vector $\boldsymbol{\phi}(t)$. $\{\omega_u, \varphi_u\}_{u=0}^k$ are learnable parameters. The sinusoidal term captures periodic patterns while the linear term accounts for non-periodic behaviors in the time series.

To construct data-driven dependency graphs for different time series, we dynamically adjust the connection of two nodes based on the learned attention coefficient sequence. We determine edge connections by summing up attention coefficients of corresponding nodes over all timestamps: $e_{ij} = \sum_{t \in \mathcal{T}} \alpha_{ij}^t / |\mathcal{T}|$.

In addition, to promote a sparse connectivity pattern and minimize redundant information, MTGNet carefully selects the top $M\%$ largest values of $\{e_{ij} \mid i, j = 1, ..., d\}$ for each sample $\boldsymbol{s}$ and prunes the edges with the bottom $(1-M\%)$ edge weights.

To determine the ideal edge-pruning proportion, we require an automated method that is adaptive to the dataset and task at hand. However, backpropagation cannot update M directly, as it does not directly impact the final classification loss. To address this issue, we developed an adaptive module that utilizes reinforcement learning (RL) to navigate the search for the optimal threshold.

Let $p_M = M\%$, we model the update process of $p_M \in [0, 1]$ as a Markov Decision Process with an infinite horizon. Specifically, given an initial p_M, the policy π in the RL agent selects whether to increase or decrease p_M between two consecutive epochs. The state space, action space, transition, reward function, and termination condition are defined as follows:

◇ **State**. At each training epoch e, the current state $s^{(e)}$ is defined as the adjacent matrix $\mathcal{E}^{(e)}$ obtained by selecting the top $M\%$ largest edge weights.

◇ **Action**. The action $a^{(e)}$ at epoch e determines how RL updates p_M based on the reward. We define the action as plus or minus a fixed value Δp from p_M.

◇ **Transition**. The transition serves as the state transition probability of the reinforcement learning environment. After updating p_M, we use $topM\big(\{e_{ij}|i, j = 1, ..., d\}\big)$ to select a new adjacent matrix in the next epoch.

◇ **Reward**. The reward evaluates whether the search mechanism is effective at the current epoch. We define the reward function to measure the improvement of classification results for each action when compared with previous epochs.

$$f(s^{(e)}, a^{(e)}) = \begin{cases} +1 & if\mathcal{ACC}^{(e)} \geq \frac{\sum_{e'=e-b}^{e-1} \mathcal{ACC}^{(e')}}{b} \\ -1 & otherwise \end{cases} \tag{3}$$

where $\mathcal{ACC}^{(e)}$ is the classification accuracy at epoch e. We use the binary reward $f\big(s^{(e)}, a^{(e)}\big)$ to guide the action policy.

◇ **Termination**. We define the terminal condition for RL as follows:

$$diff\big(\{p_M^{(e-10)}, ..., p_M^{(e)}\}\big) \leq \Delta p \tag{4}$$

where $diff$ is the difference between the maximum and minimum values of p_M over the last ten epochs. When the change is no more than Δp, it indicates the RL module has found the optimal threshold p_M^*.

The Bellman optimality equation can be used to approximate the action-value function for the finite horizon MDP described above, which can be learned through *Q-learning* [37]:

$$Q^*(s^{(e)}, a^{(e)}) = f(s^{(e)}, a^{(e)}) + \gamma_\pi \max_{a'} Q_\pi(s^{(e+1)}, a') \tag{5}$$

where γ_π is a discount factor. We exploit the ϵ-greedy policy to select the action $a^{(e)}$ $w.r.t$ Q^*, and the policy π is obtained as follows:

$$\pi(a^{(e)}|s^{(e)}, Q^*) = \begin{cases} random\ action & w.p.\ \ \epsilon \\ \arg\max_a Q^*(s^{(e)}, a) & w.p.\ \ 1-\epsilon \end{cases} \tag{6}$$

The RL agent and classification model can be jointly trained in an end-to-end manner. Once the RL has converged, p_M^* remains fixed during the next training process until the classification model has also converged.

3.2 Correlation-Aware Neighborhood Aggregation

The measurements in IS-MTS are often correlated with one another both within and across timestamps. To capture the topological structure and node features of its neighbors for enriching the representation of each node, we assume that the node's representation at time t ($t_{\text{-}0}$) not only depends on its neighboring nodes at the same time but also is influenced by its neighbors at previous time $t_{\text{-}1}, ..., t_{\text{-}R}$ in our model.

$$\begin{aligned} \boldsymbol{m}_i^{t_{\text{-}r},(l)} &= \sum\nolimits_{v_i \in \mathcal{N}_{t_{\text{-}r}}(v_j)} \gamma_{ij}^{t_{\text{-}r},(l)} \boldsymbol{h}_i^{t_{\text{-}r},(l)} && \text{(a)} \\ \boldsymbol{h}_j^{t,(l+1)} &= \sigma\big(\boldsymbol{W}^{(l)} \boldsymbol{h}_j^{t,(l)} + \sum\nolimits_{r=0}^{R} \boldsymbol{W}_r^{(l)} \boldsymbol{m}_i^{t_{\text{-}r},(l)}\big) && \text{(b)} \end{aligned} \tag{7}$$

This assumption is motivated by the data correlation between blood pressure and heart rate described in the introduction section. To achieve this, we propose a special graph convolution module with R-step Markov property that models within and across time dependencies and learns temporal and structural information from adjacent graph snapshots. Specifically, for node v_j at time t in layer l, its embedding is updated according to Eq. 7, where $\mathcal{N}_{t_{\text{-}r}}(v_j)$ denotes the neighboring nodes of v_j at time $t_{\text{-}r}$, and $\gamma_{ij}^{t_{\text{-}r},(l)}$ represents the attention score between node v_j at time t and its $t_{\text{-}r}$ neighbor v_i in layer l. We use a neural network with the softmax function to determine these attention scores as follows:

$$\beta_{ij}^{t_{\text{-}r},(l)} = \sigma\Big(\boldsymbol{b}^T\big(\boldsymbol{W}_\gamma \boldsymbol{h}_i^{t_{\text{-}r},(l)} || \boldsymbol{W}_\gamma \boldsymbol{h}_j^{t,(l)}\big)\Big); \ \gamma_{ij}^{t_{\text{-}r},(l)} = \frac{exp\big(\beta_{ij}^{t_{\text{-}r},(l)}\big)}{\sum_{v_{i'} \in \mathcal{N}_{t_{\text{-}r}}(v_j)} exp\big(\beta_{i'j}^{t_{\text{-}r},(l)}\big)} \tag{8}$$

The proposed graph convolution module, as shown in Eq. 7, computes the node embedding by accumulating transformed features via a normalized sum of neighbors from both the current and previous R-step graph snapshots as well as itself. Multiple such graph convolution modules (i.e., L layers) can be stacked to extract topological and attributed information from multiple hop neighborhoods. The final feature embedding of node v_i at time t for data sample $\boldsymbol{s}$ is denoted as $\boldsymbol{h}_i^{t,(L)}$. Unlike the aggregation strategy used in typical spatial-temporal-aware GNNs [31,32], which separately employ spatial and temporal aggregators and combine them sequentially, the proposed correlation-aware neighborhood aggregation module considers both within and across time dependencies and fuses temporal and structural information from graph snapshots simultaneously.

3.3 Masked Time-Aware Self-Attention

The objective of the time-aware self-attention module is to generate the node-level representation for a univariate time series variable, given a sequence of embeddings $\{\boldsymbol{h}_i^{t_1,(L)}, ..., \boldsymbol{h}_i^{t_{|\mathcal{T}|},(L)}\}$ from $\mathcal{T}$ graph snapshots. The standard self-attention mechanism makes an assumption of a constant time interval between time steps, which is not the case in IS-MTS data. To address this issue and consider the timestamp context and interval irregularity when calculating the correlation between two items, we employ a novel time-aware self-attention aggregator. Initially, we construct a scaled time interval matrix $\boldsymbol{\Delta} \in \mathbb{R}^{|\mathcal{T}|\times|\mathcal{T}|}$, where each entry $\boldsymbol{\Delta}_{op}$ represents the scaled time interval $\lfloor|t_o - t_p|/\delta\rfloor$ between embedding $\boldsymbol{h}_i^{t_o,(L)}$ and $\boldsymbol{h}_i^{t_p,(L)}$. Here, δ is the minimum time interval (except 0) between two items: $\delta = \min\{|t_o - t_p| \mid o, p = 1, ..., |\mathcal{T}|\}$. We then append time encoding $\boldsymbol{\phi}(t)$ to embedding $\boldsymbol{h}_i^{t,(L)}$ to include information of the absolute timestamp. The proposed time-aware self-attention can be expressed as:

$$\boldsymbol{U}_i = softmax\Big((\tilde{\boldsymbol{H}}_i^T \boldsymbol{W}_Q \boldsymbol{W}_K^T \tilde{\boldsymbol{H}}_i + \boldsymbol{w}_\delta \cdot \boldsymbol{\Delta})/\sqrt{d_h + d_t}\Big)\tilde{\boldsymbol{H}}_i^T \boldsymbol{W}_V \tag{9}$$

where $\boldsymbol{W}_V \in \mathbb{R}^{(d_h+d_t)\times d_v}$, $\boldsymbol{W}_Q \in \mathbb{R}^{(d_h+d_t)\times d_q}$ and $\boldsymbol{W}_K \in \mathbb{R}^{(d_h+d_t)\times d_q}$ are projection matrix for a value, query and key respectively. $\boldsymbol{w}_\delta \in \mathbb{R}$ is a learnable parameter for embedding time intervals, and $\tilde{\boldsymbol{H}}_i = [\boldsymbol{h}_i^{t_1,(L)}||\boldsymbol{\phi}(t_1), ..., \boldsymbol{h}_i^{t_{|\mathcal{T}|},(L)}||\boldsymbol{\phi}(t_{|\mathcal{T}|})]$ $\in \mathbb{R}^{(d_h+d_t)\times|\mathcal{T}|}$ allows the model to include absolute timestamps information. The proposed module is capable of focusing on the most informative embeddings. We then calculate the masked average of column entries of $\boldsymbol{U}_i$ as follows:

$$\boldsymbol{u}_i = \hat{\boldsymbol{U}}_i^T \overrightarrow{\boldsymbol{1}}/N_{k,i}; \quad \hat{\boldsymbol{U}}_i = \boldsymbol{U}_i \odot \boldsymbol{M}_i; \quad \boldsymbol{M}_i^T = [\boldsymbol{m}_i^{t_1}, ..., \boldsymbol{m}_i^{t_{|\mathcal{T}|}}] \tag{10}$$

where $\odot$ denotes the element-wise product, $\overrightarrow{\boldsymbol{1}} \in \mathbb{R}^{|\mathcal{T}|}$ represents a column vector of ones, and $\boldsymbol{M}_i$ is a $(0, 1)$ matrix indicating the missingness, e.g., $\boldsymbol{m}_{k,i}^{t_1} = \overrightarrow{\boldsymbol{1}} \in \mathbb{R}^{d_v}$ if $x_{k,i}^{t_1}$ is observed, $\boldsymbol{m}_{k,i}^{t_1} = \overrightarrow{\boldsymbol{0}} \in \mathbb{R}^{d_v}$ otherwise. We adopt $\boldsymbol{u}_i$ as the ultimate representation of the node-level for the univariate time series variable $\boldsymbol{s}_i$.

3.4 Graph-Level Learning Module

For samples that contain static attributes $\boldsymbol{x}_0$ (specific examples will be provided in the experimental section), a separate nonlinear transformation model is used to extract stable raw factors: $\boldsymbol{a} = \sigma(\boldsymbol{W}_0\boldsymbol{x}_0)$, where $\boldsymbol{a} \in \mathbb{R}^d$. In contrast to temporal factors, static factors remain constant across all snapshots. Based on all of the above, we aggregate the information of d node-level embeddings to obtain the graph-level representation for IS-MTS $\boldsymbol{s}$ as follows:

$$\boldsymbol{g} = Aggregate(\boldsymbol{u}_1, \boldsymbol{u}_2, ..., \boldsymbol{u}_d, \boldsymbol{a}) \tag{11}$$

where the aggregation function we use is a concatenation operator. To predict the sequence-level label, we employ a collection of interleaved fully-connected layers with softmax activation to transform the graph-level embedding $\boldsymbol{g}$ to the target $\hat{y} = \rho(\boldsymbol{g})$. Our multivariate temporal graph model is trained by minimizing the cross-entropy loss under the available training data

$$\mathcal{L} = -\frac{1}{N_{train}} \sum\nolimits_k \sum\nolimits_{c=1}^{C} [y_k^c \log \hat{y}_k^c] + \lambda_\theta ||\Theta||^2 \tag{12}$$

where $||\Theta||^2$ denotes the regularization term and hyperparameter λ_θ is utilized to balance the degree of regularization.

4 Experiments

In this section, we present the results of experiments conducted on three real-life datasets for IS-MTS classification tasks. Our model is compared with nine representative and state-of-the-art baselines.

4.1 Datasets

The PhysioNet/CinC Challenge 2012 (PNC12) dataset [11] comprises multivariate clinical time series data with 36 temporal variables (e.g., *Albumin*, *Glucose*, *pH*) and 6 static patient descriptors (e.g. *Age*, *RecordID*, *ICUType*) extracted from Intensive Care Unit (ICU) records. Each record contains irregularly sampled multivariate time series collected during the first 48 h after patients' admission to the ICU. Our method is trained and evaluated on the binary mortality prediction task of whether a patient will die during the hospital stay. The mortality labels are imbalanced, with an approximate ratio of 1:6.

The PhysioNet/CinC Challenge 2019 (PNC19) dataset [12] contains physiological records of patients in two-week hourly time windows. It consists of 34 time-dependent clinical variables and four static demographic descriptions (e.g., *Gender*). Similar to PNC12, PNC19 is highly imbalanced, with only 5% of patients developing sepsis. We compare methods to identify a patient's risk of developing sepsis and make a positive or negative prediction from the clinical records. To evaluate the model performance on these highly imbalanced datasets, we use the Area Under the ROC Curve (AUROC) and Area Under the Precision-Recall Curve (AUPRC) metrics.

The Physical Activity (PAMAP2) dataset [13] includes recordings of 18 different physical activities (e.g.,*Cycling, Playing soccer*), performed by 9 subjects wearing 3 inertial measurement units and a heart rate monitor. We followed the data preprocessing steps outlined in [14], resulting in a dataset of 5,333 irregularly sampled sequences with 17 channels and 600 temporal observations in each sequence. We randomly selected 40% of the sample observations to create irregular time intervals. Our task is to predict the multi-class label for each activity. Since the PAMAP2 dataset has approximately balanced samples, we evaluate models using metrics such as Accuracy, Precision, Recall, and F1 score.

4.2 Competitors

Based on the survey conducted by Shukla et al. [25], there are five main primitives for modeling IS-MTS: discretization, recurrence, interpolation, attention, and structural invariance. For our experiments, we choose representative and state-of-the-art methods from each category as competitors for comparison.

- **MRE** [28]: It discretizes IS-MTS into non-overlapping intervals within a fixed time length and utilizes a multi-resolution ensemble model for prediction.
- **ATTAIN** [29]: It proposes a time-aware LSTM network that incorporates attention and decay weights for modeling the time irregularity between events.

Table 1. Classification performance (%) on PNC12, PNC19 and PAMAP2 datasets.

Methods	PNC12		PNC19		PAMAP2			
	AUROC	AUPRC	AUROC	AUPRC	Accuracy	Precision	Recall	F1 score
MRE	$64.3_{\pm 2.5}$	$91.2_{\pm 0.9}$	$87.0_{\pm 1.2}$	$42.4_{\pm 2.7}$	$67.8_{\pm 2.4}$	$69.2_{\pm 1.7}$	$60.7_{\pm 3.5}$	$64.6_{\pm 2.3}$
GRU-D	$69.1_{\pm 1.3}$	$93.2_{\pm 1.0}$	$91.0_{\pm 1.0}$	$46.9_{\pm 3.5}$	$71.1_{\pm 1.3}$	$73.0_{\pm 2.0}$	$71.8_{\pm 2.8}$	$71.7_{\pm 1.9}$
VRIN	$70.6_{\pm 1.7}$	$94.4_{\pm 0.8}$	$91.4_{\pm 0.6}$	$47.3_{\pm 2.0}$	$72.6_{\pm 0.8}$	$75.8_{\pm 2.9}$	$72.0_{\pm 1.1}$	$73.3_{\pm 1.8}$
mTAND	$60.1_{\pm 3.4}$	$93.3_{\pm 0.8}$	$80.7_{\pm 1.7}$	$35.1_{\pm 3.3}$	$65.3_{\pm 0.9}$	$68.1_{\pm 4.1}$	$63.2_{\pm 2.3}$	$65.6_{\pm 3.6}$
L-ODE	$70.2_{\pm 1.4}$	$94.0_{\pm 0.7}$	$90.6_{\pm 0.8}$	$46.3_{\pm 3.0}$	$72.2_{\pm 2.0}$	$74.8_{\pm 2.7}$	$71.9_{\pm 1.9}$	$73.0_{\pm 2.5}$
ATTAIN	$73.1_{\pm 3.7}$	$95.5_{\pm 1.1}$	$89.2_{\pm 2.0}$	$46.8_{\pm 3.2}$	$81.0_{\pm 4.2}$	$82.1_{\pm 3.6}$	$84.9_{\pm 2.8}$	$83.1_{\pm 3.5}$
DATA	$72.0_{\pm 1.9}$	$96.7_{\pm 0.6}$	$88.5_{\pm 1.0}$	$46.4_{\pm 2.0}$	$80.8_{\pm 2.9}$	$81.9_{\pm 2.8}$	$83.5_{\pm 2.6}$	$82.4_{\pm 2.7}$
SeFT	$67.8_{\pm 3.2}$	$96.0_{\pm 1.1}$	$82.2_{\pm 1.1}$	$38.5_{\pm 5.1}$	$64.5_{\pm 1.7}$	$67.6_{\pm 2.3}$	$57.9_{\pm 1.8}$	$60.7_{\pm 1.9}$
RainDrop	$72.4_{\pm 1.5}$	$96.9_{\pm 0.6}$	$88.8_{\pm 0.4}$	$49.3_{\pm 3.8}$	$83.6_{\pm 1.8}$	$85.3_{\pm 1.7}$	$84.3_{\pm 1.8}$	$84.5_{\pm 1.9}$
MTGNet	$\mathbf{77.6}_{\pm 1.1}$	$\mathbf{97.7}_{\pm 0.5}$	$\mathbf{91.7}_{\pm 0.9}$	$\mathbf{56.8}_{\pm 2.6}$	$\mathbf{87.4}_{\pm 1.6}$	$\mathbf{88.7}_{\pm 1.2}$	$\mathbf{88.2}_{\pm 1.9}$	$\mathbf{88.3}_{\pm 1.4}$

- **GRU-D** [2]: It modifies the GRU cell by decaying the previous hidden state $h_{t\text{-}1}$ with a factor γ_h and utilizing it to compute the new hidden state h_t. It also decays the input variable over time toward the empirical mean.
- **L-ODE** [35]: It proposes a latent variable time series model in which the generative model and recognition network are defined by a neural ODE and an ODE-RNN, respectively.
- **VRIN** [7]: It proposes a novel variational-recurrent imputation network to exploit temporal relations and uncertainties in estimating missing values in MTS for the downstream prediction task.
- **mTAND** [26]: It presents an interpolation-based approach with learnable temporal similarity functions followed by a VAE-based model for learning from irregularly sampled data.
- **DATA** [27]: It proposes a dual-attention structure to handle missing values and estimates diversity in the unreliability of different data so that the imputed data inferred from sparse observations are less reliable than those from dense observations.
- **SeFT** [6]: It utilizes differentiable set function learning to represent the irregularly sampled time series data.
- **RainDrop** [14]: It uses message passing and self-attention to acquire a sensor dependency graph in MTS.

4.3 Setups and Results

Our MTGNet model is configured with an initial feature vector dimension of $F = 4$ and time embedding size of $d_t = 12$. For correlation-aware neighborhood aggregation, we set $R = 2$ and $L = 2$, and the weight vector dimension $\boldsymbol{c}$ is set to 6. In the RL module, we initialize the value $p_M = 0.5$ and set the action step size Δp to 0.03, $b = 1$ in Eq. (3), $\gamma_\pi = 0.9$ in (5) and $\epsilon = 0.6$ in (6). The weight matrix $\boldsymbol{W}_*^{(l)}$ for neighborhood aggregation operation has a shape of

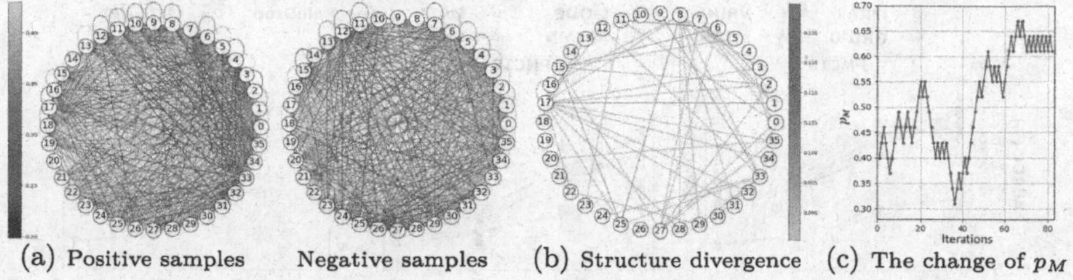

(a) Positive samples Negative samples (b) Structure divergence (c) The change of p_M

Fig. 3. Visualization of the learned dependency graphs and the updating process of p_M. Each node represents a physiological signal used in PNC12 and each edge represents the weighted connection (e.g. Node 0 denotes the enzyme Alkaline phosphatase).

4×4, while the projection matrix $\boldsymbol{W}_Q, \boldsymbol{W}_K$ and $\boldsymbol{W}_V$ for the masked time-aware self-attention have the same shape of 16×16. The classifier ρ has a neuron structure of 100-$C(No.\ of\ classes)$. We set the regularization hyperparameter $\lambda_\theta = 0.001$. Our model is implemented in PyTorch, and trained using the Adam optimizer with a learning rate of 0.0001. We randomly select 70% of instances as the training set and use the remaining 10% and 20% for validation and test sets, respectively. We repeat each experiment five times and report the average performance by mean and standard deviation. For all competitors, we set the models' parameters and hyper-parameters and choose the downstream classifiers based on their respective papers or implemented source code, and carefully tune any not mentioned to yield competitive results. The code for our model can be found in the supplementary materials.

Table 1 presents the predictive results of all models on three benchmark datasets. The results indicate that the proposed model consistently yields the highest average score across all metrics. Baseline models that do not consider structural dependencies among IS-MTS data, such as MRE, GRU-D, L-ODE, VRIN, DATA, SeFT and mTAND, show noticeably lower classification performance compared to graph-based competitors like RainDrop and MTGNet. This observation suggests that incorporating intrinsic structural information among variables is critical and should be taken into account for the IS-MTS prediction task. Furthermore, compared to RainDrop, which fails to leverage informative missing patterns, ignores within and across time structural dependencies between adjacent graph snapshots, and discards time interval information in node-level representation learning, our model takes advantage of all these benefits and performs significantly better. To illustrate the learned structural inter-dependencies among time series variables, Fig. 3a visualizes the graph connectivity on the PNC12 dataset. Since MTGNet learns a specific graph for each sample, we take the average of the learned structures for the positive and negative samples, respectively. Different colors in the visualization represent different connection weight values between nodes. We observe that there exist distinctive patterns across the learned dependency graphs of positive and negative samples. We further calculate their graph structure divergence and present the top 50

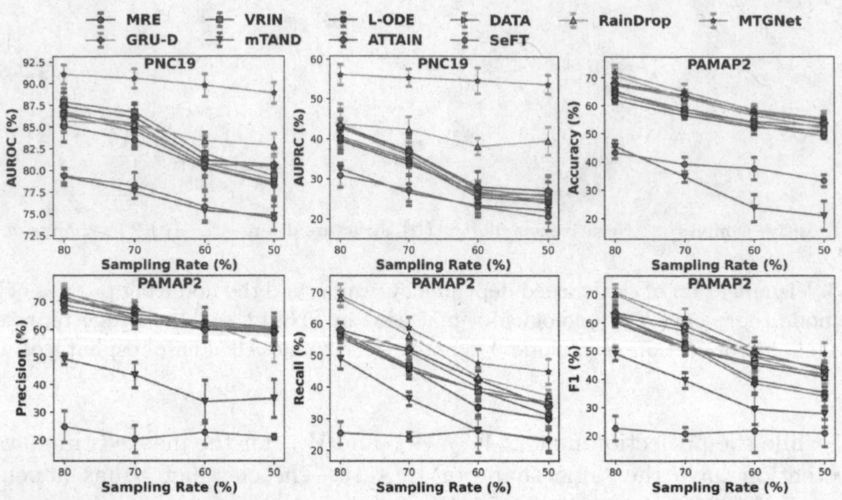

Fig. 4. Classification performance (%) on PNC19 and PAMAP2 datasets with randomly selected time series variables.

most distinctive edges in Fig. 3b. Our analysis reveals that the connection from Node 6 (*Cholesterol*) to Node 11 (*Glucose*) is helpful in differentiating samples. This data-driven observation aligns with the association between glucose and cholesterol metabolism studied in health professionals [24]. The updating process of p_M on PNC12 dataset is visualized in Fig. 3c, with the initial value randomly set to 0.4. It can be observed that the RL environment experiences fluctuation in the beginning, as the RL agent is jointly learned with other modules. However, after 60 training iterations, the RL algorithm gradually satisfies the terminal condition specified in Eq. (4), and the edge selector p_M eventually converges to a stable range of 0.60–0.65.

The observation process may sometimes be restricted in practice, leading to the total absence of certain variables (e.g., due to broken sensors, data transmission failure, or damaged storage). A robust model should be able to utilize informative structural dependencies among time series variables and appropriately compensate for missing variable observations. To investigate the impact of missing variables, we conducted experiments on the PNC19 and PAMAP2 datasets, where only a subset of time series variables was available. Since experimental studies on data collected from ICU patients, PNC12 and PNC19, show similar sorts of outcomes, we report only the experimental results of PNC19. In particular, we randomly selected a fraction of time series variables in each sample and marked the remaining variables as unobserved in both the validation and test sets. Figure 4 shows the comparison of classification performance among all the models. We observed that MTGNet consistently achieved better performance than the baselines in most of the evaluation metrics when the time series variable sampling rate decreased from 80% to 50%.

Table 2. Results (%) of the ablation study on PNC12, PNC19 and PAMAP2 datasets.

Methods	PNC12		PNC19		PAMAP2			
	AUROC	AUPRC	AUROC	AUPRC	Accuracy	Precision	Recall	F1 score
w/o Auxiliary imputation	$73.7_{\pm 1.8}$	$96.3_{\pm 0.6}$	$90.5_{\pm 1.4}$	$53.2_{\pm 3.2}$	$84.6_{\pm 1.5}$	$85.0_{\pm 1.7}$	$84.6_{\pm 1.2}$	$84.8_{\pm 1.3}$
w/o Within time correlation	$76.6_{\pm 1.3}$	$97.6_{\pm 0.4}$	$90.7_{\pm 0.7}$	$56.3_{\pm 1.7}$	$84.5_{\pm 0.8}$	$85.1_{\pm 0.2}$	$86.4_{\pm 1.6}$	$85.7_{\pm 0.9}$
w/o Across time correlation	$76.3_{\pm 2.0}$	$97.0_{\pm 0.5}$	$90.9_{\pm 0.8}$	$55.4_{\pm 2.2}$	$86.8_{\pm 1.6}$	$87.6_{\pm 1.7}$	$87.9_{\pm 1.3}$	$87.6_{\pm 1.3}$
w/o Time interval matrix	$75.6_{\pm 1.5}$	$97.4_{\pm 0.5}$	$89.8_{\pm 1.3}$	$46.9_{\pm 2.2}$	$83.3_{\pm 1.4}$	$85.6_{\pm 1.9}$	$82.9_{\pm 2.6}$	$83.9_{\pm 2.0}$
w/o Masking matrix	$65.5_{\pm 1.6}$	$95.7_{\pm 1.0}$	$83.6_{\pm 1.1}$	$38.8_{\pm 3.5}$	$80.5_{\pm 1.3}$	$83.2_{\pm 1.1}$	$79.6_{\pm 2.7}$	$80.8_{\pm 1.8}$
Full Model	$77.6_{\pm 1.1}$	$97.7_{\pm 0.5}$	$91.7_{\pm 0.9}$	$56.8_{\pm 2.6}$	$87.4_{\pm 1.6}$	$88.7_{\pm 1.2}$	$88.2_{\pm 1.9}$	$88.3_{\pm 1.4}$

To further examine the impact of the core components in our proposed model, we perform an ablation study on MTGNet by systematically removing one module at a time. The Table 2 summarizes the results of our study. In the *w/o* Auxiliary imputation setup, we remove the decayed imputer and replace the data encoding strategy in Sect. 3.1 with the generating embedding method used in Raindrop [14]. In '*w/o* across time correlation', we disregard information from previous R time steps neighborhoods. Similarly, '*w/o* within time correlation' signifies the absence of the structural information at the current time. In '*w/o* time interval matrix', we use a standard self-attention and do not consider the influence of time interval irregularity. In '*w/o* masking matrix', we directly use the last column of output $\boldsymbol{U}_i$ as the final node-level representation for univariate time series variable. Based on the ablation results, we note the following: 1) integrating observation and auxiliary imputer yields improved prediction scores as a result of capturing the overall pattern of missingness across time series; 2) the proposed model, built with correlation-aware neighborhood aggregation, outperforms '*w/o* within/across time correlation' in all datasets, indicating the importance of the proposed aggregation method in modeling within and across time dependencies and structural interactions to derive a more comprehensive representation of IS-MTS for more accurate predictions; 3) similarly, considering irregular time intervals and introducing a masking matrix help determine reasonable attention weights and distinguish the influence of embeddings on the final node-level representation, leading to improved prediction performance.

5 Conclusion

This paper proposes a novel multivariate temporal graph network for the modeling and classification of irregularly sampled multivariate time series. The proposed model is capable of handling the challenging data characteristics of IS-MTS, accommodating asynchronous sampling rates and irregular intervals, capturing the temporal dependency, and extracting the graph structure relation in a data-driven manner. Extensive experiments and analyses are conducted on various datasets, demonstrating superior performance compared to existing competitors. An interesting avenue for future research could involve extending our graph model to a probabilistic setting, allowing for sensible propagation of natural uncertainty arising from observation sparsity into predictive components.

Acknowledgement. This research is supported by the National Key R&D Program of China (Grant No. 2022YFF0608000), the Natural Science Foundation of China (No. 62172372, No. 62272487, No. 62076178), Zhejiang Provincial Natural Science Foundation (No. LZ21F030001) and Zhejiang Lab (K2023KG0AC02).

References

1. Shi, X., Chen, Z., Wang, H., Yeung, D.Y., Wong, W.K., Woo, W.C.: Convolutional LSTM network: a machine learning approach for precipitation nowcasting. In: Advances in Neural Information Processing Systems, vol. 28 (2015)
2. Che, Z., Purushotham, S., Cho, K., Sontag, D., Liu, Y.: Recurrent neural networks for multivariate time series with missing values. Sci. Rep. **8**(1), 6085 (2018)
3. Baytas, I.M., Xiao, C., Zhang, X., Wang, F., Jain, A.K., Zhou, J.: Patient subtyping via time-aware LSTM networks. In: Proceedings of the 23rd ACM SIGKDD International Conference on Knowledge Discovery and Data Mining, pp. 65–74 (2017)
4. Hong, S., et al.: Holmes: health online model ensemble serving for deep learning models in intensive care units. In Proceedings of the 26th ACM SIGKDD International Conference on Knowledge Discovery & Data Mining, pp. 1614–1624 (2020)
5. Wang, Q., et al.: BiT-MAC: mortality prediction by bidirectional time and multi-feature attention coupled network on multivariate irregular time series. Comput. Biol. Med. **155**, 106586 (2023)
6. Horn, M., Moor, M., Bock, C., Rieck, B., Borgwardt, K.: Set functions for time series. In: International Conference on Machine Learning, pp. 4353–4363. PMLR (2020)
7. Mulyadi, A.W., Jun, E., Suk, H.I.: Uncertainty-aware variational-recurrent imputation network for clinical time series. IEEE Trans. Cybern. **52**(9), 9684–9694 (2021)
8. Wang, Y., Min, Y., Chen, X., Wu, J.: Multi-view graph contrastive representation learning for drug-drug interaction prediction. In: Proceedings of the Web Conference, pp. 2921–2933 (2021)
9. Li, J., et al.: Predicting path failure in time-evolving graphs. In: Proceedings of the 25th ACM SIGKDD International Conference on Knowledge Discovery & Data Mining, pp. 1279–1289 (2019)
10. Huang, Z., Sun, Y., Wang, W.: Coupled graph ode for learning interacting system dynamics. In: The 27th ACM SIGKDD International Conference on Knowledge Discovery and Data Mining (2021)
11. Silva, I., Moody, G., Scott, D.J., Celi, L.A., Mark, R.G.: Predicting in-hospital mortality of ICU patients: the physionet/computing in cardiology challenge 2012. In: 2012 Computing in Cardiology, pp. 245–248. IEEE (2012)
12. Reyna, M.A., et al.: Early prediction of sepsis from clinical data: the PhysioNet/Computing in Cardiology Challenge 2019. In: 2019 Computing in Cardiology. IEEE (2019)
13. Reiss, A., Stricker, D.: Introducing a new benchmarked dataset for activity monitoring. In: 2012 16th International Symposium on Wearable Computers, pp. 108–109. IEEE (2012)

14. Zhang, X., Zeman, M., Tsiligkaridis, T., Zitnik, M.: Graph-guided network for irregularly sampled multivariate time series. In: International Conference on Learning Representations (2022)
15. Clark, J.S., Bjørnstad, O.N.: Population time series: process variability, observation errors, missing values, lags, and hidden states. Ecology **85**(11), 3140–3150 (2004)
16. Sezer, O.B., Gudelek, M.U., Ozbayoglu, A.M.: Financial time series forecasting with deep learning: a systematic literature review: 2005–2019. Appl. Soft Comput. **90**, 106181 (2020)
17. Ma, F., Chitta, R., Zhou, J., You, Q., Sun, T. and Gao, J. Dipole: Diagnosis prediction in healthcare via attention-based bidirectional recurrent neural networks. In: Proceedings of the 23rd ACM SIGKDD International Conference on Knowledge Discovery And Data Mining, pp. 1903–1911 (2017)
18. Shickel, B., Tighe, P.J., Bihorac, A., Rashidi, P.: Deep EHR: a survey of recent advances in deep learning techniques for electronic health record (EHR) analysis. IEEE J. Biomed. Health Inform. **22**(5), 1589–1604 (2017)
19. Cao, D., Wang, Y., Duan, J., Zhang, C., Zhu, X., Huang, C., Tong, Y., Xu, B., Bai, J., Tong, J., Zhang, Q.: Spectral temporal graph neural network for multivariate time-series forecasting. Adv. Neural. Inf. Process. Syst. **33**, 17766–17778 (2020)
20. Wang, D., et al.: Temporal-aware graph neural network for credit risk prediction. In: Proceedings of the 2021 SIAM International Conference on Data Mining (SDM), pp. 702–710. Society for Industrial and Applied Mathematics (2021)
21. Veličković, P., Cucurull, G., Casanova, A., Romero, A., Lió, P., Bengio, Y.: Graph attention networks. In: International Conference on Learning Representations (2018)
22. Chen, Z., Villar, S., Chen, L., Bruna, J.: On the equivalence between graph isomorphism testing and function approximation with GNNs. In: Advances in Neural Information Processing Systems, vol. 32 (2019)
23. Pei, H., Wei, B., Chang, K.C.C., Lei, Y., Yang, B.: Geom-GCN: geometric graph convolutional networks. In: International Conference on Learning Representations (2020)
24. Hallikainen, M., et al.: Interaction between cholesterol and glucose metabolism during dietary carbohydrate modification in subjects with the metabolic syndrome. Am. J. Clin. Nutr. **84**(6), 1385–1392 (2006)
25. Shukla, S.N., Marlin, B.M.: A survey on principles, models and methods for learning from irregularly sampled time series. arXiv preprint arXiv:2012.00168 (2020)
26. Shukla, S.N., Marlin, B.: Multi-time attention networks for irregularly sampled time series. In: International Conference on Learning Representations (2020)
27. Tan, Q., et al.: Data-GRU: dual-attention time-aware gated recurrent unit for irregular multivariate time series. Proc. AAAI Conf. Artif. Intell. **34**(01), 930–937 (2020)
28. Bahadori, M.T., Lipton, Z.C.: Temporal-clustering invariance in irregular healthcare time series. arXiv preprint arXiv:1904.12206 (2019)
29. Zhang, Y.: ATTAIN: attention-based time-aware LSTM networks for disease progression modeling. In: Proceedings of the 28th International Joint Conference on Artificial Intelligence, pp. 4369–4375, Macao, China (2019)
30. Yin, C., Liu, R., Zhang, D., Zhang, P.: Identifying sepsis subphenotypes via time-aware multi-modal auto-encoder. In: Proceedings of the 26th ACM SIGKDD International Conference on Knowledge Discovery & Data Mining, pp. 862–872 (2020)
31. Yang, S., et al.: Financial risk analysis for SMEs with graph-based supply chain mining. In: Proceedings of the Twenty-Ninth International Conference on International Joint Conferences on Artificial Intelligence, pp. 4661–4667 (2021)

32. Wang, X., et al.: Traffic flow prediction via spatial temporal graph neural network. In: Proceedings of the Web Conference, pp. 1082–1092 (2020)
33. Yan, C., Gao, C., Zhang, X., Chen, Y., Malin, B.: Deep imputation of temporal data. In: 2019 IEEE International Conference on Healthcare Informatics (ICHI), pp. 1–3. IEEE (2019)
34. Kidger, P., Morrill, J., Foster, J., Lyons, T.: Neural controlled differential equations for irregular time series. Adv. Neural. Inf. Process. Syst. **33**, 6696–6707 (2020)
35. Rubanova, Y., Chen, R.T., Duvenaud, D.K.: Latent ordinary differential equations for irregularly-sampled time series. In: Advances in Neural Information Processing Systems, vol. 32 (2019)
36. Schirmer, M., Eltayeb, M., Lessmann, S., Rudolph, M.: Modeling irregular time series with continuous recurrent units. In: International Conference on Machine Learning, pp. 19388–19405. PMLR (2022)
37. Watkins, C.J., Dayan, P.: Q-learning. Mach. Learn. **8**, 279–292 (1992)
38. Sun, Z., Sun, Z., Dong, W., Shi, J., Huang, Z.: Towards predictive analysis on disease progression: a variational Hawkes process model. IEEE J. Biomed. Health Inform. **25**(11), 4195–4206 (2021)
39. De Brouwer, E., Simm, J., Arany, A., Moreau, Y.: GRU-ODE-Bayes: continuous modeling of sporadically-observed time series. In: Advances in Neural Information Processing Systems, vol. 32 (2019)
40. Oskarsson, J., Sidén, P., Lindsten, F.: Temporal graph neural networks for irregular data. In: International Conference on Artificial Intelligence and Statistics. PMLR (2023)

Weighted Multivariate Mean Reversion for Online Portfolio Selection

Boqian Wu[1], Benmeng Lyu[2,3], and Jiawen Gu[2(✉)]

[1] University of Twente, Enschede, The Netherlands
b.wu@utwente.nl
[2] Southern University of Science and Technology, Shenzhen, China
benmeng@connect.hku.hk,gujw@sustech.edu.cn
[3] The University of Hong Kong, Hong Kong, Hong Kong

Abstract. Portfolio selection is a fundamental task in finance and it is to seek the best allocation of wealth among a basket of assets. Nowadays, Online portfolio selection has received increasing attention from both AI and machine learning communities. Mean reversion is an essential property of stock performance. Hence, most state-of-the-art online portfolio strategies have been built based on this. Though they succeed in specific datasets, most of the existing mean reversion strategies applied the same weights on samples in multiple periods and considered each of the assets separately, ignoring the data noise from short-lived events, trend changing in the time series data, and the dependence of multi-assets. To overcome these limitations, in this paper, we exploit the reversion phenomenon with multivariate robust estimates and propose a novel online portfolio selection strategy named "Weighted Multivariate Mean Reversion" (WMMR) (Code is available at: https://github.com/boqian333/WMMR).. Empirical studies on various datasets show that WMMR has the ability to overcome the limitations of existing mean reversion algorithms and achieve superior results.

Keywords: portfolio selection · online learning · multivariate robust estimates

1 Introduction

Portfolio selection, which has been explored in both finance and quantitative fields, is concerned with determining a portfolio for allocating the wealth among a set of assets to achieve some financial objectives such as maximizing cumulative wealth or risk-adjusted return, in the long run. There are two main mathematical theories for this problem: the mean-variance theory [22] and the Kelly investment [17]. Mean-variance theory proposed by Markowitz trades off between the expected return (mean) and risk (variance) of a portfolio in a single-period framework. Contrarily, the Kelly investment aims to maximize the expected log return in a multi-period setting. Online portfolio selection (PS), which follows

B. Wu and B. Lyu—Equal contribution.

D. Koutra et al. (Eds.): ECML PKDD 2023, LNAI 14173, pp. 255–270, 2023.
https://doi.org/10.1007/978-3-031-43424-2_16

the Kelly investment and investigates the sequential portfolio selection strategies, is attracting increasing interest from AI and machine learning communities. Based on the Kelly investment model, some state-of-the-art online PS strategies [10] assume that current best-performing stocks would also perform well in the next trading period. However, empirical evidence indicates that such assumptions may often be violated especially in the short term. This observation of an asset's price tends to converge to the average price over time, leading to strategies of buying poor-performing stocks and selling those with good performance. This trading principle is known as the "mean reversion" principle.

In recent years, by exploiting the multi-period mean reversion principle, several online PS strategies [5,13,18] have been proposed and achieved encouraging results when applied to many datasets. However, the existing studies ignored the data noise from short-lived events, trend changes in the time series data, and the dependence of multi-assets [18,21], while these are important properties of stock movements. To overcome these drawbacks, different methods have been proposed [26]. For instance, a new PS strategy has been proposed, which more accurately estimates parameters via subset resampling. This approach is particularly useful when the number of assets is large. An ensemble learning method has also been proposed for Kelly's growth optimal portfolio to mitigate estimation errors [24]. Additionally, [28] introduced a novel Relation-aware Transformer (RAT) method to simultaneously model complex sequential patterns and varying asset correlations for PS.

In this paper, we propose a multi-period online PS strategy named "Weighted Multivariate Mean Reversion" (WMMR) without requiring subset resampling demanding thousands of loops or model training requiring sufficient data. The basic idea of WMMR is to update the next price prediction via robust multivariate estimates with exponential decay. By capturing the correlation between multiple assets, robust multivariate estimates could reduce or remove the effect of outlying data points, which are produced by the short-lived events in the financial market and may lead to incorrect forecasts or predictions. We determine the portfolio selection strategies via online learning techniques. The experimental results show that WMMR can achieve greater profits than several existing algorithms. Moreover, it is robust to different parameter values and its performance is consistently well when considering reasonable transaction costs.

2 Problem Setting

Let us consider a financial market with m assets for n periods. On the tth period, the assets' prices are represented by a close price vector $\mathbf{p}_t \in \mathbb{R}_+^m$ and each element $p_{t,i}$ represents the close price of asset i. The changes of asset prices for n trading periods are represented by a sequence of non-negative, non-zero price relative vectors $\mathbf{x}_1, \ldots, \mathbf{x}_n \in \mathbb{R}_+^m$. Let us use $\mathbf{x}^n = \{\mathbf{x}_1, \ldots, \mathbf{x}_n\}$ to denote such a sequence of price relative vectors for n periods and $x_{t,i} = \frac{p_{t,i}}{p_{t-1,i}}$. Thus, an investment in asset i on the tth period increases by a factor of $x_{t,i}$.

At the beginning of the tth period, we diversify our capital among the m assets specified by a portfolio vector $\mathbf{b}_t = (b_{t,1}, \ldots, b_{t,m})$, where $b_{t,i}$ represents the proportion of wealth invested in asset i. Typically, we assume the portfolio is self-financed and no short selling is allowed, which means each entry of a portfolio is non-negative and adds up to one, that is, $\mathbf{b}_t \in \Delta_m$, where $\Delta_m = \{\mathbf{b}_t : \mathbf{b}_t \in \mathbb{R}_+^m, \sum_{i=1}^m b_{t,i} = 1\}$. The investment procedure is represented by a portfolio strategy, that is, $\mathbf{b}_1 = \frac{1}{m}\mathbf{1}$ and following sequence of mappings $f : \mathrm{R}_+^{m(t-1)} \to \Delta_m, t = 2, 3, \ldots$, where $\mathbf{b}_t = f(\mathbf{x}_1, \ldots, \mathbf{x}_{t-1})$ is the tth portfolio given past market sequence $\mathbf{x}^{t-1} = \{\mathbf{x}_1, \ldots, \mathbf{x}_{t-1}\}$. Let us denote $\mathbf{b}^n = \{\mathbf{b}_1, \ldots, \mathbf{b}_n\}$ as the portfolio strategy for n trading period.

On the tth trading period, an investment according to portfolio $\mathbf{b}_t$ results in a portfolio daily return s_t, that is, the wealth increases by a factor of $s_t = \mathbf{b}_t^T \mathbf{x}_t = \sum_{i=1}^m b_{ti} x_{ti}$. Since we reinvest and adopt price relative, the portfolio wealth would grow multiplicatively. Thus, after n trading periods, the investment according to a portfolio strategy $\mathbf{b}_n$ results in portfolio cumulative wealth S_n, which increases the initial wealth by a factor of $\prod_{t=1}^n \mathbf{b}_t^T \mathbf{x}_t$, that is,

$$S_n = S_0 \prod_{t=1}^{n} \mathbf{b}_t^T \mathbf{x}_t, \tag{1}$$

where S_0 denotes the initial wealth and is set to \$1 for convenience.

Finally, let us formulate the online portfolio selection problem as a sequential decision problem. In this task, the portfolio manager is a decision maker whose goal is to make a portfolio strategy $\mathbf{b}^n$ on financial markets to maximize the portfolio cumulative wealth S_n. He computes the portfolios sequentially. On each trading period t, the portfolio manager has access to the sequences of previous price relative vectors $\mathbf{x}^{t-1} = \{\mathbf{x}_1, \cdots, \mathbf{x}_{t-1}\}$, and previous sequences of portfolio vectors $\mathbf{b}^{t-1} = \{\mathbf{b}_1, \ldots, \mathbf{b}_{t-1}\}$. Based on historical information, the portfolio manager computes a new portfolio vector $\mathbf{b}_t$ for the next price relative vector $\mathbf{x}_t$, where the decision criterion varies among different managers. The resulting portfolio $\mathbf{b}_t$ is scored based on the portfolio period return of S_t. The procedure repeats until the end of trading periods and the portfolio strategy is finally scored by the cumulative wealth S_n.

3 Related Work and Motivation

3.1 Related Work

Following the principle of the Kelly investment [17], many kinds of portfolio selection methods have been proposed. Online learning portfolio selection maximizes the expected return with sequential decision-making. The most common and well-known benchmark is the *Buy-And-Hold* (BAH) strategy, that is, one invests his/her wealth in the market with an initial portfolio and holds it within his/her investment periods. The BAH strategy with a uniform initial portfolio $\mathbf{b}_1 = (1/m, 1/m, \ldots, 1/m)^T$ is called uniform BAH strategy, which is adopted as market strategy producing the market index in our study. Contrary to the static nature of the BAH strategy, active trading strategies usually change portfolios regularly during trading periods. A classical active strategy is *Constant Rebalanced Portfolios* (CRP) [6], which rebalances a fixed portfolio every trading period. The Best CRP (BCRP) is the best CRP strategy over the entire trading period, which is only a high-sight strategy.

Several portfolio strategies assume that past well-performing securities would still perform well in the future. These strategies are called momentum strategies, which approximate the expected logarithmic cumulative return of BCRP. The portfolio in *Universal portfolios* (UP) [5] is the historical performance weighted average of all possible CRP experts. The Semi-Universal Portfolio(SUP) strategies with transaction cost [14] consider Cover's moving target portfolio with occasional rebalancing. *Exponential Gradient* (EG) [12] is based on multiplicative updates.

Empirical evidence indicates that opposite trends may often happen in the financial market, which is a common and famous principle called mean reversion. Based on the idea of mean reversion, [3] proposed the *Anticorrelation* (Anticor) strategy. It calculates a cross-correlation matrix between two specific market windows and transfers the wealth from winning assets to losing assets, and adjusts the corresponding amounts based on the cross-correlation matrix. [21] proposed the *Passive Aggressive Mean Reversion* (PAMR) strategy, which only considers the single periodical mean reversion property. [9] proposed the *Passive Aggressive Combined Strategy* (PACS), which combines price reversion and momentum via a multipiece-wise loss function. [18] proposed the *Online Moving Average Reversion* (OLMAR) strategy, which exploits mean reversion's multi-period nature via moving average prediction. [13] proposed the *Robust Median Reversion* (RMR) strategy which exploits the reversion phenomenon by robust L_1-median estimator. All in all, mean reversion is crucial for designing online portfolio selection strategies.

3.2 Motivation

The existing moving average reversion strategies, i.e. OLMAR [18] and RMR [13], exploits the mean reversion in the following ways. OLMAR assumes that the stock price of $(t+1)^{th}$ period will revert to the moving average (mean) of the prices in the previous periods with a w-window, that is, the update for prediction becomes $\hat{\mathbf{p}}_{t+1} = \frac{1}{w}\sum_{i=t-w+1}^{i=t} \mathbf{p}_i$. Considering the noises and outliers in real market data, RMR exploits the multi-period reversion property via the robust median reversion, that is,

$$\hat{\mathbf{p}}_{t+1} = \arg\min_{\boldsymbol{\mu}} \sum_{i=t}^{t-w+1} \|\mathbf{p}_t - \boldsymbol{\mu}\|, \tag{2}$$

where $\|\cdot\|$ denotes the Euclidean norm. The robust median is a L_1-median in statistics [27], which is of less sensitivity to the outliers and noisy data compared to the mean. Empirical results of RMR on various datasets are significantly better than OLMAR, which inspires us to explore the robust estimates [1,15,16] in online portfolio selection.

We assume that the stock prices $\mathbf{p}_t$ satisfy $\mathbf{p}_t = \boldsymbol{\mu}_t + \boldsymbol{\sigma}_t \odot \boldsymbol{u}_t$, where $\boldsymbol{\mu}_t = (\mu_{t,1}, ..., \mu_{t,m}) \in \mathbb{R}^m$ and $\boldsymbol{u}_t = (u_{t,1}, ..., u_{t,m}) \in \mathbb{R}^m$ represent the real price behind and the noise contaminating the real price respectively. It is noticed that $\odot$ represents the element-wise multiplication. Let $u_{t,1}, ..., u_{t,m}$ for $t = 1, ..., n$ are i.i.d with the density f. $\boldsymbol{\sigma}_t = (\sigma_{t,1}, ..., \sigma_{t,m}) \in \mathbb{R}_+^m$ is the unknown parameter to measure the contamination scale on the corresponding asset. Thus, the density of $\mathbf{p}_t$ can be defined as $\frac{1}{\boldsymbol{\sigma}_t} f\left(\frac{\mathbf{p}_t - \boldsymbol{\mu}_t}{\boldsymbol{\sigma}_t}\right)$. Note that $\mathbf{p}_t$, $\boldsymbol{\mu}_t$ and $\boldsymbol{\sigma}_t$ are all vectors and the above operations are element-wise. The maximum likelihood estimation (MLE) of $\boldsymbol{\mu}_t$ and $\boldsymbol{\sigma}_t$ is:

$$\begin{aligned}(\hat{\boldsymbol{\mu}}_t, \hat{\boldsymbol{\sigma}}_t) &= \arg\max_{\boldsymbol{\mu}_t, \boldsymbol{\sigma}_t} \frac{1}{\boldsymbol{\sigma}^n} \prod_{i=t-w+1}^{t} f\left(\frac{\mathbf{p}_i - \boldsymbol{\mu}_t}{\boldsymbol{\sigma}_t}\right) \\ &= \arg\min_{\boldsymbol{\mu}_t, \boldsymbol{\sigma}_t} \left\{\frac{1}{n} \sum_{i=t-w+1}^{t} \rho\left(\frac{\mathbf{p}_i - \boldsymbol{\mu}_t}{\boldsymbol{\sigma}_t}\right) + \log \boldsymbol{\sigma}_t\right\},\end{aligned} \tag{3}$$

where $\rho(.) = -\log f(.)$, since $f(.)$ is everywhere positive and the logarithm is an increasing function. If $\rho(.)$ is differentiable and $\rho''(0)$ exists, first order optimization for (3) yields:

$$\begin{cases}\hat{\boldsymbol{\mu}}_t = (\sum_{i=t-w+1}^{t} \mathbf{p}_i W_1(\frac{\mathbf{p}_i - \hat{\boldsymbol{\mu}}_t}{\hat{\boldsymbol{\sigma}}_t}))/(\sum_{i=t-w+1}^{t} W_1(\frac{\mathbf{p}_i - \hat{\boldsymbol{\mu}}_t}{\hat{\boldsymbol{\sigma}}_t})), \\ \hat{\boldsymbol{\sigma}}_t^2 = \frac{1}{w} \sum_{i=t-w+1}^{t} W_2\left(\frac{\mathbf{p}_i - \hat{\boldsymbol{\mu}}_t}{\hat{\boldsymbol{\sigma}}_t}\right)(\mathbf{p}_i - \hat{\boldsymbol{\mu}}_t)^2,\end{cases} \tag{4}$$

$$\text{where} \begin{cases} W_1(x) = \begin{cases} -\rho'(x)/x & \text{if} \quad x \neq 0 \\ -\rho''(0) & \text{if} \quad x = 0 \end{cases}, \\ W_2(x) = \begin{cases} -\rho'(x)/x & \text{if} \quad x \neq 0 \\ -\rho''(0)/2 & \text{if} \quad x = 0 \end{cases}. \end{cases}$$

We use $\hat{\boldsymbol{\mu}}_t$ as the updated prediction for $\mathbf{p}_{t+1}$. It's noted that $\frac{\mathbf{p}_i - \hat{\mu}_t}{\hat{\sigma}_t}$ is the outlyingness measure adjusting the weights on sample $\mathbf{p}_{t+1}$ in i-th period and the next estimated stock price as a weighted mean. In general $W(x)$ is a non-increasing function of $|x|$, so outlying observations will receive smaller weights. It is worth noting that $W_1(x)$ and $W_2(x)$ are equal except when $x = 0$.

In most cases of interest, it is known or assumed that some form of dependence between stocks exists, and hence that considering each of them separately would entail a loss of information. In the univariate case, $\frac{\mathbf{p}_i - \hat{\mu}_t}{\hat{\sigma}_t}$ measures the univariate outlyingness. In the multivariate case,

Table 1. Examples of $W(d_i)$ functions

	$W(d_i)$
HUBER	$\begin{cases} k/\sqrt{d_i}, & \sqrt{d_i} \le k \\ 1, & \sqrt{d_i} > k \end{cases}$
BISQUAR	$\begin{cases} (1 - \frac{d_i}{k^2})^2, & \sqrt{d_i} \le k \\ 0, & \sqrt{d_i} > k \end{cases}$
SHR	$\begin{cases} 1, & d_i \le 4 \\ q(d_i), & 4 < d_i \le 9 \\ 0, & d_i > 9 \end{cases}$
	$q(d) = -1.944 + 1.728d - 0.312d^2 + 0.016d^3$

the squared Mahalanobis Distance [7] between the vectors $\mathbf{p}_i$ and $\boldsymbol{\mu}_t$ with respect to the covariance matrix $\boldsymbol{\Sigma}_t$ is used to measure the multivariate outlyingness, which is defined as $d_i(\mathbf{p}_i, \boldsymbol{\mu}_t, \boldsymbol{\Sigma}_t) = (\mathbf{p}_i - \boldsymbol{\mu}_t)^T \boldsymbol{\Sigma}_t^{-1}(\mathbf{p}_i - \boldsymbol{\mu}_t)$, that is, the normalized squared distance between $\mathbf{p}_i$ and $\boldsymbol{\mu}_t$. In general, the dependence of multiple assets is taken into consideration and we derive the updated prediction for the mean and covariance matrix of return by MLE.

Assumption 1 *Suppose that:* ***i.*** *The observations* $\mathbf{p}_i$ *are the i.i.d samples from multivariate probability density* $f(\mathbf{p}_i, \boldsymbol{\mu}_t, \boldsymbol{\Sigma}_t)$. ***ii.*** *The probability density* $f(\mathbf{p}_i, \boldsymbol{\mu}_t, \boldsymbol{\Sigma}_t)$ *has the form of* $f(\mathbf{p}_i, \boldsymbol{\mu}_t, \boldsymbol{\Sigma}_t) = \frac{1}{\sqrt{|\boldsymbol{\Sigma}_t|}} h(d_i(\mathbf{p}_i, \boldsymbol{\mu}_t, \boldsymbol{\Sigma}_t))$, *where* $|\boldsymbol{\Sigma}_t|$ *is the determinant of* $\boldsymbol{\Sigma}_t$. ***iii.*** $\ln f$ *is differentiable.*

Theorem 1. *Under Assumption 1, the updated prediction is given by:*

$$\begin{cases} \hat{\boldsymbol{\mu}}_t = \sum_{i=t-w+1}^{t} W(d_i)\mathbf{p}_i / \sum_{i=t-w+1}^{t} W(d_i), \\ \hat{\boldsymbol{\Sigma}}_t = \frac{1}{w} \sum_{i=t-w+1}^{t} W(d_i)(\mathbf{p}_i - \hat{\boldsymbol{\mu}}_t)(\mathbf{p}_i - \hat{\boldsymbol{\mu}}_t)^T, \end{cases} \tag{5}$$

where $W(d_i) = (-2\ln h(d_i))'$ *and* $d_i(\mathbf{p}_i, \hat{\boldsymbol{\mu}}_t, \hat{\boldsymbol{\Sigma}}_t) = (\mathbf{p}_i - \hat{\boldsymbol{\mu}}_t)^T \hat{\boldsymbol{\Sigma}}_t^{-1}(\mathbf{p}_i - \hat{\boldsymbol{\mu}}_t)$, *which are different from the univariate case.*

Proof. Let $\mathbf{p}_i$ are the i.i.d sample from $f(\mathbf{p}_i, \boldsymbol{\mu}_t, \boldsymbol{\Sigma}_t) = \frac{1}{\sqrt{|\boldsymbol{\Sigma}_t|}} h(d_i(\mathbf{p}_i, \boldsymbol{\mu}_t, \boldsymbol{\Sigma}_t))$, for $i = t - w + 1, ..., t$. The MLE of $\boldsymbol{\mu}_t$ and $\boldsymbol{\Sigma}_t$ is

$$\hat{\boldsymbol{\mu}}_t, \hat{\boldsymbol{\Sigma}}_t = \underset{\boldsymbol{\mu}_t, \boldsymbol{\Sigma}_t}{\operatorname{argmax}} \frac{1}{|\boldsymbol{\Sigma}_t|^{w/2}} \prod_{i=t-w+1}^{t} h(d_i(\mathbf{p}_i, \boldsymbol{\mu}_t, \boldsymbol{\Sigma}_t)). \tag{6}$$

It is noted that Since h is everywhere positive and the logarithm is an increasing function, thus, Eq. 6 can be written as

$$\hat{\boldsymbol{\mu}}_t, \hat{\boldsymbol{\Sigma}}_t = \underset{\boldsymbol{\mu}_t, \boldsymbol{\Sigma}_t}{\operatorname{argmin}}\, w \ln |\hat{\boldsymbol{\Sigma}}_t| + \sum_{i=t-w+1}^{t} \rho(d_i), \tag{7}$$

where $\rho(d_i) = -2\ln h(d_i)$ and $d_i = d\left(\mathbf{p}_i, \hat{\boldsymbol{\mu}}_t, \hat{\boldsymbol{\Sigma}}_t\right) = (\mathbf{p}_i - \boldsymbol{\mu}_t)^T \boldsymbol{\Sigma}_t^{-1}(\mathbf{p}_i - \boldsymbol{\mu}_t)$. Differentiating with respect to $\boldsymbol{\mu}_t$ and $\boldsymbol{\Sigma}_t$ yields

$$\sum_{i=t-w+1}^{t} W(d_i)(\mathbf{p}_i - \hat{\boldsymbol{\mu}}_t) = \mathbf{0}, \frac{1}{w} \sum_{i=t-w+1}^{t} W(d_i)(\mathbf{p}_i - \hat{\boldsymbol{\mu}}_t)(\mathbf{p}_i - \hat{\boldsymbol{\mu}}_t)^T = \hat{\boldsymbol{\Sigma}}_t$$

with $W(d_i) = \rho'(d_i)$. If we knew $f(.)$ exactly, the $W(d_i)$ would be "optimal", but since we only know $f(.)$ approximately, our goal is to find estimators that are "nearly optimal". For simplicity, we will consider two cases:

- Multivariate Normal: $f(\mathbf{p}_i, \boldsymbol{\mu}_t, \boldsymbol{\Sigma}_t) = \frac{exp(-\frac{1}{2}d_i)}{\sqrt{|\Sigma|}}$, then $W(di)$ is a constant.

- m (the number of stocks) multivariate Student distribution with v degrees: $f(\mathbf{p}_i, \boldsymbol{\mu}_t, \boldsymbol{\Sigma}_t) = \frac{exp(-\frac{1}{2}(m+v))}{(d_i+v)\sqrt{|\Sigma|}}$, then $W(d_i) = (m+v)/(d_i+v)$. If the value of v is large, then $W(d_i)$ is a constant; v is 0, then $W(d_i) = m/d_i$.

In our paper, we use classical functions (Huber [2], Bisquare [11], and the weighting function (we shall use SHR here) employed for time series estimation [23]) in robust regression to approximate the true $W(d_i)$ under unknown $f(.)$, as in Table 1. These functions assign smaller weights to outlying observations, and some may even be removed (except for the Huber function). In a time series of financial data, there will be trend changes that cannot be ignored even in a short period. Thus, the exponential decay is adopted in Eq. 5, that is,

$$\begin{cases} \hat{\boldsymbol{\mu}}_t = (\sum_{i=t-w+1}^{t} (1-\alpha)^{t-i} \mathbf{p}_i W(d_i))/(\sum_{i=t-w+1}^{t} (1-\alpha)^{t-i} W(d_i)), \\ \hat{\boldsymbol{\Sigma}}_t = \frac{1}{w} \sum_{i=t-w+1}^{t} W(d_i) (\mathbf{p}_i - \hat{\boldsymbol{\mu}}_t) (\mathbf{p}_i - \hat{\boldsymbol{\mu}}_t)^T, \end{cases} \tag{8}$$

where α is the decaying factor. $\hat{\boldsymbol{\mu}}_t$ is the predicted price vector for the $(t+1)^{th}$ period.

4 Multi-variate Robust Mean Reversion

4.1 Formulation

The proposed formulation, WMMR, is to find the optimal portfolio by weighted multivariate mean reversion and passive-aggressive online learning. The basic idea is to obtain the estimate of the next price relative $\mathbf{x}_{t+1}$ via robust multivariate estimates, and then maximize the expected return $\mathbf{b}^T\mathbf{x}_{t+1}$ with the hope that the new portfolio is not far away from the previous one.

Most of $W(d_i)$ in Table 1 depend on the constant $k \in R$. Here a rescaled d_i, i.e., d_i/S is applied to the $W(d_i)$, that is,

$$\begin{cases} \hat{\boldsymbol{\mu}}_t = (\sum_{i=t-w+1}^{t} (1-\alpha)^{t-i} \mathbf{p}_i W(d_i/S))/(\sum_{i=t-w+1}^{t} (1-\alpha)^{t-i} W(d_i/S)), \\ \hat{\boldsymbol{\Sigma}}_t = 1/w \sum_{i=t-w+1}^{t} (1-\alpha)^{t-i} W(d_i/S) (\mathbf{p}_i - \hat{\boldsymbol{\mu}}_t) (\mathbf{p}_i - \hat{\boldsymbol{\mu}}_t)^T, \end{cases} \tag{9}$$

where $S = \mathbf{MED}([d_{t-w+1}, ..., d_t])$ and $d_i(\mathbf{p}_i, \hat{\boldsymbol{\mu}}_t, \hat{\boldsymbol{\Sigma}}_t) = (\mathbf{p}_i - \hat{\boldsymbol{\mu}}_t)^T \hat{\boldsymbol{\Sigma}}_t^{-1} (\mathbf{p}_i - \hat{\boldsymbol{\mu}}_t)$. In this formulation of WMMR, different $W(d_i)$ and $\hat{\boldsymbol{\Sigma}}_t$ are discussed as follows:

- **Case 1**: $W(d_i) \equiv 1$, $\hat{\boldsymbol{\Sigma}}_t$ is not considered and $\alpha \equiv 0$.
- **Case 2**: $W(d_i) = \frac{1}{\sqrt{d_i}}$, $\hat{\boldsymbol{\Sigma}}_t \equiv \boldsymbol{I}$ and $\alpha \equiv 0$.
- **Case 3**: $W(d_i)$ is the HUBER weighting function, $\hat{\boldsymbol{\Sigma}}_t$ is computed via Eq. 5 and α is a parameter.
- **Case 4**: $W(d_i)$ is the BISQUA weighting function, $\hat{\boldsymbol{\Sigma}}_t$ is computed via Eq. 5 and α is a parameter.
- **Case 5**: $W(d_i)$ is the SHR weighting function, $\hat{\boldsymbol{\Sigma}}_t$ is computed via Eq. 5 and α is a parameter.

Algorithm 1 . WMMR($\mathbf{p}_t$, $\mathbf{p}_{t-1}$, . . . , $\mathbf{p}_{t-w+1}$,τ, k, α)

Input: Current stock price sequence $\mathbf{p}_t$, $\mathbf{p}_{t-1}$, . . . , $\mathbf{p}_{t-w+1}$; Toleration level τ; Iteration maximum K; Decaying factor α.
Output: estimated $\hat{\mathbf{x}}_{t+1}$
Procedure:
Initialize $j \leftarrow 0$, $\hat{\boldsymbol{\mu}}_t \leftarrow \frac{1}{m}\mathbf{1}$ and $\hat{\boldsymbol{\Sigma}}_t = \mathbf{1}$
The estimation of next period price: $\hat{\mathbf{p}}_{t+1} \leftarrow \hat{\boldsymbol{\mu}}_t$
while $j < K$ **do**
  Calculate the following variables:
  The multivariate outlyingness: $d_i \leftarrow (\mathbf{p}_i - \hat{\boldsymbol{\mu}}_t)^T \hat{\boldsymbol{\Sigma}}_t^{-1} (\mathbf{p}_i - \hat{\boldsymbol{\mu}}_t)$ (i = t-w+1,...,t)
  The error scale: $S \leftarrow \mathbf{MED}([d_{t-w+1}, ...d_t])$
  The weight: $W_i \leftarrow W(d_i/S)$ (i = t-w+1,...,t)
  The estimation of $\hat{\boldsymbol{\mu}}_t$ in j^{th} iteration :

$$\hat{\boldsymbol{\mu}}_t \leftarrow \sum_{i=t-w+1}^{t} (1-\alpha)^{t-i} W_i \mathbf{p}_i / \sum_{i=t-w+1}^{t} (1-\alpha)^{t-i} W_i$$

  The estimation of $\hat{\boldsymbol{\Sigma}}_t$ in j^{th} iteration :

$$\hat{\boldsymbol{\Sigma}}_t \leftarrow \frac{1}{w} \sum_{i=t-w+1}^{t} W_i \left(\mathbf{p}_i - \hat{\boldsymbol{\mu}}_t\right) \left(\mathbf{p}_i - \hat{\boldsymbol{\mu}}_t\right)^T$$

  if $|\hat{\boldsymbol{\mu}}_t - \hat{\mathbf{p}}_{t+1}| < \tau |\hat{\boldsymbol{\mu}}_t|$ **then** break
  end if
  $\hat{\mathbf{p}}_{t+1} \leftarrow \hat{\boldsymbol{\mu}}_t$
end while
The price relative vectors in $(t+1)^{th}$period: $\hat{\mathbf{x}}_{t+1} \leftarrow \hat{\mathbf{p}}_{t+1} / \mathbf{p}_t$

Note that in Case 1, $\hat{\boldsymbol{\mu}}_t = \frac{1}{w} \sum_{i=t-w+1}^{t} \mathbf{p}_i$, which is the moving average mean used in OLMAR; In Case 2, $\hat{\boldsymbol{\mu}}_t$=$(\sum_{i=t-w+1}^{t} \frac{\mathbf{p}_i}{\sqrt{\|\mathbf{p}_i - \hat{\boldsymbol{\mu}}_t\|_2}})/(\sum_{i=t-w+1}^{t} \frac{1}{\sqrt{\|\mathbf{p}_{t-i} - \hat{\boldsymbol{\mu}}_t\|_2}})$, which is the robust median used in RMR. OLMAR and RMR strategies are subsamples of WMMR. In this paper, the effectiveness of Case 3, Case 4, and Case 5 are mainly explored, which are denoted by WMMR-HUBER, WMMR-BIS, and WMMR-SHR respectively.

4.2 Online Portfolio Selection

$$\mathbf{b}_{t+1} = \arg\min_{\mathbf{b}} \frac{1}{2} \|\mathbf{b} - \mathbf{b}_t\|^2 + \frac{\theta}{2} \|\mathbf{b}\|^2 \text{ s.t. } \begin{cases} \mathbf{b}^T \hat{\mathbf{x}}_{t+1} \geq \epsilon, \\ \mathbf{b}^T \mathbf{1} = \mathbf{1} \end{cases} \tag{10}$$

where $\hat{\mathbf{x}}_{t+1}$ is the price relative estimated via weighted multivariate mean reversion and $\theta > 0$ is the regularization parameter and is manually tuned. The above formulation attempts to find a portfolio satisfying the condition of $\mathbf{b}^T \hat{\mathbf{x}}_{t+1} \geq \epsilon$ while not far away from the last portfolio. On one side, when the expected return is larger than a threshold ϵ, the investment strategy will passively keep the last portfolio. On another side, when the constraint $\mathbf{b}^T \hat{\mathbf{x}}_{t+1} \geq \epsilon$ is not satisfied, the portfolio will be aggressively updated by forcing expected return is larger than the threshold ϵ. By adding the regularization $\|\mathbf{b}\|^2$ under the constrain $\mathbf{b}^T\mathbf{1} = \mathbf{1}$, we push the new portfolio move forward to $\frac{\mathbf{1}}{m}$ and prevent the solution from over-fitted.

Algorithm 2 . Online Portfolio Selection(ϵ, w, $\hat{\mathbf{x}}_{t+1}$, $\mathbf{b}_t$)

1: **Input:** Reversion threshold: $\epsilon > 1$; Window size: w; Predicted price relatives :$\hat{\mathbf{x}}_{t+1}$; Current portfolio: $\mathbf{b}_t$.
2: **Output:** Next portfolio $\mathbf{b}_{t+1}$.
3: **Procedure:** Calculate the following variables:
4: $\eta_{t+1} = \mathbf{max}(0, \frac{(1+\theta)\epsilon - \hat{\mathbf{x}}_{t+1}^T(\mathbf{b}_t+\theta\mathbf{1})}{\|\hat{\mathbf{x}}_{t+1} - \bar{x}_{t+1}\mathbf{1}\|^2}))$
5: Update the portfolio: $\mathbf{b} = \frac{1}{1+\theta}[\mathbf{b}_t + \eta_{t+1}(\hat{\mathbf{x}}_{t+1} - \bar{x}_{t+1}\mathbf{1})] + \frac{\theta}{(1+\theta)}\frac{\mathbf{1}}{m}$
6: Normalize $\mathbf{b}_t$: $\mathbf{b}_{t+1} = \underset{\mathbf{b}\in\Delta_m}{\arg\min}\|\mathbf{b} - \mathbf{b}_{t+1}\|^2$

Algorithm 3 . Portfolio Selection with WMMR

1: **Input:** Reversion threshold: $\epsilon > 1$; Window size: w; Iteration maximum k; Toleration level τ; Decaying factor α; Market Sequence $\mathbf{P}^n$.
2: **Output:** Cumulative wealth after n^{th} periods
3: **Procedure:**
4: Initialization: Initial portfolio: $b_1 = \frac{1}{m}\mathbf{1}$; Initial wealth: $S_0 = 1$.
5: **for** $t = w$ **to** n **do**
6: Predict next price relative vector according **Algorithm** 1: $\hat{\mathbf{x}}_{t+1} \leftarrow$ WMMR($\mathbf{p}_t$, $\mathbf{p}_{t-1}$, . . . , $\mathbf{p}_{t-w+1}$,τ, k, α).
7: Update the portfolio according **Algorithm** 2: $\mathbf{b}_{t+1} \leftarrow$ Online Portfolio Selection(ϵ, w, $\hat{\mathbf{x}}_{t+1}$, $\mathbf{b}_t$).
8: Receive stock price: $\mathbf{P}_{t+1}$.
9: Update cumulative return: $S_{t+1} \leftarrow S_t \times \left(\mathbf{b}_{t+1}{}^T \frac{\mathbf{p}_{t+1}}{\mathbf{p}_t}\right)$.
10: **end for**

4.3 Algorithms

From the formulation of WMMR(Eq. 9), the weights $W(d_i/S)$ depend also on $\hat{\boldsymbol{\mu}}_t$ and $\hat{\boldsymbol{\Sigma}}_t$, hence Eq. 9 is not an explicit expression for $\hat{\boldsymbol{\mu}}_t$ and $\hat{\boldsymbol{\Sigma}}_t$. The solution of weighted multivariate estimation could be calculated through iteration, and the iteration process is described in **Algorithm** 1. Once the constraint $\|\boldsymbol{\mu}_{t+1} - \boldsymbol{\mu}_t\|_1 \leq \tau \|\boldsymbol{\mu}_t\|_1$ is satisfied, or the number of iteration is larger than the threshold k, the iteration is terminated, where τ is a toleration level and k is the maximum iteration number.

The constrained optimization problem (10) can be solved by the technique of convex optimization [4]. The solution of (10) without considering the non-negativity constraint is

$$\mathbf{b}_{t+1} = \frac{1}{1+\theta}[\mathbf{b}_t + \eta(\hat{\mathbf{x}}_{t+1} - \bar{x}_{t+1}\mathbf{1})] + \frac{\theta}{(1+\theta)}\frac{\mathbf{1}}{m}, \tag{11}$$

where $\eta = \mathbf{max}(0, \frac{(1+\theta)\epsilon - \hat{\mathbf{x}}_{t+1}^T(\mathbf{b}_t+\theta\mathbf{1})}{\|\hat{\mathbf{x}}_{t+1} - \bar{x}_{t+1}\mathbf{1}\|^2})$.

Proof. Define the Lagrangian of the problem (10) to be:

$$\mathcal{L}(\mathbf{b},\eta,\lambda) = \frac{1}{2}\left\|\mathbf{b}-\mathbf{b}_t\right\|^2 + \frac{1}{2}\theta\left\|\mathbf{b}\right\|^2 - \eta\left(\hat{\mathbf{x}}_{t+1}^T\mathbf{b}-\epsilon\right) + \lambda(\mathbf{1}^T\mathbf{b}-1). \tag{12}$$

Setting the partial derivatives of $\mathcal{L}$ with respect to the elements of $\mathbf{b}$ to zero, yields:

$$0 = \frac{\partial\mathcal{L}}{\partial\mathbf{b}} = ((\theta+1)\mathbf{b}-\mathbf{b}_t) - \eta\hat{\mathbf{x}}_{t+1} + \lambda\mathbf{1}. \tag{13}$$

Multiplying both sides of Eq. 13 with $\mathbf{1}^T$, and $\mathbf{1}^T\mathbf{b}=1$, $\mathbf{1}^T\mathbf{1}=m$, we can get $\lambda = -\frac{\theta}{m} + \frac{\eta}{m}\mathbf{1}^T\hat{\mathbf{x}}_{t+1}$. Define $\bar{x}_{t+1} = \frac{\mathbf{1}^T\hat{\mathbf{x}}_{t+1}}{m}$ as the mean of the price relatives in the period $(t+1)^{th}$. Then, λ can be rewritten as $\lambda = -\frac{\theta}{m} + \eta\bar{x}_{t+1}$, and the solution for $\mathcal{L}$ is

$$\mathbf{b} = \frac{\mathbf{b}_t}{1+\theta} + \frac{\theta\mathbf{1}}{(1+\theta)m} + \frac{\eta}{1+\theta}(\hat{\mathbf{x}}_{t+1} - \bar{x}_{t+1}\mathbf{1}). \tag{14}$$

Plugging Eq. 14 to $\frac{\partial\frac{1}{2}\|\mathbf{b}-\mathbf{b}_t\|^2}{\partial\eta} + \frac{\partial\frac{\theta}{2}\|\mathbf{b}\|^2}{\partial\eta}$, noting that, $\frac{1}{m}\mathbf{1}^T(\hat{\mathbf{x}}_{t+1} - \bar{x}_{t+1}\mathbf{1}) = 0$, yields: Thus,

$$\frac{\partial\frac{1}{2}\left\|\mathbf{b}-\mathbf{b}_t\right\|^2}{\partial\eta} + \frac{\partial\frac{\theta}{2}\left\|\mathbf{b}\right\|^2}{\partial\eta} = \frac{1}{(1+\theta)}\eta\|\hat{\mathbf{x}}_{t+1} - \bar{x}_{t+1}\mathbf{1}\|^2 \tag{15}$$

Plugging Eq. 14 to $\frac{\partial\eta(\hat{\mathbf{x}}_{t+1}^T\mathbf{b}-\epsilon)}{\partial\eta}$, yields

$$\frac{\partial\eta(\hat{\mathbf{x}}_{t+1}^T\mathbf{b}-\epsilon)}{\partial\eta} = \hat{\mathbf{x}}_{t+1}^T(\frac{\mathbf{b}_t}{1+\theta} + \frac{\theta\mathbf{1}}{1+\theta}) - \epsilon + \frac{2}{1+\theta}\eta\|\hat{\mathbf{x}}_{t+1} - \bar{x}_{t+1}\mathbf{1}\|^2 \tag{16}$$

Plugging the expression of λ and Eq. 14 to $\frac{\partial\lambda(\mathbf{1}^T\mathbf{b}-1)}{\partial\eta}$, we get,

$$\frac{\partial\lambda(\mathbf{1}^T\mathbf{b}-1)}{\partial\eta} = 0, \tag{17}$$

From Eq. 15, Eq. 16 and Eq. 17, we get,

$$0 = \frac{\partial\mathcal{L}}{\partial\eta} = \epsilon - \hat{\mathbf{x}}_{t+1}^T(\frac{\mathbf{b}_t}{1+\theta} + \frac{\theta\mathbf{1}}{1+\theta}) - \frac{\eta}{(1+\theta)}\|\hat{\mathbf{x}}_{t+1} - \bar{x}_{t+1}\mathbf{1}\|^2, \tag{18}$$

then,

$$\eta = \frac{(1+\theta)\epsilon - \hat{\mathbf{x}}_{t+1}^T(\mathbf{b}_t+\theta\mathbf{1})}{\|\hat{\mathbf{x}}_{t+1} - \bar{x}_{t+1}\mathbf{1}\|^2}. \tag{19}$$

It is noted that $\eta > 0$, so

$$\eta = \mathbf{max}(0, \frac{(1+\theta)\epsilon - \hat{\mathbf{x}}_{t+1}^T(\mathbf{b}_t+\theta\mathbf{1})}{\|\hat{\mathbf{x}}_{t+1} - \bar{x}_{t+1}\mathbf{1}\|^2}) \tag{20}$$

For simplicity, the non-negativity constraint of portfolio $\mathbf{b}$ is not considered in the above formulation. It is possible that the resulting portfolio calculated from Eq. 11 is not non-negative. Thus, the projection of the solution to the simplex domain [8] is necessary, as shown in **Algorithm** 2. Finally, the online portfolio selection algorithm based on the Weighted Multivariate Mean Reversion is described in **Algorithm** 3. Unlike the regret minimization approaches, the WMMR strategy takes advantage of the statistical properties (mean reversion) of the financial market, which is difficult to provide a traditional regret bound. [3] failed to provide a regret bound for the Anticor strategy, which passively exploits the mean reversion idea. Although we cannot prove the traditional regret bound, the proposed algorithms do provide strong empirical evidence, which sequentially advances the state of the art.

5 Experiments

The effectiveness of the proposed portfolio strategies is tested on four public datasets from real markets, whose information is summarized in Table 2. NYSE(O), which is a benchmark dataset pioneered by [5]. Considering amalgamation and bankruptcy, the second dataset NYSE(N) consists of 23 stocks from dataset NYSE(O) including 36 stocks and was collected by Li et al. [19]. The third dataset is DJIA collected by Borodin et al. [3]. MSCI is a dataset that is collected from global equity indices that constitute the MSCI World Index. Several research studies and the state-of-art model RMR also utilize these four datasets in their experiments.

Table 2. Summary of the four real datasets in our numerical experiments.

dataset	Market	Region	Time frame	Trading days	Assets
NYSE(o)	Stock	US	Jul.3rd 1962-Dec.31st 1984	5651	36
NYSE(N)	Stock	US	Jan.1st 1985-Jun.30th 2010	6431	23
DJIA	Stock	US	Jan.14th 2001-Jan.14th 2003	507	30
MSCI	Index	Global	Apr.1st 2006-Mar.31st 2010	1043	24

Cumulative wealth is the most common and significant metric and is used to measure investment performance in this paper. To be consistent comparison with other different methods, we implement the proposed WMMR-HUBER (with $k = 0.95$), WMMR-BIS (with $k = 3.85$), WMMR-SHR and set the parameters empirically without tuning for each dataset separately as follows: $w = 5$, $\epsilon = 100$, $\alpha = 0.85$ and $\theta = 0.1$. It is worth noting that choices of parameters are not always optimal for WMMR, though these parameters can be tuned to obtain optimal results. The sensitivities of these parameters will be evaluated in the next section. It is necessary to note that the parameters in Algorithm 1, iteration maximum K, are fixed to 50.

5.1 Cumulative Wealth

The cumulative wealth achieved by various methods is summarized in Table 3. On dataset NYSE(O), NYSE(N) and DJIA, WMMR (WMMR-HUBER, WMMR-BISQUARE, and WMMR-SHR) outperform the state-of-the-art. On dataset MSCI, WMMR beats the existing algorithm RMR. By tuning different values of parameter w, ϵ, α, and θ for the corresponding dataset, we also refer to the best performance (in hindsight) shown as WMMR(max) in Table 3. Besides, WMMR(max) is showing the potential of the proposed method by tuning the optimal parameter.

Finally, Table 4 shows some statistics of WMMR. We only present the results achieved by WMMR-HUBER since the effect of WMMR-BISQUARE and WMMR-SHR, are quite similar to that of WMMR. From the results, a small p-value reveals that WMMR's excellent performance is owed to the strategy principle but not due to luck.

Table 3. Cumulative wealth achieved by various strategies on the four datasets.

Methods	NYSE(O)	NYSE(N)	DJIA	MSCI
Market	14.50	18.06	0.76	0.91
Best-stock	54.14	83.51	1.19	1.50
BCRP	250.60	120.32	1.24	1.51
UP	26.68	31.49	0.81	0.92
EG	27.09	31.00	0.81	0.93
ONS	109.91	21.59	1.53	0.86
B^k	1.08E+09	4.64E+03	0.68	2.64
BNN	3.35E+11	6.80E+04	0.88	13.47
CORN	1.48E+13	5.37E+05	0.84	**26.19**
Anticor	2.41E+08	6.21E+06	2.29	3.22
PAMR	5.14E+15	1.25E+06	0.68	15.23
CWMR	6.49E+15	1.41E+06	0.68	17.28
OLMAR	4.04E+16	2.24E+08	2.05	16.33
RMR	1.64E+17	3.25E+08	2.67	16.76
TCO	1.35E+14	9.15E+06	2.01	9.68
WMMR-HUBER	4.14E+17	**4.11E+08**	**3.14**	17.65
WMMR-BIS	**4.53E+17**	3.75E+08	2.91	17.02
WMMR-SHR	3.0E+17	3.43E+08	3.10	17.42
WMMR(max)	5.83E+17	3.02E+09	3.15	25.82

5.2 Computational Time

It is widely known that computational time is important to certain trading environments, we evaluate the computational time on one core of an Intel Core i5 2.3 GHz processor with 16GB, using Python on MacBook Pro. Experiments show that it takes 57.38s, 101.65s, 526.2s, and 443.3s for DJIA, MSCI, NYSE(O), and NYSE(N) respectively, which means that the computational time for each of trading periods is less than 0.1s. The computational time is acceptable even in the scenario of high-frequency trading, which occurs in fractions of a second. Such time efficiency supports WMMR's large-scale real applications.

5.3 Parameter Sensitivity

Table 4. Statistical test of our algorithms.

Stat. Attr	NYSE(O)	NYSE(N)	DJIA	MSCI
Size	5651	6431	507	1043
MER(WMMR)	0.0078	0.0037	0.0028	0.0030
MER(Market)	0.0005	0.0005	-0.0004	0.0000
t-statistics	15.2249	7.1985	2.2059	3.9214
p-value	0.0000	0.0000	0.0278	0.0000

Firstly, the effect of sensitivity parameter w on cumulative wealth is evaluated, in Fig. 1. It is obvious that in most cases, except NYSE(N), the cumulative wealth decreases with increasing w. Secondly, the effect of sensitivity parameter ϵ on cumulative wealth is evaluated. From Fig. 2, The growth of cumulative wealth is sharp as ϵ increases and turns flat when ϵ exceeds a threshold. Finally, the effect of sensitivity parameter θ and α on cumulative wealth are evaluated in Fig. 3 and Fig. 4. From the above observation, it is clear that WMMR is robust for different parameters and it is convenient to choose satisfying parameters.

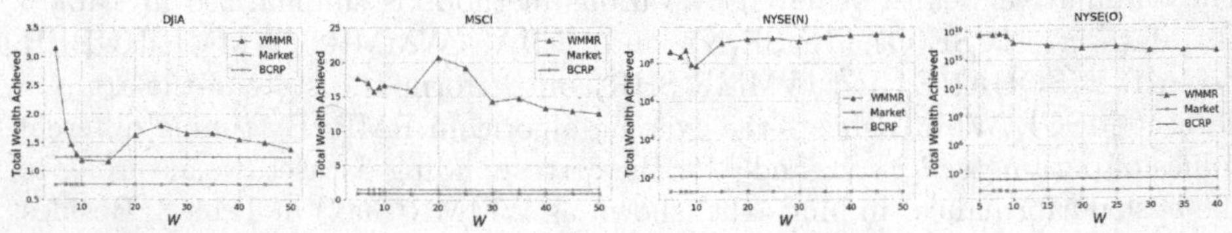

Fig. 1. Parameter sensitivity of WMMR w.r.t. w with fixed $\epsilon = 100, \alpha = 0.85, \theta = 0.1$

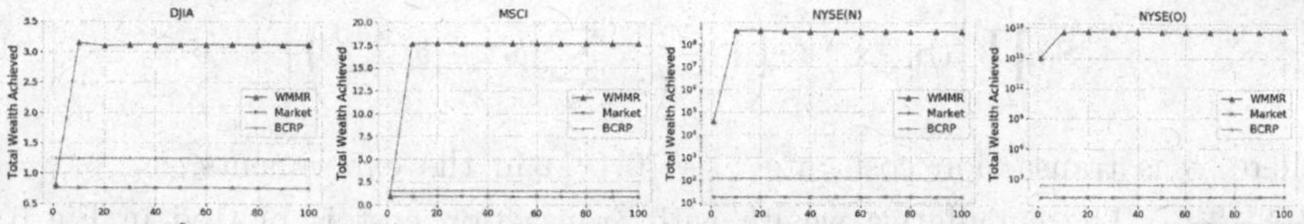

Fig. 2. Parameter sensitivity of WMMR w.r.t. ϵ with fixed $w = 5, \alpha = 0.85, \theta = 0.1$

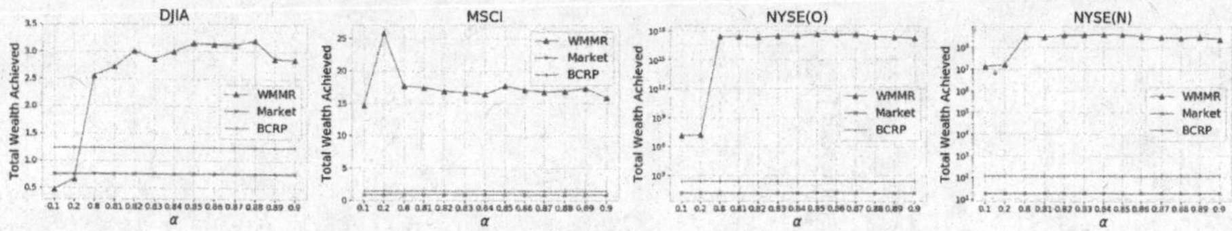

Fig. 3. Parameter sensitivity of WMMR w.r.t. α with fixed $w = 5, \epsilon = 100, \theta = 0.1$

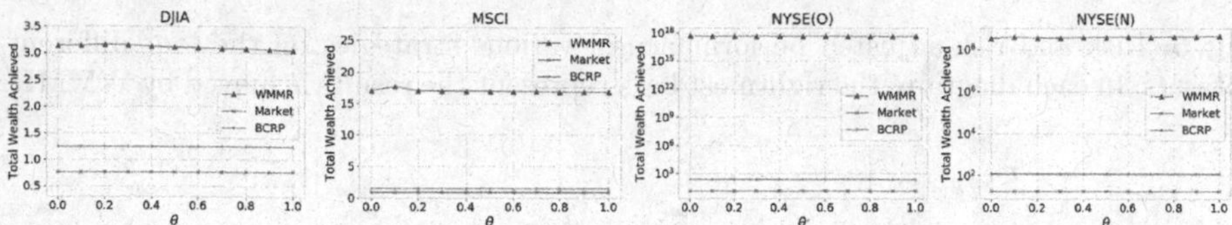

Fig. 4. 4Parameter sensitivity of WMMR w.r.t. θ with fixed $w = 5, \epsilon = 100, \alpha = 0.85$

5.4 Risk-Adjusted Returns

The risk in terms of volatility risk and drawdown risk and the risk-adjusted return in terms of annualized Sharpe ratio are evaluated in the experiment, taking two benchmarks (Market and BCRP) and two state-of-the-art algorithms (OLMAR and RMR) for comparison. The result of Risk-Adjusted Returns is shown in Fig. 5. Though the high return is associated with high risk, WMMR achieves the best performance in terms of the Sharpe ratio.

5.5 Transaction Cost Scalability

For a real-world application, the transaction cost is an important practical issue for portfolio selection. Ignoring this cost may lead to aggressive trading and bring biases into the estimation of returns. [25] proposed an approximate dynamic programming (ADP) method to tackle the multi-asset portfolio optimization problems with proportional transaction costs. [20] proposed a novel online portfolio selection framework, named Transaction Cost Optimization(TCO) to trade-off between maximizing expected log return and minimizing transaction costs. Here, the proportional transaction cost model proposed in [3] is adopted to compute the cumulative wealth:

$$\mathbf{S}_0 \prod_{t=1}^{n} \left[(\mathbf{b}_t \cdot \mathbf{x}_t) \times \left(1 - \frac{\gamma}{2} \times \sum_i \left| b_{t,i} - \hat{b}_{t-1,i} \right| \right) \right],$$

where, γ is transaction cost rate $\gamma \in (0, 0.1)$ in the experiments, $\hat{b}_{(t-1,i)} = \frac{b_{t-1,i} x_{t-1,i}}{\mathbf{b}_{t-1}^T \cdot \mathbf{x}_{t-1}}$. The cumulative wealth with transaction cost is plotted in Fig. 6. From Fig. 6, we can observe that WMMR can withstand reasonable transaction cost rates, and can beat the two benchmarks in most cases.

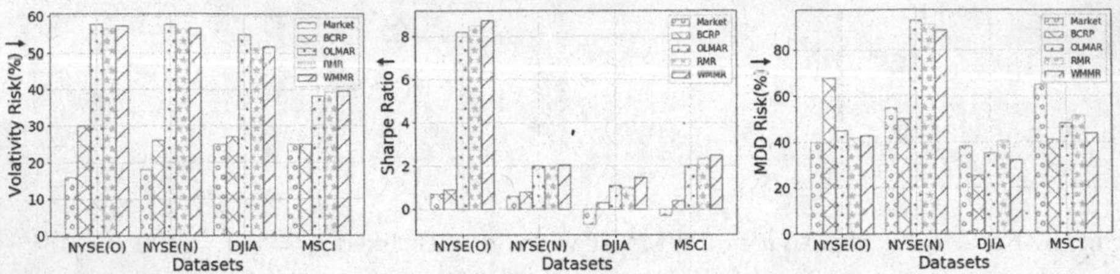

Fig. 5. Risk and risk-adjusted performance of various strategies on the four different datasets. In each diagram, the rightmost bars represent the results achieved by WMMR.

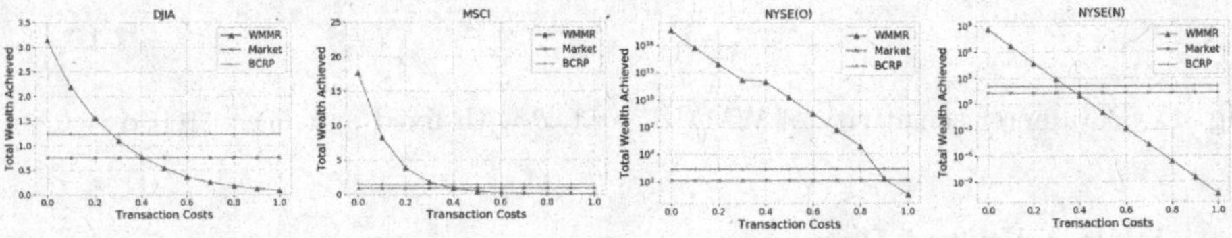

Fig. 6. Scalability of the total wealth achieved by WMMR with respect to transaction cost rate

6 Conclusion

Based on the robust multivariate estimates and PA online learning, a novel online portfolio selection strategy named "Weighted Multivariate Mean Reversion" (WMMR) is proposed in this paper. In the exploitation of "Multi-period Multivariate Average Reversion", WMMR takes data noise, trend changes, and the dependence of multi-assets into full consideration. Several cases of weighting functions with exponential decay are investigated, and the results demonstrate the effectiveness of WMMR. Moreover, extensive experiments on the real market show that the proposed WMMR can achieve satisfying performance with an acceptable run time.

Acknowledgement. J.W. Gu was supported in part by NSFC Grant 11801262, Guangdong Basic and Applied Basic Research Foundation 2023A1515030197, Shenzhen Humanities & Social Sciences Key Research Bases. We thank Qiao Xiao for helping to draw figures.

References

1. Andrews, D.F., Hampel, F.R.: Robust Estimates of Location: Survey and Advances. Princeton University Press (2015)
2. Bickel, P.J.: One-step Huber estimates in the linear model. J. Am. Stat. Assoc. **70**(350), 428–434 (1975)
3. Borodin, A., El-Yaniv, R., Gogan, V.: Can we learn to beat the best stock. J. Artif. Intell. Res. **21**, 579–594 (2004)
4. Boyd, S., Vandenberghe, L.: Convex Optimization. Cambridge University Press, Cambridge (2004)
5. Cover, T.M.: Universal portfolios. Math. Financ. **1**(1), 1–29 (1991)
6. Cover, T.M., Gluss, D.H.: Empirical Bayes stock market portfolios. Adv. Appl. Math. **7**(2), 170–181 (1986)
7. De Maesschalck, R., Jouan-Rimbaud, D., Massart, D.L.: The mahalanobis distance. Chemom. Intell. Lab. Syst. **50**(1), 1–18 (2000)
8. Duchi, J., Shalev-Shwartz, S., Singer, Y., Chandra, T.: Efficient projections onto the l 1-ball for learning in high dimensions. In: Proceedings of the 25th International Conference on Machine Learning, pp. 272–279 (2008)
9. Gao, L., Zhang, W., Tang, Q.: Passive aggressive algorithm for online portfolio selection with piecewise loss function. In: Motoda, H., Wu, Z., Cao, L., Zaiane, O., Yao, M., Wang, W. (eds.) ADMA 2013. LNCS (LNAI), vol. 8347, pp. 360–371. Springer, Heidelberg (2013). https://doi.org/10.1007/978-3-642-53917-6_32
10. Györfi, L., Lugosi, G., Udina, F.: Nonparametric kernel-based sequential investment strategies. Math. Financ. Int. J. Math. Statist. Financ. Econ. **16**(2), 337–357 (2006)
11. Heiberger, R.M., Becker, R.A.: Design of an s function for robust regression using iteratively reweighted least squares. J. Comput. Graph. Stat. **1**(3), 181–196 (1992)
12. Helmbold, D.P., Schapire, R.E., Singer, Y., Warmuth, M.K.: On-line portfolio selection using multiplicative updates. Math. Financ. **8**(4), 325–347 (1998)
13. Huang, D., Zhou, J., Li, B., HOI, S., Zhou, S.: Robust median reversion strategy for on-line portfolio selection (2013). In: Proceedings of the Twenty-Third International Joint Conference on Artificial Intelligence: IJCAI 2013: Beijing, 3–9 August 2013 (2012)
14. Huang, D., Zhu, Y., Li, B., Zhou, S., Hoi, S.C.: Semi-universal portfolios with transaction costs (2015)
15. Huber, P.J.: Robust estimation of a location parameter. In: Kotz, S., Johnson, N.L. (eds.) Breakthroughs in Statistics. Springer Series in Statistics. Springer, New York (1992). https://doi.org/10.1007/978-1-4612-4380-9_35
16. Huber, P.J.: Robust Statistics, vol. 523. John Wiley & Sons, New York (2004)
17. Kelly, J., Jr.: A new interpretation of information rate. Bell Syst. Tech. J. **35**(4), 917–926 (1956)
18. Li, B., Hoi, S.C.: On-line portfolio selection with moving average reversion. In: Proceedings of the Twenty-Ninth International Conference on Machine Learning: June 26–July 1, Edinburgh, Scotland. Citeseer (2012)
19. Li, B., Hoi, S.C., Zhao, P., Gopalkrishnan, V.: Confidence weighted mean reversion strategy for online portfolio selection. ACM Trans. Knowl. Disc. Data (TKDD) **7**(1), 1–38 (2013)
20. Li, B., Wang, J., Huang, D., Hoi, S.C.: Transaction cost optimization for online portfolio selection. Quant. Financ. **18**(8), 1411–1424 (2018)

21. Li, B., Zhao, P., Hoi, S.C., Gopalkrishnan, V.: PAMR: passive aggressive mean reversion strategy for portfolio selection. Mach. Learn. **87**(2), 221–258 (2012)
22. Markowitz, H.: Portfolio selection (1959)
23. Muler, N., Yohai, V.J.: Robust estimates for arch processes. J. Time Ser. Anal. **23**(3), 341–375 (2002)
24. Shen, W., Wang, B., Pu, J., Wang, J.: The Kelly growth optimal portfolio with ensemble learning. In: Proceedings of the AAAI Conference on Artificial Intelligence, vol. 33, pp. 1134–1141 (2019)
25. Shen, W., Wang, J.: Transaction costs-aware portfolio optimization via fast Lowner-John ellipsoid approximation. In: Proceedings of the AAAI Conference on Artificial Intelligence, vol. 29 (2015)
26. Shen, W., Wang, J.: Portfolio selection via subset resampling. In: Proceedings of the AAAI Conference on Artificial Intelligence, vol. 31 (2017)
27. Vardi, Y., Zhang, C.H.: The multivariate l1-median and associated data depth. Proc. Natl. Acad. Sci. **97**(4), 1423–1426 (2000)
28. Xu, K., Zhang, Y., Ye, D., Zhao, P., Tan, M.: Relation-aware transformer for portfolio policy learning. In: IJCAI (2020)

H^2-Nets: Hyper-hodge Convolutional Neural Networks for Time-Series Forecasting

Yuzhou Chen[1(✉)], Tian Jiang[2], and Yulia R. Gel[2,3]

[1] Temple University, Philadelphia, PA 19122, USA
yuzhou.chen@temple.edu
[2] University of Texas at Dallas, Richardson, TX 75080, USA
{tian.jiang,ygl}@utdallas.edu
[3] National Science Foundation, Alexandria, VA 22314, USA

Abstract. Hypergraphs recently have emerged as a new promising alternative to describe complex dependencies in spatio-temporal processes, resulting in the newest trend in multivariate time series forecasting, based semi-supervised learning of spatio-temporal data with Hypergraph Convolutional Networks. Nevertheless, such recent approaches are often limited in their capability to accurately describe higher-order interactions among spatio-temporal entities and to learn hidden interrelations among network substructures. Motivated by the emerging results on simplicial convolution, we introduce the concepts of Hodge theory and Hodge Laplacians, that is, a higher-order generalization of the graph Laplacian, to hypergraph learning. Furthermore, we develop a novel framework for hyper-simplex-graph representation learning which describes complex relationships among both graph and hyper-simplex-graph simplices and, as a result, simultaneously extracts latent higher-order spatio-temporal dependencies. We provide theoretical foundations behind the proposed hyper-simplex-graph representation learning and validate our new Hodge-style Hyper-simplex-graph Neural Networks (H^2-Nets) on 7 real world spatio-temporal benchmark datasets. Our experimental results indicate that H^2-Nets outperforms the state-of-the-art methods by a significant margin, while demonstrating lower computational costs.

Keywords: Hypergraph · Higher-order network · Simplicial complex · Spatio-temporal forecasting

1 Introduction

Spatio-temporal forecasting has a wide variety of applications, from human mobility assessment to biosecurity risk zoning to index-based insurance in agriculture. One of the key challenges in modeling such spatio-temporal processes is that they typically exhibit a highly complex non-stationary and non-separable dependence structure which might be infeasible to accurately address with more

D. Koutra et al. (Eds.): ECML PKDD 2023, LNAI 14173, pp. 271–289, 2023.
https://doi.org/10.1007/978-3-031-43424-2_17

traditional statistical tools. (By non-separability here, we mean that spatial dependence among observed entities depends on time and vice versa.) However, in recent years, there has emerged a number of studies, showing that such complex spatio-temporal dependencies can be successfully tackled by representing spatio-temporal data as a graph structure and explicitly modeled graph neural networks (GNNs). Applications of GNN-based models on spatio-temporal datasets include, e.g., spatio-temporal forecasting of road traffic [16,36], renewable energy [18,33] and COVID-19 spread [13,21]. While recent GNN-based models achieve promising results, they often fail to capture spatio-temporal cross-dependencies among multidimensional data, especially under sparse and heterogeneous data scenarios. A promising alternative way here is to encode complex spatial-temporal dynamics into a hypergraph representation which enables for systematic capturing of cross-wise heterogeneous patterns. As a result, in the last year, Hypergraph Neural Networks have become one of the newest trends in deep learning for spatio-temporal forecasting, demonstrating a high potential in such diverse domains as crime analytics [57], taxi demand forecasting [62], and visual event ratiocination [68]. Nevertheless, Hypergraph Neural Networks are limited in their abilities to describe higher-order interactions in multidimensional spatio-temporal data, that is, properties beyond pairwise relations among nodes in a hypergraph representation. Such higher-order interactions may include, for instance, joint response in taxi demand and supply to the upcoming thunderstorm among multiple city zones. In case of simple graphs, such multi-node relations can be modelled using the simplicial convolution [12,15,19,22] which is one recent direction in graph learning which generalizes the idea of convolutional architectures from node space to simplicial complexes based on the discrete Hodge theory and Hodge-Laplacian concepts [38,46]. However, there exists no analogue of the Hodge theory for hypergraphs.

Here we propose to merge the two newest trends in graph learning, that is, Hypergraph Neural Networks and Hodge-Laplacian based simplicial convolutions, for spatio-temporal forecasting tasks. In particular, we develop a novel Hodge-style framework for hyper-simplex-graph representation learning which describes complex inter-relationships among both graph and hyper-simplex-graph simplices.

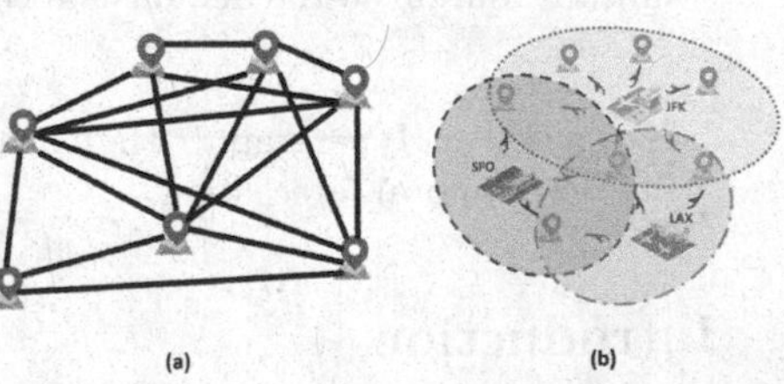

Why Hypergraphs and What New Do They Bring to Spatio-Temporal Forecasting? Suppose we are interested in the taxi price between locations A and B. It will be impacted by demand and supply in locations A and B as well as demand and supply for adjacent routes AC, CD, DB etc. (As in the case of planes, the arriving plane from JFK to SFO is then used for SFO-LAX, resulting in various higher order relations among airports; if NYC area is affected by a thunderstorm, all airports EWR, LGA, and JFK are impacted and can be viewed as a hypernode; a similar mechanism applies to cabs). The Hodge theory on hypergraphs allows us to describe those higher order demand and supply relationships. That is, we describe message propagation to AB via A and B, as well as to AB via higher order simplices formed by AC, CD, DE, EB etc., including the case when C, D, and E are viewed as a hypernode. The Figure above depicts (a) a graph representation of the network, where nodes represent cities; and (b) a hypergraph representation of the network. That is, more complicated and higher level relationships among cities can be described by a hypergraph. By introducing simplices into the problem setting, we can develop the Hodge k-Laplacian convolution which is used to capture the important higher-order structures in spatial dimension. The new time-aware learning approach **H**odge-style **H**yper-simplex-graph Neural Networks (H^2-Nets) simultaneously evaluates latent higher-order spatio-temporal dependencies, and hence allows us to achieve significant gains in forecasting performance of heterogeneous processes compared with the state-of-the-art methods. Significance and novelty of our contributions can be summarized as follows:

- H^2-Nets is the first approach to introduce simplicial convolutions to hypergraph learning, time-aware learning, and spatio-temporal forecasting.
- We develop a new hyper-simplex-graph representation for describing diffusion over higher-order hypergraph substructures and derive theoretical foundations behind the proposed framework.
- Our experiments show that H^2-Nets significantly outperforms all state-of-the-art methods in multivariate spatio-temporal forecasting tasks, often requiring noticeably less training data. These findings highlight the role of latent time-conditioned higher-order interactions for the learning task performance in heterogeneous multidimensional time-evolving data.

2 Related Work

Time-Series Forecasting with Graph Neural Networks. A natural deep learning solution to sequential data modeling consists of Recurrent Neural Networks (RNNs) and its successors such as Long-Short-Term-Memory (LSTM) networks and Gated Recurrent Unit (GRU) networks. GNNs effectively incorporate spatial dependencies in the RNN framework, especially in traffic prediction problem on road network graphs [65]. DCRNN [36] integrates diffusion graph convolutional layer into a GRU network for long-term traffic forecasting. In turn, [26] further employ attention mechanism to learn spatial and temporal dependencies, while [56] develop a self-adaptive adjacency matrix to perform graph convolutions without predefined graph structure. STSGCN [49] simultaneously captures the localized spatial-temporal correlations by localized spatial-temporal graphs.

Hypergraph Neural Networks and Simplicial Neural Networks. Convolutional neural networks (CNNs) and RNNs show excellent performance on Euclidean data. Intrinsic graph structure in many applications such citation network challenges conventional deep learning frameworks. Graph neural networks are designed for graph-based tasks, such as Graph Convolutional Network (GCN) [34], Diffusion

CNN [3] and GraphSAGE [28]. [11,55] provide detailed reviews of graph neural networks. Recently, hypergraph learning has raised a surge of interests from researches, which represents high order relation in the graph. HGNN [23] first implements GCN on hypergraphs via clique expansion. HyperGCN [58] defines a hypergraph Laplacian with linear number of nodes via mediators, while [32] constructs graph dynamically on each layer to capture hidden structure in the data. HyperSAGE [2] extends GraphSAGE by considering propagation in and between hyperedges. In turn, [31] proposes a unified framework for graph and hypergraph models. There are also some applications in sequential hypergraph data such as music composition [30], node classification in citation networks [51], power system classification [14], metro passenger flow prediction [53], and stock price prediction [45,64]. More recently, higher-order (sub)structures have been introduced in geometric deep learning framework to solve the limited representation power of traditional GNNs. Inspired by graph signal processing in electric, transportation and neuroscience systems [6,7], HodgeNet [44] is the first approach to feed neural networks with Hodge Laplacian based on discrete Hodge theory. Simplicial Neural Network (SNNs) [22] is a simplicial Laplacian-based neural networks used for missing data imputation on complexes. [27] introduces cell complex and intercellular message passing scheme to enhance representational learning on graphs. [9] proposes Message Passing Simplicial Networks (MPSNs) and shows its power over traditional GNN on some challenging graph classification tasks. Similarly, SCoNe [43] considers orientation equivariance and improves neural network architecture on simplicial complexes for trajectory prediction. [17] further employ block Hodge-Laplacian to extract interactions among multiple high order substructures. However, there yet exists no SNNs for hypergraphs.

3 Higher-Order Structures on Graph

We denote a graph $\mathcal{G} = (\mathcal{V}, \mathcal{E})$ with the node set $\mathcal{V} = \{v_i\}_{i=1}^{N}$ (i.e., a set containing N nodes) and edge set $\mathcal{E} = \{e_i\}_{i=1}^{M}$ (i.e., a set containing M edges). Adjacency matrix $\boldsymbol{A} \in \mathbb{R}^{N \times N}$ presents connectivity of the graph. For a weighted graph, each edge is assigned a weight by function $w : \mathcal{E} \mapsto \mathbb{R}_{+}$. Then the weighted adjacency matrix $\boldsymbol{A}$ is defined by $a_{ij} = w(\{v_i, v_j\})$ if nodes i and j are connected by an edge $e = \{v_i, v_j\}$ and 0, otherwise. Incidence matrix $\boldsymbol{H} \in \mathbb{R}^{N \times M}$ is an alternative representation of connectivity, where $h_{ij} = 1$ if node i is incident to edge j. We have $\boldsymbol{HWH}^\top = \boldsymbol{D} + \boldsymbol{A}$, where $\boldsymbol{W} \in \mathbb{R}^{M \times M}$ is a diagonal matrix of edge weight $\{w(e_1), \ldots, w(e_M)\}$ and $\boldsymbol{D}$ is a diagonal matrix of node degrees $d(v_i) = \sum_{j \neq i} a_{ij} = \sum_{k=1}^{M} w(e_k) h_{ik}$. Diffusion from node to node on a graph can be described using graph Laplacian matrix, $\boldsymbol{L} = \boldsymbol{D} - \boldsymbol{A} = 2\boldsymbol{D} - \boldsymbol{HWH}^\top$. For these two forms with respect to adjacency matrix and incidence matrix [1], normalized Laplacian matrix can be defined by either $\bar{\boldsymbol{L}} = \boldsymbol{I} - \boldsymbol{D}^{-1/2}\boldsymbol{A}\boldsymbol{D}^{-1/2}$ or $\bar{\boldsymbol{L}} = \boldsymbol{I} - \frac{1}{2}\boldsymbol{D}^{-1/2}\boldsymbol{HWH}^\top\boldsymbol{D}^{-1/2} = \boldsymbol{D}^{-1/2}\left[\frac{1}{2}(\boldsymbol{D} - \boldsymbol{A})\right]\boldsymbol{D}^{-1/2}$ (i.e., in terms of the vertex-edge incidence relation), respectively, where the difference is a factor of 0.5. The incidence approach is convenient for hypergraph, where edges can contain more than two nodes. For convenience, we list the preliminary notations in Table 1 in Appendix A.3.

3.1 Hyper-k-Simplex-Network Learning Statement

Given a graph $\mathcal{G} = (\mathcal{V}, \mathcal{E})$, we propose a novel variant of hypergraph, i.e., hyper-k-simplex-graph, which is a natural extension of hypergraph structure, and can be efficiently used for simplicial complexes of different dimensions (i.e., higher-order interactions) representation learning. For instance, in molecule network, each node represents an atom and each edge is a bond connecting two atoms. The bond (i.e., edge) features include bond type, ring status, molecular charge, etc. In fact, if a bond type has more instances, the deep learning model can more easily learn chemical knowledge such as molecule generation, molecular property – where the number of instances largely depend on the type of atom. Next, we introduce the notations and definition of hyper-k-simplex-network throughout this section.

Definition 1 (Hyper-k-simplex-graph). *A hyper-k-simplex-graph based on k-simplex of graph $\mathcal{G}$ can be defined as $\mathcal{H}_k = (\mathcal{S}^k_{\mathcal{G}}, \mathcal{S}^{k'}_{\mathcal{H}_k})$. Here $\mathcal{S}^k_{\mathcal{G}} = \{s^k_{i;\mathcal{G}}\}_{i=1}^P$ is a set of k-simplices in graph $\mathcal{G}$ and $\mathcal{S}^{k'}_{\mathcal{H}_k} = \{s^{k'}_{i;\mathcal{H}_k}\}_{i=1}^Q$ is a set of hyper-k′-simplices, where $k, k' \in \mathbb{Z}_{\geq 0}$ and $k \neq k'$. The hyper-k-simplex-graph allows for more than two k-simplices to be connected by a hyper-k′-simplex. For any hyper-k′-simplex $s^{k'}_{\mathcal{H}_k} \in \mathcal{S}^{k'}_{\mathcal{H}_k}$, it can be denoted as $s^{k'}_{\mathcal{H}_k} := \{s^k_{i_1;\mathcal{G}}, s^k_{i_2;\mathcal{G}}, \cdots, s^k_{i_p;\mathcal{G}}\} \subseteq \mathcal{S}^k_{\mathcal{G}}$. The relationship between k-simplices and hyper-k′-simplices can be represented by an incidence matrix $\boldsymbol{H}_{\mathcal{H}_k} \in \mathbb{R}^{\phi_k \times \phi_{k'}}$ (ϕ_k and $\phi_{k'}$ represent the number of k-simplices and k′-simplices respectively) with entries defined as*

$$h^{\mathcal{H}_k}(s^k_{\mathcal{G}}, s^{k'}_{\mathcal{H}_k}) = \begin{cases} 1, & \text{if } s^k_{\mathcal{G}} \in s^{k'}_{\mathcal{H}_k} \\ 0, & \text{otherwise.} \end{cases}$$

Fig. 1 in Appendix illustrates a toy example of the constructions of hyper-0-simplex-graph (i.e., hypergraph) and hyper-1-simplex-graph (i.e., hyper-line-graph).

Hypergraph Revisited. From Definition 1 of hyper-k-simplex-graph, we can generate a hypergraph $\mathcal{H}_0 = (\mathcal{V}, \mathcal{E}_{\mathcal{H}_0})$ by setting $k = 0$ and $k' = 1$ (i.e., $\mathcal{S}^0_{\mathcal{G}} = \mathcal{V}$ and $\mathcal{S}^1_{\mathcal{H}_0} = \mathcal{E}_{\mathcal{H}_0}$), which is widely used in studying high-order and complex relations. The hyperedges $e^{\mathcal{H}_0} \in \mathcal{E}_{\mathcal{H}_0}$ generalize edge to non-empty subset of node set $\mathcal{V}$ in graph $\mathcal{G}$. In what follows, subscript $\mathcal{H}_0$ is used for hypergraph counterparts with respect to a graph. We now state incidence matrix $\boldsymbol{H}_{\mathcal{H}_0}$, hyperedge weight $w^{\mathcal{H}_0}$ and node degree $d(v)$. Further, we also have hyperedge degree for number of nodes in each hyperedge $\delta(e^{\mathcal{H}_0}) = |e^{\mathcal{H}_0}| = \sum_{v \in \mathcal{V}} h^{\mathcal{H}_0}(v, e^{\mathcal{H}_0})$. To distinguish these two degree measures, we denote $\boldsymbol{D}_v$ and $\boldsymbol{D}_{e^{\mathcal{H}_0}}$ as corresponding diagonal matrices respectively. A hypergraph can be k-uniform for an integer $k \geq 2$ if $|\delta(e^{\mathcal{H}_0})| = k$ for all $e^{\mathcal{H}_0} \in \mathcal{E}_{\mathcal{H}_0}$. (Note that a graph is just a 2-uniform hypergraph.) Based on [10]'s Laplacian for unweighted hypergraph, we introduce a hypergraph Laplacian $\boldsymbol{L}_{\mathcal{H}_0} = \boldsymbol{D}_v - \boldsymbol{H}_{\mathcal{H}_0} \boldsymbol{W}_{\mathcal{H}_0} \boldsymbol{D}^{-1}_{e^{\mathcal{H}_0}} \boldsymbol{H}^{\top}_{\mathcal{H}_0}$.

Then, normalized hypergraph Laplacian is defined via incidence matrix, $\bar{\boldsymbol{L}}_{\mathcal{H}_0} = \boldsymbol{I} - \boldsymbol{D}_v^{-1/2}\boldsymbol{H}_{\mathcal{H}_0}\boldsymbol{W}_{\mathcal{H}_0}\boldsymbol{D}_{e^{\mathcal{H}_0}}^{-1}\boldsymbol{H}_{\mathcal{H}_0}^{\top}\boldsymbol{D}_v^{-1/2}$. For 2-uniform hypergraph, it reduces to normalized graph Laplacian. Further, as the next Lemma shows, hypergraph graph Laplacian shares similar important properties of graph Laplacian. In turn, the derived range of spectrum can be used to shed light on the numerical stability of the associated propagation [34].

Lemma 1. *(i) $\boldsymbol{L}_{\mathcal{H}_0} > 0$, $\boldsymbol{L}_{\mathcal{H}_0}^T = \boldsymbol{L}_{\mathcal{H}_0}$ and $\bar{\boldsymbol{L}}_{\mathcal{H}_0} > 0$, $\bar{\boldsymbol{L}}_{\mathcal{H}_0}^T = \bar{\boldsymbol{L}}_{\mathcal{H}_0}$; (ii) $\boldsymbol{L}_{\mathcal{H}_0}$ is a diagonally dominant matrix; (iii) $\mathbf{1}$ is an eigenvector of $\boldsymbol{L}_{\mathcal{H}_0}$ for eigenvalue 0. $\mathbf{D}_v^{1/2}\mathbf{1}$ is an eigenvector of $\bar{\boldsymbol{L}}_{\mathcal{H}_0}$ for eigenvalue 0; (iv) Diagonal elements of $\boldsymbol{L}_{\mathcal{H}_0}$ and $\bar{\boldsymbol{L}}_{\mathcal{H}_0}$ arc non negative and their off-digonal elements are non-positive; (v) For eigenvalues λ_i's of $\bar{\boldsymbol{L}}_{\mathcal{H}_0}$, $\lambda_i \in [0, 2)$.*

Additional theoretical results in Appendix A relate the spectrum of the hypergraph Laplacians to the higher order properties as k-normalized cut.

Hyper-Line-Graph. Inspired by hypergraph, we introduce a novel variant of hypergraph based on the hyper-k-simplex-graph scheme with the setting $\{k = 1, k' = 0\}$, i.e., hyper-line-graph. The main intuition behind hyper-line-graph stems from hypernode, which is an analog of hyperedge on edge of graph, that is, more complicated and hidden relationships among edges can be captured. We denote a hyper-line-graph as $\mathcal{H}_1 = \{\mathcal{E}, \mathcal{V}_{\mathcal{H}_1}\}$ with the edge set $\mathcal{E} = \{e_i\}_{i=1}^M$ in graph $\mathcal{G}$ and hypernode set $\mathcal{V}_{\mathcal{H}_1}$. To extract the edge information, different from hyperedges based on the nodes of graph $\mathcal{G}$, we define the hypernode set by clustering similar edges, where hypernode $v^{\mathcal{H}_1}$ is an aribitrary subset of $\mathcal{E}$. We define "incidence matrix" $\boldsymbol{H}_{\mathcal{H}_1}$ such that $h^{\mathcal{H}_1}(e, v^{\mathcal{H}_1}) = 1$ if $e \in v^{\mathcal{H}_1}$ and 0, otherwise. Suppose we have a hypernode weight $w^{\mathcal{H}_1} : \mathcal{V}_{\mathcal{H}_1} \to \mathbb{R}_+$. Then the edge degree of hyper-line-graph is $\delta(e) = \sum_{v^{\mathcal{H}_1} \in \mathcal{V}_{\mathcal{H}_1}} w^{\mathcal{H}_1}(v^{\mathcal{H}_1}) h^{\mathcal{H}_1}(e, v^{\mathcal{H}_1})$, while the hypernode degree $d(v^{\mathcal{H}_1}) = |v^{\mathcal{H}_1}| = \sum_{e \in \mathcal{E}} h^{\mathcal{H}_1}(e, v^{\mathcal{H}_1})$. A similar argument following the discussion about hypergraph establishes a hyper-line-graph Laplacian (see Appendix A for more details).

3.2 Preliminaries on Hodge Theory

As discussed above and in Appendix A, graph and hyper-k-simplex graph Laplacian measure diffusion among graph substructures (nodes, edges and their derived objects such as hyperedges and hypernodes). Given the role of higher interactions in a simple graph, our ultimate goal is to evaluate diffusion dynamics on high order substructures of hypergraphs. The Hodge-de Rham theory provides a general solution to study graph substructures in terms of *simplicial complexes* [38,46,47].

Definition 2 (Simplicial complex). *A collection Δ of finite non-empty subsets of a set $\mathcal{V}$ is an abstract simplicial complex if it is closed under taking subset, that is, for any $\sigma \in \Delta$ and any non-empty subset $\tau \subseteq \sigma$, we have $\tau \in \Delta$. Element $\sigma \in \Delta$ is called a k-simplex if $|\sigma| = k + 1$.*

That is, k-simplex is a convex hull of $(k+1)$ points of $\mathcal{V}$. Specifically, it corresponds to $(k+1)$ clique in graph, that is, we refer to the 0-simplices as nodes, 1-simplices as edges, 2-simplices as triangles on the graph. Let $\mathcal{S}^k_{\mathcal{G}}$ be the set of k-simplices of graph $\mathcal{G}$, node set $\mathcal{V} = \mathcal{S}^0_{\mathcal{G}}$, and edge set $\mathcal{E} = \mathcal{S}^1_{\mathcal{G}}$. Then we define a k-cochain on $\mathcal{S}^k_{\mathcal{G}}$, that is, an alternating function $f : \mathcal{V}^{k+1} \mapsto \mathbb{R}$ such that it is invariant under even permutation of the $(k+1)$ nodes and takes opposite sign, otherwise. Let $C(\mathcal{S}^k_{\mathcal{G}})$ be the Hilbert space of k-cochains. Coboundary operator connects adjacent order simplexes.

Definition 3. *A linear map $\delta_k : C(\mathcal{S}^{k-1}_{\mathcal{G}}) \rightarrow C(\mathcal{S}^k_{\mathcal{G}})$ is a k-coboundary operator such that $(\delta_k f)(v_{i_0}, \ldots, v_{i_{k+1}}) = \sum_{l=0}^{k+1}(-1)^l f(v_{i_0}, \ldots, \hat{v}_{i_l}, \ldots, v_{i_{k+1}})$, where $\hat{v}_l$ is omitted. Hodge k-Laplacian operator $\mathcal{L}_k : C(\mathcal{S}^k_{\mathcal{G}}) \mapsto C(\mathcal{S}^k_{\mathcal{G}})$ is a linear transform such that $\mathcal{L}_k = \delta_{k-1}\delta^*_{k-1} + \delta^*_k\delta_k$.*

In terms of matrix representation, adjoint δ^*_k of a linear map is the transpose operator and δ^*_k is the incidence matrix connecting k-simplex and $(k+1)$-simplex. (More technical discussion can be found in Appendix A.) Formally, Hodge k-Laplacian matrix $\boldsymbol{L}_k \in \mathbb{R}^{\phi_k \times \phi_k}$ and normalized Hodge k-Laplacian $\bar{\boldsymbol{L}}_k \in \mathbb{R}^{\phi_k \times \phi_k}$ (ϕ_k is the number of k-simplices in the set $\mathcal{S}^k_{\mathcal{G}}$) can be written as

$$\boldsymbol{L}_k = \boldsymbol{B}_k^\top \boldsymbol{B}_k + \boldsymbol{B}_{k+1}\boldsymbol{B}_{k+1}^\top \tag{1}$$

$$\bar{\boldsymbol{L}}_k = \boldsymbol{D}_{k+1}\boldsymbol{B}_k^\top \boldsymbol{D}_k^{-1}\boldsymbol{B}_k + \boldsymbol{B}_{k+1}\boldsymbol{D}_{k+2}\boldsymbol{B}_{k+1}^\top \boldsymbol{D}_{k+1}^{-1} \tag{2}$$

where $\boldsymbol{B}_k$ is the k-simplex-to-$(k-1)$-simplex incidence matrix with $\boldsymbol{B}_0 = \boldsymbol{0}$, and $\boldsymbol{D}_k$ is the diagonal matrix computed from $\boldsymbol{B}_k$.

4 The H²-Nets Methodology

Let $\boldsymbol{X}_{\tau,\mathcal{G}} \in \mathbb{R}^{N \times F}$ be node features at time τ, where F is the feature dimension of each node. The problem of time-series forecasting can be described as: given the historical graph signals of past ω periods $\{\boldsymbol{X}_{t-\omega,\mathcal{G}}, \boldsymbol{X}_{t-\omega+1,\mathcal{G}}, \ldots, \boldsymbol{X}_{t-1,\mathcal{G}}\} \in \mathbb{R}^{\omega \times N \times F}$, our aim is to learn a map $\mathscr{F}$ that is able to forecast ω' future graph signals $\{\boldsymbol{X}_{t,\mathcal{G}}, \boldsymbol{X}_{t+1,\mathcal{G}}, \ldots, \boldsymbol{X}_{t+\omega',\mathcal{G}}\}$.

Self-adaptive k-Simplex Convolution. In reality, the network structure may change over time, that is, the connection strengths of different nodes or the node-wise relationships can vary due to external factors. To overcome the limitation of the fixed graph structure, we propose a novel k-simplex representation learning scheme: self-adaptive k-simplex convolution (SSC), which utilizes a learnable k-simplex embedding dictionaries $\boldsymbol{E}_k \in \mathbb{R}^{\phi_k \times d_c}$ (where ϕ_k is the number of k-simplices $\mathcal{S}^k_{\mathcal{G}}$ and $d_c \geq 1$ is the dimension of embedding) to construct a learned graph $\boldsymbol{\Xi}_k$, and then obtain the k-simplex representation by applying convolution operation on it. We define the self-adaptive k-simplex convolution for k-simplices of the graph as follows

$$\boldsymbol{\Xi}_k = \text{softmax}(\text{ReLU}(\boldsymbol{E}_k\boldsymbol{E}_k^\top)),$$

$$\dot{\boldsymbol{Z}}^{(\ell+1)}_{\tau,\mathcal{S}^k_{\mathcal{G}}} = \psi(\boldsymbol{\Xi}_k \dot{\boldsymbol{Z}}^{(\ell)}_{\tau,\mathcal{S}^k_{\mathcal{G}}} \boldsymbol{\Theta}^{\text{SSC}}_{\mathcal{S}^k_{\mathcal{G}}}),$$

where the softmax and ReLU functions are used to normalize the similarity scores across k-simplices and preserve the strong connections and distance patterns, respectively, $\Theta^{\text{SSC}}_{\mathcal{S}^k_{\mathcal{G}}}$ denotes the trainable parameters of SSC, and $\psi(\cdot)$ is a non-linear activation function such as ReLU. Finally, $\dot{\boldsymbol{Z}}^{(\ell+1)}_{\tau,\mathcal{S}^k_{\mathcal{G}}} \in \mathbb{R}^{\phi_k \times C^{out;\text{SSC}}_{\mathcal{S}^k_{\mathcal{G}}}}$ is the activations of SSC to the (ℓ+1)-th layer (where $C^{out;\text{SSC}}_{\mathcal{S}^k_{\mathcal{G}}}$ is the output dimension of SSC) and $\dot{\boldsymbol{Z}}^{(0)}_{\tau,\mathcal{S}^k_{\mathcal{G}}} = \boldsymbol{X}_{\tau,\mathcal{S}^k_{\mathcal{G}}}$.

Hodge k-Laplacian Convolution. To better capture *pre-defined* spatial dependencies between k-simplices (where $k = \{0, 1, 2, \cdots\}$), in this work, we consider using the Hodge k-Laplacian to learn the k-simplex specific patterns in the spatial dimension. Compared with regular graph Laplacian, the (normalized) Hodge k-Laplacian is more efficient and powerful for graph representation learning, that is, it not only explicitly incorporates topological dependencies among simplices from different dimensions, but can handle spatio-temporal graph data with abundant structure information. Furthermore, to diffuse signals more efficiently from k-simplices to their multi-hop neighbors, we introduce random walk operation into normalized Hodge k-Laplacian, yielding the powered normalized Hodge k-Laplacian with power exponent r, that is, $\bar{\boldsymbol{L}}^r_k$ where $r \geq 1$. Then, k-Hodge convolution (HC) is formulated as

$$\ddot{\boldsymbol{Z}}^{(\ell+1)}_{\tau,\mathcal{S}^k_{\mathcal{G}}} = \psi(\bar{\boldsymbol{L}}^r_k \ddot{\boldsymbol{Z}}^{(\ell)}_{\tau,\mathcal{S}^k_{\mathcal{G}}} \boldsymbol{\Theta}^{\text{HC}}_{\mathcal{S}^k_{\mathcal{G}}}), \tag{3}$$

where $\bar{\boldsymbol{L}}_k \in \mathbb{R}^{\phi_k \times \phi_k}$ is the r-th power of normalized Hodge k-Laplacian, $\ddot{\boldsymbol{Z}}^{(\ell)}_{\tau,\mathcal{S}^k_{\mathcal{G}}} \in \mathbb{R}^{\phi_k \times C^{\ell;\text{HC}}_{\mathcal{S}^k_{\mathcal{G}}}}$ is the activations of HC layer to the ℓ-th layer at time τ (here $C^{\ell;\text{HC}}_{\mathcal{S}^k_{\mathcal{G}}}$ is the length of features at the ℓ-th layer) and $\ddot{\boldsymbol{Z}}^{(0)}_{\tau,\mathcal{S}^k_{\mathcal{G}}} = \boldsymbol{X}_{\tau,\mathcal{S}^k_{\mathcal{G}}} \in \mathbb{R}^{\phi_k \times C^{in;\text{HC}}_{\mathcal{S}^k_{\mathcal{G}}}}$ (here $C^{in;\text{HC}}_{\mathcal{S}^k}$ is the number of channels in input), $\boldsymbol{\Theta}^{\text{HC}}_{\mathcal{S}^k_{\mathcal{G}}} \in \mathbb{R}^{C^{\ell;\text{HC}}_{\mathcal{S}^k_{\mathcal{G}}} \times C^{\ell+1;\text{HC}}_{\mathcal{S}^k_{\mathcal{G}}}}$ is a trainable weight matrix (here $C^{\ell+1;\text{HC}}_{\mathcal{S}^k_{\mathcal{G}}}$ is the number of channels in $(\ell+1)$-layer).

Hyper-k-Simplex-Graph Convolution. Here, we introduce our proposed hypergraph variant convolution operation to enable updating k-simplex-wise feature matrix. Inspired by [58,62], the hypergraph structure can be treated as a flexible and natural modeling tool to deal with complex data. For example, in a hypergraph, a hyperedge can connect more than two nodes simultaneously and, hence, the information of hidden dependencies and higher level relationships among nodes can be captured in a more systematic manner. We also provide a theoretical justification behind our hypergraph model, revealing its expressive power (see Lemma 2 in Appendix A.2 for details). In particular, we develop a hyper-k-simplex-graph convolution (HSGC) operation based on Definition 1, which can fully explore and utilize both the features of k-simplices and graph structure information. The key of our proposed HSGC operation is to aggregate k-simplex features from hyper-k'-simplex (where a hyper-k'-simplex can be treated as a "*transporter*" that provides connection among k-simplices beyond pairwise relations)

$$\boldsymbol{Z}^{\text{HSGC}}_{\tau,\mathcal{S}^{k'}_{\mathcal{H}_k}} = \text{HSGC}_{\mathcal{S}^k_{\mathcal{G}}}(\boldsymbol{X}_{\tau,\mathcal{S}^k_{\mathcal{G}}}; \mathcal{H}^k), \tag{4}$$

$$\bar{\boldsymbol{Z}}^{\text{HSGC}}_{\tau,\mathcal{S}^k_{\mathcal{G}}} = \text{HSGC}_{\mathcal{S}^{k'}_{\mathcal{H}_k}}(\boldsymbol{Z}^{\text{HSGC}}_{\tau,\mathcal{S}^{k'}_{\mathcal{H}_k}}, \mathcal{H}^k), \tag{5}$$

where $\mathcal{H}_k = (\mathcal{S}^k_{\mathcal{G}}, \mathcal{S}^{k'}_{\mathcal{H}_k})$ represents a hyper-k-simplex-graph (i.e., $\mathcal{S}^k_{\mathcal{G}}$ is a set of k-simplices in graph $\mathcal{G}$ and $\mathcal{S}^{k'}_{\mathcal{H}_k}$ is a set of hyper-k'-simplices, and $k \neq k'$; see more details in Definition 1), and $\text{HSGC}_{\mathcal{S}^k_{\mathcal{G}}}$ and $\text{HSGC}_{\mathcal{S}^{k'}_{\mathcal{H}_k}}$ are encoder and decoder of HSGC for $\mathcal{S}^k_{\mathcal{G}}$, respectively. That is, the HSGC convolution updates k-simplex representations as

$$\boldsymbol{z}^{\text{HSGC}}_{s^{k'}_{i;\mathcal{H}_k}} = \text{SUM}(\{\psi(\boldsymbol{\Theta}^{\text{HSGC}}_{\mathcal{S}^k_{\mathcal{G}}} \boldsymbol{x}_{s^k_{j;\mathcal{G}}}), \forall s^k_{j;\mathcal{G}} \in s^{k'}_{i;\mathcal{H}_k}\}),$$

$$\bar{\boldsymbol{z}}^{\text{HSGC}}_{s^k_{j;\mathcal{G}}} = \text{SUM}(\{\psi(\boldsymbol{\Theta}^{\text{HSGC}}_{\mathcal{S}^{k'}_{\mathcal{H}_k}} \boldsymbol{z}^{\text{HSGC}}_{s^{k'}_{q;\mathcal{H}_k}}), \forall s^k_{j;\mathcal{G}} \in s^{k'}_{q;\mathcal{H}_k}\}),$$

where $\psi(\cdot)$ is a non-linear activation function, $\boldsymbol{\Theta}^{\text{HSGC}}_{\mathcal{S}^k_{\mathcal{G}}}$ and $\boldsymbol{\Theta}^{\text{HSGC}}_{\mathcal{S}^{k'}_{\mathcal{H}_k}}$ are learnable matrices, and SUM represents an element-wise summation. (For simplicity, we omit time notation τ.) After the HSGC operation, we can get the final k-simplex embedding as

$$\dddot{\boldsymbol{Z}}^{\text{HSGC}}_{\tau,\mathcal{S}^k_{\mathcal{G}}} = \boldsymbol{\Theta}^{\text{Update}}_{\mathcal{S}^k_{\mathcal{G}}}([\bar{\boldsymbol{Z}}^{\text{HSGC}}_{\tau,\mathcal{S}^k_{\mathcal{G}}}, \boldsymbol{X}_{\tau,\mathcal{S}^k_{\mathcal{G}}}]) + \boldsymbol{b}^{\text{Update}}_{\mathcal{S}^k_{\mathcal{G}}}, \tag{6}$$

where $\boldsymbol{\Theta}^{\text{Update}}_{\mathcal{S}^k_{\mathcal{G}}}$ and $\boldsymbol{b}^{\text{Update}}_{\mathcal{S}^k_{\mathcal{G}}}$ are learnable weight and bias for k-simplex updating, respectively.

Traversable Operation from k-Simplex-to-$\tilde{k}$-Simplex. To transfer the knowledge learned from k-simplex representation to $\tilde{k}$-simplex level, we propose a traversable operation $\mathscr{T}$, formalized as follows

$$\boldsymbol{Z}^{(\ell+1)}_{\tau,\mathcal{S}^k_{\mathcal{G}}} = \mathscr{T}(\dddot{\boldsymbol{Z}}^{\text{HSGC}}_{\tau,\mathcal{S}^k_{\mathcal{G}}}) = \begin{cases} \boldsymbol{B}^{\top}_{\tilde{k}}(\dddot{\boldsymbol{Z}}^{\text{HSGC}}_{\tau,\mathcal{S}^k_{\mathcal{G}}}) & k = \tilde{k} - 1, \\ \boldsymbol{B}_k(\dddot{\boldsymbol{Z}}^{\text{HSGC}}_{\tau,\mathcal{S}^k_{\mathcal{G}}}) & k = \tilde{k} + 1. \end{cases} \tag{7}$$

That is, we consider both (i) transformation from lower-dimension to higher-dimension, i.e., by multiplying $\boldsymbol{B}^{\top}_{\tilde{k}}$ by $\dddot{\boldsymbol{Z}}^{\text{HSGC}}_{\tau,\mathcal{S}^k_{\mathcal{G}}}$ and (ii) transformation from higher-dimension to lower-dimension, i.e., by multiplying $\boldsymbol{B}_k$ by $\dddot{\boldsymbol{Z}}^{\text{HSGC}}_{\tau,\mathcal{S}^k_{\mathcal{G}}}$. For instance, based on hyper-1-simplex-graph convolution, we learn the relationships among edges via hypernodes; however, the task of multivariate time-series forecasting aims to predict the 0-simplex (i.e., node) values in a multivariate temporal graph, hence, we can utilize the traverable operation $\mathscr{T}$ to transform the edge embedding to node embedding, by leveraging incidence matrix $\boldsymbol{B}_1$.

As a result, our final k-simplex level embedding $\tilde{\boldsymbol{Z}}^{(\ell+1)}_{\tau,\mathcal{S}^k_{\mathcal{G}}}$ based on above three convolution operations can be formulated as

$$\tilde{\boldsymbol{Z}}^{(\ell+1)}_{\tau,\mathcal{S}^k_{\mathcal{G}}} = [\dot{\boldsymbol{Z}}^{(\ell+1)}_{\tau,\mathcal{S}^k_{\mathcal{G}}}, \ddot{\boldsymbol{Z}}^{(\ell+1)}_{\tau,\mathcal{S}^k_{\mathcal{G}}}, \dddot{\boldsymbol{Z}}^{\text{HSGC}}_{\tau,\mathcal{S}^k_{\mathcal{G}}}],$$

where $[\cdot,\cdot,\cdot]$ denotes the concatenation operation. Note that, in this work, we argue that the essential higher-order information of spatio-temporal graph structure mainly exists in nodes and edges, and hence our method aims to learn feature representations from 0-dimensional and 1-dimensional graph substructures and interactions. Since the task of (multivariate) time-series forecasting aims to predict the node values, we need to transform the learned k-simplex (where $k = 1$ in our case) into node-level. Finally, we combine both 0-simplex (i.e., node) embedding and 1-simplex (i.e., edge) embedding to obtain the final embedding $\tilde{\tilde{\boldsymbol{Z}}}^{(\ell+1)}_{\tau} = [\tilde{\boldsymbol{Z}}^{(\ell+1)}_{\tau,\mathcal{S}^0_{\mathcal{G}}}, \mathscr{T}(\tilde{\boldsymbol{Z}}^{(\ell+1)}_{\tau,\mathcal{S}^1_{\mathcal{G}}})]$.

Gate Recurrent Unit with H^2-Nets. Following the work of [36], equipped with the final embedding $\tilde{\tilde{\boldsymbol{Z}}}^{(\ell+1)}_{\tau}$, we employ Gated Recurrent Units (GRU) to learn the spatio-temporal correlations among time series and predict the attributes at each node at a future timestamp,

$$\mathfrak{R}_t = \psi\left(\boldsymbol{W}_{\mathfrak{R}}\left[\boldsymbol{\Omega}_{t-1}, \tilde{\tilde{\boldsymbol{Z}}}^{(\ell+1)}_{\tau}\right] + \boldsymbol{b}_{\mathfrak{R}}\right),\ \mathfrak{I}_t = \psi\left(\boldsymbol{W}_{\mathfrak{I}}\left[\boldsymbol{\Omega}_{t-1}, \tilde{\tilde{\boldsymbol{Z}}}^{(\ell+1)}_{\tau}\right] + \boldsymbol{b}_{\mathfrak{I}}\right),$$

$$\boldsymbol{\Omega}_t = \tanh\left(\boldsymbol{W}_{\Omega}\left[\mathfrak{I}_t \odot \boldsymbol{\Omega}_{t-1}, \tilde{\tilde{\boldsymbol{Z}}}^{(\ell+1)}_{\tau}\right] + \boldsymbol{b}_{\Omega}\right),\ \tilde{\boldsymbol{\Omega}}_t = \mathfrak{R}_i \odot \boldsymbol{\Omega}_{t-1} + (1 - \mathfrak{R}_t) \odot \boldsymbol{\Omega}_t,$$

where $\psi(\cdot)$ is an activation function (e.g., ReLU, LeakyReLU), $\odot$ is the elementwise product, $\mathfrak{R}_t$ is the update gate and $\mathfrak{I}_i$ is the reset gate. $\boldsymbol{b}_{\mathfrak{R}}$, $\boldsymbol{b}_{\mathfrak{I}}$, $\boldsymbol{b}_{\Omega}$, $\boldsymbol{W}_{\mathfrak{R}}$, $\boldsymbol{W}_{\mathfrak{I}}$, and $\boldsymbol{W}_{\Omega}$ are learnable parameters. $\left[\boldsymbol{\Omega}_{t-1}, \boldsymbol{Z}^{(\ell+1)}_{\tau}\right]$ and $\boldsymbol{\Omega}_t$ are the input and output of GRU model, respectively. Then, we can obtain $\tilde{\boldsymbol{\Omega}}_t$ which contains both the spatio-temporal and time-aware information. Figure 1 illustrates our H^2-Nets model framework.

5 Experiments

Datasets and Baselines. In this section, we evaluate the proposed framework on (i) three real-world traffic flow datasets: NYC-Taxi [60], NYC-Bike [60], and BJ-Taxi [37], (ii) the spread of coronavirus disease COVID-19 at county-level in states of California (CA) and Pennsylvania (PA), (iii) YouTube video network: VevoMusic [54], and (iv) the largest dynamic network of time series: WikiTraffic [52]. Statistics of datasets are described in Table 2 in Appendix B.2. More details of datasets can be found in Appendix B.2. Appendix B.7 provides a comprehensive visualization of Hyperedges and Hypernodes on NYC-Taxi, NYC-Bike, and BJ-Taxi. We compare our model H^2-Nets with the following 26 state-of-the-art baselines (SOAs): (i) statistical time series model: ARIMA; (ii)

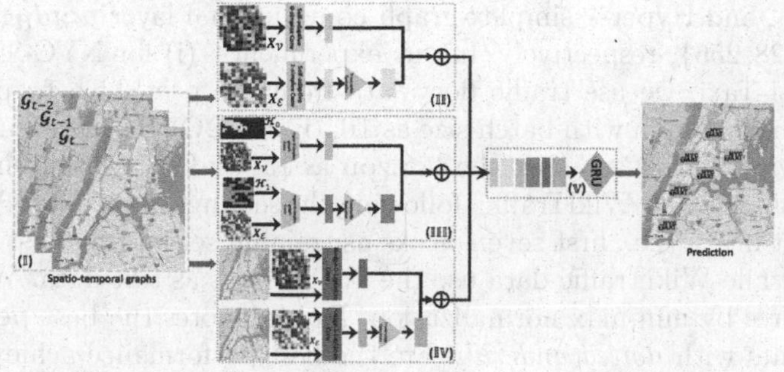

Fig. 1. H^2-Nets overview (see Appendix B.4 for more details).

Table 1. Performance on NYC-Taxi and NYC-Bike datasets.

Datasets	NYC-Taxi				NYC-Bike			
Metrics Model	RMSE		MAPE (%)		RMSE		MAPE (%)	
	In	Out	In	Out	In	Out	In	Out
ARIMA	27.25 ± 0.02	36.53 ± 0.03	20.91 ± 0.06	22.21 ± 0.04	11.25 ± 0.02	11.53 ± 0.01	25.79 ± 0.07	26.53 ± 0.06
SVR	26.15 ± 0.05	34.67 ± 0.03	18.22 ± 0.05	20.93 ± 0.02	10.12 ± 0.03	11.01 ± 0.07	23.45 ± 0.04	23.99 ± 0.03
Fuzzy+NN	26.01 ± 0.34	34.54 ± 0.31	18.97 ± 0.27	21.55 ± 0.29	11.33 ± 0.30	11.86 ± 0.28	24.69 ± 0.27	25.13 ± 0.34
RNN	30.18 ± 0.56	38.33 ± 0.55	26.24 ± 0.49	26.89 ± 0.51	13.55 ± 0.48	15.37 ± 0.47	27.03 ± 0.43	27.61 ± 0.50
LSTM	29.99 ± 0.47	37.52 ± 0.49	25.93 ± 0.50	26.48 ± 0.49	13.67 ± 0.48	15.90 ± 0.50	27.18 ± 0.47	27.89 ± 0.46
DeepST	23.61 ± 0.23	26.84 ± 0.19	22.39 ± 0.33	22.41 ± 0.35	7.62 ± 0.19	9.15 ± 0.20	22.77 ± 0.26	23.17 ± 0.23
ST-ResNet	21.76 ± 0.24	26.35 ± 0.32	21.16 ± 0.46	21.28 ± 0.50	8.87 ± 0.16	9.84 ± 0.16	23.01 ± 0.42	23.11 ± 0.37
DMVST-Net	20.66 ± 0.42	25.83 ± 0.24	17.23 ± 0.30	17.46 ± 0.40	8.73 ± 0.21	9.30 ± 0.19	21.73 ± 0.41	22.36 ± 0.33
STDN	19.35 ± 0.27	24.25 ± 0.22	16.48 ± 0.23	16.62 ± 0.21	8.29 ± 0.18	8.99 ± 0.16	21.25 ± 0.31	22.27 ± 0.31
HGC-RNN	79.45 ± 0.07	25.45 ± 0.06	40.11 ± 0.30	16.30 ± 0.02	10.06 ± 0.03	14.68 ± 0.10	21.36 ± 0.06	22.99 ± 0.11
DCRNN	18.55 ± 0.16	24.15 ± 0.25	16.25 ± 0.20	16.30 ± 0.15	8.19 ± 0.20	8.82 ± 0.11	21.22 ± 0.18	22.15 ± 0.15
AGCRN	22.78 ± 0.65	26.67 ± 0.40	15.92 ± 0.27	16.46 ± 0.53	8.33 ± 0.14	9.13 ± 0.12	21.64 ± 0.23	22.57 ± 0.25
MPNN	20.15 ± 0.31	27.75 ± 0.42	16.55 ± 0.25	16.68 ± 0.22	8.35 ± 0.10	9.67 ± 0.12	21.74 ± 0.34	22.89 ± 0.16
H²-Nets (ours)	******18.08*** ± 0.19	*****23.64*** ± 0.25	******14.66*** ± 0.06	******14.68*** ± 0.08	**7.50** ± 0.02	******8.35*** ± 0.06	******19.72*** ± 0.03	******20.68*** ± 0.07

machine learning time series model: SVR; (iii) deep neural networks-based models: Fuzzy+NN [50], DeepST [67], ST-ResNet [66], TCN [5], LSTNet [35], DeepGLO [48], UrbanFM [37], and N-BEATS [39]; (iv) RNN-based models: RNN, LSTM [29], DMVST-Net [61], DeepState [41], STDN [60], ST-MetaNet [40], and Radflow [52]; (v) GCN-based models: DCRNN [36], GraphWaveNet [56], AGCRN [4], MPNN [25], ST-GCN [59], ST-MGCN [24], and StemGNN [13]; (vi) hypergraph-based model: HGC-RNN [62]; and (vii) topological-based model: Z-GCNETs [20]. Further details of baselines are contained in Appendix B.3.

Experiment Settings. We implement our H²-Nets with Pytorch framework on NVIDIA GeForce RTX 3090 GPU. We optimize all the models by Adam optimizer for maximum of 200 epochs. The learning rate is searched in $\{0.001, 0.003, 0.005, 0.01, 0.05\}$ with weight decay rate of 0.3, the embedding dimension (i.e., d_c in $\boldsymbol{E}_k$) is searched in $\{1, 2, 3, 5, 10, 15\}$, and the power order r of normalized Hodge k-Laplacian (in Eq. 3) is searched in $\{1, 2, 3\}$. For the Hyper-k-simplex-network construction, the range of grid search space for hyperparameters k and k' is in $\{0, 1, 2, 3\}$. We search the hidden layer dimensions in self-adaptive k-simplex convolutional layer $nhid_{\text{SSC}}$, k-Hodge convolutional layer $nhid_{\mathrm{HC}}$, and Hyper-k-simplex-graph convolutional layer $nhid_{\mathrm{HSGC}}$ among $\{16, 32, 64, 128, 256\}$, respectively. In our experiments, (i) for NYC-Taxi, NYC-Bike, and BJ-Taxi, we use traffic flow data from the past 2.5 h to predict the flow for the next 30 min with batch size as 16; (ii) for COVID-19 biosurveillance, we set the window size as 5, set the horizon as 15, and set the batch size as 5; (iii) for VevoMusic and WikiTraffic, following the settings in [52], i.e., VevoMusic data are split in 7:2 (i.e., first seven weeks as training set and the last two weeks as test set) while WikiTraffic data use the last 28 days as test data. We normalize the features by min-max normalization. **Bold** denotes the best performance and the results with *dotted underline* are the best performance achieved by the next best competitors. We also perform a one-sided two-sample t-test between the best result and the best performance achieved by the next best competitor, where *, **, *** denote p-value $< 0.1, 0.05, 0.01$ (i.e., denote significant, statistically significant, highly statistically significant results, respectively. The code and datasets have been released at: https://github.com/ecmlpkddh2nets/H2NETs.git.

Results and Discussion. Table 1 summarizes all results of SOAs and our H^2-Nets on both NYC-Taxi and NYC-Bike datasets. All experiments are repeated 10 times, and we report the average performance and standard deviation with Root Mean Square Error (RMSE) and Mean Absolute Percentage Error (MAPE). As demonstrated in Table 1, our model H^2-Nets consistently outperforms SOAs on both NYC-Taxi and NYC-Bike. Moreover, for both NYC-Taxi and NYC-Bike, (i) the improvement gain of H^2-Nets over the runner-ups ranges from 2.16% to 5.63% in inflow/outflow-RMSE and (ii) the improvement gain of H^2-Nets over the runner-ups ranges from 7.11% to 11.03% in inflow/outflow-MAPE. Table 3 (*left*) shows the demand forecasting performance on BJ-Taxi in terms of RMSE and MAPE. We can see that our H^2-Nets outperforms all SOAs on all evaluation metrics, where our model achieves a relative gain of up to 25.56% over the runner-up in terms of MAPE. Table 3 (*right*) presents COVID-19 hospitalization prediction results on CA and PA, and we find that our proposed H^2-Nets achieves state-of-the-art performance on both datasets; for instance, our model yields 2.74%, 1.21% relative gains in RMSE over the runner-ups (including both GCN-based and topological-based methods) on CA and PA respectively. Moreover, on two large dynamic networks, i.e., VevoMusic and WikiTraffic, as shown in Table 2, we observe that H^2-Nets outperforms all baselines on both VevoMusic and WikiTraffic networks with relative gains of 4.49% and 5.26% compared to the runner-up (i.e., Radflow), respectively. Note that, through analyzing the results in Tables 2, 1, and 3, we can draw the following conclusions (i) our H^2-Nets successfully outperforms all RNN-based models and deep neural networks across all the evaluation metrics, i.e., only taking

Table 2. Experimental results (mean SMAPE) on VevoMusic and WikiTraffic.

Model	VevoMusic	WikiTraffic
Seasonal ARIMA	9.67	19.6
LSTM	8.68	16.6
N-BEATS	8.64	16.6
Radflow	8.37	16.0
H^2-Nets (ours)	**8.01**	**15.2**

temporal information into consideration is not enough to capture and model the correlations among different time series; (ii) compared with GCN-based models, our H^2-Nets model has two advantages: (1) it uses hyper-k-simplex-graph (in our experiments, we use both hypergraph and hyper-line-graph) to capture the beyond pairwise relations; (2) our H^2-Nets includes higher-order interactions representation learning (e.g., in edge- and triangle-level) by using k-Hodge convolution and thus boosts the graph learning ability; and (iii) our H^2-Nets shows overwhelming enhancement over hypergraph-based model (i.e., HGC-RNN) and the improvements can be owed to the hyper-line-graph learning framework, demonstrating that beyond node-level hyper-structure (i.e., hypergraph) representation learning is necessary for high-order data relation modeling with neural network architecture. Furthermore, while there exists no universal measure to assess higher order substructures, mean clique counts (MCl), along with global clustering coefficient (GCC) [63], appears a reasonable choice to assess the potential role of multi-node interactions H^2-Nets focuses on. We find that the higher MCl and GCC tend to be associated with higher forecasting gains H^2-Nets can bring. For instance, GCC of CA is more than twice higher than GCC of PA (1.91 *vs.* 0.87), while MCl for 3-node clique of CA is 6.23% higher than that of PA (4.09 *vs.* 3.85); in turn, the gains of H^2-Nets on both CA and PA *vs.* the next best competitors are 2.74% and 1.21% (in RMSE). Such phenomena can be explained by substantially more heterogeneous socio-demographic patterns of CA *vs.* PA and almost a twice higher Social Vulnerability Index (SVI) of CA [8,42], which leads to non-trivial nonstationary high-order spatio-temporal interactions in COVID-19 hospitalizations. Similar findings on the dynamics of gains in RMSE are observed in other datasets, particularly, in the mobility networks, e.g., NYC-Bike has the highest 3-node MCl of 20.08, follows by 10.67 for NYC-Taxi and 4.65 for BJ-Taxi (for more discussions on traffic flow datasets, see Table 4 in Appendix B.6). Hence, we postulate that when such heterogeneous higher-order interactions manifest, H^2-Nets may be the preferred approach for spatio-temporal forecasting. This indicates the necessity to consider both higher-order interactions and hyper-simplex-graph representation learning for node-level forecasting in multivariate time-series.

Table 3. Performance on BJ-Taxi demand (*left*) and COVID-19 hospitalizations in CA and PA (*right*).

Datasets	BJ-Taxi	
Model/Metrics	RMSE	MAPE (%)
ARIMA	23.96 ± 0.07	32.21 ± 0.02
SVR	22.07 ± 0.06	22.31 ± 0.04
Fuzzy+NN	23.02 ± 0.33	22.83 ± 0.35
RNN	27.93 ± 0.53	24.79 ± 0.51
LSTM	27.52 ± 0.55	24.13 ± 0.43
DeepST	21.02 ± 0.42	22.53 ± 0.41
ST-ResNet	22.32 ± 0.24	23.77 ± 0.43
DMVST-Net	17.12 ± 0.30	23.09 ± 0.31
STDN	18.62 ± 0.20	22.14 ± 0.19
UrbanFM	18.45 ± 0.15	20.89 ± 0.27
ST-MetaNet	18.28 ± 0.25	20.77 ± 0.28
ST-GCN	18.33 ± 0.17	20.75 ± 0.22
ST-MGCN	18.27 ± 0.19	20.73 ± 0.19
H^2-Nets (ours)*	**18.20** ± 0.15*	**16.51** ± 0.17

Model	CA		PA	
	RMSE	MAPE (%)	RMSE	MAPE (%)
ARIMA	497.75	63.08	110.95	71.38
LSTM	512.23 ± 6.00	72.64 ± 5.39	109.71 ± 1.82	74.11 ± 4.69
DCRNN	492.10 ± 2.96	69.83 ± 5.57	107.21 ± 1.63	67.15 ± 3.94
LSTNet	480.61 ± 3.91	67.72 ± 2.17	105.67 ± 1.76	72.33 ± 4.21
ST-GCN	470.52 ± 3.06	69.73 ± 5.69	106.78 ± 1.87	69.36 ± 4.59
TCN	492.82 ± 3.54	70.00 ± 6.92	105.07 ± 1.90	69.86 ± 4.91
DeepState	469.15 ± 3.71	68.24 ± 5.79	107.61 ± 2.31	67.69 ± 4.21
GraphWaveNet	394.83 ± 3.35	67.61 ± 5.36	109.41 ± 1.91	69.39 ± 4.27
DeepGLO	455.80 ± 3.18	67.35 ± 5.99	103.74 ± 2.07	68.71 ± 4.09
AGCRN	448.27 ± 2.78	66.30 ± 5.17	103.79 ± 3.08	63.45 ± 4.00
StemGNN	377.25 ± 3.91	67.90 ± 5.94	103.15 ± 1.87	63.47 ± 4.11
Z-GCNETs	356.35 ± 3.20	62.81 ± 5.75	106.22 ± 1.27	65.89 ± 4.66
H^2-Nets (ours)*	**346.83 ± 2.80**	**56.13 ± 5.61**	**101.92 ± 1.53**	**62.05 ± 4.53**

Ablation Study and Computational Complexity. To evaluate the performance of different components in our H^2-Nets model, we perform extensive ablation studies on NYC-Taxi (in outflow), NYC-Bike (in outflow), BJ-Taxi, CA, and PA, and results are presented in Table 4 (for the sake of brevity, we only report results for the NYC-Taxi and CA datasets; for further results on other datasets, please refer to Table 3 in Appendix B.5). We develop three variants of H^2-Nets, i.e., (i) H^2-Nets without hyper-k-simplex representation learning, (ii) H^2-Nets without self-adaptive k-simplex convolution, and (iii) H^2-Nets without k-Hodge convolution. The results demonstrate that, when ablating the above three components, both RMSE and MAPE increase significantly. For all datasets, hyper-k-simplex representation learning significantly improves the results as it learns hidden higher-order interactions representations beyond the node-space. Moreover, we show that H^2-Nets outperforms H^2-Nets without k-Hodge convolution due to the fact that it takes into account locality of data living over higher-dimensional structures and allows us to consider richer data structure information. Furthermore, we observe that self-adaptive k-simplex convolution always improve the performance – the reason is that self-adaptive k-simplex convolution can capture the hidden dependency across different dimensions in the data. For incidence matrices $\boldsymbol{B}_1$ and $\boldsymbol{B}_2$ can be calculated efficiently with the computational complexity $\mathcal{O}(N+M)$ and $\mathcal{O}(M+Q)$ respectively, where Q is the number of 2-simplices. If there is no predefined hyper-k-simplex structures in graph data, we can use the method described in the Appendix B to construct them of appropriate size. It takes computation of order $\mathcal{O}(N+C^2)$, where C is maximal number of candidate hyper-k-simplexes before selection.

Table 4. Ablation study for H^2-Nets.

	Architecture	RMSE	MAPE
NYC-Taxi	**H^2-Nets**	*****23.64**	*****14.68**
	W/o Hyper-k-simplex learning	28.05	15.53
	W/o Self-adaptive k-simplex convolution	25.47	15.31
	W/o k-Hodge convolution	27.05	16.38
CA	**H^2-Nets**	*****346.83**	**56.13**
	W/o Hyper-k-simplex	364.04	68.76
	W/o Self-adaptive k-simplex convolution	358.51	60.12
	W/o k-Hodge convolution	401.43	78.99

6 Conclusion

Inspired by the recent advances on applications of the discrete Hodge theory to graph learning, we have proposed the first hypergraph-simplicial neural network for spatio-temporal forecasting. We have shown that similarly to simple graphs, higher-order interactions among hypergraph substructures play important roles in the knowledge representation and learning mechanisms. In the future, we will advance the ideas of simplicial convolution on hypergraphs to node and subgraph classification in conjunction with resiliency quantification of cyber-physical systems.

Acknowledgements. This work was supported by the NASA grant # 21-AIST21_2-0059 and the ONR grant # N00014-21-1-2530. The views expressed in the article do not necessarily represent the views of the NASA and ONR.

Ethical Statement. The H^2-Nets approach and, more generally, the ideas of Hodge theory open a new pathway for learning the key multi-node interactions in many domains associated with spatio-temporal data analysis where such critical higher-order interactions are typically neglected. Such applications range from wildfire plume tracking in complex terrains to bio-threat surveillance to human mobility monitoring. While we do not anticipate any negative societal impacts of the proposed H^2-Nets ideas and the concepts of the Hodge theory, it is important to emphasise that we currently lack any formal inferential tools to quantify the uncertainties associated with learning high-order interactions, which limits our abilities in risk quantification as well as interpretability and explainability.

References

1. Agarwal, S., Branson, K., Belongie, S.: Higher order learning with graphs. In: Proceedings of the International Conference on Machine Learning, pp. 17–24 (2006)
2. Arya, D., Gupta, D.K., Rudinac, S., Worring, M.: Hypersage: generalizing inductive representation learning on hypergraphs. arXiv preprint arXiv:2010.04558 (2020)
3. Atwood, J., Towsley, D.: Diffusion-convolutional neural networks. In: Advances in Neural Information Processing Systems, vol. 29. Curran Associates, Inc. (2016)
4. Bai, L., Yao, L., Li, C., Wang, X., Wang, C.: Adaptive graph convolutional recurrent network for traffic forecasting. In: Larochelle, H., Ranzato, M., Hadsell, R., Balcan, M.F., Lin, H. (eds.) Advances in Neural Information Processing Systems, vol. 33, pp. 17804–17815. Curran Associates, Inc. (2020)
5. Bai, S., Kolter, J.Z., Koltun, V.: An empirical evaluation of generic convolutional and recurrent networks for sequence modeling. arXiv preprint arXiv:1803.01271 (2018)
6. Barbarossa, S., Sardellitti, S., Ceci, E.: Learning from signals defined over simplicial complexes. In: IEEE Data Science Workshop. IEEE (2018)
7. Benson, A.R., Abebe, R., Schaub, M.T., Jadbabaie, A., Kleinberg, J.: Simplicial closure and higher-order link prediction. Proc. Natl. Acad. Sci. USA **115**(48), E11221–E11230 (2018)
8. Bilal, U., Jemmott, J.B., Schnake-Mahl, A., Murphy, K., Momplaisir, F.: Racial/ethnic and neighbourhood social vulnerability disparities in COVID-19 testing positivity, hospitalization, and in-hospital mortality in a large hospital system in Pennsylvania: a prospective study of electronic health records. Lancet Reg. Health-Am. **10**, 100220 (2022)
9. Bodnar, C., et al.: Weisfeiler and lehman go topological: message passing simplicial networks. In: ICLR 2021 Workshop on Geometrical and Topological Representation Learning (2021)
10. Bolla, M.: Spectra, euclidean representations and clusterings of hypergraphs. Discret. Math. **117**(1–3), 19–39 (1993)
11. Bronstein, M.M., Bruna, J., Cohen, T., Veličković, P.: Geometric deep learning: grids, groups, graphs, geodesics, and gauges (2021)

12. Bunch, E., You, Q., Fung, G., Singh, V.: Simplicial 2-complex convolutional neural networks. In: NeurIPS 2020 Workshop on Topological Data Analysis and Beyond (2020)
13. Cao, D., et al.: Spectral temporal graph neural network for multivariate time-series forecasting. In: Advances in Neural Information Processing Systems (2020)
14. Chen, Y., Jiang, T., Heleno, M., Moreira, A., Gel, Y.R.: Evaluating distribution system reliability with hyperstructures graph convolutional nets. In: IEEE International Conference on Big Data, pp. 1793–1800 (2022)
15. Chen, Y., Batsakis, S., Poor, H.V.: Higher-order spatio-temporal neural networks for COVID-19 forecasting. In: IEEE International Conference on Acoustics, Speech and Signal Processing, pp. 1–5. IEEE (2023)
16. Chen, Y., Gel, Y., Poor, H.V.: Time-conditioned dances with simplicial complexes: zigzag filtration curve based supra-hodge convolution networks for time-series forecasting. Adv. Neural. Inf. Process. Syst. **35**, 8940–8953 (2022)
17. Chen, Y., Gel, Y.R., Poor, H.V.: BScNets: block simplicial complex neural networks. In: Proceedings of the AAAI Conference on Artificial Intelligence (2022)
18. Chen, Y., Heleno, M., Moreira, A., Gel, Y.R.: Topological graph convolutional networks solutions for power distribution grid planning. In: Pacific-Asia Conference on Knowledge Discovery and Data Mining, pp. 123–134 (2023)
19. Chen, Y., Jacob, R.A., Gel, Y.R., Zhang, J., Poor, H.V.: Learning power grid outages with higher-order topological neural networks. IEEE Trans. Power Syst. (2023)
20. Chen, Y., Segovia, I., Gel, Y.R.: Z-GCNETs: time zigzags at graph convolutional networks for time series forecasting. In: Proceedings of the International Conference on Machine Learning, pp. 1684–1694 (2021)
21. Chen, Y., Segovia-Dominguez, I., Coskunuzer, B., Gel, Y.: Tamp-s2gcnets: coupling time-aware multipersistence knowledge representation with spatio-supra graph convolutional networks for time-series forecasting. In: International Conference on Learning Representations (2022)
22. Ebli, S., Defferrard, M., Spreemann, G.: Simplicial neural networks. In: Topological Data Analysis and Beyond workshop at Advances in Neural Information Processing Systems (2020)
23. Feng, Y., You, H., Zhang, Z., Ji, R., Gao, Y.: Hypergraph neural networks. In: Proceedings of the AAAI Conference on Artificial Intelligence, vol. 33, pp. 3558–3565 (2019)
24. Geng, X., et al.: Spatiotemporal multi-graph convolution network for ride-hailing demand forecasting. In: Proceedings of the AAAI Conference on Artificial Intelligence, vol. 33, pp. 3656–3663 (2019)
25. Gilmer, J., Schoenholz, S.S., Riley, P.F., Vinyals, O., Dahl, G.E.: Neural message passing for quantum chemistry. In: Precup, D., Teh, Y.W. (eds.) Proceedings of the International Conference on Machine Learning. Proceedings of Machine Learning Research, vol. 70, pp. 1263–1272. PMLR (2017)
26. Guo, S., Lin, Y., Feng, N., Song, C., Wan, H.: Attention based spatial-temporal graph convolutional networks for traffic flow forecasting. In: Proceedings of the AAAI Conference on Artificial Intelligence, vol. 33, pp. 922–929 (2019)
27. Hajij, M., Istvan, K., Zamzmi, G.: Cell complex neural networks. In: NeurIPS 2020 Workshop on Topological Data Analysis and Beyond (2020)
28. Hamilton, W.L., Ying, R., Leskovec, J.: Inductive representation learning on large graphs. In: Advances in Neural Information Processing Systems (2017)
29. Hochreiter, S., Schmidhuber, J.: Long short-term memory. Neural Comput. **9**(8), 1735–1780 (1997)

30. Hsiao, W.Y., Liu, J.Y., Yeh, Y.C., Yang, Y.H.: Compound word transformer: learning to compose full-song music over dynamic directed hypergraphs. In: Proceedings of the AAAI Conference on Artificial Intelligence, pp. 4503–4511 (2021)
31. Huang, J., Yang, J.: UniGNN: a unified framework for graph and hypergraph neural networks. In: Proceedings of the International Joint Conference on Artificial Intelligence (2021)
32. Jiang, J., Wei, Y., Feng, Y., Cao, J., Gao, Y.: Dynamic hypergraph neural networks. In: Proceedings of the International Joint Conference on Artificial Intelligence (2019)
33. Karimi, A.M., Wu, Y., Koyuturk, M., French, R.H.: Spatiotemporal graph neural network for performance prediction of photovoltaic power systems. In: Proceedings of the AAAI Conference on Artificial Intelligence, vol. 35, pp. 15323–15330 (2021)
34. Kipf, T.N., Welling, M.: Semi-supervised classification with graph convolutional networks. In: Proceedings of the International Conference on Learning Representations (2017)
35. Lai, G., Chang, W.C., Yang, Y., Liu, H.: Modeling long-and short-term temporal patterns with deep neural networks. In: ACM SIGIR Conference on Research & Development in Information Retrieval, pp. 95–104 (2018)
36. Li, Y., Yu, R., Shahabi, C., Liu, Y.: Diffusion convolutional recurrent neural network: data-driven traffic forecasting. In: Proceedings of the International Conference on Learning Representations (2018)
37. Liang, Y., et al.: UrbanFM: inferring fine-grained urban flows. In: Proceedings of the ACM SIGKDD International Conference on Knowledge Discovery & Data Mining. ACM (2019)
38. Lim, L.H.: Hodge laplacians on graphs. SIAM Rev. **62**(3), 685–715 (2020)
39. Oreshkin, B.N., Carpov, D., Chapados, N., Bengio, Y.: N-beats: neural basis expansion analysis for interpretable time series forecasting. In: Proceedings of the International Conference on Learning Representations (2019)
40. Pan, Z., Liang, Y., Wang, W., Yu, Y., Zheng, Y., Zhang, J.: Urban traffic prediction from spatio-temporal data using deep meta learning. In: Proceedings of the ACM SIGKDD International Conference on Knowledge Discovery & Data Mining. ACM (2019)
41. Rangapuram, S.S., Seeger, M.W., Gasthaus, J., Stella, L., Wang, Y., Januschowski, T.: Deep state space models for time series forecasting. In: Advances in Neural Information Processing Systems, vol. 31 (2018)
42. Reitsma, M.B., et al.: Racial/ethnic disparities in COVID-19 exposure risk, testing, and cases at the subcounty level in California: study examines racial/ethnic disparities in COVID-19 risk, testing, and cases. Health Aff. **40**(6), 870–878 (2021)
43. Roddenberry, T.M., Glaze, N., Segarra, S.: Principled simplicial neural networks for trajectory prediction. In: Meila, M., Zhang, T. (eds.) Proceedings of the 38th International Conference on Machine Learning. Proceedings of Machine Learning Research, vol. 139, pp. 9020–9029. PMLR (2021)
44. Roddenberry, T.M., Segarra, S.: HodgeNet: graph neural networks for edge data. In: The 53rd Asilomar Conference on Signals, Systems, and Computers. IEEE (2019)
45. Sawhney, R., Agarwal, S., Wadhwa, A., Derr, T., Shah, R.R.: Stock selection via spatiotemporal hypergraph attention network: a learning to rank approach. In: Proceedings of the AAAI Conference on Artificial Intelligence, vol. 35, pp. 497–504 (2021)

46. Schaub, M.T., Benson, A.R., Horn, P., Lippner, G., Jadbabaie, A.: Random walks on simplicial complexes and the normalized hodge 1-laplacian. SIAM Rev. **62**(2), 353–391 (2020)
47. Schaub, M.T., Zhu, Y., Seby, J.B., Roddenberry, T.M., Segarra, S.: Signal processing on higher-order networks: livin'on the edge... and beyond. Signal Process. **187**, 108149 (2021)
48. Sen, R., Yu, H.F., Dhillon, I.S.: Think globally, act locally: a deep neural network approach to high-dimensional time series forecasting. In: Advances in Neural Information Processing Systems, vol. 32 (2019)
49. Song, C., Lin, Y., Guo, S., Wan, H.: Spatial-temporal synchronous graph convolutional networks: A new framework for spatial-temporal network data forecasting. In: Proceedings of the AAAI Conference on Artificial Intelligence, vol. 34, no. 01, pp. 914–921 (2020)
50. Srinivasan, D., Chan, C.W., Balaji, P.: Computational intelligence-based congestion prediction for a dynamic urban street network. Neurocomputing **72**(10–12), 2710–2716 (2009)
51. Sun, X., et al.: Heterogeneous hypergraph embedding for graph classification. In: Proceedings of the ACM International Conference on Web Search and Data Mining, pp. 725–733 (2021)
52. Tran, A., Mathews, A., Ong, C.S., Xie, L.: Radflow: a recurrent, aggregated, and decomposable model for networks of time series. In: Proceedings of the International World Wide Web Conference, pp. 730–742 (2021)
53. Wang, J., Zhang, Y., Wei, Y., Hu, Y., Piao, X., Yin, B.: Metro passenger flow prediction via dynamic hypergraph convolution networks. IEEE Trans. Intell. Transp. Syst. **22**(12), 7891–7903 (2021)
54. Wu, S., Rizoiu, M.A., Xie, L.: Estimating attention flow in online video networks. Proc. ACM Hum.-Comput. Interact. **3**, 1–25 (2019)
55. Wu, Z., Pan, S., Chen, F., Long, G., Zhang, C., Yu, P.S.: A comprehensive survey on graph neural networks. IEEE Trans. Neural Netw. Learn. Syst. **32**(1), 4–24 (2021)
56. Wu, Z., Pan, S., Long, G., Jiang, J., Zhang, C.: Graph WaveNet for deep spatial-temporal graph modeling. In: Proceedings of the International Joint Conference on Artificial Intelligence. International Joint Conferences on Artificial Intelligence Organization (2019)
57. Xia, L., Huang, C., Xu, Y., Dai, P., Bo, L., Zhang, X., Chen, T.: Spatial-temporal sequential hypergraph network for crime prediction with dynamic multiplex relation learning. In: Proceedings of the International Joint Conference on Artificial Intelligence (2021)
58. Yadati, N., Nimishakavi, M., Yadav, P., Nitin, V., Louis, A., Talukdar, P.: Hypergcn: a new method of training graph convolutional networks on hypergraphs. In: Advances in Neural Information Processing Systems, pp. 1511–1522 (2019)
59. Yan, S., Xiong, Y., Lin, D.: Spatial temporal graph convolutional networks for skeleton-based action recognition. In: Proceedings of the AAAI Conference on Artificial Intelligence (2018)
60. Yao, H., Tang, X., Wei, H., Zheng, G., Li, Z.: Revisiting spatial-temporal similarity: a deep learning framework for traffic prediction. In: Proceedings of the AAAI Conference on Artificial Intelligence (2019)
61. Yao, H., et al.: Deep multi-view spatial-temporal network for taxi demand prediction. In: Proceedings of the AAAI Conference on Artificial Intelligence (2018)

62. Yi, J., Park, J.: Hypergraph convolutional recurrent neural network. In: Proceedings of the ACM SIGKDD International Conference on Knowledge Discovery & Data Mining August 2020. ACM (2020)
63. Yin, H., Benson, A.R., Leskovec, J.: Higher-order clustering in networks. Phys. Rev. E **97**(5), 052306 (2018)
64. Yin, N., et al.: Dynamic hypergraph convolutional network. In: IEEE International Conference on Data Engineering (2022)
65. Yu, B., Yin, H., Zhu, Z.: Spatio-temporal graph convolutional networks: a deep learning framework for traffic forecasting. In: Proceedings of the International Joint Conference on Artificial Intelligence. International Joint Conferences on Artificial Intelligence Organization (2018)
66. Zhang, J., Zheng, Y., Qi, D.: Deep spatio-temporal residual networks for citywide crowd flows prediction. In: Proceedings of the AAAI Conference on Artificial Intelligence, pp. 1655–1661 (2017)
67. Zhang, J., Zheng, Y., Qi, D., Li, R., Yi, X.: DNN-based prediction model for spatio-temporal data. In: Proceedings of the ACM SIGSPATIAL International Conference on Advances in Geographic Information Systems. ACM (2016)
68. Zheng, W., Yan, L., Gou, C., Wang, F.Y.: Two heads are better than one: hypergraph-enhanced graph reasoning for visual event ratiocination. In: Proceedings of the International Conference on Machine Learning, vol. 139, pp. 12747–12760 (2021)

Transfer and Multitask Learning

Overcoming Catastrophic Forgetting for Fine-Tuning Pre-trained GANs

Zeren Zhang[1], Xingjian Li[2], Tao Hong[1], Tianyang Wang[3], Jinwen Ma[1(✉)], Haoyi Xiong[2], and Cheng-Zhong Xu[4]

[1] School of Mathematical Sciences, Peking University, Beijing 100871, China
jwma@math.pku.edu.cn
[2] Baidu Inc., Beijing, China
[3] University of Alabama at Birmingham, Birmingham, AL 35294, USA
[4] University of Macau, Macau, China

Abstract. The great transferability of DNNs has induced a popular paradigm of "pre-training & fine-tuning", by which a data-scarce task can be performed much more easily. However, compared to the existing efforts made in the context of supervised transfer learning, fewer explorations have been made on effectively fine-tuning pre-trained Generative Adversarial Networks (GANs). As reported in recent empirical studies, fine-tuning GANs faces the similar challenge of catastrophic forgetting as in supervised transfer learning. This causes a severe capacity loss of the pre-trained model when adapting it to downstream datasets. While most existing approaches suggest to directly interfere parameter updating, this paper introduces novel schemes from another perspective, i.e. inputs and features, thus essentially focuses on data aspect. Firstly, we adopt a trust-region method to smooth the adaptation dynamics by progressively adjusting input distributions, aiming to avoid dramatic parameter changes, especially when the pre-trained GAN has no information of target data. Secondly, we aim to avoid the loss of the diversity of the generated results of the fine-tuned GAN. This is achieved by explicitly encouraging generated images to encompass diversified spectral components in their deep features. We theoretically study the rationale of the proposed schemes, and conduct extensive experiments on popular transfer learning benchmarks to demonstrate the superiority of the schemes. The code and corresponding supplemental materials are available at https://github.com/zezeze97/Transfer-Pretrained-Gan.

Keywords: Transfer Learning · Generative Adversarial Networks

1 Introduction

Deep Neural Networks have illustrated not only a success on learning from large-scale datasets, but also a great transferability on various downstream tasks. This

Z. Zhang and X. Li—Equal contribution.

D. Koutra et al. (Eds.): ECML PKDD 2023, LNAI 14173, pp. 293–308, 2023.
https://doi.org/10.1007/978-3-031-43424-2_18

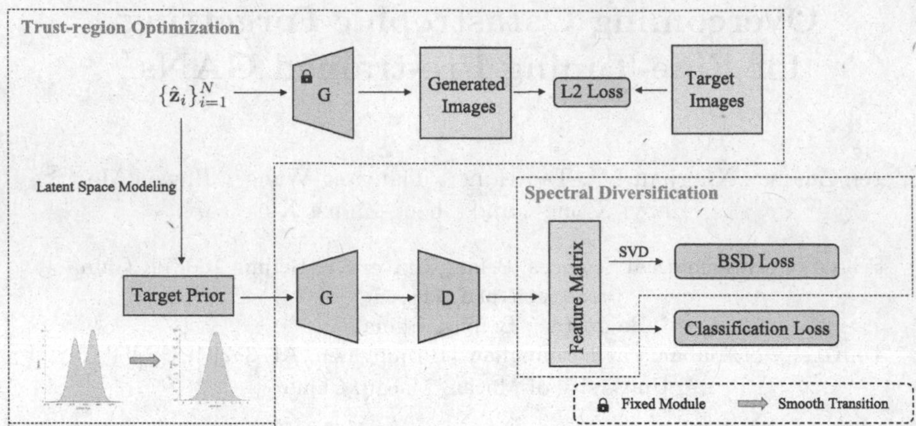

Fig. 1. Overview of our schemes in GAN fine-tuning. The Trust-Region Optimization scheme models input distributions based on target data, and dynamically adjusts input distributions by progressively aligning them with the standard Gaussian distribution (Smooth Transition). The Spectral Diversification module is designed to improve the diversity of generated data, aiming to address mode collapse.

property facilitates a highly practical learning fashion, in which one can firstly initialize a target model with a publicly available checkpoint, well-trained over rich upstream data, and then adapt the model to a target dataset by fine-tuning. While much effort has been arguably made on discriminative transfer learning, e.g. in image classification, very little work has focused on how to effectively fine-tuning GANs. To our best knowledge, [27] pioneered the first systematic study of fine-tuning pre-trained GANs, and confirmed its superiority over training from scratch.

Generally, fine-tuning makes learning with small target datasets much easier. However, directly using a pre-trained GAN to initialize a target model may still result in a poor performance, i.e. suffering from the notorious issue of mode collapse, which can be attributed to *catastrophic forgetting* [7]. To mitigate this issue, most existing works suggest to explicitly restrict the model parameter change within a small scope of the starting point, inspired by the similar practices in supervised fine-tuning [6,13]. However, we observe that such a scheme is much less effective for GAN fine-tuning, as it tends to hinder a full adaptation to the target distribution. In order to address the catastrophic forgetting in GAN fine-tuning, we need to answer the following two fundamental questions.

Q1. Why does catastrophic forgetting occur? While existing studies have recognized catastrophic forgetting as a common issue in DNNs, we aim to explore particular reasons related to GAN fine-tuning. We argue that one primary reason is because of the **discrepancy** between the initial outputs of pre-trained GANs and target data distributions in raw pixel space. Unlike supervised transfer learning, GANs perform mapping from a low-dimensional dense variable $\mathbf{z}$

to a high-dimensional sparse space $\mathcal{X}$. Consequently, without properly adjusting $\mathbf{z}$, there will be such a discrepancy, which could result in aggressive and unexpected parameter changes at early fine-tuning stages, since the generator has no sufficient clues of target data at these stages. As a result, existing transferable knowledge is subject to being destroyed due to this discrepancy.

Q2. How to detect and prevent catastrophic forgetting in GAN fine-tuning? As widely acknowledged, the manifestation of catastrophic forgetting in GAN fine-tuning can be easily recognized (many duplicate images observed). However, automatically detecting such duplicates is quite challenging in a high-dimensional and complex raw pixel space. To address this challenge, we propose to quantify the degree of diversity (a higher diversity degree indicates a less severe mode collapse) by using the approximate rank of the feature matrix w.r.t. a set of generated images. The rationale of using the approximate rank is theoretically demonstrated in Sect. 3.2, and an empirical analysis can be found in Fig. 4. In terms of diversity, although the existence of catastrophic forgetting can be confirmed, we still need an efficient approach to suppress the duplicate generations in an end-to-end fashion during fine-tuning.

Following the understanding of the two aforementioned questions, we propose two learning schemes, described as follows, aiming to overcome catastrophic forgetting in GAN fine-tuning. We illustrate the roles of the two schemes for GAN fine-tuning in Fig. 1.

Trust-Region Optimization. To prevent model parameters from being unstably updated, we adopt the classical idea of trust-region based optimization [4], which has been successfully applied on training deep NLP models [1,10]. For GAN fine-tuning, we firstly re-model the input distribution, instead of using the default Gaussian $\mathcal{N}(\mathbf{0}, \mathbf{I})$, to find an initial trust-region for updating GAN's parameters. Specifically, we model the input prior with a Gaussian Mixture Model (GMM), of which parameters are determined by an inverse projection from the target image X to the latent vector $\mathbf{z}$. As fine-tuning proceeds, we progressively align the input distribution with $\mathcal{N}(\mathbf{0}, \mathbf{I})$, which is widely acknowledged as being friendly to neural network computing [9,25]. By using this scheme, we adjust the input distribution based on the knowledge learned in pre-trained GANs, to fully leverage the information in source data.

Spectral Diversification. To efficiently monitor and handle the occurrence of mode collapse in an end-to-end fashion, we perform Singular Value Decomposition (SVD) on a stochastic batch of examples, following the similar practice in discriminative fine-tuning [3]. Then, we involve a regularizer to increase the smallest singular value of the feature matrix, rather than directly approximating the matrix rank. Intuitively, the matrix will tend to have a higher rank, i.e. including more basic features, if the tail spectral components cannot be ignored. This scheme is particularly beneficial when the target dataset is small.

We conduct extensive experiments on three popular transfer learning benchmarks. The promising results demonstrate the superiority of our schemes in fine-tuning pre-trained GANs. More importantly, our schemes focus on data aspect (input and feature), leading to its architecture-agnostic nature.

2 Background and Related Work

2.1 Deep Transfer Learning

Our work is largely motivated by deep transfer learning for classification, but we solve a very different problem. This section is discussed in detail in the Appendix A.1.

2.2 Generative Adversarial Networks (GANs)

Generative Adversarial Network (GAN) is originally proposed to generate data of which distribution is expected to be the same as that of the real data used in training. Modern GANs are capable of generating rather realistic high-resolution images [2]. Formally, GAN takes a latent vector $\mathbf{z}$ as the input, sampled from a prior distribution $p_{\mathbf{z}}$, and outputs an image $\mathbf{x} = G(\mathbf{z})$, which is learned to lie in a distribution that is ideally the same as the distribution of real data p_{data}. In addition to the generator G, a discriminator D is also needed to leverage the gaming theory (Nash equilibrium). The two networks compete with each other to achieve an improved performance for both. Denoting the parameters of G and D with θ_G and θ_D respectively, the goal is to solve the following minmax optimization objective

$$\begin{aligned} \theta_G, \theta_D = \min_{G} \max_{D} & \mathbb{E}_{\mathbf{x}\sim p_{data}}[\log D(\mathbf{x})] \\ & + \mathbb{E}_{\mathbf{z}\sim p_{\mathbf{z}}}[\log(1 - D(G(\mathbf{z}))]. \end{aligned} \tag{1}$$

One big challenge in training GANs is the notorious *mode collapse* issue, i.e. lacking diversity in generated data. This is primarily due to the fact that the learning objective is incapable of successfully modeling the entire data distribution. Existing works aim to address this issue by refining network architectures [11,23] or designing novel loss functions [8,20]. While these methods yield better performance on classical GAN training, very little work focuses on the issue in GAN fine-tuning. To leverage the pre-learned knowledge in the context of transfer learning, we propose a novel scheme to preserve the information of diversity learned by pre-trained GANs.

2.3 Transfer Learning for GANs

Following the pioneering work TransGAN [27] that initiates the research of GAN-based transfer learning, several studies make efforts to overcome catastrophic forgetting for GAN fine-tuning. Most of them attempt to freeze several parts of pre-trained GANs, and only fine-tune the other parts or involve additional adapters. Specifically, BSA [19] proposes to only fine-tune the parameters in batch normalization and freeze all the other parameters of the generator. FreezeD [16] instead freezes the shallower layers of the discriminator and updates the others. AdaFM [31] adopts a similar idea of freezing several shallow layers, but further incorporates adaptive filter modules for a better adaptation to target tasks.

MineGAN [26] also introduces additional modules to mine knowledge from one or several pre-trained GANs. In general, these methods can be categorized into two groups, namely *with additional modules* and *without additional modules*. In this paper, we select one representative from each group for experimental comparison. For the first group, we choose AdaFM [31], and for the second, we choose FreezeD [16].

In addition to the aforementioned comprehensive GAN-based transfer learning literature, there are several other works focusing on a particular learning fashion customized for GANs, such as few-shot [12,14,21,29,32], one-shot [30], and zero-shot [28] learning for GANs. In such scenarios, the target dataset could include 0, 1, or only a few (typically fewer than 10) training samples. Rather than special cases, our work focuses on general scenarios of GAN fine-tuning, in which the amount of the training samples in a target dataset could range from dozens to thousands.

3 Approach

To overcome the issue of catastrophic forgetting in GAN fine-tuning, we propose two learning schemes, namely trust-region optimization and spectral diversification. They address the issue from two perspectives, but serve the same goal. The use of one scheme will not directly impact the use of the other, and each of them can be used independently for GAN fine-tuning. We describe the two schemes in Sect. 3.1 and 3.2, respectively.

3.1 Trust-Region Optimization

In this section, we firstly introduce the basic idea and form of trust-region optimization in Sect. 3.1. Then we present our implementation of the trust-region optimization for fine-tuning pre-trained GANs. The core at our implementation includes target prior initialization (Sect. 3.1) and alternate parameter updating (Sect. 3.1).

Preliminary and Motivation

Trust region algorithms [4] attempt to search for the optimal point near a currently estimated solution, and they can be traced back to the Levenberg-Marquardt method [17] for solving nonlinear equations. For deep transfer learning, a typical example is the Bregman Proximal Point Optimization [24], which has been successfully applied in fine-tuning BERT-based NLP models [1,10]. Let us denote a general supervised learner by $f(\mathbf{x};\theta)$ with $\mathbf{x} \in X$ as its input and θ as its parameters. L denotes the Empirical Risk Minimizer (ERM), and D_{KL} denotes the symmetric KL-divergence. At each iteration t, Bregman Proximal Point Optimization (BPPO) treats the region near the current solution θ^t as the *trust region*, leading to a regularized learning objective

$$\theta^{t+1} = \arg\min_{\theta} L(\theta) + \lambda L_{Breg}(\theta, \theta^t), \tag{2}$$

where λ adjusts the contribution of the regularizer and L_{Breg} is defined as

$$L_{Breg}(\theta, \theta^t) = \sum_{\mathbf{x} \in X} D_{KL}(f(\mathbf{x}; \theta), f(\mathbf{x}; \theta^t)). \tag{3}$$

While using supervised pre-trained models can obtain good initial outputs for downstream tasks (e.g. linear probing is an acceptable way to directly reuse pre-trained feature extractor), it is not a typical solution for transferring GANs due to the large discrepancy in raw pixel space (i.e. high-dimensional images).

To adapt trust-region methods to GAN fine-tuning, we propose to find a good starting point for optimizing θ_G by aligning the input prior with a better $p^*_{\mathbf{z}}$. Analogical to the BPPO regularizer in Eq. (3), our trust-region scheme for GAN fine-tuning can be regarded as incorporating an implicit inductive bias in minimizing

$$\mathbb{E}_{\mathbf{z} \sim p^*_{\mathbf{z}}}[D_{Pix}(G(\mathbf{z}; \theta), G(\mathbf{z}; \theta^0_G))], \tag{4}$$

where D_{Pix} is the pixel-wise Euclidean distance, and $G(\mathbf{z}; \theta^0_G)$ with $\mathbf{z} \sim p^*_{\mathbf{z}}$ serves as an initial solution of the *trust region*. In the following two sections, we describe the initial computation and progressive updates for $p^*_{\mathbf{z}}$.

Target Prior Initialization

Computing Optimal Latent Vectors. Let $X = \{\mathbf{x}_i\}_{i=1}^N$ denote a training dataset, where N is the number of the training examples. In GAN fine-tuning, a generator G with its pre-trained parameters θ^0_G is available. Then we can compute the optimal latent vector $\hat{\mathbf{z}}_i$ for each data $\mathbf{x}_i$ as

$$\hat{\mathbf{z}}_i = \arg\min_{\mathbf{z}} \|G(\mathbf{z}; \theta^0_G) - \mathbf{x}_i\|^2_2. \tag{5}$$

To solve the GAN inversion problem [34], we freeze θ^0_G and perform gradient descent on $\mathbf{z}$, resulting in target-adapted latent vectors $Z = \{\hat{\mathbf{z}}_i\}_{i=1}^N$, which lead to the lowest error when using $G(\mathbf{z}; \theta^0_G)$ to approximate a x_i.

Initializing Target Prior with GMM. To generalize the prior information extracted by a pre-trained generator, we assume that the optimal latent variable conforms to a probabilistic distribution. Specifically, we employ the classical Gaussian Mixture Model (GMM) to approximate the target prior. Therefore, the initial distribution of $\mathbf{z}$, denoted by $p^0(\mathbf{z})$, can be formalized by a GMM with K independent components as

$$p^0(\mathbf{z}) = \sum_{k=1}^{K} \phi_k \mathcal{N}(\mathbf{z} | \mu^0_k, \mathbf{\Sigma}^0_k), \tag{6}$$

where ϕ_k is the k-th coefficient satisfying $\sum_{k=1}^K \phi_k = 1$, and $\mu^0_k, \mathbf{\Sigma}^0_k$ are the mean vector and covariance matrix of the k-th component. In practice, the number of the components K can be empirically chosen, and we observe that $K = 5$ is appropriate for most cases, as demonstrated in our experiments. The parameters $\{\phi_k, \mu^0_k, \mathbf{\Sigma}^0_k\}_{k=1}^K$ are solved by using the Expectation-maximization (EM) algorithm, in which the E-step computes the expectation of the component assignments given current parameters, and the M-step maximizes this expectation by updating $\{\phi_k, \mu^0_k, \mathbf{\Sigma}^0_k\}_{k=1}^K$.

Alternate Updating Between z and G
Although the GMM prior $p^0(\mathbf{z})$ provides better initial generated results and smoother parameter updates for the generator, the shifted input distribution is less friendly to neural network computing [9,25], compared with the zero-mean Gaussian input. Therefore, we implement a progressive process that moves the input distribution from the GMM prior $p^0(\mathbf{z})$ to the standard Gaussian distribution, alternating with the updates of GAN's parameters θ_G and θ_D. Specifically, denoting by T the total number of iterations for gradient updates, at each iteration $t = 1, 2, ...T$, the mean vector and covariance matrix of the input distribution $p^t(\mathbf{z})$ are adjusted by

$$\begin{aligned} \mu_k^t &= \mu_k^0 - \frac{t}{T}\mu_k^0, \\ \mathbf{\Sigma}_k^t &= \mathbf{\Sigma}_k^0 - \frac{t}{T}(\mathbf{\Sigma}_k^0 - \mathbf{I}). \end{aligned} \tag{7}$$

In this way, the parameters θ_G and θ_D are optimized near the trust regions within the entire optimization trajectory, and the input distribution progressively fits the computing-friendly region. At the end of fine-tuning, $p^T(\mathbf{z})$ reaches the standard Gaussian distribution $\mathcal{N}(\mathbf{0}, \mathbf{I})$. It can be easily validated that each intermediate $\mathbf{\Sigma}_k^t$ is also a valid covariance matrix. The proof is presented in Appendix A.2.

3.2 Spectral Diversification

Our scheme of spectral diversification is established on the theory of low-rank approximation. Specifically, in Sect. 3.2 we introduce truncated SVD as a theoretically guaranteed metric (i.e. rank of the embedding matrix) to identify mode collapse. Then, in Sect. 3.2 we describe our efficient implementation, namely Batch Spectral Diversification (BSD), for improving the diversity of generated data.

Identifying Mode Collapse with Low-Rank Approximation
In this section, we propose a metric, which can be computed by leveraging truncated SVD on feature embeddings, to measure the degree of mode collapse. Moreover, we also theoretically demonstrate the rationale and reliability of this metric.

Data Representation by Feature Matrix. Suppose we have a batch of M samples generated by a trained generator G, we use $\{\tilde{\mathbf{x}}_i\}_{i=1}^M$ to denote the set of these samples. Due to the large discrepancy in raw pixel space, we utilize the trained discriminator D to help represent these generated samples, rather than directly using the high-dimensional images. For a classical discriminator D, except the last several layers which work for binary classification, the other layers actually serve as a feature extractor. In this paper, we use F to denote such a feature extractor, and for each $\tilde{\mathbf{x}}_i$ we obtain its feature embedding $e_i = F(\tilde{\mathbf{x}}_i; \theta_D) \in \mathbb{R}^d$ by performing a regular feed-forward operation. Then we compose an embedding matrix $E = [e_1, e_2, ..., e_M] \in \mathbb{R}^{d \times M}$, for all the generated images. Since D is trained to distinguish real and fake images and F is part of D, it is reasonable to expect F to extract informative features that are sufficient for detecting near-duplicate images, generated by G.

Rank Approximation with Truncated SVD. It is well known that, if the embedding matrix $E \in \mathbb{R}^{d \times M}$ includes duplicate vectors, the rank of E will be definitely lower than $min(d, M)$. However, for those generated images, it is very rare for the corresponding E to have exactly duplicate row or column vectors due to the existence of small perturbations. Therefore, we define an *approximate rank* based on Truncated SVD.

Definition 1 (Approximate Rank). *Denoting a general matrix by $E \in \mathbb{R}^{m \times n}$ and a pre-defined approximation error rate by δ, the approximate rank of E is defined as the minimum r satisfying that, there exists a $B \in \mathbb{R}^{m \times n}$ of rank-r, such that $\|B - E\|_F \leq \delta \|E\|_F$.*

Intuitively, Definition 1 estimates the rank of a matrix by finding a surrogate matrix (with a controlled approximation error) of which rank is as lower as possible. While this definition provides a reasonable metric, it is infeasible to traverse all the matrices in the space $\mathbb{R}^{m \times n}$ to compute the approximate rank. Fortunately, this rank can be easily computed by applying Truncated SVD. Specifically, we present the following theorem.

Theorem 1. *Denoting a general matrix by $E \in \mathbb{R}^{m \times n}$, $E = USV^T$ is the Singular Value Decomposition, with the singular values in a descending order, i.e. $s_1 \geq s_2 \geq ... \geq s_{\min(m,n)}$. Given a pre-defined approximation error rate δ, the approximate rank of E defined in Definition 1 is the minimum r satisfying $\|US_rV^T - E\|_F \leq \delta \|E\|_F$, where S_r is the truncated S with only the top r singular values.*

Theorem 1 can be proved by applying the Eckart-Young theorem [5], and we show our proof in Appendix A.3.

Efficient Implementation for Spectral Diversification
Based on the above analyses, we aim to design an efficient implementation to enhance the diversity of generated data in GAN fine-tuning. While Theorem 1 provides a rigorous metric to quantify the approximate rank, it cannot be directly employed as a learning objective in an end-to-end manner. Inspired by the idea in supervised transfer learning [3] which performs batch spectral shrinkage (BSS) to suppress noisy features, during GAN fine-tuning we focus on the minimum singular value s_{-1} of the embedding matrix (E_B) which corresponds to a stochastic batch. This leads to an efficient implementation to increase the approximate rank, named as Batch Spectral Diversification (BSD). Specifically, BSD performs SVD on E_B and incorporates a regularizer R to optimize the generator as

$$R(\theta_G) = \lambda_{BSD} \frac{1}{\|s_{-1}\|^2 + C}, \tag{8}$$

where λ_{BSD} is the coefficient of the regularizer and C is a constant to avoid division by zero.

It is worth noting that regarding the BSD loss $R(\theta_G)$, we calculate gradients and update parameters only on the generator. This is because our goal is to encourage G to generate diverse images, rather than requiring D to extract diverse deep features.

4 Experiment

We conduct extensive experiments to demonstrate the superior performance of the proposed schemes in GAN fine-tuning. In this section, we firstly introduce the adopted datasets and the baseline methods, and then present comprehensive analyses for the experimental observations. We use Pytorch for all the implementations, and our source code is included in the supplementary materials.

Dataset. Following the common practices in classical transfer learning literature [16,19,27,31], we adopt three datasets, namely Flowers [18], Cathedral [33] and Pets [22]. In addition, we also consider the extreme scenarios in which there are very few data samples, to validate the robustness of our schemes. This is because one important way to evaluate a transfer learning method is to validate it on small-scale datasets. Specifically, we select 1000, 100 and 25 samples from these datasets respectively to build new subsets, namely Flowers-1K, Flowers-100, Flowers-25, Cathedral-1K, Cathedral-100, Cathedral-25, Pets-1K, Pets-100, and Pets-25. All these subsets consist of randomly selected samples, except Flowers-25 for which we choose the first 25 passion flower images from the Flowers dataset, following the suggestions in [19].

Pre-trained Model and Implementation. We utilize the GP-GAN [15] as the backbone model, pretrained on ImageNet with a resolution of 128×128. Since the pre-trained version involves class information, the class embedding layer and fully connected layer in the generator and discriminator need to be re-initialized during fine-tuning. All the training images are resized to keep compatible with the pre-trained model. We use the Adam optimizer with a learning rate of 2.5×10^{-5}. We use a batch size of 32 for all the experiments, except for the ones in which we only use 25 sampled images and a batch size of 16 to increase the randomness of each batch. For the discriminator, gradient penalty on real samples is adopted with the regularization parameter $\gamma = 10.0$.

Baselines. We compare our method with three benchmark transfer learning methods proposed for GANs, namely TransGAN [27], FreezeD [16], and AdaFM [31]. TransGAN is a pioneering work that explores GAN-based transfer learning, while FreezeD and AdaFM are the representatives of the two mainstream fashions in GAN-based transfer learning. Specifically, FreezeD is a typical work of the fashion in which *no additional modules* are used, whereas AdaFM is a typical method of the fashion which requires *additional modules.* Note that in all the tables and figures, **TrustOPT** refers to our Trust-Region Optimization scheme, whereas **TrustOPT**$^-$ refers to a simplified implementation in which we

Table 1. The comparison of the methods on the full-scale datasets. Performance is measured in FID (lower is better). † marks the results reported in [31].

Method/Dataset	Flowers	Cathedral	Pets
TransGAN	20.92	15.29	47.42
FreezeD	24.90	15.59	46.09
AdaFM	22.13	16.62	88.27
AdaFM†	16.76	15.78	-
TrustOPT$^-$ (Ours)	**19.15**	14.43	44.38
TrustOPT (Ours)	20.31	**14.23**	**44.37**

do not progressively align the re-modeled input distribution with $\mathcal{N}(\mathbf{0}, \mathbf{I})$ during fine-tuning. **BSD** refers to our Batch Spectral Diversification scheme with GMM used for modeling input distribution, while **BSD**$^-$ is a simplified version in which the standard Gaussian distribution is used for input.

4.1 Performance on the Full Datasets

Here, the experiments are conducted on the full-scale datasets. As demonstrated in Table 1, our methods yield superior results on all the three datasets. For Flowers, as shown in Fig. 2a, our TrustOPT is on par with our TrustOPT$^-$ at the earlier fine-tuning stages, however, TrustOPT shows a more stable performance at the later stages, at which TrustOPT$^-$ suffers from overfitting. This demonstrates the necessity of progressively aligning the re-modeled input distribution with $\mathcal{N}(\mathbf{0}, \mathbf{I})$ during fine-tuning. The FID scores in Table 1 can also reflect the difficulty level of a task. For instance, all the methods on the Pets dataset yield much higher FID scores than the scores obtained on the other datasets, indicating that Pets is the most challenging dataset among the three. Therefore, the results in the table also demonstrate that our methods can achieve superior performance regardless of the difficulty level of a dataset. In addition, AdaFM shows a FID surge on Pets, whereas our methods maintain stable performance across all the datasets, further demonstrating its reliability. It is worth noting that all the three datasets have around 8000 images respectively, so the catastrophic forgetting is not evident in such a scenario due to the relatively large size of the dataset. A simple straightforward fine-tuning (TransGAN) can still yield acceptable results. The methods designed for small datasets such as AdaFM and FreezeD show marginal improvements or even worse performance. On the contrary, our methods consistently outperform the others by a decent margin, demonstrating a good generalization ability.

4.2 Performance on the Subsets of 1K Samples

To investigate the robustness of each method, we compare them on the smaller datasets, including Flowers-1K, Cathedral-1K, and Pets-1K. As shown in Table 2,

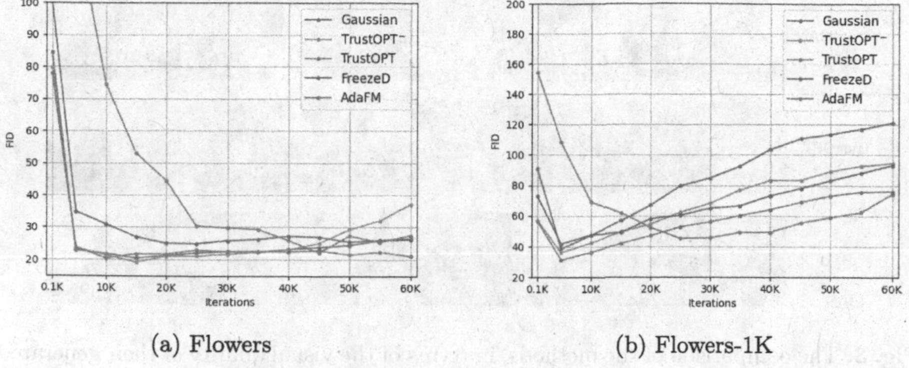

(a) Flowers (b) Flowers-1K

Fig. 2. The variation trend of the FID score with the number of iterations during fine-tuning. The comparisons are conducted on the (a) Flowers and (b) Flowers-1K dataset, respectively.

Table 2. The comparison of the methods on the three small-scale subsets, each of which consists of 1000 samples. Performance is measured in FID. † marks the results reported in [31].

Method/Dataset	Flowers-1K	Cathedral-1K	Pets-1K
TransGAN	34.36	28.74	70.86
FreezeD	41.01	27.39	69.20
AdaFM	45.03	36.03	120.90
AdaFM†	43.05	35.88	-
TrustOPT^{-} (Ours)	33.64	26.70	67.04
TrustOPT (Ours)	**30.38**	**25.13**	**66.55**

our methods significantly outperform the others on all these datasets, demonstrating the advantages of our methods for small-scale datasets. Moreover, our TrustOPT yields the best results, providing another evidence of the rationale of adjusting input distributions. Figure 2b shows how the FID scores vary with the number of iterations. As can be seen, the convergence speed of AdaFM is significantly slower than that of the others. This is because AdaFM is a typical method that modifies the structures of the shallow layers of the pre-trained generator. Such a structural modification could destroy the pre-learned knowledge, resulting in a much slower convergence, especially at the earlier fine-tuning stages. On the other hand, the methods, which do not require structural modifications, tend to suffer from overfitting. As illustrated in the figure, it can be greatly mitigated by leveraging our TrustOPT, once again indicating the necessity of adjusting input distributions.

Fig. 3. The comparison of the methods, in terms of the visual quality of their generated images. The experiment is conducted on the Cathedral-25 dataset.

Table 3. The comparison of the methods on the three small-scale subsets, each of which consists of 100 samples. Performance is measured in FID.

Method/Dataset	Flowers-100	Cathedral-100	Pets-100
TransferGAN	74.68	62.08	111.50
FreezeD	76.68	51.20	111.02
AdaFM	70.52	58.42	105.38
TrustOPT$^-$ (Ours)	69.40	38.80	103.61
BSD (Ours)	**59.12**	**34.20**	**94.00**

4.3 Performance on the Subsets of 100 and 25 Samples

GAN fine-tuning can easily suffer from the notorious issue of mode collapse when there are very few training samples in a target dataset. For example, as illustrated in Fig. 3, TransGAN tends to generate the same images when the pre-trained model is only fine-tuned on a very small dataset, namely Cathedral-25. Our TrustOPT$^-$ brings a notable improvement in terms of the diversity of the generated images. As described in Sect. 3.2, we propose the BSD scheme (Batch Spectral Diversification) to enhance diversity to address the mode collapse issue. Compared with the others, our BSD generates highly diverse images, eventually leading to much lower FID scores (Tables 3 and 4).

Moreover, since collapse of approximate rank is directly related to mode collapse as analyzed in Sect. 3.2, we conduct an experiment to investigate the effectiveness of each method on handling collapse of approximate rank, and show the results in Fig. 4. As can be seen, the vanilla fine-tuning incurs an immediate rank collapse after fine-tuning begins, whereas our TrustOPT$^-$ and BSD$^-$ to some extent mitigate the rapid collapse at the early fine-tuning stages. Our BSD achieves the best result, and such an observation is consistent with the results shown in Table 4, indicating the rationale of our analyses in Sect. 3.2.

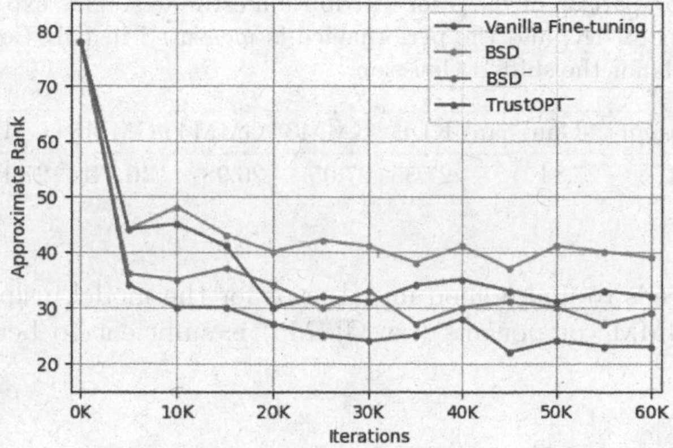

Fig. 4. This figure illustrates how approximate rank changes with the number of iterations during fine-tuning (higher is better). The experiment is conducted on the Cathedral-25 dataset.

Table 4. The comparison of the methods on the three small-scale subsets, each of which consists of 25 samples. Performance is measured in FID. † marks the results reported in [31].

Method/Dataset	Flowers-25	Cathedral-25	Pets-25
TransferGAN	125.90	91.59	123.45
FreezeD	134.59	80.62	121.19
AdaFM	**82.74**	71.18	113.76
AdaFM †	85.40	-	-
BSD$^-$ (Ours)	110.22	82.71	115.84
TrustOPT$^-$ (Ours)	98.64	54.71	114.87
BSD (Ours)	90.02	**51.65**	**105.72**

4.4 Ablation Study

In our Trust-Region Optimization scheme, we need to estimate the prior distribution of the latent space, after computing the optimal latent vectors. Various methods can be employed for such an estimation. Depending on whether additional parameters will be needed, these methods can be categorized into two groups, namely *parametric estimation* and *non-parametric estimation*. In this ablation study, we investigate the methods from both groups to present a comprehensive analysis. Specifically, for the parametric group, we adopt the multivariate Gaussian distribution and GMM. For the non-parametric group, we utilize the Kernel Density Estimation (KDE) with the Gaussian kernel for convenient sampling. As shown in Table 5, all the other methods outperform the original Gaussian method, and our schemes (based on GMM) yield the best results, regardless of the number of the components used in GMM. Moreover,

Table 5. The comparison of the prior distribution estimates. This experiment is conducted on Cathedral-1K, and the performance is measured in FID (lower is better). s-Gaussian stands for the shifted Gaussian.

Gaussian	s-Gaussian	KDE	GMM3	GMM4	GMM5	GMM6
28.74	27.84	27.55	27.05	26.98	**26.70**	27.12

since it only needs to find a good initial prior for the model, using a moderate number of 5 GMM components (i.e. GMM5) is sufficient to benefit the fine-tuning.

4.5 Limitation and Future Work

Although our BSD scheme can significantly improve the diversity of generated images when there is a small amount of training samples in a target dataset, the effect is not obvious when a target dataset includes a relatively large amount of training samples. In this case, global diversity cannot be accurately estimated via a small batch of data samples. Exploring advanced methods that are capable of retaining and utilizing global information could be a promising direction.

5 Conclusion

In this paper, we firstly analyze the primary cause and manifestation of the catastrophic forgetting issue in GAN fine-tuning, and then propose two schemes to overcome the issue. The first scheme, namely TrustOPT, can prevent an aggressive update of model parameters by properly adjusting input distributions. The second scheme, namely BSD, can significantly mitigate the mode collapse issue by enhancing the diversity of generated data, achieved by diversifying feature space. Unlike traditional methods that focus on model itself, our schemes pay attention to input and feature which are the core of data aspect. We theoretically analyze the rationale and correctness of the schemes, and empirically demonstrate their superiority by extensive experiments.

Acknowledgments. This work was support by the National Key Research and Development Program of China under grant 2018AAA0100205.

References

1. Aghajanyan, A., Shrivastava, A., Gupta, A., Goyal, N., Zettlemoyer, L., Gupta, S.: Better fine-tuning by reducing representational collapse. In: International Conference on Learning Representations (2021)
2. Brock, A., Donahue, J., Simonyan, K.: Large scale GAN training for high fidelity natural image synthesis. arXiv preprint arXiv:1809.11096 (2018)

3. Chen, X., Wang, S., Fu, B., Long, M., Wang, J.: Catastrophic forgetting meets negative transfer: batch spectral shrinkage for safe transfer learning. In: Advances in Neural Information Processing Systems, pp. 1906–1916 (2019)
4. Conn, A.R., Gould, N.I., Toint, P.L.: Trust region methods. SIAM (2000)
5. Eckart, C., Young, G.: The approximation of one matrix by another of lower rank. Psychometrika **1**(3), 211–218 (1936)
6. Gouk, H., Hospedales, T., et al.: Distance-based regularisation of deep networks for fine-tuning. In: International Conference on Learning Representations (2021)
7. Grigoryev, T., Voynov, A., Babenko, A.: When, why, and which pretrained GANs are useful? In: International Conference on Learning Representations (2022)
8. Gulrajani, I., Ahmed, F., Arjovsky, M., Dumoulin, V., Courville, A.C.: Improved training of Wasserstein GANs. In: Advances in Neural Information Processing Systems, vol. 30 (2017)
9. Ioffe, S., Szegedy, C.: Batch normalization: accelerating deep network training by reducing internal covariate shift. In: Proceedings of the 32nd International Conference on International Conference on Machine Learning, ICML 2015, vol. 37, pp. 448–456. JMLR.org (2015)
10. Jiang, H., He, P., Chen, W., Liu, X., Gao, J., Zhao, T.: Smart: robust and efficient fine-tuning for pre-trained natural language models through principled regularized optimization. In: Proceedings of the 58th Annual Meeting of the Association for Computational Linguistics, pp. 2177–2190 (2020)
11. Karras, T., Aila, T., Laine, S., Lehtinen, J.: Progressive growing of GANs for improved quality, stability, and variation. In: International Conference on Learning Representations (2018)
12. Li, K., Zhang, Y., Li, K., Fu, Y.: Adversarial feature hallucination networks for few-shot learning. In: Proceedings of the IEEE/CVF Conference on Computer Vision and Pattern Recognition, pp. 13470–13479 (2020)
13. Li, X., Grandvalet, Y., Davoine, F.: Explicit inductive bias for transfer learning with convolutional networks. In: Thirty-Fifth International Conference on Machine Learning (2018)
14. Li, Y., Zhang, R., Lu, J.C., Shechtman, E.: Few-shot image generation with elastic weight consolidation. Adv. Neural. Inf. Process. Syst. **33**, 15885–15896 (2020)
15. Mescheder, L., Geiger, A., Nowozin, S.: Which training methods for GANs do actually converge? In: International Conference on Machine Learning, pp. 3481–3490. PMLR (2018)
16. Mo, S., Cho, M., Shin, J.: Freeze the discriminator: a simple baseline for fine-tuning GANs. arXiv preprint arXiv:2002.10964 (2020)
17. Moré, J.J.: The Levenberg-Marquardt algorithm: implementation and theory. In: Watson, G.A. (ed.) Numerical Analysis. LNM, vol. 630, pp. 105–116. Springer, Heidelberg (1978). https://doi.org/10.1007/BFb0067700
18. Nilsback, M.E., Zisserman, A.: Automated flower classification over a large number of classes. In: 2008 Sixth Indian Conference on Computer Vision, Graphics & Image Processing, pp. 722–729. IEEE (2008)
19. Noguchi, A., Harada, T.: Image generation from small datasets via batch statistics adaptation. In: Proceedings of the IEEE/CVF International Conference on Computer Vision, pp. 2750–2758 (2019)
20. Nowozin, S., Cseke, B., Tomioka, R.: F-GAN: training generative neural samplers using variational divergence minimization. In: Advances in Neural Information Processing Systems, vol. 29 (2016)

21. Ojha, U., et al.: Few-shot image generation via cross-domain correspondence. In: Proceedings of the IEEE/CVF Conference on Computer Vision and Pattern Recognition, pp. 10743–10752 (2021)
22. Parkhi, O.M., Vedaldi, A., Zisserman, A., Jawahar, C.: Cats and dogs. In: 2012 IEEE Conference on Computer Vision and Pattern Recognition, pp. 3498–3505. IEEE (2012)
23. Radford, A., Metz, L., Chintala, S.: Unsupervised representation learning with deep convolutional generative adversarial networks. arXiv preprint arXiv:1511.06434 (2015)
24. Raskutti, G., Mukherjee, S.: The information geometry of mirror descent. IEEE Trans. Inf. Theory **61**(3), 1451–1457 (2015)
25. Santurkar, S., Tsipras, D., Ilyas, A., Madry, A.: How does batch normalization help optimization? In: Bengio, S., Wallach, H., Larochelle, H., Grauman, K., Cesa-Bianchi, N., Garnett, R. (eds.) Advances in Neural Information Processing Systems, vol. 31. Curran Associates, Inc. (2018)
26. Wang, Y., Gonzalez-Garcia, A., Berga, D., Herranz, L., Khan, F.S., Weijer, J.V.D.: Minegan: effective knowledge transfer from GANs to target domains with few images. In: Proceedings of the IEEE/CVF Conference on Computer Vision and Pattern Recognition, pp. 9332–9341 (2020)
27. Wang, Y., Wu, C., Herranz, L., van de Weijer, J., Gonzalez-Garcia, A., Raducanu, B.: Transferring GANs: generating images from limited data. In: Proceedings of the European Conference on Computer Vision (ECCV), pp. 218–234 (2018)
28. Xian, Y., Lorenz, T., Schiele, B., Akata, Z.: Feature generating networks for zero-shot learning. In: Proceedings of the IEEE Conference on Computer Vision and Pattern Recognition, pp. 5542–5551 (2018)
29. Xiao, J., Li, L., Wang, C., Zha, Z.J., Huang, Q.: Few shot generative model adaption via relaxed spatial structural alignment. In: Proceedings of the IEEE/CVF Conference on Computer Vision and Pattern Recognition, pp. 11204–11213 (2022)
30. Xie, Y., Fu, Y., Tai, Y., Cao, Y., Zhu, J., Wang, C.: Learning to memorize feature hallucination for one-shot image generation. In: Proceedings of the IEEE/CVF Conference on Computer Vision and Pattern Recognition, pp. 9130–9139 (2022)
31. Zhao, M., Cong, Y., Carin, L.: On leveraging pretrained GANs for generation with limited data. In: International Conference on Machine Learning, pp. 11340–11351. PMLR (2020)
32. Zhao, Y., Ding, H., Huang, H., Cheung, N.M.: A closer look at few-shot image generation. In: Proceedings of the IEEE/CVF Conference on Computer Vision and Pattern Recognition, pp. 9140–9150 (2022)
33. Zhou, B., Lapedriza, A., Xiao, J., Torralba, A., Oliva, A.: Learning deep features for scene recognition using places database. In: Advances in Neural Information Processing Systems, vol. 27 (2014)
34. Zhu, J., Shen, Y., Zhao, D., Zhou, B.: In-domain GAN inversion for real image editing. In: Vedaldi, A., Bischof, H., Brox, T., Frahm, J.-M. (eds.) ECCV 2020. LNCS, vol. 12362, pp. 592–608. Springer, Cham (2020). https://doi.org/10.1007/978-3-030-58520-4_35

Unsupervised Domain Adaptation via Bidirectional Cross-Attention Transformer

Xiyu Wang[1,2], Pengxin Guo[1], and Yu Zhang[1,3](✉)

[1] Department of Computer Science and Engineering, Southern University of Science and Technology, Shenzhen, China
yu.zhang.ust@gmail.com, 12032913@mail.sustech.edu.cn
[2] School of Computer Science, Faculty of Engineering, University of Sydney, Camperdown, Australia
[3] Peng Cheng Laboratory, Shenzhen, China

Abstract. Unsupervised Domain Adaptation (UDA) seeks to utilize the knowledge acquired from a source domain, abundant in labeled data, and apply it to a target domain that contains only unlabeled data. The majority of existing UDA research focuses on learning domain-invariant feature representations for both domains by minimizing the domain gap using convolution-based neural networks. Recently, vision transformers have made significant strides in enhancing performance across various visual tasks. In this paper, we introduce a Bidirectional Cross-Attention Transformer (BCAT) for UDA, which is built upon vision transformers with the goal of improving performance. The proposed BCAT employs an attention mechanism to extract implicit source and target mixup feature representations, thereby reducing the domain discrepancy. More specifically, BCAT is designed as a weight-sharing quadruple-branch transformer with a bidirectional cross-attention mechanism, allowing it to learn domain-invariant feature representations. Comprehensive experiments indicate that our proposed BCAT model outperforms existing state-of-the-art UDA methods, both convolution-based and transformer-based, on four benchmark datasets.

Keywords: Unsupervised Domain Adaptation · Transformer · Cross-Attention

1 Introduction

Deep Neural Networks (DNNs) have achieved remarkable success on a variety of computer vision problems [5,11,14,18,37]. However, such achievement heavily relies on a large amount of labeled training data, which is difficult to obtain in many real-world applications [4,38]. To handle the labeled data scarcity problem, Unsupervised Domain Adaptation (UDA) [42] has been proposed to transfer the knowledge learned from a source domain with ample label data to help learn

D. Koutra et al. (Eds.): ECML PKDD 2023, LNAI 14173, pp. 309–325, 2023.
https://doi.org/10.1007/978-3-031-43424-2_19

in a target domain with unlabeled data only. The core idea of UDA is to learn a domain-invariant feature representation, which could be both transferable to narrow the domain discrepancy and discriminative for classification in the target domain. To achieve this goal, in past decades many UDA methods have been proposed and they can be classified into two main categories: *domain alignment* methods [2,19,31] and *adversarial learning* methods [7,34].

Transformers have achieved remarkable success in Natural Language Processing (NLP) [32] and have recently garnered significant attention in the computer vision community. This is evidenced by the development of Vision Transformer (ViT) [5], Data-efficient Image Transformers (DeiT) [30], and Swin Transformer (Swin) [18]. In contrast to Convolutional Neural Networks (CNNs), which operate on local receptive fields of images, transformers utilize the self-attention mechanism to model long-range dependencies among visual features across an image. Owing to their superior context modeling capabilities, vision transformers have demonstrated outstanding performance in various vision tasks, such as image classification [10,18,30,36], object detection [1], dense prediction [25,27], and video understanding [8,22,26].

Several studies [21,39–41] have explored the application of transformers to address UDA problems. Some of these works [21,40,41] directly apply vision transformers, but they overlook the unique properties of UDA problems. To adapt vision transformers for UDA tasks, Xu *et al.* [39] proposed a Cross-Domain Transformer (CDTrans), which comprises a weight-sharing triple-branch transformer that employs both self-attention and cross-attention mechanisms for feature learning and domain alignment. However, the CDTrans model only considers one-directional cross-attention from the source domain to the target domain, neglecting the cross-attention from the target domain to the source domain. Moreover, during the training process, the CDTrans model requires that the data in a mini-batch consist of source and target images from the same class. This constraint introduces additional challenges in accurately determining pseudo labels for unlabeled target data and limits the model's applicability.

To address these limitations, we propose a Bidirectional Cross-Attention Transformer (BCAT) to effectively learn domain-invariant feature representations. In BCAT, we implement bidirectional cross-attention to enhance the transferability of vision transformers. This bidirectional cross-attention naturally accommodates knowledge transfer between the source and target domains in both directions, facilitating implicit feature mixup between domains. The proposed BCAT model integrates bidirectional cross-attention and self-attention within quadruple transformer blocks, enabling the learning of two augmented feature representations. These quadruple transformer blocks can comprehensively focus on both intra- and inter-domain features, thus blurring the boundary between the two domains. By minimizing the Maximum Mean Discrepancy (MMD) [9] between the learned feature representations in both domains, BCAT effectively reduces the domain gap and learns domain-invariant feature representations.

In summary, our contributions are three-fold:

- We propose a quadruple transformer block that combines both self-attention and cross-attention mechanisms, enabling the learning of augmented feature representations for both source and target domains.
- Building on the quadruple transformer block, we introduce the BCAT model within the Unsupervised Domain Adaptation (UDA) framework to effectively learn domain-invariant feature representations.
- The proposed BCAT model surpasses state-of-the-art baseline methods in performance across four benchmark datasets.

2 Related Work

2.1 Unsupervised Domain Adaptation

Unsupervised Domain Adaptation (UDA) refers to the process of transferring knowledge from a source domain, where there is a large amount of labeled data, to a target domain where there is only unlabeled data. The goal of UDA is to learn both domain-invariant and discriminative feature representations to overcome the difference between the source and target domains. Over the past few decades, various methods have been proposed to achieve this goal. For instance, Tzeng *et al.* [31] introduced the concept of Deep Domain Confusion (DCC) which learns domain-invariant feature representations by minimizing the Maximum Mean Discrepancy (MMD) [9]. Another approach was proposed by Ganin *et al.*[7] who used adversarial learning to learn domain-invariant feature representations. This method involves a domain discriminator and models the objective function as a minimax problem.

2.2 Vision Transformers

The Transformer architecture was first introduced in [32] for modeling sequential text data in the field of NLP. The idea of using Transformers for computer vision was first explored by Dosovitskiy *et al.* [5] who proposed ViT, a transformer-based model that processes sequences of image patches. Since then, several variants of ViT [10,18,27,30] have been proposed and have shown promising results on various computer vision tasks, outperforming their CNN counterparts. In particular, Liu *et al.* [18] proposed the Swin Transformer, which incorporates local attention within a window and uses a shifted window partitioning approach for cross-window connections.

2.3 Vision Transformer for Unsupervised Domain Adaptation

There have been efforts to apply vision transformers to address UDA challenges. For instance, Yang *et al.* [40] integrated the Transformer architecture into a CNN to concentrate on critical regions. Xu *et al.* [39] proposed a weight-sharing triple-branch Transformer that leverages self-attention and cross-attention mechanisms for both feature learning and domain alignment. Yang *et al.* [41] designed the Transferable Vision Transformer (TVT), which enforces ViT to focus on both transferable and discriminative features by incorporating learned transferability into the attention blocks. Zhang *et al.* [43] introduced a hybrid attention module that explicitly identifies hard-aligned features for inter-domain alignment using a single discriminator.

3 The BCAT Method

In a UDA problem, we are provided with a labeled source dataset $\mathcal{D}_s = \{(x_s^i, y_s^i)\}_{i=1}^{n_s}$ and an unlabeled target dataset $\mathcal{D}_t = \{x_t^i\}_{i=1}^{n_t}$, where n_s and n_t denote the number of instances in the source and target domains, respectively. These two domains exhibit a domain shift, leading to different data distributions, i.e., $p_s(x_s) \neq p_t(x_t)$. However, they share the same label space, i.e., $\mathcal{Y}_t = \mathcal{Y}_s$. The objective of the UDA problem is to train a model that leverages the useful knowledge in the source domain $\mathcal{D}_s$ to improve learning in the target domain $\mathcal{D}_t$.

3.1 Quadruple Transformer Block

As shown in Fig. 1, the BCAT method combines two cross-attention modules with two self-attention modules to design a quadruple transformer block.

Specifically, for the self-attention, N image patches are first transformed into queries $Q \in \mathbb{R}^{N \times d_k}$, keys $K \in \mathbb{R}^{N \times d_k}$, and values $V \in \mathbb{R}^{N \times d_v}$, where d_k and d_v indicate their dimensions. The queries and the corresponding keys calculate weights assigned to each value by a compatibility function, while a weighted sum of the values is the output of self-attention. The self-attention for image patches $\mathbf{x}$ can be computed as

$$\mathrm{Attn}_{\mathrm{self}}(\mathbf{x}) = \mathrm{softmax}\left(\frac{QK^T}{\sqrt{d_k}}\right)V, \tag{1}$$

where softmax$(\cdot)$ denotes the softmax function.

Unlike the self-attention module, the cross-attention module computes pairwise relationships between different images. We use the cross-attention module to create mixup features that blur the distinction between the source and target domains. Specifically, we define bidirectional cross-attention as executing the cross-attention between the source and target domains in both directions, as illustrated in the middle of Fig. 1. The formulation is as follows:

$$\mathrm{Attn}_{\mathrm{bidir}}(x_s, x_t) = \mathrm{Attn}_{\mathrm{cross}}(x_t, x_s) + \mathrm{Attn}_{\mathrm{cross}}(x_s, x_t),$$

$$\mathrm{Attn}_{\mathrm{cross}}(x_t, x_s) = \mathrm{softmax}\left(\frac{Q_t K_s^T}{\sqrt{d_k}}\right)V_s, \tag{2}$$

$$\mathrm{Attn}_{\mathrm{cross}}(x_s, x_t) = \mathrm{softmax}\left(\frac{Q_s K_t^T}{\sqrt{d_k}}\right)V_t, \tag{3}$$

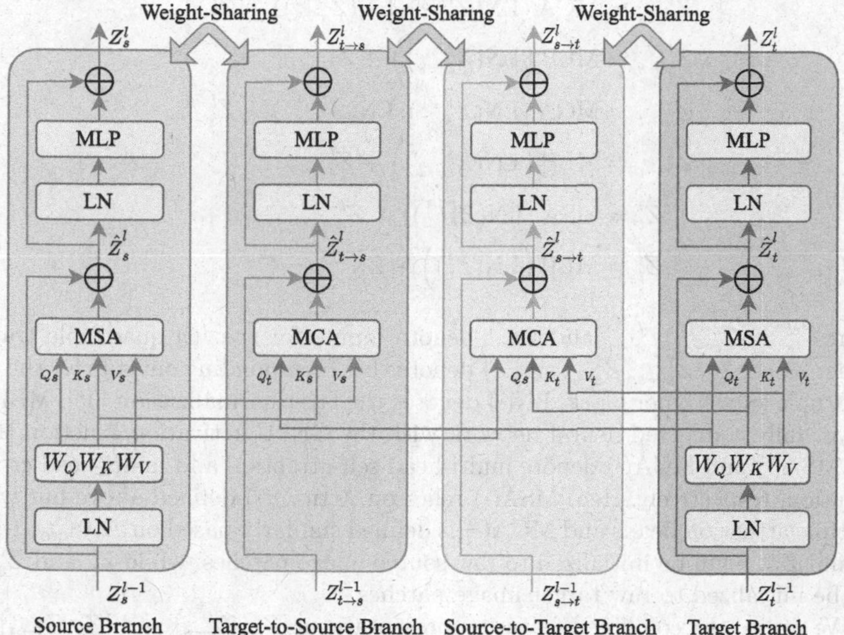

Fig. 1. A quadruple transformer block with two self-attention modules and a bidirectional cross-attention module. 'MSA' and 'MCA' denote the multi-head self-attention and multi-head cross-attention, respectively. 'LN' denotes the layer normalization. 'MLP' denotes a multi-layer perceptron. W_Q, W_K, and W_V denote transformation parameters to generate queries, keys, and values, respectively.

where x_s denotes patches of a source image, x_t denotes patches of a target image, and Q, K, and V with subscripts s and t denote queries, keys, and values based on the source and target image patches, respectively.

The quadruple transformer block consists of two self-attention modules and a bidirectional cross-attention module, as depicted in Fig. 1. The four weight-sharing transformers in the block are named from left to right as the source branch, target-to-source branch, source-to-target branch, and target branch. The source and target branches independently extract the source feature representation Z_s and target feature representation Z_t using transformer blocks with Multi-head Self-Attention (MSA) modules and Multi-Layer Perceptron (MLP) modules, respectively. The source-to-target branch and target-to-source branch, in contrast, use bidirectional cross-attention modules to learn intermediate feature representations between the source and target domains. The mathematical formulation of a quadruple transformer block is as follows:

$$\hat{Z}_s^l = \text{MSA}\left(\text{LN}(Z_s^{l-1})\right) + Z_s^{l-1},$$
$$Z_s^l = \text{MLP}\left(\text{LN}(\hat{Z}_s^l)\right) + \hat{Z}_s^l,$$

$$\hat{Z}_{t\to s}^{l} = \text{MCA}\left(\text{LN}(Z_t^{l-1}), \text{LN}(Z_s^{l-1})\right) + Z_{t\to s}^{l-1},$$
$$Z_{t\to s}^{l} = \text{MLP}\left(\text{LN}(\hat{Z}_{t\to s}^{l})\right) + \hat{Z}_{t\to s}^{l},$$
$$\hat{Z}_{s\to t}^{l} = \text{MCA}\left(\text{LN}(Z_s^{l-1}), \text{LN}(Z_t^{l-1})\right) + Z_{s\to t}^{l-1},$$
$$Z_{s\to t}^{l} = \text{MLP}\left(\text{LN}(\hat{Z}_{s\to t}^{l})\right) + \hat{Z}_{s\to t}^{l},$$
$$\hat{Z}_t^{l} = \text{MSA}\left(\text{LN}(Z_t^{l-1})\right) + Z_t^{l-1},$$
$$Z_t^{l} = \text{MLP}\left(\text{LN}(\hat{Z}_t^{l})\right) + \hat{Z}_t^{l},$$

where Z_s^{l-1}, $Z_{t\to s}^{l-1}$, $Z_{s\to t}^{l-1}$ and Z_t^{l-1} denote inputs for the lth quadruple transformer block, Z_s^l, $Z_{t\to s}^l$, $Z_{s\to t}^l$ and Z_t^l denote the corresponding outputs for the lth quadruple transformer block, LN$(\cdot)$ denotes the layer normalization [35], MLP is 2-layer fully connected neural network with the GELU activation function [12], and MSA$(\cdot)$ and MCA$(\cdot)$ denote multi-head self-attention and multi-head cross-attention, respectively. Here MSA$(\cdot)$ relies on $\text{Attn}_{\text{self}}(\cdot)$ defined above but with multiple attention heads and MCA$(\cdot)$ is defined similarly based on $\text{Attn}_{\text{cross}}(\cdot,\cdot)$. Z_s^0 and $Z_{t\to s}^0$ will be initialized to raw source image patches, while Z_t^0 and $Z_{s\to t}^0$ will be initialized to raw target image patches.

We utilize the combined feature representations $[Z_s, Z_{t\to s}]$ and $[Z_t, Z_{s\to t}]$ as the enhanced feature representations for the source and target domains, respectively. The representation $[Z_s, Z_{t\to s}]$ is considered a source-dominant feature representation, while the representation $[Z_t, Z_{s\to t}]$ is viewed as a target-dominant feature representation.

3.2 Bidirectional Cross-Attention as Implicit Feature Mixup

The bidirectional cross-attention mechanism used in the proposed quadruple transformer block is highly effective for UDA, as illustrated in Fig. 2. As shown in the figure, Z_s and Z_t are significantly different, presenting a major challenge for UDA. The bidirectional cross-attention mechanism generates $Z_{t\to s}$ and $Z_{s\to t}$, which can be seen as a mixup of Z_s and Z_t with varying proportions. Unlike direct mixup on images from the source and target domains, each image patch is weighted by all image patches from the other domain, making the mixup smoother and more robust. $Z_{t\to s}$ is closer to Z_s, while $Z_{s\to t}$ is closer to Z_t. Since the difference between $Z_{t\to s}$ and $Z_{s\to t}$ is smaller than the difference between Z_s and Z_t, $Z_{t\to s}$ and $Z_{s\to t}$ can act as a bridge to connect Z_s and Z_t, reducing the domain discrepancy. Minimizing the domain discrepancy between the source-dominant feature representation (i.e., $[Z_s, Z_{t\to s}]$) and the target-dominant feature representation (i.e., $[Z_t, Z_{s\to t}]$) is thus easier than directly minimizing the source and target feature representations (i.e., Z_s and Z_t). The results in Sect. 4.4 provide empirical evidence for the effectiveness of the bidirectional cross-attention mechanism in reducing the domain discrepancy and facilitating domain adaptation.

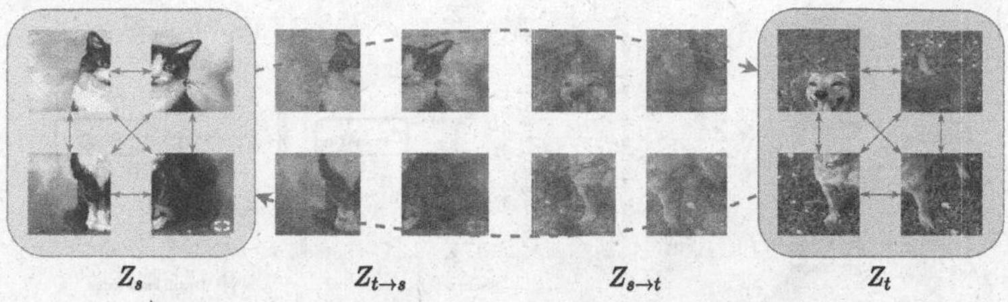

Fig. 2. An illustration of the bidirectional cross-attention mechanism to perform implicit feature mixup.

3.3 Loss Functions

For a UDA problem, in this section, we introduce how to utilize quadruple transformer blocks in the proposed BCAT method and how to construct the objective function.

As shown in the top of Fig. 3, the overall architecture of the BCAT method consists of a patch partition layer, multiple quadruple transformer blocks, and the classification layer. The patch partition layer is responsible of dividing an image $I \in \mathbb{R}^{H\times W\times 3}$ into a sequence of flattened 2D patches $\mathbf{x} \in \mathbb{R}^{N\times 3P^2}$, where (P, P) is the size of each split image patch, and $N = HW/P^2$ is the total number of patches. Multiple quadruple transformer blocks are stacked together to learn augmented feature representations for both domains. The classification layer is to do the classification given the output of the last quadruple transformer block. For notation simplicity, in the following formulations, we assume that there is only one quadruple transformer block.

To align the source-dominant and target-dominant features in two domains, MMD is utilized to define the transfer loss as

$$\mathcal{L}_{\texttt{transfer}} = \text{MMD}^2([G_s(x_s), G_c(x_t, x_s)], [G_s(x_t), G_c(x_s, x_t)])$$

where x_s and x_t represent the source and target data, $G_s(\cdot)$ denotes the output of the source or target branch in the quadruple transformer block due to the weight sharing mechanism, and $G_c(\cdot, \cdot)$ denotes the output of the target-to-source or source-to-target branch in the quadruple transformer block since these two branches share weights.

The classification layer is implemented as a 2-layer fully connected neural network. For the labeled source domain, we adopt the cross-entropy loss, which is defined as

$$\mathcal{L}_{\texttt{cls}_s} = \text{CE}(F([G_s(x_s), G_c(x_t, x_s)]), y_s),$$

where $F(\cdot)$ denotes the classification layer and $\text{CE}(\cdot, \cdot)$ denotes the cross-entropy loss. For unlabeled target data, we assign each instance a pseudo label in a way similar to the ATDOC method [17]. Specifically, we use the average of predicted class probabilities of nearest neighbors for a target instance as its predicted class probability and choose the class with the largest probability as its pseudo label.

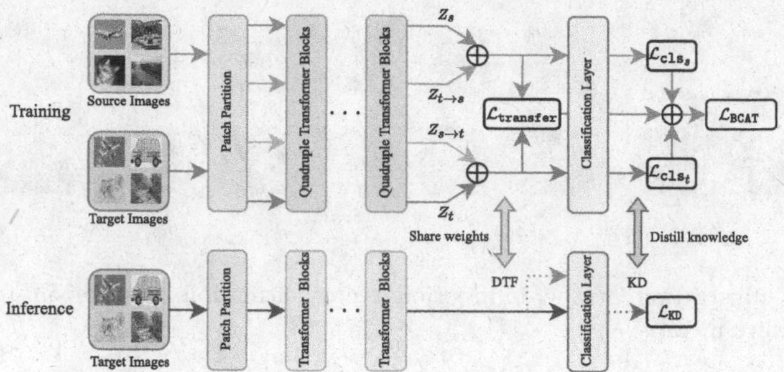

Fig. 3. Top: the architecture of the proposed BCAT method. Bottom: the two inference models introduced in Sect. 3.4.

Then the classification loss on the target domain is formulated as

$$\mathcal{L}_{\texttt{cls}_t} = -\frac{1}{N_t}\sum_{i=1}^{N_t} \hat{q}_{i,\hat{y}_i} \log p_{i,\hat{y}_i},$$

where $\hat{y}_i = \arg\max_j \hat{q}_{i,j}$ denotes the assigned pseudo label for the corresponding target instance, and $p_i = F([G_s(x_t), G_c(x_s, x_t)])$ denotes the K-dimensional prediction with K as the number of classes and $p_{i,\hat{y}_i}$ as its entry in the $\hat{y}_i$th dimension. By combining those two loss functions, the total classification loss is formulated as

$$\mathcal{L}_{\texttt{cls}} = \mathcal{L}_{\texttt{cls}_s} + \epsilon\mathcal{L}_{\texttt{cls}_t},$$

where ϵ is the ratio of the current epoch over the total number of epochs to reduce the effect of unreliable pseudo labels produced during the early training stage.

The total loss function of the BCAT method is formulated as

$$\mathcal{L}_{\texttt{BCAT}} = \mathcal{L}_{\texttt{cls}} + \beta\mathcal{L}_{\texttt{transfer}}, \tag{4}$$

where β is a hyper-parameter.

3.4 Inference for Target Domain

During the inference process for the target domain, we can use the training model to make the prediction. However, this inference approach needs to utilize source data, which brings additional storage costs to access source data. In the following, we present two inference models, which do not require to utilize source data.

Knowledge Distillation (KD). The first inference model is based on knowledge distillation [13]. Here the training model is used as a teacher, and an inference model with self-attention only is used as the student. We define the distillation loss with "softmax-T" as:

$$\mathcal{L}_{\text{KD}} = \alpha T^2 \sum\nolimits_N p_i \log q_i + \epsilon(1-\alpha)\text{CE}\left(F_S(G_{Ss}(x_t)), \hat{y}_t\right),$$

where $G_{Ss}(\cdot)$ denotes the feature extractor with self-attention in the student model, $F_S(\cdot)$ denotes the classification layer in the student network, and q_i and p_i are "softmax-T" probabilities of logit outputs of the student network and teacher network, respectively, i.e., $\frac{\exp(z_i/T)}{\sum_j \exp(z_j/T)}$.

Double Target Feature (DTF). Another inference model for the target domain without using the source data is to use only the target branch in BCAT. Since we cannot compute the target-dominant feature representation without source data, we combine the target feature with itself as the target-dominant feature representation, i.e., $[Z_t, Z_t]$, as the input of the classification layer during the inference. Thus, the predicted output is formulated as $F\left([G_s(x_t), G_s(x_t)]\right)$.

The above two inference models have no requirement to access source data during the inference. In experiments, we will compare those two inference models.

4 Experiments

In this section, we evaluate the proposed BCAT method.

4.1 Setups

Datasets. We conduct experiments on four benchmark datasets, including Office-31 [29], Office-Home [33], DomainNet [23], and VisDA-2017 [24]. By following [39], we construct transfer tasks on those four datasets.

Baseline Methods. We compare the proposed BCAT method with state-of-the-art UDA methods on respective datasets, including Calibrated Multiple Uncertainties (CMU) [6], Source HypOthesis Transfer (SHOT) [16], Domain Consensus Clustering (DCC) [15], Transferable Vision Transformer (TVT) [41], and Cross-Domain Transformer (CDTrans) [39], where TVT and CDTrans are based on transformers and other models are based on ResNet [11]. We use 'Source-only' to denote a baseline model trained on source data only with its backbone depending on the context. The BCAT method with the KD inference model is denoted by BCAT-KD, and that with the DTF inference model is denoted by BCAT-DTF.

Implementation Details. For all the UDA tasks, we use the ViT-B and Swin-B pretrained on the ImageNet dataset [3] as the backbone network for the proposed BCAT method, and hence 12 quadruple transformer blocks for ViT-B and 24 quadruple transformer blocks for Swin-B are used in the BCAT method, respectively. For the BCAT method built on the ViT-B, we use the SGD method [28]

Table 1. Accuracy (%) on the Office-31 dataset. The best results built on the ResNet and ViT are marked in box and the best results built on all the architectures (i.e., ResNet, ViT, and Swin transformer) are shown in bold.

Method		A→W	D→W	W→D	A→D	D→A	W→A	Avg.
Source-only	ResNet	68.4	96.7	99.3	68.9	62.5	60.7	76.1
SHOT		90.1	98.4	99.9	94.0	74.7	74.3	88.6
FixBi		96.1	99.3	100.0	95.0	78.7	79.4	91.4
Source-only	ViT	89.2	98.9	100.0	88.8	80.1	79.8	89.5
CDTrans		97.6	99.0	100.0	97.0	81.1	81.9	92.8
TVT		96.4	99.4	100.0	96.4	84.9	86.1	93.8
BCAT-KD (ours)		96.9	98.7	100.0	97.5	85.5	86.0	94.1
BCAT-DTF (ours)		96.1	99.1	100.0	97.5	84.9	85.8	93.9
Source-only	Swin	89.2	94.1	100.0	93.1	80.9	81.3	89.8
BCAT-KD (ours)		**99.4**	**99.5**	**100.0**	**99.8**	**85.7**	**86.1**	**95.1**
BCAT-DTF (ours)		99.2	**99.5**	**100.0**	99.6	**85.7**	**86.1**	95.0

with a momentum of 0.9 and a weight decay of 5×10^{-4} as the optimizer. We use a base learning rate of 8×10^{-3} for the Office-31, Office-Home, and DomainNet datasets and 8×10^{-4} for the VisDA-2017 dataset. For the BCAT method based on the Swin-B, the AdamW method [20] with a momentum of 0.9 and a weight decay of 0.05 is used as the optimizer. We use a base learning rate of 5×10^{-6} for the Office-31, Office-Home, and DomainNet datasets and 5×10^{-7} for the VisDA-2017 dataset. For all the datasets, we set the batch size to 64 and train the model in 20 epochs. α, β, and T in the proposed BCAT method are set to 0.8, 3, and 2, respectively, for all the UDA tasks.

4.2 Results

The results presented in Tables 1, 2, 3 and 4 indicate that transformer-based UDA models outperform ResNet-based UDA models, demonstrating the superior capacity of transformers compared to ResNet. In some datasets (e.g., Office-31, Office-Home, and DomainNet), the transformer-based 'Source-only' model exhibits comparable or even better performance than state-of-the-art ResNet-based UDA models. These findings highlight the advantages of vision transformers over ResNet for UDA tasks.

Office-31. According to Table 1, the proposed ViT-based BCAT method outperforms the other UDA method based on ViT, and it achieves the best average accuracy of 94.1%. Moreover, on some transfer tasks (e.g., A → W, A → D, and D → A), the proposed BCAT method performs better than CDTrans and TVT, which demonstrates the effectiveness of the proposed BCAT method.

Table 2. Accuracy (%) on the Office-Home dataset. The best results built on the ResNet and ViT are marked in box and the best results built on all the architectures (i.e., ResNet, ViT, and Swin transformer) are shown in bold.

Method		Ar→Cl	Ar→Pr	Ar→Rw	Cl→Ar	Cl→Pr	Cl→Rw	Pr→Ar	Pr→Cl	Pr→Rw	Rw→Ar	Rw→Cl	Rw→Pr	Avg.
Source-only	ResNet	34.9	50.0	58.0	37.4	41.9	46.2	38.5	31.2	60.4	53.9	41.2	59.9	46.1
SHOT		57.1	78.1	81.5	68	78.2	78.1	67.4	54.9	82.2	73.3	58.8	84.3	71.8
FixBi		58.1	77.3	80.4	67.7	79.5	78.1	65.8	57.9	81.7	76.4	62.9	86.7	72.7
Source-only	ViT	66.2	84.3	86.6	77.9	83.3	84.3	76.0	62.7	88.7	80.1	66.2	88.6	78.8
CDTrans		68.8	85.0	86.9	81.5	87.1	87.3	79.6	63.3	88.2	82.0	66.0	90.6	80.5
TVT		74.9	86.8	89.5	82.8	88.0	88.3	79.8	71.9	90.1	85.5	74.6	90.6	83.6
BCAT-KD (ours)		74.6	**90.8**	90.9	85.2	**91.5**	90.4	84.5	74.3	91.0	85.5	74.8	92.4	85.5
BCAT-DTF (ours)		74.2	90.6	90.9	84.2	90.9	89.9	84.1	**74.5**	90.8	85.7	74.8	92.2	85.2
Source-only	Swin	64.5	84.8	87.6	82.2	84.6	86.7	78.8	60.3	88.9	82.8	65.3	89.6	79.7
BCAT-KD (ours)		**75.4**	90.0	92.8	88.0	90.4	**92.8**	87.1	74.1	92.4	86.2	**75.8**	**93.5**	86.5
BCAT-DTF (ours)		75.3	90.0	**92.9**	**88.6**	90.3	92.7	**87.4**	73.7	**92.5**	**86.7**	75.4	**93.5**	**86.6**

Table 3. Accuracy (%) on the DomainNet dataset. The best results built on the ResNet and ViT are marked in box and the best results built on all the architectures (i.e., ResNet, ViT, and Swin transformer) are shown in bold.

Method		P→R	R→P	P→S	S→P	R→S	S→R	Avg.
Source-only	ResNet	30.1	28.3	27.0	27.0	26.9	29.7	28.2
CMU		50.8	52.2	45.1	44.8	45.6	51.0	48.3
DCC		56.9	50.3	43.7	44.9	43.3	56.2	49.2
Source Only	ViT	64.4	47.2	41.8	44.8	31.5	57.5	47.9
CDTrans		69.8	47.8	49.6	54.6	33.5	68.0	53.9
BCAT-KD (ours)		80.4	63.4	52.5	61.9	52.4	79.6	65.0
BCAT-DTF (ours)		79.2	62.8	52.7	62.2	52.7	78.5	64.7
Source-only	Swin	72.7	60.2	47.4	53.2	50.0	66.7	58.4
BCAT-KD (ours)		**81.2**	67.5	59.7	65.8	**60.9**	80.8	69.3
BCAT-DTF (ours)		81.1	**67.7**	**60.4**	**66.8**	60.7	**80.9**	**69.6**

Office-Home. As shown in Table 2, the proposed ViT-based BCAT method has the highest average accuracy of 85.5%. Compared with the best performant baseline method (i.e., the TVT method), the proposed BCAT method significantly improves the performance in almost all the transfer tasks. Although transferring to the Cl domain is an arduous task as each method has the lowest average accuracy on such transfer tasks than other transfer tasks, we use the same settings of hyper-parameters as other transfer tasks to achieve comparable or better performance, which in some extent demonstrates the good generalization ability of the proposed BCAT method.

DomainNet. According to the results on the DomainNet dataset shown in Table 3, the proposed ViT-based BCAT method achieves performance at a brand-new level with the average accuracy of 65.0%. Especially for transfer tasks P→R, R→P, R→S, and S→R, the proposed BCAT method has a performance

Table 4. Accuracy (%) on the VisDA-2017 dataset. The best results built on the ResNet and ViT are marked in box and the best results built on all the architectures (i.e., ResNet, ViT, and Swin transformer) are shown in bold.

Method		aero	bicycle	bus	car	horse	knife	motor	person	plant	skate	train	truck	Avg.
Source-only	ResNet	55.1	53.3	61.9	59.1	80.6	17.9	79.7	31.2	81.0	26.5	73.5	8.5	52.4
SHOT		94.3	88.5	80.1	57.3	93.1	94.9	80.7	80.3	91.5	89.1	86.3	58.3	82.9
FixBi		96.1	87.8	**90.5**	**90.3**	96.8	95.3	92.8	**88.7**	97.2	94.2	90.9	25.7	87.2
Source-only	ViT	98.2	73.0	82.5	62.0	97.3	63.5	96.5	29.8	68.7	86.7	**96.7**	23.6	73.2
TVT		92.9	85.6	77.5	60.5	93.6	**98.2**	89.4	76.4	93.6	92.0	91.7	55.7	83.9
CDTrans		97.1	90.5	82.4	77.5	96.6	96.1	93.6	88.6	**97.9**	86.9	90.3	62.8	88.4
BCAT-KD (ours)		99.0	**92.5**	87.4	74.8	98.2	98.5	93.6	67.7	89.0	96.4	95.8	**69.8**	88.5
BCAT-DTF (ours)		98.9	91.3	87.4	73.8	97.9	98.1	94.2	64.0	88.9	**97.4**	96.0	60.7	87.4
Source-only	Swin	98.7	63.0	86.7	68.5	94.6	59.4	**98.0**	22.0	81.9	91.4	**96.7**	25.7	73.9
BCAT-KD (ours)		**99.1**	91.5	86.8	72.4	98.6	98.1	96.5	82.1	94.4	96.0	93.9	61.1	**89.2**
BCAT-DTF (ours)		**99.1**	91.6	86.6	72.3	**98.7**	97.9	96.5	82.3	94.2	96.0	93.9	61.3	**89.2**

improvement of 10.6%, 15.6%, 19.2%, and 11.6%, respectively, over the CDTrans method that is also built on ViT. Results on this dataset again verify the effectiveness of the proposed BCAT method.

VisDA-2017. As shown in Table 4, the performance of the proposed ViT-based BCAT method on the VisDA-2017 dataset achieves the best average accuracy of 88.5%. Moreover, the proposed BCAT method achieves the best performance on five classes, including 'aeroplane', 'bicycle', 'horse', 'skate', and 'truck', than other ViT-based methods such as CDTrans and TVT.

4.3 BCAT for Other Vision Transformers

The proposed BCAT method is applicable to other vision transformers than ViT, and in Tables 1, 2, 3 and 4 we show the performance of the BCAT method built on the Swin transformer. According to the results, we can see that the proposed BCAT method built on the Swin transformer has better performance than ViT-based UDA methods and achieves the best average accuracy of 95.1%, 86.6%, 69.6%, and 89.2% on Office-31, Office-Home, DomainNet and VisDA-2017 dataset, respectively. Those results imply that the proposed BCAT method not only takes effect on the global attention mechanism as in ViT but also works on the local attention mechanism as in the Swin transformer. Moreover, the Swin-based BCAT method has a larger improvement over its 'Source-only' counterpart than CDTrans and TVT, which demonstrates the effectiveness of the BCAT method.

4.4 Ablation Study

In Table 5, we conduct ablation studies to study the effects of three loss functions: $\mathcal{L}_{\texttt{cls}_s}$, $\mathcal{L}_{\texttt{cls}_t}$, and $\mathcal{L}_{\texttt{transfer}}$, on the Office-Home dataset. For each loss function, we consider two choices: using only the self-attention (denoted by 'self'), and

Table 5. Ablation study on the Office-Home dataset in terms of the accuracy (%) based on the ViT and Swin transformer.

$\mathcal{L}_{cls_s}$	$\mathcal{L}_{cls_t}$	$\mathcal{L}_{transfer}$		Ar→Cl	Ar→Pr	Ar→Rw	Cl→Ar	Cl→Pr	Cl→Rw	Pr→Ar	Pr→Cl	Pr→Rw	Rw→Ar	Rw→Cl	Rw→Pr	Avg.
slef	–	–	ViT	66.2	84.3	86.6	77.9	83.3	84.3	76.0	62.7	88.7	80.1	66.2	88.6	78.8
slef	slef	slef		73.5	90.4	89.9	84.6	89.7	90.7	83.4	73.0	90.9	85.8	73.9	91.7	84.8
cross	–	–		66.9	87.1	89.8	82.7	89.1	89.5	79.4	65.4	90.4	82.4	65.0	91.0	81.5
cross	cross	–		73.8	91.2	90.4	85.4	90.4	90.2	84.3	73.5	90.3	84.5	74.2	92.1	85.0
cross	–	cross		72.1	87.2	89.4	83.7	89.3	89.4	81.8	72.7	90.0	84.0	73.0	91.1	83.6
cross	cross	cross		74.6	90.8	90.9	85.2	91.5	90.4	84.5	74.3	91.0	85.5	74.8	92.4	85.5
slef	–	–	Swin	64.5	84.8	87.6	82.2	84.6	86.7	78.8	60.3	88.9	82.8	65.3	89.6	79.7
slef	slef	slef		72.6	90.0	91.8	86.9	89.6	91.8	84.9	71.9	92.2	87.6	74.3	92.9	85.5
cross	–	–		67.9	84.0	88.0	82.9	85.1	86.5	76.0	64.3	87.9	81.9	66.1	89.8	80.0
cross	cross	–		71.5	90.1	92.6	87.4	91.2	93.2	85.4	72.1	92.4	85.6	74.1	92.7	85.7
cross	–	cross		68.3	85.3	89.6	84.5	85.4	88.2	83.5	66.8	89.8	85.9	70.4	90.8	82.4
cross	cross	cross		75.4	90.1	92.8	88.0	90.4	92.8	87.1	74.1	92.4	86.2	75.8	93.5	86.5

using both the self-attention and cross-attention (denoted by 'cross') during the feature extraction process. In this study, the BCAT-KD inference model is used.

Comparing the first and second rows in Table 5, we can see that both the pseudo labeling and MMD are effective for transformer-based backbones in UDA tasks. The comparison between the fourth and fifth rows shows that the MMD and pseudo labeling method still work for cross-attention based feature augmentation. According to the first and third rows, the bidirectional cross-attention shows better performance than self-attention, which could support the usefulness of the proposed bidirectional cross-attention which is to conduct the implicit feature mixup. Compared with the second row, the proposed BCAT method corresponding to the last row performs better, which demonstrates the effectiveness of the bidirectional cross-attention mechanism used in BCAT.

4.5 Comparison Between Inference Models

As shown in Tables 1, 2, 3 and 4, the two inference models proposed in Sect. 3.4 have comparable performance on the four benchmark datasets. This result suggests that the cross-attention feature $Z_{s\rightarrow t}$ with source and target information is close to the self-attention feature Z_t with only target information after training, which may imply that the proposed BCAT method could learn domain-invariant feature representations. In Table 6, we also compare two inference models with pure BCAT, whose inference model is identical to the training model by utilizing source data, based on ViT and Swin transformer in terms of the classification accuracy on each task and average, occupied GPU memory, and frames per second (FPS) for inference on each image. According to the results, we can see that the proposed KD and DTF inference methods occupy less memory and process images faster than pure BCAT with comparable and even better performance. Those results show that the proposed inference models are both effective and efficient.

Table 6. Accuracy (%), occupied GPU memory, and FPS on the Office-Home dataset for the three inference models.

Method		Ar→Cl	Ar→Pr	Ar→Rw	Cl→Ar	Cl→Pr	Cl→Rw	Pr→Ar	Pr→Cl	Pr→Rw	Rw→Ar	Rw→Cl	Rw→Pr	Avg	GPU Mem	FPS
BCAT	ViT	75.1	90.5	90.6	85.1	91.2	90.1	84.5	74.5	90.8	86.0	75.3	92.3	85.5	2241MB	78.6
BCAT-KD		74.6	90.8	90.9	85.2	91.5	90.4	84.5	74.3	91.0	85.5	74.8	92.4	85.5	1780MB	276.2
BCAT-DTF		74.2	90.6	90.9	84.2	90.9	89.9	84.1	74.5	90.8	85.7	74.8	92.2	85.2	1780MB	267.2
BCAT	Swin	74.1	89.8	90.1	88.1	89.5	92.5	87.3	73.3	92.3	88.4	74.2	92.5	86.0	4087MB	74.2
BCAT-KD		75.4	90.0	92.8	88.0	90.4	92.8	87.1	74.1	92.4	86.2	75.8	93.5	86.5	2871MB	263.9
BCAT-DTF		75.3	90.0	92.9	88.6	90.3	92.7	87.4	73.7	92.5	86.7	75.4	93.5	86.6	2871MB	253.1

Fig. 4. Attention maps of images from two classes (i.e., 'bicycle' and 'TV') in the Office-Home dataset and two classes (i.e., 'airplane' and 'cruise ship') in the DomainNet dataset. The hotter the color, the higher the attention.

4.6 Visualization of Attention Maps

As illustrated by the attention maps in Fig. 4, the proposed ViT-based BCAT method is more adept at capturing important regions than the 'Source-only' baseline, while paying less attention to the background. For instance, compared to the 'Source-only' baseline, the BCAT method focuses almost exclusively on the bicycle in the first image and exhibits more pronounced attention areas on the target objects for the second to fourth images.

5 Conclusion

In this paper, we introduce the BCAT, which is built upon the proposed quadruple transformer block. By bidirectionally learning cross-attention between different domains to generate intermediate feature representations, the combination of bidirectional cross-attention and self-attention effectively enhances domain alignment. Experimental results demonstrate that our proposed BCAT surpasses existing state-of-the-art ResNet-based and transformer-based UDA methods on four benchmark datasets. In future research, we plan to explore the application of BCAT to other computer vision tasks such as semantic segmentation.

Acknowledgments. This work is supported by NSFC key grant under grant no. 62136005, NSFC general grant under grant no. 62076118, and Shenzhen fundamental research program JCYJ20210324105000003.

References

1. Carion, N., Massa, F., Synnaeve, G., Usunier, N., Kirillov, A., Zagoruyko, S.: End-to-end object detection with transformers. In: Vedaldi, A., Bischof, H., Brox, T., Frahm, J.-M. (eds.) ECCV 2020. LNCS, vol. 12346, pp. 213–229. Springer, Cham (2020). https://doi.org/10.1007/978-3-030-58452-8_13
2. Chen, C., Chen, Z., Jiang, B., Jin, X.: Joint domain alignment and discriminative feature learning for unsupervised deep domain adaptation. In: Proceedings of the AAAI Conference on Artificial Intelligence, vol. 33, pp. 3296–3303 (2019)
3. Deng, J., Dong, W., Socher, R., Li, L.J., Li, K., Fei-Fei, L.: Imagenet: a large-scale hierarchical image database. In: 2009 IEEE Conference on Computer Vision and Pattern Recognition, pp. 248–255. IEEE (2009)
4. Dong, M., Wang, Y., Chen, X., Xu, C.: Towards stable and robust addernets. Adv. Neural Inf. Process. Syst. **34**, 13255–13265 (2021)
5. Dosovitskiy, A., et al.: An image is worth 16×16 words: transformers for image recognition at scale. arXiv preprint arXiv:2010.11929 (2020)
6. Fu, B., Cao, Z., Long, M., Wang, J.: Learning to detect open classes for universal domain adaptation. In: Vedaldi, A., Bischof, H., Brox, T., Frahm, J.-M. (eds.) ECCV 2020. LNCS, vol. 12360, pp. 567–583. Springer, Cham (2020). https://doi.org/10.1007/978-3-030-58555-6_34
7. Ganin, Y., Lempitsky, V.: Unsupervised domain adaptation by backpropagation. In: International Conference on Machine Learning, pp. 1180–1189. PMLR (2015)
8. Girdhar, R., Carreira, J., Doersch, C., Zisserman, A.: Video action transformer network. In: Proceedings of the IEEE/CVF Conference on Computer Vision and Pattern Recognition, pp. 244–253 (2019)
9. Gretton, A., Borgwardt, K., Rasch, M., Schölkopf, B., Smola, A.: A kernel method for the two-sample-problem. Adv. Neural Inf. Process. Syst. **19**, 513–520 (2006)
10. Han, K., Xiao, A., Wu, E., Guo, J., Xu, C., Wang, Y.: Transformer in transformer. Adv. Neural Inf. Process. Syst. **34**, 1–12 (2021)
11. He, K., Zhang, X., Ren, S., Sun, J.: Deep residual learning for image recognition. In: Proceedings of the IEEE Conference on Computer Vision and Pattern Recognition, pp. 770–778 (2016)
12. Hendrycks, D., Gimpel, K.: Gaussian error linear units (gelus). arXiv preprint arXiv:1606.08415 (2016)
13. Hinton, G., Vinyals, O., Dean, J.: Distilling the knowledge in a neural network. arXiv preprint arXiv:1503.02531 (2015)
14. Krizhevsky, A., Sutskever, I., Hinton, G.E.: Imagenet classification with deep convolutional neural networks. Adv. Neural Inf. Process. Syst. **25**, 1–9 (2012)

15. Li, G., Kang, G., Zhu, Y., Wei, Y., Yang, Y.: Domain consensus clustering for universal domain adaptation. In: Proceedings of the IEEE/CVF Conference on Computer Vision and Pattern Recognition, pp. 9757–9766 (2021)
16. Liang, J., Hu, D., Feng, J.: Do we really need to access the source data? source hypothesis transfer for unsupervised domain adaptation. In: International Conference on Machine Learning, pp. 6028–6039. PMLR (2020)
17. Liang, J., Hu, D., Feng, J.: Domain adaptation with auxiliary target domain-oriented classifier. In: Proceedings of the IEEE/CVF Conference on Computer Vision and Pattern Recognition, pp. 16632–16642 (2021)
18. Liu, Z., et al.: Swin transformer: hierarchical vision transformer using shifted windows. In: Proceedings of the IEEE/CVF International Conference on Computer Vision, pp. 10012–10022 (2021)
19. Long, M., Cao, Y., Wang, J., Jordan, M.: Learning transferable features with deep adaptation networks. In: International Conference on Machine Learning, pp. 97–105. PMLR (2015)
20. Loshchilov, I., Hutter, F.: Decoupled weight decay regularization. arXiv preprint arXiv:1711.05101 (2017)
21. Munir, F., Azam, S., Jeon, M.: Sstn: self-supervised domain adaptation thermal object detection for autonomous driving. In: 2021 IEEE/RSJ International Conference on Intelligent Robots and Systems (IROS), pp. 206–213. IEEE (2021)
22. Neimark, D., Bar, O., Zohar, M., Asselmann, D.: Video transformer network. arXiv preprint arXiv:2102.00719 (2021)
23. Peng, X., Bai, Q., Xia, X., Huang, Z., Saenko, K., Wang, B.: Moment matching for multi-source domain adaptation. In: Proceedings of the IEEE/CVF International Conference on Computer Vision, pp. 1406–1415 (2019)
24. Peng, X., Usman, B., Kaushik, N., Hoffman, J., Wang, D., Saenko, K.: Visda: the visual domain adaptation challenge. arXiv preprint arXiv:1710.06924 (2017)
25. Qiu, Z., Yang, H., Fu, J., Fu, D.: Learning spatiotemporal frequency-transformer for compressed video super-resolution. In: Computer Vision-ECCV 2022: 17th European Conference, Tel Aviv, Israel, 23–27 October 2022, Proceedings, Part XVIII. pp. 257–273. Springer, Heidelberg (2022). https://doi.org/10.1007/978-3-031-19797-0_15
26. Qiu, Z., Yang, H., Fu, J., Liu, D., Xu, C., Fu, D.: Learning spatiotemporal frequency-transformer for low-quality video super-resolution. arXiv preprint arXiv:2212.14046 (2022)
27. Ranftl, R., Bochkovskiy, A., Koltun, V.: Vision transformers for dense prediction. In: Proceedings of the IEEE/CVF International Conference on Computer Vision, pp. 12179–12188 (2021)
28. Robbins, H., Monro, S.: A stochastic approximation method. Ann. Math. Stat. **22**, 400–407 (1951)
29. Saenko, K., Kulis, B., Fritz, M., Darrell, T.: Adapting visual category models to new domains. In: Daniilidis, K., Maragos, P., Paragios, N. (eds.) ECCV 2010. LNCS, vol. 6314, pp. 213–226. Springer, Heidelberg (2010). https://doi.org/10.1007/978-3-642-15561-1_16
30. Touvron, H., Cord, M., Douze, M., Massa, F., Sablayrolles, A., Jégou, H.: Training data-efficient image transformers & distillation through attention. In: International Conference on Machine Learning, pp. 10347–10357. PMLR (2021)
31. Tzeng, E., Hoffman, J., Zhang, N., Saenko, K., Darrell, T.: Deep domain confusion: maximizing for domain invariance. arXiv preprint arXiv:1412.3474 (2014)
32. Vaswani, A., et al.: Attention is all you need. Adv. Neural Inf. Process. Syst. **30**, 1–11 (2017)

33. Venkateswara, H., Eusebio, J., Chakraborty, S., Panchanathan, S.: Deep hashing network for unsupervised domain adaptation. In: Proceedings of the IEEE Conference on Computer Vision and Pattern Recognition, pp. 5018–5027 (2017)
34. Wang, J., Chen, Y., Feng, W., Yu, H., Huang, M., Yang, Q.: Transfer learning with dynamic distribution adaptation. ACM Trans. Intell. Syst. Technol. (TIST) **11**(1), 1–25 (2020)
35. Wang, Q., Li, B., Xiao, T., Zhu, J., Li, C., Wong, D.F., Chao, L.S.: Learning deep transformer models for machine translation. In: ACL (2019)
36. Wang, Y., Du, B., Xu, C.: Multi-tailed vision transformer for efficient inference. arXiv preprint arXiv:2203.01587 (2022)
37. Wang, Y., Wang, X., Dinh, A.D., Du, B., Xu, C.: Learning to schedule in diffusion probabilistic models. In: Proceedings of the 29th ACM SIGKDD Conference on Knowledge Discovery and Data Mining (2023)
38. Wang, Y., Xu, C., Du, B., Lee, H.: Learning to weight imperfect demonstrations. In: Proceedings of the 38th Annual International Conference on Machine Learning (2021)
39. Xu, T., Chen, W., Wang, P., Wang, F., Li, H., Jin, R.: Cdtrans: cross-domain transformer for unsupervised domain adaptation. arXiv preprint arXiv:2109.06165 (2021)
40. Yang, G., et al.: Transformer-based source-free domain adaptation. arXiv preprint arXiv:2105.14138 (2021)
41. Yang, J., Liu, J., Xu, N., Huang, J.: Tvt: transferable vision transformer for unsupervised domain adaptation. arXiv preprint arXiv:2108.05988 (2021)
42. Yang, Q., Zhang, Y., Dai, W., Pan, S.J.: Transfer Learning. Cambridge University Press, Cambridge (2020)
43. Zhang, J., Huang, J., Luo, Z., Zhang, G., Lu, S.: Da-detr: domain adaptive detection transformer by hybrid attention. arXiv preprint arXiv:2103.17084 (2021)

Multiple-Source Adaptation Using Variational Rényi Bound Optimization

Dana Zalman (Oshri)[1,2(✉)] and Shai Fine[2]

[1] School of Computer Science, Reichman University, Herzliya, Israel
dana.oshri@post.runi.ac.il

[2] Data Science Institute, Reichman University, Herzliya, Israel
shai.fine@runi.ac.il

Abstract. Multiple Source Adaptation (MSA) is a problem that involves identifying a predictor which minimizes the error for the target domain while utilizing the predictors from the source domains. In practice, the source domains typically exhibit varying probability distributions across the input space and are unknown to the learner. Consequently, accurate probability estimates are essential for effectively addressing the MSA problem. To this end, variation inference is an attractive approach that aims to approximate probability densities. Traditionally, it is done by maximizing a lower bound for the likelihood of the observed data (evidence), i.e. maximizing the Evidence Lower BOund (ELBO). Recently, researchers have proposed optimizing the Variational Rényi bound (VR) instead of ELBO, which can be biased or difficult to approximate due to high variance. To address these issues, we propose a new upper bound called Variational Rényi Log Upper bound (VRLU). Unlike existing VR bounds, the VRLU bound maintains the upper bound property when using the Monte Carlo (MC) approximation. Additionally, we introduce the Variational Rényi Sandwich (VRS) method, which jointly optimizes an upper and a lower bound, resulting in a more accurate density estimate. Following this, we apply the VRS density estimate to the MSA problem. We show, both theoretically and empirically, that using VRS estimators provides tighter error bounds and improved performance, compared to leading MSA methods.

Keywords: Multiple-Source Adaptation · Variational Inference · Rényi Divergence

1 Introduction

Traditional Machine Learning aims to learn a model on a set of training samples to find an objective function with minimum error on unseen test data. Most research in machine learning, both theoretical and empirical, assumes that models are trained and tested using data drawn from some fixed distribution. That is, the same distribution is shared among the training and test sets with similar joint probability distributions. This single-domain setting has been well studied,

D. Koutra et al. (Eds.): ECML PKDD 2023, LNAI 14173, pp. 326–340, 2023.
https://doi.org/10.1007/978-3-031-43424-2_20

and uniform convergence theory guarantees that a model's empirical training error is close to its true error under such assumptions.

In real-world applications, this assumption breaks down easily, since training and test sets can originate from different distributions of the feature space. For instance, the statistical properties of a domain can evolve in time, or new samples can be collected from various sources, causing domain shifts. To overcome the breakdown, researchers proposed a new research area in machine learning called domain adaptation. In this setting, training and test sets are termed as the source and the target domains, respectively.

Specifically, domain adaptation is a scenario that arises when we aim to learn from a source data distribution, a well-performing model on a different (but related) target data distribution. A real-world example of domain adaptation is the common spam filtering problem. This problem consists of adapting a model from one user (the source distribution) to a new user who receives significantly different emails (the target distribution). In the problem of multiple-source domain adaptation (MSA), we ask whether the learner can combine relatively accurate predictors available for each source domain and derive an accurate predictor for any new mixture target domain.

A number of algorithms have been suggested in previous work [2,5] to resolve the domain adaptation problem. However, most of them assume knowledge of the source domains' data distribution. In general, estimating the data distribution is a difficult task, and achieving an accurate approximation might be intractable.

In many real-world problems, we are faced with probability distributions which are difficult to compute. This happens, in particular, when a distribution involves latent variables. Accordingly, strategies to approximate such distributions are required.

Variational inference (VI) is an attractive method to approximate posteriors in complex latent variables models [6]. It can handle intractable and possibly high-dimensional posteriors, and it makes Bayesian inference computationally efficient and scalable to large datasets. To this end, VI defines a simple distribution family, called the variational family, and then finds the member of the variational family that is closest to the true posterior distribution. This transforms the posterior inference into an optimization problem concerning the variational distribution.

One of the most successful applications of VI in the deep neural network realm is Variational Autoencoder (VAE) [8], which is a deep generative model that implements probabilistic model and variational Bayesian inference. Many techniques have been suggested to improve the accuracy and efficiency of variational methods [17]. Recent trends in variational inference have been dealing with the following aspects: scalability, accuracy, generalization and amortization.

In this work, we focus on the accuracy of the VAE model. A central part of the VI modeling approach is the choice of the divergence method used, which regularize the approximation of the posterior. Thus, the choice of the divergence measure can affect the accuracy of the approximation. Furthermore, using the selected divergence measure, one can devise lower and upper bounds for the likelihood of the observed data (evidence), and estimate the true posterior. Following the work of Li and Turner [9], we suggest to use the Rényi divergence (a.k.a α divergence), and we make the following contributions:

- We present an upper bound for the evidence, called the Variational Rényi Log Upper bound (VRLU), which is based on the Variational Rényi bound [9], and preserves the upper bound property.
- We devise a (sandwiched) upper-lower bound variational inference method, termed VRS, to jointly optimize the Rényi upper and lower bounds. The VRS loss function combines the VR lower bound (with positive α) and VRLU, the new upper bound (with negative α), thus providing a tighter estimate for the log evidence.
- We link The VRS estimates to the MSA objective and provide tighter theoretical error bounds.
- We provide two algorithmic implementations, Difference of Convex (DC) programming and Stochastic Gradient Descent (SGD), that solve the MSA problem using the VRS density estimates.

2 Multiple-Source Adaptation

The MSA problem was first formalized and analyzed theoretically by Mansour, Mohri, and Rostamizadeh. In their paper [11], they presented the multiple sources domain adaptation problem setup and proved that for any target domain, there exists a hypothesis, referred to as the distribution weighted combining rule (h_w^η), that achieves a low error rate with respect to the target domain. Nonetheless, it should be noted that the authors did not provide a method to determine or to learn the aforementioned hypothesis. Additionally, we note that the scope of the paper is limited to regression models and does not extend to the realm of probability models.

In a following paper by Hoffman, Mohri and Zhang [5], the authors extended the definition of the weighted combination rule h_w^η to solve probabilistic models as well, using cross-entropy loss. They also proposed an iterative algorithm using DC programming, to find the vector w which is a crucial component of the hypothesis h_w^η. Even so, this algorithm assumes knowledge of the probabilities of the data points or at least requires accurate estimates for them. To assess the quality of their model, the authors used the Rényi divergence to measure the divergence between the true distribution and the approximated one [12]. Thus, the quality of their model is determined by the quality of the approximations of the probabilities.

In order to avoid the need for good estimates, Cortes et al. [2] proposed a discriminative technique using an estimate of the conditional probabilities $p(i|x)$ for each source domain $i \in \{1, ..., k\}$ (that is, the probability that point x belongs to source i). To do so, they had to modify the DC algorithm proposed in [5], to comply with their new distribution calculations.

2.1 MSA Problem Setup

We refer to a probability model where there is a distribution over the input space X. Each data point $x \in X$ has a corresponding label $y \in Y$, where Y denotes the space of labels. The objective function, $f : X \to Y$, describes the correspondence between the data point and its label.

We will focus on the adaptation problem with k source domains and a single target domain. For each domain $i \in \{1, ..., k\}$, we have a source distribution $p_i(x)$ and a corresponding probability hypothesis $h_i(x, y) \to [0, 1]$. More precisely, h_i returns the probability that $f(x) = y$.

Let $L : [0, 1] \to R$ be a loss function penalizing errors with respect to f. The loss of hypothesis h with respect to the objective function f and a distribution p is denoted by $\mathcal{L}(h, p, f)$ and defined as:

$$\mathcal{L}(h, p, f) := E_p[L(h, f)] = \sum_{x \in X} p(x) L\left(h(x, f(x))\right) \tag{1}$$

We will refer to $L\left(h(x, f(x))\right)$ as $L(h, f)$ for simplicity. We will assume that the following properties hold for the loss function L:

- L is non-negative: $\forall a \in [0, 1] : \; L(a) \geq 0$
- L is convex.
- L is bounded: $\exists M \geq 0 \; s.t. \; \forall a \in [0, 1] : \; L(a) \leq M$
- L is continuous in both arguments.
- L is symmetric.

We will assume that for each domain i, the hypothesis h_i is a relatively accurate predictor for domain i with the distribution p_i; i.e. there exists $\epsilon > 0$ such that:

$$\forall i \in \{1, ..., k\}, \; \mathcal{L}(h_i, p_i, f) \leq \epsilon \tag{2}$$

We will denote the simplex: $\Delta = \{\lambda : \lambda_i \geq 0 \wedge \sum_{i=1}^{k} \lambda_i = 1\}$. The distribution of the target domain p_T is assumed to be a mixture of the k source distributions $p_1, ..., p_k$, that is:

$$p_T(x) = \sum_{i=1}^{k} \lambda_i p_i(x) \; (\text{for } \lambda \in \Delta) \tag{3}$$

2.2 Existence of a Good Hypothesis

The goal of solving the MSA problem is to establish a good[1] predictor for the target domain, given the source domain's predictors. A common assumption is that there is some relationship between the target domain and the distribution of the source domains.

Previous research [11] has shown that standard convex combinations of source predictors can perform sub-optimally in certain cases. Specifically, it has been

[1] A good predictor: a predictor that provides a small error with respect to the target domain.

shown that even when the source predictors have zero loss, no convex combination can achieve a loss below a certain constant for a uniform mixture of the source distributions.

Alternatively, Mansour, Mohri, and Rostamizadeh [11] proposed a distribution-weighted solution and defined the distribution-weighted combination hypothesis for a regression model. Hoffman and Mohri [5] extended the distribution-weighted combination hypothesis to a probabilistic model, as follows:

Definition 1. *(distribution-weighted combination hypothesis)*
For any $\lambda \in \Delta, \eta > 0$ *and* $(x, y) \in X \times Y$*:*

$$h_w^\eta(x,y) = \sum_{i=1}^{k} \frac{w_i p_i(x) + \eta \frac{U(x)}{k}}{\sum_{j=1}^{k}(w_j p_j(x)) + \eta U(x)} h_i(x,y) \tag{4}$$

Where $U(x)$ *is the uniform distribution over* X*.*

In the probabilistic model case, we will use L as the binary cross entropy loss: $L(h, f) = -\log h(x, f(x))$, which maintain all the required properties stated in Sect. 2.1.

Theorem 1. *For any target function* $f \in \{f{:}\forall i \in \{1, ..., k\}, \mathcal{L}(h_i, p_i, f) \leq \epsilon\}$ *and for any* $\delta > 0$*, there exist* $\eta > 0$ *and* $w \in \Delta$ *such that* $\mathcal{L}(h_w^\eta, p_\lambda, f) \leq \epsilon + \delta$ *for any mixture parameter* λ*.*

Thus, for any fixed target function f, the distribution-weighted combination hypothesis is a good hypothesis for the target domain (The proof of Theorem 1 is detailed in [11], and provided in Appendix[2] A).

It should be noted that h_w^η is calculated based on the p_i distributions. However, in real-world scenarios, the learner may not have access to the true distributions p_i and would have to rely on estimated distributions $\hat{p}_i$, obtained from the available data. We would like to address the construction procedure of h_w^η when the true distributions are unknown. We propose to use a variational inference method to estimate the true distributions, and apply these estimates, in turn, when solving the MSA problem.

3 Variational Inference

In probabilistic modeling, we aim to devise a probabilistic model, p_θ, that best explains the data. This is commonly done by maximizing the log-likelihood of the data (a.k.a *log evidence*), with respect to the model's parameter θ.

For many latent models, the log evidence integral is unavailable in closed form or it is too complex to compute. A leading approach to handle such intractable cases is Variational Inference (VI). One of the most successful applications of VI in the deep neural network realm is Variational Autoencoder (VAE).

[2] https://github.com/DanaOshri/Multiple-Source-Adaptation-using-Variational-R-nyi-Bound-Optimization/blob/main/Appendix.pdf.

3.1 Variational Autoencoder

A variational autoencoder (VAE), is a deep generative model that implements probabilistic model and variational Bayesian inference. Introduced by Kingma and Welling [8], a VAE model is an autoencoder, designed to stochastically encode the input data into a constrained multivariate latent space (encoder), and then to reconstruct it as accurately as possible (decoder).

As we mentioned before, the integral of the marginal likelihood $p_\theta(x) = \int p_\theta(x|z)p_\theta(z)dz$ is intractable. The intractability of $p_\theta(x)$, is related to the intractability of the posterior distribution $p_\theta(z|x)$ (By Bayes' theorem: $p_\theta(z|x) = \frac{p_\theta(x|z)p_\theta(z)}{p_\theta(x)}$). To turn the posterior inference into a solvable problem, we aim to approximate it with a variational distribution $q_\phi(z|x)$ (most commonly a Gaussian distribution) that minimize the KL divergence between them.

Definition 2. *Kulback-Leibler (KL) divergence [3,10]: For discrete probability distributions p and q, defined on the same probability space, the KL divergence from q to p is defined as follows:*

$$D_{KL}(p||q) = \sum_x p(x) \log\left(\frac{p(x)}{q(x)}\right) \tag{5}$$

The KL divergence between the variational distribution q_ϕ and the true distribution p_θ can be expressed as follows:

$$\begin{aligned} D_{KL}(q_\phi(z|x)||p_\theta(z|x)) &= -E_{z\sim q_\phi(z|x)}\left[\log\left(\frac{p_\theta(z|x)}{q_\phi(z|x)}\right)\right] \\ &= -E_{z\sim q_\phi(z|x)}\left[\log\left(p_\theta(z,x)\right) - \log\left(q_\phi(z|x)\right)\right] + \log p_\theta(x) \end{aligned} \tag{6}$$

Define the Evidence Lower BOund (ELBO):

$$\textbf{ELBO} := E_{z\sim q_\phi(z|x)}\left[\log\left(p_\theta(z,x)\right) - \log\left(q_\phi(z|x)\right)\right] \tag{7}$$

It follows that:

$$\log p_\theta(x) = D_{KL}(q_\phi(z|x)||p_\theta(z|x)) + \textbf{ELBO} \tag{8}$$

We note that the KL divergence is non-negative, thus, maximizing the ELBO results with the minimization of the KL divergence between $q_\phi(z|x)$ and the true, intractable, posterior $p_\theta(z|x)$.

ELBO optimization is a well-known method that has been studied in depth, and is applicable in many models, especially in VAE [15]. Nevertheless, using the ELBO can give rise to some drawbacks. For instance, the KL divergence does not always lead to best results - it tends to favour approximating distributions q_ϕ that underestimate the entropy of the true posterior.

3.2 Rényi divergence

Another divergence method that measures the distance between two distribution, is the Rényi divergence (a.k.a α divergence).

Definition 3. *For discrete probability distributions p and q, defined on the same probability space, the Rényi divergence from q to p is defined as follows:*

$$D_\alpha(p||q) = \frac{1}{\alpha - 1} \log \left(\sum_x \frac{p(x)^\alpha}{q(x)^{\alpha-1}} dx \right) \tag{9}$$

Rényi divergence was originally defined for $\alpha \in \{\alpha > 0, \alpha \neq 1\}$. This definition was extended to $\alpha = 0, 1, +\infty$ by continuity. There are certain α values for which Rényi divergence has wider application than the others, of particular interest are the values 0, 1/2, 1, 2, and ∞ (specified in Table 3 Appendix B). We note that for $\alpha \to 1$: $\lim_{\alpha \to 1} D_\alpha(p||q) = D_{KL}(p||q)$, i.e. the KL divergence is recovered. This fact forms a connection between Rényi divergence and KL divergence.

The definition of Rényi divergence was extended to $\alpha < 0$ as well. However, not all properties are preserved, and some are inverted. For example, Rényi divergence for negative orders is *non-positive* and *concave* in its first argument (cf. Fig. 2a) (Many other properties are described in Appendix B).

Definition 4. *We will denote by $d_\alpha(p||q)$ the exponential of Rényi divergence:*

$$d_\alpha(p||q) = e^{D_\alpha(p||q)} = \left(\sum_{x \in X} \frac{p(x)^\alpha}{q(x)^{\alpha-1}} \right)^{\frac{1}{\alpha-1}} \tag{10}$$

3.3 Variational Rényi

Consider approximating the evidence $p_\theta(x)$ by minimizing Rényi's α-divergence between $q_\phi(z|x)$ and the true posterior $p_\theta(z|x)$, for some selected $\alpha > 0$. Extending the posterior $p_\theta(z|x)$ and using Bayes' theorem, we get:

$$\begin{aligned} D_\alpha(q_\phi(z|x)||p_\theta(z|x)) &= \frac{1}{\alpha - 1} \log \left(E_{z \sim q_\phi(z|x)} \left[\left(\frac{q_\phi(z|x)}{p_\theta(z|x)} \right)^{\alpha-1} \right] \right) \\ &= \log p_\theta(x) + \frac{1}{\alpha - 1} \log \left(E_{z \sim q_\phi(z|x)} \left[\left(\frac{p_\theta(z,x)}{q_\phi(z|x)} \right)^{1-\alpha} \right] \right) \end{aligned} \tag{11}$$

Define the Variational Rényi (VR) bound [9] :

$$\mathbf{VR}_\alpha := \frac{1}{1 - \alpha} \log \left(E_{z \sim q_\phi(z|x)} \left[\left(\frac{p_\theta(z,x)}{q_\phi(z|x)} \right)^{1-\alpha} \right] \right) \tag{12}$$

It follows that:

$$\log p_\theta(x) = D_\alpha(q_\phi(z|x)||p_\theta(z|x)) + \mathbf{VR}_\alpha \tag{13}$$

The VR bound can be extended for $\alpha < 0$. As $D_\alpha(p||q) \geq 0$ for $\alpha \geq 0$ and $D_\alpha(p||q) \leq 0$ for $\alpha \leq 0$ (see Fig. 2a), we can conclude that for $\alpha \geq 0$, $\mathbf{VR}_\alpha$ is a lower bound for $\log p_\theta(x)$, and for $\alpha \leq 0$, $\mathbf{VR}_\alpha$ is an upper bound for $\log p_\theta(x)$.

3.4 Monte Carlo Approximation

Both the ELBO and the Rényi bounds require empirical estimations. This is commonly done by sampling and averaging, i.e. a Monte Carlo (MC) approximation [13]. The MC approximation of the KL divergence is unbiased, which ensures the convergence of the ELBO optimization process. However, the MC approximation for the Rényi bound is biased, underestimating the true expectation. For positive α, it means that the bound will be less tight, but it should still work. For negative α, this becomes a real problem since it is an underestimate of an upper bound. More precisely, the MC approximation for the Rényi bound is:

$$\widehat{\mathbf{VR}}_\alpha = \frac{1}{1-\alpha}\log\left(\frac{1}{K}\sum_{i=1}^{K}\left(\frac{p_\theta(z_i,x)}{q_\phi(z_i|x)}\right)^{1-\alpha}\right) \tag{14}$$

For this to be unbiased, the expectation should be equal to the true value,

$$E_{z\sim q_\phi(z|x)}\left[\widehat{\mathbf{VR}}_\alpha\right] = \frac{1}{1-\alpha}E_{z\sim q_\phi(z|x)}\left[\log\left(\frac{1}{K}\sum_{i=1}^{K}\left(\frac{p_\theta(z_i,x)}{q_\phi(z_i|x)}\right)^{1-\alpha}\right)\right] \tag{15}$$

By Jensen's inequality:

$$\begin{aligned} &\le \frac{1}{1-\alpha}\log\left(E_{z\sim q_\phi(z|x)}\left[\frac{1}{K}\sum_{i=1}^{K}\left(\frac{p_\theta(z_i,x)}{q_\phi(z_i|x)}\right)^{1-\alpha}\right]\right) \\ &= \frac{1}{1-\alpha}\log\left(E_{z\sim q_\phi(z|x)}\left[\left(\frac{p_\theta(z,x)}{q_\phi(z|x)}\right)^{1-\alpha}\right]\right) \end{aligned} \tag{16}$$

Thus the approximation is actually an underestimate of the true bound. This characteristic was also discussed in [9,13], where the authors suggested improving the approximation quality by using more samples and using negative α values to improve the accuracy, at the cost of losing the upper-bound guarantee.

4 Rényi Bounds Optimization

4.1 Variational Rényi log upper bound (VRLU)

We suggest a different approach for estimating the upper bound while preserving the upper bound property. Consider the following inequalities:

$$1-\frac{1}{x} \le \log x \le x-1 \tag{17}$$

Where equality holds on both sides if and only if $x=1$.

Definition 5. *Variational Rényi Log Upper bound (VRLU):*

$$\mathbf{VRLU}_\alpha := \frac{1}{1-\alpha}\left(E_{z\sim q_\phi(z|x)}\left[\left(\frac{p_\theta(z,x)}{q_\phi(z|x)}\right)^{1-\alpha}\right]-1\right) \tag{18}$$

For negative α, $\widehat{\mathbf{VRLU}}_\alpha$ is an estimation of the Rényi upper bound, and an upper bound of the log evidence:

$$\begin{aligned} E_{z\sim q_\phi(z|x)}\left[\widehat{\mathbf{VRLU}}_\alpha\right] &= E_{z\sim q_\phi(z|x)}\left[\frac{1}{1-\alpha}\left(\left(\frac{1}{K}\sum_{i=1}^{K}\left(\frac{p_\theta(z_i,x)}{q_\phi(z_i|x)}\right)^{1-\alpha}\right)-1\right)\right] \\ &\geq \frac{1}{1-\alpha}\log\left(E_{z\sim q_\phi(z|x)}\left[\frac{1}{K}\sum_{i=1}^{K}\left(\frac{p_\theta(z_i,x)}{q_\phi(z_i|x)}\right)^{1-\alpha}\right]\right) \\ &= \frac{1}{1-\alpha}\log\left(E_{z\sim q_\phi(z|x)}\left[\left(\frac{p_\theta(z_i,x)}{q_\phi(z_i|x)}\right)^{1-\alpha}\right]\right) \end{aligned} \tag{19}$$

Note that the inequalities in (17) become tighter as the argument of the log is closer to 1. In the Rényi bound approximation (14), this argument is: $1/k\sum(p_\theta(z,x)/q_\phi(z|x))^{1-\alpha}$. Thus, the approximation becomes tighter as the variational distribution, q_ϕ, is getting closer to the true distribution p_θ (the lower the divergence, the tighter the approximation), which is exactly the goal of the optimization.

Figure 1 shows the bias of MC approximations for both bounds, $\mathbf{VR}_\alpha$ and $\mathbf{VRLU}_\alpha$, over a range of negative α values. We can see that the MC approximations for $\mathbf{VR}_\alpha$ are biased and get better as the sample size K increases. On the other hand, the MC approximation for $\mathbf{VRLU}_\alpha$ preserves the upper bound property and has a relatively low variance. Therefore, $\mathbf{VRLU}_\alpha$ is a more suitable choice as an upper bound for negative α and may be used as an objective for risk minimization.

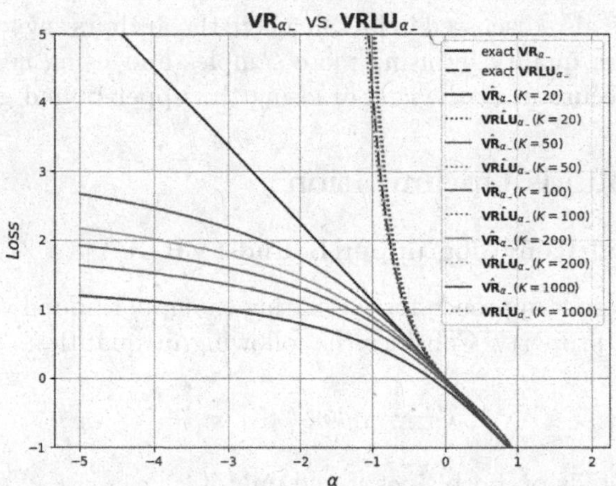

Fig. 1. $\mathbf{VR}_\alpha$ and $\mathbf{VRLU}_\alpha$, vs. their Monte Carlo approximations with different sample sizes, K, over a range of negative α values, using fixed distributions: $p \sim N(0,1)$ and $q \sim N(1.5,1)$.

4.2 Upper-Lower Bound Optimization

Using the new upper bound, $\mathbf{VRLU}_{\alpha}$, we devised $\mathbf{VRS}_{\alpha_+,\alpha_-}$, a (sandwiched) upper-lower bound variational inference algorithm for jointly minimizing Rényi upper and lower bounds. $\mathbf{VRS}_{\alpha_+,\alpha_-}$ combined both the upper and lower Rényi bounds, where the lower bound $\mathbf{VR}_{\alpha}$ is computed as in equation (14) for a constant positive α, and the upper bound $\mathbf{VRLU}_{\alpha}$ is computed as in equation (18) for a constant negative α. The overall $\mathbf{VRS}_{\alpha_+,\alpha_-}$ loss is the average of both terms, i.e.

$$\mathbf{VRS}_{\alpha_+,\alpha_-} := \frac{(\mathbf{VRLU}_{\alpha_-} + \mathbf{VR}_{\alpha_+})}{2} \tag{20}$$

Since $\mathbf{VR}_{\alpha_+} \leq \log p_{\theta}(x) \leq \mathbf{VR}_{\alpha_-} \leq \mathbf{VRLU}_{\alpha_-}$, our sandwiched loss provides a beneficial estimate for the log-likelihood of the evidence. (See VRS experiments in Appendix C).

5 MSA with Estimated Probabilities

In the MSA problem setting, it is assumed that each domain hypothesis has a small error on its domain (see equation (2)). Previous researches [5,12] showed that for each domain $i \in \{1, ..., k\}$, the loss of hypothesis h_i with respect to the objective function f and the estimated distribution $\hat{p}_i$ is bounded.

Corollary 1. [3]*Let* $\hat{p}_i$ *be an estimation of the original domain distribution* p_i. *The following inequality holds for any* $\alpha > 1$:

$$\mathcal{L}(h_i, \hat{p}_i, f) \leq [d_{\alpha}(\hat{p}_i || p_i)\epsilon]^{\frac{\alpha-1}{\alpha}} M^{\frac{1}{\alpha}} \tag{21}$$

To estimate the density using our VRS method, positive and negative α values must be used. Thus, using $\alpha < 1$, we derived a new lower bound for $\mathcal{L}(h_i, \hat{p}_i, f)$. This lower bound can be used to confirm that the use of approximated probabilities does not result in an excessive error. Additionally, using both upper and lower bounds we can achieve a more accurate estimate of the loss.

Corollary 2. *Let* $\hat{p}_i$ *be an estimation of the original domain distribution* p_i. *The following inequality holds for any* $\alpha < 1$:

$$\mathcal{L}(h_i, \hat{p}_i, f) \geq (d_{\alpha}(\hat{p}_i || p_i))^{\frac{\alpha-1}{\alpha}} \psi \tag{22}$$

Where $\psi = \left[\sum_{x \in X} p_i(x) L(h_i, f)^{\frac{\alpha}{\alpha-1}}\right]^{\frac{\alpha-1}{\alpha}}$

Let's set $\mathcal{L}_{\alpha}(\hat{p}, p) := (d_{\alpha}(\hat{p}||p))^{\frac{\alpha-1}{\alpha}}$. Figure 2b presents an example of different $\mathcal{L}_{\alpha}(\hat{p}, p)$ values. The figure shows that as the estimated distribution $\hat{p}$ approaches the true distribution p, the bounds on the loss function become increasingly similar.

Using Theorem 1 and Corollary 1, one can derive Corollary 3:

[3] Proofs for Corollaries 1, 2, and 3 are detailed in Appendix D.

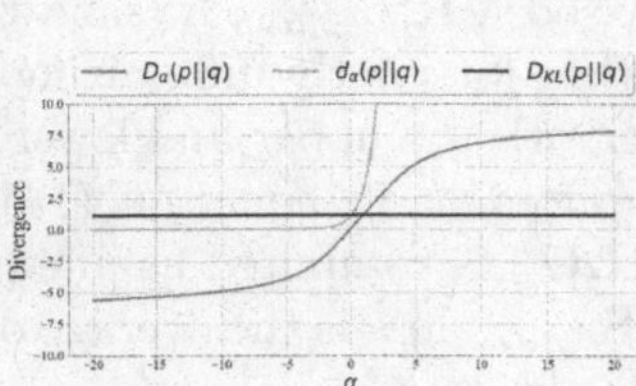

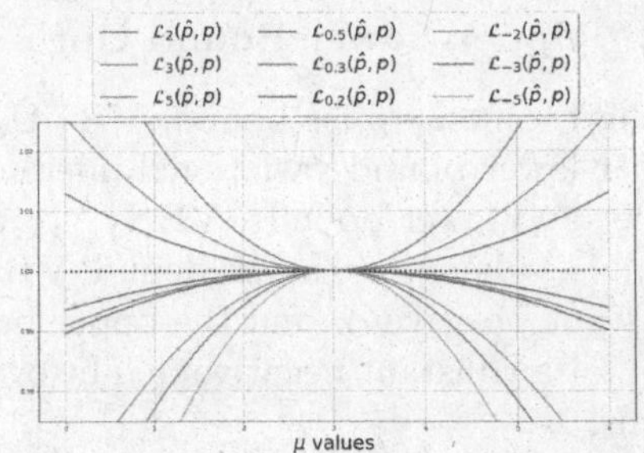

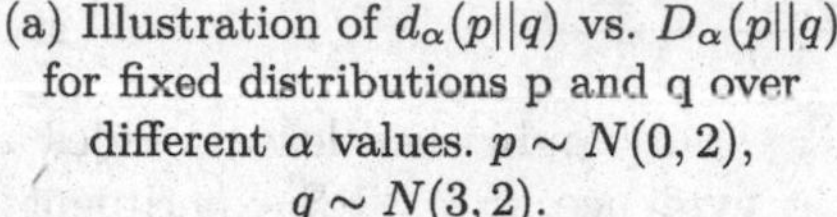

(a) Illustration of $d_\alpha(p||q)$ vs. $D_\alpha(p||q)$ for fixed distributions p and q over different α values. $p \sim N(0, 2)$, $q \sim N(3, 2)$.

(b) Comparison between $\mathcal{L}_\alpha(\hat{p}, p)$ with different α values over fixed distribution $p \sim N(3, 10)$, and distribution $\hat{p} \sim N(\mu, 10)$, where $0 < \mu < 6$.

Fig. 2. Comparing divergence measures for fixed distributions.

Corollary 3. *Let p_T be an arbitrary target distribution. For any $\delta > 0$, there exists $\eta > 0$ and $w \in \Delta$, such that the following inequality holds for any $\alpha > 1$ and any mixture parameter λ:*

$$\mathcal{L}(\hat{h}_w^\eta, p_T, f) \leq [(\epsilon^* + \delta) d_\alpha(p_T||\hat{p}_\lambda)]^{\frac{\alpha-1}{\alpha}} M^{\frac{1}{\alpha}} \tag{23}$$

Where $\epsilon^* = \max_{i\in\{1,\ldots,k\}} [d_\alpha(\hat{p}_i||p_i)\epsilon]^{\frac{\alpha-1}{\alpha}} M^{\frac{1}{\alpha}}$, $\hat{p}_\lambda = \sum_{i=1}^k \lambda_i \hat{p}_i(x)$ (for $\lambda \in \Delta$) and $\hat{h}_w^\eta$ is our good hypothesis defined in Definition 1 but calculated with $\hat{p}_i$.

In summary, we have shown in this section that estimated distributions can be effectively used to calculate a reliable distribution-weighted combining rule. We have also demonstrated that the error arising from the use of estimated distributions is bounded. Thus, we can address the MSA problem in real-world applications, when the true distributions are unknown.

6 Results

In this section[4], we report on a series of experiments designed to evaluate our methods for solving MSA problem using real-world datasets, and utilizing the VRS model to estimate the probabilities $\hat{p}_i$. We term the technique described above **VRS-MSA**.

6.1 Digit Experiment

In the following experiment, we used the MNIST, USPS, and SVHN datasets as our source domains, all of which contain digit images (See Fig. 3b).

[4] All experiments were conducted using PyTorch; https://github.com/DanaOshri/Multiple-Source-Adaptation-using-Variational-R-nyi-Bound-Optimization.

Table 1. Digit Dataset Accuracy (s - SVHN, m - MNIST and u - USPS.) Previous results were taken from [2].

Models	Test datasets							
	s	m	u	mu	su	sm	smu	mean
CNN-s	92.3	66.9	65.6	66.7	90.4	85.2	84.2	78.8
CNN-m	15.7	**99.2**	79.7	96.0	20.3	38.9	41.0	55.8
CNN-u	16.7	62.3	**96.6**	68.1	22.5	29.4	32.9	46.9
GMSA	91.4	98.8	95.6	**98.3**	91.7	93.5	93.6	94.7
VAE-MSA	72.1	97.7	94.6	96.0	92.3	95.7	95.7	92.0
$VRS_{2,-2}$-MSA	74.2	99.1	94.7	96.5	89.3	**96.1**	**95.6**	92.2
$VRS_{0.5,-0.5}$-MSA	76.0	99.1	94.6	96.5	89.4	95.8	95.4	92.4
$VRS_{2,-2}$-SGD	93.7	99.0	94.7	**98.3**	93.8	95.2	95.2	**95.7**
$VRS_{0.5,-0.5}$-SGD	**93.9**	98.4	94.9	97.8	**94.0**	95.2	95.2	95.6

For each source domain we trained a convolutional neural network (CNN) with the same setup as in [4] and used the output from the softmax score layer as our base predictors h_i. We also trained VRS models for each domain over the domain's training set. We used these trained models to approximate the domains' distributions $\hat{p}_i$.

For our DC programming algorithm, we used 1,000 image-label pairs from each domain, thus a total of 3,000 labeled pairs to learn the parameter w. We compared our VRS-MSA algorithm against the results presented in [2]. Since the training and testing datasets are fixed, we simply report the numbers from the original paper. We measured the performance of these baselines on each of the three test datasets, on combinations of two test datasets, and on all test datasets combined. We compared our VRS-MSA model against each source predictor (CNN for MNIST, USPS and SVHN), the GMSA model that uses kernel density estimation to approximate p_i [5], and the original VAE. The results are reported in Table 1 (full table provided in Appendix E).

Our VRS-MSA model demonstrates competitive performance, with particularly strong results on the union of SVHN and MNIST test set and the union of SVHN, MNIST and USPS test set. However, the performance on the SVHN domain is lower in comparison to the other classifiers. Analysis of the weights vector $w = (w_{MNIST} : 0.73, w_{USPS} : 0.19, w_{SVHN} : 0.08)$ provided by the DC programming method revealed that the value for the SVHN domain, represented by w_{SVHN}, is quite small at 0.08. Since the distribution weighted combining rule is a weighted combination of all source hypotheses with weights w, this indicates that the SVHN domain has a minimal impact on the result of h_w^η.

Furthermore, we devised a method that uses Stochastic Gradient Descent (SGD), rather than DC programming, to get a good classifier for the target domain. For each image x, every possible label $y_1, ..., y_c$, and every source domain, we created the following input: $< p_1(x, y_1), ..., p_1(x, y_c), ..., p_k(x, y_1), ...,$

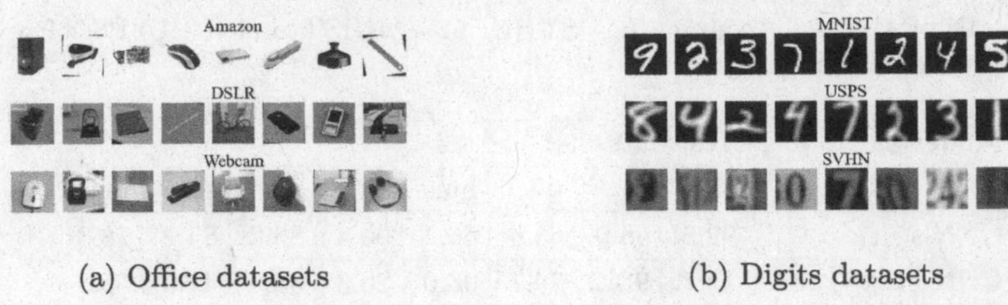

(a) Office datasets (b) Digits datasets

Fig. 3. Datasets visualization

$p_k(x, y_c), h_1(x, y_1), ..., h_1(x, y_c), ..., h_k(x, y_1), ..., h_k(x, y_c) >$. Given image x, the SGD model learns a matching between the input vector above and the true label of x. This method is termed **VRS-SGD**. Similarly to VRS-MSA, we used 1000 images from each domain to train the SGD model. The results of the VRS-SGD are reported at the last section of Table 1.

The SGD score for the SVHN test set stands out as the highest, leading to an improvement in the combined test set that includes both SVHN and USPS. One advantage of the VRS-SGD method is its ability to overcome the issue of misalignment among different VRS models by adjusting its learned weights to match the input scale. This makes the VRS-SGD method particularly valuable when working with source domains where the probabilities are smaller compared to other domains.

6.2 Office Experiment

In the following experiment, we used the Office31 dataset, which is used mainly in domain adaptation scenarios. The Office31 dataset includes 31 object categories in three domains: Amazon, DSLR, and Webcam (see Fig. 3a).

We divided each dataset into two splits, following the setting in [14]. For the training data, we used 20 samples per category for Amazon and 7 for both DSLR and Webcam. We used the rest of the samples as test sets. For each domain, we used ResNet50 architecture, pre-trained on ImageNet, and trained it using the domain's training set. We extracted the penultimate layer output from ResNet50 architecture and trained our VRS model on this pre-trained feature, to approximate the distributions p_i. For our predictors h_i, we extracted the output from ResNet50 architecture and used softmax layer to calculate the probabilities.

We compared our VRS-MSA model against previous results presented by Cortes et al. [2]. While Cortes et al. only provided results for individual test sets, we additionally present results for various combinations of test sets, providing a more comprehensive comparison of the performance of our VRS model. The results are reported in Table 2 (full table provided in Appendix E).

Our VRS-MSA model demonstrates competitive scores, with particularly strong results on the test set DSLR. We note that the DSLR's high score comes

Table 2. Office Dataset Accuracy (a - Amazon, w - Webcam, d - DSLR) Previous results were taken from [2].

Models	Test datasets							
	a	w	d	aw	ad	wd	awd	mean
GMSA	82.1	**96.8**	96.7	–	–	–	–	–
VAE-MSA	76.6	93.4	98.6	81.0	79.8	95.0	82.7	86.7
$VRS_{2,-2}$-MSA	81.6	92.2	98.6	84.5	84.0	94.3	86.0	88.7
$VRS_{0.5,-0.5}$-MSA	81.7	92.4	**98.6**	84.6	84.2	94.5	86.1	88.9
$VRS_{2,-2}$-SGD	92.2	95.0	96.8	92.7	92.7	95.6	93.1	94.0
$VRS_{0.5,-0.5}$-SGD	**92.2**	95.0	96.8	**92.8**	**92.7**	**95.6**	**93.2**	**94.0**

at the expense of Amazon and Webcam's high scores. This is mainly because the vector $w = (w_{Amazon} : 0.25, w_{DSLR} : 0.71, w_{Webcam} : 0.04)$ learned in the DC programming algorithm determined high weight to DSLR. Likewise, the VRS-SGD method achieved competitive scores compared to the models using the DC algorithm. We can see that the VRS-SGD score for the Amazon test set is the highest and as a result, the scores on test sets that include Amazon were also improved.

7 Summary

In this study, we reviewed and analyzed the MSA problem, and established the need for accurate density estimations. We presented a new upper bound for the log evidence, termed VRLU, in which its MC approximation preserves the upper bound property, and used it to devise a new (sandwiched) upper-lower bound method termed VRS. We demonstrated the usage of VRS in MSA applications, where the true distributions are unknown.

To this end, we devised two methods, VRS-MSA and VRS-SGD. In the empirical evaluation, both methods demonstrated competitive performances, and in certain instances even surpassed the performance of models reported in previous studies.

Our current efforts are directed to further enhance and extend the VRS-MSA method. Specifically, in this work, we haven't formed a connection between the latent variables of each VRS model of the different domains. It will be interesting to see how such a connection (of normalization, scaling of the probability measurements, or latent space alignment) will affect the resulting solution for the MSA problem. This direction is left for future research efforts.

Ethical Statement: There are no ethical issues.

References

1. Cheung, W.: Generalizations of hölders inequality. Sciences **26**(1), 7–10 (2001)
2. Cortes, C., Mohri, M., Suresh, A.T., Zhang, N.: A discriminative technique for multiple-source adaptation. In: International Conference on Machine Learning, pp. 2132–2143. PMLR (2021)
3. Csiszár, I.: I-divergence geometry of probability distributions and minimization problems. Ann. Probab., 146–158 (1975)
4. French, G., Mackiewicz, M., Fisher, M.: Self-ensembling for visual domain adaptation. In: International Conference on Learning Representations (2018)
5. Hoffman, J., Mohri, M., Zhang, N.: Algorithms and theory for multiple-source adaptation. In: Advances in Neural Information Processing Systems, vol. 31 (2018)
6. Jordan, M.I., Ghahramani, Z., Jaakkola, T.S., Saul, L.K.: An introduction to variational methods for graphical models. Mach. Learn. **37**(2), 183–233 (1999)
7. Kingma, D.P., Ba, J.: Adam: a method for stochastic optimization. arXiv preprint arXiv:1412.6980 (2014)
8. Kingma, D.P., Welling, M.: Auto-encoding variational bayes. Stat **1050**, 1 (2014)
9. Li, Y., Turner, R.E.: Rényi divergence variational inference. In: Advances in Neural Information Processing Systems, vol. 29 (2016)
10. MacKay, D.J.: Information Theory, Inference and Learning Algorithms. Cambridge University Press, Cambridge (2003)
11. Mansour, Y., Mohri, M., Rostamizadeh, A.: Domain adaptation with multiple sources. In: Advances in Neural Information Processing Systems, vol. 21 (2008)
12. Mansour, Y., Mohri, M., Rostamizadeh, A.: Multiple source adaptation and the Rényi divergence. In: Proceedings of the Twenty-Fifth Conference on Uncertainty in Artificial Intelligence, pp. 367–374 (2009)
13. Poole, B., Ozair, S., Van Den Oord, A., Alemi, A., Tucker, G.: On variational bounds of mutual information. In: International Conference on Machine Learning, pp. 5171–5180. PMLR (2019)
14. Saenko, K., Kulis, B., Fritz, M., Darrell, T.: Adapting visual category models to new domains. In: Daniilidis, K., Maragos, P., Paragios, N. (eds.) ECCV 2010. LNCS, vol. 6314, pp. 213–226. Springer, Heidelberg (2010). https://doi.org/10.1007/978-3-642-15561-1_16
15. Shekhovtsov, A., Schlesinger, D., Flach, B.: VAE approximation error: Elbo and exponential families. In: International Conference on Learning Representations (ICLR) (2021)
16. Van Erven, T., Harremos, P.: Rényi divergence and Kullback-Leibler divergence. IEEE Trans. Inf. Theory **60**(7), 3797–3820 (2014)
17. Zhang, C., Bütepage, J., Kjellström, H., Mandt, S.: Advances in variational inference. IEEE Trans. Pattern Anal. Mach. Intell. **41**(8), 2008–2026 (2018)

Match-And-Deform: Time Series Domain Adaptation Through Optimal Transport and Temporal Alignment

François Painblanc[1], Laetitia Chapel[2], Nicolas Courty[2], Chloé Friguet[2], Charlotte Pelletier[2], and Romain Tavenard[1(✉)]

[1] Université Rennes 2, LETG, IRISA, Rennes, France
romain.tavenard@univ-rennes2.fr

[2] Université Bretagne Sud, IRISA, UMR CNRS 6074, Vannes, France

Abstract. While large volumes of unlabeled data are usually available, associated labels are often scarce. The unsupervised domain adaptation problem aims at exploiting labels from a source domain to classify data from a related, yet different, target domain. When time series are at stake, new difficulties arise as temporal shifts may appear in addition to the standard feature distribution shift. In this paper, we introduce the Match-And-Deform (MAD) approach that aims at finding correspondences between the source and target time series while allowing temporal distortions. The associated optimization problem simultaneously aligns the series thanks to an optimal transport loss and the time stamps through dynamic time warping. When embedded into a deep neural network, MAD helps learning new representations of time series that both align the domains and maximize the discriminative power of the network. Empirical studies on benchmark datasets and remote sensing data demonstrate that MAD makes meaningful sample-to-sample pairing and time shift estimation, reaching similar or better classification performance than state-of-the-art deep time series domain adaptation strategies.

Keywords: domain adaptation · time series · optimal transport · dynamic time warping

1 Introduction

A standard assumption in machine learning is that the training and the test data are drawn from the same distribution. When this assumption is not met, trained models often have degraded performances because of their poor generalization ability. Domain adaptation (DA) is the branch of machine learning that tackles this generalisation problem when the difference in distribution can be expressed

---

Supplementary Information The online version contains supplementary material available at https://doi.org/10.1007/978-3-031-43424-2_21.

D. Koutra et al. (Eds.): ECML PKDD 2023, LNAI 14173, pp. 341–356, 2023.
https://doi.org/10.1007/978-3-031-43424-2_21

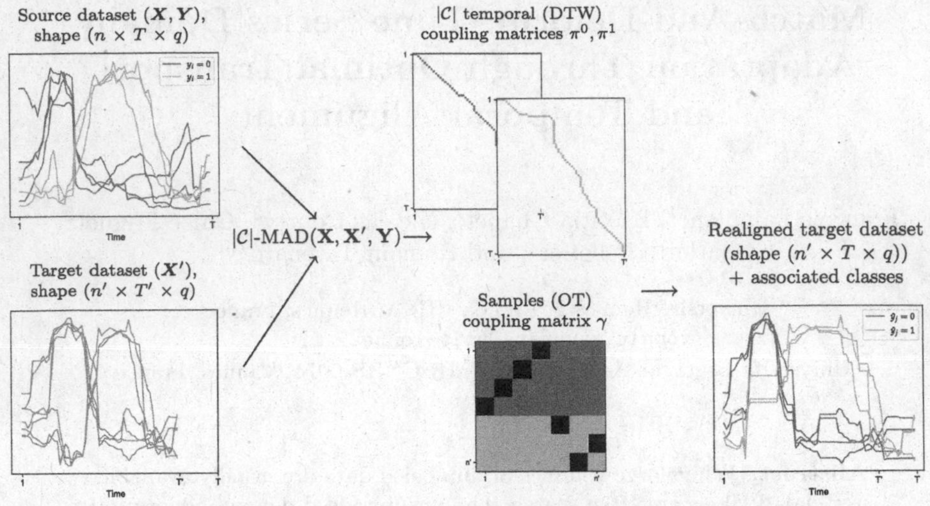

Fig. 1. Match-And-Deform ($|\mathcal{C}|$-MAD) takes two time series datasets as inputs: a source (labelled) dataset and a target (unlabelled) dataset. It jointly computes an optimal transport (OT) coupling matrix γ and $|\mathcal{C}|$ class-wise dynamic time warping (DTW) paths $\{\boldsymbol{\pi}^{(c)}\}_{c \in \mathcal{C}}$. The OT cost is derived from the pairwise distances yielded by the DTW paths while the DTW cost is weighted by the OT plan. These outputs are then used to improve classification in the target dataset.

as a shift, allowing for improving task efficiency on a target domain by using all available information from a source domain. When dealing with time series data, that are ubiquitous in many real-world situations, being able to learn across time series domains is a challenging task as temporal deformations between domains might occur in addition to the feature distribution shift.

Most of the literature in DA focuses on bridging the distribution shift, either by aligning distributions or by finding a common representation space [16,20]. In unsupervised DA frameworks, training is performed on the source domain data relying on this common representation so that effective performance on the target domain can be expected. A standard approach consists in using adversarial training to push a deep neural network model into learning domain-invariant intermediate representations [7]. This approach has been extended to the time series context by using dedicated network architectures. In VRADA [15], variational recurrent neural networks are considered while in the state-of-the-art method CoDATS [21], the feature extraction block is made of convolutional layers. However, these methods operate on pooled features in which the time dimension has vanished and, as such, ignore the impact of potential temporal dynamics across multiple yet related time series.

Optimal transport (OT) is an efficient tool for DA, in both unsupervised and semi-supervised learning. It can be used to evaluate the distribution shift as a non-linear function [3] or, as done in more recent works, it can help design deep neural network losses that take into account the dissimilarity between the domains [4]. OT-based DA methods have proven useful in many applications but do not encode any temporal coherence that should be kept when dealing with time series data.

The approach presented in this paper, coined Match-And-Deform (MAD), combines OT with dynamic time warping (DTW) to achieve time series matching and timestamp alignment. This yields a dissimilarity measure that relies on a temporally realigned sample-to-sample matching. In other words, MAD evaluates the feature distribution shift between domains up to a global temporal alignment. MAD can then be used as a loss function in a neural network to learn a domain-invariant latent representation.

In the following, the background on DTW and OT are introduced. MAD and its use as a loss for DA are then presented and experimentally compared to standard competitors, considering classification tasks on benchmark time series datasets but also on remote sensing time series datasets as an application framework. Finally, we discuss related works and present perspectives.

2 Background

In the sequel, we aim at finding a coupling between samples of two datasets, up to a global temporal shift. For that purpose, we jointly solve two alignment problems: (i) a temporal realignment (of the timestamps) of the datasets and (ii) a matching between time series (samples). Both rely on related linear optimization problems that differ in the nature of the coupling involved.

In a general way, the optimisation problem for comparing two objects (either time series or distributions) $\mathbf{x}$ and $\mathbf{x}'$ can be stated as:

$$J\Big(\mathbf{C}(\mathbf{x}, \mathbf{x}'), \Pi\Big) = \underset{\boldsymbol{\pi} \in \Pi}{\arg\min} \Big\langle \mathbf{C}(\mathbf{x}, \mathbf{x}'), \boldsymbol{\pi} \Big\rangle, \tag{1}$$

in which Π is a set of admissible couplings. A coupling will either be a temporal alignment if $\mathbf{x}$ and $\mathbf{x}'$ are time series or a matching between samples if they are distributions, with appropriate constraint sets, as detailed later in this section. The solution $J(\cdot, \cdot)$ of the optimization problem is called the optimal coupling matrix. The cost matrix $\mathbf{C}(\mathbf{x}, \mathbf{x}') = \big\{d(x^i, x'^j)\big\}_{ij}$ stores distances $d(x^i, x'^j)$ between atomic elements x^i and x'^j, respectively from $\mathbf{x}$ and $\mathbf{x}'$.

Dynamic Time Warping (DTW) is an instance of problem (1) whose goal is to match two (multivariate) time series $\mathbf{x} \in \mathbb{R}^{T \times q}$, and $\mathbf{x}' \in \mathbb{R}^{T' \times q}$ as:

$$\mathrm{DTW}(\mathbf{x}, \mathbf{x}') = J\Big(\mathbf{C}(\mathbf{x}, \mathbf{x}'), \mathcal{A}(T, T')\Big). \tag{2}$$

Here, $\mathbf{C}(\mathbf{x}, \mathbf{x}')$ stores Euclidean distances between q-dimensional atomic elements and $\mathcal{A}(T, T')$ is the set of admissible timestamps alignments between series of respective lengths T and T'. An admissible alignment $\boldsymbol{\pi} \in \mathcal{A}(T, T')$ is a binary $T \times T'$-matrix that matches timestamps between time series $\mathbf{x}$ and $\mathbf{x}'$. Its non-zero entries should form a connected path between cells $(1, 1)$ and (T, T'). This definition allows for efficient computation in quadratic time using dynamic programming [18]. Note that DTW can be seen as seeking a temporal transformation (in the form of repeated samples) such that the Euclidean distance between transformed series is minimized.

Optimal Transport (OT) is another instance of the same general optimization problem (1) that defines a distance between two probability measures. The discrete probability measures $\mathbf{X}$ and $\mathbf{X}'$ are sets of weighted samples in $\mathbb{R}^q$: $\{(\mathbf{x}^i, w^i)\}_{i=1}^n$ with $\sum_i w^i = 1$ and $\{(\mathbf{x}'^j, w'^j)\}_{j=1}^{n'}$ with $\sum_j w'^j = 1$. When no prior information is available, weights are set uniformly. OT defines a distance between $\mathbf{X}$ and $\mathbf{X}'$ by seeking the transport plan $\gamma \in \Gamma(\mathbf{w}, \mathbf{w}')$ that minimises the transport cost:

$$\mathrm{OT}(\mathbf{X}, \mathbf{X}') = J\Big(\mathbf{C}(\mathbf{X}, \mathbf{X}'), \Gamma(\mathbf{w}, \mathbf{w}')\Big). \tag{3}$$

$\Gamma(\mathbf{w}, \mathbf{w}')$ is the set of admissible transport plans, *i.e.* the set of linear transports such that all the mass from $\mathbf{X}$ is transported toward all the mass of $\mathbf{X}'$:

$$\Gamma(\mathbf{w}, \mathbf{w}') = \Big\{\boldsymbol{\gamma} | \boldsymbol{\gamma} \geq \mathbf{0}, \boldsymbol{\gamma}\mathbf{1}_{n'} = \mathbf{w}, \boldsymbol{\gamma}^\top \mathbf{1}_{n} = \mathbf{w}'\Big\}$$

with $\mathbf{1}_n$ a n-vector of ones. The transport plan $\boldsymbol{\gamma}$ is a $n \times n'$-matrix whose elements γ_{ij} indicate the amount of mass *transported* from x^i to x'^j. The transport plan is sparse, with at most $n + n' - 1$ elements that are non-zeros. The most common algorithmic tools to solve the discrete OT problem are borrowed from combinatorial optimisation and linear programming (see [14] for a thorough review).

3 Match-And-Deform (MAD)

In an unsupervised time series domain adaptation context, let us consider a source dataset $(\mathbf{X}, \mathbf{Y}) \in \mathbb{R}^{n \times T \times q} \times \mathcal{C}^n$ and a dataset from a target domain $\mathbf{X}' \in \mathbb{R}^{n' \times T' \times q}$. $\mathbf{X} = (x_1^i; \ldots; x_T^i)_{i=1}^n$ and $\mathbf{X}' = (x_1'^j; \ldots; x_{T'}'^j)_{j=1}^{n'}$ represent multidimensional time series data ($q \geq 1$) with lengths T and T', respectively. Both domains share the same label space $\mathcal{C}$ but only source labels $\mathbf{Y}$ are observed. Our goal is to classify target data, using knowledge transferred from source data.

Despite its widespread use, DTW is limited to finding a temporal alignment between two single time series $\mathbf{x} \in \mathbb{R}^{T \times q}$, and $\mathbf{x}' \in \mathbb{R}^{T' \times q}$, without any consideration for the alignment of sets of series. On the other hand, OT is designed to match datasets regardless of any temporal dimension. A simple approach to combine both matchings is to use DTW as the inner cost $\mathbf{C}(\mathbf{X}, \mathbf{X}')$ of an OT problem. However, we argue that this would result in spurious matchings, due to the many degrees of freedom introduced by individual DTW computations (see Experiments section). Instead, we introduce a new metric, coined Match-And-Deform (MAD), that jointly optimizes a global DTW alignment and an OT coupling to match two sets of time series, as illustrated in Fig. 1. Let us therefore define MAD as:

$$\begin{aligned}\mathrm{MAD}(\mathbf{X}, \mathbf{X}') &= \underset{\substack{\gamma \in \Gamma(\mathbf{w}, \mathbf{w}') \\ \pi \in \mathcal{A}(T, T')}}{\arg\min} \ \langle \mathbf{L}(\mathbf{X}, \mathbf{X}') \otimes \boldsymbol{\pi}, \boldsymbol{\gamma} \rangle \\ &= \underset{\substack{\gamma \in \Gamma(\mathbf{w}, \mathbf{w}') \\ \pi \in \mathcal{A}(T, T')}}{\arg\min} \sum_{i,j} \sum_{\ell,m} d(x^i_\ell, x'^j_m) \pi_{\ell m} \gamma_{ij}.\end{aligned} \tag{4}$$

Here, $\mathbf{L}(\mathbf{X}, \mathbf{X}')$ is a 4-dimensional tensor whose elements are $L^{i,j}_{\ell,m} = d(x^i_\ell, x'^j_m)$, with $d : \mathbb{R}^q \times \mathbb{R}^q \to \mathbb{R}^+$ being a distance. $\otimes$ is the tensor-matrix multiplication. $\boldsymbol{\pi}$ is a global DTW alignment between timestamps and $\boldsymbol{\gamma}$ is a transport plan between samples from $\mathbf{X}$ and $\mathbf{X}'$.

By combining metrics that operate between time series and samples in a single optimization problem, MAD gets the best of both worlds: it seeks a transport plan $\boldsymbol{\gamma}$ that matches samples up to a global temporal transformation $\boldsymbol{\pi}$ (in the form of repeated samples, see the DTW presentation in Background section), hence defining a metric between datasets that is invariant to dataset-wide time shifts. Note that MAD seeks for a global temporal alignment between datasets, which implies that all series inside a dataset have the same length, otherwise matching timestamps through $\boldsymbol{\pi}$ would be meaningless.

The optimization problem in Eq. (4) can be further extended to the case of distinct DTW mappings for each class c in the source data. This results in the following optimization problem, coined $|\mathcal{C}|$-MAD:

$$|\mathcal{C}|\text{-MAD}(\mathbf{X}, \mathbf{X}', \mathbf{Y}) = \underset{\substack{\gamma \in \Gamma(\mathbf{w}, \mathbf{w}') \\ \forall c, \pi^{(c)} \in \mathcal{A}(T, T')}}{\arg\min} \sum_{i,j} \sum_{\ell,m} L^{i,j}_{\ell,m} \pi^{(y^i)}_{\ell m} \gamma_{ij}\,. \tag{5}$$

In that case, $|\mathcal{C}|$ DTW alignments are involved, one for each class c. $\boldsymbol{\pi}^{(y^i)}$ denotes the DTW matrix associated to the class y^i of x^i. This more flexible formulation allows adapting to different temporal distortions that might occur across classes.

Properties. Let us now study some of the properties of this new similarity measure. Our first property links Optimal Transport, MAD and $|\mathcal{C}|$-MAD problems.

Property 1. Let $\mathbf{X} \in \mathbb{R}^{n \times T \times q}$ and $\mathbf{X}' \in \mathbb{R}^{n' \times T' \times q}$ be time series datasets. Let $\mathrm{OT}_{\mathrm{DTW}}(\mathbf{X}, \mathbf{X}')$ be the solution of the OT problem with cost $\mathbf{C}(\mathbf{X}, \mathbf{X}') = \{\mathrm{DTW}(\mathbf{x}, \mathbf{x}')\}_{\mathbf{x}, \mathbf{x}' \in \mathbf{X}, \mathbf{X}'}$, and let us denote $\mathrm{cost}(\cdot)$ the cost associated to a solution of any optimization problem. We have:

$$\mathrm{cost}\Big(\mathrm{OT}_{\mathrm{DTW}}(\mathbf{X}, \mathbf{X}')\Big) \leq \mathrm{cost}\Big(|\mathcal{C}|\text{-MAD}(\mathbf{X}, \mathbf{X}', \mathbf{Y})\Big) \leq \mathrm{cost}\Big(\mathrm{MAD}(\mathbf{X}, \mathbf{X}')\Big)$$

Moreover, MAD inherits properties from the OT field. Typically, the transport plans $\boldsymbol{\gamma}$ resulting from MAD and $|\mathcal{C}|$-MAD are sparse. If $n = n'$ and uniform weights are considered, there always exists a transport plan solution of the MAD (resp. $|\mathcal{C}|$-MAD) problem that is a permutation matrix, as stated in the following property.

Algorithm 1. $|\mathcal{C}|$–MAD optimization via BCD

Input: weighted time series datasets $\mathbf{X}$ and $\mathbf{X}'$, initial DTW paths $\{\boldsymbol{\pi}^{(c)}\}$
repeat
  Compute $\mathbf{C}_{\mathrm{OT}}(\mathbf{X}, \mathbf{X}', Y, \{\boldsymbol{\pi}^{(c)}\}_c)$ using Eq. (6)
  $\gamma \leftarrow J\Big(\mathbf{C}_{\mathrm{OT}}(\mathbf{X}, \mathbf{X}', Y, \{\boldsymbol{\pi}^{(c)}\}_c), \Gamma(\mathbf{w}, \mathbf{w}')\Big)$
  for c = 1 .. $|\mathcal{C}|$ **do**
    Compute $\mathbf{C}^c_{\mathrm{DTW}}(\mathbf{X}, \mathbf{X}', \gamma)$ using Eq. (7)
    $\boldsymbol{\pi}^{(c)} \leftarrow J\Big(\mathbf{C}^c_{\mathrm{DTW}}(\mathbf{X}, \mathbf{X}', \gamma), \mathcal{A}(T, T')\Big)$
  end for
until convergence

Property 2. Let $\mathbf{X}$ and $\mathbf{X}'$ be datasets each composed of n time series, and let us assume uniform weights, *i.e.* $\mathbf{w} = \mathbf{w}' = (1/n, \cdots, 1/n)$. There exists a transport plan solution to the MAD (resp. $|\mathcal{C}|$-MAD) problem that is a one-to-one matching, *i.e.* each sample from $\mathbf{X}$ is matched to exactly one sample in $\mathbf{X}'$ (and conversely).

Proofs for these properties are provided as Supplementary Material.

Optimization. Let us consider the joint optimization problem introduced in Eq. (5), which involves $|\mathcal{C}|$ finite sets of admissible DTW paths and a continuous space with linear constraints for the OT plan. Extension to solving the problem of Eq. (4) is straightforward. We perform a Block Coordinate Descent (BCD) to optimize the corresponding loss. BCD is a simple iterative algorithm for non-convex optimization problems in which one set of parameters is optimized while the others are held fixed at each step; this algorithm has already been used in similar contexts, e.g. in [17]. In our case, one of the involved maps is optimized with all the other ones fixed, giving $|\mathcal{C}|+1$ intertwined optimization problems in the form of Eq. (1). Indeed for a given set of DTW paths $\{\boldsymbol{\pi}^{(c)}\}_{c=1}^{|\mathcal{C}|}$, the problem in Eq. (5) boils down to a linear OT problem with a cost matrix defined as:

$$\mathbf{C}_{\mathrm{OT}}(\mathbf{X}, \mathbf{X}', \mathbf{Y}, \{\boldsymbol{\pi}^{(c)}\}_c) = \left\{ \sum_{\ell,m} L^{i,j}_{\ell,m} \pi^{(y^i)}_{\ell m} \right\}_{i,j} . \tag{6}$$

Similarly, for a fixed transport plan $\boldsymbol{\gamma}$, solving the problem in Eq. (5) with respect to a given class-specific DTW path $\boldsymbol{\pi}^{(c)}$ is a DTW problem in which the cost matrix is:

$$\mathbf{C}^c_{\mathrm{DTW}}(\mathbf{X}, \mathbf{X}', \gamma) = \left\{ \sum_{i \text{ s.t. } y^i = c, j} L^{i,j}_{\ell,m} \gamma_{ij} \right\}_{\ell,m} . \tag{7}$$

Hence, it leads to optimizing independently $|\mathcal{C}|$ DTW alignment problems.

The resulting BCD optimization is presented in Algorithm 1. Note that in each update step, we get an optimal value for the considered map given the other ones fixed, hence the sequence of $|\mathcal{C}|$-MAD losses is both decreasing and lower bounded by zero, thus converging to a local optimum.

4 Neural Domain Adaptation with a MAD Loss

OT has been successfully used as a loss to measure the discrepancy between source and target domain samples embedded into a latent space. Similarly to DeepJDOT [4], our proposal considers a deep unsupervised temporal DA model that relies on MAD or $|\mathcal{C}|$-MAD as a regularization loss function.

The deep neural network architecture of DeepJDOT is composed of two parts: (i) an embedding function g_Ω that maps the inputs into a given latent space, and (ii) a classifier f_θ that maps the latent representation of the samples into a label space shared by both source and target domains. OT is applied on the output of the embeddings such that g_Ω yields a discriminant yet domain invariant representation of the data. When dealing with temporal data, we minimize the following overall loss function over $\{\boldsymbol{\pi}^{(c)}\}_c$, γ, Ω and θ:

$$\mathcal{L}(\mathbf{X},\mathbf{Y},\mathbf{X}') = \overbrace{\frac{1}{n}\sum_i \mathcal{L}_s(y^i, f_\theta(g_\Omega(\mathbf{x}^i)))}^{(A)} + \sum_{i,j}\gamma_{ij}\Big(\underbrace{\alpha\sum_{\ell,m}\pi^{(y^i)}_{\ell m} L\left(g_\Omega(\mathbf{X}), g_\Omega(\mathbf{X}')\right)^{i,j}_{\ell,m}}_{(B)} + \beta\,\underbrace{\mathcal{L}_t(y^i, f_\theta(g_\Omega(\mathbf{x}'^j)))}_{(C)}\Big) \tag{8}$$

where $\mathcal{L}_s(\cdot,\cdot)$ and $\mathcal{L}_t(\cdot,\cdot)$ are cross entropy losses, γ (resp. $\{\boldsymbol{\pi}^{(c)}\}_c$) is the transport plan (resp. the set of DTW paths) yielded by $|\mathcal{C}|$-MAD. The first part (A) of the loss is a classification loss on the source domain; (B) and (C) rely on the OT plan γ_{ij}: (C) seeks to align the labels of the source time series with the predicted labels of their matched ($\gamma_{ij} > 0$) target time series. The difference with DeepJDOT lies in the term (B) of Eq. (8). This part aims at aligning the latent representations of the time series from the source and target domains that have been matched, the main difference here is that the embeddings of $\mathbf{x}^i$ and $\mathbf{x}'^j$ are additionally temporally realigned thanks to the DTW mapping $\boldsymbol{\pi}^{(y^i)}$. Finally, α and β are hyper-parameters to balance terms (B) and (C) in the global loss.

This loss can be minimized to zero if (i) the classifier achieves perfect accuracy on source data, (ii) the distribution of features at the output of the embedding for the source and target domains match up to a global temporal alignment per class, and (iii) source labels and target predictions are matched by the MAD transport plan.

Optimization. The loss function described in Eq. (8) is optimized over two groups of parameters: (i) the neural network parameters θ and Ω and (ii) MAD transport plan γ and DTW paths $\{\boldsymbol{\pi}^{(c)}\}_c$. Similar to what is done in [4], we use an approximate optimization procedure that relies on stochastic gradients. For each mini-batch, a forward pass is performed during which mini-batch-specific γ and $\{\boldsymbol{\pi}^{(c)}\}_c$ maps are estimated using Algorithm 1, for fixed network blocks g_Ω and f_θ. While the DTW cost matrix presented in Eq. (7) remains unchanged, the OT cost gets an extra term from the cross-domain label mapping:

$$\left\{\alpha \sum_{\ell,m} \pi_{\ell m}^{(y^i)} L\left(g_\Omega(\mathbf{X}), g_\Omega(\mathbf{X}')\right)_{\ell,m}^{i,j} + \beta \mathcal{L}_t\Big(y^i, f_\theta(g_\Omega(\mathbf{x}'^j))\Big)\right\}_{i,j}.$$

To initialize the learning process, we use random DTW paths and, when repeating this process for consecutive mini-batches of data, we use the DTW paths from the previous mini-batch as initializers. Note that even though stochastic optimisation can be expected to converge towards optimal parameters Ω and θ, it is not the case for the MAD parameters: it is known from the OT literature [8] that the expected value of the OT plan over the mini-batches does not converge to the full OT coupling. However, authors of [4] claim that the resulting non-sparse estimated plan can act as a regularizer to enforce mass sharing between similar samples.

Complexity. Assuming time series lengths in both datasets are comparable, and relying on the sparsity of γ and $\boldsymbol{\pi}^{(c)}$, computing the cost matrices $\mathbf{C}_{\text{OT}}$ and $\{\mathbf{C}^c_{\text{DTW}}\}_c$ can be done in $O(b^2Te + bT^2e)$ where b is the number of series in a mini-batch and e is the dimension of the embedding $g_\Omega(\cdot)$. Given a pre-computed cost matrix, each DTW computation is of complexity $O(T^2)$ and similarly, the complexity for the OT solving step is $O(b^3 \log b)$. The overall complexity for each iteration of Algorithm 1 is then $O(b^2(b \log b + Te) + (be + |\mathcal{C}|)T^2)$. We observe in practice that, in all our experiments, a few iterations were sufficient to reach convergence (characterised by DTW paths not evolving anymore).

5 Experiments

The use of MAD and $|\mathcal{C}|$-MAD as losses for neural domain adaptation is now assessed considering a real remote sensing dataset, for which there exists a known global temporal shift between the (classes of the) domains due to different weather conditions. We further study its use in a motion capture context.[1]

Backbone Architecture. In order to evaluate the impact of the MAD regularization loss for domain adaptation, we use the exact same deep neural network architecture as in CoDATS [21]. The feature extractor g_Ω is composed of a stack of 3 convolutional layers followed by batch normalization. The classification head f_θ then consists of a global average pooling followed by a single fully-connected layer, as shown in Fig. 2. The first layer of the feature extractor has 128 filters of size 8, the second layer has 256 filters of size 5 and the third layer has 128 filters of size 3. Note that, for CoDATS, the domain adversarial classification head is plugged after the pooling operator.

Hyper-parameters. For a fair comparison, and for all the experiments, we choose a single learning rate (0.0001) and batch size ($b = 256$) for both the CoDATS baseline and our approach. The MAD loss in Eq. (8) introduces two extra hyper-parameters; their values are set to $\alpha = 0.01$ and $\beta = 0.01$ for all

[1] Code, supplementary material and datasets are available at https://github.com/rtavenar/MatchAndDeform.

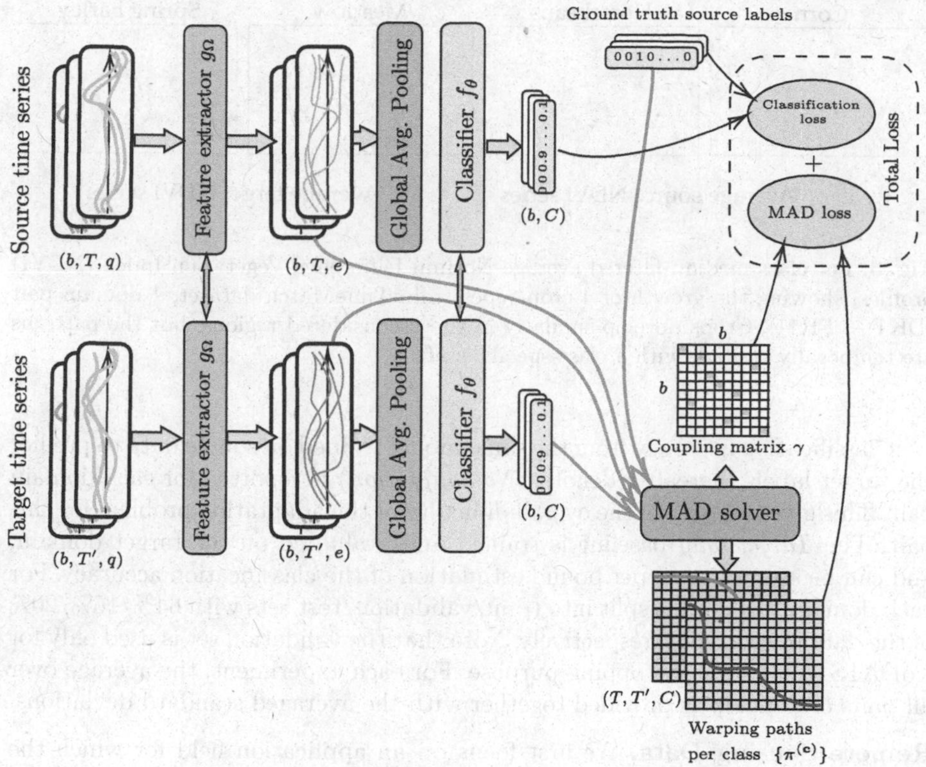

Fig. 2. Backbone architecture and schematic view of the loss computation for $|\mathcal{C}|$-MAD.

the experiments. In practice, we observe that a large range of values give similar performances (a deeper investigation is provided as Supplementary Material).

Experimental Setup. Our proposed method MAD and its variant $|\mathcal{C}|$-MAD are compared to CoDATS, which extends the domain adversarial neural network (DANN, [7]) framework to time series data and has been shown to reach state-of-the-art performance. As in [21], the proportion of each class in the target domain is assumed to be known during the learning phase. This corresponds to the CoDATS-WS variant. As an OT for DA baseline, we furthermore compare to DeepJDOT-DTW, considering DeepJDOT [4] adapted for time series: individual DTW between pairs of series are considered as transport cost matrix $C(\boldsymbol{X}, \boldsymbol{X}') = \{\text{DTW}(\boldsymbol{x}, \boldsymbol{x}')\}_{\boldsymbol{x}, \boldsymbol{x}' \in \boldsymbol{X}, \boldsymbol{X}'}$.

In MAD and DeepJDOT-DTW, the weights $\mathbf{w}$ from the source mini-batches are set such that they reflect the proportion of the classes in the target domain; uniform weights $\mathbf{w}'$ are used for target mini-batches. Note that integrating this extra information could be avoided by using unbalanced optimal transport [6], which is left for future work. For the sake of fairness, all competing methods are trained and tested on the same data splits with the same backbone architecture.

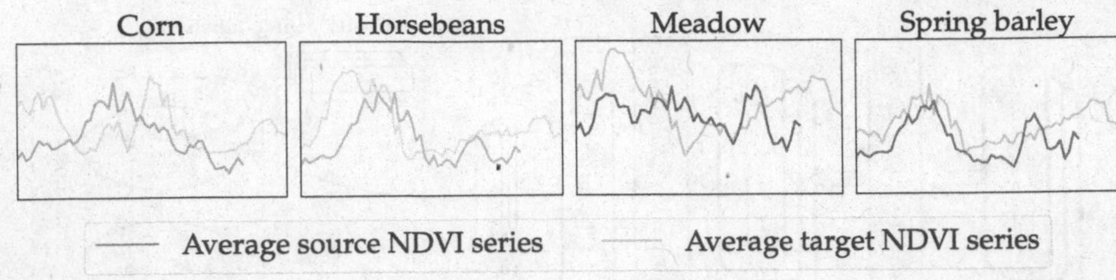

Fig. 3. Per-class median-filtered average Normal Difference Vegetation Index (NDVI) profiles, showing the growth of 4 crop types (miniTimeMatch dataset, 1 domain pair (DK1 → FR1)). Crops develop similarly in the 2 considered regions, but the patterns are temporally shifted, with a class-specific shift.

Classification accuracy from the same model trained on source data to predict the target labels (hereafter denoted *No adaptation*) is reported for each domain pair. This gives a proxy of the overall difficulty of the adaptation problem for this pair. The *Target only* baseline is trained and evaluated on the target domain, and can be seen as an upper bound estimation of the classification accuracy. For each domain, the data is split into train/validation/test sets with 64%/16%/20% of the data in each split, respectively. Note that the validation set is used only for CoDATS-WS for early stopping purpose. For each experiment, the average over all pairs of domains is provided together with the averaged standard deviations.

Remote Sensing Data. We first focus on an application field for which the temporal shift between domains has already been documented. In Earth observation, and especially for land cover mapping applications, the differences in weather, soil conditions or farmer practices between study sites are known to induce temporal shifts in the data that should be dealt with, as discussed in [13] for example. Moreover, these temporal shifts can be global to the study sites or class specific (see Fig. 3), which is the setup for which MAD and $|\mathcal{C}|$-MAD are designed.

TimeMatch dataset [13] is a crop-type mapping dataset covering four different geographical areas in Austria, Denmark, and France. It contains time series of multi-spectral measurements from satellite imagery at each geo-location. Labels are available at a parcel level: hence we consider a modified version of TimeMatch, referred to as miniTimeMatch in the following, in which measurements are averaged over agricultural parcels. The aim is to recognize parcels' crop type, such as corn or wheat. Domains correspond to different geographical areas, with their own characteristics. Moreover, we remove data from classes that are not observed in all domains, or with less than 200 agricultural fields in at least one domain. We also remove the "unknown" class that gathers crops from many types. Finally, we sample $n_{\min}$ series per class in each domain, where $n_{\min}$ is the minimum frequency of the class across all domains. This results in a dataset of 28, 858 time series and 8 classes per domain, each being described by 10 features per timestamp. The same domain pairs as in [13] are considered for the evaluation.

Observations from the miniTimeMatch dataset may be noisy, with some measurements corresponding to cloudy observations. Moreover, the time series of the different domains have different temporal sampling due to the filtering of highly cloudy images (see Fig. 3). Then, we introduce a new domain adaptation problem, considering another land crop mapping dataset called TarnBrittany, in which observations from cloudy images are removed. It is built from Sentinel-2[2] time series for the year 2018, and is composed of two domains: (Brittany) in the mid-west of France on tile T30UVU and (Tarn) in the southwest of France on tile T31TDJ. We collect 72 images for Tarn and 58 images for the cloudier Brittany. Images have been orthorectified and corrected from atmospheric effects by using the MAJA processing chain [11] to yield Level-2A surface reflectance images. As for miniTimeMatch, we average the reflectance values over the agricultural fields to obtain multivariate time series of 10 spectral bands. Labels are obtained from the French land parcel identification system (IGN RPG[3]) for the year 2018. We keep only the five main crops present in both areas. A total of 5,743 series is sampled in each area with similar class proportions in source and target domains. The two domain pairs are considered for the evaluation.

Motion Capture (MoCap) Data. We further evaluate MAD and $|\mathcal{C}|$-MAD on a MoCap setup: Human Activity Recognition (HAR) dataset [5], in which no temporal shift is documented. As such, we do not expect MAD and $|\mathcal{C}|$-MAD to behave better than state-of-the-art algorithms. The dataset contains time series (128 timestamps, 9 features, 6 classes) of movements recorded thanks to mobile sensors such as accelerometer or gyroscope; the aim is to recognize human activities such as walking or sitting. Domains correspond to different persons with their own characteristics. The same 10 domain pairs as in [21] are considered for the evaluation. Details on the dataset are provided as Supplementary Material.

Results. Table 1 shows that, on HAR dataset, MAD and $|\mathcal{C}|$-MAD reach similar performance to CoDATS-WS. In more details, MAD and $|\mathcal{C}|$-MAD outperform CoDATS-WS in five out of ten situations, achieving a slightly better average performance. Table 2 provides classification accuracy for remote sensing datasets, on which MAD and $|\mathcal{C}|$-MAD are expected to work better thanks to their ability to handle (per class) time shifts. The discrepancies between performances of models trained only on source data (*No adaptation*) and those only trained on target data (*Target only*) also point out that all domain pairs constitute a more challenging adaptation problem compared to HAR dataset. One can notice that MAD and $|\mathcal{C}|$-MAD outperform CoDATS-WS in 5 out of the 7 problems, sometimes with an important improvement (see DK1 → FR1 for example), even in the presence of noise (that is present in the miniTimeMatch dataset). This illustrates the fact that MAD and $|\mathcal{C}|$-MAD are of prime interest when global or class-specific temporal deformations occur between domains (see Fig. 3). For each set of datasets, a one-sided Wilcoxon signed-rank test is performed to assert if the results of MAD and $|\mathcal{C}|$-MAD are statistically greater than those of

[2] https://theia-ide.org/.
[3] https://geoservices.ign.fr/rpg.

Table 1. HAR dataset: classification performance (% accuracy, avg over 3 runs ± std).

Problem	No adapt.	CoDATS-WS	DeepJDOT-DTW	MAD	$\|\mathcal{C}\|$-MAD	Target only
2 → 11	83.3 ± 0.7	81.3 ± 4.4	**99.5 ± 0.7**	98.4 ± 1.3	99.0 ± 1.5	100 ± 0.0
7 → 13	89.9 ± 3.6	94.4 ± 2.6	88.4 ± 0.7	**100.0 ± 0.0**	**100 ± 0.0**	100 ± 0.0
12 → 16	41.9 ± 0.0	**64.0 ± 0.6**	56.8 ± 3.8	**64.0 ± 0.6**	**64.0 ± 0.6**	100 ± 0.0
12 → 18	90.0 ± 1.7	**100 ± 0.0**	94.5 ± 0.0	99.5 ± 0.6	99.5 ± 0.7	100 ± 0.0
9 → 18	31.1 ± 1.7	**78.1 ± 4.9**	51.6 ± 10.0	71.7 ± 0.6	71.2 ± 1.1	100 ± 0.0
14 → 19	62.0 ± 4.3	**99.5 ± 0.7**	64.4 ± 1.3	83.3 ± 2.3	84.3 ± 2.4	100 ± 0.0
18 → 23	89.3 ± 5.0	89.8 ± 0.6	97.3 ± 0.0	**98.2 ± 0.6**	97.8 ± 0.6	100 ± 0.0
6 → 23	52.9 ± 2.3	95.1 ± 3.5	60.9 ± 2.7	**97.8 ± 0.6**	**97.8 ± 0.6**	100 ± 0.0
7 → 24	94.4 ± 2.7	99.6 ± 0.6	98.3 ± 1.2	**100.0 ± 0.0**	**100 ± 0.0**	100 ± 0.0
17 → 25	57.3 ± 5.5	95.5 ± 4.6	73.6 ± 3.2	**96.3 ± 2.0**	95.5 ± 1.2	100 ± 0.0
Average	69.2 ± 2.8	89.7 ± 2.3	78.5 ± 2.4	**90.9 ± 0.9**	**90.9 ± 0.9**	100 ± 0.0

Table 2. Remote sensing datasets: classification performance (% accuracy, avg over 3 runs ± std).

Problem	No adapt.	CoDATS-WS	DeepJDOT-DTW	MAD	$\|\mathcal{C}\|$-MAD	Target only
Tarn → Brittany	88.5 ± 3.7	96.0 ± 1.6	89.4 ± 2.2	98.8 ± 0.3	**98.9 ± 0.4**	99.7 ± 0.1
Brittany → Tarn	48.9 ± 0.6	**93.6 ± 0.1**	47.6 ± 1.4	92.0 ± 0.2	90.6 ± 1.1	98.6 ± 0.2
Average	68.7 ± 1.7	94.8 ± 0.9	68.5 ± 1.8	**95.4 ± 0.2**	94.7 ± 0.8	99.2 ± 0.1
DK1 → FR1	69.2 ± 1.3	74.8 ± 1.5	79.0 ± 1.6	**88.4 ± 0.4**	88.3 ± 0.9	95.8 ± 0.9
DK1 → FR2	62.2 ± 3.5	**87.0 ± 3.4**	76.6 ± 2.5	82.5 ± 1.1	81.0 ± 1.1	94.2 ± 1.7
DK1 → AT1	73.9 ± 0.2	71.6 ± 15.4	78.6 ± 0.6	**93.1 ± 1.2**	92.3 ± 2.2	96.7 ± 0.7
FR1 → DK1	61.9 ± 5.2	78.0 ± 10.7	71.3 ± 2.9	**88.2 ± 0.3**	**88.2 ± 0.5**	96.2 ± 0.3
FR1 → FR2	78.8 ± 0.9	82.1 ± 8.2	77.1 ± 1.3	**90.5 ± 0.2**	89.6 ± 0.4	94.2 ± 1.7
Average	69.2 ± 2.2	78.7 ± 7.8	76.5 ± 1.8	**88.5 ± 0.6**	87.9 ± 1.0	95.4 ± 1.1

CoDATS-WS and deepJDOT-DTW. Significant results ($\alpha = 0.05$) are obtained for MAD and $|\mathcal{C}|$-MAD over CoDATS-WS ($p = 0.005$ and $p = 0.01$, respectively), and over DeepJDOT-DTW ($p = 3.10^{-6}$ and $p = 6.10^{-6}$, respectively), confirming the superiority of our approaches. There is no significant difference ($p = 0.18$) between CODATS-WS and deepJDOT-DTW performances.

$|\mathcal{C}|$-MAD As a Trade-Off Between MAD **and DeepJDOT-DTW.** $|\mathcal{C}|$-MAD can be seen as an intermediate configuration between MAD (in which a single global DTW alignment is performed) and DeepJDOT-DTW (which allows individual alignments between each pair of series). The good performance of $|\mathcal{C}|$-MAD compared to DeepJDOT-DTW show that it successfully manages the specific intra-class global alignments. By computing pair-to-pair DTW alignments, DeepJDOT-DTW allows for too many degrees of freedom that lead to spurious matchings. On the contrary, ($|\mathcal{C}|$-)MAD acts as a regularizer (see Property 1), allowing to meaningfully constrain the alignments for better performance.

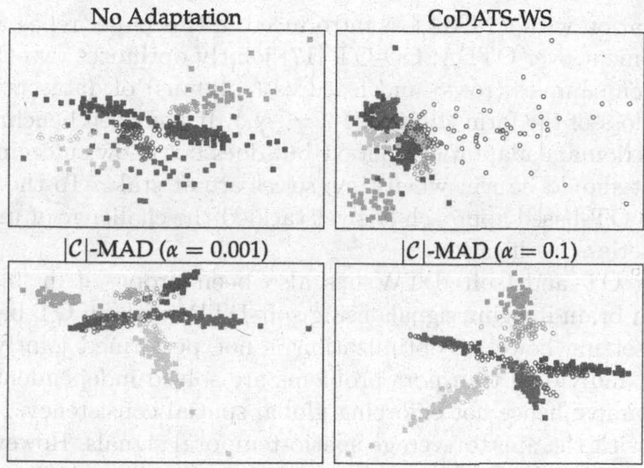

Fig. 4. Multi-Dimensional Scaling (MDS) representation of the latent space for several models on the Tarn (empty circles) → Brittany (squares) adaptation problem: each colour represents a different class.

Latent Space Visualization. To further investigate the internal properties of the models, we use Multi-Dimensional Scaling (MDS) to visualize the latent space of the compared models. To do so, we focus on the models learned for the "Tarn → Brittany" adaptation problem and visualize $g_\Omega(\mathbf{X})$ and $g_\Omega(\mathbf{X}')$ jointly for a model trained on source data only, as well as for CoDATS-WS and $|\mathcal{C}|$-MAD that aim at learning a domain-invariant representation. While Euclidean distance is used to feed MDS for both baselines, we use the distances resulting from the DTW paths for $|\mathcal{C}|$-MAD (as stored in $\mathbf{C}_{\text{OT}}$), in order to account for the temporal realignment on which our method relies. The resulting visualizations presented in Fig. 4 show a significant shift in distributions from target to source domain, when no DA strategy is employed. CoDATS-WS also fails to align domains in the presence of time shifts, whereas $|\mathcal{C}|$-MAD successfully clusters series by class.

6 Related Work

Several approaches proposed in the literature share some common ground with MAD, either because they aim at aligning complex objects to perform domain adaptation tasks or because they deal with the problem of aligning (sets of) time series.

Using OT for domain adaptation has been initially proposed in OTDA [2], which aims at aligning the source and target domains using OT. It relies on the hypothesis that the distribution shift between the two domains is an affine transformation and uses the transport plan to evaluate its coefficients. Classification is then performed on the realigned samples. DeepJDOT [4], on which the neural domain adaptation with a MAD loss introduced in this paper relies, can be seen as an improvement over OTDA. CO-OT [17] jointly optimizes two OT plans γ_s and γ_f between samples (rows) and features (columns) of datasets $\mathbf{X}$ and $\mathbf{X}'$, resulting in a loss of the form $\langle \mathbf{L}(\mathbf{X}, \mathbf{X}') \otimes \gamma_s, \gamma_f \rangle$. It has been benchmarked in a heterogeneous domain adaptation context but does not allow enforcing temporal coherence that should be met when time series are at stake. To the best of our knowledge, no OT-based approach has yet tackled the challenge of unsupervised DA for time series classification.

Combining OT and (soft-)DTW has also been proposed in [9] where the goal is to align brain imaging signals using soft-DTW with an OT-based ground cost. In this setting however, optimization is not performed jointly on γ and π but, rather, individual transport problems are solved independently for each pair of timestamps, hence not enforcing global spatial consistency. [10] propose an extension with the aim to average spatio-temporal signals. However, none of these works consider the DA scenario.

In the same line of work, [1] use a Gromov-Wasserstein-like similarity measure to compare time series that may not lie in the same ambient space (*e.g.* that do not share the same features). They solve a problem of the form $\langle \mathbf{L}(\mathbf{X}, \mathbf{X}') \otimes \boldsymbol{\pi}, \boldsymbol{\pi} \rangle$ (in which $\boldsymbol{\pi}$ is a coupling matrix that meets the DTW alignment constraints), coined Gromov-dynamic time warping. Optimization also relies on a BCD, however its convergence is not guaranteed. Moreover, it does not allow taking into account the temporal distortion that occurs between *sets* of time series.

7 Conclusion and Perspectives

In this paper, we introduce Match-And-Deform (MAD) that combines optimal transport and dynamic time warping to match time series across domains given global temporal transformations. We embed MAD as a regularization loss in a neural domain adaptation setting and evaluate its performance in different settings: on MoCap datasets, MAD gives similar performance to state-of-the-art DA time series classification methods; when a temporal deformation is at stake (such as in a remote sensing scenario), we show that MAD reaches better performance, thanks to its ability to capture temporal shifts.

The $|\mathcal{C}|$-MAD variant presented in this paper relies on source domain classes to form groups of temporally coherent series, yet an unsupervised strategy to form groups based on time series content alone is a worthy track for future works. Moreover, inspired by [19], time series weights could be learned instead of set *a priori*, in order to decrease the sensitivity to outliers. Finally, the use of MAD in other tasks, such as cross-domain missing data imputation [12], can also be considered.

Acknowledgements. François Painblanc and Romain Tavenard are partially funded through project MATS ANR-18-CE23-0006. Nicolas Courty is partially funded through project OTTOPIA ANR-20-CHIA-0030. Laetitia Chapel is partially funded through project MULTISCALE ANR-18-CE23-0022.

References

1. Cohen, S., Luise, G., Terenin, A., Amos, B., Deisenroth, M.: Aligning time series on incomparable spaces. In: International Conference on Artificial Intelligence and Statistics, pp. 1036–1044 (2021)
2. Courty, N., Flamary, R., Tuia, D., Rakotomamonjy, A.: Optimal transport for domain adaptation. IEEE Trans. Pattern Anal. Mach. Intell. **39**, 1853–1865 (2016)
3. Courty, N., Flamary, R., Habrard, A., Rakotomamonjy, A.: Joint distribution optimal transportation for domain adaptation. In: Advances in Neural Information Processing Systems, vol. 30 (2017)
4. Damodaran, B.B., Kellenberger, B., Flamary, R., Tuia, D., Courty, N.: DeepJDOT: deep joint distribution optimal transport for unsupervised domain adaptation. In: Ferrari, V., Hebert, M., Sminchisescu, C., Weiss, Y. (eds.) ECCV 2018. LNCS, vol. 11208, pp. 467–483. Springer, Cham (2018). https://doi.org/10.1007/978-3-030-01225-0_28
5. Dua, D., Graff, C.: UCI machine learning repository (2017). https://archive.ics.uci.edu/ml
6. Fatras, K., Séjourné, T., Flamary, R., Courty, N.: Unbalanced minibatch optimal transport; applications to domain adaptation. In: International Conference on Machine Learning, pp. 3186–3197 (2021)
7. Ganin, Y., et al.: Domain-adversarial training of neural networks. J. Mach. Learn. Res. **17**(1), 2030–2096 (2016)
8. Genevay, A., Peyré, G., Cuturi, M.: Learning generative models with Sinkhorn divergences. In: International Conference on Artificial Intelligence and Statistics, pp. 1608–1617 (2018)
9. Janati, H., Cuturi, M., Gramfort, A.: Spatio-temporal alignments: optimal transport through space and time. In: International Conference on Artificial Intelligence and Statistics, pp. 1695–1704 (2020)
10. Janati, H., Cuturi, M., Gramfort, A.: Averaging spatio-temporal signals using optimal transport and soft alignments. arXiv:2203.05813 (2022)
11. Lonjou, V., et al.: MACCS-ATCOR joint algorithm (MAJA). In: Remote Sensing of Clouds and the Atmosphere XXI, vol. 10001, p. 1000107 (2016)
12. Muzellec, B., Josse, J., Boyer, C., Cuturi, M.: Missing data imputation using optimal transport. In: International Conference on Machine Learning, pp. 7130–7140. PMLR (2020)
13. Nyborg, J., Pelletier, C., Lefèvre, S., Assent, I.: TimeMatch: unsupervised cross-region adaptation by temporal shift estimation. ISPRS J. Photogramm. Remote. Sens. **188**, 301–313 (2022)
14. Peyré, G., Cuturi, M.: Computational optimal transport. Found. Trends® Mach. Learn. **11**(5–6), 355–607 (2019)
15. Purushotham, S., Carvalho, W., Nilanon, T., Liu, Y.: Variational recurrent adversarial deep domain adaptation. In: International Conference on Learning Representations (2017)
16. Redko, I., Habrard, A., Morvant, E., Sebban, M., Bennani, Y.: Advances in Domain Adaptation Theory. ISTE Press, London (2019)
17. Redko, I., Vayer, T., Flamary, R., Courty, N.: Co-optimal transport. In: Advances in Neural Information Processing Systems, NeurIPS (2020)
18. Sakoe, H., Chiba, S.: Dynamic programming algorithm optimization for spoken word recognition. IEEE Trans. Acoust. Speech Signal Process. **26**(1), 43–49 (1978)

19. Vincent-Cuaz, C., Flamary, R., Corneli, M., Vayer, T., Courty, N.: Semi-relaxed Gromov-Wasserstein divergence and applications on graphs. In: International Conference on Learning Representations (2022). https://openreview.net/forum?id=RShaMexjc-x
20. Wilson, G., Cook, D.: A survey of unsupervised deep domain adaptation. ACM J. **11**, 1–46 (2020)
21. Wilson, G., Doppa, J.R., Cook, D.J.: Multi-source deep domain adaptation with weak supervision for time-series sensor data. In: ACM SIGKDD International Conference on Knowledge Discovery & Data Mining, pp. 1768–1778 (2020)

Bi-tuning: Efficient Transfer from Pre-trained Models

Jincheng Zhong, Haoyu Ma, Ximei Wang, Zhi Kou, and Mingsheng Long(✉)

School of Software, BNRist, Tsinghua University, Beijing, China
{zjc22,mhy22,kz19}@mails.tsinghua.edu.cn, messixmwang@tencent.com,
mingsheng@tsinghua.edu.cn

Abstract. It is a *de facto* practice in the deep learning community to first pre-train a deep neural network from a large-scale dataset and then fine-tune the pre-trained model to a specific downstream task. Recently, both supervised and unsupervised pre-training approaches to learning representations have achieved remarkable advances, which exploit the discriminative knowledge of labels and the intrinsic structure of data, respectively. It follows the natural intuition that both the discriminative knowledge and the intrinsic structure of the downstream task can be useful for fine-tuning. However, existing fine-tuning methods mainly leverage the former and discard the latter. A natural question arises: How to fully explore the intrinsic structure of data for boosting fine-tuning? In this paper, we propose *Bi-tuning*, a general learning approach that is capable of fine-tuning both supervised and unsupervised pre-trained representations to downstream tasks. Bi-tuning generalizes the vanilla fine-tuning by integrating two heads upon the backbone of pre-trained representations: a classifier head with an improved contrastive cross-entropy loss to better leverage the label information in an instance-contrast way, and a projector head with a newly-designed categorical contrastive learning loss to fully exploit the intrinsic structure of data in a category-consistent way. Comprehensive experiments confirm that Bi-tuning achieves state-of-the-art results for fine-tuning tasks of both supervised and unsupervised pre-trained models by large margins.

Keywords: Transfer Learning · Fine-Tuning · Contrastive Learning

1 Introduction

In the last decade, remarkable advances in deep learning have been witnessed in diverse applications across many fields, such as computer vision, robotic control, and natural language processing in the presence of large-scale labeled datasets. However, in many practical scenarios, we may have only access to a small labeled dataset, making it impossible to train deep neural networks from scratch. Therefore, it has become increasingly common within the deep learning community to

Supplementary Information The online version contains supplementary material available at https://doi.org/10.1007/978-3-031-43424-2_22.

D. Koutra et al. (Eds.): ECML PKDD 2023, LNAI 14173, pp. 357–373, 2023.
https://doi.org/10.1007/978-3-031-43424-2_22

first *pre-train* a deep neural network from a large-scale dataset and then *fine-tune* the pre-trained model to a specific downstream task. Fine-tuning requires fewer labeled data, enables faster training, and usually achieves better performance than training from scratch [17]. This two-stage style of pre-training and fine-tuning lays as the transfer learning foundation of various deep learning applications.

In the *pre-training* stage, there are mainly two approaches to pre-train a deep model: supervised pre-training and unsupervised pre-training. Recent years have witnessed the success of numerous supervised pre-trained models, e.g. ResNet [18] and EfficientNet [36], by exploiting the discriminative knowledge of manually-annotated labels on a large-scale dataset like ImageNet [6]. Meanwhile, unsupervised representation learning is recently changing the field of natural language processing by models pre-trained with a large-scale corpus, e.g. BERT [7] and GPT [33]. In computer vision, remarkable advances in unsupervised representation learning [3,16,40], which exploit the intrinsic structure of data by contrastive learning [15], have also changed the field dominated chronically by supervised pre-trained representations.

In the *fine-tuning* stage, transferring a model from supervised pre-trained models has been empirically studied in [21]. During the past years, several sophisticated fine-tuning methods were proposed, including L2-SP [24], DELTA [23] and BSS [5]. These methods focus on leveraging the discriminative knowledge of labels from the downstream task by a cross-entropy loss and the implicit bias of pre-trained models by a regularization term. However, the intrinsic structure of data in the downstream task is generally discarded during fine-tuning. Further, rare attention has been paid to fine-tuning efficiently from an unsupervised pre-trained model. In a prior study, we empirically observed that unsupervised pre-trained representations focus more on the intrinsic structure, while supervised pre-trained representations explain better on the label information, as shown in Fig. 4. This implies that fine-tuning unsupervised pre-trained representations [16] would be more difficult and deserves further investigation.

Regarding to the success of supervised and unsupervised pre-training approaches, it follows a natural intuition that both *discriminative knowledge* and *intrinsic structure* of the downstream task can be useful for fine-tuning. A question arises: How to fully explore the intrinsic structure of data for boosting fine-tuning? To tackle this major challenge of deep learning, we propose **Bi-tuning**, a general learning approach that is capable of fine-tuning both supervised and unsupervised pre-trained representations to downstream tasks. Bi-tuning generalizes the vanilla fine-tuning by integrating two specific heads upon the backbone of pre-trained representations:

- A classifier head with an improved contrastive cross-entropy loss to better leverage the label information in an instance-contrast way, which is the dual view of the vanilla cross-entropy loss and is expected to achieve a more compact intra-class structure.
- A projector head with a newly-designed categorical contrastive learning loss to fully exploit the intrinsic structure of data in a category-consistent way, resulting in a more harmonious cooperation between the supervised and unsupervised fine-tuning mechanisms.

Designed as a general-purpose fine-tuning approach, Bi-tuning can be applied with a variety of backbones without any additional assumptions. Comprehensive experiments confirm that Bi-tuning achieves state-of-the-art results for fine-tuning tasks of both supervised and unsupervised pre-trained models by large margins. We justify through ablations and analyses the effectiveness of the proposed two-heads fine-tuning architecture with their novel loss functions. Code is available at https://github.com/thuml/Transfer-Learning-Library.

2 Related Work

2.1 Pre-training

During the past years, supervised pre-trained models achieve impressive advances by exploiting the inductive bias of label information on a large-scale dataset like ImageNet [6], such as GoogleNet [35], ResNet [18], DenseNet [19], EfficientNet [36] and ViT [10], to name a few. Meanwhile, unsupervised representation learning is recently shining in the field of natural language processing by models pre-trained with a large-scale corpus, including GPT [33], BERT [7] and XLNet [41]. Even in computer vision, recent advances in unsupervised representation learning [3,16,40], which exploit the inductive bias of data structure, are shaking the long-term dominated status of representations learned in a supervised way. Further, a wide range of handcrafted pretext tasks have been proposed for unsupervised representation learning, such as relative patch prediction [8], solving jigsaw puzzles [29], colorization [43], multi-modal prediction [32], etc.

2.2 Contrastive Learning

Specifically, a variety of unsupervised pretext tasks are based on some forms of contrastive learning, in which the instance discrimination approach [3,16,40] is one of the most general forms. Other variants of contrastive learning methods include contrastive predictive learning (CPC) [30] and colorization contrasting [37]. Recent advances of deep contrastive learning benefit from contrasting positive keys against *very large* number of negative keys. Therefore, how to efficiently generate keys becomes a fundamental problem in contrastive learning. To achieve this goal, [9] explored the effectiveness of in-batch samples, [40] proposed to use a memory bank to store all representations of the dataset, [16] further replaced a memory bank with the momentum contrast (MoCo) to be memory-efficient, and [3] showed that a brute-force huge batch of keys works well. A new branch of works [4,13] explores contrastive learning without negative keys.

2.3 Fine-Tuning

Fine-tuning a model from supervised pre-trained models has been empirically explored in [21] by launching a systematic investigation with grid search of the hyper-parameters. During the past years, a line of fine-tuning methods have been proposed to exploit the inductive bias of pre-trained models: L2-SP [24] drives the weight parameters of target task to the pre-trained values by imposing L2 constraint based on the inductive bias of parameter; DELTA [23] computes channel-wise discriminative knowledge to reweight the feature map regularization with an attention mechanism based on the inductive bias of behavior; BSS [5] penalizes smaller singular values to suppress nontransferable spectral components based on singular values.

Other fine-tuning methods including learning with similarity preserving [20] or learning without forgetting [25] also work well on some downstream classification tasks. However, the existing fine-tuning methods mainly focus on leveraging the knowledge of the downstream labels with a cross-entropy loss. Intuitively, encouraging a model to capture the label information and intrinsic structure simultaneously may help the model transition between the upstream unsupervised models to the downstream classification tasks. In natural language processing, GPT [33,34] has employed a strategy that jointly optimizes unsupervised training criteria while fine-tuning with supervision. However, we empirically found that trivially following this kind of force-combination between supervised learning loss and unsupervised contrastive learning loss is beneficial but limited. The plausible reason is that these two loss functions will contradict with each other and result in a very different but not discriminative feature structure compared to that of the supervised cross-entropy loss, as revealed by a prior study shown in Fig. 3.

3 Backgrounds

It is worth noting that the principles of contrastive learning actually can date back very far [1,14,15]. The key idea of contrastive learning is to maximize the likelihood of the input distribution $p(\mathbf{x}|D)$ conditioned on the dataset D contrasting to the artificial noise distribution $p_n(\mathbf{x})$, also known as noise-contrastive estimation (NCE). Later, [12] pointed out the relations between generative adversarial networks and noise-contrastive estimation. Meanwhile, [30] revealed that contrastive learning is related to mutual information between a query and the corresponding positive key, which is known as InfoNCE. Considering a query $\mathbf{q}$ with a large key pool $\mathcal{K} = \{\mathbf{k}_0, \mathbf{k}_1, \mathbf{k}_2, \cdots, \mathbf{k}_{|\mathcal{K}|}\}$ where $|\mathcal{K}|$ is the number of keys, the kind of non-parametric form [30,40] of contrastive loss can be defined as

$$L_{\text{InfoNCE}} = -\log \frac{\exp(\mathbf{q} \cdot \mathbf{k}_0/\tau)}{\sum_{i=0}^{|\mathcal{K}|} \exp(\mathbf{q} \cdot \mathbf{k}_i/\tau)}, \tag{1}$$

where τ is the temperature hyper-parameter. Note that $\mathbf{k}_0$ is the only positive key that $\mathbf{q}$ matches while negative keys $\{\mathbf{k}_1, \mathbf{k}_2, \cdots, \mathbf{k}_{|\mathcal{K}|}\}$ are selected from a dynamic queue which iteratively and progressively replaces the oldest samples by the newly-generated keys. Intuitively, contrastive learning can be defined as a query-key pair matching problem, where a contrastive loss is a $(|\mathcal{K}| + 1)$-way cross-entropy loss to distinguish $\mathbf{k}_0$ from a large key pool. A contrastive loss is to maximize the similarity between the query and the corresponding positive key $\mathbf{k}_0$ since they are extracted from different views of the same data example.

4 Methods

In inductive transfer learning, a.k.a. fine-tuning, we have access to a target dataset $\mathcal{D} = \{(\mathbf{x}_i, y_i)\}_{i=1}^N$ with N labeled examples and a pre-trained model $\mathcal{M}$ attained on a large-scale source dataset. Instantiated as a deep neural network, $\mathcal{M}$ usually consists of a pre-trained backbone f_0 and a pre-trained head g_0 whose fine-tuned ones are denoted by f and g, respectively. Following the common practice of fine-tuning, f is initialized as f_0. Contrarily, g is usually a randomly initialized fully-connected layer parameterized by $\mathbf{W}$, since the target dataset usually has a label space of size C different from that of pre-trained models.

4.1 Vanilla Fine-Tuning of Pre-trained Representations

For each query sample $\mathbf{x}_i^{\mathrm{q}}$ from the target dataset, we can first utilize a pre-trained feature encoder $f(\cdot)$ to extract its pre-trained representation as $\mathbf{h}_i^{\mathrm{q}} = f(\mathbf{x}_i^{\mathrm{q}})$. Without any additional assumptions, the pre-trained feature encoder $f(\cdot)$ can be commonly used network backbones according to the downstream tasks, including ResNet [18] and DenseNet [19] for supervised pre-trained models, and MoCo [16] and SimCLR [3] for unsupervised pre-trained models.

Given a pre-trained representation $\mathbf{h}_i^{\mathrm{q}}$, a fundamental step of vanilla fine-tuning is to feedforward the representation $\mathbf{h}_i^{\mathrm{q}}$ into a C-way classifier $g(\cdot)$, in which C is the number of categories for the downstream classification task. Denote the parameters of the classifier $g(\cdot)$ as $\mathbf{W} = [\mathbf{w}_1, \mathbf{w}_2, \cdots, \mathbf{w}_C]$, where $\mathbf{w}_j$ corresponds to the parameter for the j-th class. Given the training dataset of the downstream task, the parameters of the classifier and the backbone can be updated by optimizing a standard cross-entropy (CE) loss as

$$L_{\mathrm{CE}} = -\sum_{i=1}^{N} \log \frac{\exp(\mathbf{w}_{y_i} \cdot \mathbf{h}_i^{\mathrm{q}})}{\sum_{j=1}^{C} \exp(\mathbf{w}_j \cdot \mathbf{h}_i^{\mathrm{q}})}. \tag{2}$$

With a CE loss on the target labeled dataset, the vanilla fine-tuning approach leverages the discriminative knowledge of labels. As later experiments revealed, the vanilla fine-tuning approach underperforms in a low data regime since it will easily suffer from heavy overfitting on the limited target labeled dataset. Regarding the success of supervised and unsupervised pre-training approaches, we realize that it is significant to further exploit the *discriminative knowledge* and *intrinsic structure* of the downstream task for fine-tuning. To achieve this, we propose a contrastive cross-entropy (CCE) loss on the classifier head to further exploit the label information and a categorical contrastive learning (CCL) loss on the projector head to capture the intrinsic structure of target data, which will be detailed orderly in the following sections.

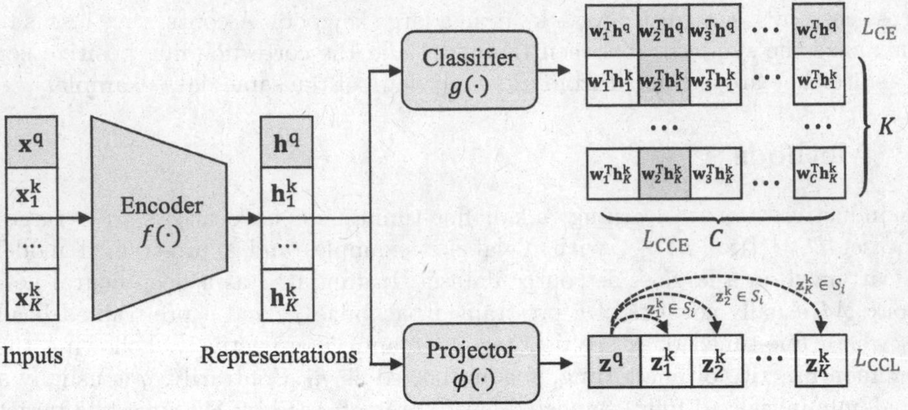

Fig. 1. The **Bi-tuning** approach, which includes an encoder for pre-trained representations, a classifer head and a projector head. Bi-tuning enables a dual fine-tuning mechanism: a contrastive cross-entropy (CCE) loss on the classifier head to exploit label information and a categorical contrastive learning (CCL) loss on the projector head to capture the intrinsic structure of target data.

4.2 Classifier Head with Contrastive Cross-Entropy Loss

First, we delve into the cross-entropy loss to figure out the mechanism of how it exploits label information. For each instance-class pair $(\mathbf{x}_i, y_i)$ on a given dataset, the predicted output of the fine-tuned model is a probability vector of size C where C is the number of categories. From another perspective, the cross-entropy loss of vanilla fine-tuning can be regarded as a *class-wise championship*, i.e., the category that is the same as the ground-truth label of each instance is expected to win the game. As revealed in Fig. 1, to find the correct class, the cross-entropy loss performs *column-wise championship* for each instance.

To further exploit the label information of the downstream task, we propose an alternative form of the conventional cross-entropy loss on the classifier head, named contrastive cross-entropy loss L_{CCE}. Correspondingly, L_{CCE} performs a *row-wise championship* for each class while L_{CE} is a *column-wise championship* for each instance. Instead of operating loss computation along the class dimension (i.e., the number of classes C), L_{CCE} operates along the key-set dimension (i.e., the number of keys $K+1$). As an instance-wise championship in L_{CCE}, the instance nearest to the prototype of each class is expected to win the game. For each sample $(\mathbf{x}_i, y_i)$ in the target dataset, the representation encoded by f is $\mathbf{h}_i$. For clarity, we focus on a particular data example $(\mathbf{x}, y)$ and omit the subscript i. The proposed L_{CCE} for each data example is formulated as

$$L_{\text{CCE}} = -\frac{1}{|\mathcal{K}_p|} \sum_{\mathbf{h}^+ \in \mathcal{K}_p} \log \frac{\exp(\mathbf{w}_y \cdot \mathbf{h}^+/\tau)}{\sum_{\mathbf{h} \in \mathcal{K}_p \cup \mathcal{K}_n} \exp(\mathbf{w}_y \cdot \mathbf{h}/\tau)}, \tag{3}$$

where $\mathcal{K}_p$ is the positive key set, $\mathcal{K}_n$ is the negative key set, and τ is the hyperparameter for temperature scaling. Note that, $\mathcal{K}_p$ consists of $\mathbf{k}_0$ and keys with the same label y where $\mathbf{k}_0$ is extracted from a differently augmented view of the query $\mathbf{q}$. On the contrary, $\mathcal{K}_n$ includes examples from other classes $\{1, 2, \cdots, C\} \backslash y$. Here, $\mathbf{h}$'s are samples from the hidden key pool produced by the key generating mechanism (except $\mathbf{h}^{\mathrm{q}}$). Without loss of generality, we adopt the key generating approach in Momentum Contrast (MoCo) [16] as our default one due to its simplicity, high-efficacy, and memory-efficient implementation. In summary, by encouraging instances in the training dataset to approach towards their corresponding class prototypes (feature center of the same-label samples), L_{CCE} further exploits the label information of the target dataset and tends to achieve a more compact intra-class structure than the vanilla fine-tuning.

4.3 Projector Head with Categorical Contrastive Learning Loss

Till now, we have proposed the contrastive cross-entropy loss on the classifier head to fully exploit the label information. However, this kind of loss function may still fall short in capturing the intrinsic structure. Inspired by the remarkable success of unsupervised pre-training, which also aims at modeling the intrinsic structure in data, we first introduce a projector $\phi(\cdot)$ which is usually off the shelf to embed a pre-trained representation $\mathbf{h}_i^{\mathrm{q}}$ into a latent metric space as $\mathbf{z}_i^{\mathrm{q}}$. Intuitively, we apply the standard contrastive learning loss (InfoNCE) defined in Eq. (1) on the target dataset to capture intrinsic structure in data. However, the InfoNCE loss assumes that there is a *single* key $\mathbf{k}_+$ (also denoted as $\mathbf{k}_0$) in the dictionary to match the given query $\mathbf{q}$, which implicitly requires every instance to belong to an individual class. In other words, it regards every sample in the key pool as a negative sample except $\mathbf{k}_+$, which requires minimizing the similarity between the query with all negative samples. Yet, from the perspective of discriminative learning, we should maximize inter-class distance but minimize intra-class distance. As a consequence, those samples with the same class as the query sample should not be treated as negative samples, and the similarity between them should be maximized.

As aforementioned, if we simply apply InfoNCE loss on the labeled downstream dataset, it will result in an extremely different but not discriminative feature structure compared with that of the supervised cross-entropy loss, making the classifier struggle. Obviously, this dilemma reveals that the naive combination of the supervised cross-entropy loss and the unsupervised contrastive loss is not an optimal solution for fine-tuning, which is also backed by our experiments in Table 3. To capture the label information and intrinsic structure simultaneously, we propose a novel categorical contrastive loss L_{CCL} on the projector head based on the following hypothesis: when we fine-tune a pre-trained model to a downstream task, it is reasonable to regard other keys in the same class as the positive keys that the query matches. In this way, L_{CCL} expands the scope of positive keys from *single instance* to *a set of instances*, resulting in more harmonious collaboration between the supervised and unsupervised learning mechanisms. Similar to the format of the InfoNCE loss, L_{CCL} is defined as

$$L_{\text{CCL}} = -\frac{1}{|\mathcal{K}_p|} \sum_{\mathbf{z}^+ \in \mathcal{K}_p} \log \frac{\exp(\mathbf{z}^{\mathrm{q}} \cdot \mathbf{z}^+ / \tau)}{\sum_{\mathbf{z} \in \mathcal{K}_p \cup \mathcal{K}_n} \exp(\mathbf{z}^{\mathrm{q}} \cdot \mathbf{z} / \tau)}, \tag{4}$$

with notations in parallel to that of Eq. (3). Note that the sum is taken over all positive keys, indicating that there may be more than one positive key for a single query, i.e., $|\mathcal{K}_p| \geq 1$.

We provide an intuitive explanation of why L_{CCL} is complementary to vanilla fine-tuning. While using the standard cross-entropy loss, we can learn a hyperplane for discriminating each class from the other classes, and the instances of each class are only required to be far away from its associated hyperplane—they are not required to form into a compact structure in the metric space. As for the proposed categorical contrastive loss, besides requiring the instances of each class to stay far away from those of the other classes, we further require that they should form a compact structure in the metric space. This is exactly the advantage of *contrast-by-metric* over *discriminate-by-hyperplane*, which better facilitates the fine-tuning on downstream task.

4.4 Optimization Objective of Bi-tuning

Finally, we reach a novel fine-tuning approach for efficient transfer from both supervised and unsupervised pre-trained models. Due to the dual-head design, the approach is coined **Bi-tuning**, which jointly optimizes the contrastive cross-entropy loss on classifier head and the categorical contrastive learning loss on projector head, as well as the standard cross-entropy loss, in an end-to-end deep architecture. The overall loss function of Bi-tuning is

$$\min_{\Theta=\{f,g,\phi\}} \quad L_{\text{CE}} + L_{\text{CCE}} + L_{\text{CCL}}, \tag{5}$$

where Θ denotes the parameters of the encoder f, the classifier head g and the projector head ϕ. Desirably, since the magnitude of the above loss terms is comparable, we empirically find that there is no need to introduce any extra hyper-parameters to trade-off them. This simplicity makes Bi-tuning easy to be applied to different datasets or tasks. The full portrait of Bi-tuning is shown in Fig. 1.

5 Experiments

We follow the common fine-tuning principle described in [42], replacing the last task-specific layer in the classifier head with a randomly initialized fully connected layer whose learning rate is 10 times of that for pre-trained parameters. Meanwhile, the projector head is set to be another randomly initialized fully connected layer. For the key generating mechanisms, we follow the style in [16], employing a momentum contrast branch with a default momentum coefficient

Table 1. Top-1 accuracy on various datasets using ResNet-50 by *supervised* pre-training.

Dataset	Method	Sampling Rates			
		25%	50%	75%	100%
CUB	Fine-tuning	61.36 ± 0.11	73.61 ± 0.23	78.49 ± 0.18	80.74 ± 0.15
	L2SP [24]	61.21 ± 0.19	72.99 ± 0.13	78.11 ± 0.17	80.92 ± 0.22
	DELTA [23]	62.89 ± 0.11	74.35 ± 0.28	79.18 ± 0.24	81.33 ± 0.24
	BSS [5]	64.69 ± 0.31	74.96 ± 0.21	78.91 ± 0.15	81.52 ± 0.11
	Bi-tuning	$\mathbf{67.47} \pm 0.08$	$\mathbf{77.17} \pm 0.13$	$\mathbf{81.07} \pm 0.09$	$\mathbf{82.93} \pm 0.23$
Cars	Fine-tuning	56.45 ± 0.21	75.24 ± 0.17	83.22 ± 0.17	86.22 ± 0.12
	L2SP [24]	56.29 ± 0.21	75.62 ± 0.32	83.60 ± 0.13	85.85 ± 0.12
	DELTA [23]	58.74 ± 0.23	76.53 ± 0.08	84.53 ± 0.29	86.01 ± 0.37
	BSS [5]	59.74 ± 0.14	76.78 ± 0.16	85.06 ± 0.13	87.64 ± 0.21
	Bi-tuning	$\mathbf{66.15} \pm 0.20$	$\mathbf{81.10} \pm 0.07$	$\mathbf{86.07} \pm 0.23$	$\mathbf{88.47} \pm 0.11$
Aircraft	Fine-tuning	51.25 ± 0.18	67.12 ± 0.41	75.22 ± 0.09	79.18 ± 0.20
	L2SP [24]	51.07 ± 0.45	67.46 ± 0.22	75.06 ± 0.45	79.07 ± 0.21
	DELTA [23]	53.71 ± 0.30	68.51 ± 0.24	76.51 ± 0.55	80.34 ± 0.14
	BSS [5]	53.38 ± 0.22	69.19 ± 0.18	76.39 ± 0.22	80.83 ± 0.32
	Bi-tuning	$\mathbf{58.27} \pm 0.26$	$\mathbf{72.40} \pm 0.22$	$\mathbf{80.77} \pm 0.10$	$\mathbf{84.01} \pm 0.33$

$m = 0.999$ and two cached queues both normalized by their L2-norm [40] with dimensions of 2048 and 128 respectively. For each task, the best learning rate is selected by cross-validation under a 100% sampling rate and applied to all four sampling rates. Queue size K is set as $8, 16, 24, 32$ for each category according to the dataset scales, respectively. Other hyper-parameters in Bi-tuning are fixed for all experiments. The temperature τ in Eq. (3) and Eq. (4) is set as 0.07 [40]. The trade-off coefficients between these three losses are kept as 1 since the magnitude of the loss terms is comparable. All tasks are optimized using SGD with a momentum 0.9. All results in this section are averaged over 5 trials, and standard deviations are provided.

5.1 Supervised Pre-trained Representations

Standard Benchmarks. We first verify our approach on three fine-grained classification benchmarks: `CUB-200-2011` [38] (with 11788 images for 200 bird species), `Stanford Cars` [22] (containing 16185 images of 196 classes of cars) and `FGVC Aircraft` [28] (containing 10000 samples 100 different aircraft variants). For each benchmark, we create four configurations which randomly sample 25%, 50%, 75%, and 100% of training data for each class respectively, to reveal the detailed effect while fine-tuning to different data scales. We choose recent fine-tuning technologies: L2-SP [24], DELTA [23], and the state-of-the-art method BSS [5], as competitors of Bi-tuning while regarding vanilla fine-tuning

Table 2. Top-1 accuracy on COCO-70 dataset using DenseNet-121 by *supervised* pre-training.

Method	Sampling Rates			
	25%	50%	75%	100%
Fine-tuning	80.01 ± 0.25	82.50 ± 0.25	83.43 ± 0.18	84.41 ± 0.22
L2SP [24]	80.57 ± 0.47	80.67 ± 0.29	83.71 ± 0.24	84.78 ± 0.16
DELTA [23]	76.39 ± 0.37	79.72 ± 0.24	83.01 ± 0.11	84.66 ± 0.08
BSS [5]	77.29 ± 0.15	80.74 ± 0.22	83.89 ± 0.09	84.71 ± 0.13
Bi-tuning	**80.68** ± 0.23	**83.48** ± 0.13	**84.16** ± 0.05	**85.41** ± 0.23

as a baseline. Note that vanilla fine-tuning is a strong baseline when sufficient data is provided. Results are averaged over 5 trials. As shown in Table 1, Bi-tuning significantly outperforms all competitors across all three benchmarks by large margins (e.g. 10.7% absolute rise on *CUB* with a sampling rate of 25%). Note that even under 100% sampling rate, Bi-tuning still outperforms others.

Large-Scale Benchmarks. Previous fine-tuning methods mainly focus on improving performance under low-data regime paradigms. We further extend Bi-tuning to large-scale paradigms. We use annotations of the COCO dataset [26] to construct a large-scale classification dataset, cropping object with padding for each image and removing minimal items (with height and width less than 50 pixels), resulting in a large-scale dataset containing 70 classes with more than 1000 images per category. The scale is comparable to ImageNet in terms of the number of samples per class. On this constructed large-scale dataset named COCO-70, Bi-tuning is also evaluated under four sampling rate configurations. Since even the 25% sampling rate of COCO-70 is much larger than each benchmark in Sect. 5.1, previous fine-tuning competitors show micro contributions to these paradigms. Results in Table 2 reveal that Bi-tuning brings general gains for all tasks. We hypothesize that the intrinsic structure introduced by Bi-tuning contributes substantially.

5.2 Unsupervised Pre-trained Representations

Representations of MoCo [16]**.** In this round, we use ResNet-50 pre-trained unsupervisedly via MoCo on ImageNet as the backbone. Since suffering from the large discrepancy between unsupervised pre-trained representations and downstream classification tasks as demonstrated in Fig. 3, previous fine-tuning competitors usually perform very poorly. Hence we only compare *Bi-tuning* to the state-of-the-art method *BSS* [5] and vanilla fine-tuning as baselines. Besides, we add two intuitively related baselines: (1) **GPT***, which follows a GPT [33,34] fine-tuning style but replaces its predictive loss with the contrastive loss; (2) **Center** loss, which introduces compactness of intra-class variations [39] that is effective in recognition tasks. As reported in Table 3, trivially borrowing fine-tuning strategy in GPT [33] or center loss brings tiny benefits, and is even

Table 3. Top-1 accuracy on various datasets using ResNet-50 *unsupervised* pre-training by MoCo.

Dataset	Method	Sampling Rates			
		25%	50%	75%	100%
CUB	Fine-tuning	38.57 ± 0.13	58.97 ± 0.16	69.55 ± 0.18	74.35 ± 0.18
	GPT* [34]	36.43 ± 0.17	57.62 ± 0.14	67.82 ± 0.05	72.95 ± 0.29
	Center [39]	42.53 ± 0.41	62.15 ± 0.51	70.86 ± 0.39	75.61 ± 0.33
	BSS [5]	41.73 ± 0.14	59.15 ± 0.21	69.93 ± 0.19	74.16 ± 0.09
	Bi-tuning	**50.54** ± 0.23	**66.88** ± 0.13	**74.27** ± 0.05	**77.14** ± 0.23
Cars	Fine-tuning	62.40 ± 0.26	81.55 ± 0.36	88.07 ± 0.19	89.81 ± 0.48
	GPT* [34]	65.83 ± 0.27	82.39 ± 0.17	88.62 ± 0.11	90.56 ± 0.18
	Center [39]	67.57 ± 0.12	82.78 ± 0.30	88.55 ± 0.24	89.95 ± 0.1
	BSS [5]	62.13 ± 0.22	81.72 ± 0.22	88.32 ± 0.17	90.41 ± 0.15
	Bi-tuning	**69.44** ± 0.32	**84.41** ± 0.07	**89.32** ± 0.23	**90.88** ± 0.13
Aircraft	Fine-tuning	58.98 ± 0.54	77.39 ± 0.31	84.82 ± 0.24	87.35 ± 0.17
	GPT* [34]	60.70 ± 0.08	78.93 ± 0.17	85.09 ± 0.10	87.56 ± 0.15
	Center [39]	62.23 ± 0.09	79.30 ± 0.14	85.20 ± 0.41	87.52 ± 0.20
	BSS [5]	60.13 ± 0.32	77.98 ± 0.29	84.85 ± 0.21	87.25 ± 0.07
	Bi-tuning	**63.16** ± 0.26	**79.98** ± 0.22	**86.23** ± 0.29	**88.55** ± 0.38

harmful on some datasets, e.g. `CUB`. Bi-tuning yields consistent gains on all fine-tuning tasks of unsupervised representations.

Other Unsupervised Pre-trained Representations. To justify Bi-tuning's general efficacy, we extend our method to unsupervised representations by other pre-training methods. Bi-tuning is applied to MoCo (version 2) [16], SimCLR [3], InsDisc [40], Deep Cluster [2], CMC [37] on `Car` dataset with 100% training data. Table 4 is a strong signal that Bi-tuning is not bound to specific pre-training pretext tasks.

Analysis on Components of Contrastive Learning. Recent advances in contrastive learning, i.e. momentum contrast [16] and memory bank [40] can be plugged into Bi-tuning smoothly to achieve similar performance and the detailed discussions are deferred to Appendix. Previous works [3,16] reveal that a large amount of contrasts is crucial to contrastive learning. In Fig. 2(a), we report the sensitivity of the numbers of sampling keys in Bi-tuning (MoCo) under 25% and 100% sampling ratio configurations. Note that CUB has various categories with a few images in each category. We let K balancedly sampled from every category to simplify our analysis here. Figure 2(a) shows that though a larger key pool is beneficial, we cannot expand the key pool due to the limit of training data, which may lose sampling stochasticity during training. This result suggests that there is a trade-off between stochasticity and a large number of keys. [3] pointed out that the dimension of the projector also has a big impact. The sensitivity of the dimension of the projector head is also presented in Fig. 2(b). Note that the unsupervised pre-trained model (e.g., MoCo) may provide an off-the-shelf

Table 4. Top-1 accuracy on Car dataset (100%) with different *unsupervised* pre-trained representations.

Pre-training Method	Fine-tuning	**Bi-tuning**
Deep Cluster [2]	83.90 ± 0.48	**87.71** ± 0.34
InsDisc [40]	86.59 ± 0.22	**89.54** ± 0.25
CMC [37]	86.71 ± 0.62	**88.35** ± 0.44
MoCov2 [16]	90.15 ± 0.48	90.79 ± 0.34
SimCLR(1×) [3]	89.30 ± 0.18	**90.84** ± 0.22
SimCLR(2×) [3]	91.22 ± 0.19	**91.93** ± 0.19

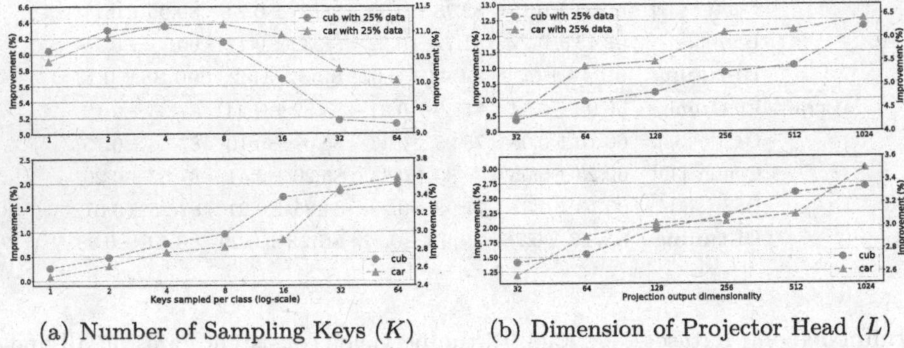

(a) Number of Sampling Keys (K) (b) Dimension of Projector Head (L)

Fig. 2. Sensitivity analysis of hyper-parameters K and L for Bi-tuning.

projector, fine-tuning or re-initializing it is almost the same (90.88 vs. 90.78 on Car when L is 128).

5.3 Collaborative Effect of Loss Functions

As shown in Table 5, using either contrastive cross-entropy (CCE) or categorical contrastive (CCL) with vanilla cross-entropy (CE) already achieves relatively good results. These experiments prove that there is collaborative effect between CCE and CCL loss empirically. It is worth mentioning that CCE and CCL can work independently of CE (see the fourth row in Table 5), while we optimize these three losses simultaneously to yield the best result. As discussed in prior sections, we hypothesize that Bi-tuning helps fine-tuning models characterize the intrinsic structure of training data when using CCE and CCL simultaneously.

5.4 Interpretable Visualization of Representations

We use a popular visualization tool proposed in [11] to give a interpretable visualization as shown in Fig. 3. Note that Fig. 3(a) is the original image, Fig. 3(b), Fig. 3(c) and Fig. 3(d) are respectively obtained from a randomly initialized

Table 5. Collaborative effect in Bi-tuning on CUB-200-2011 using ResNet-50 pre-trained by MoCo.

Loss Function			Sample Rate			
CE	CCE	CCL	25%	50%	75%	100%
✓	✗	✗	38.57 ± 0.13	58.97 ± 0.16	69.55 ± 0.18	74.35 ± 0.18
✓	✓	✗	45.42 ± 0.11	64.33 ± 0.28	71.56 ± 0.30	75.82 ± 0.21
✓	✗	✓	41.09 ± 0.23	60.77 ± 0.31	70.30 ± 0.29	75.30 ± 0.20
✗	✓	✓	47.70 ± 0.41	64.77 ± 0.15	71.69 ± 0.11	76.54 ± 0.24
✓	✓	✓	**50.54** ± 0.23	**66.88** ± 0.13	**74.27** ± 0.05	**77.12** ± 0.23

(a) Original (b) Random (c) Supervised (d) MoCo (e) Bi-tuning

Fig. 3. Interpretable visualization of learned representations via various training methods.

model, a supervised pre-trained model on ImageNet, and an unsupervised pre-trained model via MoCov1 [16]. We infer that supervised pre-training will obtain representations focusing on the discriminative part and ignoring the background part. In contrast, unsupervised pre-training pays uninformative attention to every location of an input image. This could be the reason that why fine-tuning unsupervised representations is harder than their supervised counterparts. Impressively, Bi-tuning in Fig. 3(e) captures both local details and global category-structures. Bi-tuning benefits from both the supervised discriminative knowledge and the unsupervised intrinsic structure. And this is the reason why Bi-tuning works well.

5.5 Visualization by t-SNE

We train the t-SNE [27] visualization model on the MoCo representations fine-tuned on Pets dataset [31]. Visualization of the validation set is shown in Fig. 4. Note that representations in Fig. 4(a) do not present good classification structures. Figure 4(c) suggests that forcefully combining the unsupervised loss as GPT [34] may cause conflict with CE and clutter the classification boundaries.

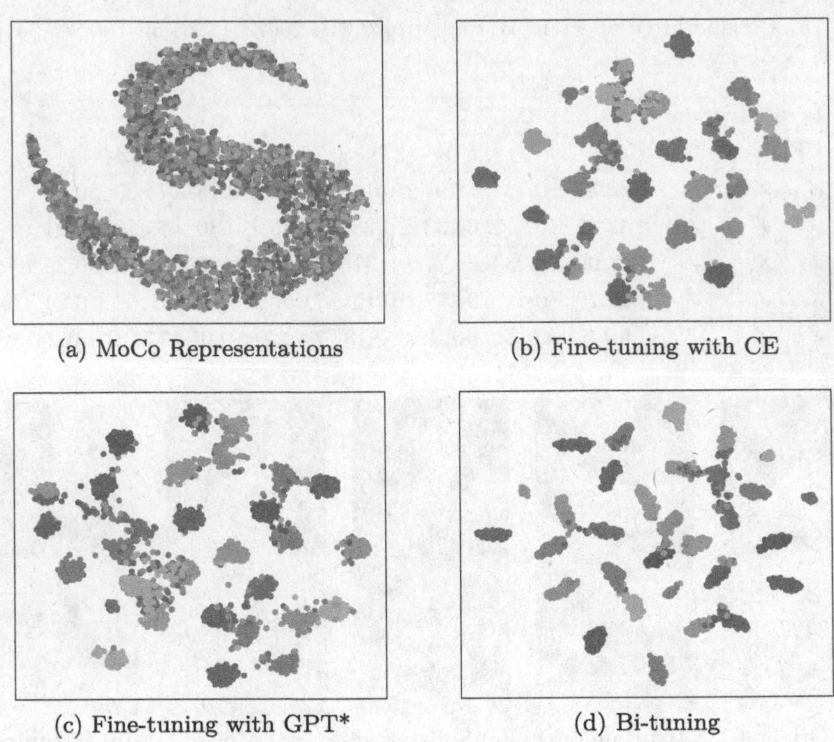

(a) MoCo Representations
(b) Fine-tuning with CE
(c) Fine-tuning with GPT*
(d) Bi-tuning

Fig. 4. T-SNE [27] of representations on Pets [31].

Figure 4(d) suggests that Bi-tuning encourages the fine-tuning model to learn better intrinsic structure besides the label information. Therefore, Bi-tuning presents the best classification boundaries as well as intrinsic structures.

6 Conclusion

In this paper, we propose a general Bi-tuning approach to fine-tuning both supervised and unsupervised representations. Bi-tuning generalizes the standard fine-tuning with an encoder for pre-trained representations, a classifier head and a projector head for exploring both the discriminative knowledge of labels and the intrinsic structure of data, which are trained end-to-end by two novel loss functions. Bi-tuning yields state-of-the-art results for fine-tuning tasks on both supervised and unsupervised pre-trained models by large margins.

Acknowledgements. This work was supported by the National Key Research and Development Plan (2020AAA0109201), National Natural Science Foundation of China (62022050 and 62021002), and Beijing Nova Program (Z201100006820041).

References

1. Becker, S., Hinton, G.E.: Self-organizing neural network that discovers surfaces in random-dot stereograms. Nature **355**(6356), 161–163 (1992)
2. Caron, M., Bojanowski, P., Joulin, A., Douze, M.: Deep clustering for unsupervised learning of visual features. In: Ferrari, V., Hebert, M., Sminchisescu, C., Weiss, Y. (eds.) Computer Vision – ECCV 2018. LNCS, vol. 11218, pp. 139–156. Springer, Cham (2018). https://doi.org/10.1007/978-3-030-01264-9_9
3. Chen, T., Kornblith, S., Norouzi, M., Hinton, G.: A Simple Framework for Contrastive Learning of Visual Representations. arXiv preprint arXiv:2002.05709 (2020)
4. Chen, X., He, K.: Exploring simple Siamese representation learning. In: Proceedings of the IEEE/CVF Conference on Computer Vision and Pattern Recognition, pp. 15750–15758 (2021)
5. Chen, X., Wang, S., Fu, B., Long, M., Wang, J.: Catastrophic forgetting meets negative transfer: batch spectral shrinkage for safe transfer learning. In: NeurIPS, pp. 1906–1916 (2019)
6. Deng, J., Dong, W., Socher, R., Li, L.J., Li, K., Fei-Fei, L.: ImageNet: a large-scale hierarchical image database. In: CVPR, pp. 248–255. IEEE (2009)
7. Devlin, J., Chang, M.W., Lee, K., Toutanova, K.: BERT: pre-training of deep bidirectional transformers for language understanding. arXiv preprint arXiv:1810.04805 (2018)
8. Doersch, C., Gupta, A., Efros, A.A.: Unsupervised visual representation learning by context prediction. In: ICCV, pp. 1422–1430 (2015)
9. Doersch, C., Zisserman, A.: Multi-task self-supervised visual learning. In: ICCV, pp. 2051–2060 (2017)
10. Dosovitskiy, A., et al.: An image is worth 16x16 words: transformers for image recognition at scale. In: International Conference on Learning Representations (2020)
11. Fong, R.C., Vedaldi, A.: Interpretable explanations of black boxes by meaningful perturbation. In: ICCV, pp. 3429–3437 (2017)
12. Goodfellow, I., et al.: Generative adversarial nets. In: NeurIPS, pp. 2672–2680 (2014)
13. Grill, J.B., et al.: Bootstrap your own latent-a new approach to self-supervised learning. Adv. Neural. Inf. Process. Syst. **33**, 21271–21284 (2020)
14. Gutmann, M., Hyvärinen, A.: Noise-contrastive estimation: a new estimation principle for unnormalized statistical models. In: AISTATS (2010)
15. Hadsell, R., Chopra, S., Lecun, Y.: Dimensionality reduction by learning an invariant mapping. In: CVPR (2006)
16. He, K., Fan, H., Wu, Y., Xie, S., Girshick, R.: Momentum contrast for unsupervised visual representation learning. In: CVPR (2020)
17. He, K., Girshick, R.B., Dollár, P.: Rethinking ImageNet pre-training. In: ICCV, pp. 4917–4926. IEEE (2019)
18. He, K., Zhang, X., Ren, S., Sun, J.: Deep residual learning for image recognition. In: CVPR, pp. 770–778 (2016)
19. Huang, G., Liu, Z., van der Maaten, L., Weinberger, K.Q.: Densely connected convolutional networks. In: CVPR. IEEE Computer Society (2017)
20. Kang, Z., Lu, X., Lu, Y., Peng, C., Xu, Z.: Structure learning with similarity preserving. arXiv preprint arXiv:1912.01197 (2019)

21. Kornblith, S., Shlens, J., Le, Q.V.: Do better ImageNet models transfer better? In: CVPR, pp. 2661–2671 (2019)
22. Krause, J., Stark, M., Deng, J., Fei-Fei, L.: 3D object representations for fine-grained categorization. In: 3dRR (2013)
23. Li, X., Xiong, H., Wang, H., Rao, Y., Liu, L., Huan, J.: DELTA: deep learning transfer using feature map with attention for convolutional networks. In: ICLR (2019)
24. Li, X., Grandvalet, Y., Davoine, F.: Explicit inductive bias for transfer learning with convolutional networks. In: Dy, J.G., Krause, A. (eds.) ICML (2018)
25. Li, Z., Hoiem, D.: Learning without forgetting. TPAMI **40**(12), 2935–2947 (2017)
26. Lin, T.-Y., et al.: Microsoft COCO: common objects in context. In: Fleet, D., Pajdla, T., Schiele, B., Tuytelaars, T. (eds.) ECCV 2014. LNCS, vol. 8693, pp. 740–755. Springer, Cham (2014). https://doi.org/10.1007/978-3-319-10602-1_48
27. Maaten, L.v.d., Hinton, G.: Visualizing data using t-SNE. J. Mach. Learn. Res. **9**, 2579–2605 (2008)
28. Maji, S., Rahtu, E., Kannala, J., Blaschko, M., Vedaldi, A.: Fine-grained visual classification of aircraft. Technical report (2013)
29. Noroozi, M., Favaro, P.: Unsupervised learning of visual representations by solving jigsaw puzzles. In: Leibe, B., Matas, J., Sebe, N., Welling, M. (eds.) ECCV 2016. LNCS, vol. 9910, pp. 69–84. Springer, Cham (2016). https://doi.org/10.1007/978-3-319-46466-4_5
30. van den Oord, A., Li, Y., Vinyals, O.: Representation learning with contrastive predictive coding (2018)
31. Parkhi, O.M., Vedaldi, A., Zisserman, A., Jawahar, C.: Cats and dogs. In: CVPR, pp. 3498–3505. IEEE (2012)
32. Radford, A., et al.: Learning transferable visual models from natural language supervision. In: International Conference on Machine Learning, pp. 8748–8763. PMLR (2021)
33. Radford, A., Sutskever, I.: Improving language understanding by generative pre-training. In: arxiv (2018)
34. Radford, A., Wu, J., Child, R., Luan, D., Amodei, D., Sutskever, I.: Language models are unsupervised multitask learners. OpenAI Blog **1**(8), 9 (2019)
35. Szegedy, C., et al.: Going deeper with convolutions. In: CVPR (2015)
36. Tan, M., Le, Q.V.: EfficientNet: rethinking model scaling for convolutional neural networks. In: ICML (2019)
37. Tian, Y., Krishnan, D., Isola, P.: Contrastive multiview coding. arXiv preprint arXiv:1906.05849 (2019)
38. Welinder, P., et al.: Caltech-UCSD Birds 200. Technical report. CNS-TR-2010-001, California Institute of Technology (2010)
39. Wen, Y., Zhang, K., Li, Z., Qiao, Yu.: A discriminative feature learning approach for deep face recognition. In: Leibe, B., Matas, J., Sebe, N., Welling, M. (eds.) ECCV 2016. LNCS, vol. 9911, pp. 499–515. Springer, Cham (2016). https://doi.org/10.1007/978-3-319-46478-7_31
40. Wu, Z., Xiong, Y., Yu, S.X., Lin, D.: Unsupervised feature learning via non-parametric instance discrimination. In: CVPR (2018)
41. Yang, Z., Dai, Z., Yang, Y., Carbonell, J.G., Salakhutdinov, R., Le, Q.V.: XLNet: Generalized autoregressive pretraining for language understanding. In: NeurIPS (2019)

42. Yosinski, J., Clune, J., Bengio, Y., Lipson, H.: How transferable are features in deep neural networks? In: Advances in Neural Information Processing Systems, pp. 3320–3328 (2014)
43. Zhang, R., Isola, P., Efros, A.A.: Colorful image colorization. In: Leibe, B., Matas, J., Sebe, N., Welling, M. (eds.) ECCV 2016. LNCS, vol. 9907, pp. 649–666. Springer, Cham (2016). https://doi.org/10.1007/978-3-319-46487-9_40

Generality-Training of a Classifier for Improved Calibration in Unseen Contexts

Bhawani Shankar Leelar(✉) and Meelis Kull

Institute of Computer Science, University of Tartu, Tartu, Estonia
{bhawani.shankar.leelar,meelis.kull}@ut.ee

Abstract. Artificial neural networks tend to output class probabilities that are miscalibrated, *i.e.*, their reported uncertainty is not a very good indicator of how much we should trust the model. Consequently, methods have been developed to improve the model's predictive uncertainty, both during training and post-hoc. Even if the model is calibrated on the domain used in training, it typically becomes over-confident when applied on slightly different target domains, e.g. due to perturbations or shifts in the data. The model can be recalibrated for a fixed list of target domains, but its performance can still be poor on unseen target domains. To address this issue, we propose a generality-training procedure that learns a modified head for the neural network to achieve better calibration generalization to new domains while retaining calibration performance on the given domains. This generality-head is trained on multiple domains using a new objective function with increased emphasis on the calibration loss compared to cross-entropy. Such training results in a more general model in the sense of not only better calibration but also better accuracy on unseen domains, as we demonstrate experimentally on multiple datasets. The code and supplementary for the paper is available (https://github.com/bsl-traveller/CaliGen.git).

Keywords: classifier calibration · distribution shift · out-of-distribution generalization

1 Introduction

Deep Neural Network (DNNs) typically produce predictions that are not calibrated, which means their predicted probabilities express confidence levels that are not reflected in accuracy. Calibration methods improve the calibration of their predictive uncertainty both during model training [1–5] and post-hoc [6–17]. These calibration methods still tend to be over-confident under distribution shift because of distribution disparity between the source (or pre-shift) and target (or post-shift) domains [18–21]. Standard methods of domain adaptation

This work was supported by the Estonian Research Council grant PRG1604 and the European Social Fund via IT Academy programme.

D. Koutra et al. (Eds.): ECML PKDD 2023, LNAI 14173, pp. 374–391, 2023.
https://doi.org/10.1007/978-3-031-43424-2_23

and transfer learning [22] can offer some but limited help because of focusing on prediction accuracy and not on calibration [23].

Table 1. Comparison between calibration generalization and related calibration paradigm

Calibration paradigm	Calibration data	Test data
Single-domain calibration	$\mathcal{D}^{source}$	$\mathcal{D}^{source}$
Multi-domain calibration	$\mathcal{D}^1, \ldots, \mathcal{D}^n$	$\mathcal{D}^1, \ldots, \mathcal{D}^n$
Calibration transfer/adaptation	$\mathcal{D}^{source}, \mathcal{D}^{target}$	$\mathcal{D}^{target}$
Calibration generalization	$\mathcal{D}^1, \ldots, \mathcal{D}^n$	$\mathcal{D}^{n+1}$

This issue is addressed in recent research about calibration across multiple domains [19–21,24–27] where the goal is to obtain calibrated probabilities in the target domain(s) using information from the source domain(s). More precisely, these methods address several different but related tasks, which we propose to categorize as follows, building on the categorization by Wang et al. [28] (see Table 1): (1) *single-domain calibration*, *i.e.*, the classical task of learning calibrated uncertainty estimates in a single domain without any shift involved; (2) *multi-domain calibration* with the goal of learning calibrated predictions for multiple domains by using some labeled data from each of these domains during learning; (3) *calibration transfer or adaptation* where a calibration learned on source domain can be transferred (might lose the calibration on source domain) or adapted (preserves calibration on source domain) to a target domain with the help of some labeled or unlabelled samples from the target domain during learning [19,20,25,27]; and (4) *calibration generalization* where there are no data available from the target domain during the learning phase, and hence the model is faced with test data from a previously unseen domain, typically a variation of the seen domain(s) due to a slight distribution shift, some perturbations to the data or a context change [21,24].

We focus on calibration generalization, and in particular on the same scenario as Gong et al. [21] where the goal is to provide calibrated predictions in an unseen domain under the assumption of having access to the following resources: (a) a model trained on training (source) domains; (b) labeled data in several calibration domains, helping to prepare for the unseen domain; (c) access to the representation layer (*i.e.*, latent space features) of the model, helping to relate test instances of the unseen domain to the training and calibration domains. In other words, the goal is very specific: having access to a model trained on source domains and access to multiple calibration domains, how can we best prepare ourselves for unseen data by using but not modifying the representation layer of the model?

The work of Gong et al. [21] builds on Temperature Scaling (TS) [16], which is a simple and commonly used calibration method where a single temperature parameter is used to adjust the confidence level of the classifier. Instead

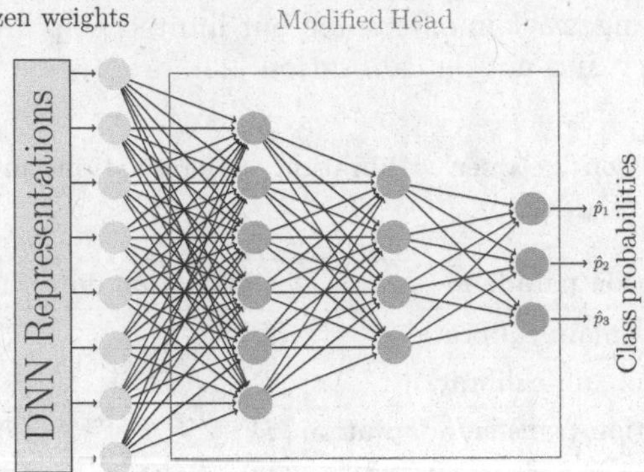

Fig. 1. Modified head of DNN. The network before the Representation layer is fixed, and after the representation layer, 2 dense hidden layers (with dimensions (1024, 512) for DomainNet, and (512, 128) for the other two datasets) and one dense logit layer (equal to the number of classes) are added. We use dropout (0.5), L2 regularizer (0.01), and ReLU activation for all layers with softmax on the last layer

of applying the same temperature on all instances, Gong et al. vary the temperature across instances. The idea is first to cluster the data of all calibration domains jointly and then learn a different temperature for each cluster. Clustering is performed in the representation space, *i.e.*, on the activation vectors of the representation layer instead of the original features. On a test instance, the temperature from the closest cluster is used (a method called *Cluster NN*), or a linear model fitted on cluster centers is used to predict the temperature to be used (a method called *Cluster LR*).

These cluster-based methods have the following limitations. First, they rely on TS to offer a suitable family of calibration transformations, while several newer calibration methods with richer transformation families have been shown to outperform TS [1–3,29]. Second, test-time inference to obtain predictions requires additional computation outside the classifier itself, thus making the solution slightly more complicated technically. While this second point is typically a minor problem, having a single classifier model to provide predictions on test data would still be advantageous.

To address these shortcomings, we propose a novel calibration method Cali-Gen (Calibration by Generality Training), to improve calibration generalization to unseen domains. We insert additional fully-connected layers to the network on top of the representation layer and train this additional structure on the calibration domains (freezing the representations, *i.e.*, the earlier part of the network, see the illustration in Fig. 1). We propose a custom objective function (see Sect. 4.1) to be used with this training process, which addresses both prediction accuracy and calibration error with a weighted combination of cross-entropy and KL-divergence. We call this process *generality-training* because its goal is to improve the model's generalizability to unseen domains. Our major contributions include the following:

- We propose a novel solution for the simultaneous generalization of a neural network classifier for calibration and accuracy in a domain generalization procedure.
- We propose a novel secondary loss function to be used with cross-entropy to encourage calibration. We have tested it in a calibration generalization setting, but it is open to finding more use cases in similar or different scenarios.
- We provide a theoretical justification for the proposed algorithm and explain its advantage in better generalization.
- We provide experimental results on real-world data to justify its advantage over existing calibration generalization methods. We show that our method generalizes better to unseen target domains with improved accuracy and calibration while maintaining well-calibrated probabilities in the source domains.

The rest of the paper is organized as follows: Sect. 2 discusses related work in calibration and multi-domain calibration. In Sect. 3, we discuss the required background to understand the paper. We propose the method in Sect. 4 and give a theoretical explanation. We discuss datasets and experimental set-up in Sect. 5. In Sect. 6, we discuss the results obtained on 3 datasets with comparison to other state-of-the-art (SOTA) methods along with an ablation study, and in Sect. 7, we give concluding remarks.

2 Related Work

2.1 Calibration

Researchers have proposed many solutions to obtain well-calibrated predictions from neural networks. These solutions can be summarised into three categories. In the first category, the primary training loss is replaced or augmented with a term that explicitly incentives calibration; examples include the AvUC loss [1], MMCE loss [2], Focal loss [3,4] and Cross-entropy loss with Pairwise Constraints [5]. Other examples include Mixup [30], Label smoothing [31], and Label Relaxation [32], which can also be interpreted as modifying the loss function and has been shown to improve calibration.

While the above methods offer to achieve calibrated probabilities during training, solutions using post-hoc calibration methods fall into the second category in which model predictions are transformed after the training by optimizing additional parameters on a held-out validation set [6–17]. One of the most popular techniques in this category is TS [16], however, it is ineffective under distribution shift in certain scenarios [18].

A third category of methods examines model changes such as ensembling multiple predictions [33,34] or multiple priors [29].

2.2 Multi-domain Calibration

All the above works aim to be calibrated in a single domain or context (in-distribution data). Still, studies have shown that existing post-hoc calibration methods are highly overconfident under domain shift [23,27]. In recent times, researchers have shifted their attention to addressing the issue of calibration under distribution shift and multi-domain calibration [19–21,24–27,35,36]. As calibration on multiple in-distribution domains, multi-domain calibration is also used in fairness [25,35,36]. Recent research on calibration adaptation considers the setting when labels are unavailable from the target domain [19,20,25,27]. However, a more challenging task of calibration generalization, when no samples from target domains are available during training or calibration, is considered by [21,24]. In particular, Wald et al. [24] extended Isotonic Regression to the multi-domain setting, which takes predictions of a trained model on validation data pooled from training domains.

Gong et al. [21] have used latent space features to predict a temperature to use in TS calibration to obtain better calibration. This work is close to our work, where calibration generalization is sought. The core idea behind the work is that instances with similar representations might require a similar temperature to achieve better-calibrated probabilities. They proposed Cluster-level Nearest Neighbour (*Cluster NN*), which uses clustering on features and then calculates the temperature for each cluster, which will be applied on the target domain based on the assigned cluster. They also proposed Cluster-level Regression (*Cluster LR*), where a linear regression model is trained on cluster centers to predict the target temperature. They use multiple domains to learn calibration to better generalize unseen domains while depending on inferred temperature for probability calibration.

3 Background

3.1 Calibration

Consider a DNN $\phi(.)$, parameterized by θ, which for any given input X predicts a probability for each of the K classes as a class probability vector $\hat{P}$. The class with the highest probability is denoted $\hat{Y}$, and the corresponding probability is known as the confidence, denoted $\hat{Q}$. The classifier is defined to be *perfectly confidence-calibrated* [16] if $\mathbb{P}(\hat{Y} = Y|\hat{Q} = q) = q, \forall q \in [0,1]$ where Y is the ground truth label. The calibration methods aim to adjust the confidence during or after the training to achieve calibrated probabilities. Expected Calibration Error (ECE) [13,16] is used to quantify the calibration capabilities of a classifier by grouping test instances into B bins of equal width based on predicted confidence values where B_m is the set of instances such that $B_m = \{i|\hat{q}_i \in (\frac{m-1}{B}, \frac{m}{B}]\}$ and $\hat{q}_i$ is the predicted confidence for the ith instance. ECE is calculated as the weighted absolute difference between accuracy and confidence across bins as:

$$\mathcal{L}_{\text{ECE}} = \sum_{m=1}^{B} \frac{|B_m|}{N} |\mathbb{A}(B_m) - \mathbb{Q}(B_m)|, \tag{1}$$

where N is the total number of instances; for each bin B_m, the accuracy is $\mathbb{A}(B_m) = \frac{1}{|B_m|}\sum_{i\in B_m} 1(\hat{y}_i = y_i)$ and the confidence is $\mathbb{Q}(B_m) = \frac{1}{|B_m|}\sum_{i\in B_m} \hat{q}_i$; and finally, $\hat{y}_i$ and y_i are the predicted and actual label for the ith instance.

Temperature Scaling Calibration. TS method for calibration is a simple and popular calibration method [16] which gives calibrated probabilities, once an optimal temperature $T^* > 0$ is calculated by minimizing negative log likelihood (NLL) loss as follows:

$$T^* = \arg\min_{T>0} \sum_{(\mathbf{x}_v,\mathbf{y}_v)\in\mathcal{D}_v} \mathcal{L}_{\mathrm{NLL}}(\sigma(\mathbf{z}_v/T), \mathbf{y}_v), \tag{2}$$

where $\mathcal{D}_v$ is the validation set, $\mathbf{z}_v$ are the logit vectors (network outputs before the softmax) obtained from a classifier trained on $\mathcal{D}_{tr}$ (the training set), $\mathbf{y}_v$ are the ground truth labels, and $\sigma(.)$ is the softmax function. Calibrated probabilities are obtained by applying T^* on test logit vectors $\mathbf{z}_{ts}$ of the test set $\mathcal{D}_{ts}$ as $\hat{\mathbf{y}}_{ts} = \sigma(\mathbf{z}_{ts}/T^*)$.

3.2 Standard Calibration-Refinement Decomposition

Following the notations from the previous Section, let $C = (C_1, \cdots, C_K)$ be the perfectly calibrated probability vector, corresponding to the classifier $\phi(.)$, where $C = \mathbb{E}[Y \mid \hat{P}]$. Consider the expected loss of $\hat{P}$ with respect to Y, *i.e.*, $\mathbb{E}[D(\hat{P}, Y)]$ where D is a proper scoring rule. According to the calibration-refinement decomposition [37,38], the expected loss can be decomposed into the sum of the expected divergence of $\hat{P}$ from C and the expected divergence of C from Y with respect to any proper scoring rule D as follows:

$$\mathbb{E}[D(\hat{P}, Y)] = \mathbb{E}[D(\hat{P}, C)] + \mathbb{E}[D(C, Y)] \tag{3}$$

These two terms are known as the *Calibration Loss (CL)* and the *Refinement Loss (RL)*. CL ($\mathbb{E}[D(\hat{P}, C)]$) is the loss due to the difference between the model estimated probability score $\hat{P}$ and the fraction of positive instances with the same output. Better calibrated models have lower CL. The loss RL ($\mathbb{E}[D(C, Y)]$) is due to the multiple class instances with the same score $\hat{P}$.

As NLL decomposes into the sum of CL and RL, training a DNNs with the objective of NLL means putting equal importance to both parts. This motivates our custom modification to the loss function, which we will describe next.

4 Calibration by Generality Training (CaliGen)

We aim to achieve better generalization of calibration and accuracy with generality-training of the classifier. To achieve the best of both, we propose a new loss function, CaliGen loss, to be used with our approach. The primary objective of classifier training with NLL (*i.e.*, the cross-entropy loss) is to increase the classification accuracy. In contrast, we want the network to produce calibrated probabilities which is hard to achieve by minimizing NLL [16]. To achieve this goal, we need to use an objective function that penalizes the situation when the model produces uncalibrated probabilities.

4.1 CaliGen Loss Function

NLL loss can be expressed as follows [3]:

$$\mathcal{L}_{\mathrm{NLL}}(\hat{P}, Y) = \mathcal{L}_{\mathrm{KL}}(\hat{P}, Y) + \mathbb{H}[Y] \tag{4}$$

where $\mathcal{L}_{\mathrm{KL}}(.)$ is the KL-divergence loss and $\mathbb{H}[Y]$ is entropy which is a constant with respect to the prediction that is being optimized. Following Eq. (3), we can decompose divergence in Eq. (4) as:

$$\mathcal{L}_{\mathrm{NLL}}(\hat{P}, Y) = \mathcal{L}_{\mathrm{KL}}(\hat{P}, C) + \mathcal{L}_{\mathrm{KL}}(C, Y) + \mathbb{H}[Y], \tag{5}$$

Our objective of generalization is to improve emphasis on CL ($\mathcal{L}_{\mathrm{KL}}(\hat{P}, C)$), that is to obtain better calibration. In other words, if we decrease emphasis on RL ($\mathcal{L}_{\mathrm{KL}}(C, Y)$), it will give more importance to CL. Mathematically, we consider a new loss function as follows:

$$\mathcal{L}(\hat{P}, Y) = \mathcal{L}_{\mathrm{KL}}(\hat{P}, C) + (1 - \rho)(\mathcal{L}_{\mathrm{KL}}(C, Y) + \mathbb{H}[Y]), \tag{6}$$

where $\rho \in [0, 1]$ is a hyperparameter, with higher values of ρ putting less emphasis on refinement and thus more emphasis on calibration. The problem in implementing such a loss function is that we cannot know the perfectly calibrated probabilities C. Thus, instead we approximate these with the probability vector $\hat{C}$ obtained by TS calibration, assuming that $\mathcal{L}_{\mathrm{KL}}(\hat{P}, \hat{C}) \approx \mathcal{L}_{\mathrm{KL}}(\hat{P}, C)$. This assumption is justified as we first fit TS on the validation set data and then use the same data to generate $\hat{C}$. Given the above approximation, we can now add a negligible term $\rho(\mathcal{L}_{\mathrm{KL}}(\hat{P}, \hat{C}) - \mathcal{L}_{\mathrm{KL}}(\hat{P}, C))$ to the loss function in Eq. (6) as:

$$\begin{aligned}
\mathcal{L}(\hat{P}, \hat{C}, Y) &= \mathcal{L}(\hat{P}, Y) + \rho(\mathcal{L}_{\mathrm{KL}}(\hat{P}, \hat{C}) - \mathcal{L}_{\mathrm{KL}}(\hat{P}, C)) \\
&= (1 - \rho)\mathcal{L}_{\mathrm{KL}}(C, Y) + \mathcal{L}_{\mathrm{KL}}(\hat{P}, C) \\
&\quad + \rho(\mathcal{L}_{\mathrm{KL}}(\hat{P}, \hat{C}) - \mathcal{L}_{\mathrm{KL}}(\hat{P}, C)) + (1 - \rho)\mathbb{H}[Y]) \\
&= (1 - \rho)\mathcal{L}_{\mathrm{KL}}(C, Y) + (1 - \rho)\mathcal{L}_{\mathrm{KL}}(\hat{P}, C) \\
&\quad + \rho\mathcal{L}_{\mathrm{KL}}(\hat{P}, \hat{C}) + (1 - \rho)\mathbb{H}[Y] \\
&= (1 - \rho)(\mathcal{L}_{\mathrm{KL}}(\hat{P}, C) + \mathcal{L}_{\mathrm{KL}}(C, Y) + \mathbb{H}[Y]) + \rho\mathcal{L}_{\mathrm{KL}}(\hat{P}, \hat{C}) \\
&= (1 - \rho)\mathcal{L}_{\mathrm{NLL}}(\hat{P}, Y) + \rho\mathcal{L}_{\mathrm{KL}}(\hat{P}, \hat{C}),
\end{aligned} \tag{7}$$

For $\rho > 0$, the loss function in Eq. (7) decreases the emphasis on $\mathcal{L}_{\mathrm{NLL}}(\hat{P}, Y)$) and adds emphasis on $\mathcal{L}_{\mathrm{KL}}(\hat{P}, \hat{C})$, which is equivalent to reducing the gap between distribution of predicted probabilities $\hat{P}$ and temperature scaled calibrated probabilities $\hat{C}$. We have $\mathcal{L}(\hat{P}, \hat{C}, Y) \approx \mathcal{L}(\hat{P}, Y)$ (using the assumption $\mathcal{L}_{\mathrm{KL}}(\hat{P}, \hat{C}) \approx \mathcal{L}_{\mathrm{KL}}(\hat{P}, C)$), hence by minimizing $\mathcal{L}(\hat{P}, \hat{C}, Y)$, we are minimizing $\mathcal{L}(\hat{P}, Y)$ with more emphasis on CL ($\mathcal{L}_{\mathrm{KL}}(\hat{P}, C)$). We call this custom loss function $\mathcal{L}(\hat{P}, \hat{C}, Y)$ as the CaliGen loss.

4.2 Generality Training

We learn calibration by generality-training of a trained network by modifying the prediction head. We insert two more layers between the representation and logit layers of the trained network, as shown in Fig. 1. The additional two layers improve the ability to realize more complex functions, as demonstrated by the ablation study in Sect. 6.3. This modified head can be considered a separate Multi-Layer Perceptron (MLP) with two hidden layers where input is the representation produced by the trained model. CaliGen loss requires 3 vectors: representation vector, ground truth label vector, and calibrated probabilities. Generality-training of this modified head is a two-stage task: (i) We consider multiple domains for calibration domain set $\mathcal{C}$, and for each domain $c \in \mathcal{C}$, we obtain T_c^* using TS calibration method given in Eq. (2). We then use it to get the calibrated probability vector $\hat{C}$ for each instance in the calibration domains. These calibrated probabilities for each calibration domain are generated once before the generality-training. We have used TS to obtain the calibrated probabilities for its simplicity. However, our method requires only calibrated probabilities, and thus, in principle, TS in generality-training can be replaced by any other post-hoc calibration method. (ii) During generality-training, all the layers are frozen till the representation layer. We use the CaliGen loss function given in Eq. (7) for optimization based on a fixed value of ρ.

Hyper-parameter Tuning. We consider different values of ρ from [0.0, 0.1, ..., 0.9, 1.0] in the CaliGen loss function Eq. (7) for optimization and use early stopping (with 20% of data allocated for validation). We select the best value of ρ using 3-fold cross-validation based on best error while restricting the selection of ρ from 0.2 to 0.8. The selection range is restricted in $[0.2, 0.8]$ to avoid extreme ρ values that do not improve calibration in our observation (see Fig. 2). The best values of ρ are given in the Supplementary material.

5 Experiments

We experiment with three datasets to test our method. These experiments aim to test our proposed method CaliGen on real datasets and compare the results with SOTA methods in the area. In the following, we give a brief description of each dataset.

5.1 Datasets

Office-Home. [39] The dataset contains around 15,500 images of different sizes from 65 categories. It is further divided into four domains: Art, Clipart, Painting, and Real World. We resize the images to 224×224 and split each domain into 80-20 subsets referred to as the *Large* subset and the *Small* subset, respectively. We use the *Large* subset for training and evaluation, whereas the *Small* subset for calibration. We use one domain for training, 2 for calibration, and 1 remaining domain for evaluation along the same lines as used in [21] and perform experiments on all possible 12 combinations of splitting the 4 domains into 1 training, 1 test, and 2 calibration domains.

DomainNet. [40] The dataset contains different size images from 6 domains across 345 categories. The domains are Clipart, Infograph, Painting, Quickdraw, Real, and Sketch. We resize the images to 224×224 and split each domain into 90–10 referred to as the *Large* subset and the *Small* subset, respectively. We use the *Large* subset for training and evaluation and the *Small* subset for calibration. We use 2 domains for training, 3 for calibration, and 1 for evaluation, similar to [21]. We perform experiments on all possible 60 combinations.

CIFAR-10-C. We used the CIFAR-10 dataset [41] and applied 15 corruptions [42,43] from level 1 (less severe) to level 5 (more severe) on it. We consider 4 corruptions (Gaussian Noise, Brightness, Pixelate, and Gaussian blur) of level 1 as well as original images as the source domains, 4 different corruptions (Fog, Contrast, Elastic Transform, and Saturate) of level 1 as the calibration domains, and the remaining 7 corruptions of all levels as the target domain. A more detailed description of this dataset is given in the supplemental material.

5.2 Experimental Setup

Generality-Training. We use ResNet101 [44] and EfficientNet V2 B0 [45] pre-trained on Imagenet and re-train it on each of the datasets listed in Sect. 5.1. For generality-training, we train a Multi-Layer Perceptron (modified head of DNN) with details given in Fig. 1 and Sect. 4.2.

Base Methods. We use TS on the held-out validation set from the source domain as a reference method. This method does not generalize to unseen domains and is called the *source only* calibration (TS). We consider an *Oracle* method where the model is calibrated with TS on the *Large* subset of the target domain. *Oracle* method is closest to the best possible calibration method within the TS family as it has access to the test data for calibration. For other base methods, we consider TS and Top Label Calibration (Histogram Binning Top Label or HB-TL) [17] by fitting these methods on calibration domains. We have also considered learning the weights by focal loss [3] instead of NLL and then applying calibration methods to improve calibration.

Calibration Adaptation Methods. There is very limited work in Calibration generalization settings; however, the work done by Park et al., Calibrated Prediction with Covariate Shift (CPCS) [19] and by Wang et al., Transferable Calibration (TransCal) [20] address the calibration adaptation by estimating the density ratio of the target domain and source domain with unlabelled instances from the target domain. We used calibration domain instances to estimate the

Table 2. Calibration performance (ECE %) evaluated on target domains of Office-Home dataset and averaged by target domains. The weights are learned by minimizing NLL (default) and focal loss (FL)

Method	Art	Clipart	Product	Real World	Average
Uncalibrated	37.61 ± 5.21	40.32 ± 0.28	29.64 ± 4.81	26.05 ± 7.48	33.41 ± 7.75
TS (Source)	18.12 ± 5.42	24.44 ± 5.38	11.64 ± 5.34	11.25 ± 0.74	16.36 ± 7.15
TS (Oracle)	*4.77 ± 0.51*	*6.06 ± 0.88*	*6.6 ± 0.9*	*6.59 ± 1.13*	*6.0 ± 1.16*
HB-TL	25.38 ± 1.73	25.99 ± 4.87	18.57 ± 5.92	14.68 ± 3.54	21.16 ± 6.4
TS	8.24 ± 3.15	15.87 ± 1.4	7.73 ± 3.09	8.77 ± 2.91	10.15 ± 4.3
CPCS	8.98 ± 3.08	15.47 ± 1.62	7.26 ± 1.88	9.32 ± 3.6	10.26 ± 4.1
TransCal	28.76 ± 14.78	23.91 ± 15.78	18.2 ± 10.44	15.5 ± 8.38	21.6 ± 13.71
Cluster NN	8.03 ± 1.79	17.08 ± 2.1	8.2 ± 2.9	7.92 ± 1.65	10.31 ± 4.47
Cluster LR	7.4 ± 0.86	17.79 ± 3.33	8.56 ± 2.81	7.48 ± 1.7	10.31 ± 4.95
Cluster En.	7.77 ± 1.81	17.15 ± 2.02	7.84 ± 2.9	7.56 ± 2.07	10.08 ± 4.66
CaliGen	**6.64 ± 1.84**	**14.61 ± 4.87**	**6.38 ± 0.93**	**7.27 ± 0.54**	**8.72 ± 4.32**
Uncalibrated (FL)	38.97 ± 3.66	40.73 ± 4.11	29.52 ± 2.17	25.54 ± 5.6	33.69 ± 7.55
TS (FL)	8.73 ± 3.18	14.81 ± 1.61	9.02 ± 1.91	9.17 ± 2.36	10.43 ± 3.45

density ratio for a fair comparison with CaliGen, assuming the target domain is unseen.

Cluster-Level Methods. As we propose the calibration generalization method, we compare our method with the current SOTA method cluster level [21]. We use K-means clustering (for *Cluster NN*) with 8 clusters for the Office-Home dataset and 9 clusters for the other two datasets. The number of clusters for Office-Home and DomainNet was selected from the paper [21] while for CIFAR-10-C, we experimented with clusters from 6 to 15 and chose 9, which gave the best results in the test dataset. We train a linear regressor (for *Cluster LR*) on cluster centers, and for the cluster ensemble method, we take the mean of logits of these two along with TS.

6 Results and Discussion

We perform experiments to test the robustness of CaliGen on different challenging tasks: (a) slight distribution shifts due to corruptions (CIFAR-10-C) and (b) major domain shifts (Office-Home, DomainNet). For this, we experimented with different calibration methods considering calibration domains (which include source domains) to compare the performance of CaliGen with other SOTA methods. Gong et al. [21] considered only calibration domain data for calibration learning, while our experiments suggest that it will lose calibration on source data if source domains are not included in calibration domains (see supplementary material). We run 20 iterations of our experiments with 500 samples from

Table 3. Calibration performance (ECE %) evaluated on target domains of DomainNet dataset and averaged by target domains

Method	Clipart	Infograph	Painting	Quickdraw	Real	Sketch
Uncalibrated	16.12 ± 3.2	28.95 ± 6.9	22.74 ± 5.24	38.33 ± 13.88	18.61 ± 3.71	22.1 ± 3.73
TS (Source)	10.98 ± 2.83	22.31 ± 5.58	15.39 ± 3.99	28.43 ± 13.09	11.26 ± 4.01	14.05 ± 2.05
Oracle (TS)	5.93 ± 0.68	4.72 ± 0.73	4.96 ± 0.78	2.44 ± 0.69	5.08 ± 0.6	5.34 ± 0.37
HB-TL	6.99 ± 1.03	17.3 ± 2.92	10.83 ± 2.29	22.34 ± 3.2	7.66 ± 1.72	10.16 ± 2.02
TS	8.02 ± 2.54	10.35 ± 4.34	6.07 ± 1.48	18.23 ± 11.84	9.06 ± 3.66	6.11 ± 1.25
CPCS	7.09 ± 1.54	13.02 ± 5.35	7.44 ± 3.07	21.5 ± 12.52	8.02 ± 1.33	6.35 ± 1.82
TransCal	**6.94 ± 1.61**	19.39 ± 7.9	11.05 ± 3.73	23.7 ± 13.04	7.2 ± 2.25	9.07 ± 3.23
Cluster NN	7.27 ± 1.33	11.67 ± 5.03	6.0 ± 1.76	19.6 ± 8.33	**6.24 ± 1.13**	6.0 ± 1.04
Cluster LR	8.43 ± 1.84	13.01 ± 7.69	6.97 ± 2.43	21.86 ± 7.04	7.62 ± 2.16	6.08 ± 0.87
Cluster En.	7.2 ± 1.48	11.55 ± 5.34	**5.66 ± 1.18**	20.27 ± 7.61	6.3 ± 1.61	**5.23 ± 0.57**
CaliGen	9.63 ± 1.3	**6.91 ± 1.81**	5.83 ± 0.62	**12.17 ± 1.56**	8.4 ± 0.86	5.81 ± 0.6

Large subset or Test subset and report mean ECE % (calculated with bin size 15) with standard deviation and mean Error % with standard deviation for each dataset.

6.1 Performance Measures

Calibration Performance. Our method CaliGen achieves SOTA results for ECE on each dataset as shown in Table 2 (Office-Home) and Table 3 (DomainNet) where we outperform all other methods on average. For the DomainNet dataset, we achieve the best results on average (8.13 ± 2.57, while the second best method is the cluster ensemble achieving ECE of 9.37 ± 6.6). Note that the high standard deviations in the table are due to considering different combinations of domains for source, calibration, and target. E.g., when Art is the target in Office-Home, then Caligen has ECE of 6.64 ± 1.84, where 6.64 and 1.84 are, respectively, the mean and standard deviation of 5.41,8.75,5.76, which are respectively the results when the source is Clipart, Product, or RealWorld. All methods other than CaliGen struggle when the task is more complex (Clipart in Office-Home, and Quickdraw in DomainNet). In contrast, CaliGen improves the uncalibrated ECE significantly. CPCS is either outperforming or comparable to cluster-based methods. In comparison, CaliGen achieves lower ECE on target domains and also on source domains (see supplementary material). DNN trained with focal loss [3] might not give better calibration on the unseen domain when compared to NLL. We have given detailed results considering the focal loss in the supplementary material.

Improvement Ratio. Improvement Ratio (IR) [21] measures the model's calibration transfer score. Given a source-only calibration and target-only (*Oracle*) calibration, one can measure how close to the oracle-level the model is, compared

Table 4. Improvement Ratio based on average ECE % scores of target domains when the classifier is trained using ResNet (R) or EfficientNet (E)

Method	CIFAR-10-C (R)	Office-Home (R)	Office-Home (E)	DomainNet (R)
CaliGen	**0.34**	**0.74**	**0.88**	**0.73**
Second best	0.26 (CPCS)	0.61 (Cl. En.)	0.78 (CPCS)	0.63 (Cl. En.)

Table 5. Error % averaged by target domains for different datasets while classifier is trained using ResNet101 (R) or EfficientNet V2 B0 (E). All TS based methods do not change error and are the same as Uncalibrated

Method	CIFAR-10-C (R)	Office-Home (R)	Office-Home (E)	DomainNet (R)
Uncalibrated	48.41 ± 14.1	68.95 ± 9.68	61.98 ± 8.8	77.93 ± 11.93
CaliGen	47.22 ± 16.13	63.49 ± 9.64	56.74 ± 10.37	76.33 ± 10.86

to the source-only level. It is measured by $IR = \frac{ECE_S - ECE}{ECE_S - ECE_T}$, where ECE_S is the source only ECE and ECE_T is the *Oracle* ECE. CaliGen achieves the best IR across all datasets (see Table 4). The detailed results on the CIFAR-10-C dataset and EfficientNet network are given in the supplementary material.

Accuracy Generalization. The generality training procedure has access to representations, ground truth labels, and calibrated probabilities of calibration domains, but the representations are learned only on source domains. During generality-training, the model tries to minimize NLL loss on ground truth labels along with minimizing divergence to calibrated probabilities which helps in better accuracy generalization (see Table 5) along with calibration generalization, given the representations learned on source domains.

6.2 Effect of ρ on ECE and Error

In our method, ρ is a hyper-parameter for which we select the best value by 3-fold cross-validation based on minimum error. Figure 2 shows the effect of changing ρ on error and ECE for both Office-Home and DomainNet datasets. We observe the best error rate when ρ is 0.2 or 0.3, and the error increases for higher values, while ECE is not monotonous for higher values of ρ. For $\rho = 0$, the objective function is NLL, and the generality-training does not minimize KL-divergence, so higher ECE and lower error are expected. Still, as we increase ρ, the error further minimizes and monotonically increases after $\rho = 0.3$.

6.3 Ablation Study

We perform an ablation study on generality training considering the effects of (i) not modifying the objective function and (ii) not modifying the head.

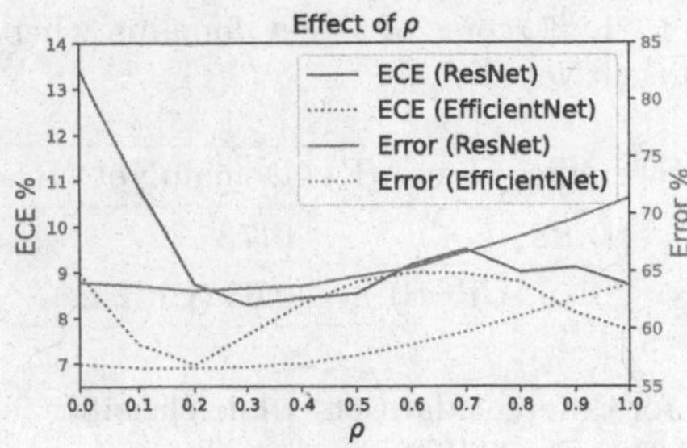

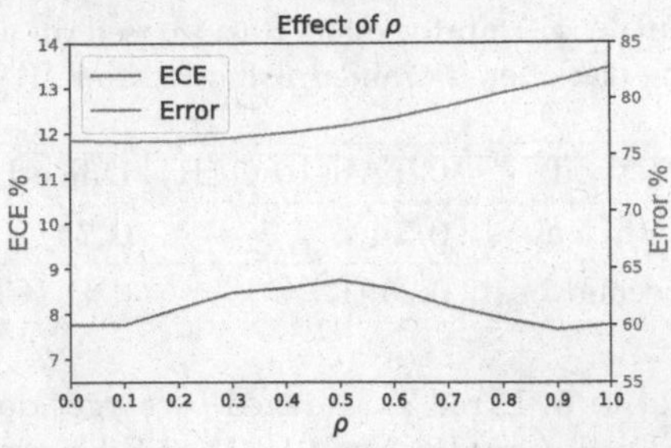

Fig. 2. Effect of ρ on ECE and Error on datasets (a) Office-Home, (b) DomainNet

Unmodified Objective Function. We test the abilities of our proposed objective function given in Eq. (7) by setting $\rho = 0$ (Only the NLL loss). We observe that when only the NLL loss is used, we do not achieve desirable results for ECE as shown in Table 6. This confirms that models trained with NLL give equal importance to CL and RL, thus struggling to produce well-calibrated probabilities.

Table 6. Calibration performance (ECE %) averaged by target domains of Office-Home dataset while fine-tuned with either unmodified loss function or unmodified head

Ablation	Art	Clipart	Product	Real World	Average
Unmodified loss	13.41 ± 4.77	21.23 ± 7.37	10.14 ± 4.83	8.93 ± 0.26	13.43 ± 6.93
Unmodified head	10.57 ± 2.05	19.14 ± 4.67	6.73 ± 0.96	$\mathbf{6.22 \pm 0.32}$	10.66 ± 5.79
CaliGen (no ablation)	$\mathbf{6.64 \pm 1.84}$	$\mathbf{14.61 \pm 4.87}$	$\mathbf{6.38 \pm 0.93}$	7.27 ± 0.54	$\mathbf{8.72 \pm 4.32}$

Unmodified Head. We justify the modification of the network head by testing our CaliGen loss function on the unmodified head. We use the same procedure without modifying the head and select the best ρ by 3-fold cross-validation. As shown in Table 6, modifying the head improves the performance on average. Adding more layers to the head gives it the ability to realize more complex functions while we use dropout (0.5) and L2 regularizer (0.01) to prevent overfitting.

6.4 Limitations

Our method gives better calibration compared to SOTA methods in calibration generalization setting, same as Gong et al. [21], where we set the representations to be fixed. We have made the assumption of fixed representations throughout the whole paper. In contrast, now we investigate what one can do if there are enough time and resources to relearn the representations as well, something that was not considered by Gong et al. [21]. Thus, we use ResNet pre-trained on Imagenet for this experiment and retrained it on source and calibration domains.

Experimental Setup. For training, we use the Office-Home dataset with an additional 50% of the *Small* subsets (10% of the whole domain) from calibration domains along with the source domain (*Large* subset, 80%). This setting redistributes the data for training and calibration such that we have the *Large* subset of source domains and *Small* subset of calibration domains available for training and calibration as discussed in Sect. 5.1. For calibration, the *Small* subset of the source domain (20%) and the remaining 50% of the *Small* subset (10%) of the calibration domains are used.

Table 7. Calibration performance (ECE %) and Error % averaged by target domains of Office-Home dataset while ResNet trained and calibrated on all combinations of 3 domains.

Domain	Trained on source and calib. domains			CaliGen (trained on source domain)		
	ECE (Uncl.)	ECE (TS)	Error	ECE (Uncl.)	ECE	Error
Art	28.67 ± 9.15	9.84 ± 0.42	68.78 ± 3.1	37.61 ± 5.21	6.64 ± 1.84	72.71 ± 2.4
Clipart	40.07 ± 4.13	15.75 ± 1.25	72.34 ± 8.61	40.32 ± 0.28	14.61 ± 4.87	71.94 ± 0.17
Product	19.7 ± 4.03	6.72 ± 1.43	47.78 ± 8.72	29.64 ± 4.81	6.38 ± 0.93	57.97 ± 1.69
RealWorld	21.58 ± 4.6	6.24 ± 0.89	52.55 ± 7.37	26.05 ± 7.48	7.27 ± 0.54	51.34 ± 5.36
Average	27.51 ± 9.92	9.64 ± 3.94	60.36 ± 12.72	33.41 ± 7.75	8.72 ± 4.32	63.49 ± 9.64

Results. Results shown in Table 7 are averaged by target domains. CaliGen obtains surprisingly better ECE than the model trained on calibration data. However, this training procedure aims to give richer representation to source and calibration domains, which helps in better accuracy generalization on unseen domains. However, CaliGen still gives slightly better errors in the Clipart and Real World domains. In a scenario where calibration domains are unavailable during training, it is more sensible to save cost by generality-training with CaliGen instead of retraining the whole network.

7 Conclusion

In this paper, we addressed the problem of calibration generalization for unseen domains. Based on the goal of improving calibration, we derived a new loss function that gives more weightage to Calibration Loss. We proposed a novel generality-training procedure CaliGen which modifies the head of the DNN and uses our proposed CaliGen loss function, which gives more weightage to Calibration Loss. Together, these two changes improve domain generalization, meaning that accuracy and calibration improve on unseen domains while staying comparable to standard training on seen domains. Similarly to several earlier works, the method assumes that all the layers until the representation layer are fixed and cannot be retrained due to limited resources. We also show that if retraining is possible, then results can be improved further.

References

1. Krishnan, R., Tickoo, O.: Improving model calibration with accuracy versus uncertainty optimization. In: Advances in Neural Information Processing Systems, vol. 33, pp. 18237–18248 (2020)
2. Kumar, A., Sarawagi, S., Jain, U.: Trainable calibration measures for neural networks from kernel mean embeddings. In: Dy, J., Krause, A. (eds.) Proceedings of the 35th International Conference on Machine Learning. Proceedings of Machine Learning Research, vol. 80, pp. 2805–2814. PMLR (2018). https://proceedings.mlr.press/v80/kumar18a.html
3. Mukhoti, J., et al.: Calibrating deep neural networks using focal loss. In: Larochelle, H., et al. (eds.) Advances in Neural Information Processing Systems, vol. 33, pp. 15288–15299. Curran Associates Inc. (2020). https://proceedings.neurips.cc/paper/2020/file/aeb7b30ef1d024a76f21a1d40e30c302-Paper.pdf
4. Lin, T.-Y., et al.: Focal loss for dense object detection. In: Proceedings of the IEEE International Conference on Computer Vision, pp. 2980–2988 (2017)
5. Cheng, J., Vasconcelos, N.: Calibrating deep neural networks by pairwise constraints. In: Proceedings of the IEEE/CVF Conference on Computer Vision and Pattern Recognition, pp. 13709–13718 (2022)
6. Platt, J., et al.: Probabilistic outputs for support vector machines and comparisons to regularized likelihood methods. Adv. Large Margin Classif. **10**(3), 61–74 (1999)
7. Zadrozny, B., Elkan, C.: Transforming classifier scores into accurate multiclass probability estimates. In: Proceedings of the Eighth ACM SIGKDD International Conference on Knowledge Discovery and Data Mining, pp. 694–699 (2002)
8. Kull, M., et al.: Beyond temperature scaling: obtaining well-calibrated multi-class probabilities with dirichlet calibration. In: Advances in Neural Information Processing Systems, vol. 32 (2019)
9. Zadrozny, B., Elkan, C.: Obtaining calibrated probability estimates from decision trees and Naive Bayesian classifiers. In: Proceedings of the Eighteenth International Conference on Machine Learning, pp. 609–616 (2001)
10. Naeini, M.P., Cooper, G.F.: Binary classifier calibration using an ensemble of near isotonic regression models. In: 2016 IEEE 16th International Conference on Data Mining (ICDM), pp. 360–369. IEEE (2016)
11. Allikivi, M.-L., Kull, M.: Non-parametric Bayesian isotonic calibration: fighting over-confidence in binary classification. In: Brefeld, U., Fromont, E., Hotho, A., Knobbe, A., Maathuis, M., Robardet, C. (eds.) ECML PKDD 2019. LNCS (LNAI), vol. 11907, pp. 103–120. Springer, Cham (2020). https://doi.org/10.1007/978-3-030-46147-8_7
12. Kull, M., Filho, T.S., Flach, P.: Beta calibration: a well-founded and easily implemented improvement on logistic calibration for binary classifiers. In: Singh, A., Zhu, J. (eds.) Proceedings of the 20th International Conference on Artificial Intelligence and Statistics. Proceedings of Machine Learning Research, vol. 54, pp. 623–631. PMLR (2017). https://proceedings.mlr.press/v54/kull17a.html
13. Naeini, M.P., Cooper, G., Hauskrecht, M.: Obtaining well calibrated probabilities using Bayesian binning. In: Twenty-Ninth AAAI Conference on Artificial Intelligence (2015)
14. Wenger, J., Kjellström, H., Triebel, R.: Non-parametric calibration for classification. In: International Conference on Artificial Intelligence and Statistics, pp. 178–190. PMLR (2020)

15. Gupta, K., et al.: Calibration of neural networks using splines. In: International Conference on Learning Representations (ICLR) (2021). https://openreview.net/forum?id=eQe8DEWNN2W
16. Guo, C., et al.: On calibration of modern neural networks. In: International Conference on Machine Learning, pp. 1321–1330. PMLR (2017)
17. Gupta, C., Ramdas, A.: Top-label calibration and multiclass-to-binary reductions. In: International Conference on Learning Representations (2022). https://openreview.net/forum?id=WqoBaaPHS-
18. Ovadia, Y., et al.: Can you trust your model's uncertainty? Evaluating predictive uncertainty under dataset shift. In: Advances in Neural Information Processing Systems, vol. 32 (2019)
19. Park, S., et al.: Calibrated prediction with covariate shift via unsupervised domain adaptation. In: Chiappa, S., Calandra, R. (eds.) Proceedings of the Twenty Third International Conference on Artificial Intelligence and Statistics. Proceedings of Machine Learning Research, vol. 108, pp. 3219–3229. PMLR (2020). https://proceedings.mlr.press/v108/park20b.html
20. Wang, X., et al.: Transferable calibration with lower bias and variance in domain adaptation. In: Larochelle, H., et al. (eds.) Advances in Neural Information Processing Systems, vol. 33, pp. 19212–19223. Curran Associates Inc. (2020). https://proceedings.neurips.cc/paper/2020/file/df12ecd077efc8c23881028604dbb8cc-Paper.pdf
21. Gong, Y., et al.: Confidence calibration for domain generalization under covariate shift. In: Proceedings of the IEEE/CVF International Conference on Computer Vision, pp. 8958–8967 (2021)
22. Weiss, K., Khoshgoftaar, T.M., Wang, D.: A survey of transfer learning. J. Big Data **3**(1), 1–40 (2016)
23. Pampari, A., Ermon, S.: Unsupervised calibration under covariate shift. CoRR, abs/2006.16405 (2020). https://arxiv.org/abs/2006.16405
24. Wald, Y., et al.: On calibration and out-of-domain generalization. In: Advances in Neural Information Processing Systems, vol. 34 (2021)
25. Pleiss, G., et al.: On fairness and calibration. In: Advances in Neural Information Processing Systems, vol. 30 (2017)
26. Kong, L., et al.: Calibrated language model fine-tuning for in- and out-of-distribution data. In: Proceedings of the 2020 Conference on Empirical Methods in Natural Language Processing (EMNLP), pp. 1326–1340. Association for Computational Linguistics (2020). https://doi.org/10.18653/v1/2020.emnlp-main.102. https://aclanthology.org/2020.emnlp-main.102
27. Tomani, C., et al.: Post-hoc uncertainty calibration for domain drift scenarios. In: Proceedings of the IEEE/CVF Conference on Computer Vision and Pattern Recognition, pp. 10124–10132 (2021)
28. Wang, J., et al.: Generalizing to unseen domains: a survey on domain generalization. IEEE Trans. Knowl. Data Eng. (2022)
29. Dusenberry, M., et al.: Efficient and scalable Bayesian neural nets with rank-1 factors. In: International Conference on Machine Learning, pp. 2782–2792. PMLR (2020)
30. Thulasidasan, S., et al.: On mixup training: improved calibration and predictive uncertainty for deep neural networks. In: Advances in Neural Information Processing Systems, vol. 32 (2019)
31. Müller, R., Kornblith, S., Hinton, G.E.: When does label smoothing help? In: Wallach, H., et al. (eds.) Advances in Neural Information Processing Systems, vol.

32. Curran Associates Inc. (2019). https://proceedings.neurips.cc/paper/2019/file/f1748d6b0fd9d439f71450117eba2725-Paper.pdf
32. Lienen, J., Hüllermeier, E.: From label smoothing to label relaxation. In: Proceedings of the AAAI Conference on Artificial Intelligence, vol. 35, pp. 8583–8591 (2021)
33. Lakshminarayanan, B., Pritzel, A., Blundell, C.: Simple and scalable predictive uncertainty estimation using deep ensembles. In: Advances in Neural Information Processing Systems, vol. 30 (2017)
34. Wen, Y., Tran, D., Ba, J.: Batchensemble: an alternative approach to efficient ensemble and lifelong learning. In: International Conference on Learning Representations (2020). https://openreview.net/forum?id=Sklf1yrYDr
35. Hébert-Johnson, U., et al.: Multicalibration: calibration for the (computationally-identifiable) masses. In: International Conference on Machine Learning, pp. 1939–1948. PMLR (2018)
36. Shabat, E., Cohen, L., Mansour, Y.: Sample complexity of uniform convergence for multicalibration. In: Advances in Neural Information Processing Systems, vol. 33, pp. 13331–13340 (2020)
37. Bröcker, J.: Reliability, sufficiency, and the decomposition of proper scores. Q. J. Roy. Meteorol. Soc. **135**(643), 1512–1519 (2009)
38. Kull, M., Flach, P.: Novel decompositions of proper scoring rules for classification: score adjustment as precursor to calibration. In: Appice, A., Rodrigues, P.P., Santos Costa, V., Soares, C., Gama, J., Jorge, A. (eds.) ECML PKDD 2015. LNCS (LNAI), vol. 9284, pp. 68–85. Springer, Cham (2015). https://doi.org/10.1007/978-3-319-23528-8_5
39. Venkateswara, H., et al.: Deep hashing network for unsupervised domain adaptation. In: Proceedings of the IEEE Conference on Computer Vision and Pattern Recognition, pp. 5018–5027 (2017)
40. Peng, X., et al.: Moment matching for multi-source domain adaptation. In: Proceedings of the IEEE International Conference on Computer Vision, pp. 1406–1415 (2019)
41. Krizhevsky, A., Nair, V., Hinton, G.: CIFAR-10 (Canadian institute for advanced research) (2009). https://www.cs.toronto.edu/~kriz/cifar.html
42. Hendrycks, D., Dietterich, T.: Benchmarking neural network robustness to common corruptions and perturbations. In: International Conference on Learning Representations (2019). https://openreview.net/forum?id=HJz6tiCqYm
43. TensorFlow Datasets Team. imagenet2012_corrupted (2020). https://github.com/tensorflow/datasets/blob/master/tensorflow_datasets/image_classification/imagenet2012_corrupted.py
44. He, K., et al.: Deep residual learning for image recognition. In: Proceedings of the IEEE Conference on Computer Vision and Pattern Recognition, pp. 770–778 (2016)
45. Tan, M., Le, Q.: Efficientnetv2: smaller models and faster training. In: International Conference on Machine Learning, pp. 10096–10106. PMLR (2021)

Informed Priors for Knowledge Integration in Trajectory Prediction

Christian Schlauch[1,2,3(✉)], Christian Wirth[2], and Nadja Klein[1,3]

[1] Chair of Statistics and Data Science at Humboldt-Universität zu Berlin, Berlin, Germany
christian.schlauch@student.hu-berlin.de
[2] Continental AG, Hannover, Germany
[3] Chair of Uncertainty Quantification and Statistical Learning at Research Center Trustworthy Data Science and Security, and Technische Universität Dortmund, Dortmund, Germany

Abstract. Informed learning approaches explicitly integrate prior knowledge into learning systems, which can reduce data needs and increase robustness. However, existing work typically aims to integrate formal scientific knowledge by directly pruning the problem space, which is infeasible for more intuitive world and expert knowledge, or requires specific architecture changes and knowledge representations. We propose a probabilistic informed learning approach to integrate prior world and expert knowledge without these requirements. Our approach repurposes continual learning methods to operationalize Baye's rule for informed learning and to enable probabilistic and multi-modal predictions. We exemplify our proposal in an application to two state-of-the-art trajectory predictors for autonomous driving. This safety-critical domain is subject to an overwhelming variety of rare scenarios requiring robust and accurate predictions. We evaluate our models on a public benchmark dataset and demonstrate that our approach outperforms non-informed and informed learning baselines. Notably, we can compete with a conventional baseline, even using only half as many observations of the training dataset.

Keywords: Autonomous Driving · Bayesian Deep Learning · Continual Learning · Informed Learning · Trajectory Prediction

1 Introduction

Deep learning approaches achieve excellent prediction performance in many domains but require an exhaustive amount of training data [23]. This training data may be challenging to obtain e.g. because relevant events are too rare or costly to observe. Informed learning (IL) [20] tries to alleviate this problem by integrating so-called prior knowledge. This means scientific, world, or expert knowledge is explicitly integrated into the learning system and not just implicitly

D. Koutra et al. (Eds.): ECML PKDD 2023, LNAI 14173, pp. 392–407, 2023.
https://doi.org/10.1007/978-3-031-43424-2_24

learned from observations. Doing so allows a reduction of the required training data, an increase in the acquired accuracy, or both. Furthermore, the system can be more robust and safe, especially when encountering unseen events [23]. These benefits are particularly interesting in the autonomous driving domain, where safety and reliability under a wide variety of complex scenarios are essential [23].

Existing IL approaches are, however, often limited to integrating formal scientific knowledge by directly reducing the problem space [20]. Reducing the problem space is less suitable for integrating world or expert knowledge for which reasonable exceptions occur. For example, in autonomous driving, we might expect most traffic participants to comply with speed regulations but must not rule out violations. IL approaches that integrate such knowledge usually require architectural changes or specific knowledge representations for careful data augmentation or loss construction to appropriately bias the learning system [20]. This limits their applicability. To address these shortcomings, we propose a probabilistic IL approach by repurposing regularization-based continual learning (CL) methods [6], thus operationalizing Bayes' rule for IL.

Such an approach, while conceptually simple, has not yet been used in IL, even though it inherits four major advantages: (1) The approach allows one to integrate prior world and expert knowledge without ruling out exceptions. (2) It does not require architectural changes and does not assume a specific representation for the prior knowledge as long as it is possible to map the prior knowledge to the prediction target. (3) The probabilistic formulation is theoretically well-motivated and allows one to infer complete predictive distributions, which enable well-calibrated, multi-modal outputs beyond simple point predictions. Probabilistic formulations lead to improved models, even if calibration and multi-modality only play a minor role [13]. (4) Potentially, the approach allows one to integrate multiple, semantically different sources of prior knowledge by updating the prior sequentially.

We study our approach by considering trajectory prediction for autonomous driving as an exemplary application. The trajectory prediction is especially challenging since well-calibrated multi-modal predictions are necessary to enable safe planning [13]. Safety-critical events, like near-collision, are exceedingly rare to observe and practically unavailable in public datasets [3,24]. Prior knowledge is, however, often readily available [23]. In our study, we integrate the prior expert knowledge that trajectories are likely to stay on-road [2], see Fig. 1. Exceptions to this expectation may occur in the formation of an emergency corridor or during evasive maneuvers. Using this single prior knowledge enables us to compare to existing work, even though it does not allow us to investigate advantage (4). We present an implementation that adapts the state-of-the-art CoverNet [17] and MultiPath [4] trajectory predictors using generalized variational continual learning (GVCL) [12]. We critically analyze our approach in multiple experiments and show that it improves existing non-informed baselines and outperforms other IL approaches like transfer learning or multi-task learning with auxiliary losses [2].

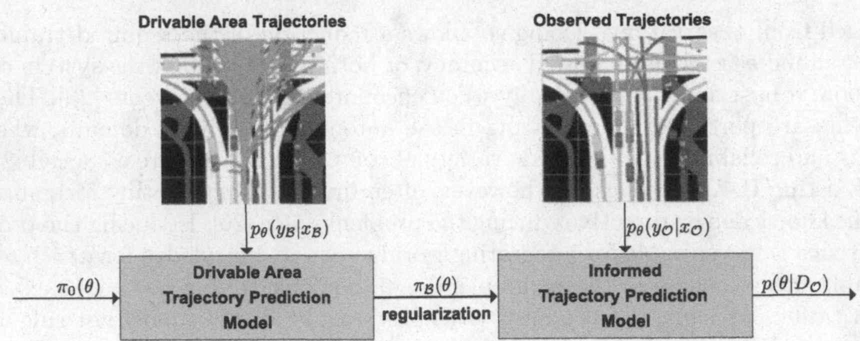

Fig. 1. Two-task example for the integration of prior expert knowledge with our probabilistic IL approach for the trajectory prediction in autonomous driving, c.f. Sect. 4.3.

In summary, our contributions are:

- A probabilistic IL approach to systematically integrate prior world and expert knowledge into deep learning models, that also enables well-calibrated multi-modal, probabilistic predictions;
- a concrete application of our approach to the trajectory prediction in autonomous driving, adapting the state-of-the-art CoverNet and MultiPath predictors; and
- an extensive evaluation, showing that we substantially improve on multiple CoverNet and MultiPath baseline variants.

The paper is structured as follows: We relate our work to the existing literature in Sect. 2. In Sect. 3, we introduce our probabilistic IL approach before we exemplify it on the CoverNet and MultiPath architecture in Sect. 4. In Sect. 5, we benchmark our method against various baseline variants and close the paper with a conclusion and discussion in Sect. 6. Our code is published on GitHub[1]

2 Related Work

The idea of integrating prior knowledge into learning systems has been a long-standing research subject, but IL is only recently emerging as a distinct field of research in the development of parsimonious and trustworthy AI [20]. Rueden et al. [20] provide a taxonomy for existing IL methods based on the type and representation of prior knowledge as well as the integration approach. In most domains, like trajectory prediction for autonomous driving, there has been a particular focus on integrating scientific knowledge about physical limitations [23]. For instance, Phan-Minh et al. [17] propose dynamically constructed scene-specific trajectory sets based on plausible dynamical models as output representation, while Cui et al. [5], Li et al. [10] define specific layer types to encode a

[1] https://github.com/continental/kiwissen-bayesian-trajectory-prediction.

dynamical model directly. In contrast, Bahari et al. [1] present a post-processing approach based on a model predictive controller.

While these methods prune the problem space, we enable the "soft constraining" integration of world and expert knowledge that can be violated. Earlier work in the same direction has been done by Wang et al. [21] using an multi-task learning approach, while Boulton et al. [2] introduce an auxiliary loss method combined with a transfer learning approach where the model is pre-trained using prior knowledge. Similar approaches have been shown to be beneficial in other domains [18]. However, transfer learning may "forget" the prior knowledge, as preservation is not enforced, while multi-task learning approaches require a single dataset with simultaneously available labels. Our approach based on CL methods can be applied without these limitations. To our knowledge, CL methods have not yet been used to realize an IL approach.

De Lange et al. [6], Parisi et al. [16] categorize existing CL methods as regularization-based, replay-based, or architectural. Architectural methods require a specific model representation, while replay-based methods typically employ replay buffers. We focus on regularization-based methods as they do not have these requirements and can be easily formulated in a probabilistic way, which is itself argued to feature robustness and safety [13]. We leverage GVCL which generalizes variational continual learning (VCL) [15] and online elastic weight consolidation (Online EWC) [9,19]. Other regularization-based methods may potentially be used instead [16]. However, GVCL is a well-established, theoretically well-motivated method and can be applied to a wide variety of model architectures without modification [with the exception of recurrent architectures for which variational reformulations are typically more involved [7].

3 A Probabilistic Informed Learning Approach

We introduce a probabilistic informed learning (IL) approach to explicitly integrate prior world and expert knowledge into deep learning systems. The basic idea is to map the prior knowledge to learning tasks. By applying Baye's rule to learn over these tasks sequentially we aggregate an informed prior before learning from actual observations. To this end, we repurpose regularization-based continual learning (CL), making our approach computationally tractable and preventing catastrophic forgetting. In the following, we formalize this idea.

3.1 The Informed Learning Problem

Our focus is on supervised learning problems, where we denote $\mathcal{D} = \{\mathcal{X} \times \mathcal{Y}\}$ as the domain over the input space $\mathcal{X}$ and the output space $\mathcal{Y}$. In the conventional setup, we draw a single labeled dataset $D = \{(x_i, y_i)\}_{i=1}^{N}$ consisting of a finite number of N conditionally independent realizations $y_i|x_i$, where $x_i \in \mathcal{X}$ and $y_i \in \mathcal{Y}$. Let $p(y|x)$ denote the true conditional distribution of Y given $X = x$ and let $\mathcal{H}$ denote a hypothesis space consisting of hypothesis (probabilistic deep learning models) $h_\theta(\cdot)$ that are defined through some model parameters

θ. Given D and $\mathcal{H}$, the *task* is to learn a final hypothesis $h_\theta(x) \in \mathcal{H}$ in form of a predictive distribution $h_\theta(x) \sim p_\theta(y|x)$ by applying a learning algorithm $\mathcal{L} : D \rightarrow \mathcal{H}$. Our goal is now to integrate prior world or expert knowledge $\mathcal{B}$ into the learning algorithm $\mathcal{L}$, thereby placing an inductive bias into the learning problem [20,23]. Following Rueden et al. [20], we call such an explicit integration of prior knowledge $\mathcal{B}$ an *informed learning problem.*

3.2 Operationalizing Bayes' Rule for Informed Learning

To tackle the IL problem, we extend the conventional setup by defining a sequence of multiple *knowledge-based* tasks $t = 1, \ldots, T-1$. In contrast to the conventional *observational* task $t = T$, we generate the respective labelled datasets $D_t = \{(x_i^{(t)}, y_i^{(t)})\}_{i=1}^{N_t}$ with N_t samples each by mapping our prior knowledge $B_t \subset \mathcal{B}$ onto our prediction target. This can be done by either generating completely synthetic data (e.g. with simulations) or leveraging semantic annotations to input data of an observational dataset. We illustrate the latter approach, which is especially cheap, in Sect. 4.1. We recursively learn over this sequence of tasks by applying Bayes' rule, allowing us to recover the posterior probability distributions $p(\theta|D_{1:T})$ with

$$p(\theta|D_{1:T}) \propto \pi_0(\theta) \prod_{t=1}^{T} p_\theta(y_t|x_t). \tag{1}$$

given the respective likelihoods $p_\theta(y_t|x_t)$ and $\pi_0(\theta)$ as the initial, uninformed prior.

In general, this approach does not require a specific model representation and can be applied to existing state-of-the-art models using a shared output representation $\mathcal{Y}$ for all tasks. The sequential approach allows reusing posteriors $\pi_{D_{1:t-1}}(\theta)$ in different sequences, expanding the sequence when new data or knowledge becomes available or reordering the tasks to form a curriculum [14]. Notably, the formulation leads to an implicit trade-off for the impact of our prior knowledge; if less observational data is available, e.g. for rare events in the input space $\mathcal{X}$, the more relevant the informed prior is.

3.3 Repurposing Continual Learning Methods

Our above learning task setup is similar to a CL task-incremental problem [6]. However, the IL context justifies stronger assumptions since more information is available. First, we can assume that the number of tasks is finite, and their identities to be known. Second, we can assume that our prior knowledge is not in conflict with the observed data since we intend to make information explicit that we assume to be implicitly contained in domain [20]. Thus, we assume no domain shift between the aggregated informed prior and our observations. However, we are still concerned with shifts *during* aggregation of our informed prior since different prior knowledge may conflict. E.g. in autonomous driving, we may require a trade-off between conflicting traffic rules. In fact, it can be advantageous to implicitly resolve rule conflicts during learning since such conflicts are often challenging to solve a priori in symbolic systems. Thus, we must minimize potential catastrophic forgetting to learn an appropriate joint posterior weight distribution that captures all prior knowledge and observations. By repurposing CL methods, we tackle this concern and make our approach computationally tractable.

We illustrate our approach with GVCL, which is a likelihood-tempered version of VCL [15] based on variational inference (VI) [22]. The likelihood-tempering has been shown to help, in VI [22], in some settings. GVCL tackles the recursion described in Eq. (1) by minimizing the likelihood-tempered log-evidence lower bound (so-called β-ELBO, $\beta \in [0, 1]$) at every task $t = 1, \ldots, T$. This yields a tractable approximate solution $q_t(\theta) \approx p(\theta|D_{1:t})$ using the approximate posterior $q_{t-1}(\theta) \approx p(\theta|D_{1:t-1})$ of the previous task $t-1$ as a prior distribution weighted by β for all t. More precisely, the β-ELBO at time t is defined by

$$\beta\text{-ELBO} = \mathbb{E}_{\theta \sim q_t(\theta)} \left[\log p_\theta(y_t|x_t)\right] - \beta D_{\mathrm{KL}}(q_t(\theta) \| q_{t-1}(\theta)), \tag{2}$$

where $D_{\mathrm{KL}}(q_t(\theta)||q_{t-1}(\theta))$ is the Kullback-Leibler (KL) divergence between two probability distributions q_t, q_{t-1}. We assume a fixed form $q_t(\theta)$ that belongs to the family $\mathcal{Q}$ of Gaussian distributions with diagonal covariance matrices. As uninformed prior $q_0(\theta) = \pi_0(\theta)$, we use a zero-mean, unit-variance normal distribution. Here, θ collects all weights and biases, and the variational parameter vector $\nu = (\mu, \sigma)^\top$ consists of the means and standard deviations of the independent Gaussian variational distributions of each model weight. Note, that we may artificially sharpen the informed prior in the D_{KL}-term as described by Loo et al. [12], which enables us to tune the effect of the prior $q_{t-1}(\theta)$.

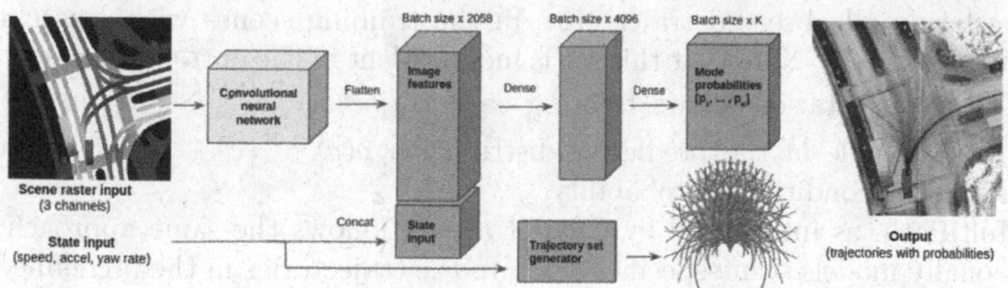

Fig. 2. Model architecture from Phan-Minh et al. [17].

4 An Application to Trajectory Prediction in Autonomous Driving

We exemplify our probabilistic IL approach by applying it to CoverNet [17] and MultiPath [4], two state-of-the-art trajectory prediction models in autonomous driving [8,11]. We integrate the prior expert knowledge, that trajectories are likely to stay on-road, by leveraging drivable area map data that is commonly available in public datasets. Boulton et al. [2] also applied this prior knowledge, allowing us to compare to existing baselines.

4.1 The Trajectory Prediction Problem

Our focus is on single-target trajectory prediction problems, where a self-driving system is assumed to observe the states in the state space $\mathcal{Y}$ of all agents $\mathcal{A}$ present in a scene on the road. Let $y_j^{(t)} \in \mathcal{Y}$ denote the state of agent $a_j \in \mathcal{A}$ at time t and let $y_j^{(t-T_o:t)} = \left(y_j^{(t-T_o)}, y_j^{(t-T_o+\delta t)}, \ldots, y_j^{(t)}\right)$ be its observed trajectory over an observation history T_o with sampling period δt. Additionally, we assume access to agent-specific maps M_i which includes semantic annotations such as the drivable area and is centered around a target agent $a_i \in \mathcal{A}$. The scene context of agent a_i consisting of map and states is then denoted as $x_i = (\{y_j^{(t-T_o:t)}\}_{j=1}^{|\mathcal{A}|}, M_i)$. Given x_i, the goal is to predict the distribution of a_i's future trajectories $p(y_i^{(t+\delta t:t+T_h)}|x_i)$ over the prediction horizon T_h.

4.2 Reviewing CoverNet and MultiPath

CoverNet [17] approaches the trajectory prediction problem with a computer vision-based architecture as shown in Fig. 2. The input consists of the current state $y_i^{(t)}$ of the target vehicle a_i and a birds-eye-view RGB rendering of the scene context x_i over a three-second observation period ($T_o = 3$ s). The output uses a predefined set $\mathcal{K}(\epsilon)$ of $n(\epsilon)$ possible trajectories

$$\mathcal{K}(\epsilon) = \left\{ y_k^{(t+\delta t:t+T_h)} \;\middle|\; k = 1, \ldots, n(\epsilon) \right\},$$

where ϵ is a coverage bound. Following Phan-Minh et al. [17], we can define $\mathcal{K}(\epsilon)$ by clustering all observed trajectories in the training scenes with ϵ as cluster distance in meter[2]. Note that this set is independent of the current scene context x_i. The representation allows treating each trajectory $y_k^{(t+\delta t:t+T_h)}$ in the set $\mathcal{K}(\epsilon)$ as a sample of the predictive distribution $p(y_i^{(t+\delta t:t+T_h)}|x_i)$, while only computing its conditional probability.

MultiPath, as introduced by Chai et al. [4], follows the same approach but additionally models scene-specific offsets to the trajectories in the predefined set $\mathcal{K}(\epsilon)$ (termed as anchor trajectories) at each time step. This offset allows a better adaption to the scene context and can be understood as conditionally independent Gaussian distributions at each time step. However, we keep the covariances of these Gaussian distributions frozen, reducing the task to a standard regression problem, as this has shown the best performance in the large-scale experiment by Chai et al. [4]. We implement the MultiPath model by extending the CoverNet architecture in Fig. 2 with an additional regression head.

[2] In general, any space-filling heuristic may be used to generate the set $\mathcal{K}(\epsilon)$, even a data-agnostic one.

4.3 Defining Our Task Setup

Given an observational dataset $D_{\mathcal{O}} = \{(x_i, y_{i,\text{true}}^{(t+\delta t:t+T_h)})\}_{i=1}^N$ with ground truth trajectories $y_{i,\text{true}}^{(t+\delta t:t+T_h)}$, we can define two tasks following our approach described in Sect. 3, see Fig. 1. The first knowledge task integrates our prior knowledge $\mathcal{B}$ that trajectories are likely to stay on-road, while the second observational task encompasses the conventional training on observations.

- **Task 1 – learning from on-road trajectories:** For each scene context x_i in $D_{\mathcal{O}}$, we label every trajectory in the predefined set $\mathcal{K}(\epsilon)$ that is contained in the drivable area of M_i over all time-steps $\tau \in (t, t+\delta t, \ldots, t+T_h)$ as positive. This results in a new $D_{\mathcal{B}} = \{(x_i, k_i)\}_{i=1}^N$, where k_i is a binary vector with multiple positive labels. We then train the CoverNet and the MultiPath models on this multi-label classification task using a binary cross-entropy loss. At this point, we do not need access to scene-specific ground truth trajectories $y_{i,\text{true}}^{(t+\delta t:t+T_h)}$ from $D_{\mathcal{O}}$.
- **Task 2 – learning from observed trajectories:** Given $\mathcal{D}_{\mathcal{O}}$, the trajectory in $\mathcal{K}(\epsilon)$ closest to $y_{i,\text{true}}^{(t+1:t+T_h)}$ is labeled as positive. Thus, for CoverNet (CN), the prediction problem is reduced to a multi-class classification with $D_{\mathcal{O}}^{\text{CN}} = \{(x_i, k_i)\}_{i=1}^N$, where k_i is a binary vector with a single positive label. Then, CoverNet is trained using a sparse categorical cross-entropy loss where the softmax function normalizes its logit transformations. MultiPath additionally considers the offset $\Delta_{i,\text{true}}^{(t+\delta t:t+T_h)}$ between the ground truth and the positively labeled (closest) trajectory $\mathcal{K}(\epsilon)$, resulting in $D_{\mathcal{O}}^{\text{MTP}} = \{(x_i, k_i, \Delta_{i,\text{true}}^{(t+\delta t:t+T_h)})\}_{i=1}^N$. The scene specif offsets are then trained with a l_2-regression loss.

This task setup can be used to train GVCL-Variants of the CoverNet and MultiPath models by applying the formalism in Sect. 3.3.

5 Experiments

We investigate the performance of our proposed informed GVCL-Variant using the NuScenes dataset of Caesar et al. [3]. In our main study we investigate the performance of our models under diminishing observation counts and in an ablation type study the effect of the coverage bound ϵ in $\mathcal{K}(\epsilon)$.

5.1 Datasets

The NuScenes dataset, our $\mathcal{D}_{\mathcal{O}}$ (see Sect. 4.3), contains 1000 scenes, each being 20 s, with two samples per second (δt = 0.5 s). We use the data split described by Phan-Minh et al. [17] with 32186/8560/9041 observations in the training/validation/test set with three second history (T_o = 3 s) and six second prediction horizons (T_h = 6 s). We employ the predefined trajectory sets $\mathcal{K}(\epsilon)$ with coverage bounds $\epsilon \in \{2, 4, 8\}$ that are distributed with the dataset from the NuScenes prediction challenge [3]. Lastly, we leverage the drivable area included in NuScenes map data to define a knowledge dataset, our $D_{\mathcal{B}}$ (see Sect. 4.3).

5.2 Baseline Variants

We consider two non-informed baseline variants:

- **Base-Variant** of the CoverNet [17] and the MultiPath model [4] (Sect. 3.3).
- **VI-Variant** as a probabilistic adaptation [22] of the Base-Variants. Like our GVCL-Variant described in Sect. 4.2, the number of parameters is doubled, in comparison to the Base-Variant, and the likelihood-temperature is set by a hyperparameter $\beta \in [0, 1]$. This baseline allows us to distinguish the effects of our probabilistic IL approach and probabilistic (uninformed) learning alone.

We also consider two informed baseline variants:

- **Loss-Variant** uses an auxiliary on-road loss as introduced by Boulton et al. [2]. The model jointly trains on on-road and observed trajectories. The trade-off between losses is controlled by a hyperparameter $\lambda_{\text{multi}} > 0$.
- **Transfer-Variant** pre-trains on on-road trajectories in a first task before training solely on observed ones, as described in Sect. 4.3. It also has been used by Boulton et al. [2]. This variant can be viewed as an ablation for our approach without regularization.

Since our GVCL-Variant has effectively doubled the parameters, we also introduce a **GVCl-Det-Variant** to allow for a fair comparison to the non-probabilistic baselines. The GVCL-Det-Variant is trained according to the GVCL method but makes non-probabilistic predictions at test time using the mean μ of the variational parameters ν only (see Sect. 4.2).

5.3 Implementation Details

All our models utilize the architecture described in Sect. 4.2 with a ResNet50 backbone. We report further implementation details, including optimizer choices, hyperparameter tuning, and settings, as well as hardware configurations, in Sec. A of our Supplemental Material (SM). Our code is published on GitHub[3].

5.4 Metrics and Evaluation

To evaluate our experiments, we report the min, max, and average results of three independent runs per experiment. We consider the following metrics commonly applied in the literature [8,11]. The average displacement error minADE_1 and final displacement error minFDE_1 evaluate the quality of the most likely trajectory, whereas minADE_5 considers the five most likely trajectories. The minADE_5 metric indirectly depends on well-calibrated, probabilistic predictions, as it evaluates the quality of the probability-based ordering. In addition, we consider the $\text{HitRate}_{5,2}$, that measures if one of the 5 most likely trajectories is "close enough" [17]. Furthermore, we consider the drivable area compliance (DAC) metric that

[3] https://github.com/continental/kiwissen-bayesian-trajectory-prediction.

determines how far the predictions conform to the prior knowledge. We report a more extensive set of metrics in Sec. B of our SM.

Note that, since the observed ground truth trajectory may not be part of the trajectory set $y_{i,\text{true}}^{(t+\delta t\,:\,t+T_h)} \notin \mathcal{K}(\epsilon)$, the CoverNet model exhibits an irreducible approximation error in displacement metrics (ADE, FDE). This is not the case for the MultiPath model due to its regression of the offset.

5.5 Results - Effect of Training Size

In this main study, we run three sets of experiments with 10%, 50%, and 100% of the available observations in the training split while using the full validation and test splits of $\mathcal{D}_{\mathcal{O}}$. However, we use the complete training split of $\mathcal{D}_{\mathcal{B}}$. This relates to real-world driving applications, where map data is substantially cheaper to obtain than observations. The 10% and 50% subsets are randomly sub-sampled, and the coverage bound is set to $\epsilon = 4$, resulting in $|\mathcal{K}(4)| = 415$ trajectories.

CoverNet Variants. Table 1 shows the performance of our GVCL-CoverNet in comparison with the baselines under varying amounts of available observations. First, we observe that our GVCL-CoverNet outperforms all baselines in all three sets of experiments across all metrics except the DAC of Transfer-CoverNet. Most notably, GVCL-CoverNet improves on the prediction performance of the other informed baselines (Transfer- and Loss-CoverNet), especially in calibration-sensitive metrics (minADE_5, $\text{HitRate}_{5,2}$) the fewer observations are available, as shown in Fig. 3. Regarding the DAC, we expect our model to only conform to the prior knowledge in so far that is beneficial for the general prediction performance, since the regularization implicitely trades off the prior knowledge and observations. In that regard Transfer-CoverNet, as non-probablistic ablation to our model, may overly bias the DAC since it performs worse than GVCL-CoverNet in all other metrics.

We also note, that the GVCL-CoverNet performance gains can only be partially attributed to the probabilistic formulation as GVCL-CoverNet again outperforms the non-informed VI-CoverNet across all metrics. A caveat to the probabilistic models is their doubled number of parameters. However, we observe that our GVCL-Det-CoverNet still achieves the best minADE_1 and minFDE_1 of all non-probabilistic models. It also achieves the same or higher $\text{HitRate}_{5,2}$ and is only outperformed by Transfer-CoverNet in the calibration-sensitive metric minADE_5 for 50% and 100% of the data. We hypothesize that the deterministic reduction leads to a substantial calibration-loss at test time loss. However, we also note that with decreasing amounts of available observations the GVCL-Det-CoverNet model becomes more competitive. In fact, we can obtain the predictive performance (in terms of minADE_1 and minFDE_1) of the Base model, with **just 50%** of the training data.

These results substantiate the relevance of the prior knowledge in our approach, which shows increasing benefits the fewer observations are available. We deem this especially relevant in open-world applications, where the available training data covers rare edge cases much less sufficiently than test examples in public datasets like NuScenes.

Table 1. Average performance with maximum deviation of three independent runs of all CoverNet variants using coverage bound $\epsilon = 4$ (**bold** as unique best result and *italic* as unique best non-probabilistic per set).

Experiment	minADE_1	minADE_5	minFDE_1	$\text{HitRate}_{5,2}$	DAC
100% Data					
Base	4.77±0.49	2.26±0.10	10.61±1.16	0.19±0.01	0.88±0.01
Transfer	4.70±0.04	*2.12±0.01*	10.15±0.06	0.19±0.00	***0.96±0.01***
Loss	4.88±0.13	2.40±0.05	10.53±0.27	0.18±0.01	0.94±0.01
VI	4.13±0.13	2.03±0.09	9.21±0.35	0.21±0.00	0.91±0.01
GVCL	**3.99±0.05**	**1.94±0.03**	**8.96±0.01**	**0.22±0.00**	0.94±0.01
GVCL-Det	*4.55±0.11*	2.26±0.05	*9.93±0.25*	0.19±0.00	0.91±0.02
50% Data					
Base	5.47±0.27	2.60±0.12	12.03±0.69	0.16±0.01	0.87±0.01
Transfer	5.24±0.11	*2.33±0.03*	11.14±0.33	0.17±0.01	***0.96±0.01***
Loss	5.84±0.15	2.68±0.04	12.61±0.25	0.15±0.00	0.91±0.01
VI	4.61±0.01	2.21±0.02	10.24±0.03	0.19±0.00	0.89±0.01
GVCL	**4.30±0.03**	**1.63±0.01**	**9.57±0.01**	**0.20±0.00**	0.92±0.00
GVCL-Det	*4.76±0.16*	2.41±0.09	*10.41±0.42*	*0.18±0.01*	0.91±0.00
10% Data					
Base	6.37±0.17	3.06±0.08	13.81±0.33	0.13±0.01	0.85±0.00
Transfer	6.41±0.14	3.14±0.10	13.41±0.19	0.13±0.00	***0.98±0.00***
Loss	6.77±0.46	3.24±0.14	14.25±0.19	0.11±0.01	0.84±0.03
VI	6.03±0.15	2.80±0.08	12.77±0.22	0.14±0.00	0.82±0.02
GVCL	**5.51±0.15**	**2.55±0.08**	**11.86±0.29**	**0.17±0.00**	0.91±0.01
GVCL-Det	*5.77±0.07*	*2.75±0.05*	*12.08±0.09*	*0.16±0.00*	0.93±0.02

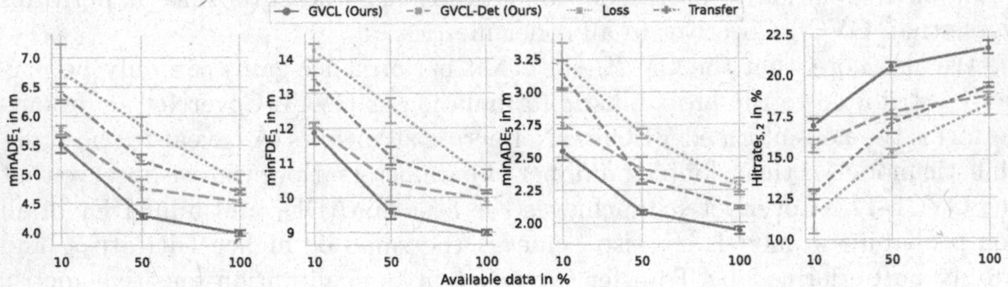

Fig. 3. Min-max performance of informed CoverNet variants using $\epsilon = 4$.

MultiPath Variants. We present in Table 2 the performance of our GVCL-MultiPath variant in comparison to the baselines under varying amounts of available observations. The results support our conclusion from the CoverNet comparison. We again observe that our GVCL-MultiPath outperforms all baselines in all three sets of experiments across all metrics except the DAC of Transfer-MultiPath (Fig. 4).

Table 2. Average performance with maximum deviation (rounded to the 2nd decimal) of three independent runs of all MultiPath variants using coverage bound $\epsilon = 4$ (**bold** as unique best result and *italic* as unique best non-probabilistic per set).

Experiment	$minADE_1$	$minADE_5$	$minFDE_1$	$HitRate_{5,2}$	DAC
100% Data					
Base	4.88±0.22	2.17±0.15	11.14±0.51	0.30±0.02	0.92±0.02
Transfer	5.07±0.01	2.15±0.10	11.05±0.05	0.28±0.01	***0.98±0.00***
Loss	*4.76±0.04*	*2.12±0.05*	10.79±0.15	*0.31±0.01*	0.94±0.00
VI	4.74±0.23	2.19±0.06	10.19±0.30	0.28±0.01	0.93±0.01
GVCL	**4.26±0.15**	**2.00±0.05**	**9.43±0.39**	**0.33±0.00**	0.94±0.01
GVCL-Det	4.87±0.27	2.54±0.15	*10.48±0.06*	0.25±0.00	0.93±0.01
50% Data					
Base	5.36±0.07	2.47±0.03	12.17±0.26	0.24±0.01	0.89±0.01
Transfer	5.70±0.09	2.53±0.012	12.20±0.21	0.23±0.02	***0.98±0.01***
Loss	*5.35±0.21*	*2.42±0.10*	12.03±0.39	0.24±0.04	0.90±0.01
VI	4.82±0.08	2.23±0.01	10.75±0.13	0.28±0.01	0.91±0.00
GVCL	**4.69±0.16**	**2.20±0.06**	**10.37±0.40**	**0.30±0.01**	0.93±0.01
GVCL-Det	5.44±0.63	2.80±0.41	*11.62±1.28*	0.21±0.01	0.91±0.03
10% Data					
Base	*6.10±0.08*	*3.08±0.07*	13.24±0.12	0.18±0.01	0.85±0.02
Transfer	6.85±0.20	3.30±0.02	14.26±0.23	0.14±0.01	***0.98±0.01***
Loss	6.71±0.13	3.38±0.14	14.42±0.38	0.16±0.02	0.85±0.03
VI	6.11±0.09	2.97±0.04	12.81±0.09	0.18±0.01	0.86±0.01
GVCL	**5.64±0.15**	**2.92±0.12**	**12.40±0.30**	**0.21±0.01**	0.91±0.02
GVCL-Det	6.15±0.28	3.11±0.16	*13.16±0.46*	0.18±0.01	0.91±0.00

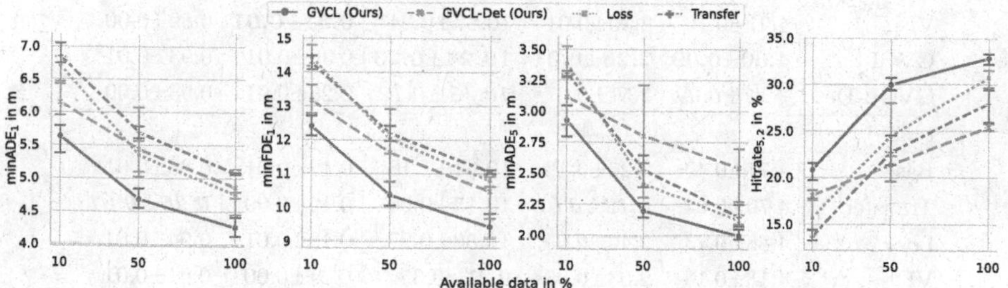

Fig. 4. Min-max performance of informed MultiPath variants using $\epsilon = 4$.

In Fig. 3 we hightlight the performance benefits in comparison to the informed MultiPath baselines. We again theorize that Transfer-MultiPath may overbias the DAC. In fact, Transfer-MultiPath shows even worse performance than Base-MultiPath ($minADE_1$, $HitRate_{5,2}$), especially with fewer observations available. This further substantiates that the Transfer-variants are not able to appropriately trade-off prior knowledge and observations.

The results also show again that the performance gains of our GVCL-MultiPath can only be partially attributed to the probabilistic formulation, as it outperforms VI-MultiPath across all metrics. Furthermore, GVCL-Det-MultiPath achieves highest minFDE_1 of all non-probablistic models and shows comparable performance in the minADE_1. Notably, it also shows a higher DAC than Base- and Loss-MultiPath while substantially outperforming Transfer-MultiPath the fewer observations are available. This further substantiates that our approach leads to a better implicit trade-off between prior knowledge and observations. However, GVCL-Det underperforms in calibration-sensitive metrics (minADE_5, $\text{HitRate}_{5,2}$), which we again attribute to a calibration-loss at test time.

5.6 Ablation - Effect of Coverage Bound ϵ

In this ablation-type study, we investigate the influence of the coverage bound on the CoverNet variants by comparing the performance for two additional coverage bounds $\epsilon \in \{2, 8\}$, corresponding to $|\mathcal{K}(2)| = 2206$ and $|\mathcal{K}(8)| = 64$ trajectories.

Table 3. Average performance of three independent runs of all CoverNet variants using the full dataset $\mathcal{D}_\mathcal{O}$ (**bold** as unique best result and *italic* as unique best non-probabilistic per set).

Experiment	minADE_1	minADE_5	minFDE_1	$\text{HitRate}_{5,2}$	DAC
ϵ=2					
Base	5.21±0.21	2.69±0.21	11.67±0.44	*0.26±0.00*	0.89±0.00
Transfer	5.38±0.13	2.54±0.04	11.50±0.28	0.25±0.00	0.97±0.00
Loss	5.09±0.04	*2.44±0.04*	10.76±0.09	0.23±0.00	0.97±0.01
VI	4.91±0.10	2.30±0.01	10.87±0.24	**0.31±0.01**	0.89±0.00
GVCL	**4.60±0.09**	**2.26±0.01**	**10.24±0.23**	0.30±0.01	0.93±0.01
GVCL-Det	*4.87±0.09*	2.57±0.07	*10.43±0.12*	0.25±0.01	0.93±0.00
ϵ=4					
Base	4.77±0.49	2.26±0.10	10.61±1.16	0.19±0.01	0.88±0.01
Transfer	4.70±0.04	*2.12±0.01*	10.15±0.06	0.19±0.00	***0.96±0.01***
Loss	4.88±0.13	2.40±0.05	10.53±0.27	0.18±0.01	0.94±0.01
VI	4.13±0.13	2.03±0.09	9.21±0.35	0.21±0.00	0.91±0.01
GVCL	**3.99±0.05**	**1.40±0.03**	**8.96±0.10**	**0.22±0.00**	0.94±0.01
GVCL-Det	*4.55±0.11*	2.26±0.05	*9.93±0.25*	0.19±0.00	0.91±0.02
ϵ=8					
Base	4.95±0.09	2.43±0.04	10.86±0.24	0.08±0.00	0.85±0.01
Transfer	4.96±0.10	2.34±0.02	10.56±0.13	0.08±0.00	0.89±0.02
Loss	4.91±0.14	2.40±0.05	10.62±0.31	0.08±0.00	0.88±0.02
VI	4.33±0.09	2.31±0.01	9.44±0.22	0.08±0.00	0.87±0.00
GVCL	**4.19±0.03**	**2.27±0.01**	**9.16±0.04**	0.08±0.00	**0.90±0.01**
GVCL-Det	*4.68±0.01*	*2.33±0.01*	*9.78±0.10*	0.08±0.00	0.89±0.01

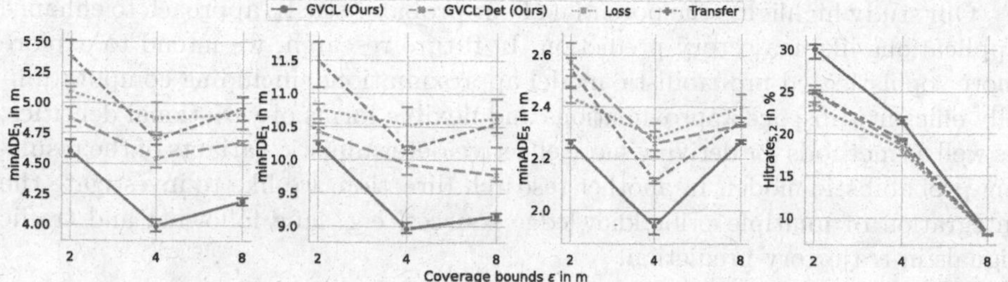

Fig. 5. Min-max performance of informed CoverNet variants using the full dataset $\mathcal{D}_{\mathcal{O}}$.

Table 3 shows the performance of our GVCL-CoverNet variant in comparison with the baselines under the different coverage bounds. Similar to before, we first observe that our GVCL-CoverNet model outperforms all baselines for each coverage bound across all metrics except the DAC of Transfer-CoverNet. Figure 5 highlights the performance improvements over the informed CoverNet baselines. As in our main study, we observe that even our GVCL-Det-CoverNet model achieves substantial performance gains with the best minADE_1 and minFDE_1 of all non-probabilistic models over all coverage bounds. We see that the calibration issues of the GVCL-Det-CoverNet model persists, with similar performance in the calibration-sensitive metrics minADE_5 and $\text{HitRate}_{5,2}$. We again conclude that it is not optimal to simply discard the variance information.

Second, we observe that all models achieve their respective best prediction performance (as measured by minADE_1, minADE_5 and minFDE_1) with a coverage bound $\epsilon = 4$. We assume that a low trajectory set resolution with a coverage bound $\epsilon = 8$ is too coarse to sufficiently cover all possible trajectories, introducing a higher approximation error, while a high resolution with coverage bound $\epsilon = 2$ poses a too difficult prediction challenge.

6 Conclusion

We propose a probabilistic IL approach that integrates prior world and expert knowledge into deep learning systems while making minimal assumptions about the model architecture and representation of the prior knowledge. We demonstrate the effectiveness of our approach by implementing two GVCL variants of the state-of-the-art CoverNet and MultiPath trajectory prediction models for autonomous driving. We integrate prior knowledge that trajectories likely stay on-road by only utilizing already available map data. As a result, we show that our approach substantially outperforms the original CoverNet and MultiPath, even when trained with only half the observations. Importantly, we outperform informed CoverNet and MultiPath variants, with increasing benefits when only limited observations are available.

Our study highlights the potential of our probabilistic IL approach to enhance applications like trajectory prediction. In future research, we intend to explore more sophisticated probabilistic model approximations, including computationally efficient subspace approximations and flexible forms of variational densities, as well as methods for deriving more effective deterministic variants of the resulting probabilistic model. In another research direction, we like to investigate the integration of multiple prior knowledge sources, e.g. lane following and traffic signals in trajectory prediction.

Acknowledgements. The research leading to these results is funded by the German Federal Ministry for Economic Affairs and Climate Action within the project "KI Wissen - Entwicklung von Methoden für die Einbindung von Wissen in maschinelles Lernen". The authors would like to thank the consortium for the successful cooperation.

References

1. Bahari, M., Nejjar, I., Alahi, A.: Injecting knowledge in data-driven vehicle trajectory predictors. Transp. Res. Part C: Emerg. Technol. **128**, 103010 (2021)
2. Boulton, F.A., Grigore, E.C., Wolff, E.M.: Motion prediction using trajectory sets and self-driving domain knowledge. arXiv preprint https://arxiv.org/abs/2006.04767 (2021)
3. Caesar, H., et al.: nuscenes: a multimodal dataset for autonomous driving. In: Proceedings of the 2020 IEEE/CVF Conference on Computer Vision and Pattern Recognition, CVPR 2020, Seattle, WA, USA (2020)
4. Chai, Y., Sapp, B., Bansal, M., Anguelov, D.: Multipath: multiple probabilistic anchor trajectory hypotheses for behavior prediction. In: Proceedings of Machine Learning Research (PMLR): 3rd Annual Conference on Robot Learning, CoRL 2019, Osaka, Japan (2019)
5. Cui, H., et al.: Deep kinematic models for kinematically feasible vehicle trajectory predictions. In: Proceedings of the 2020 IEEE International Conference on Robotics and Automation, ICRA 2020, Paris, France (2020)
6. De Lange, M., et al.: A continual learning survey: defying forgetting in classification tasks. IEEE Trans. Pattern Anal. Mach. Intell. **44**, 3366–3385 (2022)
7. Gal, Y., Ghahramani, Z.: A theoretically grounded application of dropout in recurrent neural networks. In: Advances in Neural Information Processing Systems 29: Annual Conference on Neural Information Processing Systems, NeurIPS 2016, Barcelona, Spain (2016)
8. Huang, Y., Du, J., Yang, Z., Zhou, Z., Zhang, L., Chen, H.: A survey on trajectory-prediction methods for autonomous driving. IEEE Trans. Intell. Veh. **7**, 652–674 (2022)
9. Kirkpatrick, J., et al.: Overcoming catastrophic forgetting in neural networks. Proc. Natl. Acad. Sci. PNAS **114**, 3521–3526 (2017)
10. Li, J., Ma, H., Tomizuka, M.: Conditional generative neural system for probabilistic trajectory prediction. In: Proceedings of the 2019 IEEE/RSJ International Conference on Intelligent Robots and Systems, IROS 2019, Macau, SAR, China (2019)
11. Liu, J., Mao, X., Fang, Y., Zhu, D., Meng, M.Q.H.: A survey on deep-learning approaches for vehicle trajectory prediction in autonomous driving. IEEE Trans. Intell. Veh. (2021)

12. Loo, N., Swaroop, S., Turner, R.E.: Generalized variational continual learning. In: Proceedings of the 9th International Conference on Learning Representations, ICLR 2021, Virtual Event (2021)
13. McAllister, R., et al.: Concrete problems for autonomous vehicle safety: advantages of bayesian deep learning. In: Proceedings of the 26th International Joint Conference on Artificial Intelligence, IJCAI 2017, Melbourne, Australia (2017)
14. Mundt, M., Hong, Y., Pliushch, I., Ramesh, V.: A wholistic view of continual learning with deep neural networks: forgotten lessons and the bridge to active and open world learning. arXiv preprint https://arxiv.org/abs/2009.01797 (2020)
15. Nguyen, C.V., Li, Y., Bui, T.D., Turner, R.E.: Variational continual learning. In: Proceedings of the 6th International Conference on Learning Representations, ICLR 2018, Vancouver, BC, Canada (2018)
16. Parisi, G.I., Kemker, R., Part, J.L., Kanan, C., Wermter, S.: Continual lifelong learning with neural networks: a review. Neural Netw. **113**, 54–71 (2019)
17. Phan-Minh, T., Grigore, E.C., Boulton, F.A., Beijbom, O., Wolff, E.M.: Covernet: multimodal behavior prediction using trajectory sets. In: Proceedings of the 2020 IEEE/CVF Conference on Computer Vision and Pattern Recognition, CVPR 2020, Seattle, WA, USA (2020)
18. von Rueden, L., Houben, S., Cvejoski, K., Bauckhage, C., Piatkowski, N.: Informed pre-training on prior knowledge. arXiv preprint https://arxiv.org/abs/2205.11433 (2022)
19. Schwarz, J., et al.: Progress & compress: a scalable framework for continual learning. In: Proceedings of the 35th International Conference on Machine Learning, ICML 2018, Stockholm, Sweden (2018)
20. von Rueden, L., et al.: Informed machine learning - a taxonomy and survey of integrating knowledge into learning systems. IEEE Trans. Knowl. Data Eng. **35**, 614–633 (2021)
21. Wang, E., Cui, H., Yalamanchi, S., Moorthy, M., Djuric, N.: Improving movement predictions of traffic actors in bird's-eye view models using gans and differentiable trajectory rasterization. In: KDD 2020: Proceedings of the 26th ACM SIGKDD Conference on Knowledge Discovery and Data Mining, KDD 2020, Virtual Event (2020)
22. Wilson, A.G., Izmailov, P.: Bayesian deep learning and a probabilistic perspective of generalization. In: Advances in Neural Information Processing Systems 33: Annual Conference on Neural Information Processing Systems, NeurIPS 2020, Virtual Event (2020)
23. Wörmann, J., et al.: Knowledge augmented machine learning with applications in autonomous driving: a survey. arXiv preprint https://arxiv.org/abs/2205.04712 (2022)
24. Zhan, W., et al.: INTERACTION dataset: an international, adversarial and cooperative motion dataset in interactive driving scenarios with semantic maps. arXiv preprint http://arxiv.org/abs/1910.03088 (2019)

CAENet: Efficient Multi-task Learning for Joint Semantic Segmentation and Depth Estimation

Luxi Wang and Yingming Li(✉)

College of Information Science and Electronic Engineering, Zhejiang University, Hangzhou, Zhejiang, China
{wangluxi,yingming}@zju.edu.cn

Abstract. In this paper, we propose an efficient multi-task method, named Context-aware Attentive Enrichment Network (CAENet), to deal with the problem of real-time joint semantic segmentation and depth estimation. Building upon a light-weight encoder backbone, an efficient decoder is devised to fully leverage available information from multi-scale encoder features. In particular, a new Inception Residual Pooling (IRP) module is designed to efficiently extract contextual information from the high-level features with diverse receptive fields to improve semantic understanding ability. Then the context-aware features are enriched adaptively with spatial details from low-level features via a Light-weight Attentive Fusion (LAF) module using pseudo stereoscopic attention mechanism. These two modules are progressively used in a recursive manner to generate high-resolution shared features, which are further processed by task-specific heads to produce final outputs. Such network design effectively captures beneficial information for both semantic segmentation and depth estimation tasks while largely reducing the computational budget. Extensive experiments across multi-task benchmarks validate that CAENet achieves state-of-the-art performance with comparable inference speed against other real-time competing methods. Code is available at https://github.com/wlx-zju/CAENet.

Keywords: Multi-task learning · Semantic segmentation · Depth estimation · Light-weight network

1 Introduction

In the multi-task learning (MTL) paradigm, multiple relevant tasks are jointly tackled to exploit their correlations to improve the generalization performance [4,9]. Recently this paradigm has enjoyed wide interest of research and encouraged lots of successful applications in computer vision [11,45] and natural language processing [16,24]. Taking the representative object detection model Fast-RCNN [14] as an example, it performs region classification and bounding box regression simultaneously to improve the object detection accuracy.

D. Koutra et al. (Eds.): ECML PKDD 2023, LNAI 14173, pp. 408–425, 2023.
https://doi.org/10.1007/978-3-031-43424-2_25

However, the impressive performance improvements by MTL often come at a price of increased runtime and memory footprint. For example, complex backbones [3,17,41] and sophisticated task interaction strategies [23,40,44] would be combined together to boost the generalization performance. In particular, some methods attempt to exploit several state-of-the-art networks for each sub-task as subnetwork to construct a multi-task network [13,26], which increases the model size and computational overhead substantially. Such way of multi-task modeling remains a hurdle to real-world applications. For example, for the sake of safety an autonomous driving system requires fast and accurate inference of full visual understanding of the scene, which includes recognizing pedestrians and vehicles of various types, and perceiving distance to these objects. To meet the real-time requirements of real-world compute-constrained applications, using a well-designed efficient network to jointly process multiple tasks has become a crucial strategy.

In this paper, we focus on the real-time joint semantic segmentation and depth estimation, which are closely related tasks and can provide essential information for indoor and outdoor scene understanding. Though different multi-task learning schemes [6,15,27] have been proposed to deal with this joint learning, how to make a balance between efficiency and accuracy on both tasks for different scenes remains an open problem. For example, DSPNet [6] exploits shared convolutional feature maps by ResNet50 [17] and provides a multi-task approach for both road segmentation and distance estimation from detected objects, but is still far from real-time speed. QuadroNet [15] introduces an additional dense pixel-wise encoder besides the RetinaNet [21] backbone to acquire more high-level semantics for segmentation and depth estimation tasks. On the other hand, several works [1,27,29] employ light-weight backbones to construct efficient encoder-decoder structures, which helps reduce memory and computational demand. Despite their fast inference speed, the generalization performance might be influenced due to the limitation of model capacity.

To further boost the performance of the light-weight multi-task encoder-decoder structure, in this work we propose a Context-aware Attentive Enrichment Network (CAENet), which builds upon a light-weight backbone and aims to fully exploit its features at multiple levels by adaptively enriching the coarse (low-resolution) feature maps with fine-grained (high-resolution) features. In particular, an Inception Residual Pooling (IRP) module is first introduced to extract rich context to enhance the semantic understanding of the coarse feature maps. It exploits both small and large receptive fields with an inception-style setup [37] to fully capture neighboring similarity and long-range connection, resulting in context-aware coarse feature maps. Further, a Light-weight Attentive Fusion (LAF) module is presented to enrich the context-aware coarse feature maps with fine-grained (high-resolution) features by a pseudo stereoscopic attention mechanism. Specifically, spatial and channel attention paths are employed in a parallel manner to comprehensively enrich the context-aware coarse feature maps. Both IRP and LAF modules are progressively used in a recursive manner to generate the final high-resolution output.

Extensive experiments are conducted on popular multi-task datasets to evaluate the proposed approach. On NYUv2 dataset [36], the best-performing CAENet (built on top of STDCNet [12] backbone) achieves 55.53% mIoU and 75.11% δ_1 accuracy on semantic segmentation and depth estimation tasks respectively. Such performance is fairly close to or even surpasses some sophisticated MTL methods, but CAENet holds considerably fewer parameters and runs at faster speed. When compared to other real-time baselines, CAENet also outperforms most competing methods with on par efficiency. Besides, on CityScapes dataset [7], consistent performance gains over other real-time baselines can also be observed. These results demonstrate the great potential of the proposed method in real-time joint semantic segmentation and depth estimation.

2 Related Work

2.1 Multi-task Learning

Multi-task learning (MTL) systems can tackle multiple tasks at once and have attracted much attention. Compared with single-task learning, such way better imitates how human beings comprehend the surroundings and exhibits stronger generalization capability by mining the inter-task relationships [9,39]. However, multi-task deep networks that achieve impressive performance usually exploit sophisticated task interaction [23,26,40,44], and thus run at high cost. Specifically, Cross-Stitch [26] and MTAN [23] interact with per-task branches from shallow layers, while PAD-Net [44] and MTI-Net [40] utilize multi-modal distillation to refine task-aware features. In contrast, we employ hard parameter sharing mechanism and focus on improving the shared representation to meet the requirements of real-time processing.

2.2 Real-Time Semantic Segmentation and Depth Estimation

Semantic segmentation and depth estimation are two fundamental visual tasks, which need to assign category label and distance value for each pixel respectively. These tasks are often involved in real-world applications such as autonomous driving and robots which require real-time processing. To deal with real-time segmentation, BiSeNet [46] and SwiftNet [31] adopt a light-weight multi-branch structure to aggregate low-level details and high-level context. The recently proposed STDCNet [12] is a deliberately designed backbone for efficient and effective segmentation. As for real-time depth estimation, FastDepth [42] and GuideDepth [34] leverage low-level features and multi-scale images respectively to help recover spatial information. There are also a handful of works [1,15,27,29] related to real-time joint segmentation and depth estimation. An et al. [1] and Neven et al. [29] use branched task-specific decoders to produce corresponding predictions. Nekrasov et al. [27] build a multi-task network on top of Light-Weight RefineNet [28] and use depthwise convolution to tighten the computational budget. QuadroNet [15] adds a series of dilated convolutions besides the backbone to

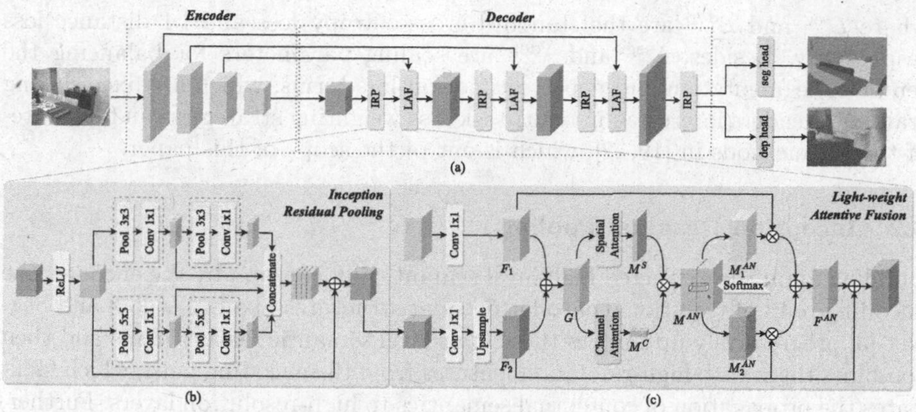

Fig. 1. Network architecture and components. (a) Overview of the proposed multi-task network; (b) Inception Residual Pooling module; (c) Light-weight Attentive Fusion module. $\oplus$ and $\otimes$ designate element-wise summation and multiplication respectively.

generate task-agnostic features, which are fed forward to a convolutional layer for task-specific channel adaptation. In this paper, we propose a light-weight network that can tackle both tasks simultaneously and reaches state-of-the-art balance between accuracy and efficiency.

3 Methodology

3.1 Architecture Overview

Following the prevalent well-performing encoder-decoder structure, a light-weight Context-aware Attentive Enrichment Network (CAENet) is proposed for real-time multi-task learning. In particular, as illustrated in Fig. 1(a), a light-weight CNN backbone is adopted for the encoder to learn high-level semantic information from gradually downsampled feature maps, which can be any off-the-shelf model. The decoder is recursively constructed by two well-designed modules, namely Inception Residual Pooling (IRP) and Light-weight Attentive Fusion (LAF), which captures context-aware coarse features and enriches them with fine-grained features via pseudo stereoscopic attention mechanism respectively.

On the other hand, the hard parameter sharing mechanism is employed for achieving parameter-efficiency, where the encoder-decoder structure is shared by the semantic segmentation and depth estimation tasks. Further, light-weight task-specific heads simply composed of two convolutional layers are appended to the shared structure to generate the corresponding segmentation and depth predictions.

The loss function for the joint training of semantic segmentation and depth estimation is formulated as follows:

$$\mathcal{L} = \lambda^{\mathrm{seg}}\mathcal{L}^{\mathrm{seg}} + \lambda^{\mathrm{dep}}\mathcal{L}^{\mathrm{dep}}, \tag{1}$$

where $\mathcal{L}^{seg}$ and $\mathcal{L}^{dep}$ are the standard cross-entropy loss and L1 distance loss respectively. Besides, λ^{seg} and λ^{dep} are scaling parameters for balancing the semantic segmentation and depth estimation loss terms, which are fixed during training. Readers interested in multi-task loss weighting strategies can find state-of-the-art methods in [19,22], which is out of the scope of this paper.

3.2 Inception Residual Pooling

Building upon the extracted high-level semantic information by the encoder, the decoding path of traditional encoder-decoder structures like U-Net [33] and SegNet [3] progressively upsamples these high-level semantic feature maps and then combines them with high-resolution features from the encoding path, which facilitates the propagation of contextual semantics to high-resolution layers. Further, since contextual information is of vital significance when it comes to semantic understanding of the scene, Chained Residual Pooling (CRP) module is introduced in RefineNet [20] to enhance the context learning for the decoding path. However, this module is designed without paying much attention to computational complexity, which may prohibit the related applications in real-world scenarios.

In this work, we consider a more efficient way to learn accurate contextual information and integrate them with high-resolution features to improve the generalization performance. Inspired by the parallel structure of Inception module [37] that can explore diverse receptive fields efficiently, an Inception Residual Pooling (IRP) module is proposed to capture rich contextual information from more comprehensive image regions with low-complexity pooling operations. The high-level feature map along the decoding path goes through IRP, as illustrated in Fig. 1(b). In order to leverage diverse receptive fields for context learning, the input feature map after ReLU activation is processed with two parallel pooling chains with 3×3 and 5×5 window size respectively, where cascaded pooling stages are employed to reuse the results from the previous stage to efficiently expand the receptive field like [20]. Each pooling stage is composed of a max-pooling layer where the stride is set to 1, followed by a convolutional layer to accommodate the weight of the extracted context. Note that the first stage in each chain reduces the dimensionality of channels. Then the pooled features from each stage are concatenated to reconstruct the feature map of original dimensionality, which is fused with the activation result. The IRP module is applied at each semantic level in the decoder and such design can efficiently extract rich contextual information to benefit the semantic understanding.

3.3 Light-Weight Attentive Fusion

Along the decoding path, the context-aware coarse features learned by IRP are upsampled and enriched with fine-grained (high-resolution) feature maps from the encoder. Typical enrichment ways are sum or concatenation of these features followed by the convolutional operation [28,30,33,42]. However, such approaches do not take into account the different importance of features from different semantic levels so that these approaches may not refine the high-level coarse features accurately. Therefore, in this work a Light-weight Attentive Fusion (LAF) module is introduced to adaptively implement the enrichment with important information, as shown in Fig. 1(c). To be specific, the element-wise feature sum $\boldsymbol{G}$ of the aligned features from different semantic levels ($\boldsymbol{F}_1$ and $\boldsymbol{F}_2$) is exploited to compute the pseudo stereoscopic attention maps by integrating the spatial and channel attention maps, which are generated respectively in a parallel manner.

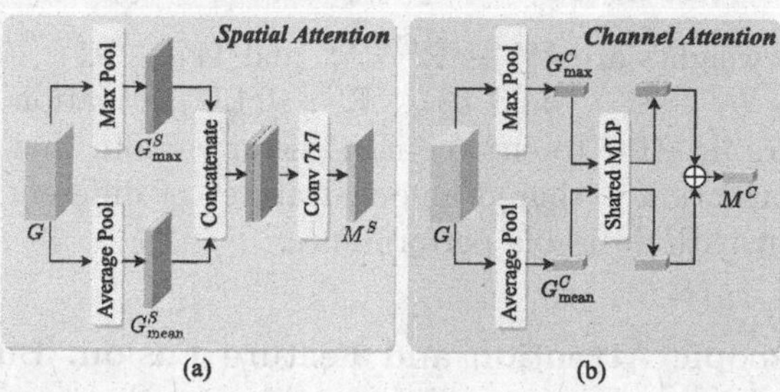

Fig. 2. Attention sub-modules that generate corresponding attention maps from the feature sum $\boldsymbol{G}$. (a) Spatial attention module; (b) channel attention module. $\oplus$ designates element-wise summation.

Spatial Attention Mechanism. The spatial attention mechanism is at the core of learning the importance of features from different semantic levels. It generates spatial attention maps which activate the regions containing beneficial information and suppress the less important, schematically depicted in Fig. 2(a).

As in [43], max- and average-pooling operations are first applied along the channel axis to get $\boldsymbol{G}^S_{\text{max}}$ and $\boldsymbol{G}^S_{\text{mean}}$. Such operations are efficient at extracting sufficient activation information. The max element over channels indicates the most prominent feature in corresponding location, while the mean value mapping provides useful information from a smoother perspective.

Then the outputs of pooling operations are concatenated and fed to a standard convolutional layer followed by batch normalization to generate spatial attention maps $\boldsymbol{M}^S \in \mathbb{R}^{2\times H\times W}$. Specifically, each channel in $\boldsymbol{M}^S$ encodes the spatial attention information for the corresponding feature level. Since a large receptive field for features can help capture rich local context information [43], the kernel size of the convolution is set to 7. Note that the dilated convolution is not chosen for the sake of computational consumption, which can lead to slower inference speed [30].

Channel Attention Mechanism. Besides spatial attention, the channel attention mechanism is also employed to assign channel-wise importance. The diagram is shown in Fig. 2(b). Analogously, max- and average-pooling operations are applied along the spatial dimension to obtain $\boldsymbol{G}^C_{\text{max}}$ and $\boldsymbol{G}^C_{\text{mean}}$.

Then both feature descriptors are forwarded to a shared multi-layer perceptron (MLP) to exploit the inter-channel relationships. There is a hidden layer in the MLP to constrain the number of parameters, where the reduction ratio is set to 8. Finally the channel-wise attention information is encoded by element-wise summation of output feature vectors. The process can be formulated as

$$\boldsymbol{M}^{C} = MLP(\boldsymbol{G}^{C}_{\max}) + MLP(\boldsymbol{G}^{C}_{\text{mean}}), \tag{2}$$

$$MLP(\boldsymbol{X}) = \boldsymbol{W}_2(\boldsymbol{W}_1\boldsymbol{X} + \boldsymbol{b}_1) + \boldsymbol{b}_2, \tag{3}$$

where the shared weights are $\boldsymbol{W}_1 \in \mathbb{R}^{C/8\times C}$ and $\boldsymbol{W}_2 \in \mathbb{R}^{C\times C/8}$, with the corresponding biases $\boldsymbol{b}_1 \in \mathbb{R}^{C/8}$ and $\boldsymbol{b}_2 \in \mathbb{R}^{C}$. ReLU activation is also inserted between two layers in MLP to enforce non-linearity. Note that the same channel attention information is shared among features of different levels, which is parameter-efficient with desirable performance.

Pseudo Stereoscopic Attention and Feature Fusion. Building upon the learned spatial and channel attention information, pseudo stereoscopic attention maps $\boldsymbol{M}^{A}$ are constructed through the element-wise multiplication of the spatial and channel attention maps after broadcasting, which simultaneously considers the spatial-wise and inter-channel dependency.

However, the direct output of multiplication may lead to unbounded value, which is detrimental to training convergence. To alleviate this problem, softmax function is adopted to normalize attention maps along the feature level axis as in [5,25]:

$$\boldsymbol{M}^{AN}_{i,c,h,w} = \frac{e^{\boldsymbol{M}^{A}_{i,c,h,w}}}{\sum_{j=1}^{2} e^{\boldsymbol{M}^{A}_{j,c,h,w}}}, i = 1, 2. \tag{4}$$

Afterwards, the unique element-wise attention maps for features from different levels are obtained and the attentive features are calculated as

$$\boldsymbol{F}^{AN} = \sum_{i=1}^{2} \boldsymbol{M}^{AN}_{i} \otimes \boldsymbol{F}_{i}. \tag{5}$$

Besides the generated attentive features $\boldsymbol{F}^{AN}$, a shortcut connection is also added from the aligned context-aware coarse feature $\boldsymbol{F}_2$ to maintain the information flow, as depicted in Fig. 1(c). This helps preserve the original information in the coarse feature and facilitate the gradient flow in backward propagation.

4 Experiments

4.1 Implementation Details

Datasets. The proposed CAENet is evaluated on two public datasets which contain labeled samples for both semantic segmentation and depth estimation tasks. The NYUv2 [36] dataset collects images from various indoor scenes, and contains 795 densely labeled images for training and another 654 for testing. The segmentation performance is evaluated on 13 classes defined in [8]. The CityScapes [7] dataset consists of 2975, 500, and 1525 fine-grained urban images for training, validation, and testing respectively. It contains 19-class segmentation annotations, together with pre-computed disparity depth maps from stereo cameras. Performance evaluation on the validation set is performed as done in [2,23,46]. As common practice for real-time networks [12,30,31], the original images are downsampled to a smaller resolution of 512×1024 to speed up training and inference.

Baselines. To verify the effectiveness of the proposed CAENet, we compare it with both real-time and non-real-time baselines. The real-time multi-task baselines include HDES-Net [1] and the network proposed by Nekrasov et al. [27]. Since existing efficient networks for joint segmentation and depth estimation learning are relatively few, for comprehensive comparison, several lightweight single-task networks are extended to deal with this joint learning. Specifically, the original segmentation models RGPNet [2] and STDC-Seg [12], and the original depth model FastDepth [42] are employed by appending an extra task head respectively. Other single-task methods which exhibit state-of-the-art efficiency-accuracy trade-off are also taken into account. For semantic segmentation, BiSeNet [46], SwiftNet [31] are included. To deal with monocular depth estimation, the network proposed by Tu et al. [38] GuideDepth [34] are included. Non-real-time multi-task approaches include PAD-Net [44], MTAN [23], and MTI-Net [40], which achieve state-of-the-art performance.

Training Setup. All our experiments are implemented by the PyTorch [32] library, and the results are obtained via the average of 3 independent trials. The backbones employed by all the networks are pre-trained on ImageNet [10]. During the training process, several standard methods of data augmentation are applied, including random cropping, rescaling, and flipping. We use the Adam [18] optimizer with the batch size of 8. The learning rate is adjusted by a poly policy $init\_lr \times (1 - \frac{epoch}{max\_epoch})^{0.9}$, where the best $init\_lr$ is searched for different methods. The number of max_epoch differs among datasets. Specifically, we train the model for 300 epochs on NYUv2 and 100 epochs on CityScapes. Besides, the scaling parameters in Eq. (1) are set as $\{\lambda^{\text{seg}} = 1, \lambda^{\text{dep}} = 1\}$ on NYUv2 and $\{\lambda^{\text{seg}} = 1, \lambda^{\text{dep}} = 0.5\}$ on CityScapes. All the baseline methods are re-implemented with the same training protocol as CAENet for fair comparison.

Evaluation Metrics. The mean Intersection over Union (mIoU) is used to measure the performance on semantic segmentation. For depth estimation, root mean square error (rmse) between the predicted depth maps and ground truth labels is computed for evaluation. The accuracy under a certain threshold [40] ($\delta_i < 1.25^i$, here only $i = 1$ is measured for concise comparison) is also computed as a quantitative criterion. The number of parameters (Params) and processed frames per second (FPS) are reported to estimate the size and efficiency of different models. In particular, FPS is measured on a GeForce GTX 1080Ti GPU with a single image as input, where the average value from 100 forward passes is computed.

4.2 Ablation Study

This section introduces ablation experiments to verify the effectiveness of each component in CAENet. All the experiments are conducted with MobileNetV2 [35] backbone on NYUv2 [36] dataset.

Table 1. Ablation Study for Module Components

No.	Component		seg	dep	
	IRP	LAF	mIoU↑(%)	rmse↓(m)	δ_1↑(%)
0			49.55	0.7259	68.46
1	✓		52.63	0.6637	73.80
2		✓	50.73	0.6981	70.67
3	✓	✓	**53.58**	**0.6551**	**74.60**

Module Components of CAENet. To investigate the effectiveness of the proposed IRP and LAF module, we carry out experiments with each module individually and then combine them together. Experimental results are listed in Table 1, which suggest adding each module can gradually boost the performance. The model with IRP surpasses that without by a large margin on both tasks, implying contextual information is essential to scene understanding. The LAF module can also push forward the performance, since it can automatically look at the more important part of multi-level features. The comparison between baseline (No. 0) and the proposed CAENet (No. 3) well demonstrates its superiority. The overall performance achieves 4.03% higher mIoU and 6.14% higher δ_1 gains.

Inception Residual Pooling. Table 2 summarizes results about different architecture configurations of the proposed IRP module. When only one type of max-pooling kernel size is involved; this module is reduced to the single-chain version. As evident, adding more stages in the single-chain case can enlarge the receptive field efficiently and arrives at higher prediction accuracy. On the other hand, when the number of stages keeps the same, the combination of different types of max-pooling kernel size can further boost the performance. This implies both small and large receptive fields can work out in a complementary way to each other. The observations above lead us to construct a double-chain module

Table 2. Ablation Study for Inception Residual Pooling

No.	Kernel Size		Stages	Channel Ratio[a]	seg	dep	
	3 × 3	5 × 5			mIoU↑(%)	rmse↓(m)	δ_1↑(%)
0			—	—	50.73	0.6981	70.67
1	✓		1	1	52.05	0.6790	72.09
2	✓		2	1/2	52.63	0.6716	72.66
3	✓		4	1/4	53.19	0.6705	73.61
4		✓	1	1	52.20	0.6748	72.70
5		✓	2	1/2	53.18	0.6629	74.15
6		✓	4	1/4	53.38	0.6627	74.44
7	✓	✓	1	1/2	52.64	0.6658	73.23
8	✓	✓	2	1/4	**53.58**	**0.6551**	**74.60**
9	✓	✓	4	1/8	53.49	0.6615	74.42

[a]"Channel Ratio" indicates the ratio of the number of output channels in each stage to input feature of IRP.

Table 3. Ablation Study for Light-weight Attentive Fusion

No.	Pooling[a]		Attention[b]			seg	dep	
	max	ave	s	c	order	mIoU↑(%)	rmse↓(m)	δ_1↑(%)
0					—	52.63	0.6637	73.80
1	✓		✓	✓	parallel	53.46	0.6626	74.03
2		✓	✓	✓	parallel	53.24	0.6572	74.25
3	✓	✓	✓		—	53.25	0.6604	73.95
4	✓	✓		✓	—	53.17	0.6698	72.80
5	✓	✓	✓	✓	s→c	53.09	0.6574	73.62
6	✓	✓	✓	✓	c→s	53.43	0.6684	73.18
7	✓	✓	✓	✓	parallel	**53.58**	**0.6551**	**74.60**

[a]The max- and average-pooling for dimension reduction are denoted with "max" and "ave".

[b]The spatial and channel attention modules are denoted with "s" and "c" respectively, and "order" is ignored when any of these modules is not applied.

with sufficient pooling stages. However, the channel dimension of each stage will reduce proportionally to the number of stages due to the inception-style setup. The performance with such low-dimension embeddings may deteriorate when adding too many stages (No. 9). Therefore, we keep only 2 stages in each chain (No. 8), which achieves the best performance.

Light-Weight Attentive Fusion. The LAF module aims to capture important information from features of different semantic levels and the ablation results are shown in Table 3. We first test the influence of pooling operations. Specifically, the max- (No. 1) and average-pooling (No. 2) both provide useful information, thus leading to superior performance separately. And it is not surprising that leveraging the above two pooling operations simultaneously can further boost the performance.

As for attention learning, both the spatial (No. 3) and channel (No. 4) modules can improve segmentation performance, while for the depth metrics, the spatial module still outperforms element-wise summation (No. 0) and the channel module deteriorates drastically. This infers that channel attention alone is not enough for depth estimation learning. Further, spatial and channel attention modules are combined to complement to each other.

We also conduct experiments with different arrangements of two attention modules. In addition to the default parallel setting, the cascaded structure can also make use of both modules. However, this inappropriate arrangement (No. 5 and 6) lead to even worse performance than each module alone. It is apparent from the last three rows of Table 3 that constructing pseudo stereoscopic attention maps by multiplication of spatial and channel maps (No. 7) achieves the best performance on both tasks.

4.3 Comparison with State-of-the-Art Methods

Table 4 and 5 exhibit the evaluation results of different methods on NYUv2 and CityScapes datasets respectively. The results show that CAENet outperforms other real-time multi-task methods in terms of efficiency and accuracy. Although HDES-Net [1] delivers relatively fast speed, its performance on both tasks is inferior to CAENet due to the lack of thorough feature refinement. The more competitive network proposed by Nekrasov et al. [27] exploits multi-level context and features to progressively restore the spatial information, but it does not pay enough attention on distinguishing the importance of features from different semantic levels during fusion, which might cause that it does not perform as well as CAENet across different datasets. The results above suggest the necessarity of the proposed IRP and LAF modules for contextual information extraction and adaptive feature enrichment.

The multi-task baselines by extending the original single-task networks commonly fail to perform well on another task. In particular, FastDepth [42] is only able to produce 47.18% and 59.07% mIoU on the segmentation task of NYUv2 and CityScapes respectively. Besides, the performance on depth estimation is also not satisfying because of its rather simple decoder structure. The original segmentation networks, namely RGPNet [2] and STDC-Seg [12], both yield competitive segmentation results compared to CAENet with the same backbone, but suffer about 1%-2% accuracy drop on depth estimation. Such performance gap implies the deficiency of task-specific design when transferred to multi-task settings.

Compared to the single-task networks, CAENet consistently generates more accurate predictions while being comparably efficient. As for segmentation, BiSeNet [46] is a fast design for real-time applications, but has rather low mIoU, especially for high-resolution images of CityScapes dataset. SwiftNet [31] produces promising results via multi-branch structure, which would introduce relatively expensive computational cost. In terms of monocular depth estimation, GuideDepth [34] and the network proposed by Tu et al. [38] exhibit sub-optimal performance in complex indoor environments of NYUv2 as they seldom exploit detailed low-level features to help restore spatial resolution.

Table 4. Experimental Results on NYUv2 Dataset

Group[a]	Method	Backbone	Tasks[b]	Efficiency		Performance		
				Params	Speed[c]	seg	dep	
				(M)	(FPS)	mIoU↑(%)	rmse↓(m)	δ_1↑(%)
①	PAD-Net [44]	ResNet50	seg, dep	42.69	5.0	56.43	0.6508	74.57
	MTAN [23]	ResNet50	seg, dep	73.47	2.8	56.94	0.6510	74.17
	MTI-Net [40]	ResNet50	seg, dep	68.53	12.0	56.99	0.6216	77.71
②	Nekrasov et al. [27]	MobileNetV2	seg, dep	3.01	71.8	52.03	0.6647	73.58
	HDES-Net [1]	MobileNetV2	seg, dep	3.37	95.0	47.82	0.7265	69.98
	FastDepth [42]	ResNet18	seg*, dep	29.16	80.4	47.18	0.7008	71.11
	RGPNet [2]	ResNet18	seg, dep*	17.76	133.7	52.17	0.6705	72.49
	STDC-Seg [12]	STDCNet	seg, dep*	13.49	88.8	<u>54.88</u>	0.6796	73.13
	Tu et al. [38]	MobileNetV2	dep	3.45	56.8	—	0.7880	63.73
	GuideDepth [34]	MobileNetV2	dep	2.52	69.1	—	0.7331	69.43
	BiSeNet [46]	ResNet18	seg	13.04	138.5	51.18	—	—
	SwiftNet [31]	ResNet18	seg	12.06	94.0	51.39	—	—
	CAENet	MobileNetV2	seg, dep	2.46	76.5	53.58	<u>0.6551</u>	<u>74.60</u>
		ResNet18		11.69	125.9	52.75	0.6688	73.72
		STDCNet		10.07	83.0	**55.53**	**0.6505**	**75.11**

[a]Non-real-time and real-time methods are categorized into group ① and ②. Note that the best performance for each task among real-time methods is highlighted in bold and the second best is underlined.
[b]The superscript "*" on specific task denotes the introduction of corresponding extra task head in addition to the original single-task network.
[c]Speed (FPS) is measured with 480 × 640 resolution.

Table 5. Experimental Results on CityScapes Dataset

Group	Method	Backbone	Tasks	Efficiency		Performance		
				Params	Speed[a]	seg	dep	
				(M)	(FPS)	mIoU↑(%)	rmse↓(m)	δ_1↑(%)
①	PAD-Net [44]	ResNet50	seg, dep	42.70	2.6	73.09	6.631	89.43
	MTAN [23]	ResNet50	seg, dep	73.47	1.6	72.77	6.669	89.11
	MTI-Net [40]	ResNet50	seg, dep	68.55	7.1	72.68	6.580	90.33
②	Nekrasov et al. [27]	MobileNetV2	seg, dep	3.02	44.7	69.10	6.987	87.81
	HDES-Net [1]	MobileNetV2	seg, dep	3.38	61.8	64.24	7.743	84.81
	FastDepth [42]	ResNet18	seg*, dep	29.16	52.6	59.07	7.091	87.62
	RGPNet [2]	ResNet18	seg, dep*	17.76	93.1	67.55	7.110	87.02
	STDC-Seg [12]	STDCNet	seg, dep*	13.49	73.9	69.20	6.943	88.16
	Tu et al. [38]	MobileNetV2	dep	3.45	34.1	—	7.267	88.08
	GuideDepth [34]	MobileNetV2	dep	2.52	44.2	—	7.032	<u>88.20</u>
	BiSeNet [46]	ResNet18	seg	13.04	94.7	66.00	—	—
	SwiftNet [31]	ResNet18	seg	12.06	81.9	69.07	—	—
	CAENet	MobileNetV2	seg, dep	2.46	49.7	**70.06**	**6.887**	88.10
		ResNet18		11.70	84.6	68.96	7.012	87.86
		STDCNet		10.08	69.4	<u>69.93</u>	<u>6.897</u>	**88.29**

[a]Speed (FPS) is measured with 512 × 1024 resolution.

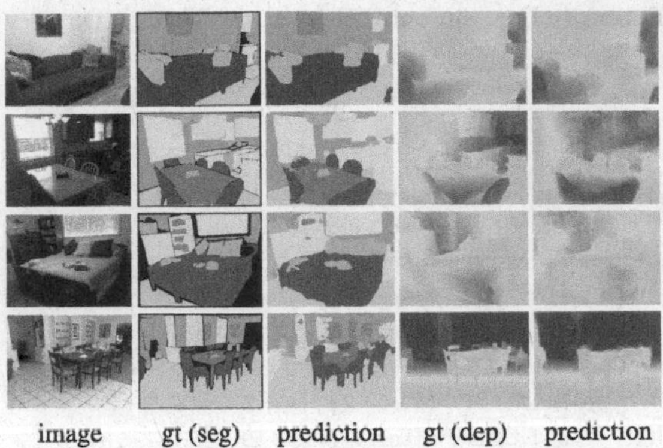

Fig. 3. Qualitative results of semantic segmentation and depth estimation tasks on the NYUv2 test set. The black pixels in gt do not have corresponding annotations, where gt denotes the ground truth.

Overall, CAENet can produce the highest accuracy on both segmentation and depth estimation tasks among real-time solutions, with competitive inference speed. This means the proposed method pushes forward the state-of-the-art trade-off between accuracy and efficiency across different datasets.

We also compare the performance against non-real-time multi-task methods, which rely on complex backbones and task interaction strategies to strengthen the learning capability. These methods commonly have better performance than CAENet, but they require much more computing resources, and thus are not suitable for resource-constrained real-world applications. With one or two orders of magnitude fewer parameters and faster inference speed, the proposed CAENet can produce competitive results to help reduce the performance gap between real-time and non-real-time methods. Specifically on NYUv2 dataset, it achieves on par or even higher depth accuracy than the sophisticated multi-task networks, such as PAD-Net [44] and MTAN [23].

4.4 Qualitative Results

Several visual examples of per-task predictions in indoor (Fig. 3) and outdoor (Fig. 4) scenes are provided to illustrate the effectiveness of CAENet.

In Fig. 3, the proposed CAENet shows excellent learning capability in complicated indoor scenes. It can capture contextual information to fulfill the semantic completeness for large objects (e.g., the sofa in the 1st row and the bed in the 3rd row). It also yields fairly coherent depth estimation on the surface of table in the 2nd row even with reflection. Besides, it can well adapt to abrupt changes in the background, such as the floor in the 4th row, producing accurate segmentation and depth predictions.

As for the outdoor dataset CityScapes (Fig. 4), CAENet generates pixel-wise results fairly close to the ground truth. It can detect all categories appearing in the image, which exhibits semantic fidelity. For depth estimation, it can extract detailed information, discriminating objects and background in between.

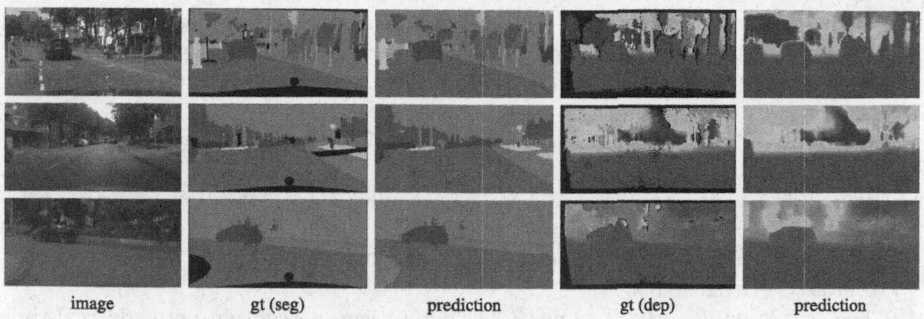

Fig. 4. Qualitative results of semantic segmentation and depth estimation tasks on the CityScapes validation set.

5 Conclusion

In this paper we propose CAENet, an efficient multi-task network for joint semantic segmentation and depth estimation, where a new Inception Residual Pooling (IRP) module is designed to efficiently extract the contextual information from the high-level features with diverse receptive fields and these context-aware features are enriched adaptively via a Light-weight Attentive Fusion (LAF) module. Such network design helps capture beneficial information for both scene understanding tasks efficiently. Extensive experimental results demonstrate the effectiveness of CAENet, which achieves state-of-the-art performance with comparable inference speed against other real-time competing methods.

Acknowledgments. This work is supported in part by NSFC (No. U20A20387) and the Key R&D Program of Zhejiang Province (No. 2021C01119).

Ethical Statement. In this paper, we mainly investigate the design of efficient multi-task learning for joint semantic segmentation and depth estimation. The research topic is not policing- or military-related, and the experiments are conducted on public datasets of indoor and outdoor scenes. We consider that the required discussion about ethic and future societal effect is not applicable for our work.

References

1. An, S., Zhou, F., Yang, M., Zhu, H., Fu, C., Tsintotas, K.A.: Real-time monocular human depth estimation and segmentation on embedded systems. In: 2021 IEEE/RSJ International Conference on Intelligent Robots and Systems (IROS), pp. 55–62 (2021). https://doi.org/10.1109/IROS51168.2021.9636518
2. Arani, E., Marzban, S., Pata, A., Zonooz, B.: RGPNet: a real-time general purpose semantic segmentation. In: 2021 IEEE Winter Conference on Applications of Computer Vision (WACV), pp. 3008–3017 (2021). https://doi.org/10.1109/WACV48630.2021.00305

3. Badrinarayanan, V., Kendall, A., Cipolla, R.: SegNet: a deep convolutional encoder-decoder architecture for image segmentation. IEEE Trans. Pattern Anal. Mach. Intell. **39**(12), 2481–2495 (2017). https://doi.org/10.1109/TPAMI.2016.2644615
4. Caruana, R.: Multitask learning. Mach. Learn. **28**, 41–75 (1997). https://doi.org/10.1023/A:1007379606734
5. Chen, L.C., Yang, Y., Wang, J., Xu, W., Yuille, A.L.: Attention to scale: scale-aware semantic image segmentation. In: 2016 IEEE Conference on Computer Vision and Pattern Recognition (CVPR), pp. 3640–3649 (2016). https://doi.org/10.1109/CVPR.2016.396
6. Chen, L., Yang, Z., Ma, J., Luo, Z.: Driving scene perception network: real-time joint detection, depth estimation and semantic segmentation. In: 2018 IEEE Winter Conference on Applications of Computer Vision (WACV), pp. 1283–1291 (2018). https://doi.org/10.1109/WACV.2018.00145
7. Cordts, M., et al.: The cityscapes dataset for semantic urban scene understanding. In: 2016 IEEE Conference on Computer Vision and Pattern Recognition (CVPR), pp. 3213–3223 (2016). https://doi.org/10.1109/CVPR.2016.350
8. Couprie, C., Farabet, C., Najman, L., LeCun, Y.: Indoor semantic segmentation using depth information. In: Bengio, Y., LeCun, Y. (eds.) 1st International Conference on Learning Representations, ICLR 2013, Scottsdale, Arizona, USA, 2–4 May 2013, Conference Track Proceedings, pp. 1–8 (2013). https://arxiv.org/abs/1301.3572
9. Crawshaw, M.: Multi-task learning with deep neural networks: a survey. CoRR abs/2009.09796 (2020). https://arxiv.org/abs/2009.09796
10. Deng, J., Dong, W., Socher, R., Li, L.J., Li, K., Fei-Fei, L.: ImageNet: a large-scale hierarchical image database. In: 2009 IEEE Conference on Computer Vision and Pattern Recognition, pp. 248–255 (2009). https://doi.org/10.1109/CVPR.2009.5206848
11. Eigen, D., Fergus, R.: Predicting depth, surface normals and semantic labels with a common multi-scale convolutional architecture. In: 2015 IEEE International Conference on Computer Vision (ICCV), pp. 2650–2658 (2015). https://doi.org/10.1109/ICCV.2015.304
12. Fan, M., et al.: Rethinking BiSeNet for real-time semantic segmentation. In: 2021 IEEE/CVF Conference on Computer Vision and Pattern Recognition (CVPR), pp. 9711–9720 (2021). https://doi.org/10.1109/CVPR46437.2021.00959
13. Gao, Y., Ma, J., Zhao, M., Liu, W., Yuille, A.L.: NDDR-CNN: layerwise feature fusing in multi-task CNNs by neural discriminative dimensionality reduction. In: 2019 IEEE/CVF Conference on Computer Vision and Pattern Recognition (CVPR), pp. 3200–3209 (2019). https://doi.org/10.1109/CVPR.2019.00332
14. Girshick, R.: Fast R-CNN. In: 2015 IEEE International Conference on Computer Vision (ICCV), pp. 1440–1448 (2015). https://doi.org/10.1109/ICCV.2015.169
15. Goel, K., Srinivasan, P., Tariq, S., Philbin, J.: QuadroNet: multi-task learning for real-time semantic depth aware instance segmentation. In: 2021 IEEE Winter Conference on Applications of Computer Vision (WACV), pp. 315–324 (2021). https://doi.org/10.1109/WACV48630.2021.00036
16. Hashimoto, K., Xiong, C., Tsuruoka, Y., Socher, R.: A joint many-task model: growing a neural network for multiple NLP tasks. In: Proceedings of the 2017 Conference on Empirical Methods in Natural Language Processing, Copenhagen, Denmark, pp. 1923–1933. Association for Computational Linguistics, September 2017. https://doi.org/10.18653/v1/D17-1206, https://aclanthology.org/D17-1206

17. He, K., Zhang, X., Ren, S., Sun, J.: Deep residual learning for image recognition. In: 2016 IEEE Conference on Computer Vision and Pattern Recognition (CVPR), pp. 770–778 (2016). https://doi.org/10.1109/CVPR.2016.90
18. Kingma, D.P., Ba, J.: Adam: a method for stochastic optimization. In: Bengio, Y., LeCun, Y. (eds.) 3rd International Conference on Learning Representations, ICLR 2015, San Diego, CA, USA, 7–9 May 2015, Conference Track Proceedings, pp. 1–15 (2015). https://arxiv.org/abs/1412.6980
19. Lin, B., YE, F., Zhang, Y., Tsang, I.: Reasonable effectiveness of random weighting: a litmus test for multi-task learning. In: Transactions on Machine Learning Research (2022)
20. Lin, G., Milan, A., Shen, C., Reid, I.: RefineNet: multi-path refinement networks for high-resolution semantic segmentation. In: 2017 IEEE Conference on Computer Vision and Pattern Recognition (CVPR), pp. 5168–5177 (2017). https://doi.org/10.1109/CVPR.2017.549
21. Lin, T.Y., Goyal, P., Girshick, R., He, K., Dollár, P.: Focal loss for dense object detection. IEEE Trans. Pattern Anal. Mach. Intell. **42**(2), 318–327 (2020). https://doi.org/10.1109/TPAMI.2018.2858826
22. Liu, B., Liu, X., Jin, X., Stone, P., Liu, Q.: Conflict-averse gradient descent for multi-task learning. In: Ranzato, M., Beygelzimer, A., Dauphin, Y., Liang, P., Vaughan, J.W. (eds.) Advances in Neural Information Processing Systems, vol. 34, pp. 18878–18890. Curran Associates, Inc. (2021)
23. Liu, S., Johns, E., Davison, A.J.: End-to-end multi-task learning with attention. In: 2019 IEEE/CVF Conference on Computer Vision and Pattern Recognition (CVPR), pp. 1871–1880 (2019). https://doi.org/10.1109/CVPR.2019.00197
24. Liu, X., He, P., Chen, W., Gao, J.: Multi-task deep neural networks for natural language understanding. In: Proceedings of the 57th Annual Meeting of the Association for Computational Linguistics, pp. 4487–4496, Florence, Italy. Association for Computational Linguistics, July 2019. https://doi.org/10.18653/v1/P19-1441. https://aclanthology.org/P19-1441
25. Liu, Y., Zhang, X.Y., Bian, J.W., Zhang, L., Cheng, M.M.: SAMNet: stereoscopically attentive multi-scale network for lightweight salient object detection. IEEE Trans. Image Process. **30**, 3804–3814 (2021). https://doi.org/10.1109/TIP.2021.3065239
26. Misra, I., Shrivastava, A., Gupta, A., Hebert, M.: Cross-stitch networks for multi-task learning. In: 2016 IEEE Conference on Computer Vision and Pattern Recognition (CVPR), pp. 3994–4003 (2016). https://doi.org/10.1109/CVPR.2016.433
27. Nekrasov, V., Dharmasiri, T., Spek, A., Drummond, T., Shen, C., Reid, I.: Real-time joint semantic segmentation and depth estimation using asymmetric annotations. In: 2019 International Conference on Robotics and Automation (ICRA), pp. 7101–7107 (2019). https://doi.org/10.1109/ICRA.2019.8794220
28. Nekrasov, V., Shen, C., Reid, I.: Light-weight refinenet for real-time semantic segmentation. In: British Machine Vision Conference 2018, BMVC 2018, Newcastle, UK, 3–6 September 2018, p. 125. BMVA Press (2018). http://bmvc2018.org/contents/papers/0494.pdf
29. Neven, D., Brabandere, B.D., Georgoulis, S., Proesmans, M., Gool, L.V.: Fast scene understanding for autonomous driving. CoRR abs/1708.02550, 1–5 (2017). https://arxiv.org/abs/1708.02550
30. Oršic, M., Krešo, I., Bevandic, P., Šegvic, S.: In defense of pre-trained imagenet architectures for real-time semantic segmentation of road-driving images. In: 2019 IEEE/CVF Conference on Computer Vision and Pattern Recognition (CVPR), pp. 12599–12608 (2019). https://doi.org/10.1109/CVPR.2019.01289

31. Oršić, M., Šegvić, S.: Efficient semantic segmentation with pyramidal fusion. Pattern Recognit. **110**, 107611 (2021). https://doi.org/10.1016/j.patcog.2020.107611. https://www.sciencedirect.com/science/article/pii/S0031320320304143
32. Paszke, A., et al.: PyTorch: an imperative style, high-performance deep learning library. In: Advances in Neural Information Processing Systems, vol. 32, pp. 1–12. Curran Associates, Inc. (2019). https://proceedings.neurips.cc/paper/2019/file/bdbca288fee7f92f2bfa9f7012727740-Paper.pdf
33. Ronneberger, O., Fischer, P., Brox, T.: U-Net: convolutional networks for biomedical image segmentation. In: Navab, N., Hornegger, J., Wells, W.M., Frangi, A.F. (eds.) MICCAI 2015. LNCS, vol. 9351, pp. 234–241. Springer, Cham (2015). https://doi.org/10.1007/978-3-319-24574-4_28
34. Rudolph, M., Dawoud, Y., Güldenring, R., Nalpantidis, L., Belagiannis, V.: Lightweight monocular depth estimation through guided decoding. In: 2022 International Conference on Robotics and Automation (ICRA), pp. 2344–2350 (2022). https://doi.org/10.1109/ICRA46639.2022.9812220
35. Sandler, M., Howard, A., Zhu, M., Zhmoginov, A., Chen, L.C.: MobilenetV 2: inverted residuals and linear bottlenecks. In: 2018 IEEE/CVF Conference on Computer Vision and Pattern Recognition, pp. 4510–4520 (2018). https://doi.org/10.1109/CVPR.2018.00474
36. Silberman, N., Hoiem, D., Kohli, P., Fergus, R.: Indoor segmentation and support inference from RGBD images. In: Fitzgibbon, A., Lazebnik, S., Perona, P., Sato, Y., Schmid, C. (eds.) ECCV 2012. LNCS, vol. 7576, pp. 746–760. Springer, Heidelberg (2012). https://doi.org/10.1007/978-3-642-33715-4_54
37. Szegedy, C., et al.: Going deeper with convolutions. In: 2015 IEEE Conference on Computer Vision and Pattern Recognition (CVPR), pp. 1–9 (2015). https://doi.org/10.1109/CVPR.2015.7298594
38. Tu, X., et al.: Efficient monocular depth estimation for edge devices in internet of things. IEEE Trans. Industr. Inf. **17**(4), 2821–2832 (2021). https://doi.org/10.1109/TII.2020.3020583
39. Vandenhende, S., Georgoulis, S., Van Gansbeke, W., Proesmans, M., Dai, D., Van Gool, L.: Multi-task learning for dense prediction tasks: a survey. IEEE Trans. Pattern Anal. Mach. Intell. **44**(7), 3614–3633 (2022). https://doi.org/10.1109/TPAMI.2021.3054719
40. Vandenhende, S., Georgoulis, S., Van Gool, L.: MTI-Net: multi-scale task interaction networks for multi-task learning. In: Vedaldi, A., Bischof, H., Brox, T., Frahm, J.-M. (eds.) ECCV 2020. LNCS, vol. 12349, pp. 527–543. Springer, Cham (2020). https://doi.org/10.1007/978-3-030-58548-8_31
41. Wang, J., et al.: Deep high-resolution representation learning for visual recognition. IEEE Trans. Pattern Anal. Mach. Intell. **43**(10), 3349–3364 (2021). https://doi.org/10.1109/TPAMI.2020.2983686
42. Wofk, D., Ma, F., Yang, T.J., Karaman, S., Sze, V.: FastDepth: fast monocular depth estimation on embedded systems. In: 2019 International Conference on Robotics and Automation (ICRA), pp. 6101–6108 (2019). https://doi.org/10.1109/ICRA.2019.8794182
43. Woo, S., Park, J., Lee, J.-Y., Kweon, I.S.: CBAM: convolutional block attention module. In: Ferrari, V., Hebert, M., Sminchisescu, C., Weiss, Y. (eds.) ECCV 2018. LNCS, vol. 11211, pp. 3–19. Springer, Cham (2018). https://doi.org/10.1007/978-3-030-01234-2_1
44. Xu, D., Ouyang, W., Wang, X., Sebe, N.: PAD-Net: multi-tasks guided prediction-and-distillation network for simultaneous depth estimation and scene parsing. In:

2018 IEEE/CVF Conference on Computer Vision and Pattern Recognition, pp. 675–684 (2018). https://doi.org/10.1109/CVPR.2018.00077

45. Yang, Y., Hospedales, T.M.: Deep multi-task representation learning: a tensor factorisation approach. In: International Conference on Learning Representations, pp. 1–12 (2017). https://openreview.net/forum?id=SkhU2fcll
46. Yu, C., Wang, J., Peng, C., Gao, C., Yu, G., Sang, N.: BiSeNet: bilateral segmentation network for real-time semantic segmentation. In: Ferrari, V., Hebert, M., Sminchisescu, C., Weiss, Y. (eds.) ECCV 2018. LNCS, vol. 11217, pp. 334–349. Springer, Cham (2018). https://doi.org/10.1007/978-3-030-01261-8_20

Click-Aware Structure Transfer with Sample Weight Assignment for Post-Click Conversion Rate Estimation

Kai Ouyang[1], Wenhao Zheng[2], Chen Tang[1], Xuanji Xiao[2](✉), and Hai-Tao Zheng[1,3](✉)

[1] Tsinghua University, Beijing, China
{oyk20,tc20}@mails.tsinghua.edu.cn, zheng.haitao@sz.tsinghua.edu.cn

[2] Shopee Inc, Shenzhen, China
wenhao.zheng@shopee.com, growj@126.com

[3] Pengcheng Laboratory, Shenzhen 518055, China

Abstract. Post-click Conversion Rate (CVR) prediction task plays an essential role in industrial applications, such as recommendation and advertising. Conventional CVR methods typically suffer from the data sparsity problem as they rely only on samples where the user has clicked. To address this problem, researchers have introduced the method of multi-task learning, which utilizes non-clicked samples and shares feature representations of the Click-Through Rate (CTR) task with the CVR task. However, it should be noted that the CVR and CTR tasks are fundamentally different and may even be contradictory. Therefore, introducing a large amount of CTR information without distinction may drown out valuable information related to CVR. This phenomenon is called the *curse of knowledge* problem in this paper. To tackle this issue, we argue that a trade-off should be achieved between the introduction of large amounts of auxiliary information and the protection of valuable information related to CVR. Hence, we propose a **C**lick-aware **S**tructure **T**ransfer model with sample **W**eight **A**ssignment, abbreviated as **CSTWA**. It pays more attention to the latent structure information, which could refine the input information related to CVR, instead of directly sharing feature representations. Meanwhile, to capture the representation conflict between CTR and CVR, we calibrate the representation layer and reweight the discriminant layer to excavate the click bias information from the CTR tower. Moreover, it incorporates a sample weight assignment algorithm biased towards CVR modeling, to make the knowledge from CTR would not mislead the CVR. Extensive experiments on industrial and public datasets have demonstrated that CSTWA significantly outperforms widely used and competitive models.

Keywords: Post-click Conversion Rate · Curse of Knowledge

K. Ouyang and W. Zheng—Equal contribution
This work was completed during Kai Ouyang's internship at Shopee, and Xuanji Xiao is the first corresponding author of this work.

D. Koutra et al. (Eds.): ECML PKDD 2023, LNAI 14173, pp. 426–442, 2023.
https://doi.org/10.1007/978-3-031-43424-2_26

1 Introduction

The Conversion Rate (CVR) prediction task is crucial for ranking systems in modern industrial applications, such as e-commerce platforms and video platforms, as it is essential for better user experience and improving revenue. Conventional CVR methods employ the same network architectures as Click-Through Rate (CTR) prediction task. However, in practice, the samples of the CVR task are usually much fewer than the CTR, with the former being only about 1% of the latter. The sparsity of training data makes CVR models suffer great difficulties in fitting, which leads to the well-known data sparsity problem of CVR [12].

Inspired by multi-task learning, recent CVR methods have introduced auxiliary tasks (*e.g.*, the CTR task) to address the above challenge [20,25]. They leverage samples of non-clicked impressions and even directly share the feature representations with auxiliary tasks. Although the introduction of substantial external knowledge alleviates the data sparsity problem to a certain extent, this approach is not perfect. On the one hand, the amount of knowledge introduced from auxiliary tasks (*e.g.*, the CTR task) far exceeds that possessed by the CVR task, which reduces the model's ability to capture user conversion behavior. On the other hand, the introduced auxiliary knowledge and the knowledge related to CVR are not clearly distinguished, which makes the model easily assimilated by the introduced external knowledge. These two reasons make it highly likely that the CVR model will be overwhelmed by a large amount of knowledge introduced (*i.e.*, CTR knowledge). This paper calls this phenomenon the *curse of knowledge* problem.

However, the CVR task is inherently different from the CTR task. In some cases, they are even contradictory. For example, item covers with sexy or erotic content tend to attract more clicks while few of them would lead to purchase. Besides, although the number of clicks on some daily needs (*e.g.*, kitchenware, toilet paper, *etc*) of a user is usually low, the purchase rate is high. Namely, there exists a huge gap between the information on the user's click behaviors (*i.e.*, the CTR knowledge) and the information needed to model the user's actual conversion behaviors. Therefore, the curse of knowledge problem in the multi-task learning-based CVR models hinders their ability to capture real conversion behaviors, resulting in suboptimal performance.

To tackle this issue, we believe that it is necessary to alleviate the curse of knowledge problem that arises while introducing a large amount of auxiliary knowledge to solve the data sparsity problem. Hence, we put forward a **C**lick-aware **S**tructure **T**ransfer model with sample **W**eight **A**ssignment algorithm, abbreviated as **CSTWA**, to protect the valuable knowledge related to CVR. We mine the task-independent information (*i.e.*, latent structure information [18]) from the CTR and construct the Structure Migrator to inject it into the CVR feature representations. Meanwhile, we design the Click Perceptron to model the click bias information, so that the CVR tower can capture the difference between clicked and non-clicked samples. Moreover, we devise a novel sample weight assignment algorithm, named Curse Escaper. It makes the model pay more attention to those samples whose CVR information and CTR information are contradictory. In this way, we can further enhance the ability to model the users' real conversion behaviors and avoid the model being overwhelmed by CTR information. We conduct extensive experiments and achieve state-of-the-art (SOTA) performance on industrial and public datasets, which demonstrates the superiority of our CSTWA.

To summarize, we mainly make the following fourfold contributions:

- We elucidate the *curse of knowledge* problem of the CVR methods based on multi-task learning. To alleviate this problem, we propose CSTWA, which can protect valuable information related to CVR while introducing auxiliary information.
- We mine latent, task-independent *item-item* and *user-user* structure information from CTR, and we utilize it to filter the knowledge related to CVR.
- We enhance the representation layer with a calibration technique and the discriminant layer with a brand-new sample weight assignment algorithm, which can explicitly mitigate the side effects of introducing knowledge of auxiliary tasks.
- Extensive experiments on industrial and public datasets demonstrate the superiority of CSTWA over competitive methods.

2 Related Work

This paper aims to alleviate the curse of knowledge problem in the CVR models based on multi-task learning. Therefore, we briefly review the most related work from the following two aspects: (a) Conversion Rate Prediction, and (b) Multi-task Learning.

2.1 Conversion Rate (CVR) Prediction

Recommender systems are highly significant in contemporary society [14,15]. Conversion Rate (CVR) prediction is critical for the ranking systems of many industrial applications, such as recommendation systems [12,17], as it is directly related to user experience and final revenue.

Although research on CTR is prosperously developing [2,3,5,7,9,19,22], there are few kinds of literature directly proposed for the CVR task [24,27]. Meanwhile, researchers often directly use the CTR prediction method to estimate the CVR, and only replace the training samples with the samples of clicked impressions. However, this causes the well-known extremely data sparsity problem [12].

To address this challenge, recently proposed methods model CVR directly over the entire space, which includes the samples of clicked and non-clicked impressions. For example, ESMM [12] introduces two auxiliary tasks of predicting the post-view click-through rate (CTR) and post-view click-through & conversion rate (CTCVR), instead of training the CVR model directly with samples of clicked impressions. ESM^2 [25] models CVR prediction and auxiliary tasks simultaneously according to the conditional probability rule defined on the user behavior graph, in a multi-task learning framework. Recently, AITM [26] proposes to adaptively learn what and how much information to transfer for different conversion stages of different users, achieving significantly better performance compared with previous methods. Moreover, ESCCM^2 [21] employs a counterfactual risk minimizer as a regularizer in ESMM [12] to address both Inherent Estimation Bias (IEB) and Potential Independence Priority (PIP) issues simultaneously.

However, they either share feature representations with the CTR tower or directly use knowledge from CTR. They overlook or fail to address the curse of knowledge caused by introducing massive external auxiliary information, which limits their ultimate performance. In contrast, when we train the CVR model using samples from the entire space, we weaken the assimilation from auxiliary knowledge and enhance valuable CVR-related knowledge through structure transfer strategy and sample weight assignment algorithm.

2.2 Multi-task Learning

To model the multi-stage nature of the user's purchasing behavior (*e.g.*, $impression \rightarrow click \rightarrow purchase$), and alleviate the model fitting difficulty caused by the data sparsity problem of the CVR task, the previous work tries to model the CVR task through a multi-task learning framework. They model one or more auxiliary tasks for the CVR task (*e.g.*, CTR task), expanding the sample space while capturing information about the multi-stage nature of the purchasing behavior [4,13]. ESMM series (ESMM [12], ESMM2 [25]) uses click signals (CTR) and post-click signals and uses shared feature-embedding layer to tackle the conversion sample sparsity. MMOE series (MMOE [11], SNR [10], PLE [20]) propose a multi-gate mixture of expert sub-networks, which provide a limited degree of sharing at the granularity of the sub-network.

These multi-task learning methods alleviate the data sparsity problem of the CVR task to a certain extent. They capture the multi-stage nature of users' purchasing behavior, achieving considerable performance improvement. However, they all ignore the fact that auxiliary tasks (*e.g.*, CTR task) and the CVR task are essentially different and even contradictory. Therefore, directly using the samples of auxiliary tasks or even directly sharing the feature representation can lead to the curse of knowledge problem, *i.e.*, the CVR model will be overwhelmed by the knowledge of auxiliary tasks.

3 Method

In this section, we define the problem and the key notations, and introduce our proposed framework CSTWA in detail.

3.1 Problem Definition

The task of Post-click Conversion Rate (CVR) prediction aims to predict the likelihood that a user will purchase an item, while the task of Click-Through Rate (CTR) prediction aims to predict the probability of a user clicking on an item. Both tasks utilize a feature set that includes user features, item features, and context features, most of which are categorical and can be represented using one-hot encoding.

We assume the observed dataset to be $\mathcal{S} = \{s_i = (x_i, y_i, z_i)\}|_{i=1}^{N}$, where $s_i = (x_i, y_i, z_i)$ denotes an impression sample, and N is the total number of impression samples. $x_i = \{f_1, \dots, f_n\}$ represents feature values of an impression sample, where f denote a feature value. The binary labels y and z indicate whether a click or conversion event occurs in the sample s_i, respectively, and can take on the values of 1 or 0.

The estimation of click-through rate (CTR) and conversion rate (CVR) involves predicting the probabilities of the following events, respectively:

$$\mathcal{P}_{\text{CTR}} = \mathcal{P}(y = 1|x), \ \mathcal{P}_{\text{CVR}} = \mathcal{P}(z = 1|y = 1, x). \tag{1}$$

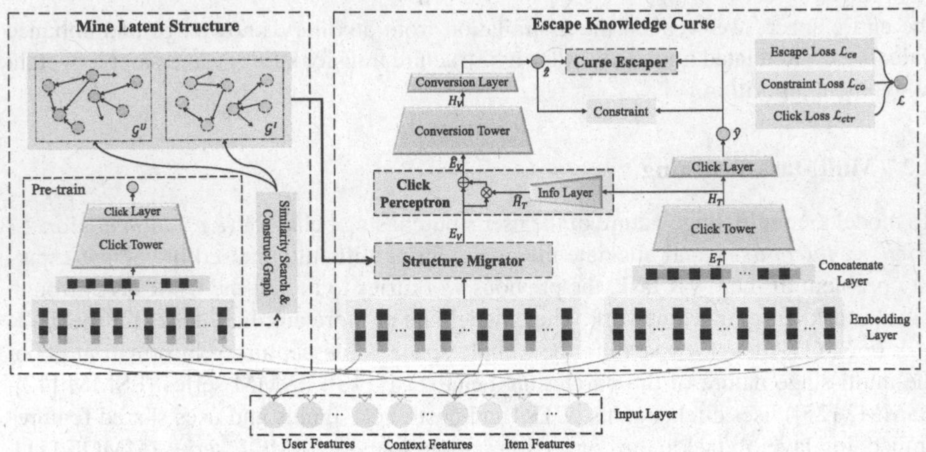

Fig. 1. The architecture of CSTWA. It could be divided into two parts. The first part is the Mine Latent Structure. The second one is the Escape Knowledge Curse, which contains three important components: Structure Migrator, Click Perceptron, and Curse Escapter.

In this paper, we define $X^U = \{x_1^U, \ldots, x_{N^U}^U\}$ and $X^I = \{x_1^I, \ldots, x_{N^I}^I\}$ as sets representing all users and items, respectively. Here, x^U and x^I represent all feature values of a user or item (identified by their unique ID), where $|x^U| = l^U$ and $|x^I| = l^I$ denote the number of features for each user or item, and N^U and N^I denote the total number of users and items, respectively.

3.2 Motivation and Architecture

As the user's purchase behavior only occurs after impressions and clicks, sufficient interactions are often needed before a purchase is made, resulting in limited training samples for CVR. This poses a serious data sparsity problem for CVR. Although utilizing knowledge of CTR can mitigate this issue, it introduces the curse of knowledge where the knowledge of CVR is overshadowed by a vast amount of CTR knowledge.

To address this problem, we propose that we should learn latent and task-independent structure information instead of directly using the feature representations of CTR. We also model the click bias information of samples to enable the model to differentiate between clicked and non-clicked samples. Furthermore, we introduce a brand-new weight assignment algorithm called Curse Escaper, which emphasizes the role of false negative samples (*i.e.*, the output of CTR tower is high, but $z = 0$) and false positive samples (*i.e.*, the output of CTR tower is low, but $z = 1$) in the training process. The above three components enable our model to escape the curse of CTR knowledge.

The architecture of CSTWA is depicted in Fig. 1. The entire framework comprises the following components, which we will elaborate on later in this section:

– Mine Latent Structure, which mines latent pairwise *user-user* and *item-item* structure information from the feature representations of the pre-trained CTR model. It generates user and item graphs;

– Escape Knowledge Curse, which relies on three components, namely, (i) Structure Migrator, (ii) Click Perceptron, and (iii) Curse Escaper, to model the CVR task and alleviate the curse of knowledge problem.

3.3 Mine Latent Structure

Previous research has shown that users are more likely to interact with items that are similar to those they have interacted with before, rather than different ones [18]. This collaborative filtering relationship, also known as structure information, is independent of the task. Therefore, the collaborative filtering knowledge discovered on the CTR task can be applied to CVR modeling as additional knowledge.

Pre-train. To capture the collaborative filtering knowledge, we pre-trained a simple CTR model that only contained a Multi-Layer Perceptron (MLP) layer. In this study, we utilized the basic MLP as the backbone structure for the CVR, CTR, and pre-trained CTR models, which is similar to previous research [26].

The pre-trained CTR model's structure is consistent with the rightmost part of Fig. 1, and it consists of five components: (a) Input Layer, where samples are input. (b) Embedding Layer, which transforms the sparse and dense features into feature embedding. (c) Concatenate Layer, which concatenates the feature embeddings. (d) Click Tower, which contains a multi-layer perceptron, the Dropout, and the ReLU activation function. (e) Click Layer, which consists of a multi-layer perceptron and the Sigmoid activation function.

We train this CTR model using impression samples and extract its Embedding Layer to capture collaborative filtering knowledge in the CTR task.

Similarity Search. To derive collaborative filtering insights from the CTR task, we compute similarities between items and between users. To begin, we concatenate the feature embeddings of a user according to their ID to generate the user representation. Similarly, we employ the same procedure for items to derive their representation:

$$r^U_{\text{pre}} = [e^U_{1,\text{pre}}||\cdots||e^U_{l^U,\text{pre}}], r^I_{\text{pre}} = [e^I_{1,\text{pre}}||\cdots||e^I_{l^I,\text{pre}}], \tag{2}$$

where $e_{\text{pre}} \in \mathbb{R}^d$ denotes the feature embedding obtained from the pre-trained CTR model, d is the embedding size, and $||$ denotes the concatenate operation. Besides, $r^U_{\text{pre}} \in \mathbb{R}^{d^U}$, $r^I_{\text{pre}} \in \mathbb{R}^{d^I}$ represent the user/item representation, where $d^U = l^U \times d$, $d^I = l^I \times d$, and l^U, l^I denote the number of features for the user and item, respectively.

To evaluate the similarity between users, we opt for the straightforward and non-parametric cosine similarity measure [23]:

$$S^U_{ij} = \frac{(r^U_{i,\text{pre}})^T r^U_{j,\text{pre}}}{||r^U_{i,\text{pre}}||\ ||r^U_{j,\text{pre}}||}, \tag{3}$$

where S^U_{ij} is scalar, which represents the semantic correlations between two users i, j. $S^U \in \mathbb{R}^{N^U \times N^U}$ denotes the similarity matrix of users. Similar to Eqs. 2 and 3, we can also obtain the similarity matrix S^I for items.

To reduce the time cost of constructing the similarity matrix, we use the Faiss[1] [6] library, which can efficiently performs similarity searches.

Construct Graph. To visualize these collaborative filtering relationships, we construct graphs according to the similarity matrix. Typically, the adjacency matrix of a graph should contain non-negative values, but in our case, the values of S_{ij} fall within the range of $[-1, 1]$. Hence, we set the negative terms of S to zeros. Additionally, we recognize that fully-connected graphs are computationally intensive and are likely to introduce noisy and unimportant edges [1], so we aim to create sparse graphs.

Specifically, we only retain edges with the top-K confidence scores for each node i, resulting in the sparsified adjacency matrix G^U:

$$G_{ij}^U = \begin{cases} S_{ij}^U, & \text{if } S_{ij}^U \in \text{top-}K(S_{i,:}^U), \\ 0, & \text{otherwise}, \end{cases} \tag{4}$$

where $S_{i,:}^U$ denotes the i-row of S^U, and G^U is the sparsified adjacency matrix.

To alleviate the exploding or vanishing gradient problem [8], we normalize the adjacency matrix as:

$$\mathcal{G}^U = (D)^{-\frac{1}{2}} G^U (D)^{-\frac{1}{2}}, \tag{5}$$

where $D \in \mathbb{R}^{d^U}$ is the diagonal degree matrix of G^U, $\mathcal{G}^U$ denotes the final graph for users. Similar to Eqs. 4 and 5, we can also obtain the sparsified adjacency matrix G^I and the final graph $\mathcal{G}^I$ for items. To reduce the storage cost of the adjacency matrix, we use the Sparse[2] library of Pytorch [16].

3.4 Escape Knowledge Curse

After obtaining the collaborative filtering information based on the CTR task (*i.e.*, $\mathcal{G}^U$ and $\mathcal{G}^I$), we implement the three components discussed in Sect. 3.2 to alleviate the problem of the curse of knowledge. To illustrate the method's overall flow, we outline the transformation process of a sample $s = (x, y, z)$ from input to output.

To begin with, we must convert the characteristics of the input sample into a feature representation through an embedding lookup. Similar to previous CVR methods that utilize multi-task learning, we train the CVR model on the entire impression space and utilize the CTR task as an auxiliary. However, we differ in that we have two separate Embedding Layers for the CVR and CTR tasks, which we refer to as V and T, respectively. Hence, the process of embedding lookup can be described as follows:

$$e_{i,V} = V(f_i),\ e_{i,T} = T(f_i), \tag{6}$$

where $e_i \in \mathbb{R}^d$ denotes the feature embedding for i-th feature f_i of the sample s, and d is the embedding size.

Then, we can obtain the representation of the sample s for the CTR tower as follows:

$$E_T = [r_{s,T}^U || r_{s,T}^I || r_{s,T}^C] = [e_{1,T}^U || \dots || e_{l^U,T}^U || e_{1,T}^I || \dots || e_{l^I,T}^I || e_{1,T}^C || \dots || e_{l^C,T}^C], \tag{7}$$

[1] https://github.com/facebookresearch/faiss.

[2] https://pytorch.org/docs/stable/sparse.html.

where $E_T \in \mathbb{R}^{d^U+d^I+d^C}$ is the input of CTR tower, $r^U_{s,T} \in \mathbb{R}^{d^U}$ is the user-side feature representation of the sample s, $r^I_{s,T} \in \mathbb{R}^{d^I}$ is the item-side feature representation, $r^C_{s,T} \in \mathbb{R}^{d^C}$ denotes the context feature representation. The value of d^C is calculated as $l^C \times d$, where l^C is the number of context features present in sample s.

Structure Migrator (SM). In this part, we migrate the task-independent structure information (*i.e.*, $\mathcal{G}^U$ and $\mathcal{G}^I$) mined from the pre-trained CTR model to the CVR model.

We repeat the Eq. 2 on the Embedding Layer V of the CVR model to obtain the user/item representation matrices:

$$R^U = \{r^U_{1,V}, \ldots, r^U_{N^U,V}\},\ R^I = \{r^I_{1,V}, \ldots, r^I_{N^I,V}\}, \tag{8}$$

where $R^U \in \mathbb{R}^{d^U \times N^U}$, $R^I \in \mathbb{R}^{d^I \times N^I}$, $r^U \in \mathbb{R}^{d^U}$, $r^I \in \mathbb{R}^{d^I}$, and N_U, N_I denote the total number of users and items, respectively.

Next, we utilize a straightforward yet efficient message propagation and aggregation process, which does not require any feature transformation or activation. This process is computationally efficient as well. The l-th layer of this process can be expressed as:

$$R^U_{(l)} = \mathcal{G}^U R^U_{(l-1)}, \tag{9}$$

where $R^U_{(l)} \in \mathbb{R}^{d^U \times N_U}$ is the l-th layer embedding matrix, and the initial $R^U_{(0)}$ is R^U. After stacking L layers, $R^U_{(L)}$ encodes the high-order user-user relationships.

Similar to Eqs. 8 and 9, we can also obtain the item's $R^I(L)$. As a result, we obtain new user/item embeddings, *i.e.*, $R^U(L)$ and $R^I(L)$, which encode collaborative filtering knowledge from CTR. To inject the collaborative filtering knowledge into CVR modeling more smoothly, we set a hyper-parameter to control the update of CVR features. In the t-th epoch ($t > 1$), the update of $R^U_{(L)}$ can be formulated as:

$$R^U_{(L,t)} = \alpha R^U_{(L,t)} + (1-\alpha) R^U_{(L,t-1)}, \tag{10}$$

where α controls the proportion of updates. Similarly, we update $R^I_{(L,t)}$ through the same process.

We then generate the representation of the sample s for the CVR tower:

$$E_V = [r^U_{s,V} || r^I_{s,V} || r^C_{s,V}] = [R^U_{(L,t)}[s] || R^I_{(L,t)}[s] || e^C_{1,V} || \cdots || e^C_{l^C,V}], \tag{11}$$

where $E_V \in \mathbb{R}^{d^U+d^I+d^C}$ is the input of CVR tower, and $R_{(L,t)}[\cdot]$ means searching for the embeddings corresponding to the user or item in the sample s from the embedding matrix $R^U_{(L,t)}$ or $R^I_{(L,t)}$.

Click Perceptron (CP). To distinguish between clicked impression samples and non-clicked impression samples during training, we incorporate the hidden representation of the CTR auxiliary task into CVR modeling as bias information for the samples.

To capture CTR knowledge in the sample, we employ Click Tower on E_T:

$$H_T = \mathrm{TW}_{\mathrm{click}}(E_T), \tag{12}$$

where $H_T \in \mathcal{R}^{d^o}$, d^o is the embedding size of the output layer of the Click tower, and $\mathrm{TW}_{\mathrm{click}}$ means the Click Tower.

Next, we construct the Info Layer to incorporate bias information while preserving the original distribution and mitigating the instability of model training. This layer comprises a multi-layer perceptron and the Sigmoid activation function:

$$\hat{H}_T = \mathrm{Sigmoid}(\mathrm{MLP}(H_T)), \tag{13}$$

where $\hat{H}_T \in \mathbb{R}^{d^U+d^I+d^C}$, which is composed of a series of numbers between $[0, 1]$. MLP represents the multi-layer perceptron. We multiply $\hat{H}_T$ by 2 to keep its mean around 1 and inject it as bias information into the modeling of CVR:

$$\hat{E}_V = E_V(1 + 2\hat{H}_T), \tag{14}$$

where $\hat{E}_V \in \mathbb{R}^{d^U+d^I+d^C}$ denotes the hidden representation of sample s in CVR modeling, which is injected with collaborative filtering knowledge and click bias information.

To extract CVR knowledge and the information introduced externally, we employ Conversion Tower on $\hat{E}_V$:

$$H_V = \mathrm{TW}_{\mathrm{conv}}(\hat{E}_V)), \tag{15}$$

where $H_V \in \mathcal{R}^{d^o}$, and $\mathrm{TW}_{\mathrm{conv}}$ means the Conversion Tower.

To estimate the probability of user click and purchase respectively, we construct the Conversion Layer and Click Layer, which are comprised of the multi-layer perceptron and Sigmoid activation function:

$$\hat{y} = \mathrm{Sigmoid}(\mathrm{MLP}(H_T)), \hat{z} = \mathrm{Sigmoid}(\mathrm{MLP}(H_V)), \tag{16}$$

where $\hat{y}, \hat{z}$ are the predicted probabilities of click and purchase behavior occurring in the sample s, respectively.

Curse Escaper (CE). To further strengthen the model's ability to model users' real conversion behavior, we add a brand-new weight assignment algorithm, named Curse Escaper, into the loss function. The loss function of CSTWA is mainly composed of three parts, as follows.

First, for the CTR task, we minimize the cross-entropy loss of it:

$$\mathcal{L}_{\mathrm{ctr}} = -\frac{1}{N}\sum_{i=1}^{N}(y_i \log \hat{y}_i + (1 - y_i)\log(1 - \hat{y}_i)), \tag{17}$$

where N is the total number of samples in the entire sample space $\mathcal{S}$, y_i is the click label of the i-th sample, and $\hat{y}_i$ is the predicted click probability.

To alleviate the curse of knowledge problem, we increase the weights of the false positive samples (*i.e.*, samples where the CTR predictive value is high but no conversion behavior actually occurs) and the false negative samples (*i.e.*, samples where the CTR predictive value is low but conversion behavior actually occurs) in the loss function.

Technically, we predefine two hyperparameters, pos and neg, which indicate the thresholds for high CTR predictive value and low CTR predictive value, respectively. Mathematically, the loss function of CVR can be formulated as:

$$\mathcal{L}_{\text{ce}} = -\frac{1}{N}\sum_{i=1}^{N}(\mathcal{A}z_i \log \hat{z}_i + \mathcal{B}(1 - z_i)\log(1 - \hat{z}_i)),$$
$$\text{where, } \mathcal{A} = \max(1, (\frac{neg}{\hat{y}_i})^{\gamma}),\ \mathcal{B} = \max(1, (\frac{\hat{y}_i}{pos})^{\gamma}), \tag{18}$$

where $\hat{y}_i$ is the CTR predictive value, z_i is the conversion label of the i-th sample, and γ controls the magnitude of weight enhancement. To prevent excessive weighting, we set upper limits for $\mathcal{A}$ and $\mathcal{B}$. During the experiment, we searched for the optimal values between 2 and 10, and ultimately restricted $\mathcal{A}$ and $\mathcal{B}$ to be below 4.

Besides, considering that the purchase behavior occurs after the click, we follow AITM [26] to set an extra loss function to constrain the CVR predictive value to be less than the CTR predictive value:

$$\mathcal{L}_{\text{co}} = \frac{1}{N}\sum_{i=1}^{N}\max(\hat{z}_i - \hat{y}_i, 0). \tag{19}$$

It outputs the positive penalty term only when $\hat{z}_i > \hat{y}_i$, otherwise, it outputs 0. Finally, the loss function of our method can be formulated as:

$$\mathcal{L} = w_1\mathcal{L}_{\text{ctr}} + w_2\mathcal{L}_{\text{ce}} + w_3\mathcal{L}_{\text{co}}, \tag{20}$$

where w_1, w_2, w_3 are weights of $\mathcal{L}_{\text{ctr}}, \mathcal{L}_{\text{ce}}, \mathcal{L}_{\text{co}}$, which are set to (1, 1, 0.6) in this paper, respectively

4 Experiments

In this section, we perform experiments to evaluate the proposed framework against various baselines on industrial and public real-world datasets, and answer the following Research Questions (RQs):

- **RQ1:** How does our method perform compared with the baseline models on the public datasets?
- **RQ2:** How do the three key components affect the final performance?
- **RQ3:** How sensitive our model is to perturbations of several key hyper-parameters?

Table 1. Statistics of the public datasets after processing, where M means million, and "%Positive" means the percentage of clicked/converted samples in the train set.

Dataset	#Users/#Items	#Train/#Validation/#Test	%Positive(%)
Industrial	30M/ 0.28M	465M/45M/44M	7.04/0.28
Public	0.2M/0.5M	38M/4.2M/43M	3.89/0.02

4.1 Experimental Settings

In this part, we introduce the benchmark dataset, the evaluation metrics, the state-of-the-art methods involved in the comparison, and the implementation details.

Datasets. We conduct extensive experiments on the following two datasets: *Industrial dataset*: The industrial dataset contains all samples of the livestream platform of our App, which is one of the largest e-commerce platform in the world, in a continuous period of time. We divide the training set, validation set and test set in chronological order. *Public dataset*: The public dataset is the Ali-CCP (Alibaba Click and Conversion Prediction) [12] dataset[3]. We follow the previous work to use all the single-valued categorical features and randomly take 10% of the train set as the validation set to verify the convergence of all models. We follow the previous work [26] to filter the features whose frequency less than 10. The statistics of datasets are shown in Table 1.

Evaluation Metrics. In the offline experiments, to comprehensively evaluate the effectiveness of our method and compare it with the baseline methods, we follow the existing works [12,20,26] to adopt the standard metric Area Under Curve (AUC), which is widely used in the recommendation and advertising systems and can reflect the ranking ability. The mean and standard deviation (std) is reported over five runs with different random seeds. We report the AUC on the auxiliary task and the focused main task (*i.e.*, click and purchase prediction task).

Baseline Methods. We compare the proposed method with the following representative and mainstream models: **MLP**: It is the base structure of our framework, which consists of the Click/Conversion Tower and Click/Conversion Layer. **ESMM** [12,25]: ESMM and ESM^2 use a unified multi-task learning framework to predict purchase and post-click behaviors over the entire space to relieve the sample selection bias problem. **OMoE** [11]: The Expert-Bottom pattern in OMoE (One-gate Mixture-of-Experts) incorporates experts by utilizing a single gate shared across all tasks. **MMoE** [11]: It is designed to integrate experts via multiple gates in the Gate Control. Moreover, it explicitly learns to model task relationships from data. **PLE** [20]: Progressive Layered Extraction (PLE) with Expert-Bottom pattern separates task-shared experts and task-specific experts explicitly. **AITM** [26]: It is a contemporaneous work that proposes the

[3] https://tianchi.aliyun.com/dataset/dataDetail?dataId=408.

Table 2. The AUC performance (mean±std) on the industrial and public datasets. The Gain means the mean AUC improvement compared with the MLP. We bold the best results and indicate the second-best results with an underline. "*" indicates that the improvement is statistically significant at p-value < 0.05 over paired samples t-test.

Dataset	Industrial Dataset				Public Dataset			
Model	Click AUC	Gain	Purchase AUC	Gain	Click AUC	Gain	Purchase AUC	Gain
MLP	0.7970±0.0020	–	0.8466±0.005	–	0.6147±0.0012	–	0.5789±0.0042	–
ESMM	0.7971±0.0012	+0.0001	0.8579±0.0031	+0.0113	0.6152±0.0023	+0.0005	0.6376±0.0050	+0.0587
OMoE	0.7969±0.0012	−0.0001	0.8520±0.0040	+0.0054	**0.6192±0.0022**	+0.0045	0.6412±0.0061	+0.0623
MMoE	<u>0.7982±0.0013</u>	+0.0012	0.8503±0.0032	+0.0037	0.6170±0.0021	+0.0023	0.6439±0.0035	+0.0650
PLE	**0.7989±0.0012**	+0.0019	0.8516±0.0022	+0.0050	0.6166±0.0015	+0.0019	0.6446±0.0026	+0.0657
AITM	0.7884±0.0014	−0.0086	<u>0.8587±0.0033</u>	+0.0121	<u>0.6183±0.0016</u>	+0.0036	<u>0.6456±0.0047</u>	+0.0667
ESCM^2	0.7973±0.0019	+0.0003	0.8505±0.0050	+0.0039	0.6176±0.0012	+0.0029	0.6427±0.0041	+0.0638
CSTWA	0.7938±0.0014	−0.0032	**0.8613±0.0024***	+0.0147	0.6160±0.0020	+0.0013	**0.6532±0.0028***	+0.0743

attention-based AIT module which can adaptively learn what and how much information to transfer for different stages of different audiences. **ESCM^2** [21]: It is devised to augment ESMM with counterfactual regularization. This is the state-of-the-art method in the CVR prediction task. To be fair, all models, including CSTWA, utilize the same fundamental network structure and hyper-parameters in their Multi-Layer Perceptron.

Implementation Details. We implemented our method using PyTorch [16]. To ensure a fair comparison, we set the embedding dimension d to 5 for all models. We used the Adam optimizer with a learning rate of 0.001, a batch size of 2000, and 10 epochs. L2 regularization is set to 1e-6. In the Expert-Bottom pattern, the dimensions of layers in the MLP-Expert are set to $[64, 32, 16]$. In the Probability-Transfer pattern, the dimensions of layers in the MLP-Tower (*i.e.*, Click/Conversion Tower) are set to $[128, 64, 32]$. That is, $d^o = 32$. The dropout rates in each layer are set to $[0.1, 0.3, 0.3]$, and the activation function used is ReLU. In addition, we perform a grid search on the validation set to find the optimal hyper-parameters. We tune the K parameter of the top-K function using values of $4, 8, 16$, and 32, ultimately setting it to 8. Meanwhile, we set L to 1. The values for α and γ were set to 0.3 and 3, respectively. For the hyper-parameters pos and neg, we set them to the 99-th and 10-th percentile of the previous 10,000 CTR predicted values, respectively.

4.2 Experimental Results

In this part, we report our experimental results and conduct a detailed analysis to investigate CSTWA framework.

Main Results (RQ1). We report the AUC scores of all models on the offline test set. The results of purchase AUC are shown in Table 2, and we can draw the following insightful observations:

Table 3. The AUC performance (mean±std) of the variants on the public dataset.

Dataset Model	Public Dataset			
	Click AUC	**Gain**	**Purchase AUC**	**Gain**
MLP	0.6147±0.0012	–	0.5789±0.0042	–
+ SM	**0.6207±0.0031**	+0.0060	0.6372±0.0022	+0.0583
+ CP	0.6159±0.0008	+0.0012	0.6357±0.0034	+0.0568
+ CE	0.6142±0.0010	-0.0005	0.6312±0.0024	+0.0523
+ CP, CE	0.6151±0.0022	+0.004	0.6423±0.0025	+0.0634
+ SM, CE	0.6162±0.0012	+0.0015	0.6422±0.0027	+0.0633
+ SM, CP	0.6154±0.0016	+0.0007	0.6503±0.0016	+0.0714
CSTWA	0.6160±0.0020	+0.0013	**0.6532±0.0028***	+0.0743

(a). Compared to the single-task model MLP, multi-task models generally exhibit better performance. This indicates that achieving satisfactory performance for the single-task model is difficult due to the extreme data sparsity. In fact, if the CVR model is trained solely with samples of clicked impressions, many of the feature embeddings may not be trained sufficiently.

(b). ESMM and ESCM^2 models based on the Probability-Transfer pattern improve slightly as they only consider simple probability information transfer between adjacent tasks. On the other hand, the models based on the Expert-Bottom pattern, regulate the shared information among tasks and perform better than many baselines.

(c). AITM enhances CVR estimation by explicitly modeling inter-task relationships, while PLE outperforms baselines by separating shared and specific task experts. This demonstrates that explicitly modeling the transfer of information between tasks can improve performance.

(d). All existing works overlook the curse of knowledge caused by too much auxiliary task information. As a result, CSTWA is the best in CVR prediction among various baselines. This shows that extracting and transferring CTR knowledge, adding sample bias information, and enhancing CVR information can boost the main task.

Ablation Study (RQ2). To investigate the importance of critical components in CSTWA, namely the Structure Migrator (SM), Click Perceptron (CP), and Curse Escaper (CE), we conduct extensive ablation experiments to examine how they affect the final performance. The experimental results are presented in Table 3.

When utilizing any of the three key components, there is a significant increase in performance. This demonstrates that introducing bias information to enable the model to capture stage information in the sample can further improve performance. Additionally, explicitly enhancing the model's understanding of conversion behavior through the use of weight enhancement algorithms in the loss function can alleviate the curse of knowledge problem. Furthermore, when utilizing the SM component, there is a noticeable performance increase, indicating that task-independent structure information is effective. The use of the CE component leads to a decrease in CTR-related metrics, as we explicitly enhance the weight of CVR-related knowledge in the samples. However, this decrease is acceptable because our main task is to model the CVR.

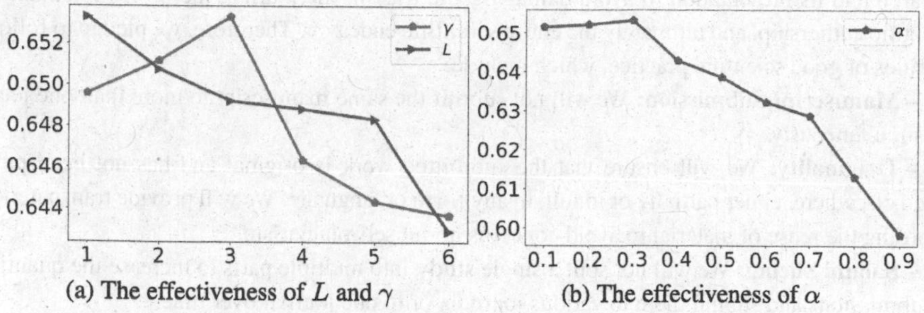

(a) The effectiveness of L and γ (b) The effectiveness of α

Fig. 2. The purchase AUC performance of ablation experiments on the public dataset.

Hyper-Parameter Study (RQ3). To explore the sensitivity of CSTWA to perturbations of different hyper-parameters, We conduct ablation experiments for hyper-parameters L, α, and γ on the public dataset. The results are shown in Fig. 2.

(a) As depicted in Fig. 2a, we vary the values of hyper-parameters L and γ to evaluate their impact on the performance. We observed that increasing the number of layers for neighborhood propagation do not improve the performance significantly. To reduce the computational burden of the graph network, we set L to 1. Additionally, we find that setting γ to 3 resulted in the best performance, beyond which the performance drop rapidly. This indicates that considering instances of information contradiction is crucial, but giving them too much weight is not desirable.

(b) To confirm the efficacy of α, we experiment with several different settings, ranging from 0.1 to 0.9, as shown in Fig. 2b. The best performance is at $\alpha = 3$. This suggests that the CTR task's structure information helps the CVR task. However, since CTR and CVR tasks are distinct, setting a higher α leads to poorer results.

5 Conclusion

In this work, we elucidate the curse of knowledge problem in CVR methods based on multi-task learning. For solving the above problem, we propose CSTWA, which contains three effective components (*i.e.*, Structure Migrator, Click Perceptron, and Curse Escaper), which can filter the input information that is more friendly for CVR, calibrate the fundamental representation layer, and reweight the discriminant layer. Specifically, our method could mine and transfer the task-independent structure information from the auxiliary task (*i.e.*, CTR task). Meanwhile, it models the click bias information of samples of the entire space. Besides, it introduces a brand-new weight assignment algorithm to explicitly reinforce CVR-related knowledge. Extensive experiments on two datasets demonstrate the superior performance of CSTWA.

In the future, we plan to explore more efficient ways of transferring structure information to make our models more cost-effective.

Acknowledgement. This research was supported by Shopee Live Algorithm team.

Ethical Statement. As authors, we acknowledge the importance of maintaining the integrity of research and its presentation to avoid damaging the trust in the journal, the professionalism of scientific authorship, and ultimately the entire scientific endeavor. Therefore, we pledge to follow the rules of good scientific practice, which include:

– **Manuscript Submission:** We will not submit the same manuscript to more than one journal simultaneously.

– **Originality:** We will ensure that the submitted work is original and has not been published elsewhere, either partially or in full, in any form or language. We will provide transparency regarding the reuse of material to avoid concerns about self-plagiarism.

– **Salami Slicing:** We will not split a single study into multiple parts to increase the quantity of submissions and submit them to various journals or to one journal over time.

– **Concurrent Publication:** If we choose to publish concurrently or secondarily, we will meet certain conditions such as translations or manuscripts intended for a different group of readers.

– **Data Presentation:** We will present our results clearly, honestly, and without fabrication, falsification, or inappropriate data manipulation. We will adhere to discipline-specific rules for acquiring, selecting, and processing data, and we will not present data, text, or theories by others as our own. Proper acknowledgments will be given for all materials, and we will secure permissions for copyrighted materials. We understand that the journal may use software to screen for plagiarism.

– **Permissions:** We will obtain permissions for the use of software, questionnaires/(web) surveys, and scales in our studies.

– **Citation:** We will cite appropriate and relevant literature to support our claims in both research and non-research articles, and we will avoid excessive and inappropriate self-citation or coordinated efforts among several authors to collectively self-cite.

– **Truthful Statements:** We will avoid making untrue statements or descriptions about an entity that could potentially be seen as personal attacks or allegations about that person.

– **Public Health and National Security:** We will clearly identify research that may be misapplied to pose a threat to public health or national security.

– **Authorship:** We will ensure that the author group, corresponding author, and order of authors are correct at submission.

All of the above guidelines are essential for respecting third-party rights such as copyright and/or moral rights. As authors, we recognize our responsibility to uphold the highest ethical standards in scientific research and publication.

References

1. Chen, Y., Wu, L., Zaki, M.: Iterative deep graph learning for graph neural networks: Better and robust node embeddings. In: Advances in Neural Information Processing Systems, vol. 33, pp. 19314–19326 (2020)
2. Cheng, H.T., et al.: Wide & deep learning for recommender systems. In: Proceedings of the 1st Workshop on Deep Learning for Recommender Systems, pp. 7–10 (2016)
3. Guo, H., Tang, R., Ye, Y., Li, Z., He, X.: DeepFM: a factorization-machine based neural network for CTR prediction. arXiv preprint arXiv:1703.04247 (2017)

4. Hadash, G., Shalom, O.S., Osadchy, R.: Rank and rate: multi-task learning for recommender systems. In: Proceedings of the 12th ACM Conference on Recommender Systems, pp. 451–454 (2018)
5. Huang, T., Zhang, Z., Zhang, J.: Fibinet: combining feature importance and bilinear feature interaction for click-through rate prediction. In: Proceedings of the 13th ACM Conference on Recommender Systems. pp. 169–177 (2019)
6. Johnson, J., Douze, M., Jégou, H.: Billion-scale similarity search with GPUs. IEEE Trans. Big Data **7**(3), 535–547 (2019)
7. Juan, Y., Zhuang, Y., Chin, W.S., Lin, C.J.: Field-aware factorization machines for CTR prediction. In: Proceedings of the 10th ACM Conference on Recommender Systems, pp. 43–50 (2016)
8. Kipf, T.N., Welling, M.: Semi-supervised classification with graph convolutional networks. arXiv preprint arXiv:1609.02907 (2016)
9. Lian, J., Zhou, X., Zhang, F., Chen, Z., Xie, X., Sun, G.: xDeepFM: combining explicit and implicit feature interactions for recommender systems. In: Proceedings of the 24th ACM SIGKDD International Conference on Knowledge Discovery & Data Mining, pp. 1754–1763 (2018)
10. Ma, J., Zhao, Z., Chen, J., Li, A., Hong, L., Chi, E.H.: SNR: sub-network routing for flexible parameter sharing in multi-task learning. In: AAAI, vol. 33, pp. 216–223 (2019)
11. Ma, J., Zhao, Z., Yi, X., Chen, J., Hong, L., Chi, E.H.: Modeling task relationships in multi-task learning with multi-gate mixture-of-experts. In: Proceedings of the 24th ACM SIGKDD International Conference on Knowledge Discovery & Data Mining, pp. 1930–1939 (2018)
12. Ma, X., et al.: Entire space multi-task model: an effective approach for estimating post-click conversion rate. In: Proceedings of the 41st International ACM SIGIR Conference on Research & Development in Information Retrieval, pp. 1137–1140 (2018)
13. Ni, Y., et al.: Perceive your users in depth: Learning universal user representations from multiple e-commerce tasks. In: Proceedings of the 24th ACM SIGKDD International Conference on Knowledge Discovery & Data Mining, pp. 596–605 (2018)
14. Ouyang, K., et al.: Mining interest trends and adaptively assigning sample weight for session-based recommendation. arXiv preprint arXiv:2306.11610 (2023)
15. Ouyang, K., Xu, X., Tang, C., Chen, W., Zheng, H.: Social-aware sparse attention network for session-based social recommendation. In: Findings of the Association for Computational Linguistics: EMNLP 2022, pp. 2173–2183 (2022)
16. Paszke, A., et al.: Automatic differentiation in PyTorch (2017)
17. Qu, Y., et al.: Product-based neural networks for user response prediction. In: 2016 IEEE 16th International Conference on Data Mining (ICDM), pp. 1149–1154. IEEE (2016)
18. Rendle, S., Freudenthaler, C., Gantner, Z., Schmidt-Thieme, L.: BPR: Bayesian personalized ranking from implicit feedback. arXiv preprint arXiv:1205.2618 (2012)
19. Song, W., et al.: AutoInt: automatic feature interaction learning via self-attentive neural networks. In: Proceedings of the 28th ACM International Conference on Information and Knowledge Management, pp. 1161–1170 (2019)
20. Tang, H., Liu, J., Zhao, M., Gong, X.: Progressive layered extraction (PLE): a novel multi-task learning (MTL) model for personalized recommendations. In: Fourteenth ACM Conference on Recommender Systems, pp. 269–278 (2020)
21. Wang, H., et al.: ESCM2: entire space counterfactual multi-task model for post-click conversion rate estimation. In: Proceedings of the 45th International ACM SIGIR Conference on Research and Development in Information Retrieval, pp. 363–372 (2022)
22. Wang, R., Fu, B., Fu, G., Wang, M.: Deep & cross network for ad click predictions. In: Proceedings of the ADKDD 2017, pp. 1–7 (2017)

23. Wang, X., Zhu, M., Bo, D., Cui, P., Shi, C., Pei, J.: AM-GCN: adaptive multi-channel graph convolutional networks. In: Proceedings of the 26th ACM SIGKDD International Conference on Knowledge Discovery & Data Mining, pp. 1243–1253 (2020)
24. Wen, H., Zhang, J., Lin, Q., Yang, K., Huang, P.: Multi-level deep cascade trees for conversion rate prediction in recommendation system. In: Proceedings of the AAAI Conference on Artificial Intelligence, vol. 33, pp. 338–345 (2019)
25. Wen, H., et al.: Entire space multi-task modeling via post-click behavior decomposition for conversion rate prediction. In: Proceedings of the 43rd International ACM SIGIR Conference on Research and Development in Information Retrieval, pp. 2377–2386 (2020)
26. Xi, D., et al.: Modeling the sequential dependence among audience multi-step conversions with multi-task learning in targeted display advertising. In: Proceedings of the 27th ACM SIGKDD Conference on Knowledge Discovery & Data Mining, pp. 3745–3755 (2021)
27. Yang, H., Lu, Q., Qiu, A.X., Han, C.: Large scale CVR prediction through dynamic transfer learning of global and local features. In: Workshop on Big Data, Streams and Heterogeneous Source Mining: Algorithms, Systems, Programming Models and Applications, pp. 103–119. PMLR (2016)

Constrained-HIDA: Heterogeneous Image Domain Adaptation Guided by Constraints

Mihailo Obrenović[1,2(✉)], Thomas Lampert[1], Miloš Ivanović[2], and Pierre Gançarski[1]

[1] ICube, University of Strasbourg, Strasbourg, France
mobrenovic@unistra.fr
[2] Faculty of Science, University of Kragujevac, Radoja Domanovica 12, 34000 Kragujevac, Serbia

Abstract. Supervised deep learning relies heavily on the existence of a huge amount of labelled data, which in many cases is difficult to obtain. Domain adaptation deals with this problem by learning on a labelled dataset and applying that knowledge to another, unlabelled or scarcely labelled dataset, with a related but different probability distribution. Heterogeneous domain adaptation is an especially challenging area where domains lie in different input spaces. These methods are very interesting for the field of remote sensing (and indeed computer vision in general), where a variety of sensors are used, capturing images of different modalities, different spatial and spectral resolutions, and where labelling is a very expensive process. With two heterogeneous domains, however, unsupervised domain adaptation is difficult to perform, and class-flipping is frequent. At least a small amount of labelled data is therefore necessary in the target domain in many cases. This work proposes loosening the label requirement by labelling the target domain with must-link and cannot-link constraints instead of class labels. Our method Constrained-HIDA, based on constraints, contrastive loss, and learning domain invariant features, shows that a significant performance improvement can be achieved by using a very small number of constraints. This demonstrates that a reduced amount of information, in the form of constraints, is as effective as giving class labels. Moreover, this paper shows the benefits of interactive supervision—assigning constraints to the samples from classes that are known to be prone to flipping can further reduce the necessary amount of constraints.

Keywords: Deep Learning · Domain Adaptation · Constraints · Remote Sensing

1 Introduction

Supervised deep learning (DL) models are heavily dependent on the existence of the large-scale labelled datasets. The process of obtaining the reference data

D. Koutra et al. (Eds.): ECML PKDD 2023, LNAI 14173, pp. 443–458, 2023.
https://doi.org/10.1007/978-3-031-43424-2_27

is however often very slow and expensive. This is especially the case in the field of remote sensing (RS), where acquiring the labels requires collecting data in the field from locations that may be complicated to reach due to inaccessibility, natural disasters, armed conflicts etc. Furthermore, the existing reference data may not be reusable for images taken at a later date due to constant changes of the Earth's surface, such as seasonal and climate changes, deforestation, growth of urban area etc. Since satellites generate huge amount of data on a daily basis, these limitations put the pace of producing reference data far behind the speed of acquiring new data.

Most of the time, existing trained supervised DL models cannot be applied to other dataset as they often generalise poorly. If the conditions during data acquisition differ, there will be a domain shift—a difference between probability distributions—between the datasets. *Domain adaptation* (DA) techniques can help with overcoming this problem. Typically, DA involves learning a model on one data distribution (named *source domain*, typically labelled), and applying it to another, different but related data distribution (called *target domain* typically unlabelled or scarcely labelled) by reducing the shift between domains. Alternatively, both domains can be given to one model at training time, yet with the labels present exclusively or primarily in the source domain.

When there is a small amount of labelled data in a mainly unlabelled target domain, semi-supervised domain adaptation (SSDA) can be employed, and methods for SSDA are specifically developed to take advantage of existing target labels. When there are no labels at all in the target domain, unsupervised domain adaptation (UDA) methods are used. These methods often try to compensate for the absence of supervision in the target domain by using pseudo-labels. Another possible way to incorporate certain knowledge about the target domain, rarely addressed in DA so far, is using the *constraints*.

Constrained clustering is a type of learning where knowledge is provided in the form of constraints rather than labels. The motivation for developing such methods was to improve upon the performance of unsupervised models by providing alternative knowledge about the problem domain in the absence of exact hard labels. Constraints are most often given between the pairs of samples in the form of must-link and cannot-link constraints. There is a growing base of constrained clustering literature, the paradigm is gaining in popularity due to the fact that it does not require classes to be defined (since constraints only act upon pairs of samples) and offers a much weaker form of supervision than labelled samples. It is much easier for an expert to express their preference that two samples should be grouped together (or not), rather than defining absolute labels. This is particularly useful when samples are hard to interpret and interactive, iterative approaches are preferable.

Constraints can be very helpful in DA, especially in situations when there is a huge domain shift. Though existing DA methods are very successful in the field of computer vision (CV), most of them assume RGB images in *both domains* (homogeneous DA). In remote sensing, however, a variety of sensors are used (Fig. 1), capturing images of different modalities, with:

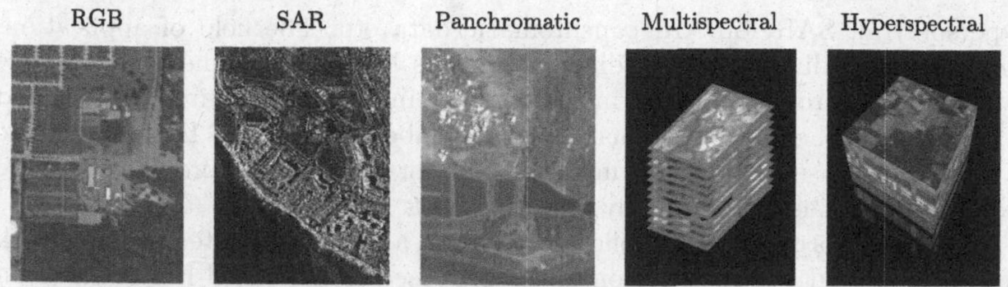

Fig. 1. Different sensors in remote sensing. Images taken from Maxar Open Data Program, Sentinel-1, WorldView-2, EuroSAT and Indian Pines datasets.

- different spatial resolution
- different, non-corresponding channels (referred to as bands in RS), and possibly different numbers of bands.

The domains in RS therefore may not lay in the same space and may have a different dimensionality, increasing still the effective 'domain shift'. Homogeneous DA approaches cannot be applied to such heterogeneous domains. Instead, heterogeneous domain adaptation (HDA) methods are used.

HDA methods show good performance in semi-supervised settings when a small amount of labelled data is also available in the target domain. The results are, however, much more limited in unsupervised HDA. The problem of class flipping occurs frequently, and it is difficult for the algorithms to associate the same-class samples between domains with such a huge domain shift without any supervision. Many works, therefore, state that a presence of at least a small amount of reference data is required to perform HDA [5,24].

In this work, we offer a new approach to HDA by introducing constraints to the learning process to reduce the labelling requirement. We hypothesise that HDA methods may greatly benefit from just a few constraints to avoid incorrectly matching classes between domains and that hard labels are not necessary to overcome the problem of large domain shifts. We present a novel method named Constrained-HIDA, a heterogeneous image domain adaptation model for the task of patch classification, in which the knowledge of the target domain is provided in the form of constraints. Constrained-HIDA extracts domain invariant features from two heterogeneous domains, where samples are forced to respect the constraints in the learned representation space through the use of contrastive loss. We show that by using a very small number of constraints, our method can match the performance of semi-supervised HDA methods, thus reducing greatly the amount of information from the target domain needed. Interactive supervision can make the method even more efficient, by assigning constraints to the samples that are known to be difficult to solve. The results show that in this manner less constraints can be used without affecting the performance.

The developed Constrained-HIDA method could be very beneficial to the RS community since the domain adaptation problem is exacerbated by large domain shifts due to the use of different modalities, e.g. RGB, multispectral, hyperspectral, SAR, LiDAR, panchromatic data etc. The field of application, however, is not limited to RS; different sensors having the same point of view can be found in robotics (depth images, radar), in medical imaging (e.g. CT and MRI) etc. Another benefit is facilitating the labelling process, Hsu et al. state that in many cases, it may be an easier task for a human to provide pair-wise relationships rather than directly assigning class labels [15].

This article is organised as follows: in Sect. 2, a review of related existing work is given, followed by a description of the proposed Constrained-HIDA model in Sect. 3. Experimental setup and results are shown in Sect. 4. Finally, the concluding remarks are given and future work is discussed in Sect. 5.

2 Literature Review

The emergence of Generative Adversarial Networks (GANs) inspired numerous homogeneous domain adaptation techniques for computer vision. Some of these models aim to extract domain invariant features such as DANN [8,9] (derived from the original GAN [10]), WDGRL [23] (derived from Wasserstein GAN [1]), DSN [4], etc. Others like CyCADA [14] aim to translate data between domains and are mostly based on image-to-image GAN architectures [32]. It is known, however, that these UDA methods do not scale well to the semi-supervised setting [22]. Methods that specifically aim to use few target labels easily outperform UDA methods [22], motivating the need for specific SSDA algorithms. When target labels are not available at all, many UDA methods fall back on pseudo-labelling [19,25].

In many cases, even if there are no hard, explicit labels, some background knowledge about the domain is available. This knowledge can be incorporated in the form of instance-level constraints. In constrained clustering, constraints on the pairs of data samples are used to guide the clustering. These constraints can be in the form of must-link or cannot-link, which state that the pair should or should not belong to the same cluster [29]. Zhang et al. propose the deep constrained clustering framework [31] which takes advantage of the benefits of deep learning to learn embedding features and clustering in an end-to-end manner.

Contrastive loss is often used with pair-wise constraints, for example in face recognition [7]. Its simple formula pushes must-link pairs closer in latent space, and cannot-link pairs farther apart. Contrastive learning is therefore a natural choice when learning features for constrained clustering. Hsu et al. used contrastive KL loss on logits of their neural network for constrained clustering [15]. An example of the contrastive loss being used together with clustering in DA is the Contrastive Adaptation Network (CAN) [16].

Constraints found their application in homogeneous DA. Liu et al. [20] pose the problem of unsupervised DA as semi-supervised constrained clustering with target labels missing. The source labels are used to create partition-level constraints. This is especially useful for preserving the structure of domains in multi-source DA. This work, however, does not explore how to use knowledge or preserve the structure in the target domain. Another interesting UDA work is assigning pairwise pseudo-constraints to samples in the target domain to facilitate the clustering process [17]. In SSDA, soft constraints are used to help tackle the problem of imbalanced classes in medical images [12]. The constraints included, however, are based on labels in the target domain that are already used by the algorithm, with the sole purpose of preserving the structure, and they do not introduce any new knowledge about the target domain.

Heterogeneous domain adaptation is much less present in the literature than homogeneous DA. Most of the heterogeneous DA methods for CV are designed to work with tabular data and focus on adapting between vectorial features extracted from the images of different sizes, such as between SURF and DeCAF [18,30] and DeCAF and ImageNet features [26], or to adapt from image to text data [5,24].

The HDA methods applicable to raw-image data of different modalities such as the ones that exist in RS are less frequent. Adversarial Discriminative Domain Adaptation (ADDA) [27] is evaluated on RGB and depth images, but the limitation of the model is that it assumes the same number of channels in the domains. This is also true for Benjdira et al.'s contribution to RS [3], which can be applied to different sensors, but the number of bands must remain the same. Another model for RS by Benjdira et al. [2] can work with a different number of channels, but it is designed for semantic segmentation, and it requires the existence of labelled segmentation masks in the target domain to be used as an intermediate space during the translation process. This approach, therefore, does not extend to classification.

CycleGAN for HDA [28] is a patch classification approach based on image-to-image translation, it is a variant of CycleGAN in which a metric loss, classification loss, and a super-resolution capability are introduced. It is designed to handle RS data of different resolutions, but it may be possible to apply it to domains with different numbers of channels[1] Another work on patch classification of RS data explores the potential of learning domain invariant features in HDA [21]. The paradigm of extracting domain-invariant features is a natural choice for our Constrained-HIDA, as applying the contrastive loss on the constraints is straightforward in the learned common latent feature space.

To the best of our knowledge, there are no other works on using the constraints in HDA, thus making Constrained-HIDA the first such method.

3 Methodology

In this section, the Constrained-HIDA model will be described. Constrained-HIDA extracts deep domain-invariant features from two heterogeneous domains. The learning of a common latent space of invariant features is guided by cross-entropy loss on available (source domain) labels for class discrimination, Wasserstein loss is used to reduce the distance between domains, and contrastive loss on constraints helps to preserve the correct local structure of domains.

[1] It is not clear in the original article [28] if the method was evaluated on the same or different numbers of channels.

Let $X^s = \{x_i^s\}_{i=1}^{n^s}$ be a labelled source dataset of n^s samples from the domain $\mathcal{D}_s$ following the data distribution $\mathbb{P}_{x^s}$ with labels y_i^s, and let $X^t = \{x_j^t\}_{j=1}^{n^t}$ be an unlabelled target dataset of n^t samples from the domain $\mathcal{D}_t$ following the data distribution $\mathbb{P}_{x^t}$. Constrained-HIDA is able to work with heterogeneous domains, i.e. $x^s \in \mathcal{X}^s$, $x^t \in \mathcal{X}^t$, $\mathcal{X}^s \neq \mathcal{X}^t$ where the dimensions d^s and d^t of spaces $\mathcal{X}^s$ and $\mathcal{X}^t$ may or may not differ.

A certain amount of domain knowledge is given in the form of pairwise constraints of two types—must-link and cannot-link. These constraints can be attached to two samples coming from the same domain or from different domains. In this paper, the focus is on the case where there are only inter-domain constraints. The set of constrained samples X^c is usually a small fraction of the whole dataset $X = X^s \cup X^t$. Let $\mathcal{C}^=$ be a set of must-link constraints $C_i^=$, where $C_i^= = (x_{i1}, x_{i2}) \in \mathcal{C}^=$ implies that x_{i1} and x_{i2} should belong to the same cluster/class, and let $\mathcal{C}^{\neq}$ be a set of cannot-link constraints, where $C_j^{\neq} = (x_{j1}, x_{j2}) \in \mathcal{C}^{\neq}$ implies that x_{j1} and x_{j2} should belong to the different cluster/class, $\mathcal{C}^=, \mathcal{C}^{\neq} \subset X^s \times X^t$, $\mathcal{C}^= \cap \mathcal{C}^{\neq} = \emptyset$.

Constrained-HIDA's architecture is presented in Fig. 2 and consists of 5 neural network components: 3 feature extractors, a domain critic, and a class discriminator, with the addition of contrastive loss over constraints on extracted features. To work with the data coming from two different spaces, possibly of different input sizes, two different input branches are needed. Therefore, Constrained-HIDA has two separate feature extractors—$FE_s : \mathcal{X}^s \to \mathbb{R}^{d_1}$ and $FE_t : \mathcal{X}^t \to \mathbb{R}^{d_1}$—these have the task of bringing the data to a feature space of the same size — $g^s = FE_s(x^s)$ and $g^t = FE_t(x^t)$. Furthermore, another invariant feature extractor $FE_i : \mathbb{R}^{d_1} \to \mathbb{R}^{d_2}$ is employed to model the similarity of the data domains and to extract domain invariant features—$h^s = FE_i(g^s)$ and $h^t = FE_i(g^t)$.

Wasserstein distance is used to measure the distance between domains. This metric is calculated by solving the optimal transport between two probability distributions μ and ν. Since this is computationally expensive, the domain critic $DC : \mathbb{R}^{d_2} \to \mathbb{R}$ is trained to approximate it instead [1,23], accelerating the training process. The loss of this component is defined such that

$$\mathcal{L}_{wd}(h^s, h^t) = \frac{1}{n^s} \sum_{i=1}^{n^s} DC(h_i^s) - \frac{1}{n^t} \sum_{j=1}^{n^t} DC(h_j^t). \tag{1}$$

In order to calculate the empirical Wasserstein distance, Eq. (1) needs to be maximised, therefore the domain critic component is trained by solving

$$\max_{\theta_{dc}} (\mathcal{L}_{wd} - \gamma \mathcal{L}_{grad}), \tag{2}$$

where θ_{dc} are the domain critic's weights and $\gamma \mathcal{L}_{grad}$ is a regularisation term enforcing the Lipschitz constraint. When training our domain critic [23], this regularisation term amounts to

$$\mathcal{L}_{grad}(\hat{h}) = \left(\left\| \nabla_{\hat{h}} DC(\hat{h}) \right\|_2 - 1 \right)^2, \tag{3}$$

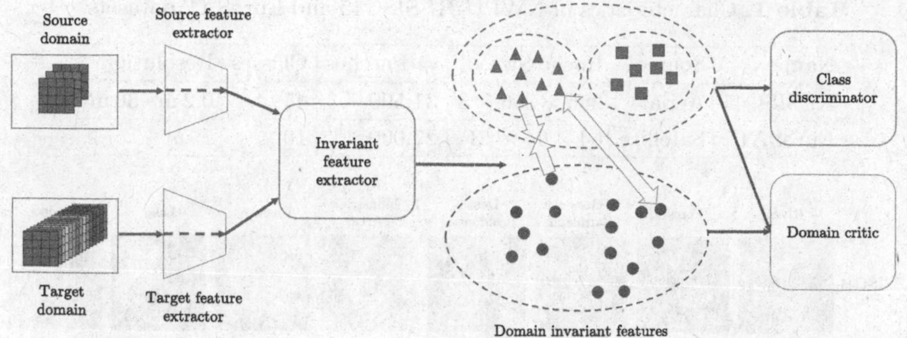

Fig. 2. Overview of the proposed method. Features of the labelled source domain samples are shown in blue, with triangles and squares representing different classes, while features of the unlabelled target domain samples are shown as red circles. Must-link constraints force samples to move towards each other (green arrows), and cannot-link constraints force samples to move apart (orange arrow). (Colour figure online)

where $\hat{h}$ is the union of source and target representation points—h^s and h^t—and the points sampled from the straight lines between coupled points of h^s and h^t. This way, we are sufficiently close to enforcing the norm of 1 on the entire space of the two domains [11].

The class discriminator $C : \mathbb{R}^{d_2} \rightarrow \mathbb{R}^c$ (where c is the number of classes) is trained on the extracted features of the labelled source samples (h^s, y^s) (and does not use the unlabelled target data). If labels y^s are one-hot encoded, the cross-entropy classification loss is used, such that

$$\mathcal{L}_c(h^s, y^s) = -\frac{1}{n^s} \sum_{i=1}^{n^s} \sum_{k=1}^{c} y^s_{i,k} \log C(h^s_i). \tag{4}$$

Contrastive loss is applied to the extracted features of the constrained pairs of samples. Let $I^=$ be an indicator function equal to one when the pair (x_i, x_j) is under must-link constraint, or equal to zero otherwise. Let also $I^{\neq}$ be an indicator function for cannot-link constraints. The contrastive loss is defined such that

$$\mathcal{L}_{con} = \sum_{i,j} I^=(x_i, x_j) ||h_i - h_j||_2^2 + I^{\neq}(x_i, x_j) \max\left(0, m - ||h_i - h_j||_2^2\right), \tag{5}$$

where h_i, h_j are the extracted features of samples x_i, x_j, and m is a threshold that prevents the cannot-link loss from moving towards infinity, i.e. the features of samples under a cannot-link constraint are limited to be a distance of m apart.

If we denote the feature extractor's weights as θ_{fe} and the class discriminator's weights as θ_c, the final min-max adversarial optimisation problem to be solved is

$$\min_{\theta_{fe}, \theta_c} \left\{ \mathcal{L}_c + \lambda_1 \max_{\theta_{wd}} \left[\mathcal{L}_{wd} - \gamma \mathcal{L}_{grad}\right] + \lambda_2 \mathcal{L}_{con} \right\}. \tag{6}$$

Table 1. Characteristics of NWPU-RESISC45 and EuroSAT datasets.

Name	Source	Image Size	# Patches	Classes	Resolution
RESISC45	Aerial	$256 \times 256 \times 3$	31,500	45	0.2 m–30 m
EuroSAT	Satellite	$64 \times 64 \times 13$	27,000	10	10 m

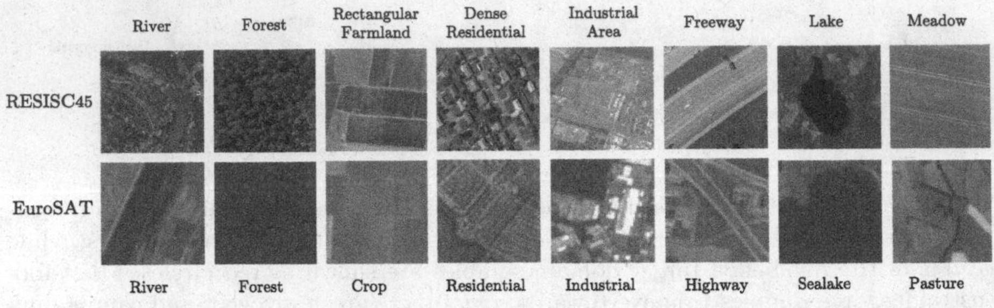

Fig. 3. Examples of chosen corresponding classes from RESISC45 and EuroSAT datasets. For EuroSAT, the RGB version of the dataset is shown.

where λ_1 and λ_2 are the weights of the contrastive loss and Wasserstein loss respectively.

4 Experimental Results

4.1 Data

The proposed approach is evaluated on the following eight corresponding classes from two heterogeneous remote sensing datasets (details given in Table 1 and examples of classes given in Fig. 3):

- NWPU-RESISC45 [6] (high-resolution aerial RGB images extracted from Google Earth)—dense residential, forest, freeway, industrial area, lake, meadow, rectangular farmland, and river.
- EuroSAT [13] (low-resolution multi-spectral images from the Sentinel-2A satellite) — residential, forest, highway, industrial, sealake, pasture, annual crop and permanent crop (two classes merged into one), river.

The problem to be solved is patch classification, with each patch having a single label. The RESISC45 dataset is composed of images taken from 100 countries and regions all over the world, throughout all seasons and all kinds of weather. The EuroSAT dataset covers 34 European countries and also consists of data from throughout the year. Both datasets, therefore, have in-domain temporal and geographic variability, making even the in-domain problem of classification very difficult.

Transfer learning brings another level of difficulty, especially with the huge domain shift that exists in the presented datasets. Figure 4 visualises some classes

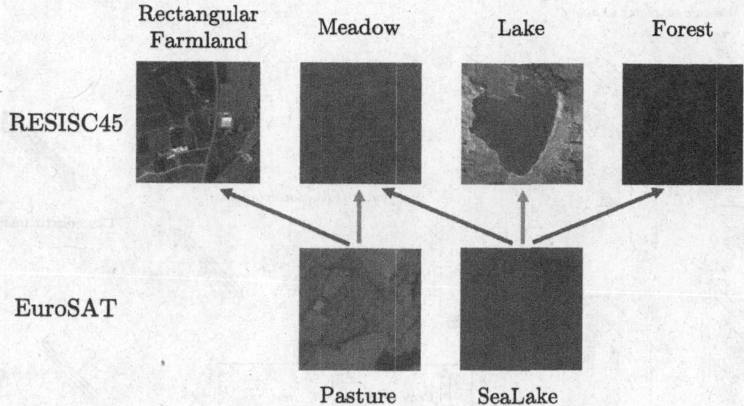

Fig. 4. Examples of issues that can arise during transfer learning between RESISC45 and EuroSAT. Green arrows show which samples should be aligned, and red arrows show which samples tend to be aligned, but should not. (Colour figure online)

that tend to be misaligned between domains. The Lake class in RESISC45 shows the entire lake with the surrounding area, whereas in EuroSAT only a patch of water is shown, making it more similar to meadow and forest which also present uniform colours. In the following experiments, we show that a huge improvement in performance can be achieved by introducing must-link and cannot-link constraints between such misaligned patches.

One advantage of the proposed Constrained-HIDA approach is that information in all channels can be used. The information provided by non-RGB channels can be discriminative but is often neglected. For example, the multispectral EuroSAT data contain, aside from the visible RGB bands, near-infrared (NIR), short-wave infrared (SWIR) and red edge bands etc.

The datasets are split into the train, validation, and test sets with the proportion of 60:20:20 while keeping the classes balanced in all sets. The test set was set aside during development and only used for the final experiments presented herein.

4.2 Implementation Details

Constrained-HIDA is a convolutional architecture. (see Fig. 5 for details). The feature extractor for RESISC45 consists of two convolutional layers with 16 and 32 filters respectively. Each convolutional layer is followed by 4×4 max-pooling. The feature extractor for EuroSAT is the same, except that it has 2×2 max-pooling after every convolutional layer. The shared invariant feature extractor has two convolutional layers with 32 and 64 filters respectively, and one fully-connected (FC) layer of 100 nodes. All of the kernels have size 5×5. The class discriminator has one FC layer with softmax activation. The domain critic (DC) has an FC layer with 100 nodes followed by an FC layer with 1 node.

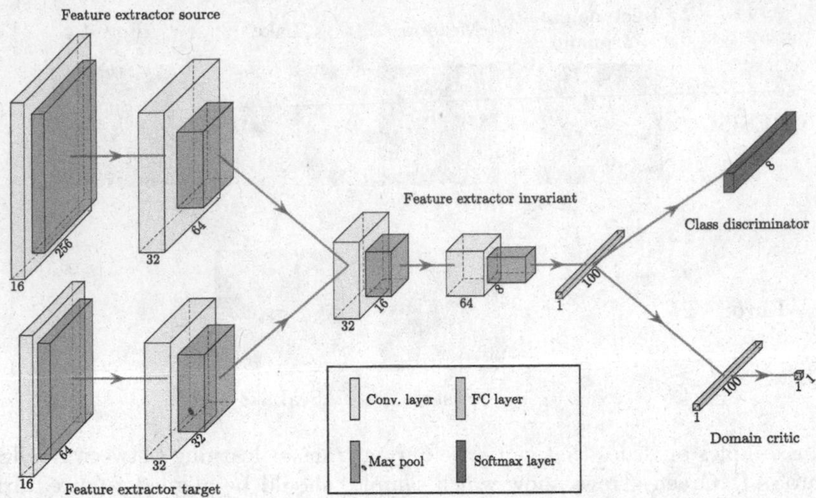

Fig. 5. The architecture of the proposed Constrained-HIDA model, specifically used for the case when the source dataset is RESISC45 and the target dataset is EuroSAT.

In each training step, the DC is trained for 10 iterations with a learning rate of 10^{-3}, the DC is then frozen and the rest of the model is trained for 1 iteration with a learning rate of 10^{-4}. The DC loss' weight λ_1 is 0.1, and the contrastive loss weight λ_2 is 0.3. The Adam optimiser is used.

The input data is standardised per channel so that each channel has a mean of 0 and a standard deviation of 1. The following augmentation transformations are used: flipping with a probability of 0.45, rotation with a probability of 0.75 for 90°, 180°, or 270°, changing contrast with the probability of 0.33 by multiplying the values of the pixels with the coefficient ranging between 0.5 and 1.5, changing brightness with the probability of 0.33 by adding the coefficient ranging between −0.3 and 0.3 scaled by the mean of pixel values per channel before standardisation, blurring with the probability of 0.33 with Gaussian filter with σ parameter values ranging from 1.5 to 1.8, and finally adding Gaussian noise with mean 0 and standard deviation between 10 and 15 with the probability of 0.33. The batch size is 32, and in each iteration, half of the training batch (16) comes from the source and the other half from the target domain. In every batch, there are always 4 pairs of source-target samples with a constraint, either must-link or cannot-link. The model is trained for 40 epochs.

The convolutional architecture used for Constrained-HIDA is not rigorously optimised but was found through initial experiments. The hyper-parameters related to the domain critic, as well as learning rates, optimiser, and loss weights, are taken from the WDGRL method [23]. Data augmentation was chosen based on remote sensing domain experience. Increasing batch size or percentage of constrained pairs per batch did not improve performance further.

The code to reproduce the Constrained-HIDA experiments presented in this article is available online[2].

4.3 Comparison Methods

To the best of our knowledge, there are no other HDA works on using constraints instead of labels in the target domain. Our method is therefore compared with HDA methods for image data in an unsupervised and semi-supervised setting. The first comparison method is CycleGAN for HDA [28], which can be used in both UDA and SSDA, a method tailored for RS and for data with different spatial resolutions. We will denote unsupervised and semi-supervised variants of the method as CycleGAN for U-HDA and CycleGAN for SS-HDA. We further compare with an unsupervised version of our method without using any constraints or any labels in the target domain (denoted U-HIDA), and with a semi-supervised version that uses labels in the target domain, but not constraints nor contrastive loss (denoted SS-HIDA). Semi-supervised methods are evaluated in the situation where 1.25% of labelled target data is available (5 labelled samples per class, 40 in total).

Our Constrained-HIDA is evaluated on a range of different amounts of constraints (40, 80, 160, 320, and 480 constrained pairs), where the ratio of must-link and cannot-link constraints is 1:7. Constraints are generated by taking pairs of samples and if their ground truth label is the same, a must-link constraint is created between them, if their ground truth labels differ, a cannot-link constraint is instead added. This is repeated until the correct number and ratio of constraints are found. Each constrained pair has one sample from the source and one from the target domain, they are all therefore inter-domain. No intra-domain constraints were used. Note that in semi-supervised DA comparison methods, the existence of 5 labels per class in the target domain, with 8 classes and 400 samples per class in training sets of each domain, implies the existence of 128,000 inter-domain constraints, and 780 intra-domain constraints in the target domain—a number far greater then what our method is using! For demonstration purposes, we also show the results of our method with all the inter-domain constraints implied by 40 labels in the target domain, (i.e. 16,000 must-link and 112,000 cannot-link), without using any intra-domain constraints, and without directly using any target labels for the training, relying solely on the contrastive loss over constraints in the target domain.

[2] https://github.com/mihailoobrenovic/Constrained-HIDA.

Table 2. Accuracy of the proposed Constrained-HIDA model with different numbers of constraints, UDA methods are shown as lower baselines and SSDA methods are shown as upper baselines. Standard deviations are shown in parentheses.

	R → E	E → R
CycleGAN for U-HDA	18.48 (8.00)	16.82 (5.74)
U-HIDA	13.61 (11.33)	17.77 (9.37)
Constrained-HIDA 40 constraints	35.52 (7.70)	33.29 (13.59)
Constrained-HIDA 80 constraints	39.09 (10.02)	40.54 (9.43)
Constrained-HIDA 160 constraints	48.59 (7.46)	49.00 (7.17)
Constrained-HIDA 320 constraints	64.68 (3.68)	56.13 (7.12)
Constrained-HIDA 480 constraints	65.27 (2.53)	59.37 (5.48)
Constrained-HIDA all constraints for 40 labels	**69.34 (3.60)**	**63.71 (2.12)**
CycleGAN for SS-HDA 40 labels	41.57 (9.20)	47.29 (1.53)
SS-HIDA 40 labels	66.14 (2.92)	62.68 (3.24)

4.4 Results

The overall accuracy of our and all the comparison methods with RESISC45 as source and EuroSAT as target (R → E) and vice-versa (E → R) are shown in Table 2.

For the R → E case, the results show that our Constrained-HIDA almost doubles the performance of unsupervised CycleGAN for HDA with as few as 40 constraints, with even higher gains over the unsupervised version of the model (U-HIDA). As more constraints are added, the better Constrained-HIDA performs. With 160 constraints, it already gains 7% over semi-supervised CycleGAN for HDA that uses 40 labels in the target domain. From 320 constraints and on, the results become comparable to the semi-supervised version of our model SS-HIDA.

For the E → R case, the findings are similar. Constrained-HIDA with 40 constraints has around 2 times stronger performance than the lower baselines. With 160 constraints it already outperforms semi-supervised CycleGAN for HDA by around 2%, with the gain growing as more constraints are added. When using 480 constraints, the results of Constrained-HIDA become comparable to SS-HIDA.

Constrained-HIDA using all of the inter-domain constraints implied by 40 labels in the target domain (i.e. 120,000 constraints) even outperforms SS-HIDA trained with 40 target labels in both cases — by more than 3% in the R → E case, and around 1% in the E → R case. This is a very interesting finding, having in mind that the classifier in Constrained-HIDA is trained only on source samples and that only the contrastive loss and Wasserstein loss were affected by target samples, while the classifier of SS-HIDA was trained with all available labelled data including from the target domain. This implies that it might be

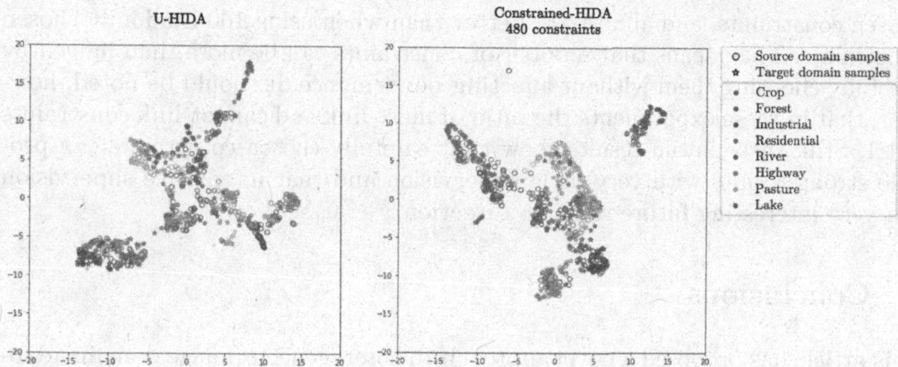

Fig. 6. PaCMAP visualisation of U-HIDA and Constrained-HIDA features in the R → E case.

more important to align the structure of the target domain with the source domain than to use (a small number of) hard target labels.

It should be noted, however, that in the case of Constrained-HIDA using 320 and 480 constraints, there are 40 and 60 must-link constraints respectively. This means that there are 40 and 60 target samples, each associated with a source sample that is labelled. One could argue that this indirectly brings information about the labels to the target domain. This information is however still weaker than a label in our experiments. The target labels are used when training the classifier in SSDA comparison methods and directly introduce the information equivalent to a huge number of must-link and cannot-link constraints, both inter-domain and intra-domain. On the other hand, in our experiments, Constrained-HIDA only applies the contrastive loss to inter-domain constraints. Furthermore, the numbers of 320 and 480 constraints still represent only 0.25%, and 0.375% respectively of the total number of 128,000 constraints implied by 40 labels in the target domains.

As shown in Fig. 6, Constrained-HIDA learns better discriminative features compared to U-HIDA. In the absence of constraints, U-HIDA tends to flip classes, for example, many target samples of the crop class are matched with the river class, a lot of forest class samples are matched with pasture etc. In contrast, Constrained-HIDA better matches classes and the spread between the domains is reduced such that the overlap is more consistent, explaining the increase in performance observed in Table 2.

Interactive supervision can further reduce the need for constraints. If constraints are manually created with prior knowledge, on samples representing classes that are known to be problematic, fewer constraints can be more effective. By identifying and adding constraints to a certain number of target samples that are misclassified by unsupervised HIDA in the R → E case, 8 such constraints are sufficient for Constrained-HIDA to achieve an accuracy of 40.92%, and 80 gives 55.36%, which is 15% better than when using the same number of randomly chosen constraints, and almost 7% better than when using 160 randomly chosen constraints. This means that number of constraints can be more than halved by carefully choosing them without affecting performance. It should be noted, however, that in these experiments the ratio of must-link and cannot-link constraints is 1:1. Still, these initial results show that carefully chosen constraints can provide strong results with very little supervision and that interactive supervision is a very interesting future research direction.

5 Conclusions

This article has proposed a novel approach to heterogeneous image domain adaptation using constraints named Constrained-HIDA. To the best of our knowledge, this is the first such method using constraints instead of labels in a semi-supervised setting. The results show that with a very small number of constraints, Constrained-HIDA strongly outperforms UDA methods, and has comparable results with SSDA methods, even outperforming them when using an equivalent amount of information. This shows that replacing labels with constraints could reduce the need for supervised information in the target domain and could facilitate the job of annotating experts for whom providing constraints might be easier and more natural than providing hard labels.

In the future, Constrained-HIDA could be further improved by introducing pseudo-labels or pseudo-constraints, with e.g. constrained clustering; this could enrich the information about the target domain. The prospect of interactive learning is another interesting direction, allowing the user to put constraints on the examples misclassified by the model, in an iterative manner, could additionally decrease the number of constraints needed. The method could also be evaluated in homogeneous DA, on domains coming from the same input space, but with a huge domain shift.

Acknowledgements. This work was granted access to the HPC resources of IDRIS under the allocation 2021-A0111011872 made by GENCI. We thank Nvidia Corporation for donating GPUs and the Centre de Calcul de l'Université de Strasbourg for access to the GPUs used for this research. Supported by the French Government through co-tutelle PhD funding and ICube's internal project funding (RL4MD).

References

1. Arjovsky, M., et al.: Wasserstein generative adversarial networks. In: ICML, pp. 214–223 (2017)
2. Benjdira, B., Ammar, A., Koubaa, A., Ouni, K.: Data-efficient domain adaptation for semantic segmentation of aerial imagery using generative adversarial networks. Appl. Sci. **10**(3), 1092 (2020)
3. Benjdira, B., et al.: Unsupervised domain adaptation using generative adversarial networks for semantic segmentation of aerial images. Remote Sens. **11**(11), 1369 (2019)
4. Bousmalis, K., et al.: Domain separation networks. In: NIPS, pp. 343–351 (2016)

5. Chen, W.-Y., Hsu, T.-M.H., Tsai, Y.-H.H., Wang, Y.-C.F., Chen, M.-S.: Transfer neural trees for heterogeneous domain adaptation. In: Leibe, B., Matas, J., Sebe, N., Welling, M. (eds.) ECCV 2016. LNCS, vol. 9909, pp. 399–414. Springer, Cham (2016). https://doi.org/10.1007/978-3-319-46454-1_25
6. Cheng, G., et al.: Remote sensing image scene classification: Benchmark and state of the art. Proc. IEEE **105**(10), 1865–1883 (2017)
7. Chopra, S., Hadsell, R., LeCun, Y.: Learning a similarity metric discriminatively, with application to face verification. In: CVPR, vol. 1, pp. 539–546. IEEE (2005)
8. Ganin, Y., Lempitsky, V.: Unsupervised domain adaptation by backpropagation. In: ICML, pp. 1180–1189 (2015)
9. Ganin, Y., et al.: Domain-adversarial training of neural networks. JMLR **17**(1), 2096–2030 (2016)
10. Goodfellow, I., et al.: Generative adversarial nets. In: NIPS, pp. 2672–2680 (2014)
11. Gulrajani, I., et al.: Improved training of Wasserstein GANs. In: NIPS, vol. 30 (2017)
12. Harada, S., et al.: Cluster-guided semi-supervised domain adaptation for imbalanced medical image classification. arXiv preprint arXiv:2303.01283 (2023)
13. Helber, P., et al.: EuroSAT: A novel dataset and deep learning benchmark for land use and land cover classification. IEEE JSTARS **12**(7), 2217–2226 (2019)
14. Hoffman, J., et al.: CyCADA: Cycle-consistent adversarial domain adaptation. In: ICML, pp. 1989–1998 (2018)
15. Hsu, Y.C., Kira, Z.: Neural network-based clustering using pairwise constraints. arXiv preprint arXiv:1511.06321 (2015)
16. Kang, G., Jiang, L., Yang, Y., Hauptmann, A.G.: Contrastive adaptation network for unsupervised domain adaptation. In: CVPR, pp. 4893–4902 (2019)
17. Li, J., Li, G., Shi, Y., Yu, Y.: Cross-domain adaptive clustering for semi-supervised domain adaptation. In: CVPR, pp. 2505–2514 (2021)
18. Li, J., et al.: Heterogeneous domain adaptation through progressive alignment. IEEE Trans. Neural Netw. Learn. Syst. **30**(5), 1381–1391 (2018)
19. Liu, H., Wang, J., Long, M.: Cycle self-training for domain adaptation. Adv. Neural Inf. Process. Syst. **34**, 22968–22981 (2021)
20. Liu, H., Shao, M., Ding, Z., Fu, Y.: Structure-preserved unsupervised domain adaptation. IEEE Trans. Knowl. Data Eng. **31**(4), 799–812 (2018)
21. Obrenovic, M., Lampert, T., Monde-Kossi, F., Gançarski, P., Ivanović, M.: SS-HIDA: Semi-supervised heterogeneous image domain adaptation. In: MACLEAN: MAChine Learning for EArth ObservatioN Workshop co-located with the European Conference on Machine Learning and Principles and Practice of Knowledge Discovery in Databases (ECML/PKDD) (2021)
22. Saito, K., et al.: Semi-supervised domain adaptation via minimax entropy. In: ICCV, pp. 8050–8058 (2019)
23. Shen, J., et al.: Wasserstein distance guided representation learning for domain adaptation. In: AAAI, pp. 4058–4065 (2018)
24. Shu, X., et al.: Weakly-shared deep transfer networks for heterogeneous-domain knowledge propagation. In: ACM Multimedia, pp. 35–44 (2015)
25. Sohn, K., et al.: Fixmatch: Simplifying semi-supervised learning with consistency and confidence. Adv. Neural Inf. Process. Syst. **33**, 596–608 (2020)
26. Titouan, V., et al.: CO-Optimal transport. In: NeurIPS, vol. 33, pp. 17559–17570 (2020)
27. Tzeng, E., et al.: Adversarial discriminative domain adaptation. In: CVPR, pp. 7167–7176 (2017)

28. Voreiter, C., et al.: A cycle GAN approach for heterogeneous domain adaptation in land use classification. In: IGARSS, pp. 1961–1964 (2020)
29. Wagstaff, K., Cardie, C., Rogers, S., Schrödl, S., et al.: Constrained k-means clustering with background knowledge. In: ICML, vol. 1, pp. 577–584 (2001)
30. Wang, X., et al.: Heterogeneous domain adaptation network based on autoencoder. J. Parallel Distrib. Comput. **117**, 281–291 (2018)
31. Zhang, H., Zhan, T., Basu, S., Davidson, I.: A framework for deep constrained clustering. Data Mining Knowl. Disc. **35**, 593–620 (2021)
32. Zhu, J.Y., et al.: Unpaired image-to-image translation using cycle-consistent adversarial networks. In: ICCV, pp. 2223–2232 (2017)

Author Index

D. Koutra et al. (Eds.): ECML PKDD 2023, LNAI 14173, pp. 459–460, 2023.
https://doi.org/10.1007/978-3-031-43424-2

Printed in the United States
by Baker & Taylor Publisher Services